Lecture Notes in Computer Science   8867

Commenced Publication in 1973
Founding and Former Series Editors:
Gerhard Goos, Juris Hartmanis, and Jan van Leeuwen

Editorial Board

David Hutchison
  Lancaster University, UK
Takeo Kanade
  Carnegie Mellon University, Pittsburgh, PA, USA
Josef Kittler
  University of Surrey, Guildford, UK
Jon M. Kleinberg
  Cornell University, Ithaca, NY, USA
Friedemann Mattern
  ETH Zurich, Switzerland
John C. Mitchell
  Stanford University, CA, USA
Moni Naor
  Weizmann Institute of Science, Rehovot, Israel
C. Pandu Rangan
  Indian Institute of Technology, Madras, India
Bernhard Steffen
  TU Dortmund University, Germany
Demetri Terzopoulos
  University of California, Los Angeles, CA, USA
Doug Tygar
  University of California, Berkeley, CA, USA
Gerhard Weikum
  Max Planck Institute for Informatics, Saarbruecken, Germany

T0212743

Ramón Hervás   Sungyoung Lee
Chris Nugent   José Bravo (Eds.)

Ubiquitous Computing and Ambient Intelligence

Personalisation and User Adapted Services

8th International Conference, UCAmI 2014
Belfast, UK, December 2-5, 2014
Proceedings

 Springer

Volume Editors

Ramón Hervás
Castilla-La Mancha University, Escuela Superior de Informática
Paseo de la Universidad 4, 13071 Ciudad Real, Spain
E-mail: ramon.hlucas@uclm.es

Sungyoung Lee
Kyung Hee University, Department of Computer Engineering
446-701, Seocheon-dong, Giheung-gu, Yongin-si, Gyeonggi-do, Korea
E-mail: sylee@oslab.khu.ac.kr

Chris Nugent
University of Ulster, Computer Science Research Institute
School of Computing and Mathematics, Jordanstown Campus
Shore Road, Newtownabbey BT37 0QB, UK
E-mail: cd.nugent@ulster.ac.uk

José Bravo
Castilla-La Mancha University, Escuela Superior de Informática
Paseo de la Universidad 4, 13071 Ciudad Real, Spain
E-mail: jose.bravo@uclm.es

ISSN 0302-9743   e-ISSN 1611-3349
ISBN 978-3-319-13101-6   e-ISBN 978-3-319-13102-3
DOI 10.1007/978-3-319-13102-3
Springer Cham Heidelberg New York Dordrecht London

Library of Congress Control Number: 2014953288

LNCS Sublibrary: SL 3 – Information Systems and Application, incl. Internet/Web
and HCI

© Springer International Publishing Switzerland 2014
This work is subject to copyright. All rights are reserved by the Publisher, whether the whole or part of
the material is concerned, specifically the rights of translation, reprinting, reuse of illustrations, recitation,
broadcasting, reproduction on microfilms or in any other physical way, and transmission or information
storage and retrieval, electronic adaptation, computer software, or by similar or dissimilar methodology
now known or hereafter developed. Exempted from this legal reservation are brief excerpts in connection
with reviews or scholarly analysis or material supplied specifically for the purpose of being entered and
executed on a computer system, for exclusive use by the purchaser of the work. Duplication of this publication
or parts thereof is permitted only under the provisions of the Copyright Law of the Publisher's location,
in ist current version, and permission for use must always be obtained from Springer. Permissions for use
may be obtained through RightsLink at the Copyright Clearance Center. Violations are liable to prosecution
under the respective Copyright Law.
The use of general descriptive names, registered names, trademarks, service marks, etc. in this publication
does not imply, even in the absence of a specific statement, that such names are exempt from the relevant
protective laws and regulations and therefore free for general use.
While the advice and information in this book are believed to be true and accurate at the date of publication,
neither the authors nor the editors nor the publisher can accept any legal responsibility for any errors or
omissions that may be made. The publisher makes no warranty, express or implied, with respect to the
material contained herein.

Typesetting: Camera-ready by author, data conversion by Scientific Publishing Services, Chennai, India

Printed on acid-free paper

Springer is part of Springer Science+Business Media (www.springer.com)

Preface

Ambient intelligence promotes environments surrounded by intelligent interfaces and ubiquitous communication embedded into everyday objects to support human activities and achieve a better quality of life. Ambient Intelligence (AmI), since the initial vision of ISTAG in 2002, has been evolving in recent years while still maintaining a holistic view: AmI focuses on users, beyond the technology. This year we celebrated a joint event for the 8th International Conference on Ubiquitous Computing and Ambient Intelligence (UCAmI 2014) and the 6th International Work-conference on Ambient Assisted Living (IWAAL 2014) in Belfast, UK. The UCAmI conference, since its inception, has evolved adapting its topics to consider new trends in AmI in addition to the inclusion of workshops targeting the most specific areas. Furthermore, in an effort to increase the visibility of the contributions of UCAmI, selected papers will be invited for submission as extended versions in the journals: *Sensors, Journal of Medical Systems, Medical Informatics and Decision Making* and the *Journal of Cognitive Computation*. As such we would like to thank the distinguished editors of these journals for providing us with these opportunities.

The program of this joint event includes the UCAmI Workshops on Ambient Intelligence for Urban Areas (AmIUA), Internet of Things Everywhere: Towards Smart Objects Everywhere (IoTE), End-User Service Provision for Ambient Intelligence (EUSPAI) and Video Soft Sensing (VSS). This year's event included keynotes from internationally recognized researchers in their fields: Dr. Michael J. McGrath from Intel Labs, Dr. Riitta Hellman from Karde AS, and Prof. Jesse Hoey from the Computational Health Informatics Laboratory (CHIL). We would like to thank our distinguish keynote speakers for their participation and contribution to this joint event.

We received an over whelming response from researchers who submitted their contributions for consideration to UCAmI 2014, with a 50% increase in manuscripts submitted compared to last year's edition of UCAmI (UCAmI 2013). In this eighth edition of UCAmI, we received 70 submissions involving 238 authors from 20 different countries. Following the review process we had an acceptance rate for long papers of 40%. A total number of 168 reviews were undertaken by 106 reviewers from 29 countries. We would like to thank all the authors who submitted their work for consideration and also the reviewers for providing their detailed and con-structive reviews in a timely manner.

Finally, we would like to express our deepest thanks to our colleagues for assisting in organizing this event, particularly Professor Chris Nugent from the

University of Ulster and Professor Jose Bravo from Castilla-La Mancha University. We would also like to thank all the Program Committee members for their time and contributions.

December 2014

Ramón Hervás
Sungyoung Lee
Chris Nugent
José Bravo

Organization

General Chairs

José Bravo   Castilla-La Mancha University, Spain
Chris Nugent   University of Ulster, UK

UCAmI PC Chairs

Ramón Hervás   Castilla-La Mancha University, Spain
Sungyoung Lee   Kyung Hee University, Korea

EUSPAI PC Chairs

Ramón Alcarria   Universidad Politécnica de Madrid, Spain
Augusto Morales   Universidad Politécnica de Madrid, Spain
Tomás Robles Valladares   Universidad Politécnica de Madrid, Spain

IoT PC Chairs

Antonio Skarmeta   University of Murcia, Spain
Antonio J. Jara   University of Applied Sciences Western
                                  Switzerland, Switzerland

AmIUA PC Chairs

Nelson Baloian   University of Chile, Chile
Hiroaki Ogata   Kyushu University, Japan
Benjamin Weyers   RWTH Aachen University, Germany

AmIUA PC Chairs

Hui Wang   University of Ulster, UK

Publicity Chairs

Vladimir Villarreal   Technological University of Panama, Panama
Jesús Fontecha Diezma   Castilla-La Mancha University, Spain

Local Organizing Chair

Ian Cleland   University of Ulster, UK

Organizing Committee

Jesús Fontecha, Spain   Mark Beattie, UK
Tania Mondéjar, Spain   Colin Shewell, UK
Vladimir Villarreal, Panama   Joseph Rafferty, UK
Gabriel Urzáiz, Mexico   Philip Hartin, UK
Iván González, Spain   Andrew Ennis, UK

Web Masters

Kyle Boyd   University of Ulster, UK
Mark Beattie   University of Ulster, UK

Program Committee

Unai Aguilera   Deusto Institute of Technology - DeustoTech,
                                     University of Deusto, Spain
Xavier Alamán   Autonomous University of Madrid, Spain
Ramón Pablo Alcarria Garrido   Technical University of Madrid, Spain
Jan Alexandersson   DFKI GmbH, Germany
Mohamed Bakhouya   University of Technology of Belfort
                                     Montbeliard, France
Mert Bal   Miami University, USA
Madeline Balaam   Newcastle University, UK
Nelson Baloian   University of Chile, Chile
Denilson Barbosa   University of Alberta, Canada
Jean-Paul Barthes   UTC, USA
Hector Bedon   Technical University of Madrid, Spain
Paolo Bellavista   University of Bologna, Italy
Daniel Biella   University of Duisburg-Essen, Germany
Francisco Javier Blaya
    Gonzálvez   University of Murcia, Spain
Andrés Lorenzo Bleda   Technical Centre of Furniture and Wood
                                     (CETEM), Spain
Stephane Bouchard   Université du Québec en Outaouais-UQO,
                                     Canada
Fatima Boujarwah   Kuwait University, Kuwait
Robin Braun   University of Technology, Sydney
Jose Bravo   Castilla La Mancha University, Spain

Ceren Budak	University of California, Santa Barbara - UCSB, USA
Yang Cai	Carnegie Mellon University, USA
Edwin Cedeño	Technical University of Madrid, Spain
Sophie Chabridon	Institut TELECOM; TELECOM Management SudParis / CNRS UMR SAMOVAR, France
Ranveer Chandra	Microsoft, USA
Ignacio Chang	Technological University of Panama, Panama
Shuwei Chen	University of Ulster, UK
Wei Chen	Eindhoven University of Technology, The Netherlands
Marcello Cinque	University of Naples Federico II, Italy
Walter Colitti	ETRO-COMO, Vrije Universiteit Brussel, Brussels
Diane Cook	Washington State University, USA
Domenico Cotroneo	University of Naples Federico II, Italy
Geoff Coulson	Lancaster University, UK
Kevin Curran	University of Ulster, UK
Carlos Dafonte	University of A Coruña, Spain
Vincenzo De Florio	University of Antwerp, Belgium
Boris De Ruyter	Philips Research, USA
Stefan Decker	National University of Ireland, Ireland
Giovanna Di Marzo Serugendo	University of Geneva, Switzerland
Simon Dobson	University of St. Andrews, UK
Charalampos Doukas	University of the Aegean, Greece
Ignacio Elicegui	University of Cantabria, Spain
Jesus Favela	CICESE, Mexico
Mohamed Fayad	San Jose State University, USA
Ana Fensel	STI Innsbruck, University of Innsbruck, Austria
Carlo Ferrari	University of Padova, Italy
Jesus Fontecha	Castilla-La Mancha University, Spain
Jonathan Freeman	i2 Media Research Ltd., UK
Leo Galway	University of Ulster, UK
Borja Gamecho	UPV/EHU, Spain
Carlo Giovannella	Università degli Studi di Roma La Sapienza, Italy
Antonietta Grasso	Xerox Research Centre Europe, France
Dan Grigoras	UCC, USA
Luis Guerrero	Universidad de Chile, Chile
Bin Guo	Institut Telecom SudParis, France
Chris Guy	University of Reading, UK
Antonio Gómez Skarmeta	University of Murcia, Spain

Maria Haritou	Institute of Communication and Computer Systems - National Technical University of Athens, Greece
Jan Havlik	Czech Technical University in Prague, Czech Republic
Riitta Hellman	Karde AS, Norway
Valeria Herskovic	Pontificia Universidad Católica de Chile, Chile
Ramón Hervás	Castilla-La Mancha University, Spain
Jesse Hoey	University of Waterloo, Canada
Eva Hornecker	University of Strathclyde, UK
Bin Hu	Birmingham City University, UK
Robert Istepanian	Kingston University, London, UK
Witold Jacak	Polytechnic University of Upper Austria, Austria
Anne James	Coventry University, UK
Antonio J. Jara	University of Murcia, Spain
Min Jing	University of Ulster, UK
Alan Jovic	University of Zagreb, Croatia
Wolfgang Kastner	Institute of Computer Aided Automation, Austria
Abdelmajid Khelil	Huawei ERC, Germany
Ryzsard Klempous	Wroclaw University of Technology, Poland
Srdjan Krco	DunavNET, Ireland
Latif Ladid	University of Luxembourg, Luxembourg
Jean-Christophe Lapayre	DISC - Université de Franche-Comté, France
Mikel Larrea	University of the Basque Country UPV/EHU, Spain
Sungyoung Lee	Kyung Hee University, Korea
Ernst Leiss	University of Houston, USA
Lenka Lhotska	Czech Technical University in Prague, Czech Republic
Suzanne Little	Dublin City University, Ireland
Jun Liu	University of Ulster, UK
Vincenzo Loia	Università degli Studi di Salerno, Italy
Tun Lu	Fudan University, China
Wolfram Luther	University of Duisburg-Essen, Germany
Diego López-De-Ipiña	DeustoTech - Deusto Institute of Technology, University of Deusto, Spain
Ricardo-J. Machado	Universidade do Minho, Portugal
Stephen Makonin	Simon Fraser University, Canada
Maria Martinez	University of A Coruña, Spain
Rene Mayrhofer	Johannes Kepler University Linz, Austria
Roc Meseguer	Universitat Politècnica de Catalunya, Spain

Peter Mikulecky	University of Hradec Králové, Czech Republic
Vittorio Miori	ISTI-CNR, Italy
Augusto Morales Domíguez	Technical University of Madrid, Spain
Ana Moreira	Center de informatica e technologies da informacao, Portugal
María Victoria Moreno Cano	University of Murcia, Spain
Philip Morrow	University of Ulster, UK
Francisco Moya	Castilla-La Mancha University, Spain
Tatsuo Nakajima	Waseda University, Japan
Michele Nati	University of Surrey, UK
David H. Nguyen	University of California, Irvine, USA
Marcos Nieto	Vicomtech-IK4, Spain
Chris Nugent	University of Ulster, UK
Sergio Ochoa	Universidad de Chile, Chile
Hiroaki Ogata	Kyushu University, Japan
George Okeyo	University of Agriculture and Technology, Kenya
Cristiano Paggetti	I+ Srl, Italy
Philippe Palanque	University of Toulouse, France
Marcello Pelillo	University of Venice, Italy
Dennis Pfisterer	University of Lübeck, Germany
Thomas Ploetz	Newcastle University, UK
Till Plumbaum	DAI-Labor, Technische Universität Berlin, Germany
Jose Antonio Pow-Sang	Pontificia Universidad Católica del Perú, Peru
Parisa Rashidi	University of Florida, USA
Patrick Reignier	ENSIMAG, France
Luis Francisco Revilla	University of Texas Austin, USA
Giuseppe Riva	Università Cattolica del Sacro Cuore, Italy
Tomás Robles	Technical University of Madrid, Spain
Joel Rodrigues	Instituto de Telecomunicações, University of Beira Interior, Portugal
Nirmalya Roy	University of Maryland Baltimore County, USA
Jerzy W. Rozenblit	University of Arizona, USA
Jonathan Ruiz-De-Garibay	DeustoTech - Deusto Institute of Technology, Spain
Rodrigo Santos	Universidad Nacional del Sur - Bahía Blanca, Argentina
Uli Sattler	The University of Manchester, UK
Markus Schneider	University of Florida, USA
Bryan Scotney	University of Ulster, UK
Boon-Chong Seet	Auckland University of Technology, New Zealand
Weiming Shen	NRC, Canada

Kenia Sousa   USI4BIZ, Luxemburg
Kåre Synnes   Luleå University of Technology, Sweden
Chantal Taconet   TELECOM Management SudParis, France
Valentina Tamma   University of Liverpool, UK
Gabriel Urzaiz   Universidad Anahuac Mayab, Mexico
Janet van der Linden   Open University, UK
Rob van Kranenburg   Sociotal, Belgium
Félix Jesús Villanueva Molina   University of Castilla-La Mancha, Spain
Natalia Villanueva-Rosales   University of Texas at El Paso, USA
Massimo Villari   University of Messina, Italy
Vladimir Villarreal   Technological University of Panama, Panama
Hui Wang   University of Ulster, UK
Nadir Weibel   UCSD, USA
Benjamin Weyers   RWTH Aachen University VR Group,
                                   Germany
Erik Wilde   EMC Corporation, USA
Hen-I Yang   Iowa State University, USA
Juan Ye   University of St. Andrews, UK
Zhiwen Yu   Northwestern Polytechnical University,
                                   P.R. China, China
Jianguo Zhang   University of Dundee, UK
Rui Zhang   IBM Research - Almaden, USA
Huiyu Zhou   Queen's University, Canada
Jing Zhou   Communication University of China, China
Gustavo Zurita   University of Chile, Chile

Additional Reviewers

Rachel Gawley, UK   Michael Craven, UK
Jonathan Synnott, UK   Giuseppe Fico, Spain
Timothy Patterson, UK   Giorgio Carpino, Italy
Alberto Calzada, UK   Jseús Fontecha, Spain
Ian Cleland, UK   Iván González, Spain
Phillip Hartin, UK

Table of Contents

Human Interaction in Ambient Intelligence (1/3)

Human Interaction in Ambient Intelligence (2/3)

Human Interaction in Ambient Intelligence (3/3)

ICT Instrumentation and Middleware Support for Smart Environments and Objects (1/2)

ICT Instrumentation and Middleware Support for Smart Environments and Objects (2/2)

Adding Intelligence for Environment Adaptation

Security and Privacy Issues in AAL

Workshop on Ambient Intelligence for Urban Areas (AmIUA)

Workshop on IoT Everywhere: Towards Smart Objects Everywhere (IoT)

Workshop on End-User Service Provision for Ambient Intelligence (EUSPAI)

Workshop on Video Soft Sensing (VSS)

Implementing a Pedestrian Tracker
Using Low-Cost Bluetooth Inertial Sensors

Alfonso Bahillo, Ander Arambarri, Ignacio Angulo, Enrique Onieva, Pilar Elejoste,
and Asier Perallos

Deusto Institute of Technology (DeustoTech), University of Deusto, Bilbao, 48007, Spain
{alfonso.bahillo,a.arambarri,ignacio.angulo,enrique.onieva,pilar.elejoste,
perallos}@deusto.es

Abstract. Foot-mounted inertial measurement units (IMUs) are becoming the basis for many pedestrian positioning systems as a component of accurate indoor navigation. However, most of solutions that implement low-cost IMUs are often connected to a laptop by a wired connection which interferes with the pedestrian movements. Moreover, nobody walks carrying a laptop but a smartphone. Smartphones are attractive platforms for researchers to collect data coming from several sensors due to their small size, low-cost, and the fact that they are already carried routinely by most people. Therefore, this paper (i) describes a custom-built foot-mounted pedestrian indoor localization system based on commercially available low-cost inertial sensors connected wirelessly (via Bluetooth) to a smartphone, and (ii) demonstrates the capability of smartphones to be used as the target of a wirelessly IMU-based positioning system where raw IMU data will be processed in real time. We have tested the pedestrian tracker with commercial devices in a five floor building with reasonable results (accumulated error lower than 1%).

1 Introduction

The use of location data to control normal day features are being more popular in recent years not only for security applications, but also for mass market applications. Applications of location data include Location-Based Services (LBS) such as pedestrian navigation in complex indoor buildings, inclusion of elders or disabled citizens in Ambient Assisted Living (AAL) scenarios, support to first-aid responders such as firemen or policemen in risky situations, the proactive supply of information at specific locations for museum visitors, or the customized advertising in shopping malls, among others [1]. Outdoors, most of the positioning applications rely on global navigation satellite systems (GNSS). However, satellite signals get severely degraded in indoor environments such as inside buildings, urban canyons or tunnels. For these indoor environments, many local positioning systems (LPS) have been developed during the past two decades based on different technologies, and utilizing many physical signals (see [2] for a LPS survey). After all this research effort, it is becoming a fact that none of these technologies clearly outperforms the others. Thus, a current trend in addressing indoor localization is to fuse already deployed technologies.

An increasing popular indoor positioning solution combines pedestrian deadreckoning (PDR), using foot-mounted inertial measurement units (IMUs), with already

R. Hervás et al. (Eds.): UCAmI 2014, LNCS 8867, pp. 1–8, 2014.
© Springer International Publishing Switzerland 2014

deployed beacon-based technologies to provide indoor and accurate long-time navigation [3, 4, 5]. Indeed, PDR is the basis for many indoor localization techniques (see [6] for a tutorial on PDR). Despite the increasing popularity of methods which use PDR techniques based on foot-mounted IMUs, most of them connect the IMU to a laptop by a wired connection (usually by USB) which interferes with the human movements. The existing commercial IMUs with wireless connectivity would solve that problem, but they are relatively high cost (e.g. MTw from Xsens Technologies). Other solutions lose the sense of mobility because of the sensors signals are proceessed on a laptop. Nevertheless, nobody walks with a laptop but with a tablet or smartphone.

Therefore, the contribution of this work is twofold: (i) making the connectivity to the IMU wireless and of lower-cost by developing a custom-built foot-mounted pedestrian indoor localization system based on commercially available low-cost inertial sensors connected via Bluetooth to a smartphone (or tablet), and (ii) processing the IMU signals in the smartphone (or tablet) at real time by developing a LPS framework on Android operating platform. Thus, you can easily, and at low cost, implement our Bluetooth foot-mounted IMU and apply the already developed techniques with minimum custom configuration.

The paper is structured as follows: Section 2 describes the low-cost IMU with Bluetooth connectivity implemented in this work. Section 3 gives a brief overview on inertial pedestrian dead-reckoning and describes the PDR method to be developed on Android and which performance will be evaluated. Section 4 shows our experimental setup and empirical positioning results. Section 5 gives some final conclusions.

2   Low-Cost Bluetooth Inertial Sensors

The low-cost IMU conected via Bluetooth to a smartphone discussed in this paper consists of three modules - an IMU with three sensors, a Bluetooth modem, and a lithium polymer (LiPo) battery - to wirelessly give the smartphone the data gathered by the IMU. In this work we have used the modules provided by SparkFun Electronics. As IMU we used the *9DOF Razor IMU* which consists of a MEMS triple-axis accelerometer (ADXL345), a triple-axis gyro (ITG-3200), and a triple-axis magnetometer (HMC5883L) to give us nine degrees of inertial measurements [7, 8, 9]. As Bluetooth modem we used the *BlueSMiRF Gold* which works wirelessly as a serial (RX/TX) pipe. Both IMU and Bluetooth modem are powered by the very slim and extremely light weight *850 mAh LiPo battery*.

To set up the hardware, we follow the online tutorial describing how to build an attitude and heading reference system (AHRS) using the SparkFun *9DOF Razor IMU* [10]. Basically, connecting the *9DOF Razor IMU* to the *BlueSMiRF Gold* modem attending their I/O header layouts. The *LiPo battery* powers the *9DOF Razor IMU* thorough an USB charger also used to charge the battery. After assembling the three modules we designed an enclosure with a 3D printer in order to mount them easier on the foot. Figure 1(a) shows the whole system. The modules are mounted one on the top of the other minimizing the space that they take up. The velcro straps are used to fix the IMU to the foot as it is shown in Figure 1(b). Therefore, with no more than 175$ (taken current SparkFun Electronics prices) you can implement a low-cost Bluetooth foot-mounted IMU for pedestrian tracking.

LiPo USB Charger
9DOF Razor IMU
BlueSMiRF Gold
LiPo battery
Enclosure
Velcro straps

(a) Low-cost Bluetooth IMU

(b) Foot-mounted IMU

Fig. 1. Pedestrian tracker. (a) Low-cost Bluetooth IMU into the enclosure, and (b) attached to the right foot.

The parametrization of the IMU is application dependent. As a result, no universal parameters can be given. However, some groups of parameters can still be identified [11]. The parameters of the hardware set-up are only the sensor placement/mounting and the sampling frequency. On the one hand, a rule of thumb is that for inertial navigation systems (INS) employing low-cost sensors, the position error is proportional to the cube of the operational time which means that free-inertial navigation is only feasible for a few seconds [12]. Therefore, we place the IMU on the foot for using the well-known zero velocity update (ZUPT) method and thus bounding the error growth. On the other hand, after an experimental analysis of human motion sampling, E. Munoz et al. noted that the limiting signals in terms of bandwidth are those from the accelerometer due to the high frequencies generated when the foot hits the floor [13]. They established that the sampling frequency should lie between 200 Hz - when using flat shoes - and 300 Hz - when high heels. In this work we used flat shoes therefore, we set the accelerometer data rate to 200 Hz. For the gyro the bandwidth needed is not greater than 50 Hz, therefore the sampling frequency would be 100 Hz [13].

The external parameters are the trajectory and the sensors output. Regarding the sensors output W.T. Faulkner et al. found that altitude errors in pedestrian-tracking systems are due to the accelerations of the foot exceeding the dynamic range of the accelerometer [14]. They noted that accelerations can reach $\pm 10g$ when walking, and $\pm 13g$ when running. Therefore, for the best results the accelerometer is configured in a 13-bit resolution $(4mg/LSB)$ to reach a range up to $\pm 13g$. Likewise, the gyro is configured with a full-scale range of $\pm 2000/s$ corresponding to a sensitivity of $0.0695/s$ per LSB. Due to we focus on indoor environments in this work, the magnetometer sensor is not used due to the indoor magnetic disturbances. Thus, the raw data to be sent wirelessly consists of 12 bytes, 6 for the accelerometer (2 by axis) at 200 Hz data rate, and 6 for the gyro (2 by axis) at 100 Hz data rate. The raw outputs of sensors are collected by the *9DOF Razor IMU* on-board *ATmega328* microcontroller and output over the serial interface to the Bluetooth modem.

3 Inertial Pedestrian Dead-Reckoning

Dead reckoning is the process of estimating an object's position by tracking its movements relative to a known starting point and attitude. There are two alternative PDR integration methods: those that estimate position by integrating step lengths (SL) and orientation estimations at each detected step [15, 16]. And, those with a foot-mounted IMU, implementing an INS on a Kalman filter [17, 18, 19, 6]. Both SL and INS-KF share the same main drawback, the drift, the accumulation of positioning errors during the dead-reckoning integration. Without resetting the drift, the velocity (position estimation) error would increase linearly (quadratically) with time. However, we can remove the velocity error applying the well-known ZUPT method which detects the *stance phase* - that is, when the IMU is stationary - and thus we can reset the estimated velocity to zero and adjust the estimated position [17]. Detecting when an IMU is stationary can be challenging, this has made foot-mounted IMU's our choice for PDR. Furthermore, INS-KF method performs better than SL since velocity and position errors are correlated, and the cross-covariances let the KF correct the position (and not only the velocity) during a ZUPT.

The article published in 2005 by E. Foxlin is probably the most cited work in this area [17]. He explains how to take advantage of correlated position/velocity errors in KF to also remove most position errors with each ZUPT. A. Jimenez et al. gives a more complete description of the implementation process, and a more recently work by C. Fischer et al. outlines a tutorial for implementing a reasonably accurate tracker using a foot-mounted IMU with minimum custom configuration [19] and [6], respectively. In this paper, we take the raw data collected by the smartphone through its Bluetooth interface and transform them into successive positions and orientations. For this transformation we implement an INS-KF method taking the standard inertial PDR method described in [6] with some variations explained below:

- *System initialization*: While the user's foot remains motionless on the floor (previous to start walking), the acceleration and rate-of-turn signals are recorded. On the one hand, the acceleration data is used to estimate the roll and pitch angles (the yaw is provided by the user) which give us the initial rotation matrix. This initial matrix is refined *a posteriori* with successive acceleration measurements on an extended Kalman filter while the foot remains motionless. On the other hand, the mean of gyro data is computed as the bias to be subtracted from successive gyro measurements.
- *Detect a stationary phase*: Instead of only using a simple threshold on the magnitude of the gyro rate-of-turn measurements, we implement a triple-condition algorithm which not only takes into account the magnitude of the gyro measurements but also the magnitude of the acceleration and its local variance [19].
- *Detect if going up/down*: Similarly to ZUPT method, we can remove the position error in altitude on the Kalman filter while the IMU remains at the same floor. Detecting if the IMU is going up/down can be accomplished by a two-condition algorithm which takes into account the local variance of the estimated position in altitude and its magnitude change within the last period of time (e.g. one second).
- *Heading drift reduction*: Heading drift still remains despite using ZUPT since the heading error is unobservable. However, the majority of buildings have dominant

directions defined by the orientation of their corridors and, a person walks most of the time along straight-line paths parallel to these dominant directions. Therefore, assuming the person walks in indoor buildings we can implement the so-called heuristic drif elimination (HDE) proposed by Borenstein and Ojeda or a more recently work by A. Jimenez et al. improving the previous one (iHDE) [20] and [21], respectively.

4 Evaluation

The pedestrian tracker using low-cost Bluetooth inertial sensors has been developed on Android, a mobile operating platform which nowadays controls most of the smartphones. As a way to verify its behaviour under a real environment it has been tested using a commercial smartphone which processes the raw IMU data in real time.

4.1 Experimental Setup

For the experimental evaluation we conducted real trials at the building of the Faculty of Engineering (Deusto University) in the city of Bilbao, whose floor map is shown in Figure 2. This five floor building is approximately 112 m long and 62 m wide. The approximately 800 m long path followed goes by three floors, starting in the 5*th* floor (at 16 m height), going down to the 3*rd* floor (at 8 m height) by the stairs, once more going down to the 2*nd* floor (at 4 m height), and finally returning to the starting point going up to the 5*th* floor. In the experiments the target is a person who walks more or less at constant speed, and carries the foot-mounted IMU detailed in section 2 and the Galaxy Nexus GT-i9250 smartphone. This smartphone incorporates the Broadcom BCM4330 single chip device providing with Bluetooth *4.0+HS* connectivity among others handheld wireless systems, and a 1.5 GHz dual core ARM-based processor which implements the pedestrian tracker algorithm in real time.

4.2 Results

We do not aim to give a precise comparison of different PDR heuristics with their optimal parameters. Rather, we want to evaluate the performance of a custom-built foot-mounted pedestrian tracker based on commercially available low-cost inertial sensors connected via Bluetooth to a smartphone which processed the raw IMU data in real time. All position estimates are relative to the initial position and heading, therefore a small error early in the path would have a significant effect later on.

Figure 2 shows the horizontal and altitude plots from our three implementations: ZUPT heuristic, ZUPT and going up/down heuristics, and ZUPT, going up/down and iHDE heuristics. All of them share the same framework, the standard inertial PDR method described in [6], using the initial transformation matrix provided by the gathered initial accelerometers data, and removing the gyro bias computed at the beginning of the trial. Acceleration and gyro data rate at 200 Hz and 100 Hz, respectively, gave the best results. Lower data rates degraded the performance, but higher rates did not bring

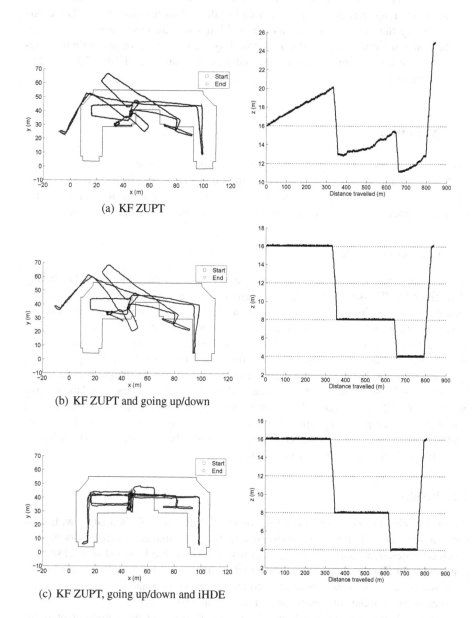

(a) KF ZUPT

(b) KF ZUPT and going up/down

(c) KF ZUPT, going up/down and iHDE

Fig. 2. Plots for a 800 m long walk through the Faculty of Engineering at the University of Deusto. Each pair of plots shows the horizontal position (left) and altitude (right) for (a) KF with ZUPT heuristic, (b) KF with ZUPT and going up/down heuristics, and (c) KF with ZUPT, going up/down and iHDE heuristics.

any noticeable improvement. The KF implementation with heading drift and altitude error elimination always provide the best results. As a way to compute the accuracy of the pedestrian tracker, the route started and finished at the same point. Therefore, the accumulated positioning error is computed as the 3D Euclidean distance between the starting and finishing positions with respect to the total traveled distance. Thus, applying iHDE and going up/down heuristics, the total accumulated error is 2 m, i.e. 0.25% of the total traveled distance. The results were reasonable (accumulated error lower than 1%) but would improve by testing different environments with different users, which probably need better tuning the KF and the parameters of the implemented heuristics.

5 Conclusions

The discussion in this paper has given an overview of the possibilities of smartphones to be used as the target of a wirelessly IMU-based positioning system. Firstly, we have described a custom-built foot-mounted IMU based on commercially available low-cost inertial sensors to be connected wirelessly to a smartphone. Secondly, we have demonstrated the capability of smartphones to process raw IMU data in real time which are received wirelessly up to 200 Hz data rate. Finally, we have tested the pedestrian tracker with commercial devices in a five floor building achieving an accumulated error lower than 1%. As future work we are going to fuse the raw IMU data with the smartphone sensors data such as WiFi and GPS trying to provide accurate and long-time navigation.

References

[1] Harle, R.: A survey of indoor inertial positioning systems for pedestrians. IEEE Communications Surveys and Tutorials 15, 1281–1293 (2013)
[2] Gu, Y., Lo, A., Niemegeers, I.: A survey of indoor positioning systems for wireless personal networks. IEEE Communications Surveys & Tutorials 11, 13–32 (2009)
[3] Zampella, F., Bahillo, A., Prieto, J., Jimenez, A.R., Seco, F.: Pedestrian navigation fusing inertial and rss/tof measurements with adaptive movement/measurement models: Experimental evaluation and theoretical limits. Sensors and Actuators A: Physical 203, 249–260 (2013)
[4] Zhang, K., Zhu, M., Retscher, G., Wu, F., Cartwright, W.: Three-dimension indoor positioning algorithms using an integrated rfid/ins system in multi-storey buildings. In: Gartner, G., Rehrl, K. (eds.) Location Based Services and TeleCartography II - From Sensor Fusion to Context Models. Lecture Notes in Geoinformation and Cartography, pp. 373–386. Springer, Heidelberg (2008)
[5] Ruiz, A.R.J., Granja, F.S., Honorato, J.C.P., Rosas, J.I.G.: Accurate pedestrian indoor navigation by tightly coupling foot-mounted imu and rfid measurements. IEEE T. Instrumentation and Measurement 61, 178–189 (2012)
[6] Fischer, C., Sukumar, P.T., Hazas, M.: Tutorial: Implementing a pedestrian tracker using inertial sensors. IEEE Pervasive Computing 12, 17–27 (2013)
[7] Analog Devices: Digital Accelerometer. ADXL345 Datasheet, pp. 1–40 (2013)
[8] InvenSense Inc.: Digital Gyroscope. ITG-3200 Product Specification, pp. 1–40 (2010)
[9] Honeywell International Inc.: Digital Compass. HMC5883L Datasheet, pp. 1–20 (2010)
[10] GitHub: Tutorial: Building an AHRS using the SparkFun "9DOF Razor IMU" or "9DOF Sensor Stick". HMC5883L Datasheet (accessed May 2014)

[11] Nilsson, J.O., Skog, I., Handel, P.: Performance characterisation of foot-mounted zupt-aided inss and other related systems. In: International Conference on Indoor Positioning and Indoor Navigation (IPIN), pp. 1–7. IEEE (2010)

[12] El-Sheimy, N., Niu, X.: The Promise of MEMS to the Navigation Community. Inside GNSS, 6+ (2007)

[13] Munoz, D., Heirich, O., Khinder, M., Robertson, P.: Optimal sampling frequency and bias error modeling for foot-mounted IMUs. In: International Conference on Indoor Positioning and Indoor Navigation (IPIN), pp. 1–9. IEEE (2013)

[14] Faulkner, W., Alwood, R., Taylor, D., Bohlin, J.: Altitude accuracy while tracking pedestrians using a boot-mounted IMU. In: Position Location and Navigation Symposium (PLANS), pp. 90–96. IEEE (2010)

[15] Ladetto, Q., Seeters, J., Sokolowski, S., Sagan, Z., Merminod, B.: Digital Magnetic Compass and Gyroscope for Dismounted Soldier Position and Navigation. Sensors and Electronics Technology Panel, NATO Research and Technology Agency Sensors, pp. 1–15 (2002)

[16] Stirling, R.: Development of a Pedestrian Navigation System Using Shoe Mounted Sensors. University of Alberta, Department of Mechanical Engineering (2004)

[17] Foxlin, E.: Pedestrian tracking with shoe-mounted inertial sensors. IEEE Comput. Graph. Appl. 25, 38–46 (2005)

[18] Feliz, R., Zalama, E., Garcia-Bermejo, G., Bohlin, J.: Pedestrian Tracking Using Inertial Sensors. Journal Physical Agents 3, 35–43 (2009)

[19] Jimenez, A.R., Granja, F.S., Prieto, J.C., Rosas, J.I.G.: Indoor pedestrian navigation using an ins/ekf framework for yaw drift reduction and a foot-mounted imu. In: Workshop on Positioning, Navigation and Communication, pp. 135–143. IEEE (2010)

[20] Borenstein, J., Ojeda, L.: Heuristic drift elimination for personnel tracking systems. Journal of Navigation 63, 591–606 (2010)

[21] Jimenez, A., Seco, F., Zampella, F., Prieto, J., Guevara, J.: Improved Heuristic Drift Elimination (iHDE) for pedestrian navigation in complex buildings. In: International Conference on Indoor Positioning and Indoor Navigation (IPIN), pp. 1–8. IEEE (2011)

A Combined Approach to the Problem of Opening a Door with an Assistant Mobile Robot

Javier Moreno, Dani Martínez, Marcel Tresanchez, Merce Teixidó,
Jordi Casanovas, and Jordi Palacín

Department of Computer Science and Industrial Engineering, University of Lleida,
Jaume II, 69, 25001 Lleida, Spain
{jmoreno,dmartinez,mtresanchez,mteixido,palacin}@diei.udl.cat,
jcasanovas@quimica.udl.cat

Abstract. This paper proposes a combined approach to the problem of opening a door with a mobile robot. In one hand, the detection of the doors and the doors handles is performed by means of a dedicated onboard camera. In the other hand, the mechanical interaction with the door handle is performed by means of a DC motor. Both devices have been designed in order to be included in the design of an assistive mobile robot. This combined proposal has been tested in a university facility where the contrast between the texture colors used in the structural elements has simplified the implementation of the visual detection procedures.

Keywords: assistive mobile robot, opening door action, door detection, doors handles detection.

1 Introduction

The problem of manipulating objects with geometrical constraints and performing actions such as opening a door has been addressed by many research works. For example, in [1] the proposal was a rescue robot equipped with a manipulator which is used for locate the door handle. In [2] a manipulator device that is able to detect a door handle, open the door and passing through was presented. Alternatively, in [3] the proposal was to learn the movements of door handle in order to reduce the forces applied.

The problem of opening a door has three main different limitations [4]. The first one is that conventional environments are designed for human interaction. The second one is the limited ability and force of the robots. The third one is the uncertainty of the environmental parameters which difficult automatic robotized operation.

This paper proposes the analysis of the problem of using a mobile robot in order to open a conventional door designed to be handled by humans. The new contribution of this paper is the development of a specialized electromechanical device that can be attached to an assistive mobile robot.

R. Hervás et al. (Eds.): UCAmI 2014, LNCS 8867, pp. 9–12, 2014.
© Springer International Publishing Switzerland 2014

2   The Problem of Opening a Door

The problem of opening a door has to deal with mobile robot constrains, types or door handles, the automatic detection of the door handle, the variability in their positioning parameters, and the torque required to open a door. In this paper the proposal is addressing the problem of opening a door in the case of using an assistive mobile robot with a circular base and a thin body. This mechanical structure simplifies the application and development of additional specialized mechanical devices.

2.1   Types of Door Handles

This section proposes a preliminary segmentation of the different door handles types found in different public buildings and flats in Lleida, Spain. The handles can be classified according their shape in three main different groups (Table 1): type A in the cases of having a stick, type B in the cases of having a circular handling, and type C in the cases of sliding doors. According the exploration performed, type A handle is the most frequent (93%) and the subtype A1 the most common (55.8%).

Figure 1 show the parameters that identify the location and position of a type A handle in a conventional door where h is the distance from the floor to the door handle, b is the distance between the door handle and next blocking object, and c is the distance between the door handle and the next transversal wall. Both parameters b and c defines the space available for mobile robot maneuvering.

Table 1. Types of door handles considered and frequency of appearance

Types	A1 	A2 	A3 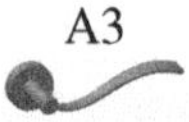	A4 	B 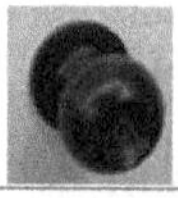	C 
Freq.	55.8%	23.3%	11.6%	2.3%	7.0%	0.0%

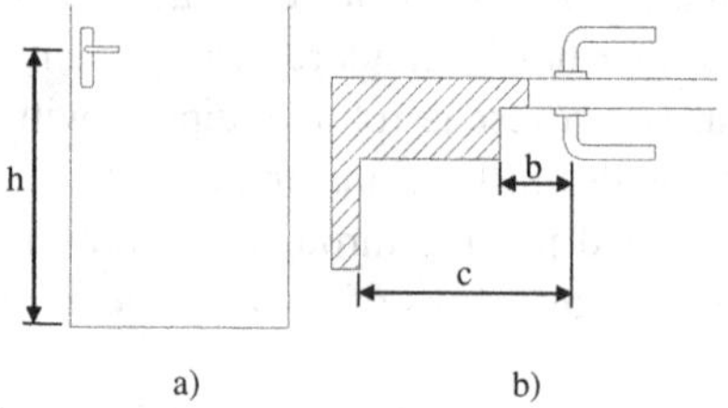

a)   b)

Fig. 1. Position of door handles, a) Front view, b) Top view

An analysis of the most frequent values of such parameters was realized. The parameter h can have values in a range from 99 cm. to 103 cm. The most frequent value in the cases analyzed was 101 cm. The parameter b can have values in a wide range with 4 cm as the lowest value and with the majority of the values located in distances higher than 35 cm (50% of the cases). Finally, the lowest value of the parameter c was 6 cm and the majority of the values were located in a distance greater than 34 cm (75% of the cases).

3   Proposed Device to Open a Door

3.1   Mechanical Device

Figure 8 shows the detail of the main part of the mechanical device proposed in order to hold a handle and open a door. This mechanical device offers at least two mechanical contact points with the handle and is directly powered with a geared DC motor that can be used to turn the handle in clockwise and anticlockwise directions. The mechanical device contains a hole for an onboard camera that will be used to control the mobile robot maneuvering while approaching to the door handle.

The effectiveness of this mechanical device requires the alignment of the center of rotation of the DC motor with the center of rotation of the handle in order to take advantage of all the torque applied by the DC motor.

Fig. 2. Mechanical procedure

3.2   Automatic Detection of the Door and the Handle

The problem of the automatic detection of the door and the door handle will be limited to the environment defined by the Polytechnic School of the University of Lleida, Spain. In this paper, the automatic detection will be performed by analyzing the image acquired by the camera attached to the mechanical device proposed to open a door. The assumption is that this camera (and the mechanical device) will be normally pointed to the ground until the mechanical device is activated or released.

The proposed procedure for object segmentation is based on a manual selection of two texture areas: door and not door (floor and walls) in one representative image. The texture color information of these two classes is represented in a three dimensional histogram with 32 bins per color. Figure 5 shows a combined lock up table (LUT) that resumes the segmentation information of the two classes selected. The table has 32x32x32 (32,768) bins which converts any RGB color intensity combination in the classes: door, not door, and not classified. Finally, the procedure proposed to detect a door handle is based on the definition of a morphological filter adapted to the characteristic shape of the handles: a thin vertical body and a thin horizontal stick. Figure 6 shows the door handle detection results obtained with different images analyzed.

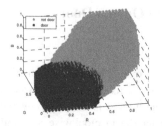

Fig. 3. RGB Classification LUT

Fig. 4. Detection results with a morphological filter

4   Conclusions

This paper addresses the problem of opening a door with a mobile robot. The paper proposes a mechanical device with an onboard camera in order to detect and guide the activation of the mechanical device. A prototype device has been applied at the Polytechnic School; University of Lleida, Spain where the texture colors of the floor, walls and doors have simplified the segmentation of the doors and door handles in acquired images by defining a histogram based segmentation LUT. Finally, a morphological filter has been proposed in order to detect de handles of the doors in the images. Future work will be focused on attaching the proposed device to an assistive mobile robot and on validating the combined system.

References

1. Kobayashi, S., Kobayashi, Y., Yamamoto, Y., Watasue, T., Ohtsubo, Y., Inoue, T., Yasuda, M., Takamori, T.: Development of a door opening system on rescue robot for search "UMRS-2007". In: Proceedings of SICE Annual Conference, Tokyo, pp. 2062–2065 (2008)
2. Nagatani, K., Yuta, S.: An experiment on opening-door-behavior by an autonomous mobile robot with a manipulator. In: Proceedings of IEEE/RSJ International Conference on Intelligent Robots and Systems (Human Robot Interaction and Cooperative Robots), Pittsburgh, PA, vol. 2, pp. 45–50 (1995)
3. Niemeyer, G., Slotine, J.-J.E.: A simple strategy for opening an unknown door. In: Proceedings of IEEE International Conference on Robotics and Automation, Albuquerque, NM, vol. 2, pp. 1448–1453 (1997)
4. Chung, W., Rhee, C., Shim, Y., Lee, H., Park, S.: Door-Opening Control of a Service Robot Using the Multifingered Robot Hand. IEEE Transactions on Industrial Electronics 56(10), 3975–3984 (2009)

Mobile Physical Rehabilitation of Patients through Intelligence Devices

Vladimir Villarreal, Abel Silvera, and Lilia Muñoz

Emergent Computational Technologies Research Lab (GITCE)
Technological University of Panama, David, Chiriquí, Panamá
{vladimir.villarreal,abel.silvera,lilia.munoz}@utp.ac.pa

Abstract. That develop solutions that facilitate the development of therapy from home are a compelling factor in our social environment. In our country mobile technology is important as a support tool in the rehabilitation of people. This paper presents a proposal that allows the development of an application that helps develop a patient physiotherapy activities, from your home, offering analysis and recommendation of your doctor. The application generates reports of the results of these physical activities both for the patient and the doctor. We integrate an ontological classification of mobile devices and a previous study of the impact of the development of this technology in our country.

Keywords: web services, software development, human computer interaction, mobile users interfaces design.

1   Introduction

Mobile devices evolve and are capable of running more demanding processes, what has unleashed an endless applications for different presentations of such devices, jumping to solve problems in different fields, such as academic, business and even staff. Given this, questions arise such as: Which advantages bring all this type of technological progress in Panama and the growing availability of Internet connection? and Are exploited in the sector health in Panama?

It is possible that the almost exponential advance mobile technology, do not allow to easily see the advantages of this mobile technology can provide at any given time. That is why that is necessary to determine the mobile technological advance in Panama, and thus have an idea clearer on how to get the most out of all these technologies, the improvement of mobile components, which help in coverage or supported medical assistance in an area not very common as it is physical therapy. Given this, we will notice the quantification of the Panamanian population who own a mobile phone, or otherwise has a smart device, which will facilitate your life, according to your need [1].

We can notice, that the realization of a mobile app of this type relating to health, could be a good way of responses from people, who need or require attention medical, since is observed at the national level there is a good percentage of people who have cell phones. remarkable that a smart device will not replace the functions that a specialist doctor, but our main goal is not to replace it, but that the device will help the patient or user, which can do exercises in the right way, and that such exercises be registered so that the patient can keep the results, in order to then have a record of the repetitions performed and which exercises. All this will happen, as assistance to the patient, given

R. Hervás et al. (Eds.): UCAmI 2014, LNCS 8867, pp. 13–16, 2014.
© Springer International Publishing Switzerland 2014

that the service of physiotherapy in Panama is composed of a gym that allows the patient to the development of treatment techniques for stimulating the movement of ambulation. A detail of the technical services held in 2012, in order to be able to determine how much population is the beneficiary of these medical processes, and many professionals are of domestic origin, who is trained to do this is shown below.

2   Development of the Application Following MoMo Framework

This application will be developed following the framework for the development of mobile applications MoMo [2][3]. The proposed development cycle allows us to obtain different functional prototypes that define each element or module that make up the final application (Figure 1). The steps of the development framework are following: Selection of the module to be applied, Definition of design patterns, Definition of functional patterns, Ontological relationship of each module, The layers relate to their respective modules, Determination of the relation between layers, Integration of all the elements, Evaluation of the prototype and Redesign of the elements for the generation of a new prototype.

To facilitate the development of the proposed application, we rely on the ontological model MoMOntology [4] [5] presenting a classification of all possible elements to be taken into account when developing mobile solutions can be adapted to any mobile device. To model the different services and elements that make up the framework, we will define each of the elements involved in the development of languages of the semantic web (OWL)-based software architecture.

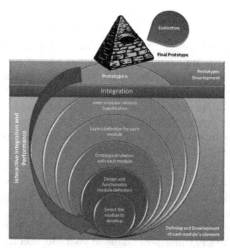

Fig. 1. Development of the application based into MOMO framework structure

Based on the steps that make up the development of the ontologies defined by METHONTOLOGY [6] [7] and for a better understanding of each of the elements of the application, we have based the development on the classification of mobile devices featuring MoMOntology. This ontology classified the devices according to your hardware, software, communication or network capabilities. These three elements are the aspects that define the functionality of the application.

3   Proposal for Mobile Rehabilitation of Patients

After evaluated all the technical and social aspects, is proposed to develop a mobile application based on the Android platform, so it works on devices with version 4.1 of Android "Jelly Bean", that has an interface that allows to know the General patient information, such as name, cedula, among others as shown in Figure 2 (a).

Given these facts, the patient will be another interface, which will ask the patient, to determine what type of need of rehabilitation is having, so the application applicable to show the patient how the exercises I should do (Figure 2 (b)). At the time that the patient knows the exercise which should make the application will define what magnitude or degree of exercise, for which applicable to indicate how many series have to do (Figure 2 (c)).

Given this device shall be in a data collection interface, counted repetitions of the exercise, since thus will tell the patient if he has managed to make the number of repetitions needed. When the patient finishes make the series or exercise routine (Figure 2 (d)), the application will show you a new interface in its results, and will be stored in real time, from the time that started the session until the moment that ended. Previously the patient should indicate at the time of filling their data, how much was the period that the specialist recommended him to do therapy. This will be done, because the application will also serve as an Assistant and remind the patient, periodically, the moment that should begin to make the session.

This application will be recommended to the patient by the professional physical therapist, who treats you at its first meeting, since depending on the degree of rehabilitation, can the professional indicate the frequency with which must attend the Centre to see the progress of the person, through outcomes remove device.

This will serve as a tool to professional, and at the same time as Assistant to the patient, since sessions have considerable economic value, and if at a certain moment it would require 20 sessions, ideally, with this application you can reduce the number of sessions, halved, and so be able to generate savings to the patient, which could be used in other treatments.

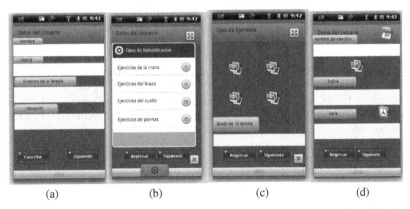

(a)   (b)   (c)   (d)

Fig. 2. a. Capture of patient data, b. capture the type of exercise, c. selection of grade or difficulty of therapy, d. capture of data resulting from the exercise: series and routine

4   Conclusions

The development of the proposed application is based on the framework for the development of applications mobile MoMo, which defines as graphical interfaces are implemented to develop applications for monitoring of patients, an ontological classification of the possible elements used and distribution in all the programmable elements in an application layer. Are confident that once implemented, our application will benefit a large number of people who often cannot attend a rehabilitation session, offering an alternate tool to this problem. There are technical, communication capabilities and operations; we have to integrate them into a single functional application and which will grow with time.

References

1. Burgos, D.A., Echeverry, H.J.: Estado del Arte del Uso de Aplicaciones en Dispositivos Móviles en el Área de Medicina, Colombia (2012), http://recursosbiblioteca.utp.edu.co/tesisd/textoyanexos/0053B957.pdf
2. Villarreal, V., Laguna, J., López, S., Fontecha, J., Fuentes, C., Hervás, R., de Ipiña, D.L., Bravo, J.: A Proposal for Mobile Diabetes Self-control: Towards a Patient Monitoring Framework. In: Omatu, S., Rocha, M.P., Bravo, J., Fernández, F., Corchado, E., Bustillo, A., Corchado, J.M. (eds.) IWANN 2009, Part II. LNCS, vol. 5518, pp. 870–877. Springer, Heidelberg (2009)
3. Villarreal, V., Bravo, J., Hervás, R., Fuentes, C., Laguna, J., Fdez, A.D., Sánchez, C., López, S.: Diabetes Patients' Care based on Mobile Monitoring. In: IADIS International Conference, Applied Computing 2009, Rome, Italy (2009)
4. Villarreal, V., Hervás, R., Fdez, A.D., Bravo, J.: Applying ontologies in the development of patient mobile monitoring framework. In: 2nd International Conference on e-Health and Bioengineering, EHB 2009. IEEE, Constata (2009)
5. Bravo, J., López-de-Ipiña, D., Fuentes, C., Hervás, R., Peña, R., Vergara, M., Casero, G.: Enabling NFC Technology for Supporting Chronic Diseases: A Proposal for Alzheimer Caregivers. In: Aarts, E., Crowley, J.L., de Ruyter, B., Gerhäuser, H., Pflaum, A., Schmidt, J., Wichert, R. (eds.) AmI 2008. LNCS, vol. 5355, pp. 109–125. Springer, Heidelberg (2008)
6. Azpírez, J.C., Gómez-Pérez, A., Lozano-Tello, A., Pinto, S.: (ONTO)2 Agent: An ontology-based WWW broker to select ontologies. In: Workshop on Applications of Ontologies and Problem-Solving Methods (ECAI 1998), Brighton, UK (1998)
7. Fernandez-Lopez, M.: Overview of Methodology for Building Ontologies. In: Workshop on Ontologies and Problem-Solving Methods: Lessons Learned and Future Trends, IJCAI 1999 (1999)

Using Ambient Intelligence
to Improve Public Transport Accessibility

Carmelo R. García, Alexis Quesada-Arencibia, Teresa Cristóbal,
Gabino Padrón, Ricardo Pérez, and Francisco Alayón

Institute for Cybernetic Science and Technology
Department of Informatics and Systems
University of Las Palmas de Gran Canaria
{rgarcia,aquesada,gpadron,rperez,falayon}@dis.ulpgc.es

Abstract. This paper described how ubiquitous computing and ambient intelligence can be applied in order to make more accessible the public road transport for people with special needs. The main goal of the proposed system is to assist to this kind of people during the trips. This system is autonomous and does not affect the common operations carried out in the public transport infrastructure; it provides useful data obtained transparently, using different sensors installed in the infrastructure.

Keywords: ambient intelligence, ubiquitous computing, ubiquitous data management, intelligent transport systems.

1   Introduction

In general, existing public transport information services consider mostly users with "normal" physical and cognitive abilities. However, people with special needs, like disable and elderly, need proper information in order to facilitate them the access to the transport network. For these groups of people, this information is critical in the case of wide transit system and dynamic transport network. Proper information implies multimedia information because this kind of information is the only understandable for these groups of people.

In the bibliography we can find many references about the requirements of the computer information for persons with specials needs [1, 2, 3] and descriptions about modification of software systems in order to improve the information accessibility (for example verbal description) and redefinitions of public databases to include useful information for this group of people (for example places with wheelchair accessibility) [4]. Many cases of information services for person with special needs in the public transport world have been reported in the bibliography [5, 6, 7], but these cases are not general solutions from different points of view (group of people affected, kinds of service provided, transportation mode, etc.). The main goal of this work is to describe how the ubiquitous computing paradigm and more specifically Ambient Intelligence can be used to develop proper and integrated information services for this group of people, assuming realistic technology scenarios of the public transport network infrastructures.

R. Hervás et al. (Eds.): UCAmI 2014, LNCS 8867, pp. 17–20, 2014.
© Springer International Publishing Switzerland 2014

2   How the Ambient Intelligence Paradigm Can Help to Improve the Public Transport Accessibility

In relation to the information accessibility, Emiliani [8] describes the main benefits provided by ambient intelligence and the challenges associated. The first is related to interactive devices; these will range from mobile personal devices to fixed and specialized devices placed in the infrastructure of the environment, providing these devices functionalities specially adapted to the user needs (voice synthesis, vibration warnings, touch screen, etc.). The second benefit is related to interaction model; this must explicit, based on the context awareness, in order to anticipate the user preferences. Finally, the third benefit consists of services: these are provided by applications with a high level of mobility, ubiquity and personal adaption, aiding to the people in the daily activities. To achieve these benefits, challenges such as: relegated interaction, to balance manual control versus automatic control, capacity to anticipate the user needs, security and privacy.

In this work we study how to provide an intelligent environment in public transport vehicles. The main goal of the system is to facilitate the access to the public road transport to people with special needs, being this goal very important for public transport operators and authorities. To achieve this objective, two important aspects must be taken into account: the safety of the traveller and the usability and accessibility of the system in order to provide a proper ambient to this kind of people.

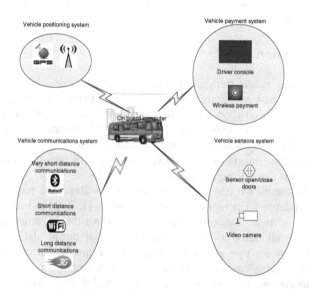

Fig. 1. Main elements of the vehicle used by the on route guidance system

3   System Description

The proposed system provides an on route guidance service for passengers with mobility problems, such as: elderly people and passengers with wheelchairs. A general description of the system is made in this section. This explanation is based on the required hardware/software elements, the main entities (ontology) and the working principles.

Nowadays, according to the real-time information requirements established by transport authorities and organisms for traveller information, the onboard equipment plays a main role in that kind of information system. A typical configuration covers the following elements: on board computer that controls all the devices of the equipment, the positioning system to provide information about the position and velocity of the vehicle, the on board payment system and finally the sensors system to control the main parameters related to safety of the vehicle (open doors sensors and cameras) or environment (for example temperature and atmosphere pollution). The main elements of the proposed system are shown in Figure 1. The architecture is a layered structure formed by four levels. The Infrastructure Level that is responsible to connect to the infrastructure installed in the public transport infrastructure. The Communication Level that is responsible of the data communication between applications (information providers and clients). The Control Level that is responsible for synchronizing the execution of services and the access to data. The Services Level where all the information providers are executed.

In order to provide interoperable services in public transport, the data models play important role. In Europe, there are some standard recommendations for the public transport reported by the European Standardization (CEN) about different aspects of the public transport. For our purposes, the recommendation named Transmodel [9] has been used, specifically the recommendations about the representation of the elements of the transport infrastructure, specifically attributes related to physical accessibility of vehicles and sites (stops and stations) and accessibility related to information services for passengers with special needs. The main entities used by the system ontology are the following: Passenger, Vehicle, Route, Bus-Stop, Interest-Point, Resource-Infrastructure, User-Device, On-Route-Server and User-Client.

In this paragraph the main aspects of the working principles of this on route travel assistant for people with mobility problem, such as people who need a wheelchair to move. In the explanation, in order to facilitate the understanding of the presented system, the different concepts introduced above are written in brackets. The traveller (Passenger), using an app (Client) executing on his mobile phone (User-Device), connects to an information service (On-Route-Service) of the transport company or transport authority, asking for information about how to travel from one geographical location to another. The information service, running in the Service Level using the resources of the Infrastructure Level, provides to the traveller app information about: the nearest stop (Stop), the line to take (Route), the time of the bus (Vehicle) adapted for passengers with wheelchairs, the stops along the journey and the destination stop (Stop). The traveller app registers the identification of the route and the bus to take, the stops along the route and the last stop made by the vehicle. This information is obtained from the service running on Infrastructure Layer.

When the selected bus arrives to the bus stop (Bus-Stop), the traveller app connects to the vehicle information services provider (On-Route-Service) to request an instance of guidance service. Identifying the kind of app, the vehicle information service provider knows that the passenger has special needs, specifically mobility problems, and therefore it actives special facilities in different elements of the system:

4   Conclusions

The main conclusion of this work is that the paradigm of ubiquitous computing and ambient intelligence can help us to solve traditional problem and to face new challenges in the field of the public transport, improving the level and quality of mobility of the citizens. To illustrate this statement, a guidance service for people with special needs has been presented. The system can autonomously control all the relevant events and elements in order to make a safety and friendly trip, identifying the relevant points of the route, providing information to the traveller using multimedia information and controlling the different element of the vehicle to ensure the safety of the passenger.

References

1. Geehan, T.: Improving Transportaion Information: Design Guidelines for Making Travel More Accessible (TP 12705E). Transportation Development Centre Transport Canada (1996)
2. Duvarci, Y., Yigitcanlar, T.: An Integrated Modeling Approach for the Transportation Disadvantaged. Journal of Urban Planning and Development 133(3), 188–200 (2007)
3. Mitchell, C.G.B., Ling Suen, S.: Urban Travel, Intelligent Transportation Systems, and the Safety of Elderly and Disabled Travelers. Journal of Urban Technology 5(1), 17–43 (1998)
4. Fink, J., Kobsa, A.: Adaptable and Adaptive Information Provision for All Users, Including Disabled and Elderly People. New Review of Hypermedia and Multimedia 4, 163–188 (1998)
5. Barbeau, S.J., et al.: The travel assistant device: Utilizing gps-enabled mobile phones to aid transit riders with special needs. In: Proc. 15th World Congress on Intelligent Transportation Systems, New York (2008)
6. Sánchez, J.H., Oyarzún, C.A.: Mobile audio assistance in bus transportation for the blind. In: Proc. 7th International Conference Series on Disability, Virtual Reality and Associated Technologies with ArtAbilitation, Maia, Portugal (2008)
7. Zhou, H., Hou, K., Zuo, D., Li, J.: Intelligent Urban Public Transportation for Accessibility Dedicated to People with Disabilities. Sensors 12, 10678–10692 (2012)
8. Emiliani, P.L., Stephanidis, C.: Universal access to ambient intelligence environments: Opportunities and challenges for people with disabilities. IBM Systems Journal 44(3), 605–619 (2005)
9. European Committee Standardization: Reference Data Model for Public Transport, Tech. Rep. CEN TC278 (2005), http://www.cenorm.be

A Social Robot in a Tourist Environment

Diego Nieto, Alexis Quesada-Arencibia,
Carmelo R. García, and Roberto Moreno-Díaz

Institute for Cybernetic Science and Technology
Department of Informatics and Systems
University of Las Palmas de Gran Canaria, Spain
diego.nieto.m@outlook.com,
{aquesada,rgarcia,rmorenoj}@dis.ulpgc.es

Abstract. In this paper, we have focused on applying robotics as a social element and an intermediary in tourism. To that end, a system has been developed that will benefit the tourist experience. To do this, every room of the hotel would have a low-cost social robot, a Karotz. This robot interacts orally with the tourist to provide him or her with news about the hotel and the best tourism activities for the user. The components of the robot were used during the development to make communication flows natural. This has enabled us to create a social robot that covers a need faced by the tourist industry. The developed prototype shows that this is a plausible field of application for social robotics.

Keywords: social robotics, robot applications, human-robot interaction, social interaction.

1 Introduction

Social robotics is a field of information technology that is still in its infancy. However, we are starting to see the appearance of the first systems that focus on interacting simply and clearly with human beings for specific tasks. We can find clear examples of social robots in the Genibo Robot Dog, Zoomer Interactive Robot Dog or Karotz [1].

1.1 Social Robots: A New Approach to Tourism

If social robotics is a totally open field, robotics applied to tourism is even more so. We propose taking a step forward in this field with a social robotics-based system aimed at tourism. To date, hotels and tourism companies have interacted with their customers in very basic ways, degrading the tourist experience as they consider the hotel and the companies offering tourism activities as distant, unrelated elements with which they have no interaction.

To overcome this barrier, we propose using robotics as the central component of interaction between hotels and tourism companies and tourists [2].

R. Hervás et al. (Eds.): UCAmI 2014, LNCS 8867, pp. 21–24, 2014.
© Springer International Publishing Switzerland 2014

1.2   The Final System with Karotz

The robot we have selected for this Project is Karotz, as it meets a set of compulsory requisites when considering using robots on a medium and large scale. These static, rabbit-shaped robots have certain functions that made them highly suitable for this project. The first of these features is their capacity for spoken communicating in up to four different languages. To this end, they have the TTS[1] and ASR[2] systems that enable them to communicate orally almost any text or phrase that fits a pre-established pattern. The second fundamental piece is that applications can be developed for the robot that can be installed in their system, so the behaviour of the robot can be adapted depending on our specific purpose. The third factor is that it can connect to the Internet to transmit data from the applications that have been installed. Finally, the cost is very low, less than $100, making it suitable for buying in large quantities.

The final system developed proposes a robot as the element that acts as intermediary between the tourist and the tourism activities companies. To attain this, there would be a Karotz robot in every hotel room connected to the Internet and fitted with the tourism application developed. This way, each user can choose from different actions such as receiving notification from the hotel they are staying in and discovering the activities offered by the hotel and nearby tourism activity companies. All these actions take place by voice communication to make the human-robot interaction as natural as possible.

2   Development and Design

Using robotics as a social element in tourism involves developing specific applications for this area. Two applications were developed to build the system described, the server application and the robot application.

2.1   Dialogue Management

Spoken interaction is something that is still in the development stage in robots. Natural language obviously still has a long way to go but the Karotz social robot is fitted with advanced tools – TTS and ASR [3]. Both can work in English, Spanish, French and German, making them an ideal tool for tourists.

The application uses the API that Karotz provides for developers. This API has been used to implement the communication logic with the server, which is divided in two:

- Delivery of phrases. For delivering phrases, Karotz the robot uses the Text to Speech function that converts any text into voice.
- Receiving phrases: Processing phrases is far more complex than delivering them, which is why there are certain restrictions. The Automated Speech Recognition system fitted in Karotz allows it to understand phrases with ABNF grammar.

---

[1]   This is the conversion of a text into an artificial voice in three phases: standardisation of the text, phonetic conversion and prosodic division.

[2]   This is voice recognition applying algorithms like Hidden Markov Models, Dynamic time warping or Neural Networks.

To talk to the robot, certain restrictions have to be respected for the robot to be able to understand the tourist:

- It requires a silent environment, with noise levels below 30-40 decibels.
- The user can be no more than 50 cm from the robot.
- The user must speak correctly and use a normal intonation for the robot to fit the phrase it hears to the pre-defined patterns.

2.2   Interaction Design

The interaction design is the fundamental part of the system as this is the part that determines how the robot interacts with the tourist through speech and the mobile and light elements it has. In our implementation, the ears were used to let the tourist know that the robot was communicating with the server. This way, the aim is to use gestures to tell the tourist that the robot has understood and that it is working on the tourist's request [4].

The next of the robot's functions that is used to indicate the flow of conversation are the colours that light up the robot. This is both a really simple element, but also very clear. Natural behaviour is something inherent to the human being. Thus, we could say that we are not determinist systems and that is something that we wanted to include in our interactions with the robot. To attain this, a range of phrases have been implemented in the communication flow with the same meaning.

Finally, the robot's most social element is that it can get to know you. The robot is capable of recommending tourism activities depending on the profile of the tourist. There is an algorithm in the server that interacts with the robot that makes recommendations based on the Collaborative Filtering technique [5]. This builds up an in-depth knowledge base that can be used individually or collectively by the robots in the hotel.

3   Results and Conclusions

The most important result is that we have managed to generate a social robotics-based system to enhance the tourist experience. The system as a whole has been developed for Karotz robots that, with this application up-loaded, can operate in any registered hotel. We have also managed to create a recommendation system whereby the robot can make recommendations customised to each user. From all the above, we can conclude that this system is a prototype of what we will probably find in the future, in one form or another, in most hotels. Finally, there is an evident need to continue developing these robots, especially the recognition of natural language, and to extend their use and applications for potential sectors such as tourism.

4   Future Work

There is undoubtedly a lot more work to be done for this project. The prototype developed only has certain functions available, but these could be extended with the addition of the more following services.

The development of applications on Karotz is not very scalable, so when the application reaches a certain size it starts to become unstable. Other more modern and robust robots like the Aisoy1, based on Raspberry Pi ROS[6] robotic software, would slightly improve the scalability, robustness and functionality of the services that the social robot could provide. This robot is fitted with an emotion engine that enables it to show expressions with movements of the eyes and eyebrows.

Finally, an improvement in the recommendation system would enrich the robot-user interaction further and make it better.

References

1. Hernández-Ramírez, J., Mendoza-Robaina, E.I., Quesada-Arencibia, A., Rodríguez-Rodríguez, J.C., García-Rodríguez, C.R., Moreno-Díaz Jr., R., Mendoza-Robaina, E.J.: Training Bioloid Robots for Playing Football. In: Moreno-Díaz, R., Pichler, F., Quesada-Arencibia, A. (eds.) EUROCAST 2013, Part II. LNCS, vol. 8112, pp. 333–340. Springer, Heidelberg (2013)
2. Mendoza-Robaina, E.I., Quesada-Arencibia, A., Rodríguez-Rodríguez, J.C., Hernández-Ramírez, J., García-Rodríguez, C.R., Moreno-Díaz Jr., R., Mendoza-Robaina, E.J.: Building a tourist assistant with a nao aldebaran. In: Moreno-Díaz, R., Pichler, F., Quesada-Arencibia, A. (eds.) EUROCAST 2013, Part II. LNCS, vol. 8112, pp. 326–332. Springer, Heidelberg (2013)
3. Alonso-Martín, F., Salichs, M.A.: Integration of a Voice Recognition System in a Social Robot. Cib. Syst. 42, 215–246 (2011)
4. Zaraki, A., Mazzei, D., Giuliani, M., De Rossi, D.: Designing and Evaluating a Social Gaze-Control System for a Humanoid Robot. IEEE Trans. H. Syst. 44, 157–168 (2014)
5. Chen, J.H., Chao, K.M., Shah, N.: Hybrid Recommendation System for Tourism. In: 10th IEEE International Conference on E-Business Engineering, pp. 156–161. IEEE, New York (2013)
6. Mayachita, I., Widyarini, R., Sono, H.R., Ibrahim, A.R., Adiprawita, W.: Implementation of Entertaining Robot on ROS Framework. In: 4th International Conference on Electrical Engineering and Informatics, vol. 11, pp. 380–387. Elsevier, Amsterdam (2013)

Prediction of Diabetes Mellitus
Based on Boosting Ensemble Modeling

Rahman Ali[1], Muhammad Hameed Siddiqi[1], Muhammad Idris[1],
Byeong Ho Kang[2], and Sungyoung Lee[1,*]

[1] Dept. of Computer Engineering, Kyung Hee University, Korea
[2] Dept. of Engineering and Technology, ICT, University of Tasmania, Australia
{rahmanali,siddiqi,idris,sylee}@oslab.khu.ac.kr,
byeong.Kang@utas.edu.au

Abstract. Healthcare systems provide personalized services in wide spread domains to help patients in fitting themselves into their normal activities of life. This study is focused on the prediction of diabetes types of patients based on their personal and clinical information using a boosting ensemble technique that internally uses random committee classifier. To evaluate the technique, a real set of data containing 100 records is used. The prediction accuracy obtained is 81.0% based on experiments performed in Weka with 10-fold cross validation.

Keywords: Knowledge Acquisition, Reasoning, Ensemble Modeling, Prediction, Diabetes, Boosting.

1 Introduction

Diabetes mellitus is a chronic disease that results from absolute or relative deficiency of insulin. At the Ubiquitous Computing Laboratory[1], our group is working on the development of a cloud-based clinical decision support system (CDSS) for chronic disease [1]. Currently, this system predicts diabetes in patients and gives recommendations using standard rule-based reasoning. We extends the system by predicting the diabetes using machine learning approach. Machine learning is an active research area and has extensively been used for different medical applications in general and prediction of diabetes mellitus in specific. A number of ensemble learning techniques have been proposed in literature for the diabetes mellitus summarized in Table 1.

In the literature, we found no such diabetes prediction system that predicts the diabetes from patients personal and clinical data. We propose the ensemble of AdaboostM1 with random committee to predict the diabetes types from patients personal and clinical data. The proposed method is supported by an architecture that integrates data management, learning and prediction components together to consider as an additional contribution of this study.

Rest of the paper is structured as section 2 describes the methodology, Section 3 focus on evaluation of the results and Section 4 concludes the work with future directions.

---

[*] Corresponding author.
[1] http://uclab.khu.ac.kr/

R. Hervás et al. (Eds.): UCAmI 2014, LNCS 8867, pp. 25–28, 2014.
© Springer International Publishing Switzerland 2014

Table 1. Ensemble learning approaches for the prediction of diabetes

S.No	Problem taken into account	Machine Learning-based Ensemble Methods
1	Risk forecasting for diabetes Type-2[2]	Gaussian NB, Log. Regression, K-NN, CART, Random Forests and SVM
2	Predicting the presence of diabetes[3]	SVM and BP NN
3	Predicting glucose level in diabetes data[4]	Linear and Bayesian ensemble model
4	Predicting psychosocial wellbeing of patients[5]	Multi-layer perceptron neural network model
5	Architecture for diabetes prediction system [6]	Fuzzy logic, NN and CBR
6	Predicting Type-2 diabetes[7]	Fisher linear discriminate analysis, SVM and DT
7	Predicting Type-2 diabetes [8]	Random forest and gradient boosting machine

2   Proposed Methodology

The methodology of the proposed approach is explained with the help of architecture shown in Fig. 1. The main focus of the study is 'diabetes knowledge acquisition and prediction engine' rather than each individual component of the architecture.

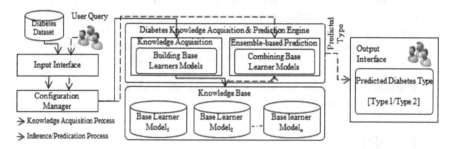

Fig. 1. Knowledge acquisition and reasoning architecture for predicting diabetes types

For the learning process, the diabetes dataset is passed through input interface to the configuration manager for preprocessing and selecting algorithms for learning. Knowledge acquisition component learns the data and stores in the knowledge base.

For the prediction process, user query is passed through the input interface to the configuration manager where an appropriate combination method (function), for combining the predictions of multiple classifiers, is selected. Based on the selection ensemble-based prediction component is activated which loads learned models from the knowledge base and combines their outputs for the final prediction sent to the output interface.

For ensemble modeling and prediction, we adapted AdaboostM1 algorithm [9] along with random committee. Random committee classifier uses random tree as the base classifier. The boosting technique repeatedly runs random tree over various distribution of training diabetes data and combines the outputs in a single random committee classifier. The final prediction is a straight average of the predictions generated by the individual random tree classifiers.

3   Results Evaluation

We acquired diabetes dataset of 100 patients records with 56 of type-1 and 44 of type-2 from a local hospital. The parameters used for evaluation are: Gender, Total Cholesterol, Triglyceride, Low-density lipoprotein, High-density lipoprotein, Occupational therapy, Physical therapy, Fasting blood sugar, Systolic blood pressure, Diastolic blood pressure, Weight, Height, Hypoglycemia, HbA1c, Diabetes type, vital-Symptoms, Sentiments, and Activities. Table 2 shows the characteristics of the dataset.

Table 2. Characteristics of the diabetes dataset

Dataset	#attributes	#instances	Missing values	#numeric attributes	#nominal attributes	#classes/instances per class	
						Type1	Type2
Diabetes	18	100	No	12	6	56	44

Experiments were performed using Intel Pentium Dual-CoreTM (2.5 GHz) desktop computer with a 4GB RAM in Weka [10] with a 10–fold cross validation scheme for splitting the data into training and testing sets. The results are shown in Table 3 and Table 4.

Table 3. Detailed accuracy (by class) of the proposed ensemble-based approach

Class	TP Rate	FP Rate	Precision	Recall	F-Measure	ROC Area
Diabetes Type 1	0.839	0.227	0.825	0.839	0.832	0.82
Diabetes Type 2	0.773	0.161	0.791	0.773	0.782	0.82
Weighted Avg.	0.81	0.198	0.81	0.81	0.81	0.82

Table 3 shows that the prediction accuracy is 81% which can be further improved by using preprocessing, feature selection and adding more data to the dataset.

Table 4. Confusion matrix for diabetes type 1 and type 2 predictions

Diabetes Type	Type 1	Type 2
Type 1	47	9
Type 2	10	34

Table 4 shows that the prediction accuracy of class type-1 is higher than the prediction accuracy of class type-2. The accuracy of class type-2 may increase if more data of type-2 is added to the training dataset.

4   Conclusion and Future Work

We have proposed a novel ensemble method (AdaboostM1 with random committee) to predict the diabetes type of patients. This work can be further extended in future by integrating it into our cloud-based CDSS system for chronic disease and adding a feedback mechanism on its top to increase the satisfaction level of the users and overall system.

Acknowledgment. This work was supported by the Industrial Strategic Technology Development Program (10035348, Development of a Cognitive Planning and Learning Model for Mobile Platforms) funded by the Ministry of Knowledge Economy (MKE, Korea).

References

[1] Hussain, M., Khattak, A.M., Khan, W.A., et al.: Cloud-based Smart CDSS for chronic diseases. Health and Technology 3(2), 153–175 (2013)

[2] Mani, S., Chen, Y., Elassy, T., Clayton, W.: Type 2 Diabetes Risk Forecasting from EMR Data using Machine learning. In: AMIA Annual Symposium Proceedings, vol. 2012, pp. 606–615. American Medical Informatics Association (2012)

[3] Zolfaghari, R.: Diagnosis of Diabetes in Female Population of Pima Indian Heritage with Ensemble of BP Neural Network and SVM. International Journal of Computational Engineering & Management 15(4) (2012)

[4] Stahl, F.: Diabetes Mellitus Glucose Prediction by Linear and Bayesian Ensemble Modeling, Sweden (2012)

[5] Narasingarao, M., Manda, R., Sridhar, G., et al.: A clinical decision support system using multilayer perceptron neural network to assess wellbeing in diabetes. The Journal of the Association of Physicians India 57, 127–133 (2009)

[6] Thirugnanam, M., Kumar, P., Srivatsan, S.V., et al.: Improving the Prediction Rate of Diabetes Diagnosis Using Fuzzy, Neural Network, Case Based (FNC) Approach. Procedia Engineering 38, 1709–1718 (2012)

[7] Chen, H., Tan, C.: Prediction of type-2 diabetes based on several element levels in blood and chemometrics. Biological Trace Element Research 147(1-3), 67–74 (2012)

[8] Sood, A., Diamond, S., Wang, S.: Type 2 Diabetes Mellitus Classification. Department of Computer Science, Stanford University (2012)

[9] Freund, Y., Schapire, R.E.: Experiments with a new boosting algorithm. In: ICML, vol. 96, pp. 148–156 (1996)

[10] Hall, M., Frank, E., Holmes, G., et al.: The WEKA data mining software: An update. ACM SIGKDD Explorations Newsletter 11(1), 10–18 (2009)

A Novel Software Architecture for Multimodal Transport Semantic Information Provision Adapted to the User Context

Asier Moreno, Asier Perallos, Diego López-de-Ipiña,
Enrique Onieva, and Itziar Salaberria

Deusto Institute of Technology (DeustoTech), University of Deusto, 48007 Bilbao, Spain
{asier.moreno,perallos,dipina,enrique.onieva,
itziar.salaberria}@deusto.es

Abstract. This paper describes a new approach for the management and exchange of information related to multimodal transportation. The publication of transport information as semantic information is established through the development of an ontology for multimodal transport and the design of a distributed architecture which allows the integration of the transport information at data level.

The advantages afforded by the proposed system due to the use of linked open data and a distributed architecture will be presented, comparing it with other existing solutions. The adequacy of the information generated in regard to the specific user's context will also be addressed.

Finally, a working solution of a semantic trip planner running on the proposed architecture will be presented, as a demonstration and validation of the system.

Keywords: Intelligent Transportation Systems, Multimodal Transport Information, Semantic Middleware, Linked Open Data, Context-aware Computing.

1   Introduction

Advances made over the last years in the application of ICT to transportation systems are extensive, constant and diverse. With regard to the software services for transport, some of the elements that have evolved the most, providing a high added value to the user, are the multimodal trip planning solutions. In this area, solutions like *Google maps* or *OpenTripPlanner* have made important progresses in facilitating trip management and planning to the users.

However, there is still a large room for improvement in this area. Existing tools are not sufficiently interoperable due to the lack of a universal and consistent format to represent transport information. Likewise, they do not take into account relevant factors, such as the user's context. Moreover, in most cases these planning tools are closed so the access to its information becomes very costly.

This paper proposes a novel software architecture to address the limitations encountered incorporating innovative technologies such as semantic middleware, context-awareness computing or linked open data which, however, have already been successfully tested in other application areas.

R. Hervás et al. (Eds.): UCAmI 2014, LNCS 8867, pp. 29–36, 2014.
© Springer International Publishing Switzerland 2014

The article is divided into four main sections. First, the state of the art is set with regard to the technologies and knowledge areas covered in the proposed solution. The following points (sections 3 and 4) develop the solution, detailing its components, functional characteristics and software architecture. The system is then validated by the deployment of a trip planning solution running on actual transport data. Finally, conclusions and future work derived from the experimentation analysis are given.

2   State of the Art

Intelligent Transportation Systems (ITS) can be defined as a set of applications within computer science, electronics and communications aimed at improving mobility, security and transport productivity, optimizing the use of infrastructures and energy consumption and improving the capacity of the transport systems [1].

Within ITS field, this work is focused on providing enriched transport information to the user, through the integration of information sources and the generation of new knowledge. Research carried out on these concepts [2,3] has been instrumental for the emergence of Advanced Traveler Information Systems (ATIS), being journey planning applications such as Google Transit[1] or Moveuskadi[2] in the private field or OpenTripPlanner[3] as free software, key software applications in this subject.

The aforementioned applications use the General Transit Feed Specification (GTFS) as data format for modelling transit information. GTFS defines a common format for public transportation data, having established itself as the de facto standard. However, the format relies on CSV (Comma-separated values) files to represent the information which is then compressed and stored. This leads to isolated and outdated data that is not easily queryable nor extensible. Table 1 shows a comparison between solutions for transit data modelling, including the one presented in this paper.

As made explicit by J.L. Campbell et al. [4], the effectiveness of transportation information systems largely depends on the ability to integrate information from diverse sources and the suitability of this information to the specific user. The work carried out by the Artificial Intelligence community showed evidence that formal ontologies could be used to specify knowledge between different entities.

Ontologies are the heart of the Semantic Web, an extension of the World Wide Web in which the meaning (semantics) of information and services is defined [5]. In ontologies, the semantic description of data, i.e., the logical relationships between data elements and other formal statements are made explicit through ontology languages such as OWL (Ontology Web Language).

This not only makes it easier for other human users to understand the specifically intended meaning of the models, but also means that other tools can use the definitions transparently [6]. Lorenz et al. [7] made a comprehensive survey on standardization efforts for geographic information and explained the ontology of a transportation network derived from the ISO Geographic Data Files. Niaraki [8] developed an

---

[1]   Google Transit, http://maps.google.com/transit/
[2]   Moveuskadi, http://moveuskadi.com/
[3]   OpenTripPlanner, http://www.opentripplanner.org/

ontology based personalized route planning system using a multi-criteria decision making. Another related work is made by Houda [9] focused on the information required by the passenger for preparing a journey, choosing the best way to move from one point to another using multimodal transportation. Gunay et al. [10] built a semantic based public transportation geoportal based on the INSPIRE (Infrastructure for Spatial Information in the European Community) data theme. The aim of this work is to investigate the use of semantics to empower the traditional GIS approach.

Along with the use of ontologies, the inclusion of contextual information also derives in the enrichment of the resulting information [11]. Examples of this are the solutions presented by G.D. Abowd [12] or D. Bujan [13] for the context management in the field of tourism applications, a similar area of application.

All the research discussed above concern ontology studies. However, each work is motivated by different objectives, methodologies or expected results. Our goal is to construct a distributed software architecture that allows, through the formalization of transit data acquired from heterogeneous sources together with the integration of relevant information, enabling software services related to multimodal mobility.

Table 1. Comparison between formats for transport information provision

	GTFS[4]	WFS[5]	Ad-hoc[6]	MTO
Classification	Open Data	Open Data	Private	Open Data
Structure	Implicit	Implicit	Implicit	Formal
Extensibility	No	No	No	Yes
Linkable	No	No	No	Yes
Queries	Programmatic	Web Service	API	Direct (SPARQL)
Data Access	Limited	Limited	Limited	Full

3   MTO: Multimodal Transport Ontology

Traditional GIS systems perform spatial queries using a keyword-based method. However, this approach remains incapable of handling intelligent queries due to a lack of geographic concepts (semantics) in the dataset [10]. This issue is very satisfactorily resolved using ontologies as demonstrated in the state of the art, so creating an ontology for transport information provision and management is conducted.

3.1   MTO Design Methodology

The design of ontologies should follow a process to guide and evaluate the model. Several studies can be found, an example is the criteria identified by Gruber [14].

---

[4] General Transit Feed Specification,
https://developers.google.com/transit/gtfs/
[5] Web Feature Service, http://www.opengeospatial.org/standards/wfs/
[6] Ad-hoc. Proprietary formats defined by agencies or institutions that manage their own data.

There are also more detailed methodologies that seek to establish a strategy for the guided development of ontologies. In 1995 Uschold and King [15] suggested a methodology based on the following phases: identify the target ontology, build, evaluate, and document it. A more ambitious approach is the so called Methontology [16] which covers the whole life cycle, matching the ontology to a software product. Noy and McGuiness [17] for their part, describe an iterative process consisting of several stages: determine the domain and scope, consider reusing existing ontologies, list the important terms, define classes and their hierarchy, define properties and constraints and create the instances. In 2009, Suarez-Figueroa [18] presents a new approach with NeOn methodology, a set of nine scenarios for building ontologies and ontology networks, emphasizing the reuse of ontological and non-ontological resources, reengineering and fusion, and considering collaboration and dynamism.

NeOn Methodology is the most suitable approach for the design of MTO, primarily due to the fact that is focused on the reuse and transformation of non-ontological resources, such as the CSV files that compose GTFS. The development is mainly ascribed to scenario 2 using adapters which allow the generation of semantic information from data sources currently available on the Internet.

Given that GTFS is currently the de facto standard for transit data representation, it has been chosen to undertake a reformulation of their CSV files to entities within the ontology. A survey of existing transportation vocabularies that could be reused for the ontology design has been conducted. Thus, widely community supported vocabularies, like Geonames[7], Geosparql[8], Time[9] or WGS84[10] have been used. Also, an adapter, a desktop portable and multiplatform application developed in Java, has been developed for the conversion from GTFS to MTO.

3.2   MTO Vocabulary

The basis for the transport data model will be taken from the GTFS specification. The main classes, properties and relationships that compose MTO are shown in Fig. 1.

One of the key characteristics for a system which aims to model transportation information is the design used to store the geographical data. In this aspect, the decisions that have been taken are based on the standardization and future extensibility and/or reusability of the designed ontology.

Regarding standardization this work has followed a twofold approach: geo-referenced points have been defined by using the widely supported properties latitude and longitude, following the WGS84 standard. *hasGeometry* property has also been defined, extending from the Geosparql ontology and allowing to perform geometric queries over ontology points, as shown in Fig. 2. It has also been decided to link the ontology with Geonames, an ontology engaged in storing geopolitical information. The link is done through the *belongsToPlace* property referencing the Geonames URI corresponding to the territory where the point of the ontology is located.

---

[7]   GeoNames Ontology, http://www.geonames.org/ontology/
[8]   GeoSPARQL, http://www.opengeospatial.org/standards/geosparql/
[9]   Time Ontology in OWL, http://www.w3.org/TR/owl-time/
[10] Basic Geo (WGS84 lat/long), http://www.w3.org/2003/01/geo/

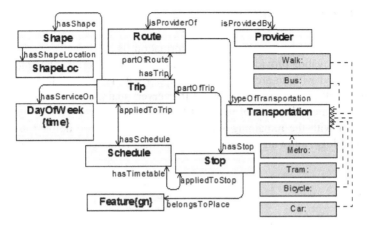

Fig. 1. Multimodal Transport Ontology main concepts and relationships

The representation of the transport-related information as an ontology facilitates the use of advantageous aspects, like the ability to link data with other data sources, which can be relevant to the specific domain. This suppose an improvement of the information by integrating in it non-quantitative aspects.

It was decided to extend MTO by linking and classifying the collaborative points of interest (POIs) provided by Linkedgeodata[11] and Geonames ontologies. Linkedgeodata uses the data collected by the OpenStreetMap project and makes it available as an RDF knowledge base according to the Linked Data principles.

```
SELECT DISTINCT ?poi ?lat ?lon WHERE {
    ?poi mto:hasLatitude ?lat; mto:hasLongitude ?lon.
    ?poi geo:hasGeometry ?g.?g geo:asWKT ?wkt.
    FILTER (geof:distance(?wkt, "LINESTRING(-2.50 42.50,
-2.60 42.60)"^^geo:wktLiteral, units:metre) < 5000)}
```

Fig. 2. SPARQL query. Selecting POIs within 5 km of a given line.

Other important topic to consider when generating more accurate and rich information is the specific context of the user. Without this context, data offered could lose interest, since no personalized information can be generated. For each query that arrives to the system, the user context is established with the purpose of filtering data according to their specific circumstances. The architecture defines, in order to build such model, a faceted search with a set of properties referred to the POIs in the route:

- Name of the point of interest to look for
- Linked data source to consult (Geonames and/or Linkedgeodata).
- Geographical location of the query. This information can be used:
    — In a geopolitical way (e.g. POIs located in Biscay).
    — In a geometric way (e.g. POIs within 5 km of a given route).
- Hierarchical classification of the POIs

---

[11] LinkedGeoData, http://linkedgeodata.org/

4   Distributed Architecture

The way in which the transportation information is represented and structured supposes an innovation provided by the present work. However, the data model has to be complemented with an architecture that supports it. This is conducted by several distributed SPARQL servers. Each one of the servers maintains its own transit information and is managed in a local way, but facilitates the interoperability by means of its connection with the remaining servers by URIs, which are defined as metadata inside the ontology, allowing so, to perform distributed queries in a transparent way.

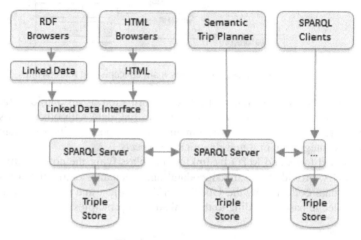

Fig. 3. System Architecture

The architecture, shown in Fig. 3, is similar to the one used by DNS to solve web domain names, facilitating the information distribution in a straightforward way. These are the two main elements of the proposed architecture:

- **Linked Data Interface.** Pubby's instance, a linked data frontend for SPARQL endpoints deployed with the aim of realizing content negotiation. It provides a data interface to RDF browsers and a simple HTML interface for HTML browsers.
- **SPARQL Servers.** Parliament, a high-performance triple store, has been used since it is compatible with the Geosparql standard, providing so, an index for geospatial queries, making it so, highly indicated in the transportation domain.

5   Validation: Semantic Trip Planner

The implementation of a semantic trip planner (Fig. 4) running on the proposed architecture was established in order to validate the developed solution. It is necessary to clarify that for the process of finding transit routes the architecture relies on the use of OpenTripPlanner (OTP). This in turn leads to an extensive modification of the tool. The following points have been accomplished:

- Load of transport data published by the Basque Government and generation of the corresponding semantic content via the developed GTFS adapter.
- Implementation of three distributed SPARQL servers, publishing as LOD semanticized transit information relating to the three Basque country provinces.
- OTP project modifications to include data provided by the supplied architecture: consuming the ontological model developed, accessing existing related information and so, providing contextualized multimodal transit information to the user.

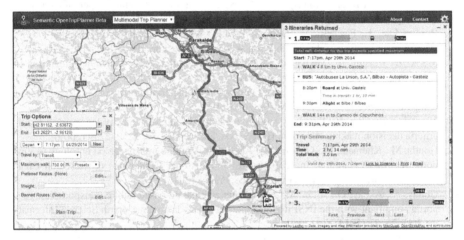

Fig. 4. Semantic Trip Planner

6   Conclusion and Future Work

The study conducted on the systems currently used to represent transport information led to the conclusion that they were not sufficiently interoperable, extensible or open. The work highlighted in this paper exposes an alternative solution, a new approach to the management of transit data, providing semantic information, formally structured and integrated. Likewise, an architecture of distributed and interoperable SPARQL servers is presented as the providers of transit data. A much more powerful and direct tool for accessing to all the available transit information, with support for advanced queries (geospatial and geopolitical) and enabling multiple data output formats.

The work done, based on the application of the linked open data principles to the field of transportation has tried to improve the quality of the provided information. This promotes the development of applications that could provide innovative services in an area, sustainable mobility, that is receiving social and institutional support given its environmentally friendly characteristics.The linked data community is very active and hence the next steps point to an extension of the ontology and the desirable appearance of an ecosystem of both applications and open transit data that supports it.

References

1. General Secretariat for Transport, Spanish Ministry of Public Works and Transport: Los Sistemas Inteligentes de Transporte (2010) ISBN: 978-84-498-0866-1
2. Caulfield, B., O'Mahony, M.: An Examination of the Public Transport Information requirements of Users. Transactions on Intelligent Transportation Systems, 21–30 (2007)
3. Boucher, S., Zimanyi, E.: An ontology-based geodatabase interoperability platform. In: Cases on Semantic Interoperability for Information Systems Integration: Practices and Applications, pp. 294–315 (2009)
4. Campbell, J.L., Carne, C., Kantowitz, B.H.: Human Factors Design Guidelines for Advanced Traveler Information Systems (ATIS) and Commercial Vehicle Operations (CVO). U.S. Department of Transportation, Technical Report FHWA-RD-98-057 (1998)
5. Berners-Lee, T., Fischetti, M., Dertouzos, M.L.: Weaving the Web: The Original Design and Ultimate Destiny of the World Wide Web by Its Inventor. HarperInformation (2000)
6. Malik, Z., Rezgui, A., Medjahed, B., Ouzzani, M., Sinha, A.K.: Semantic integration in geosciences. Int. J. Semant. Comp. 4 (2010)
7. Lorenz, B., Ohlbach, H.J., Yang, L.: Ontology of transportation networks. Department of computer science, University of Munich (2005)
8. Niaraki, A.S., Kim, K.: Ontology based personalized route planning system using a multi-criteria decision making approach. Expert Syst. and Applic. 36, 2250–2259 (2009)
9. Houda, M., Khemaja, M., Oliveira, K., Abed, M.: A public transportation ontology to support user travel planning. In: 2010 Fourth International Conference on Research Challenges in Information Science (RCIS), Nice, France (2010)
10. Gunay, A., Akcay, O., Altan, M.O.: Building a semantic based public transportation geoportal compliant with the INSPIRE transport network data theme. Earth Science Informatics 7(1), 25–37 (2014)
11. Dey, A.K., Abowd, G.: The context toolkit: Aiding the development of context-aware applications. In: Workshop on Soft. Engineering for Wearable and Pervasive Computing (2000)
12. Abowd, G.D., Atkeson, C.G., Hong, J., Long, S., Kooper, R., Pinkerton, M.: Cyberguide: A mobile context-aware tour guide. Wireless Networks 3(5), 421–433 (1997)
13. Buján, D., Martín, D., Torices, O., López-de-Ipiña, D., Lamsfus, C., Abaitua, J., Alzua-Sorzabal, A.: Context Management Platform for Tourism Applications. Sensors 13 (2013)
14. Gruber, T.R.: Toward principles for the design of ontologies used for knowledge sharing. International Journal of Human-Computer Studies 43(5), 907–928 (1995)
15. Uschold, M., King, M.: Towards a Methodology for Building Ontologies. In: Workshop on Basic Ontological Issues in Knowledge Sharing, Stockholm, Sweden (1995)
16. Fernández, M., Gómez, A., Juristo, N.: Methontology: From ontological art towards ontological engineering. In: Spring Symposium on Ontological Engineering, California (1997)
17. Noy, N.F., McGuinness, D.L.: Ontology Development 101: A Guide to Creating Your First Ontology: Knowledge Systems Laboratory (2001)
18. Suárez-Figueroa, M.C.: NeOn Methodology for building Ontology Networks: Specification, scheduling and reuse. PhD Thesis. Universidad Politécnica de Madrid (2010)

Ambient Gamification of Automobile Driving to Encourage Safety Behaviors

Marcela D. Rodríguez[1], Jorge E. Ibarra[1], José Ruben Roa[2],
Cecilia M. Curlango[1], Luis Felipe Bedoya[1], and Héctor Daniel Montes[1]

[1] School of Engineering, Autonomous University of Baja California, UABC, Mexicali, Mexico
[2] School of Architecture, Autonomous University of Baja California, UABC, Mexicali, Mexico
```
{marcerod,Jorge.ibarra,rube.roa,curlango,
felipe.bedoya,dmontes}@uabc.edu.mx
```

Abstract. Unsafe driving has a negative effect on society and its citizens since it leads to traffic accidents. Most states penalize unsafe driving; however, this potential for penalization does not change how people drive and alternate ways must be found. With the aim of persuading people to change how they drive, we propose to gamify the driving activity through ambient devices that provide drivers with awareness about their driving behavior. In this paper, we present the design of ambient devices that we propose to offer a seamless drivers' interaction with a game that challenge players to avoid risky driving behaviors.

Keywords: gamification, behavior change, ambient displays, context-awareness.

1 Introduction

Unsafe driving is a behavior that has a negative effect on society and its citizens since it leads to traffic accidents. According to the WHO [1], about 1.24 million people die each year on the world's roads, and 62% of these deaths occur in 10 countries, including: India, China, the US, and Mexico. Among the key risk factors are speeding and drivers' distracted behaviors as a result of using mobile phones. Technology in cars is now taking over certain aspects of driving for increasing drivers' safety, and the efficiency and enjoyment of the in-car user interfaces [2]. Today's vehicles allow for many more functions and provide more information; so vehicle interfaces face similar user experience issues as computers. To offer a pleasing user experience while promoting driver's safety behaviors, we propose to gamify the driving activity through ambient devices. Gamify refers to *"the use of game design elements in non-game contexts to motivate and increase user activity and retention"* [3]. In section 2 we present related work of applications proposed for this context; section 3 describes the workshops conducted to design ambient devices; section 4 presents the system design, section 5 describes the system architecture; and section 6 concludes.

2 Related Work

The use of applications that seek to persuade people to change how they drive is an alternate approach to persuade citizens to respect transit laws. As Fogg (2002) points

R. Hervás et al. (Eds.): UCAmI 2014, LNCS 8867, pp. 37–43, 2014.
© Springer International Publishing Switzerland 2014

out, people can be influenced by computer products and this fact provides an opportunity to use such products to change people's behavior [4]. Currently, the Axa Insurance company, offers a mobile phone application to encourage users improve their driving. It provides an analysis of their driving actions (e.g. how they accelerate), rewards their good driving behavior through points and medals, and allows users to share their accomplishments with their social networks [5]. Other games have been proposed to modify different aspects of the manner in which people drive. For instance, EcoChallenge provides challenges to drivers so that their fuel consumption is reduced while at the same time trying not to impact their driving style in a negative way [6]. And the I-GEAR application tries to convince drivers to help avoid causing traffic congestion by suggesting they take alternate routes or leave at a later time, and providing incentives for following the suggestions made, such as a free parking at a mall [7]. Finally, Driving Miss Daisy is an application in which the player is challenged to drive a virtual passenger in a smooth and safe manner. Audible feedback is provided during the drive, and at the end of a drive the player is provided with a summary of his performance and is able to see how it compares to that of other players on the same route [8]. A problem with applications that seek to modify users' driving behavior is that they can place such demands on users that they become distractions. Therefore, apps should refrain from sending text messages to drivers while their vehicle is in motion [9]. Our approach strives for the gamification of driving activity through ambient displays with the aim to support a seamlessly user interaction with the game application.

3   Design Workshops

Figure 1 represents that the methodology we followed consisted of two design workshops conducted with the project's designers, who were 2 students and 1 professor from the Computer Engineering Department, and 2 students and 1 professor from the Graphic Design Department. The first workshop (DW1) enabled us to abstract the most relevant aspects of players' interaction with game systems that influence game adoption. To reach this end, the Computer Engineers team conducted interviews of 12 students before the workshop. Thus, during the workshop, designers categorized the responses from the interviews by using the Affinity Diagram technique [10]. It presented on its top-level, the common game design elements that became requirements for our game, e.g. a game model based on challenges, enabling the game personalization based on a redeeming scheme, and supporting socialization and competition.

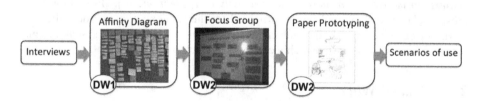

Fig. 1. Method followed for designing ambient games

The aim of the second workshop (DW2) was to design ambient game prototypes for providing drivers a safety and pleasurable user experience. This consisted of a focus group session in which 2 mixed teams were formed with members of both Departments. At the beginning of the session, they were presented with the system requirements for designing a game according to the expected context of use, such as: the game should be location-aware, behavior-aware, support implicit interactions, and based on ambient objects in order to provide peripheral information. With this in mind, each team proceeded to post design ideas for addressing the videogames design elements abstracted in the DW1. Finally, each team devised a game paper prototype. We merged both of the designs through scenarios of use, resulting in a system comprised of a head up ambient display and an ambient accessory for the car's rearview mirror. These devices interface with a mobile phone application, which infers users' driving behavior and manage the game.

4   System Design

The system proposed aims to gamify the driving activity by challenging users to follow traffic rules and avoid risky behaviors (e.g. texting), while competing with their social network. On a daily basis, it will present gamers with driving challenges indicating the transit rule to follow, which whenever they are accomplished will give the user a reward; for instance: "When driving by a school zone, you should not exceed the 15mph speed limit in order to get 800 coins". The ambient devices proposed to support driving gamification are:

- **m-HCAR (mirror-Hanging Accessory for Reflection).** This is a mirror-hanging accessory as shown in Fig. 2c. It is digitally augmented to provide peripheral feedback regarding the driver's compliance of the traffic rules during his driving route, while promoting reflection regarding his driving behavior. Thus, while driving, the user realizes he is infringing a traffic rule in a timely manner.
- **GHUD (Game-notification Head Up Display).** It presents information on a display, which might be the rearview mirror (as depicted in Fig. 2b). This shows notifications regarding the game progress, such as accomplished challenges, driver expertise level, and gained incentives. To provide information in an unobtrusive manner avoiding unsafe distractions, GHUD displays notifications when the car stops, such as during red traffic lights or when parked.
- **Mobile phone application.** It was designed to be used when the user is not driving since it enables him to consult detailed information regarding his progress (such as consulting rankings), to configure and personalize the game (e.g. to redeem their rewards for improving the m-HCAR), and to receive notifications about new challenges to accomplish.

4.1   Driving Behavior Awareness

In this scenario, we illustrate how ambient devices provide awareness about the risks associated with drivers' distracted behavior caused by using mobile phones while driving.

Scenario: *Before Tony, an executive of a marketing company, leaves his home to go to work, he takes his phone to check his messages, and then, notices that he has a new driving challenge. As shown in Fig. 2a, it indicates that when he makes up to 15 full stops, he will win 500 coins. As he leaves his home to drive the office 5 minutes later then usual, he drives by exceeding the allowed speed limit. Tony's behavior causes the m-HCAR (mirror-Hanging Accessory for Reflection) to start buzzing to provide him with an initial awareness of this infringement. However, he decides to ignore it; additionally, he takes his phone to send a message to his secretary to inform her that he will arrive late for the morning-scheduled meeting. As Tony did not present good driving behavior, the m-HCAR represents it by a dented front fender, as shown in Fig 2c. Thus, when he parks, the head-up display presents that his avatar is still in the novice level, he did not completed any of his challenges, and finally, he is notified of his infringements as seen in Fig. 2b.*

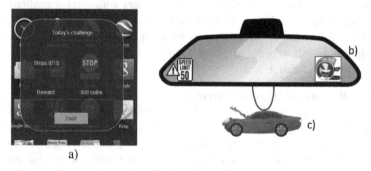

a)

b)

c)

Fig. 2. Ambient game comprised of: a) a mirror-Hanging Accessory for Reflection (m-HCAR) b) a Game-notification Head Up Display (GHUD) c) a Game Application for mobile phone

4.2   Social Driving Challenges

In countries like Mexico, 45% of the infringements correspond to unsafe driving actions, and third of them are for not obeying traffic lights. The following scenario illustrates how the system enables users to socialize and compete to cope with this behavior.

Scenario: *It's Saturday morning, and Bob is going to meet with his friends for playing football. While taking his breakfast, Bob checks which of his friends may be on the way to the football park by consulting the game's social roster from his mobile phone, since those that are driving appear with the online status (see Fig. 3a). He realizes that Phil is not driving yet. So, Bob decides to challenge Phil to obey traffic lights as* *shown in Fig. 3b. Phil accepts the challenge, and then, he is presented with the rules to follow, such as: 'The yellow light is not the end of the green light phase, it is the beginning of the red light phase. You must STOP on a yellow light' (see Fig. 3b). When Phil and Bob stop at a traffic light, the head-up presents their challenge progress. As Bob wins this challenge, his head-up display shows he has incremented his coins, which later are used to improve his avatar".*

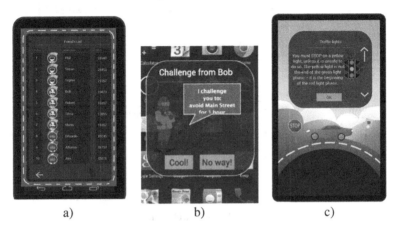

a)   b)   c)

Fig. 3. Mobile phone game application presenting: a) the user's social network roster, b) a challenge notification send by other user, c) aids for following a traffic rule

5 System Implementation

Figure 4 presents the system architecture representing the components that implement the system.

5.1 Mobile Phone Application

The *Mobile Phone* application consist of two sub-systems or nodes:

a) The *Game_app* sub-system contains components for managing the game (e.g. generating challenges), accessing the social network, and a repository of the user's driving challenges.

b) The *Behavior Aware* sub-system relies on the motion and position sensors built inside the Android phone. It measures parameters such as driving speed, braking distance and proper braking; makes use of the GPS for location awareness; and integrates a set of driving rules into the app to keep track of and evaluate driving performance. We are currently assessing the use of On-Board Diagnostics System (OBD), which connects directly to the car computer to get more accurate measurements.

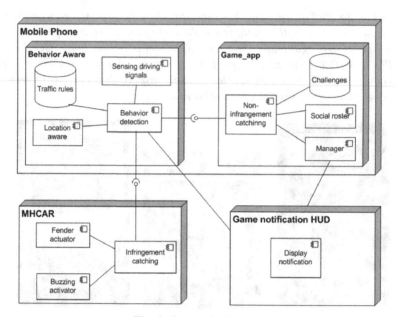

Fig. 4. System Architecture

5.2   m-HCAR Ambient Device

The *m-HCAR* node has the *Infringement catching* component, which receives notifications by the *Behavior detection* component when the driver breaks a transit rule. The m-HCAR hardware module is implemented using the IOIO board, which is a programmable interface controller to allow Android devices to interface with external hardware via Bluetooth. We selected the IOIO over other devices such as Arduino, since there is no requirement for extra shields to interface with Android devices, which saves space on the module. The *Buzzing activator* component controls a miniature vibration motor to make the m-HCAR buzz to provide immediate awareness when a traffic infringement is detected. If the driver does not correct his behavior, the car aspect will be modified to represent his infringement. For doing this, a set of servomotors with magnets attached to their shafts is controlled by the IOIO board through its actuator software components (e.g. *Fender actuator*). By shifting the position of each magnet, bumps and cracks, for instance, appear on the car surface.

5.3   Game Notification Head-up Display

The *Game Notification HUD* node contains the *Display notification* component, which displays the driver's game progress sent by the *Manager* component of the *Mobile phone*. The GHUD hardware module consists of a transparent display embedded in the rearview mirror. It is controlled wirelessly by the game-app of the Mobile Phone, which sends updated data and signals to turn the display on only when the car is not moving, which is detected by the *Behavior aware* component. The rearview mirror was considered the least intrusive technology among several that were initially considered. We are reviewing other alternatives, such as smart glasses, which might provide information to the driver in a private manner.

6   Conclusions and Future Work

In this paper, we argue that ambient devices are appropriate to gamify driving activity. We plan to implement a proof of concept of these devices to conduct an in-lab usability evaluation by using a driving simulator. This will enable us to gather evidence regarding the users' experience in a safety setting in order to assess whether the awareness supported by each device is adequate for supporting unwanted and safe distractions, and for promoting good driving behaviors.

Acknowledgements. Our thanks to the students for participating in the design workshop.

References

1. Global status report on road safety 2013 (2013), http://www.who.int/ violence_injury_prevention/road_traffic/en/
2. Walker, G.H., Stanton, N.A., Young, M.S.: Where is computing driving cars? International Journal of Human Computer Interaction 13(2), 203–229 (2001)
3. Deterding, S., Dixon, D., Khaled, R., Nacke, L.: From game design elements to gamefulness: Definiung "gamification". In: ACM Academic MindTrek Conference, pp. 9–15 (2011)
4. Fogg, B.J.: Persuasive technology: Using computers to change what we think and do. Ubiquity (December 2002)
5. AXA Application available at, http://axadrive.mx/
6. Ecker, R., Holzer, P., Broy, V., Butz, A.: Ecochallenge: A race for efficiency. In: ACM Conf. on Human Computer Interaction with Mobile Devices and Services, pp. 91–94 (2011)
7. McCall, R., Koenig, V.: Gaming concepts and incentives to change driver behaviour. In: Ad Hoc Networking Workshop (Med-Hoc-Net), pp. 146–151. IEEE (2012)
8. Shi, C., Lee, H.J., Kurczal, J., Lee, A.: Routine driving infotainment app: Gamification of performance driving. In: Adjunct Proc. of the 4th International Conference on Automotive User Interfaces and Interactive Vehicular Applications, pp. 181–183 (2012)
9. Rouzikhah, H., King, M., Rakotonirainy, A.: Examining the effects of an eco-driving message on driver distraction. Accident Analysis & Prevention 50, 975–983 (2013)
10. Holtzblatt, K., Wendell, J.B., Wood, S.: Rapid contextual design, p. 320. Morgan Kaufman/Elsevier, San Francisco (2005)

Towards a Non-intrusive Self-management System for Asthma Control Using Smartphones

Iván González[1], Cristian Carretón[1], Sergio F. Ochoa[2], and José Bravo[1]

[1] MAmI Research Lab, University of Castilla-La Mancha Paseo de la Universidad, Ciudad Real, Spain
ivan.gzdiaz@gmail.com, cristian.carreton@alu.uclm.es, Jose.Bravo@uclm.es
[2] Computer Science Department, University of Chile, Santiago de Chile, Chile
sochoa@dcc.uchile.cl

Abstract. A noise-robust algorithm for segmentation of breath events during continuous speech is presented. The built-in microphone of a smartphone is used to capture the speech signal (voiced and breath frames) under conditions of a relatively noisy background. A template matching approach, using mel-cepstrograms, is adopted for constructing several similarity measurements to distinguish between breath and non-breath frames. Breath events will be used for lung function regression.

Keywords: asthma control, breath detection, MFCC, mel-cepstrogram, lung function.

1 Introduction

Asthma control refers to a set of procedures to describe the extent to which external symptoms of respiratory chronic condition (*asthma severity*) are minimized through preventive medical intervention and personal care of asthma.

In the last two decades there have been numerous advances that have allowed a better understanding of asthma by improving the methods of diagnosis and the effectiveness of the medication to prevent exacerbations. However, studies have been less focused in asthma control. In this sense, they have materialized in the development of management guidelines e.g. [1]. These asthma management guidelines emphasize the nature of the disease, which is subject to numerous predisposition factors, triggers and heterogeneous symptomatology. Therefore, the evaluation of the extent of asthma severity (and asthma control consequently) is considered a complex and multidimensional task. In order to give some instrumental support for self-management asthma control, *portable spirometers* have become the most widely used tool, providing daily and objective measurements of lung function like: *FEV1* (*Forced Expiratory Volume in 1 sec*), *FVC* (*Forced Vital Capacity*), ... ; and also holding and history of recent past records for the patient which is so useful to analyse asthma severity state and progression.

However, portable spirometers have some shortcomings that impede its popular implantation as a support tool for self-management asthma control. For example, they require manual steps for setting and some sort of training

R. Hervás et al. (Eds.): UCAmI 2014, LNCS 8867, pp. 44–47, 2014.
© Springer International Publishing Switzerland 2014

in order to get accurate measurements and these are serious inconvenients for some patients (e.g. elderly or children). In addition, forced spirometry requires explicit interaction in an invasive way, since a long exhalation is needed. In order to deal with the disadvantages of forced spirometry and its dedicated devices, some active areas of research like m-Health [2] have plenty of opportunities. The main goal of this area is *health monitoring without intrusion*. That is, receive feedback about vital signs and process it, trying to achieve minimal interaction and reducing embedded sensors everything possible.

In this paper we present an ongoing study in the context of m-Health which is part of a bigger framework for asthma control. Here we propose a noise-robust algorithm for segmentation of breath events (inhalations and exhalations) during continuous speech through the built-in microphone, while the smartphone is in conversation position (speaker near the ear and microphone near the mouth). Once breath sounds are exactly delimited, next step will be extract some features from them in order to build a regression model to estimate some lung functions.

2   Previous Work

Before adopting the noise-robust segmentation of breath events as our development line, we tried to use the microphone to capture the acoustic signal of a forced expiration, with the intention of modelling the patient's vocal tract and the reverberation of sound around his head and finally estimate some lung functions using regression. In other words, make a transformation of audio samples of a forced expiration, captured through the microphone like uncalibrated signals of pressure, into measures of airflow which are useful to construct a regression model of some lung functions. This procedure was founded on SpiroSmart app [3]. The first phase of this previous approach was to calculate the spectrogram from the acoustic signal of the forced expiration (Fig. 1a). After it, two different filters were applied in order to discard low energy frequencies in each FFT frame (filter over columns, Fig. 1b) and to preserve only relative large resonances (filter over rows, Fig. 1c). After spectrogram filtration, finally the average resonance magnitude in each FFT frame was calculated to be used for feature extraction of flow rate over time. Each of these features would become a input for the lung function regression model. Although SpiroSmart's authors achieved good results with this approach, we gave up that research line as part of our

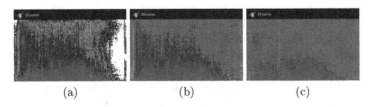

(a)   (b)   (c)

Fig. 1. *(a)* Original spectrogram of a forced expiration; *(b)* After discarding low energy frequencies (black&green points); *(c)* After removing short noise resonances ($< 300ms$)

framework for asthma control. The main reason was that the spectrogram was strongly influenced for air blowing distance, saturating the microphone (if the blow is too close); and losing important energy in some frequencies (if the blow is far away). Also, it was to sensitive to background noise.

3   Case of Use: Noise-Robust Segmentation Algorithm

Here we show a general view of the algorithm developed for the exactly demarcation of breath sounds during continuous speech in a relatively noisy environment. The outcome of this algorithm (in terms of delimited acoustic frames which are part of inhalations or exhalations time events) will feed a feature extraction algorithm as previous step for lung function regression.

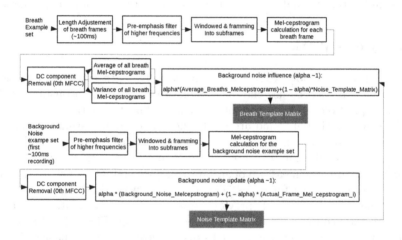

Fig. 2. Template matrices for: *breath example set* (top) & *noise example* (bottom)

In order to be able to differentiate between *breath* and *non-breath* frames a template matching approach, focused on Mel-cepstrogram calculation like the proposed in [4], has been used. In addition, we have extended this template matching procedure to distinguish between *weak breath frames* and *only background noise frames*, due to their similarity. To address this last task, the template matching procedure is also used as *similarity measurement* and again MFCC extraction is needed to build a Mel-cepstrogram of the first $100ms$ of the recording (which are representative of background noise). This method has some steps in common with the MFCC *Voice Activity Detection* (VAD) algorithm in [5]. Fig. 2 show a schematic block view describing the construction of the *template matrices* which will be used like similarity measurements for the *breath example set* (top) and for the *background noise example* (bottom) respectively. Both template matrices share several calculation steps. After selection of some representative isolated frames for breath set and first $100ms$ of the recording for the background noise example, pre-emphasis filter is used, then *Hamming* windowing and framing into subframes ($10ms$) are obtained as previous step for Mel-cepstrogram calculation of each frame and DC removal. Finally, each template matrix is updated under background noise influence using a formula and alpha factor as in [5]. An actual frame can be classified as *breath/non-breath* using a similarity coefficient Sc formed by its Mel-cepstrogram $M(i)$, the variance matrix of breath set V and the breath template matrix T:

$$Sc = \frac{1}{\sum_{rows} \sum_{columns} \mid \frac{M(i)-T}{V} \mid^2}; \quad Lower\ Sc \Longrightarrow less\ similarity \quad (1)$$

Other time domain features like: *short-time energy* and *ZCR* can be added to improve the breath/non-breath classification. For frames already classified as breath, a second similarity coefficient (like the first one but using the noise template matrix instead) must be used to discard some false positives considered as breath frames, but in fact they are background noise frames.

4   Conclusion

The algorithm proposed is giving us good results for breath segmentation in relatively noisy environment with very few false negatives. However, the false positive rate (in silence/noisy environment) must be reduced a little more, for example, taking into account what is happening around the detected breath events and not considering them like independent frames. Once this is done, we will work in the feature extraction from breath events.

Acknowledgment. This work is conducted in the context of the FRASE MINECO project (TIN2013-47152-C3-1-R). Also, we appreciate the support of UBIHEALTH project under International Research Staff Exchange Schema (MC-IRSES 316337).

References

1. The global initiative for asthma (GINA), http://www.ginasthma.org/
2. Bravo, J.: m-Health: Mobile Computing and Health Monitoring. J. of Computation in Biosciences and Engineering
3. Larson, E.C., Goel, M., Boriello, G., Helthe, S., Rosenfeld, M., Patel, S.N.: SpiroSmart: Using a microphone to measure lung function on a mobile phone. In: UbiComp, pp. 280–289 (2012)
4. Ruinskiy, D., Lavner, Y.: An Effective Algorithm for Automatic Detection and Exact Demarcation of Breath Sounds in Speech and Song Signals. IEEE Transactions on Audio, Speech, and Language Processing 15(3), 838–850 (2007)
5. Hongzhi, W., Yuchao, X., Meijing, L.: Study on the MFCC similarity-based voice activity detection algorithm. In: AIMSEC, pp. 4391–4394 (2011)

Powerchord: Towards Ambient Appliance-Level Electricity Use Feedback through Real-Time Sonification

Dan Lockton[1], Flora Bowden[2], Clare Brass[2], and Rama Gheerawo[1]

[1] Helen Hamlyn Centre for Design, Royal College of Art, London SW7 2EU, UK
[2] Sustain RCA, Royal College of Art, London SW7 2EU, UK
{dan.lockton,flora.bowden,clare.brass,rama.gheerawo}@rca.ac.uk

Abstract. Feedback on energy use mainly uses visual, numerical interfaces. This paper introduces an alternative: energy *sonification*, turning real-time electricity use data from appliances into ambient sound. *Powerchord*, a work in progress prototype developed through co-creation with householders, is detailed.

1   Background: Householder Research Around Energy

Influencing energy use through behaviour change [e.g. 10, 15], is a major research topic across multiple technological and social science disciplines. Feedback displays for electricity or gas, and *smart meters*, which enable additional networked functionality, such as adaptive pricing changes, have shown some influence on behaviour, [e.g. 8], but the situation is complex: simple numerical feedback may not take account of the realities of household life [3, 5, 6] or people's understanding of units and quantities [18], nor link people to wider understanding of the energy system [1]. Some *persuasive technology* work [e.g. 4, 14] has sought to bring an 'ambient' approach.

As part of a European project, designers have carried out in-depth research with householders [9, 11], including co-creation workshops and a hackday, focused on energy use. One theme emerging was the *invisibility of energy* as an issue in householders' lack of understanding, contributing to energy waste. One householder told us:

> "I worked out that through gas and electricity every year, the average house gets the equivalent of a bit over three tons of coal delivered completely silently and without any mess. And go back a hundred years ago and everyone would have a really good quantitative understanding of how much energy they used because they had to physically shovel the stuff."

This issue suggested opportunities for visualisation beyond numbers, but also non-visually, for example *sonification* [19]. In co-creation with householders, it was suggested that being able to 'listen' to whether appliances were switched on, the relative magnitude and characteristics of their energy use, and what state they were in (e.g. listening to a washing machine will give a good idea as to where it is in its cycle), was potentially useful. There are echoes of early work in calm technology and ubiquitous computing, such as Natalie Jeremijenko's *Live Wire (Dangling String)* [20], and the concept of *soundscapes* [e.g. 12]. Sonification offers benefits for ambient, peripheral comprehension of data with multiple dimensions, including pattern recognition and detecting state changes [16]. To explore energy sonification, CurrentCost electricity monitors, as supplied to many UK utility customers, were chosen. The CurrentCost

R. Hervás et al. (Eds.): UCAmI 2014, LNCS 8867, pp. 48–51, 2014.
© Springer International Publishing Switzerland 2014

'ecosystem' includes a bridge connecting to a router and posting data to a website, and individual appliance monitors (IAMs) wirelessly connected to the base unit, enabling disaggregated data. CurrentCost has been used in a number of Internet of Things (IoT) academic studies [e.g. 17].

2   Sound of the Office

An initial 'IoT' energy sonification *parameter-mapping* experiment was carried out in a university office. Three CurrentCost IAMs monitored electricity use of a kettle, a laser printer, and a gang socket for a row of desks, sending data to the website from where it was exported as a CSV file. Data for 12 hours—from midnight on a Sunday to midday Monday—were scaled [2] and converted into a three-track 30-second MIDI file[1] using csvmidi, with *lower* pitches representing *higher* power, and vice versa (a householder suggestion), and hourly drumbeat 'ticks' [19]. MIDI instruments represented appliances: a tenor sax is the kettle (up to 1.5kW in use); a synth brass is a Kyocera laser printer (background whine of 10W on standby, deepening to 300W-500W in use); and a polysynth is the gang socket, with laptops (15W-50W) plugged in during the day and a charger (1W) otherwise. As the audio starts, over the printer's whine, the kettle comes on as a security guard makes himself a 1.00am cup of tea. Then, early in the morning, the cleaners used the kettle—twice quickly (reboiling?) and then again. Suddenly, at 9.30am, as staff arrive, the kettle goes on, laptops are plugged in, the printer starts up and the energetic hubbub of office life appears. The approach is similar to [7]—a summary 'gist', presented after the fact.

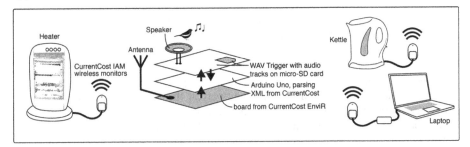

Fig. 1. Diagram of the Powerchord system

3   Powerchord (Work in Progress)

While summary sonification provided an interesting auditory display of multiple appliance power use over time, (near-)real-time 'closed loop' feedback offers advantages, e.g. a householder could change appliance use directly [16]. To achieve this, it was decided to do processing locally (i.e. not really 'IoT'). Building on others' code[2], *Powerchord* was developed: an Arduino-based system (Figs. 1 and 2) which parses CurrentCost XML output every 6s, extracting the IAM power figures for individual appliances, and

---

[1] The file, titled *Sound of the Office*, can be heard at http://v.gd/officesound
[2] E.g. by Colin R Williams: http://www.crwilliams.co.uk/projects/
arduino-currentcost-lcd

mapping these figures to ranges defined in code, and linked to a Robertsonics *WAV Trigger*, enabling polyphonic playback for multiple audio files simultaneously. For each power range (from <10W up to >2kW), for each appliance, a particular audio track is played, and looped until the power range changes. The system supports up to nine IAMs.

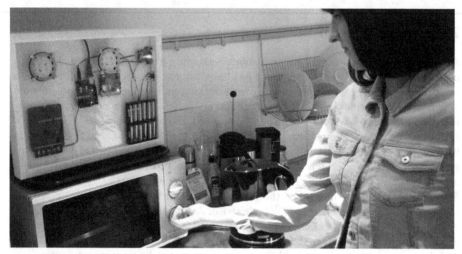

Fig. 2. A Powerchord prototype in use, monitoring a microwave oven and kettle

Any audio tracks can be used, including tones, sound effects or music—on a user-replaceable micro SD card. Powerchord can thus act as a platform for different kinds of ambient energy sonification research. For this demonstration prototype, *birdsong*[3] has been used—blackbirds, house sparrows and herring gulls—edited so that different intensities of song (number of birds, agitation level) map to power ranges, with different birds for each appliance[4]. The idea is to embed ambient energy feedback, in this case using birdsong as a metaphor, within the existing framework of the soundscapes of daily routines, such that rather than being part of the "increasing clutter of beeps and bleeps" [16] of feedback, a familiar ambient sound is 'repurposed' with an extra layer of information—very much *calm* technology [20], or *blended sonification* [13].

This is work in progress; at the time of writing, a Powerchord prototype has been informally trialled in offices and researchers' homes, to understand how in practice people make use of it, and to refine the design before a larger deployment in a field study over autumn 2014, with volunteer householders in London and south-east England, the interim results of which will be reported at UCAmI 2014.

References

1. Boucher, A., Cameron, D., Jarvis, N.: Power to the People: Dynamic Energy Management through Communal Cooperation. In: Proceedings of DIS 2012, Newcastle (2012)
2. Brown, L.M., Brewster, S.A., Ramloll, R., Burton, M., Riedel, B.: Design guidelines for audio presentation of graphs and tables. In: Proceedings of International Conference on Auditory Display (ICAD 2003), Boston, MA (2003)

---

[3] From those available under Creative Commons licences at http://xeno-canto.org
[4] Videos, schematics, code and updates on the project are at http://v.gd/powerchord

3. Brynjarsdóttir, H., Håkansson, M., Pierce, J., Baumer, E.P.S., Di Salvo, C., Sengers, P.: Sustainably unpersuaded: How persuasion narrows our vision of sustainability. In: Proceedings of CHI 2012, Austin, Texas (2012)
4. Casado-Mansilla, D., Lopez-de-Armentia, J., Garaizar, P., López-de-Ipiña, D.: To switch off the coffee-maker or not: that is the question to be energy-efficient at work. In: Proceedings of CHI 2014 Extended Abstracts, Toronto (2014)
5. van Dam, S., Bakker, C.A., van Hal, J.D.M.: The mediating role of home energy management systems. In: Proceedings of First European Conference on Energy Efficiency and Behaviour, Maastricht (2009)
6. Hargreaves, T., Nye, M., Burgess, J.: Keeping energy visible? Exploring how householders interact with feedback from smart energy monitors in the longer term. Energy Policy 52, 126–134 (2013)
7. Hermann, T., Drees, J.M., Ritter, H.: Broadcasting auditory weather reports—A pilot project. In: Proceedings of International Conference on Auditory Display (ICAD 2003), Boston, MA (2003)
8. Kobus, C.B.A., Mugge, R., Schoormans, J.P.L.: Washing when the sun is shining! How householders interact with a household energy management system. Ergonomics 56(3), 451–462 (2012)
9. Lockton, D., Bowden, F., Greene, C., Brass, C., Gheerawo, R.: People and energy: A design-led approach to understanding everyday energy use behaviour. In: Proceedings of EPIC 2013: Ethnographic Praxis in Industry Conference, London (2013)
10. Lockton, D., Nicholson, L., Cain, R., Harrison, D.: Persuasive Technology for Sustainable Workplaces. Interactions 21(1), 58–61 (2014)
11. Lockton, D., Renström, S., Bowden, F., Rahe, U., Brass, C., Gheerawo, R.: Energy storytelling through annotating everyday life. In: Proceedings of BEHAVE 2014: 3rd European Conference on Behaviour and Energy Efficiency, Oxford (2014)
12. Mackrill, J.B., Jennings, P., Cain, R.: Improving the hospital 'soundscape': A framework to measure individual perceptual response to hospital sounds. Ergonomics 56(11), 1687–1697 (2013)
13. Tünnermann, R., Hammerschmidt, J., Hermann, T.: Blended Sonification: Sonification for Casual Information Interaction. In: Proceedings of International Conference on Auditory Display (ICAD 2013), Łódź, Poland (2013)
14. Ruge, L., Schrader, A.: Persuasion Mobility in Ambient Intelligence. In: Proceedings of AMBIENT 2013, Porto, Portugal (2013)
15. Selvefors, A., Karlsson, I.C.M., Rahe, U.: Use and adoption of interactive energy feedback systems. In: Proceedings of IASDR 2013, Tokyo (2013)
16. Serafin, S., Franinovic, K., Hermann, T., Lemaitre, G., Rinott, M., Rocchesso, D.: Sonic Interaction Design. In: Hermann, T., Hunt, A., Neuhoff, J.G. (eds.) The Sonification Handbook, pp. 87–110. Logos, Berlin (2011)
17. Smeaton, A.F., Doherty, A.R.: Persuading consumers to reduce their consumption of electricity in the home. In: Berkovsky, S., Freyne, J. (eds.) PERSUASIVE 2013. LNCS, vol. 7822, pp. 204–215. Springer, Heidelberg (2013)
18. Strengers, Y.: Designing Eco-Feedback Systems for Everyday Life. In: Proceedings of CHI 2011, Vancouver (2011)
19. Walker, B.N., Nees, M.A.: Theory of Sonification. In: Hermann, T., Hunt, A., Neuhoff, J.G. (eds.) The Sonification Handbook, pp. 9–39. Logos, Berlin (2011)
20. Weiser, M., Brown, J.S.: Designing calm technology (1995), http://www.ubiq.com/hypertext/weiser/calmtech/calmtech.htm

Collaborative E-Learning Framework for Creating Augmented Reality Mobile Educational Activities

Javier Barbadillo, Nagore Barrena, Víctor Goñi, and Jairo R. Sánchez

Vicomtech-IK4, Paseo Mikeletegi 57, 20009 Donostia-San Sebastián, Spain
{jbarbadillo,nbarrena,vgoni,jrsanchez}@vicomtech.org
http://www.vicomtech.org

Abstract. This work introduces an Augmented Reality based framework for e-learning platforms that allows the creation of collaborative activities for mobile devices. The easy-to-use authoring tool is Web3D based and can be integrated with e-learning platforms as a plug-in resource. The Augmented Reality content can be added to a real scenario visualiser, building a sequence of scenes and events. The students can download any activity with a mobile device and play it in a multiplayer collaborative mode. The presented framework solves the problem of standard integration of Augmented Reality applications in education offering a distributed framework which is e-learning compliant.

Keywords: Augmented Reality, Collaborative Learning.

1 Introduction

The use of new technologies is rising and its alignment with knowledge is setting a new reality in which the connectivity, interactions and the visualisation of all the activities are not centralized, but distributed, collaborative and interactive. In addition, it is very important to improve the educational process taking advantage of science, new technologies and resources that can enhance learning. In that way, nowadays, the use of IT tools to support education is a reality which is optimizing the teaching and learning processes.

The use of electronic media and IT tools for educational purposes is known as e-learning. According to [3] e-learning has to move beyond platforms such as Learning Management Systems (LMS) to get students to do collaborative activities using actively the IT resources.

Furthermore, IT tools such as Augmented Reality (AR) could bring benefits to teaching-learning processes, by means of an intuitive way for interaction and collaboration between real and augmented objects. Such an approach is not possible for instance, adopting Virtual Reality, where a complete simulated world is deployed and interaction with real world does not exist [6].

In this context, the main goal of the system presented in this paper is to integrate both AR and LMS technologies to create a powerful collaborative educational system, i.e to develop a set of computer tools focused on collaborative

R. Hervás et al. (Eds.): UCAmI 2014, LNCS 8867, pp. 52–59, 2014.
© Springer International Publishing Switzerland 2014

and interactive learning through AR contents. With this purpose, an authoring tool integrated in a collaborative LMS platform has been developed. The application generated by the authoring tool and located in the LMS can be run by students in an interactive way on mobile devices, with learning purposes.

As an example, a natural science teacher could take advantage of mobile devices and AR technologies to teach The Earth's layers creating an interactive exercise. Moreover, the application should be available in the LMS. In order to achieve these targets, the main contributions of this paper are:

1. An **authoring-tool** which allows non-expert users to generate a whole AR application easily.
2. The development of an architecture that allows the **integration** of the authoring tool **in LMS**.
3. An **AR engine** with a **distributed architecture** among The Cloud and mobile devices that allows creating AR applications.
4. **AR collaborative** applications which allow the **interaction among students**.

2   Related Work

Thanks to the emergence of new mobile devices, AR technologies have been quickly developed. New mobiles have all the features needed to launch AR applications in a single device. They are equipped with high speed Internet connection, good computational power, cameras, as well as sensors such as GPS. As a consequence, the use of AR has received a lot of attention in education [13]. There is no doubt on the potential of AR content for improving motivation and learning as showed in studies like [11] and [13], but the lack of standards drags out the integration in educational environments.

Currently, AR based educational systems still don't offer a standard solution that gathers all the functionalities previously mentioned in the Introduction. One of the first approaches to an educational platform with AR was presented in [8]. They took advantage of the first versions or Web3D technologies to introduce a web-based editor for creating 3D content and a viewer for educational purposes. Although the idea was innovative the installation of specific plug-ins was required and it was intended for a tabletop environment.

Some works use AR for a particular educational application. For example [12] work proposes a simple interface for examination applications that allows user interaction with the finger. This approach limits the user to say yes or no, and still no standards are applied for integration with LMS. Also the system in [5] uses an authoring tool to develop AR applications for industrial sequential procedures. Despite the sequential application is a considerable improvement it is required to use specific hardware and software.

An AR based mobile software that provides 3D and multimedia e-learning material for complementing books or other educational support is presented in [7]. Markers embedded on books or other supports can be used to launch the AR tracking for enriching the education content. Although this work proposes the integration with LMS tools it is quite limited as there is no general authoring tool for creating the content.

An improvement was made in [2] by presenting a Web3D based authoring tool for designing an AR scene using a textured marker and a reference image of the real world. Once the scene is created the application is available to download in a mobile device that will render the scene as designed. The strong point is that standard web technologies are used but still this is limited to a single scene and no integration with educational platforms is presented.

In this paper, based on the aspects that a teaching AR framework must cover according to [9], a framework for creating sequential AR applications for mobile devices is proposed. An easy-to-use authoring tool integrates with LMS so the applications are shown as activities in LMS courses. Students can remotely download the applications.

3   System Architecture

The AR framework consists of three principal modules that make it possible to create, distribute and execute an AR mobile application. The architecture of the main modules is shown in Fig. 1a and can be described as follows:

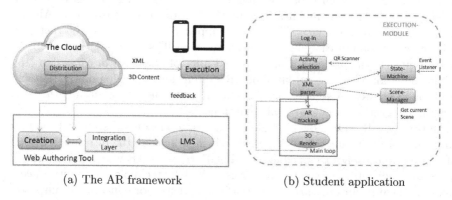

(a) The AR framework   (b) Student application

Fig. 1. The Creation Module schema and the Execution Module schema

- **Creation module:** It is a Web3D authoring tool that allows the creation of an AR activity. A non-expert user can create an AR application by setting sequences of scenes and events.
- **Distribution module:** A server on The Cloud stores the multimedia content, the applications, an AR engine and the different user's data. This way the created content and applications are available to download remotely.
- **Execution module:** The mobile application is able to select and download any activity created with the authoring tool. Once the content is downloaded the mobile application launches the tracking process.

In order to make possible the integration with LMS, the integration layer must be also developed. Section 4 is dedicated to analyse this layer. Besides, in the next paragraphs the different modules of the framework are explained in detail.

Creation Module

The module for creating AR educational applications is a Web3D based authoring tool. The web interface consists of a state-machine editor, a scene editor, an action and event editor. See Fig. 2.

Going back to the previously mentioned example, the AR application should do the following: when a specific textured image is captured by the camera in the mobile device a 3D model of The Earth must appear augmented in the scene. Some questions about The Earth's layers will be asked to the student, who must answer by clicking with the finger in the right area of the model rendered. If the answer is correct the application will change to the next AR scenario. The state-machine editor represents this whole AR exercise using a flowchart (Fig 2a). The teacher can build the flowchart by placing boxes and arrows in the graphic interface. Each box is a state and the arrows represent the conditions for passing from one state to another. The teacher may select a box to configure the scene associated, which is done in the scene editor.

The scene editor allows configuring the states of the exercise. Each state is represented by an augmented scene composed by 3D object and a textured marker that will be recognized by the AR engine. The user must select a textured marker image and a picture of the real world in which that textured marker appears. The pair of images is sent to the remote AR engine, which returns the 3D camera position. This position is used to overlay the augmented content on the picture. The user can rotate, translate and scale any object (Fig 2b).

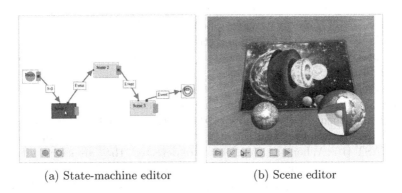

(a) State-machine editor   (b) Scene editor

Fig. 2. The AR Web3D authoring tool

The multimedia objects available can be images, videos or 3D models. After an object is placed in the scene the action editor will show a list of actions for that object, like "show", "launch animation" or "hide".

The event editor is used to define the transitions between connected states. It is enabled when the user selects an arrow on the state-machine editor. The event editor shows the list of objects in the source scene and the available events for each object: "click", "end", "animation", "timer". At least one event must be selected for any of the objects. If more than one event is selected both will trigger the transition. For example, a change of scene may be triggered by either clicking on a 3D model or when an animation finishes.

Once the activity is finished it may be saved and exported as an XML file. The document encodes the state-machine, the URL for the multimedia content and the position matrix for every element at each scene. The XML file is stored in The Cloud so any student can download it remotely.

Distribution Module

The functionalities of this module are to separate the AR processing from the authoring tool, to store the multimedia content and to manage students' interactions and feedback. A server on The Cloud controls all these tasks.

In order to augment extra information in the environment the position and orientation of the mobile device must be estimated in real-time. Mobile devices already offer position and orientation information, using some internal sensors such as GPS, compass and accelerometers. Nevertheless the position obtained using those sensors is not accurate enough to insert 3D augmented elements in the real scene. However, using vision-based algorithms and the camera of the mobile device is sufficient to calculate the localization of the device accurately.

The AR engine developed in this paper implements vision-based algorithms that use a previously known marker to locate the device. The marker is an specific textured image chosen by the user through the authoring-tool, and must be trained previously. When the AR application is running, using the camera of the device, the marker can be recognized in the environment and consequently the localization of the device can be calculated easily and fast.

For this reason the AR engine is distributed between The Cloud, where the training process is done, and the mobile device, where the tracking process is done in real-time using the camera.

The AR engine trainer is listening for the Creation Module's petitions. When a pair of images marker-scene is sent to the AR engine, the detection and training process is launched. Feature points of the marker, named *KeyPoints* must be detected. In this case, the features are detected using a corner detector algorithm named FAST [10]. When the *KeyPoints* are detected, they are saved with their position in the image, and their descriptors. Descriptors are vectors that encode their appearance of each point. In this case the descriptors used are FREAK [1] owing to the agility to process them.

When the AR application is launched in a mobile device, a tracking process is launched locally. The main goal of this process is to recognize the textured marker in the environment and calculate the position of the device.

The Cloud module also stores the applications created, which are encoded as an XML file. The document encodes data from each scene, actions, events, and the 3D position of multimedia content, the URLs of downloadable content and the course associated in the LMS.

The server also has functionality for collaborative activities. Several students can run an activity in their own devices remotely, in a similar way a multiplayer game is played. The server controls a unique state-machine and event handler for all the students and shares it via TCP connection. When a device reports an event, the server checks if it is valid for a change of state and propagates the new state to the rest of the devices. All the students will see synchronized scenes at their respective devices.

Execution Module

It is necessary to install a mobile application to play the created activities. The goal of the application is to be as general as possible so it can cope with any kind of activity. To achieve this, the application implements an XML parser, a state-machine interpreter and a scene manager. (Fig. 1b).

At the beginning a log-in screen verifies the user credentials against the LMS. Next there is a screen for selecting the desired activity. This is done by scanning a QR from the course web page, which encodes the URL of the XML file. Also the user can invite other logged users to play the activity in a collaborative way. This means that the AR activity can be done by more than one student together, i.e they do the activity jointly from different mobile devices.

Once the activity is launched the mobile downloads the XML file from The Cloud, as well as the multimedia content. The application creates the state-machine and the scene manager, and starts detecting markers in the scene.

The scene manager renders scenes associated to the current state. When a texture marker is detected in the real world, the current scene is rendered until a trigger event occurs. The multimedia content is displayed according to the actions set by the teacher for the scene (See Fig 3b).

In the tracking process the features of the image must be detected as it is done in training process. Then, calculating Hamming distance between *KeyPoints* of the current and training image the match of points is gotten to extract the 3D pose of the camera using a homography calculation. [4].

4   Use Case: Integration Layer with Moodle

The potential of the proposed framework is in part thanks to the integration of the authoring tool in a LMS. In this section the particular case for the integration layer with Moodle is explained.

It was necessary to develop a Moodle plugin for the integration. Moodle automatically detects the new AR module and adds it to the list of resources. A teacher may add an AR activity in a similar way a Youtube video is embedded.

If an AR activity is added to a course the teacher will see an embedded authoring tool for configuring the application (Fig. 3a). Once the application is saved it will be encoded as an XML file and stored in The Cloud. The student's view of the course page will show an embedded QR code with the URL of the

XML file. The student can download any application by simply scanning the QR with the mobile device.

The AR activity is associated to the course by a unique ID. As any other Moodle's resource, the AR plugin can handle information of user's privileges and credentials and it is able to retrieve qualifications.

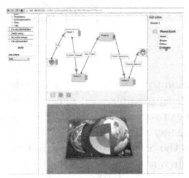 

(a) Authoring tool in Moodle   (b) AR application in a mobile devices

Fig. 3. Moodle and the application in mobile device

5   Conclusions and Future Work

We have presented a framework for creating, distributing and executing AR collaborative activities that completely integrates with any LMS. The activities can be easily designed by a non-expert teacher just by browsing the LMS course web page. Multimedia content can be added and used again and activities can be stored and re-edited later. This novel contribution allows the complete integration of LMS and AR.

Students can play the activities remotely since they have got a smart phone with internet connection. All the technologies are standard and multiplatform so the integration with the educational environment is as simple as possible.

Currently the AR framework is able to design augmented scenes based on the desired texture marker. A less intrusive approach would be the tracking of any 3D textured object instead of the restriction to a 2D texture marker. Also a 3D reconstruction module would allow the handling of occlusions between virtual and real objects, which will become a substantial improvement in practical tutorials with machinery, for example.

Although our approach achieves the main aspects mentioned in [9], it still lacks of geoposition awareness. While for an activity based on a texture marker this is not relevant it would be interesting for outdoor tutorials or courses where the student position is needed.

Acknowledgments. This work has been partially funded by the Spanish Ministry of Economy and Competitiveness under the project ELASTRACK (TIN2012-33879).

References

1. Alahi, A., Ortiz, R., Vandergheynst, P.: Freak: Fast retina keypoint. In: 2012 IEEE Conference on Computer Vision and Pattern Recognition (CVPR), pp. 510–517. IEEE (2012)
2. Barbadillo., J., Sánchez, J.R.: A web3d authoring tool for augmented reality mobile applications. In: Web3D, p. 206. ACM (2013)
3. Dalsgaard, C.: Social software: E-learning beyond learning management systems. European Journal of Open, Distance and E-Learning 2006(2) (2006)
4. Hartley, R., Zisserman, A.: Multiple view geometry in computer vision. Cambridge university press (2003)
5. Orduña, J.M., Fernández, M., Gimeno, J., Morillo, P.: An advanced authoring tool for augmented reality applications in industry. XXIII Jornadas de Paralelismo, 586–591 (2010)
6. Kaufmann, H.: Collaborative augmented reality in education. Institute of Software Technology and Interactive Systems, Vienna University of Technology (2003)
7. Kose, U., Koc, D., Yucesoy, S.A.: An augmented reality based mobile software to support learning experiences in computer science courses. In: VARE. Procedia Computer Science, vol. 25, pp. 370–374. Elsevier (2013)
8. Liarokapis, F., Mourkoussis, N., White, M., Darcy, J., Sifniotis, M., Petridis, P., Basu, A., Lister, P.F.: Web3d and augmented reality to support engineering education. World Transactions on Engineering and Technology Education, UICEE 3(1), 11–14 (2004)
9. Dede, C., Dunleavy, M.: Augmented reality teaching and learning. In: Handbook of Research on Educational Communications and Technology, pp. 735–745 (2014)
10. Rosten, E., Drummond, T.: Machine learning for high-speed corner detection. In: Leonardis, A., Bischof, H., Pinz, A. (eds.) ECCV 2006, Part I. LNCS, vol. 3951, pp. 430–443. Springer, Heidelberg (2006)
11. Di Serio, A., Ibáñez, M.B., Kloos, C.D.: Impact of an augmented reality system on students' motivation for a visual art course. Computers and Education 68, 586–596 (2013)
12. Wang, M.-J., Tseng, C.-H., Shen, C.-Y.: An easy to use augmented reality authoring tool for use in examination purpose. In: Forbrig, P., Paternó, F., Mark Pejtersen, A. (eds.) HCIS 2010. IFIP AICT, vol. 332, pp. 285–288. Springer, Heidelberg (2010)
13. Wu, H.-K., Lee, S.W.-Y., Chang, H.-Y., Liang, J.-C.: Current status, opportunities and challenges of augmented reality in education. Computers & Education 62, 41–49 (2013)

Mobile Augmented Reality to Support Teachers of Children with Autism

Lizbeth Escobedo and Monica Tentori

Computer Science Department, CICESE Research Center, Ensenada, México
lizbeth.escobedo@gmail.com, mtentori@cicese.mx

Abstract. The visual supports teachers use during the object discrimination therapies of children with autism are not interactive, and children with autism lose concentration and motivation, resulting in increasing the workload of teachers during therapies. We hypothesize that augmented reality (AR) could offer a new type of "augmented visual support" capable of providing the visual support and interactivity teachers need to engage children with autism during therapies. We present a deployment study of MOBIS to understand if mobile AR technologies could reduce the burden and workload of teachers during therapies. We analyze a data-set of 8-weeks deployment study of the use of MOBIS in three classrooms of students with autism (n=21, 7 teachers and 14 students with autism). We found that MOBIS enables multitasking, and reduces teachers' burden and workload. We close discussing directions for future work.

Keywords: Autism, Social issues, Technology Enhanced Learning, Cognitive assistive technologies, Pervasive computing.

1 Introduction

Autism is a cognitive disability associated with impairments in attention, information processing and memory [1]. Due to these problems most of the children with autism must need a caregiver to help them when executing the activities of daily living. The role of caregivers in day-to-day life is key to a successful and satisfying life for persons with cognitive disabilities. Caring for someone with cognitive disabilities is a stressful and challenging task [2]. The variety of activities accomplished by caregivers covers all the work required to respond to the physical, psychological, and social needs of the person requiring support. Discrimination training is a type of cognitive therapy, teachers use to empower children with autism cognitive learning [3]. Teachers use paper-based visual support during the cognitive therapies (*e.g.*, discrimination training) to provide students with the support they need to reach their goals. Perform the therapy with a student with autism is an overwhelming task, for example, during our study we found out teachers can't take notes when conducting the therapy and they often wait until the therapy is over or the end of the day. So teachers often make mistakes when taking notes. Also, during discrimination therapies teachers need to constantly prompt students[1] and give away rewards to engage them, while caring from them and maintaining a detailed record of their achievements and behavior. Those

---

[1] For simplicity of reading, we will regularly refer as student to a child with autism.

R. Hervás et al. (Eds.): UCAmI 2014, LNCS 8867, pp. 60–67, 2014.
© Springer International Publishing Switzerland 2014

visual supports used in cognitive therapies help to reduce teachers' burden and workload while maintaining to the student engage during classes. However, paper-based visual supports are not interactive and students frequently lose motivation, adding an extra burden and workload to already overwhelmed teachers.

Augmented Reality (AR) with the potential of augmenting the physical form of a traditional object with the visual support teachers use during therapies could help to reduce the burden and workload associated with the multitasking between conducting the therapy constantly prompting students while giving away rewards, and taking notes.

In previous work [4], we focused on the design and development of MOBIS, and in the analysis and evaluation of the impact among students. In this paper, we focus to evaluate how augmented reality could be used to help teachers to reduce the burden and workload they experienced when conducting therapies while enabling students to use the physical objects during therapies. In this research we present an analysis of an 8-week deployment study of MOBIS an AR application that enables teachers to annotate digital information on physical objects to help students during the object discrimination therapy. The results of the analysis of the data-set demonstrate how MOBIS reduces the burden and workload of teachers during therapies.

2 Related Work

For more than five years, research in ubiquitous computing has explored how to support teachers or caregivers to capture and access relevant data to inform the monitoring of students progress using natural interfaces without significant effort [5]. Pervasive computing technologies for creating and manipulating "interactive visual supports" have demonstrated this new visual support help students remediate their speech and language disabilities (*e.g.,* MOCOTOS [6]), improve their social skills (*e.g.,* MOSOCO [7]), and manage their schedules (*e.g.,* vSked [8]). These works show that there is great potential to use pervasive computing that provide interactive visual support in helping students' training; however, none of these efforts have investigated how to help teachers to train students during therapies while avoiding the workload of teachers and at the same time maintain engage to the students.

AR is attractive to support teachers during therapies, and helping students to take full advantage of visual support, improving their interactivity and attractiveness. The visual support provides help to students during therapies, but there is a lack of mechanisms to reduce teachers' burden and workload while engaging student in the therapy. This opens research questions about how AR technologies could be used to enhance the visual support to provide help to teachers during real time structured lessons.

3 Visual Support Used during the Discrimination Therapies of Students

To understand the characteristics of the visual support teachers use during discrimination therapies and to supplement our understanding from our literature review, we conducted a qualitative study at Pasitos –a specialized clinic were around 15 psychologists-teachers attend to close to 50 low functioning students. Teachers at Pasitos use the combined blocking procedure [3] to teach a student how to discriminate different objects. This method demands the student to conduct trials to learn how to discrimination of one object. Teachers conduct a task composed of 10 trials. During each trial teachers struggle to keep students on task (e.g., engaged in the therapy), so teachers have to invest a lot of effort in helping students during discrimination training (e.g., prompting students and giving away rewards, while maintaining a detailed record of students' progress, and "keeping an eye" on the other students).

4   MOBIS (Mobile Object Identification System)

MOBIS is an AR system that brings interactivity, engagement, and provides visual support during the cognitive therapies of students. MOBIS enables the direct annotation of digital content on physical objects including scribbles, audio, text, or figures. MOBIS automatically prompts and provides rewards to students when appropriate. Also, MOBIS records students' activities and interactions, enabling the teacher to stay focused "on the student" instead of being fixated in the notebook recording information. Details on architecture and functionality can be found in [4].

5   Field Study

MOBIS was deployed (Fig. 1 right) in 3 classrooms of Pasitos, with 14 students and 7 teachers (n=21). All students that have participated in the study were between 3 and 7 years old (m=5.08, sd=0.90). The evaluation study followed three conditions: pre-deployment (2 weeks), deployment (5 weeks), and post-deployment (1 week).

Fig. 1. Participants using MOBIS during the evaluation study. A teacher setting up the therapy (left). A student using MOBIS as a "visor" to identify a giraffe painted in the wall (right).

During pre-deployment, students participated in a standard (e.g., in the desktop) object discrimination therapy including direct instruction from teachers and the use of paper-based visual supports. Then researchers installed MOBIS and gave 3 training lessons to the participants (e.g., teachers and students) in the study. During the deployment phase students and teachers used MOBIS during therapies (Fig. 1). Finally, in the post-deployment phase, participants returned to the first condition, and MOBIS was not available.

5.1 Data Collection

Participants were video recorded during therapies inside classrooms. Researchers observed the therapies during the three conditions of the study for a total time of observation of just under 54 hours (pre-deployment: 27 hr. 11 min., deployment: 15 hr. 18 min., post-deployment: 12 hr. 2 min.). We conducted weekly interviews across each study phase with the teachers participating in the study. Interviews were individually, face-to-face, and semi-structured. Interviews were recorded and lasted about 30 minutes (m=0:43:10 sd=01:10:05). These data-set corresponds to a previous study, and for this study we conducted 5 additional semi-structured interviews. During interviews we asked about the impact of the use of MOBIS in the workload of teachers. At the end of the study, the teaching staff and students completed surveys about their experiences with MOBIS and took part in a 60-minute group interview. Recorded interviews and videos were transcribed to facilitate their analysis.

5.2 Analysis of Data

All field notes, interview transcripts, and videos were inspected together using a mixed-methods approach. The dataset from both deployments and the latest collected data were analyzed for evidence of the efficacy of MOBIS to support teachers during therapies. Researchers followed a qualitative approach to analyze data using open coding [9] and multi-phased affinity analysis [10] to uncover emergent themes from the interview data. For our particular case, the qualitative technique of analysis involved constant sense making of the data collected. The analysis was complemented with discussions among the researchers to validate issues and refine ideas. We then developed a coding scheme focused on activities of teachers. This coding scheme was cross-analyzed during discussions among the research team to validate and refine its categories and properties. Videos were coded using a coding scheme that was developed specifically for this project using LSA [11]. Each video were coded twice from the perspective of the teacher and of the student. A quantitative analysis with the new data-set was conducted to estimate the time teachers spent in different activities during therapies. Videos were transcribed into spreadsheets with columns for time stamps, description of actions, subjects involved in the actions, artifacts used and codes. Inter-observer reliability was acceptable (r=.92). Finally, an ANOVA with repeated measures test was used to compare teachers' activities.

6 Results

MOBIS had a positive impact on teachers' burden and workload. MOBIS helped teachers to reduce the time they spend giving prompts, and taking notes, and enabled teachers to attend multiple students at one time.

6.1   Use and Adoption

Teachers found MOBIS "useful and easy to use". Teachers rapidly learned how to use MOBIS with a few hours of training and with no support.*"For me was very easy, I like the technology, I feel [MOBIS] is easy and practical. And I find [MOBIS] super easy to use, and besides [MOBIS] let me to do more things during a therapy"* (Belinda, Teacher). Teachers used MOBIS for the object discrimination therapy, to setup the therapy (e.g., student, object, trials, rewards, and prompts), monitor the therapy (e.g., trials done and to do, trials with prompts), take notes (e.g., if teachers want to add a particular note), and also print reports about a particular student and/or therapy. *"Everything is faster, because if I am doing another activity [not engaged in the therapy], MOBIS alerts me when the student finishes or if the student needs a prompt"* (Ale, teacher). Teachers felt less stressed about engaging a student in a therapy. *"Additionally I felt myself more independent, in the way that I was able to take care of other students and at the same time looked at the student in the therapy, just observing if the student needs help "* (Ale, teacher). These results demonstrate MOBIS worked as a truly assistive support for teachers during therapies.

6.2   Multi-tasking

MOBIS helped teachers to attend multiple-students (n>1) during the therapy (before-MOBIS: 00:00:13; using-MOBIS: 00:03:09; and after-MOBIS: 00:00:09, Fig. 2 left), without adding an extra burden to teachers. *"[with MOBIS] I felt more independent and free, in the way that I can handle another student in other activity, and at the same time supervising the student using MOBIS".* (Lucy, Teacher)

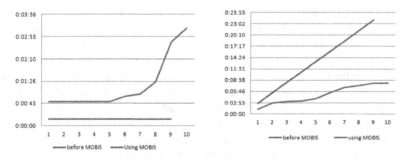

Fig. 2. Cumulative distribution comparing the average time per therapy teachers remained attending more than one student (left), and giving physical prompts (right)

These results highlight that the capabilities of MOBIS for giving away prompts and rewards on behalf of teachers increases teachers' opportunity to improve their performance by managing more than one student at a time (Fig. 2 left). These results are very important because usually cognitive therapies involved individual work –i.e., one teacher attending one student-, and as the rest of the class is unattended. As a consequence classroom activities became more difficult and complicated. Attending multiple students at a time could also contribute to improve classroom transitions increasing consistency in school schedules.

6.3   Burden and Workload

Our results indicate MOBIS reduced teachers' burden and workload in two ways: for taking notes and in their efforts in prompting students to keep them engaged during the therapy. We found out teachers significantly reduced the number of given-prompts when using MOBIS (Fig. 2 right, before-MOBIS: 18.28; using-MOBIS: 9.58; and after-MOBIS: 17.54, p=0.01, df=2). *"[using MOBIS] I don't have to tell the student what to do, over and over again, because MOBIS does it for me, and also because MOBIS helped the student to identify the object" (Angelina, Teacher).*

Table 1. Prompts during the study

Average prompts	before-MOBIS	using-MOBIS
Physical	4.93 (sd=7.52)	1.82 (sd=4.95)
To use MOBIS	NA	5.32 (sd=7.57)
Verbal	13.35 (sd=6.72)	7.76 (sd=7.87)

*NA=Not Applicable

Students needed less educator-initiated prompts (Table 1) and speed up the way classroom activities were executed, reducing teachers' burden and workload. Analyzing the information per type of prompt, we found out teachers spent less time giving away physical prompts when using MOBIS (Fig. 2 right). This shows that this technology is also important because as teachers were less time prompting, that made faster each therapy (Fig. 2 right), and this allowed other students to take the therapy, as there are limited school hours. However, although teachers' prompts during the use of MOBIS were almost absent, we found out teachers did spend a considerable amount of time prompting students to help them learn how to use MOBIS, and specially the smartphone (Table 1). Even though this new type of prompting dedicated to teach students how to use the technology appeared teachers felt less stressed, and they explain to us that after students learn how to use MOBIS the completely faded out these prompts about technology-usage.

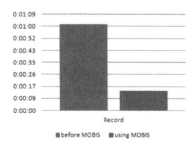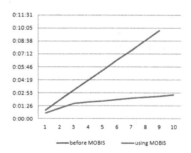

Fig. 3. Average time teachers spend taking notes (left), and cumulative distribution comparing the average time per therapy teachers were taking notes (right)

MOBIS also reduced the time teachers spent taking notes (Fig. 3 left, before-MOBIS: 00:01:02; using-MOBIS: 00:00:14; and after-MOBIS: 00:00:56, p=0.01, df=2) making the therapy smoother as there were less interruptions. This result allowed teachers to be multitasking, attending more than one student at the same time. *"[... using MOBIS] I don't have to worry about taking notes in the correct line, because [MOBIS] does this task for me, and [MOBIS] do it right, it is much better"* *(Ale, Teacher).*These results highlight the importance to support the record keeping (Fig. 3) during therapies when designing augmented reality technology. Supporting teachers in record keeping makes them less stressed about events related to the student during therapies. *"[When using MOBIS] I was observing how the student was working in the therapy. As I know, notes are safe and the student is doing the therapy without my prompts, [now] I can focus in observing how the student works. [I can reflect] about the impact of the therapy and how the student is reacting to treatment"* *(Anna, Teacher).* This automatic record-keeping allowed teachers to have safe and accurate notes, because teachers don't have to wait until the end of the therapy or the day to capture notes. Teachers can have real data in real time about each therapy. *"For us, doing the therapy is a hard work, trying to engage the student and taking notes. Because we lose things [...], while we are taking notes. [Using MOBIS] I can see the student; I can see how functional the student is"* *(Anna, Teacher).* Altogether, these results demonstrate that augmented reality systems are important to teachers helping them to reducing the workload associated to taking notes and giving prompts to students.

7   Conclusions and Future Work

AR is important for teachers of children with autism during cognitive therapies. We present how MOBIS is useful to reduce the workload of teachers, helping them to give less prompts and rewards, facilitating record-keeping and letting teachers to attend more than one student at the same time during therapies. We also demonstrate how these positive' results on teachers also impacted the behavior and engagement of the students during therapies. Rather than distracting and increasing errors during the therapy, MOBIS helped students to be engaged towards people and objects –these were the main problems teachers encountered before using MOBIS. We did observed the application evolved from a "toyish" application to a truly assistive support indicating novelty did not play a central role, and that in fact some novelty aspects wore off after the training sessions made prior the deployment condition.

As future work we are analyzing how MOBIS supports skills generalization after withdrawing MOBIS inside classrooms and in real-life situations. We leave open questions as to how an "appropriate AR visor" could impact in the prompts teachers give to children with autism.

Acknowledgments. We thank the participants in this work, the grant MSR Faculty Fellowship Gift, MSR-LACCIR, SEP-CONACYT, and CONACYT for students' fellowships.

References

1. Quill, K.: Instructional Considerations for Young Children with Autism: The Rationale for Visually Cued Instruction. Journal of Autism and Developmental Disorders 27(6) (1997)
2. Guberman, N.: Caregivers: Their Role in Rehabilitation. In: International Encyclopedia of Rehabilitation, Center for International Rehabilitation Research Information and Exchange (CIRRIE), Buffalo, NY (2010)
3. Williams, G., Pérez-González, L.A., Muller, A.: Using a combined blocking procedure to teach color discrimination to a child with autism. Journal of Applied Behavior Analysis 38(4), 555–558 (2005)
4. Escobedo, L., et al.: Integrating the physical and the digital world to increase the attention of children with autism. IEEE Pervasive Computing (to appear, 2014)
5. Abowd, G.D., Mynatt, E.D.: Charting Past, Present, and Future Research in Ubiquitous Computing. ACM Transactions on Computer-Human Interaction (TOCHI) 7(1), 29–58 (2000)
6. Monibi, M., Hayes, G.: Mocotos: Mobile Communications Tools for Children with Special Needs. In: IDC 2008. ACM, Chicago (2008)
7. Escobedo, L., et al.: MOSOCO: A Mobile Assistive Tool to Support Children with Autism Practicing Social Skills in Real-Life Situations. In: CHI 2012. ACM, Austin (2012)
8. Hayes, G.R., et al.: Interactive Visual Supports for Children with Autism. Personal and Ubiquitous Computing 14(7) (2010)
9. Strauss, A., Corbin, J.: Basics of Qualitative Research: Techniques and procedures for developing grounded theory. Sage, Thousand Oaks (1998)
10. Kuniavsky, M.: Observing the user experience: A practitioner's guide to user research. Morgan Kaufmann, San Francisco (2003)
11. Mintzberg, H.: Structured Observation as a Method to Study Managerial Work. The Journal of Management Studies 7(1), 87–104 (1970)

Conquest - Outdoor Based Games Enhanced with Sensors

Mikael Åhlén, Martin Winbjörk, and Simon Hietala

Department of Computer Science, Electrical and Space Engineering
LTU – Luleå University of Technology
Luleå, Sweden
{mikhln-9,winmar-9,simhie-9}@student.ltu.se

Abstract. This paper presents Conquest, a game platform in the class of trans-reality games in pervasive gaming that combines old classical outdoor games that have been introduced in computer games with the possibilities of today's technology to enhance outdoor based games. The proposed platform use Near Field Communication (NFC), location-awareness with Global Positioning System (GPS) and mobile communication to support three game types that are similar and share a common foundation in the context of sensors and user interaction. Finally, we present a prototype with the usage of the Actor model to efficiently map each physical CPU-powered device to a virtual actor in the back-end.

Keywords: Pervasive games, trans-reality games, Near Field Communication, location-awareness, mobile communication.

1 Introduction

Pervasive gaming have been into researchers' interest with different kind of games and approaches. Magerkurth et al. [1] discuss pervasive gaming and states that computer games are nowdays a highly interactive form of entertainment, and one of the goals with pervasive gaming is to engage the players on a higher level than traditional computer and board games, both physically and socially. Computer games lets the player immerse in a imaginative virtual world with sound and graphics which is carried over to pervasive games. Fantasy, challenge and curiosity are the three main elements to motivate players. All of these elements are present in pervasive games and enhanced. In this paper, we describe Conquest, a game platform in the class of trans-reality games primary developed for outdoor usage where the key concept is to combine old classical outdoor games that have been introduced in computer games, such as capture the flag, and bring some of the possibilities of computer games back to the outdoor environment by sensors and mobile communication. The platform is developed so any Internet-enabled device with the required sensors should be possible to use as a client, such as smartphones, tablets, laptops or general microcontrollers with Near Field Communication (NFC), location-awareness with Global Positioning System (GPS) and mobile communication. We present three game types, *conquest, king of the*

R. Hervás et al. (Eds.): UCAmI 2014, LNCS 8867, pp. 68–71, 2014.
© Springer International Publishing Switzerland 2014

hill and *capture the flag*, that share a common foundation and give suggestions on the design and implementation of each game type respectively in the context of the sensors and usage.

The main objective in this paper is to explore the possibilities of outdoor games that are enhanced with sensors. A second and minor objective is to use the Actor model [2] to enable highly-concurrent systems in this type of games and evaluate the resulting system architecture. The prototype client is implemented as an application on the Android platform whilst the back-end is implemented in the programming language Scala on the JVM that provides an Actor model implementation via the Akka toolkit.

The remainder of this paper is organized as follows: Section 2 describes related work, Section 3 describes the background and game types, Section 4 the resulting implementation and technology used in the prototype and in Section 5 we conclude and discuss future work.

2   Related Work

Location-based games in the area of pervasive gaming have many studies [3,4,5,6,7] with similar ideas and concepts, namely that they use the player's smartphone or similar device as location tracker to enhance the physical world with digital technologies and use virtual objects, such as opponents or flags, that the players should capture. Smith et al. [6] implement virtual objects in a game called *The Drop* with some characteristics related to the capture the flag game type described in section 3. They discuss and reason about physical devices but conclude that a physical device have some disadvantages such as that the physical device has to be location-aware and thus require a CPU-powered device with sensors and thus, brings extra costs to the game. Cheok et al. [7] design and implement a capture the flag game with smartphones that players in the real-world outdoor environment are using to track location, whilst remote players with PC's interact with the game in a virtual world in 3D. To represent these flags they use a Linux-based device with bluetooth. Tutzschke and Zukunft [8] implement a generic framework for pervasive games that is close to our approach, and give an example of a prototype of a game called *King of Location* that is similar our presented game type *conquest* and use the player's location to take over bases.

In our review in previous research in this area we have found similar ideas and implementations [7,8], but not with our approach with physical devices and communication over NFC to interact with bases and flags. Neither mentions about any usage of the Actor model and how it fits in this kind of games.

3   Game Types

Different classical outdoor games that have been introduced in computer games often share a common foundation, such as two team-based, with the usage of flags or similar physical and movable objects in the game-play. To bring the computer game types back to the physical and outdoor environment we represent these flags or movable objects with some type of CPU-powered device and designed to be as generic as possible to support a wide range of games with the same device type and tools. With these ideas in mind, we decided that three classical outdoor games that have been introduced in computer games was possible to enhance with modern and digital technology to the outdoor environment. After identifying these three games, the shared components necessary to implement the platform was Near Field Communication (NFC), location-awareness with Global Positioning System (GPS) and mobile communication to allow communication between clients and the server. The *conquest* game type is played by two teams and at least two bases, with the goal for each team to hold and supervise the bases to increase the score of its team. *King of the hill* is a game type that is played by two teams but only one base that each team wants to hold and supervise. In this game type the scoring is similar to the conquest type, and based on base takeovers that increase its own team score, but can also be used with timed scoring, and ends when the games time limit is reached. *Capture the flag* is the most different game type and require the most advanced implementation as well. Capture the flag (CTF) is based on two teams and two bases and each team wants to bring its opponents flag to its own base at the same time as its own flag is in its own base to increase its team score. CTF requires four devices, two as bases with fixed position, and two as movable flags.

All game types share that the base takeovers are made over NFC by players with NFC cards, which could be a smartphone or device with the same required specification to provide host card emulation, which is the the case of CTF.

4   Technology and System Design

The client for the prototype is based on the Android platform running on a smartphone with 3G or LTE, NFC and GPS but designed to support other type of devices, such as tablets, laptops but particular microcontrollers such as Arduino with the required sensors. A minor purpose of this paper was to see how the Actor model fits this kind of system and for this we used the Scala language with the Akka toolkit to enable design of event-driven and scalable back-end applications where its Actor model implementation is one of the core components. The Actor model can briefly be described as objects with an inbox (represented as a FIFO queue) that share its own state by communicating with other actors mailboxes via asynchronous messages to enable highly-concurrent systems. The core Actor in the system is a *Game master* that is responsible for all external communication, such as handle messages passed from the HTTP-based RESTful API used by clients or front-end. The *game master* supervise a set of running *game actors*, that share a general interface for all game types. Each *game actor* supervise its own set of *virtual devices* that maps each physical device used in the game and stores its own state, such as when the device was last synchronized with the server. We see that the advantage of using the Actor model with no shared-state over other shared-state concurrency paradigms is that we can model a highly-concurrent system that makes it easy to reason about concurrency and application logic. To test the system without hardware for clients a simple simulation engine on Actor models was built as well. The testing was performed with moderate load on a single machine, but could transparently scale out to multiple machines with the support of remote Actors provided by the Akka toolkit.

5 Conclusions and Future Work

In this paper we have presented the initial work of the Conquest platform and with this prototype looked at the possibilities with sensors, especially NFC and GPS and mobile communication to enhance classical outdoor games such as capture the flag and king of the hill. We can conclude that the system architecture modeled with actors enabled us to write a highly-concurrent system and think that applications written as agents or similarly to our approach fits the Actor model well. In the future we see that an arduino-based device/client will be developed and analyze what limitations and possibilities that platform has in relation to the Android OS. We also suggest that more lightweight protocols than the HTTP built for sensors and the era of the Internet-of-Things and Machine-to-Machine such as the Constrained Application Protocol (CoAP) or MQTT should be evaluated.

References

1. Magerkurth, C., et al.: Pervasive games: bringing computer entertainment back to the real world. Computers in Entertainment (CIE) 3(3), 4 (2005)
2. Hewitt, C., Bishop, P., Steiger, R.: A universal modular actor formalism for artificial intelligence. In: Proceedings of the 3rd International Joint Conference on Artificial Intelligence. Morgan Kaufmann Publishers Inc. (1973)
3. Broll, W., et al.: Meeting technology challenges of pervasive augmented reality games. In: Proceedings of 5th ACM SIGCOMM Workshop on Network and System Support for Games. ACM (2006)
4. Peitz, J., Saarenpää, H., Björk, S.: Insectopia: Exploring pervasive games through technology already pervasively available. In: Proceedings of the International Conference on Advances in Computer Entertainment Technology. ACM (2007)
5. Stach, C.: Gamework–A Framework Approach for Customizable Pervasive Applications. International Journal of Computer Information Systems and Industrial Management Applications 4, 66–75 (2012) ISSN 2150-7988
6. Smith, I., Consolvo, S., LaMarca, A.: The Drop: Pragmatic problems in the design of a compelling, pervasive game. Computers in Entertainment (CIE) 3(3), 4 (2005)
7. Cheok, A.D., et al.: Capture the flag: Mixed-reality social gaming with smart phones. IEEE Pervasive Computing 5(2), 62–69 (2006)
8. Tutzschke, J.-P., Zukunft, O.: Frap: A framework for pervasive games. In: Proceedings of the 1st ACM SIGCHI Symposium on Engineering Interactive Computing Systems. ACM (2009)

The Brightnest Web-Based Home Automation System

Benjamin Planche, Bryan Isaac Malyn,
Daniel Buldon Blanco, and Manuel Cerrillo Bermejo

Luleå University of Technology, Luleå, Sweden
http://www.ltu.se

Abstract. Brightnest is a generic and user-friendly web-based Home Automation System. Its interface provides users with information on the whole system or with control over the devices and their rules. The architecture is based on web-services and their REST API, implemented using *node.js*. New types of devices can also be easily integrated into the system thanks to an innovative architecture using "JS Drivers", imitating the way a computer usually handles new devices. To demonstrate our solution, various devices were employed, such as *SunSPOTs* and *Philips HUE Lights*.

Keywords: Home Automation, Domotic, Sensors, Actuators, Sunspot, Hue Light, Web-Interface, Webserver, Driver.

1 Introduction

More and more commercial solutions or open-source projects related to Home Automation are available. The objective of this paper is to present *Brightnest*, a light-weight web-based automation system which embraces the idea of flexibility without giving up on simplicity, using recent Web technologies.

The paper is structured as follows: Section 2 presents the current state of Home Automation, while Section 3 states our own approach and its features. The architecture is covered in Section 4, before the conclusion in Section 5.

2 Related Work

A large bibliography exists dedicated to Smart Homes, and many automation systems already exist on the market. [1,2]

The previous years have also seen the development of various affordable and interesting devices, such as micro-computers like the *Raspberry Pi* or sensor platforms like the *Arduino*. Following this evolution, open-source home automation projects — e.g. *OHS*[1] or *OSA*[2] — started appearing, taking advantage of

---

[1] OpenHomeAutomation, 2013, *GitHub Repository - open-home-system*,
https://github.com/openhomeautomation/open-home-system, April 2014
[2] Rupp, V., Woodworth, B., 2014, *Open Source Automation - Automation software for the home and more*, http://www.opensourceautomation.com, April 2014

R. Hervás et al. (Eds.): UCAmI 2014, LNCS 8867, pp. 72–75, 2014.
© Springer International Publishing Switzerland 2014

those to develop alternative solutions. Various scientific projects emerged too, trying to bring together Smart Homes and Web of Things. [3,4] However, such initiatives still lack visibility and diffusion, as formalized by some user studies and reviews. [5,6] They can at first seem too complex to install and manage by inexperienced users.

Current systems can especially be considered as either:

- Too complex, i.e. too technical or experimental, and thus difficult to grasp for users without technical backgrounds;
- Too rigid, especially when attempts were made to improve the user experience, losing in abstraction in the process.

We thus decided to work on an approach to Home Automation which could be easily extended by the open-source community while empowering the end-users with simple tools.

3   Global Features

A major and early designing choice was to put the web-server at the center of our architecture, in such a way that every operation could be done through its REST API. This choice had also for consequence to facilitate the implementation of a Web interface, using the latest HTML5 features to interact with the system and present the data. In order to meet our requirement related to user-friendliness, special efforts were put in the documentation of the system and in the implementation of scripts to ease the installation and configuration steps.

Our second main requirement was to keep *Brightnest* flexible, to preserve as much abstraction as possible. As a result, various features were developed: not only known devices can be added/removed in one click, but the integration of new kinds of sensors/actuators has been simplified as much as possible. The only requirement is to push a small *node.js* "driver" in order to let the server know how to communicate with the new devices. The behavior of the automation system can also be entirely configured, through the definition of simple rules binding sensors and actuators.

To demonstrate our solution, *SunSPOTs* were used as sensors (temperature, light, and proper acceleration). As for the actuators, we worked with *Philips HUE lights* as well as external programs. Configuration requests were sent to the programmable lights through their base station; while thanks to the implementation of a wrapper, applications such as *vlc* could be launched with pre-defined parameters (checked to prevent malicious attacks).

4   Architecture

To keep a clear, easy to improve, architecture, we opted for a *Model View Controller* (MVC) architecture, as shown in Fig. 1.

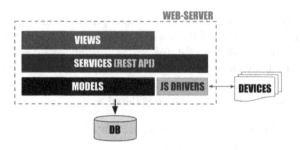

Fig. 1. Webserver Architecture

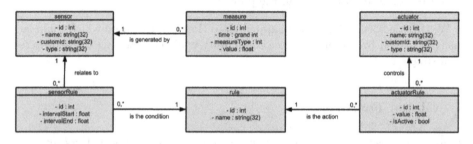

Fig. 2. Entity–Relationship Model

4.1 Models

The entities our system has to deal with and their relations are straightforwardly identifiable, as proved in Fig 2. Though *sensors* and *actuators* are currently modeled the same way (a user-friendly *name*, a *type* and a *customId* used by the drivers), the choice to distinguish them was made due to their different semantics and behaviors.

Measures are timestamped values, with a *type* to differentiate the numerous signals one sensor can generate.

The rest is used by the inference engine, based on customizable *rules*. These rules are composed of two parts:

– *sensorRules*, the conditions to be met by the measures of one sensor each;
– *actuatorRules*, the actions to be taken when all the conditions are met.

4.2 Web-Services

Using *express*[3], a *node.js* web application framework, a clear and effective REST API was implemented. It covers both the services required by the sensors themselves (to push their measures) and those called by the users (to control the devices, manage the rules, or visualize the data). They interact with the models using normalized *CRUD* operations.

---

[3] Holowaychuk, T., 2014, *Express - node.js web application framework*, http://expressjs.com, April 2014

4.3 Views

The views are HTML pages, dynamically filled and updated through Ajax requests. Using some of the HTML5 features, such as the Canvas API or the semantic elements, they offer a clean and ergonomic layout, with an emphasis put on semantics and responsiveness.

4.4 JS Drivers

"*JS Driver*" is the name given to an innovative solution to allow the integration of new kinds of devices into the system. These drivers are lightweight *node.js* modules which contain the necessary methods for the web-server to communicate with the devices they are dedicated to. Drivers for either sensors or actuators must implement an interface of 3 functions — to *add* and *remove* a device to the system, or *update* its definition — though those for actuators must also define a method to *apply* a request. The drivers should simply be placed inside folders defined beforehand, and they will automatically taken into account by the web-server at launch time.

5 Conclusion

While our system isn't polished yet, it provides the basis of a Smart Home. It is simple in design and in use, and thus easy to upgrade. It allows users to quickly and straightforwardly create drivers to run their devices whilst automatically integrating them into the system.

The work that still needs to be done will only further improve its usability (interface, drivers integration, etc.), efficiency (*websockets* instead of Ajax, improved inference algorithms, etc.), and security (authentication, SSL protocol, etc.).

References

1. Brumitt, B., Meyers, B., Krumm, J., Kern, A., Shafer, S.: EasyLiving: Technologies for intelligent environments. In: Thomas, P., Gellersen, H.-W. (eds.) HUC 2000. LNCS, vol. 1927, pp. 12–29. Springer, Heidelberg (2000)
2. Mozer, M., Dodier, R., Miller, D., Anderson, M., Anderson, J., Bertini, D., Bronder, M., Colagrosso, M., Cruickshank, R., Daugherty, B., et al.: The adaptive house. In: IEE Seminar Digests, vol. 11059, pp. v1–v39. IET (2005)
3. Kamilaris, A., Pitsillides, A., Trifa, V.: The smart home meets the web of things. International Journal of Ad Hoc and Ubiquitous Computing 7(3), 145–154 (2011)
4. Aiello, M.: The role of web services at home. In: International Conference on Internet and Web Applications and Services/Advanced International Conference on Telecommunications, AICT-ICIW 2006, pp. 164. IEEE (2006)
5. Davidoff, S., Lee, M.K., Yiu, C., Zimmerman, J., Dey, A.K.: Principles of smart home control. In: Dourish, P., Friday, A. (eds.) UbiComp 2006. LNCS, vol. 4206, pp. 19–34. Springer, Heidelberg (2006)
6. Chan, M., Estève, D., Escriba, C., Campo, E.: A review of smart homes present state and future challenges. Computer Methods and Programs in Biomedicine 91(1), 55–81 (2008)

A Service for Semantic Enrichment of Smartphone Photographs

Andrew Ennis[1], Chris Nugent[1], Philip Morrow[2], Liming Luke Chen[3],
George Ioannidis[4], and Alexandru Stan[4]

[1] School of Computing and Mathematics, University of Ulster, UK
ennis-a1@email.ulster.ac.uk, cd.nugent@ulster.ac.uk
[2] School of Computing and Information Engineering, University of Ulster, UK
pj.morrow@ulster.ac.uk
[3] School of Computer Science and Informatics, De Montfort University, Leicester, UK
liming.chen@dmu.ac.uk
[4] IN2 Search Interfaces Development Ltd
{gi,as}@in-two.com

Abstract. This paper describes an approach to model data extracted from several geospatial data sources based on the geo-metadata from a smartphone photograph. The model enables the geospatial data sources to be cross referenced and inferences made about the relationships between the data and the photograph. The service provided by our system takes a photograph and generates semantic geospatial enrichments that can be annotated to the photograph.

Keywords: Geospatial data, Semantic enrichment, Spatial ontology, Smartphone photograph.

1   Introduction

With the increasing abundance of smart devices for creating and consuming media, such as smartphones, tablets and smart digital cameras, it has become effortless to create vast amounts of information. In 2012 the number of smartphones globally exceeded 1 billion and this is expected to double by 2015 [1]. Gartner predicts that by 2015 80% of mobile handsets sold globally will be smartphones and these will outweigh PCs as the most common device to access the web [2]. The ease with which media can be captured and uploaded online results in vast amounts of information being created and stored online daily. There are also an increasing number of online information sources and tools being made publicly available, such as DBpedia[1], Flickr[2] and YouTube[3]. With this information deluge it has become increasingly time-consuming to decipher actionable information upon which informed decision making can be based. This is particularly the case for multimedia content, such as photographs and videos where a means to better organize, categorize and make searchable

---

[1] http://dbpedia.org/
[2] https://www.flickr.com/
[3] https://www.youtube.com/

R. Hervás et al. (Eds.): UCAmI 2014, LNCS 8867, pp. 76–79, 2014.
© Springer International Publishing Switzerland 2014

the generated media is required. Users are subsequently suffering from information overload and struggle to discriminate relevant from irrelevant information. To solve this problem there is a need to have more detailed and useful metadata attached (e.g. to photographs), to facilitate and improve organization and categorization to facilitate relevant searches. During media capture, limited metadata is attached to the media. Recently, with the increased use of smart digital cameras, Global Positioning System (GPS) coordinates embedded in the metadata can be used for searching and categorization. In addition by analyzing the image pixels it is possible to determine if a photograph was taken indoors or outdoors, and its location based on the photometric effects of shadows [3]. There is, however, a specific lack of semantic geospatial information in the form of metadata. The remainder of this paper is organized as follows. Section 2 discusses related work; Section 3 describes the proposed geospatial data model; Section 4 discusses the Conclusions and Future Work.

2   Related Work

The majority of related work in the media enrichment research area involves automatic image annotation based on extracted semantic features from the image pixel data. Ballan *et al* discuss an approach to video annotation and retrieval using ontologies and rule learning [4]. Their approach uses semantic concept classifiers and Semantic Web Rule Language (SWRL) to determine what concepts are in the video and then generate annotations based on these concepts. Relevant to work in the current paper is their use of ontologies and rules to automatically determine appropriate annotations. However, their method uses a predefined set of trained concepts to search for in a given image. This limits the annotations only to those that the system has been trained to recognize. In contrast the proposed approach in this paper to geospatial semantic annotation uses the information and concepts extracted from various datasets to then construct an ontology that enables further semantic inferences to be made based on a set of rules. Bannour and Hudelot discuss the use of ontologies for image annotation and highlight that in order to enable complete high-level semantic annotations the use of several knowledge sources is needed and inferences must be made across the knowledge sources [5]. Yi discusses the use of ontologies for the fusion of multiple geographic data sources and entity matching [6]. The work discusses what information is considered relevant and useful in an ontology based on the different points of view of the different research communities. Given that this makes the process of fusing several ontologies together challenging, the paper proposes a graph model based ontology method to facilitate fusion of multiple geographic ontologies [6]. The approach matches entities; however it lacks the ability to determine geospatial relationships between the entities which are a particular media requirement for our geospatial model.

Taking into consideration related work it is clear that there are still many gaps in media enrichment which have not been addressed, in particular the area of geospatial semantic enrichment of media. This paper proposes to address these issues by developing a way to fuse several geospatial data sources together and model this data such that it can easily be used for searching and retrieval of the media.

3   Geospatial Data Modeling

In our previous work we extracted geospatial information from multiple geospatial data sources [7], [8]. We used the GPS coordinates in a photograph to extract different items of information and fused the result sets together. This data needs to be analyzed and interpreted so that an understanding of how the data relates to the media can be established in an automatic way. To do this the data needs to be modeled such that inferences can be made across the data, thus enabling relationships between the extracted data and the media to be determined. The model needs to be able to store links back to the original data source in order to enable verification and provenance of the data. Given that some of the data sources are part of the linked data cloud, this link to the original data source can be used by applications as an entry point to the linked cloud. Applications can then further follow the linked cloud links and gather more information beyond the scope of the extracted geospatial data. In the following sections we discuss the approach taken to model the data extracted from several geospatial data sources and how to automatically infer the relationships between the data and the media.

3.1   Data Model

For our data model to handle all the criteria described above we choose to model the data in an ontology. This has many benefits and extra features which enables our system to reason over the extracted data and infer relationships between the data. To handle the data model we modified our system architecture [7], [8] so that in the extraction layer we create sets of triples representing the extracted objects and their attributes such as latitude, longitude, place name and place feature (building, statue, etc). These triples represent subject-predicate-object. During the model population phase, we calculate predefined attributes, such as the distance to each Point Of Interest (POI) from the photograph. This pre-calculation enables faster processing in our model. We then run SWRL rules against the model to enable inference of further information. Our system permanently stores this inferred information and so avoids the recalculation of this information, thus speeding up the annotation generation process. The intention is that our system will begin to learn more accurately what relevant annotations to associate with a given location.

3.2   SWRL Rules

We apply SWRL rules to the model to infer further information and relationships, in particular that of the POIs to the photograph. Due to the complexity of geospatial calculations we developed several custom SWRL built-ins, for example to calculate compass bearing, distance between two GPS coordinates and name similarity. These built-ins then supply values back to the rule which can be used for comparisons or in the result of the rule. An example is shown below, where one of the rules is to calculate if the POI is in the direction the photograph was taken. This coupled with the distance from the photograph, enables a query easily to determine what the photograph is looking at and so adds additional semantic context to the photograph.

This rule determines if a POI lies within +/- 20° of the photographs compass and so implies that the photograph is looking in the direction of the POI. 40° is assumed to be a reasonable field of view that's likely to contain the main subject of the photograph.

```
poi(?p) ∧ photograph(?photo) ∧ latitude(?p, ?poilat) ∧ longi-
tude(?p, ?poilon) ∧ latitude(?photo, ?photolat) ∧ longi-
tude(?photo, ?photolon) ∧ compass(?photo, ?photocompass) ∧
p1:IsLookingInDirection(?poilat, ?poilon, ?photolat, ?photolon,
?photocompass, 20) → islookingindirection(?photo, ?p)
```

4   Conclusions and Future Work

In conclusion our semantic enrichment model provides a way to model geospatial information extracted from many datasets and infer relationships between the extracted information and a photograph. It also enables conflict resolution between the extracted information, such as the city location of the photograph. The model requires further refinement with regard to what the most appropriate relationships are that could be inferred using SWRL rules. Future work will also look at linking and embedding the model into a photograph to enable sharing.

References

1. Yang, J.: Smartphones in Use Surpass 1 Billion, Will Double by 2015 (2012), http://www.bloomberg.com/news/2012-10-17/smartphones-in-use-surpass-1-billion-will-double-by-2015.html (accessed: May 29, 2014)
2. Pettey, C.: Gartner Identifies the Top 10 Strategic Technology Trends for 2013 (2012), http://www.gartner.com/newsroom/id/2209615 (accessed: May 15, 2013)
3. Zheng, Y.-T., Zha, Z.-J., Chua, T.-S.: Research and applications on georeferenced multimedia: A survey. Multimed. Tools Appl. 51(1), 77–98 (2010)
4. Ballan, L., Bertini, M., Del Bimbo, A., Serra, G.: Video annotation and retrieval using ontologies and rule learning. IEEE Multimed. 20(17), 2–10 (2010)
5. Bannour, H., Hudelot, C.: Towards ontologies for image interpretation and annotation. In: 2011 9th Int. Work. Content-Based Multimed. Index., pp. 211–216 (June 2011)
6. Yi, S.: Learning ontologies for geographic entity matching and multi-sources data fusion. In: 21st Int. Conf. Geoinformatics, pp. 1–5 (2013)
7. Ennis, A., Chen, L., Nugent, C., Ioannidis, G., Stan, A.: A System for Real-Time High-Level Geo-Information Extraction and Fusion for Geocoded Photos. In: Proc. Int. Conf. Adv. Mob. Comput. Multimed., MoMM 2013, pp. 75–84 (2013)
8. Ennis, A., Chen, L., Nugent, C., Ioannidis, G., Stan, A.: High-level geospatial information discovery and fusion for geocoded multimedia. Int. J. Pervasive Comput. Commun. 9(4), 367–382 (2013)

Notifications for Collaborative Documents Editing

An Augmented Object Approach

Gustavo López and Luis A. Guerrero

CITIC, ECCI, Universidad de Costa Rica, San José Costa Rica
gustavo.lopez_h@ucr.ac.cr, luis.guerrero@ecci.ucr.ac.cr

Abstract. In a collaborative writing session one of the most important activities is the notification to all the collaborators about changes in documents (data awareness). In this paper we propose the use of an augmented object as the mechanism to notify changes in shared documents. In this way, collaborators can be aware of modifications even if they are not in front of the computer. A prototype was implemented and evaluated. The augmented object prototype can be used with the Google Docs suite, which permits the collaborators to work in a distributed and asynchronous way.

Keywords: Collaborative writing, Augmented objects, Awareness, Notifications.

1   Introduction

When working with other people on a document using a collaborative editor, the focus is normally the document itself instead of the people that is working on it. Users want to know whether the document has been changed or reviewed since they last view it.

Since the invention of computers different applications have been developed to support document writing and editing, and thanks to the Internet, these applications have been expanding to support collaborative work. Many strategies for collaborative writing have been described in the literature [1] [2]. According to these strategies the collaborative work can be parallel or sequential. Either way, direct communication is needed in order to complete the work efficiently.

In this research paper we propose the use of augmented objects to keep track of changes in documents being processed in collaboration with other people; such notifications are based on the writing strategies presented by Lowry et al. [1].

As the collaboration tool we decided to use Google Drive because it is one of the most used tools nowadays. In 2010 Google launched Google Docs, an office suite for text, spreadsheets and slides processing. This service allows real-time collaboration on documents by a large number of users. One of the main characteristics of Google Drive is that it allows tracking notifications in real time, providing graphical feedback to users. Google Drive strongly relies on graphical user interfaces via Web browsers to provide user interaction and access to the stored data [3].

R. Hervás et al. (Eds.): UCAmI 2014, LNCS 8867, pp. 80–87, 2014.
© Springer International Publishing Switzerland 2014

We have been working with Google Drive since 2011 and through usability testing and user feedback, we have identified a need for automatic notifications of changes on files.

Recent modifications on Google's software allow the user to keep track of the history of changes made to files. History reviewing also relies on the Graphical User Interface so if the user wants to know if a document has been changed he/she has to access the software tool.

We found the possibility to address the notification needed via an augmented object by applying Ubiquitous Computing principles to alert Google Docs users about changes in the documents. In a previous work we created an augmented object that uses post-it notes to alert users of incoming important mail [4]. Now we propose an adaptation of this object in order to support data awareness.

In order to be able to discern when to notify a user, a writing strategy must be defined. The solution we propose supports all collaborative writing strategies presented by Lowry et al. [1].

To illustrate this need, consider the following hypothetical scenario: three researchers are working on a paper, two of them are the main authors and the other one is a reviewer. The reviewer does not want to know anything about the paper unless is ready to be reviewed, and both authors want to know if the other one is working on the paper. Our system will deliver notifications to the authors every time the other one access and changes the shared document. When both authors finish writing the document a property set by the authors triggers the notification to the reviewer. Using the same mechanism the reviewer can trigger a notification to the authors in order to check the proposed improvements when finished.

This paper is organized as follows: in the next section we discuss some aspects related to collaborative writing. Section 3 shows some related works. Section 4 presents our prototype. Finally, Section 5 shows some conclusions and further work.

2   Collaborative Document Editing

Collaborative document editing tools allow people to share and work synchronously or asynchronously on documents via Internet. Most collaborative editing tools rely on visual features of graphical user interfaces. Some examples of collaborative editing tools are: Box [5] that allows users to view, edit and work with documents in collaboration with other users; Google Drive [6] that is a file storage and synchronization service provided by Google; and Collabedit [7] that works similar to the above but supporting collaboration on software programming.

On this research we use Google Drive as the tool for collaboration. The main activities that Google Drive supports are: (1) moving or removing, (2) renaming, (3) uploading, (4) sharing, and (5) editing and commenting. This tool has an activity-tracking panel, which uses a Graphical User Interface. The users need to login in order to check out if there's been any changes in the documents.

In 2013 a Google Drive update allowed email notifications of changes on spreadsheets. Even though this feature is helpful still requires the user to check the changes in order to determine whether an action on his/her part is required. A similar problem was described by López et al. focused on notifications for important emails [4].

The possibilities to define an alert in the actual Google tool are the following: alert when changes are made; alert when one spreadsheet is modified; alert when any of the following cells are modified; alert when a collaborator is added or eliminated.

The possible granularities are: email me immediately or email me a daily digest. Google also allows pushing notifications that are considered for following iterations of the system. The following is an example of the mail send by Google Docs when a notification rule is triggered.

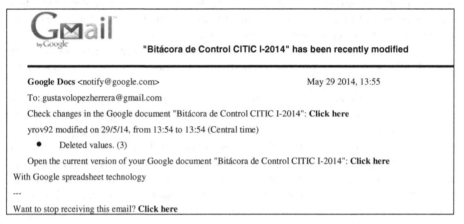

Fig. 1. An email sent by notify@google.com with a notification of a change

Figure 1 shows a notification email received when the document has been changed, it also shows who performed the change and when. There are two links in the email one allows the user to see the changes performed and the other one allows seeing the current document. At this moment, this technology is only available for spreadsheets.

3   Related Work

It is known that notifications are an important part of the collaborative work. The people that collaborate require to stay up to date with the work that has been done, this feature is also known as data awareness. The notification system in a collaborative tool can significantly improve the system's flexibility.

Shen & Sun described a flexible notification framework that guides the design of notification components for collaborative systems [8]. The framework has two types of notifications: the outgoing and incoming. Authors also defined two parameters: the frequency and granularity of the notification. These parameters are used to define when the notifications are going to be delivered and what kind of changes will trigger a notification.

Nowadays, even though many online tools for collaborative document editing are available, many of those tools, known as versioning mechanisms, do not allow users to easily keep track of changes made in the documents. Awareness has actually been addressed for many years especially in large scale editing systems.

Birnholtz & Ibara [9] performed an interview to understand how people work with others using commercial collaborative writing tools. The data presented by the authors help us to understand how these systems are used. Authors conclude that the way in which changes are presented and visualized by users can affect their interpretation.

Other frameworks are present in the literature but they are focused on change awareness based on graphical user interfaces. However, some of the critical aspects of the research also apply to physical notifications through any tangible user interface. The framework presented by Tam & Greenberg [10] includes data like: Who performed the change? What changed? When did changes occur?, among others.

This framework can be used both to inform about and critique change awareness tools. The framework describes high level questions that should be answered in order to remain aware of the document status [10]: (1) Where have changes been made?, (2) Who has made the changes?, (3) What changes were made?, (4) How were things changed?, (5) When did the changes take place?, (6) Why were the changes made? Our system described in the next section focuses on some of these questions and applies them through an automatic detection of changes in Google Drive documents.

4   System Overview

This section presents an overview of the software architecture used to allow physical notification of changes in shared documents using Google Drive suite. We use the taxonomy presented by Lowry et al. [1] in which authors describe several types of strategies for collaborative writing processes. For each possible writing strategy we present a model to support collaboration. For this purpose we assume that the frequency and granularity of the notifications are always the same, any change triggers the notification and the systems verify changes in established time periods.

4.1   Tangible User Interfaces

There is a trend on physical notifications for different systems in current ubiquitous computing research. In this project, we use an augmented object based on an adhesive post-it note metaphor to display the notification of changes in a document being edited collaboratively. Our prototype is based on the one presented by López et al. where authors used Phidgets and a case to hook the augmented post-it note behind a surface and allow it to display the note somewhere in the workspace of the user [4].

Even though we evaluated the prototype using this tangible user interface the front end of the system could be changed with other context aware notification tools applying context-aware and self-adaptations like the ones presented by Ruiz-López et al. [11].

Fig. 2. Notifications shown in context for two different documents and the case with Phidgets that contains the servo that moves the pos-it note (appear and disappear)

Figure 2 shows the notifications being displayed for document changes made by a user. Using this post-it note augmented object (located behind the monitor or the phone) a co-writer can be aware about modifications in the document made by others.

Our main goal for a second version of the prototype is to display a LCD screen instead of a single paper in order to be able to dynamically change the user name and show the date of the change. All this data is already gathered by the system but since we do not have the LCD screen available for this prototype, we only display the notification with a generic note.

In the next section we will discuss different scenarios based on Lowry's et al. writing strategies [1]. For each case, we defined when and what should be notified to users.

4.2   Writing Strategies

This section defines the writing strategies considered in the construction of the notification system and how the software adapts depending on the strategy the group members are implementing.

Lowry et al. [1] present a taxonomy in which they describe various writing strategies for collaboration in the creation of documents. The strategies are: Single-author writing, Sequential single writing, Parallel writing by horizontal division, and Parallel writing by stratification.

In the *group single writing* strategy a group is collaborating, however, only one of the members can edit the document. Notifications are only required when the shared document has been modified by the writer. The granularity of our solution for this case is an immediate notification. The system starts monitoring the documents since they are created. Collaborator can view the document but cannot edit it. The notification is sent when the writer finishes editing.

In the *sequential writing* strategy each writer starts working after the previous one finishes. In this case, the notification is required depending on the previous author. For this kind of notification we established an immediate notification granularity. This means that one of the writers finishes, the next one receives the notification immediately. In this scenario, order parameters must be established in the configuration to set the order in the delivery of the notifications.

Parallel writing occurs when a team divides the work into discrete units and the co writers work in parallel. In this scenario, the group must set the granularity of the notifications because no order can be established in advance.

We did not focus too much on this writing strategy since there is no interdependence between the coworkers and the notifications. It is difficult to set this scenario automatically. Lowry et al. define a variation of this strategy as the *horizontal division*. In this scenario co-writers create subdocuments and afterwards one of the authors is in charge of merging the sub-documents. In this case, the notification is only delivered to the author in charge of merging the whole document once all the sub-documents are finished; and all the members are notified once the merging author finishes the full document. Horizontal-division writing is the most common form of parallel writing in which each participant is responsible for a particular section of a document.

In the *Stratified-division writing* strategy three roles must be set: the Editor, the Author and the Reviewer. The author or writer is responsible of writing a portion of the content. The editor is the person who has the responsibility and ownership for the overall content of product. The reviewer is a person who provides specific content feedback but is not involved in the changes.

In this scenario the author works on the document and when he finishes either a part or the totality of the document the reviewer starts working, hence, he receives a notification. After the review process the author receives the notification and accepts or rejects the reviews by modifying the document and finally the editor makes sure that the final product is satisfactory.

4.3   Google API and the Software behind the Scenes

We designed and developed a specific software tool for change's tracking in collaborative writing processes that uses the Google API to access the shared documents. We use OAuth protocol 2.0 for authentication. The software was designed to use an XML file as configuration. The XML file contains the information about the applied strategy, the document(s) being monitored, the sampling time and the security credentials.

Once the system configuration is ready and data is loaded when the time threshold is achieved the system connects with Google´s servers to check if any changes have been made to the monitored files if a status change is detected the required notifications are triggered. The following are the Google API methods we use in our prototype [6]:

- **Description and MarkedViewedByMeDate** methods are used to allow the system to know if the reviewer finishes his/her revision or the status of the document.
- **ExplicitlyTrashed** method is used when a file has been explicitly trashed, as opposed to recursively trashed. This property is only a check to determine if the file was erased and by whom.
- **FileSize** method gives us the size of the file in bytes. This property is used to determine in parallel work if somebody changed the document, since in this writing strategy it is very difficult to determine some kind of order, this property allows a fine history tracking of changes by measuring the file size.
- **LastModifyingUser, ModifiedByMe, ModifiedDate and ModifiedByMeDate** methods are used depending on the strategy used, since we know each user role and the last modifications made to the document we can discern if a notification is in order and who needs to receive it.
- **LastViewedByMeDate** and version properties help us distinguish if any changes have been performed to the document since the last time the user watched it.

5   Evaluation of the Prototype

We evaluated the writing strategies using the prototype showed in Figure 2 in various real collaboration scenarios. For single-author writing we installed the system in all collaborators' computers in order to display notifications when the author finishes editing. The edition was triggered when the author specified in the description property.

This test showed us that the notification system was functional. The first test also showed that the granularity in which Google commits changes to the server was between 2 and 4 minutes. The granularity to commit changes affects directly the speed of the notification.

Second scenario was the writing of a research paper. The order was pre-established and constituted on the configuration file. When an author closes the document the next one gets a notification. This test allowed us to detect that closing the document (closing browser window) was not a correct action to send this notification.

In a third scenario, a parallel writing strategy was tested for functionality. Four collaborators work in parallel. Every time the document was modified the notification was displayed. This evaluation showed that notifications were not that useful. On parallel work everybody works at any time and since there is no pre-established order, notification was confusing.

The final scenario was for stratified division writing. The document was a simple letter. The author drafted a letter that his boss needed to check, modify and send to her secretary (the final editor). The author wanted to know when the letter was checked by the reviewer (the boss). Once the trigger is sent, establishing the end of the review, the author checks the suggested changes and triggers the editor's notification by changing the document's description. In this case, the system works fine.

6   Conclusions and Future Work

Data awareness is still an open problem in the collaborative work area, particularly in the design of collaborative writing tools. In this paper we proposed an augmented object solution for defining notifications strategies. Using this prototype, authors working in the same document can be aware of changes in the document even if their computer is off. In this way, we integrated the notification system (data awareness system) to the user environment, using a natural metaphor: a post-it note with a message about changes in the document.

Using our prototype we can support awareness mechanisms (notifications) for all the collaborative writing strategies defined in the literature. We can have data awareness about the team work even if the software tool is not running in our computer.

More information can be showed to the co-writers. Our prototype captures more information than the one we can show in a post-it note. In a future prototype we will use a small LCD screen in order to provide more information to the user, for instance, how many changes the document has, the user that made the changes and the time and date, what section of the document was changed, etc.

References

1. Lowry, P.B., Curtis, A., Lowry, M.: Building a Taxonomy and Nomenclature of Collaborative Writing to Improve Interdisciplinary Research and Practice. Journal of Business Communication, 66–99 (2004)
2. Onrubia, J., Engel, A.: Strategies for collaborative writing and phases of knowledge construction in CSCL environments. Computers & Education, 1256–1265 (2009)
3. Herrick, D.R.: Google This!: Using Google Apps for Collaboration and Productivity. In: Proceedings of the 37th ACM Communication and Collaboration, New York, USA (2009)
4. Herrera, G.L., López, M., Guerrero, L.A.: Development and Evaluation of an Augmented Object for Notifications of Particular Emails. In: Nugent, C., Coronato, A., Bravo, J. (eds.) IWAAL 2013. LNCS, vol. 8277, pp. 128–131. Springer, Heidelberg (2013)
5. Box: Box (2014),
   https://www.box.com/personal/online-collaboration
6. Google: Google Drive, Google (2014), http://drive.google.com
7. Collabedit: Collabedit simple collaborative text (2014), http://collabedit.com/
8. Shen, H., Sun, C.: Flexible Notification for Collaborative Systems. In: Proceedings of the 2002 ACM Conference on Computer Supported Cooperative Work, New York, USA (2002)
9. Birnholtz, J., Ibara, S.: Tracking Changes in Collaborative Writing: Edits, Visibility and Group Maintenance. In: Proceedings of the ACM 2012 Conference on Computer Supported Cooperative Work, New York, USA (2012)
10. Tam, J., Greenberg, S.: A framework for asynchronous change awareness in collaborative documents and workspaces. International Journal of Human-Computer Studies, 583–898 (2006)
11. Ruiz-López, T., Rodríguez-Domínguez, C., Rodríguez, M.J., Ochoa, S.F., Garrido, J.L.: Context-Aware Self-adaptations: From Requirements Specification to Code Generation. In: Urzaiz, G., Ochoa, S.F., Bravo, J., Chen, L.L., Oliveira, J. (eds.) UCAmI 2013. LNCS, vol. 8276, pp. 46–53. Springer, Heidelberg (2013)

Design and Evaluation of an Ambient Lighting Interface of HRV Biofeedback System in Home Setting

Bin Yu, Jun Hu, and Loe Feijs

Department of Industrial Design,
Eindhoven University of Technology Eindhoven, The Netherlands
{B.YU,J.Hu,L.M.G.Feijs}@tue.nl

Abstract. Chronic stress puts individuals at an increasing risk of numerous health problems. In this study, we present an ambient lighting interface of a biofeedback system that helps users to self-regulate their breathing pattern in a home environment. To evaluate the usability and functionality of the ambient lighting interface, an experiment was conducted with 12 participants. The results suggest that users would be able to use ambient lighting biofeedback to regulate their breathing with the purpose of improving heart rate variability. Moreover, the lighting interface designed in the study is more acceptable than a traditional graphic interface for home use. We discuss these results as well as design implications for the interface of future biofeedback systems.

Keywords: Stress, Ambient intelligence, Pervasive healthcare, Biofeedback.

1   Introduction

Chronic stress has a number of negative effects on individual health and well-being. Without relief between stresses in everyday life, such stress would increase the risk of diseases such as depression, heart attacks and even cancer [1]. Biofeedback techniques have demonstrated efficacy in coping with stress [2]. Heart rate variability (HRV), the variation between heart-beat intervals, represents one of the most promising markers of the autonomic nervous system (ANS). Due to the chronic stress, the autonomic nervous system tends to be thrown out of balance. Heart rate variability (HRV) biofeedback is a powerful tool for coping with chronic stress. During HRV biofeedback training, individuals will be able to restore overall autonomic balance by following the feedback information and using breathing and relaxation techniques[3].

Pervasive healthcare enables individuals to increase awareness about their health condition through bio-sensing. By integrating computer interfaces into the real environment, a user can obtain health information from the surrounding environment and interact with it. The combination of decorative and informative aspects makes intelligent lighting both pleasant and helpful for users. Based on this hypothesis, we believe that ambient lighting could be a ubiquitous interface in biofeedback systems. In clinical settings, most of biofeedback systems utilize numeric or graphic interfaces as shown in figure 1(b), which may not apply to the average people for home use. Therefore, in this study, we designed a HRV biofeedback system which integrates ambient lighting, assisting users in regulating breathing patterns for stress reduction at

R. Hervás et al. (Eds.): UCAmI 2014, LNCS 8867, pp. 88–91, 2014.
© Springer International Publishing Switzerland 2014

home. In our system, heart-beat data are recorded by a pulse sensor in a bio-sensing unit and transmitted to a data processing unit; then, heart rate variability value is calculated and fed back to users through the changes of ambient light. The feasibility of ambient lighting interface in presenting biofeedback information was evaluated in an experiment with 12 participants. Based on the results, we discuss our findings for the design of future biofeedback system interfaces in the context of pervasive healthcare.

2   System Design

In this study, we designed an ambient lighting interface for a HRV biofeedback system of home use. Users do not have to sit in front of a computer and stare at the screen, but they can perform biofeedback training in the living room, the bedroom or even the bathroom. The intensity and color of light are selected to represent two variables of heart-beats: beat-to-beat intervals and real-time heart rate variability, as shown in Figure 1(a). Light intensity is controlled directly by beat-to-beat intervals while light color is controlled by heart rate variability in real-time.

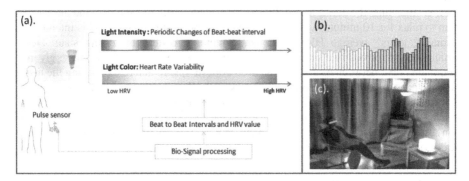

Fig. 1. (a). Ambient lighting responses to HRV (b). Traditional graphic interface

In HRV biofeedback training, the individual can learn to consciously influence the HRV with changing ambient lighting. Firstly, beat-to-beat intervals guide users to adjust their breath to fit in their resonant breathing frequency for example; secondly, actual HRV value would make users be aware of the training effects, which helps to enhance their confidence in a training process. With the user's breathing becoming slow and deep, the beat-beat intervals change in an approximate sinusoidal pattern, and accordingly, the light changes from dark to bright and back to the dark periodically. Depending on the improvement of HRV, the light color changes from warm tone (orange) to calming tone (blue), indicating the degree of users' training effects. The system consists of three parts: a bio-sensing unit, a data processing unit, and a "Hue" intelligent light (*Phillips, the Netherlands*). The heart beat data is measured by a PPG sensor placed on the left index finger. In the signal acquisition unit, the beat-to-beat interval data is calculated and transmitted to the PC's data processing program through a USB serial port. The Hue's intensity and color is controlled by the beat-to-beat interval and heart rate variability via a Wi-Fi wireless connection.

3   Experiment

12 volunteers employed in research positions in Eindhoven University of Technology were involved in the experiment. Subjects' physiological data (pulse and respiration) were collected by a bio-signal acquisition device designed at TU/e and a set of the ANT system (*ANT, the Netherlands*) respectively. All participants complete two biofeedback tests: one with a traditional graphic interface and the other one with the lighting interface, see figure 1(c). Before the experiment, the instructions were given to all participants. In the graphic biofeedback test, the instructions were: "*the waveform represents beat-to-beat intervals, which is related to your breathing. Try to make the waveform in a smooth sinusoidal form by adjusting your breath slowed-down and deeper.*" In the lighting biofeedback test, the instructions were: "*the intensity of light represents beat-to-beat intervals, which is related to your breathing. Try to make the light change from dark to bright and then to dark periodically by regulating your breath. You breathe more slowly and deeply, the changes of light become more smooth and regular. The colors of light indicate the heart rate variability, when it turns from orange into blue, which means your heart rate variability is being improved.*"

After finishing the tutorial, we fitted participants with bio-sensors and instructed them to relax for 10 minutes with eyes closed. This pre-test resting period is intended to normalize users' average HRV value and breathing pattern in resting state. Next, participants performed two biofeedback tests in a random order and they were given a 10-minute break between each test to answer a questionnaire and relax. During the tests, pulse signal was recorded throughout this period. The participants' perceptions were collected using a questionnaire survey. The questionnaire consisted of 21 questions, which were partly adopted from Lund's USE Questionnaire [4]. One-way ANOVA was then used to analyze whether there were any significant differences in HRV and participant's perceptions between the lighting interface and the graphic interface.

4   Results and Discussion

There were twelve participants in this study; however two participants, who did not finish the biofeedback tests, were eliminated. The final effective sample size was thus ten, with five males and five females. In Table 1, the result of questionnaire survey showed that there was no significant difference on user evaluation between ambient lighting and graphic interfaces. In the satisfaction dimension, the feedback of lighting biofeedback test (M=0.53) was positive compared to graphic test (M=0.03). We received more detailed feedback from the open-ended questions. Specifically, more than 80% participants were interested in ambient lighting interface and emphasized that the ambient lighting was very convenient due to fewer restrictions on place of use. Moreover, they found ambient lighting made them feel more comfortable and relaxed during the training. The improvement of HRV throughout graphic and lighting biofeedback tests was calculated as shown in Table 2. Compared to the value before the tests, the average HRV were improved in both tests. The improvement was significant in the graphic test (M= 37%, F=9.11, p < 0.05). In the lighting test, average HRV was also improved by 30%. There was no significant difference on improvement of HRV between the lighting and graphic biofeedback tests.

Table 1. Mean scores of participant's perceptions between graphic and lighting interface

Dimensions	Graphic interface (n=10)		Lighting interface (n=10)		ANOVA	
	M	SD	M	SD	F	P
Ease of use	0.85	1.08	0.74	0.87	0.07	0.797
Ease of learning	1.34	1.00	1.11	0.76	0.39	0.540
Satisfaction	0.03	1.24	0.53	0.92	1.05	0.319

Table 2. The improvement of heart rate variability in the graphic and lighting biofeedback tests

HRV Improvement (%)	Graphic interface (n=10)		Lighting interface (n=10)		ANOVA	
	M	SD	M	SD	F	P
	37*	0.39	30	0.52	0.14	0.72

* p<0.05   HRV improvement: Graphic bio-test vs. Pre-test

Based on these results, we think that ambient lighting interfaces could be a new ubiquitous interface of biofeedback system. In future work, we are interested in involving audio or haptic interface in biofeedback system, which enable users to perform training sessions with eyes closed. In our view, the timeliness, accuracy and stability of feedback interface is crucial to provide a pleasant user experience during biofeedback training. We will reconsider the mapping from physiological information and the properties of ambient lighting, making it clearer and easier to learn. Combining these results with qualitative feedback from participants, we concluded that ambient lighting holds a promise for becoming a good interface to present biofeedback information to users in home settings; specifically for the purpose of relaxation, ambient lighting also has a great potential in setting the ambiance.

References

1. Chandola, T., Brunner, E., Marmot, M.: Chronic stress at work and the metabolic syndrome: Prospective study. BMJ 332(7540), 521–525 (2006)
2. McCraty, R., Tomasino, D.: Heart rhythm coherence feedback: A new tool for stress reduction, rehabilitation, and performance enhancement. In: The First Baltic Forum on Neuronal Regulation and Biofeedback, pp. 2–4 (2014)
3. Lehrer, P.M., Vaschillo, E., Vaschillo, B.: Resonant frequency biofeedback training to increase cardiac variability: Rationale and manual for training. Applied Psychophysiology and Biofeedback 25(3), 177–191 (2000)
4. Lund, A.M.: Measuring usability with the USE questionnaire. Usability Interface 8(2), 3–6 (2001)

A Hybrid Evaluation Methodology
for Human Activity Recognition Systems

Gorka Azkune[1], Aitor Almeida[1], Diego López-de-Ipiña[1],
and Liming Luke Chen[2]

[1] Deusto Institute of Technology – DeustoTech, University of Deusto, Bilbao, Spain
[2] School of Computer Science and Informatics, De Montfort University,
Leicester, UK

Abstract. Evaluating human activity recognition systems usually implies following expensive and time consuming methodologies, where experiments with humans are run with the consequent ethical and legal issues. We propose a hybrid evaluation methodology to overcome the enumerated problems. Central to the hybrid methodology are surveys to users and a synthetic dataset generator tool. Surveys allow capturing how different users perform activities of daily living, while the synthetic dataset generator is used to create properly labelled activity datasets modelled with the information extracted from surveys. Sensor noise, varying time lapses and user erratic behaviour can also be simulated using the tool. The hybrid methodology is shown to have very important advantages that allow researchers carrying out their work more efficiently.

Keywords: Evaluation, Activity Recognition, Synthetic Dataset Generator, Activity Survey.

1 Introduction

Human activity recognition has become a very important research topic, since it is a key technology in applications such as surveillance-based security, ambient assisted living, social robotics and pervasive and mobile computing. Even though activity recognition is very diverse in terms of sensor approaches and algorithmic choices, evaluation is usually carried out applying a very well known methodology:

1. Choose a target environment and deploy sensors to acquire and process information about human activities.
2. Select a group of persons who can perform target activities in the prepared environment.
3. Select a dataset labelling system so datasets generated by users can be used as a ground truth.
4. Run experiments with users and label obtained activity datasets.
5. Use the same datasets to test the activity recognition system and store the labels produced by it.
6. Compare the labels of the activity recognition system with the ground truth using appropriate metrics.

R. Hervás et al. (Eds.): UCAmI 2014, LNCS 8867, pp. 92–99, 2014.
© Springer International Publishing Switzerland 2014

Each of the enumerated steps may vary depending on the activity recognition approach and the available resources. The described methodology, which will be called *standard methodology* for the rest of the paper, is the reference for any group working on human activity recognition.

Nevertheless, there are some problems that make very difficult to implement the standard methodology. For instance, (i) it is not always possible to own an environment and install sensors and processing systems, due to economic reasons, (ii) running experiments with human beings imply ethical and legal issues that can slow down the research process, and (iii) dataset labelling systems are not perfect, since most of them rely on users' memory or discipline to annotate every activity carried out.

This paper presents a novel evaluation methodology to overcome the enumerated problems. The methodology has been named *hybrid* because it combines real users' inputs and simulation tools. The key idea is to circulate surveys among target users with the objective of capturing how they perform certain activities of daily living. Using the information collected by surveys, individual scripts are prepared, which are then processed by a synthetic dataset generator tool to simulate arbitrary number of days and generate perfectly labelled datasets of activities. To get as close as possible to real world settings, the synthetic dataset generator uses probabilistic sensor noise models and probabilistic time lapses.

The paper is structured as follows: Section 2 shows the related work. Section 3 describes in detail the proposed methodology. Section 4 introduces the survey designed to capture how different users perform activities of daily living, while Section 5 presents the synthetic dataset generator tool developed to implement the hybrid methodology. Section 6 discusses the advantages and disadvantages of the proposed methodology. Finally, Section 7 presents the conclusions and provides some insights for future work.

2   Related Work

Evaluation methodologies for activity recognition systems are usually explained in research papers whose objective is to present contributions related to activity recognition rather than the evaluation methodology itself. There are many papers that follow the standard methodology introduced in Section 1, such as [13], [9] or [14]. Other authors use public datasets provided by research groups which own special installations and share the collected data. That is the case of [7] and [1]. The major drawback of such an approach is that those datasets cannot be controlled by researchers and that they may not be appropriate for concrete objectives.

A common problem shared by those methodologies refer to dataset labelling methods. Many research works show experimental methodologies where participants have to manually annotate the activities they are performing [14], [12] and [10]. Wren et al. show in [15] experiments where an expert had to go through raw sensor data to find activities and annotate them. Manual annotation methods are prone to human errors, which results in imperfect ground truth datasets. Alternatives to manual annotation can be found in [9], where a bluetooth headset is used to allow residents tag activities while they are performing them and in [8], where a mobile phone application has been developed to annotate activities.

Annotation problems can be avoided using synthetic dataset generators or simulators. Okeyo et al. provide a good example of how synthetic dataset generators can be used for evaluation purposes in [11]. Their tool is not very complex regarding activity modelling, as authors are mainly interested in time relations between actions. The DiaSim [2] simulator executes pervasive computing applications, but it is mainly focused on applications such as fire situations, intrusions, etc. instead of activities of daily living. Finally, Persim [6] and its enhanced version Persim 3D [5] offer a complete simulation tool for human activity recognition, but they lack a way to model sensor noise and virtual character behaviour.

Inspired on those methodologies, our approach aims at providing a complex and realistic synthetic dataset generator, where user inputs are taken into account through surveys, minimising researchers' bias and combining effectively real users and advanced simulation tools.

3   Hybrid Evaluation Methodology Approach

The hybrid evaluation methodology has been specially designed for activity recognition systems which assume the **dense sensing paradigm** introduced by Chen et al. in [3], where an action of a user interacting with an object is detected through the sensor attached to the object. Even though the methodology itself is not limited to concrete scenarios, the implementation presented in this paper works for single user - single activity scenarios, i.e. only one user is considered and concurrent or interleaved activities are not taken into account.

Based on those constraints, the hybrid evaluation methodology has the following steps (see Figure 1):

1. Design activity survey: to capture how users perform activities, a proper survey has to be designed. A detailed explanation of how surveys are designed can be found in Section 4.
2. Select target users: depending on the objectives of the research, several user groups can be selected. For example, if the system aims at providing help to elderly people, selecting members of that target group is recommended.
3. Distribute survey: a suitable way to distribute surveys has to be used, which guarantees users' anonymity. The distribution method can also be influenced by target users. For example, using web-based surveys can be a bad idea if surveys are directed to elderly people, who can be unfamiliar with those technologies.
4. Translate surveys to scripts: this step is critical. Appropriate criteria have to be adopted to translate the answers obtained from surveys to scripts for synthetic dataset generator. It is very important not to alter or lose the information provided by users.
5. Model sensor noise: sensor noise has to be modelled in order to achieve realistic activity datasets.

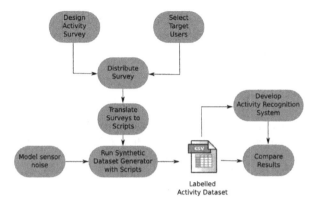

Fig. 1. The hybrid evaluation methodology steps depicted in a flowchart

6. Run synthetic dataset generator: using the scripts obtained from surveys and sensor error models, the synthetic dataset generator is executed. The output of the tool is a labelled activity dataset which will serve as the ground truth for evaluation.
7. Develop the activity recognition system: researchers have to develop the activity recognition system in order to be tested. Notice that datasets generated by the synthetic dataset generator can also be used in this step, specially for data-driven activity recognition systems.
8. Compare results: finally, the results obtained by the activity recognition system have to be compared with the ground truth, using appropriate metrics.

4   Survey for Activities of Daily Living

The survey to capture how activities are performed by users has two main parts. The first part is devoted to capture what activities are performed in different days. The second part, on the other hand, asks users about how they perform those activities based on user-object interactions. An example of a survey used by us in some projects can be found in the web[1].

For the first part, users are asked to describe their week days in terms of activities. They are expected to provide information about time slots and activity sequences performed in those time slots. Users might also be asked to provide time relations between two consecutive activities. For example, between 7:00 and 7:30 AM a user might make a coffee and ten minutes later might brush teeth.

The second part is longer. Target activities are presented one by one. For each activity, several questions are asked to users, to capture the locations of activities, the ways activities are performed, the objects used for each activity, a description of how those objects are used and duration estimations.

---

[1] http://goo.gl/etCNyi

In our current experiments, Google Forms[2] are used to circulate the surveys, because they can be sent by e-mail to target users, users' answers are anonymous and it offers convenient ways to collect and manage received answers.

5   Synthetic Dataset Generator

The synthetic dataset generator tool is central to the hybrid evaluation methodology. The tool has been implemented in Python 2.7[3]. The input to the synthetic dataset generator is a script called *ADL script*.

The first part of the *ADL script* is for defining *sensor activation patterns* for activities. Sensor activation patterns are used to describe how activities are performed in terms of sensor activations. An activity can have an arbitrary number of sensor activation patterns, which are specified with an occurrence probability and a sequence of sensor activations with relative time lapses. An example of sensor activation patterns for activity *MakeCoffee* can be found in Figure 2.

```
MakeCoffee  2
0.50  storeSens@0  mugSens@5  fridgeSens@10  smilkSens@5  afcoffeeSens@5
      coffeePotSens@15  potSens@20  microwaveSens@20
0.50  storeSens@0  cupSens@5  fridgeSens@10  smilkSens@5  afcoffeeSens@5
      coffeePotSens@15  potSens@20  microwaveSens@20
```

Fig. 2. Sensor activation patterns for *MakeCoffee* activity. The activity has two activation patterns with equal probability.

The values that come after the '@' symbol represent the time in seconds between the previous sensor activation and the current one. The synthetic dataset generator establishes a time lapse with a Gaussian random generator whose mean value is the value specified in the script and the standard deviation is the 25% of the mean. This way, time lapses between two consecutive sensor activations are realistic.

The second part of the *ADL script* defines the so called *activity patterns*, which represent different days of the user in terms of performed activities. Two kinds of activity patterns are defined: (i) *sequences*, where a time slot is given with a sequence of activities and time lapses between two consecutive activities, and (ii) *alterations*, where a probability value is assigned to an activity to be performed in a concrete time slot. An example is depicted in Figure 3, where a typical day of a user is described, with an occurrence probability of 0.29, since the activity pattern describes a weekend day ($2/7 \simeq 0.29$). In this case, the user reported that (s)he sometimes reads a book in the afternoon. Alterations allow modelling this kind of behaviour.

---

[2] http://www.google.com/google-d-s/createforms.html
[3] https://www.python.org/

```
Prob 0.29  4
S  9:00 − 10:00  MakeCoffee@0  BrushTeeth@1800  ReadBook@120
S  13:30 − 14:30  MakePasta@0  BrushTeeth@600
S  22:00 − 23:00  BrushTeeth@0  WashHands@10
A  18:00 − 20:00  ReadBook  0.5
```

Fig. 3. An example of an activity pattern, which has an occurrence probability of 0.29 and it is composed of three sequences (*S*) and an alteration (*A*)

The third part of the script is to define *positive sensor noise*, which models the probability for a concrete sensor to get activated in an hour interval independently of ongoing activities. Positive sensor noise is used to model sensor errors and user's erratic behaviour. Erratic behaviour refers to user-object interactions that are not part of an activity. Imagine a user wants to prepare some pasta. Once the store has been open, to grab pasta a coffee recipient has to be moved. This interaction will be registered by the sensor attached to the coffee recipient, but it is not part of the activity. To model sensor positive noise, a probability is assigned to concrete sensors. Synthetic activity generator will use those probabilities to produce noise each hour, using a uniform probability distribution.

But to model sensor errors, positive sensor noise is not enough. Sometimes, sensors that should get activated, fail. To model those errors another file is used: the context model file. This file is a *Json*[4] file where objects of the environment, attached sensors and sensor error models are defined. The file is used to acquire sensor error models, which in our case, have been obtained from the analysis given in [4]. Using this information, synthetic dataset generator introduces a failing probability to any sensor that has to be activated, achieving more realistic datasets.

Using the *ADL script* and the context model file, the synthetic dataset generator creates a CSV file where each sensor activation has an associated time-stamp and is labelled with an activity name or with special label *None* if it is caused by noise. Additionally, activity start and end time are marked in the dataset.

6 Discussion

The hybrid methodology presented in this paper has several advantages over the standard methodology explained in Section 1:

1. The hybrid methodology is cheap and fast: it does not need to acquire or build any special environment, which can be an important investment.
2. A lot of users' information can be used: as it is based on surveys, it is generally easy to achieve a great number of users for the tests.
3. Ethical and legal issues are much softer: in contrast with the standard methodology, there are no experiments with human beings. The only important point to be considered is the anonymity of users.

---

[4] http://www.json.org/

4. Datasets can be generated on demand: using the synthetic dataset generator, arbitrary number of datasets can be generated as needed.
5. Perfectly labelled datasets can be obtained: the synthetic dataset generator labels all sensor activations according to the given script and sensor error models. In consequence, the generated dataset is a perfect ground truth.
6. The influence of researchers is minimised: using surveys, researchers cannot write their own scripts with their bias. Even though researchers are still responsible of writing the scripts, following appropriate survey-script translation criteria, researchers' influence in the datasets is minimised.
7. Any kind of scenarios can be implemented: the synthetic dataset generator allows preparing experiments where no sensor noise exist, where only a concrete kind of sensor noise exists or where conditions are as close as possible to realistic settings. The chance of implementing all those varieties of scenarios allows researchers test deeper their activity recognition systems, since they can see the influence of any factor they consider relevant.

However, there are some disadvantages also. For example, modelling user erratic behaviour is not easy. Although synthetic dataset generator offers a way to model this kind of interaction, it cannot capture it accurately. Another disadvantage refers to the information provided in surveys. Some users are very precise in their answers, but some are not. Sometimes, important details of activities are omitted by users in their answers, hence the precise way of performing activities cannot always be captured.

7   Conclusions and Future Work

A novel evaluation methodology for activity recognition systems has been presented in this paper. It has been shown that the methodology has several advantages over the standard methodology used by the community. However, we do not pretend to substitute the standard methodology. Our approach can be seen as a good complement to boost research and to let researchers who cannot afford following the standard methodology make good science. The hybrid methodology is a good methodology to evaluate research works on activity recognition.

For future work, two main areas have been identified: (i) research on more complex and accurate methods to model user erratic behaviour and (ii) adaptation of surveys and synthetic dataset generator to implement single user - concurrent activities scenario. Advances on those two areas would allow simulating more realistic experiments.

Acknowledgements. This work has been supported by the Spanish Government under the FRASEWARE project: TIN2013-47152-C3-3-R.

References

1. Aztiria, A., Augusto, J.C., Basagoiti, R., Izaguirre, A.: Accurate temporal relationships in sequences of user behaviours in intelligent environments. In: Augusto, J.C., Corchado, J.M., Novais, P., Analide, C. (eds.) ISAmI 2010. AISC, vol. 72, pp. 19–27. Springer, Heidelberg (2010)

2. Bruneau, J., Jouve, W., Consel, C.: DiaSim: A parameterized simulator for pervasive computing applications. In: 6th Annual International Mobile and Ubiquitous Systems: Networking & Services, MobiQuitous 2009, pp. 1–10. IEEE (2009)
3. Chen, L., Hoey, J., Nugent, C.D., Cook, D.J., Yu, Z.: Sensor-based activity recognition. IEEE Transactions on Systems, Man, and Cybernetics-Part C 42(6), 790–808 (2012)
4. Chen, L., Nugent, C.D., Wang, H.: A knowledge-driven approach to activity recognition in smart homes. IEEE Transactions on Knowledge and Data Engineering 24(6), 961–974 (2012)
5. Helal, A., Cho, K., Lee, W.: 3D modeling and simulation of human activities in smart spaces. In: 2012 9th International Conference on Ubiquitous Intelligence & Computing and 9th International Conference on Autonomic & Trusted Computing (UIC/ATC), pp. 112–119. IEEE (2012)
6. Helal, S., Lee, J.W., Hossain, S.: Persim-Simulator for human activities in pervasive spaces. In: 2011 7th International Conference on Intelligent Environments (IE), pp. 192–199. IEEE (2011)
7. Helaoui, R.: Recognizing interleaved and concurrent activities: A statistical-relational approach. In: 2011 IEEE International Conference on Pervasive Computing and Communications (PerCom), Seattle, USA, pp. 1–9. IEEE (2011)
8. Huynh, T., Fritz, M., Schiele, B.: Discovery of activity patterns using topic models. In: Proceedings of the 10th International Conference on Ubiquitous Computing, pp. 10–19. ACM (2008)
9. Van Kasteren, T., Noulas, A.: Accurate activity recognition in a home setting. In: Proceedings of the 10th International Conference on Ubiquitous Computing, pp. 1–9 (2008)
10. Liao, L., Fox, D., Kautz, H.: Location-based activity recognition. In: Advances in Neural Information Processing Systems, vol. 18, p. 787 (2006)
11. Okeyo, G., Chen, L., Wang, H., Sterritt, R.: Dynamic sensor data segmentation for real-time knowledge-driven activity recognition. Pervasive and Mobile Computing (December 2012)
12. Philipose, M., Fishkin, K.P.: Inferring activities from interactions with objects. Pervasive Computing 3(4), 50–57 (2004)
13. Rashidi, P., Cook, D.J.: Discovering activities to recognize and track in a smart environment. IEEE Transactions on Knowledge and Data Engineering 23(4), 527–539 (2011)
14. Tapia, E.M., Intille, S.S., Larson, K.: Activity Recognition in the Home Using Simple and Ubiquitous Sensors. In: Ferscha, A., Mattern, F. (eds.) PERVASIVE 2004. LNCS, vol. 3001, pp. 158–175. Springer, Heidelberg (2004)
15. Wren, C.R., Tapia, E.M.: Toward scalable activity recognition for sensor networks. In: Hazas, M., Krumm, J., Strang, T. (eds.) LoCA 2006. LNCS, vol. 3987, pp. 168–185. Springer, Heidelberg (2006)

Real-Time Monitoring of User Physical Activity and Position in an Outdoor Public Space

Leon Foster[1,*], Mathieu Gielen[2], Mark Beattie[3], and Simon Goodwill[1]

[1] Sheffield Hallam University, Centre for Sports Engineering Research, Collegiate Crescent, Sheffield, S10 2BP, UK
[2] Delft University of Technology, Faculty of Industrial Design Engineering, Landbergstraat 15, 2628 CE Delft, The Netherlands
[3] University of Ulster, Shore Road, Newtownabbey, Co Antrim, UK
{l.i.foster,s.r.goodwill}@shu.ac.uk, M.A.Gielen@tudelft.nl,
Beattie-M3@email.ulster.ac.uk

Abstract. A primary aim of the ProFit FieldLab project is to encourage physical activity through innovations in products, services and ICT systems. User interactions with newly installed prototype play and exercise equipment within a FieldLab needs to be monitored so that its value and effectiveness can be assessed. Real-time feedback of activity level and location is important to associate user activity with specific pieces of equipment and video capture data. However, there is no current off-the-shelf solution for this. The aim of this study was to create a low-cost, real-time activity and location monitoring system based around a smartphone. The system incorporates accelerometer, heart rate, GPS and Wi-Fi RSSI values. Initial testing of the system has shown that user activity level and movement on a specific item of play equipment in the Delft FieldLab can be recorded alongside targeted video capture.

Keywords: Activity monitoring, Participant tracking, Wi-Fi proximity, GPS logging, ProFit FieldLab.

1 Introduction

ProFit is a collaborative European Union funded project that aims to support product innovation and novel ICT system development in sport, exercise and play. Public recreational spaces in four European cities are now hosts to FieldLabs, which serve as end-user locations for research and development of product and ICT innovations. The cities that currently host a FieldLab are: Sheffield in the UK, Delft and Eindhoven in the Netherlands and Kortrijk in Belgium [1]. The unique attribute of a Fieldlab is that it enables the study of products in the natural environment of target user groups. However, a potential downside of operating outside a laboratory is the reduced ability to control research conditions [2]. The development of measurement systems in Fieldlabs reflected the balance between allowing for natural behaviour and the collection of valid data.

---

* Corresponding author.

R. Hervás et al. (Eds.): UCAmI 2014, LNCS 8867, pp. 100–107, 2014.
© Springer International Publishing Switzerland 2014

The Delft FieldLab is located in a children's playground, and is the initial location for the examination of play equipment. The 'Memo' circle, developed by Yalp™ (Fig. 1) was the first piece of equipment studied. This equipment consists of a set of seven poles, each with an interactive and touch-sensitive multi-coloured LEDs. There are currently two games that require participants to chase and hit the changing co-loured surfaces as these move from one LED screen to the next. The Yalp™ Memo is aimed at encouraging play interaction between children and their grandparents. This collaboration between business and university is driven by the role of design in social innovation; looking to reduce the disconnection between children and older people through play.

As part of the ProFit project, information regarding the performance of prototype equipment installed in FieldLabs is fed back to manufacturers. This is part of the product development process, and acts as an incentive for companies to test and eva-luate novel products in a FieldLab. For the Memo, research data is required in two areas: (1) user physical activity level and (2) qualitative feedback on user interaction with the product and other users. Physical activity data can be gained from ICT moni-toring systems, while qualitative data comes from questionnaires and video analysis of users interacting with the equipment. Therefore, in order to monitor the effective-ness of innovations within a FieldLab, user interactions with equipment around the site needs be monitored. One method of doing this is with positional tracking and filming of participants. This will enable the collection of targeted interaction videos, avoid the collection of excessive video data, and monitor the physical activity levels of individual participants.

(a)   (b)

Fig. 1. (a) Overview of the Delft FieldLab (b) Yalp™ Memo circle play equipment

The manual filming of FieldLab participants using traditional fixed or hand-held video cameras is difficult to do on a large scale, and can disrupt a user's natural beha-viour. Any video footage gained in this manner is unlikely to give a true indication of typical user interaction with the site and other users. Unobtrusive monitoring and filming of participants is required to gain a more accurate understanding of user activ-ity. Knowing the position of a user within a FieldLab can enable the autonomous filming in areas of interest, assuming that suitable cameras are used, such as pan-tilt-zoom (PTZ) cameras. Activity monitoring systems such as those based on the Acti-Graph™ wGT3X-BT sensors are designed for longitudinal studies and as such it is difficult to stream live data from them. Additionally the ActiGraph™ sensors do not currently provide positional data. The tracking and monitoring of multiple athletes within the field of play or training environments is becoming common place for elite team based sports. Tracking technology within systems such as Catapult's MiniMax and equivalents are based around Global Positioning System (GPS) receivers and accelerometers. A limitation of existing tracking systems is that they are bespoke and expensive (costing up to £2,700 per sensor unit for a typical system) [3]. This generally makes these systems unsuitable for use in a public recreational environment, such as a FieldLab site. Another limitation of the elite tracking and monitoring systems is the accuracy of the GPS data. In ideal unobstructed outdoor environments GPS has a reported accuracy of less than 1 m [4], but in typical city environments this accuracy is generally lower than quoted figures due to signal obstruction by buildings and trees. In an initial scoping study in Delft it was found that GPS positional data was not accurate enough in a FieldLab environment to distinguish when a user was in close proximity to specific equipment. Therefore, an alternative positioning system would be required to identify when a user was in close proximity to a piece of equipment of interest.

Currently there is no off-the-shelf single system which provides all the information required to accurately track and monitor users in a FieldLab, and to enable the video capture of user interaction with equipment. A custom tracking and monitoring system based around typical smartphones as processing and sensing units (typical unit cost of £150) is described in this paper. The use of typical smartphones enables the system to be flexible, low cost with the ability to augment the system with additional sensors, such as heart rate monitors or blood flow sensors [5]. The sensors employed as part of a smartphone activity/tracking system are as follows: (1) proximity – Wi-Fi, (2) location – GPS/GLONASS, (3) activity – accelerometers and (4) heart rate – peripheral Bluetooth 4.0 wrist strap.

2   Systems Overview

2.1   Agent Software Model – Centralized Database

Given the collaborative nature of the ProFit project, an agent software model was considered to be appropriate. An agent model allows the separate development of software agents or applications that then communicate with each other through a central data storage medium. This enables software to be developed independently at different sites using any development environment. Within the ProFit project all software created for use on FieldLab sites follows a standardised database structure. In this way each FieldLab site has its own individual database based on this universal structure.

The database was constructed and managed through Microsoft™ SQL Server 2012, and runs on a local server. It is accessible by any device or agent software, providing that the correct permissions have been granted and a local area network link has been obtained. For the purposes of this study all activity, location and camera information was stored in this central database. Communication between client and server was via ASP.NET web services.

2.2   Smartphone Activity Monitoring System

Smartphones are now produced with a variety of in-built sensors such as GPS receivers, accelerometers, gyroscopes, digital compasses and optical sensors. These sensors coupled with the processing, storage and connectivity of standard smartphones make them an ideal candidate to form the basis of a low-cost live activity monitoring system for research applications within a FieldLab. There are three main types of smartphone currently on the market, all with advantages and disadvantages: (1) iPhones, manufactured by Apple™, (2) Android™ smartphones, made by a variety of manufacturers and (3) Windows™ phones also from a variety of manufacturers. Due to the widespread availability, lower cost and features available with Android™ based smartphones, these were the logical starting point for development of a low-cost activity monitoring and tracking system.

2.3   Bluetooth 4.0 Connectivity

Bluetooth is a wireless technology standard for exchanging data over short distances. The latest standard, Bluetooth 4.0 or LE (low energy) is used by new body worn sensors such as heart rate monitors to stream live data. Therefore, only phones with this new Bluetooth standard and with the latest version of the Android™ operation system (v4.4) are suitable for use in a system where heart rate needs to be captured.

2.4   Tracking, Wi-Fi Proximity and Activity Monitoring Solution

Global Positioning System (GPS) uses an array of satellites to determine the position of a receiver. Gray et al. [6] showed that GPS is useful for tracking athletes over a set distance but positional accuracy can vary greatly when non-linear paths are measures. Therefore the zigzagging paths envisaged to be used by people in a FieldLab environment will not be accurately monitored by GPS alone. An alternative positional monitoring system based on radio frequency signal strength and time-of-flight of Wi-Fi and Bluetooth enabled devices are the basis of Local Positioning Measurements systems (LPM). These have a reported positional absolute error of 0.234 m [7]. The main advantages of these types of system are that they do not require the use of the GPS, and have higher accuracy. Therefore, it was decided that using Wi-Fi RSSI values from an access point in the centre of a piece of equipment would give sufficient positional accuracy to identify when users were in close proximity. Bluetooth proximity protocols and software development kits are not currently widely available and initial testing with these types of devices have shown them to be unstable when used in conjunction with other Bluetooth devices such as heart rate monitors. Therefore, it was decided a proximity system based on basic Wi-Fi signal strength would be preferable.

2.5 Android Smartphone Application

A bespoke Android™ application called ProFit HRM (Fig. 3a) was created. This had the capability to stream live data back to the central database, comprising: GPS coordinates, accelerometer data, Wi-Fi RSSI values (from the nearest access point), and heart rate data from a Bluetooth 4.0 peripheral. All data was sent at 1 Hz to the central server, to minimise bandwidth and increase battery life. The accelerometer was sampled on board at 100 Hz but an average acceleration value over one second was streamed. The application was developed within the Android Studio integrated development environment and the Android™ software development kit [8]. Once started, this application ran in the background on the smartphone's operating system and the device was given to a participant to be worn in a secure holder on their lower back. Using the in-built Wi-Fi hardware the Android™ smartphone connected to the local server via the wireless connection provided at the FieldLab. It is envisaged that in the future, as the relevant hardware becomes available, this application could be developed further to send other sensor data such as blood pressure, blood flow rates and body temperature. The Android™ application can be deployed on any number of Bluetooth 4.0 smartphones, from Android™ operating system 4.4 upwards.

2.6 Zone Monitoring and Video Recording Trigger

A video and audio based recording system was developed to be used in conjunction with the position and proximity monitoring system. This system took the live GPS positional data and Wi-Fi proximity information from an Android™ smartphone and enabled the recording of audio and video streams. The system was based around an agent piece of software called ProFit Zone (created in Microsoft™ Visual Studio 2012, and written in VB.NET). This agent monitored the database at 1 Hz for the positional and proximity information being fed back by the smartphones and compared this information to pre-set values containing zone information and Wi-Fi threshold values. The Wi-Fi RSSI value of the nearest access point to the smartphone was used only as a measure of proximity and a unique SSID was used to identify the piece of equipment. A RSSI threshold value was setup to indicate when a user was in the vicinity of that piece of equipment. This threshold value can be tailored for specific equipment and environmental conditions. A "start recording" commanded was issued back to the central database when a user with a smartphone was in close proximity to the piece of equipment (below the threshold value). When the user left the piece of equipment and a timeout value was reached a "stop recording" command was issued. A separate recording agent was employed to capture the video and audio streams from cameras in view (Fig. 3c). Video clips were saved on a central server and associated trial information stored in the database. A schematic of the data flow in this system and the agent applications required is shown in Fig. 2 with a screen shot of the ProFit Zone software shown in Fig. 3b. The database structure is shown in Fig. 4. From initial testing it was found that GPS information alone was not accurate or stable enough to measure proximity to a piece of equipment and therefore only logged to be analysed at a later date.

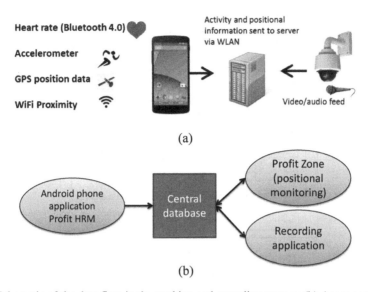

(a)

(b)

Fig. 2. Schematic of the data flow in the tracking and recording system; (b) Agent applications required for positional/proximity monitoring and recording of participants

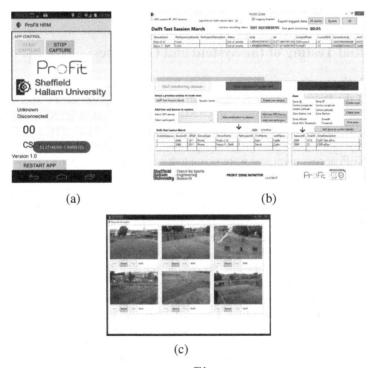

(a)   (b)

(c)

Fig. 3. Screen shots of (a) ProFit HRM Android™ application, (b) ProFit Zone agent application and (c) ProFit capture recording software

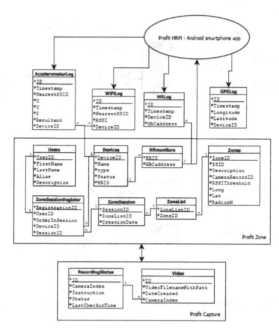

Fig. 4. Database structure and related software applications

3   Initial Testing of the System and Outcomes

The activity/tracking system to monitor user-interaction with different equipment was installed in the Delft FieldLab in March 2014. An access point with a specific SSID was installed in the centre of the Yalp™ Memo circle, to act as a proximity beacon. Database and software applications were also installed on a local server on the LAN. Smartphones running the ProFit HRM application connected to the LAN through a separate Wi-Fi access point and were given to a small number of participants.

An initial test of the system on this single piece of equipment showed that activity and positional data of the participants could be streamed live to the server. Wi-Fi RSSI allowed proximity information to the Memo equipment to be monitored at sufficient accuracy to control the video recordings. The RSSI threshold value was adjusted based upon a small-scale calibration procedure, but this process needs to be refined to accurately define the radius of detection. Activity levels of the participants were logged within the system and accessible through the database. Findings and observations from pilot-tests were reported back to Yalp™. This has lead to various changes in the Memo circle, such as menu set-up and hardware. Some videos were shown to the company to illustrate findings; however, no videos have been transferred, because of privacy and ethical considerations. Players' physical activity levels were also reported, but it was noted that these were provisional measurements with a small sample size. In cases when children opted for cooperative instead of competitive play, the activity levels differed from what was expected. One game was changed by Yalp™ to raise the physical activity level of players.

4   Future Work

The next steps required for the future development of the system include: testing the reliability of the Wi-Fi RSSI threshold values and proximity system; development of a research plan and methodologies to incorporate the system; scoping studies with increased numbers of participants; and also expand the system to work on multiple pieces of equipment. Some initial work has been carried out to demonstrate the validity of activity measurement through the use of smartphones, which has shown good correlation to existing activity monitoring systems. However, this works needs to be expanded and incorporated in to the development of this activity monitoring system.

5   Conclusion

The activity and tracking system presented in this paper demonstrates a novel way of monitoring physical activity and user-interactions within a public open space. The ability to accurately monitor when users are in proximity to a single piece of equipment enabled the live capture of appropriate videos for qualitative analysis. This type of low-cost system enhances the ability of a ProFit FieldLab to collect real world activity data within outdoor recreational environment, but further testing and validation is required to show that the system is equivalent to current activity research tools.

References

1. ProFit 2013. FieldLAB: An opportunity for internation cooperation in sports innovation, http://www.fieldlabs.eu/ (last accessed on November 01, 2013)
2. Markopoulos, P., Read, J.C., MacFarlane, S., Höysniemi, J.: Evaluating Children's Interactive Products: Principles and Practices for Interaction Designers. Morgan Kaufman, Burlington (2008)
3. Catapult (2013), http://www.catapultsports.com/ (last accessed on November 01, 2013)
4. Bajaj, R., Ranaweera, S.L., Agrawal, D.P.: GPS: location-tracking technology. Computer 35(4), 92–94 (2002)
5. Depari, A., Flammini, A., Rinaldi, S., Vezzoli, A.: Multi-sensor system with Bluetooth connectivity for non-invasive measurements of human body physical parameters. Sensors and Actuators A: Physical 202, 147–154 (2013)
6. Gray, A.J., Jenkins, D., Andrews, M.H., Taaffe, D.R., Glover, M.L.: Validity and reliability of GPS for measuring distance travelled in field-based team sports. J. Sport. Sci. 28(12), 1319–1325 (2010)
7. Ogris, G., Leser, R., Horsak, B., Kornfeind, P., Heller, M., Baca, A.: Accuracy of the LPM tracking system considering dynamic position changes. J. Sport. Sci. 30(14), 1503–1511 (2012)
8. Kemper, H.C.G., Ooijendijk, W.T.M., Stiggelbout, M.: Consensus over de Nederlandse norm voor gezond bewegen. (TSG: Tijdschrift voor gezondheidswetenschappen, vol. 78(3), pp. 180-183 (2000)). Vereniging voor Volksgezondheid en Wetenschap, Utrecht

Use of Tangible Interfaces to Support a Literacy System in Children with Intellectual Disabilities

Janio Jadán-Guerrero[1,3], Gustavo López[2], and Luis A. Guerrero[1,2]

[1] Doctoral Program in Computer Science, Universidad de Costa Rica, San José, Costa Rica
[2] Centro de Investigaciones en Tecnologías de la Información y Comunicación, CITIC
Universidad de Costa Rica, San José, Costa Rica
[3] Universidad Tecnológica Indoamérica
Av. Machala y Sabanilla, Quito, Ecuador
{janio.jadan,gustavo.lopez_h}@ucr.ac.cr,
luis.guerrero@ecci.ucr.ac.cr

Abstract. People with intellectual disabilities should develop reading and writing skills since children. Otherwise, they will have additional difficulties in their daily life activities, as buying in a store, taking medicaments or getting a job. In this paper we present a prototype that uses tangible interfaces and augmented objects to support a literacy method for children with intellectual disabilities. The prototype was evaluated and the preliminary results showed that the system can not only assists teachers in the classroom, but also helps to better manage the interaction with children and non-traditional interfaces.

Keywords: Non-traditional interfaces, Literacy, Tangible interfaces, Augmented objects.

1   Introduction

Literacy development in people with intellectual disabilities is a key factor to ensure their integration into society. This paper is focused on Down Syndrome. People with mild or moderate level of the syndrome often have additional difficulties to read and develop daily life activities, such as buy in a store, take medications, take a bus or get a job [1].

Reading and writing are very important skills that people with intellectual disabilities should development since children. Children with intellectual disabilities like others grow up and live in their community surrounded by technology e.g., laptops, tablets, smart phones, smart TVs, videogame consoles and other non-traditional devices [2]. In this scenery, caregivers or teachers try to take advantage of some mobile applications. However, most of the programs and technology aids are designed with language and cultural considerations that vary considerably from the needs and requirements of native Spanish speaking users [3].

Designing technologies for children with disabilities is highly complex due to the diversity of needs involved in their daily lives. However, educational technologies have emerged rapidly in recent years due to the growth of Internet access and mobile devices [4].

R. Hervás et al. (Eds.): UCAmI 2014, LNCS 8867, pp. 108–115, 2014.
© Springer International Publishing Switzerland 2014

As we know, the purpose of education is to prepare children for life in the real world, and technology helps to strengthen the teaching and learning process, particularly in special education where it plays a significant role in a child´s life [4] [5].

Our goal in this research project is to help children with special needs to recognize and associate real world objects with pictograms or photographs. There are educational methods specially designed to consider the characteristics for teaching children with intellectual disabilities. Troncoso and Del Cerro´s method is one of them. We attempt to apply this method jointly with tangible objects to enhance the literacy process for children with intellectual disabilities [5].

The rest of this paper is organized as follows: Background and related work of tangible interfaces used for teaching reading is presented in Section 2, as well as the method to teach children with Down syndrome how to read. Section 3 describes the system architecture of the implemented prototype. The information obtained from a preliminary evaluation is detailed in Section 4. Finally, the conclusions and future work are described in Section 5.

2   Background and Related Work

Literacy is one of the crucial elements of early childhood education. It starts with parents and other caregivers that begin preparing the child to read with some activities at home [6]. However, due to the diminished intellectual capabilities of children with intellectual disabilities, different ways of learning basic reading and writing skills are required in comparison with other children of the same age [5] [7]. In the next section we present the most important methods used with those children and some computer systems based on tangible objects for support literacy.

2.1   Literacy Methods

Literacy methods can be classified into two categories: *synthetic* or ascending, that begins with sublexical units such as letters, syllables ending in the word; and *global* or down, that starts with the word or phrase ending in syllables and letters. The two most widely used teaching methods for reading in Spanish are the *syllabic* and *phonics* methods [8]. In the case of children with intellectual disabilities, who have difficulties with syllable recognition there is not a unique method. However, therapists suggest a *global reading method.*

One of these methods was published in the book "Down Syndrome: Reading and writing" by María Victoria Troncoso and Mercedes Del Cerro [9]. The pedagogical approach that the method applies is the discriminative-perceptual learning. This approach focuses on teaching a kid to perceive sounds and relate them to actions or objects.

The method emphases in the development of five abilities: memory, attention, association, discrimination and denomination. For each one of them the method is taught with cards and pictures. The purpose of these cards is that the child can relate a word to an image and associate the both concepts. Figure 1 shows some samples of those cards.

Fig. 1. Troncoso's Method cards for a key and a ball (in Spanish)

2.2   Computer-Supported Literacy Systems

In the literature review, we found that in the past five years, some applications were developed for teaching reading skills using tangible interfaces. Some of these projects are mentioned below.

E-du box is an educational multimedia platform including a tangible companion that helps children in reading activities. The system has a tangible interface that uses familiar and everyday lives objects such as wood and tissues. Using a Bluetooth connection children interact with a pen-shaped mouse that vibrates according to some situations defined by the educator. Feedback is provided by a tangible, interactive and animated e-du agent, who is able to move and speak to children [10].

Reading Glove is a wearable RFID (Radio Frequency IDentification) reader that engages readers in an audio-based interactive narrative by allowing them to "extract memories" from tagged physical objects [11].

T-maze is a tangible programming tool for children. Authors use a camera to catch the sequence of wooden blocks in real time, which will be used to analyze the sequence and enable the children to receive feedbacks immediately [12].

Table Top is a Troncoso's method application using inversed projection with a videobeam. Authors use a tangible interface that uses objects with external tags recognized by a camera. The tangible interfaces are physical objects that represent the images or words presented to the children with Down Syndrome [5].

Co-StiCap (Stimulating Collaborative Cognitive Capabilities) is a multi-device based on distributed user interfaces and games systems. It aims to provide cognitively stimulating activities for children with Attention Deficit Hyperactivity Disorder. It shows the use of a laptop, a smartphone and tangible object coded by NFC labels [13].

RoyoBlocks is a toy set that provides children an opportunity to develop fundamental literacy skills. The study concludes that when a child is playing, they bring to the interaction an array of existing cognitive and emotional associations [7].

Lit Kit is a portable, cyber-physical artifact supporting children's picture-book reading. It creates room-scaled, audio-visual and spatial effects to both contextualize language and provide feedback during dialogical interactions between a child and an adult reader [14]. Figure 2 shows the picture of the systems described above.

| E-du box | Table Top | T - maze | |
| Reading Glove | Co-StiCap | Lit Kit | RoyoBlock |

Fig. 2. Tangible computer supported literacy systems

All the systems mentioned offer an environment to practice the educational concepts of learning by doing, which can enhance the efficiency of children's learning [12] [15]. Children's literacy can be advanced in a tangible, co-creative environment that is both physical and digital. Our solution differs with the presented above in the use of Wi-Fi technology enabling long distance communications and portability. It also differs because we avoid using external tags or signs that can modify the external appearance of the objects. We accomplish this by applying a digitalization and rapid manufacturing process i.e., 3D scanning and printing to redesign the objects and embed the required tags.

3   System Architecture

The system architecture is shown in Figure 3. The system prototype consists of three main components: a tangible user interface that uses RFID recognition, a processing unit, and a mobile user interface that displays the object abstractions (an image and a word). The whole process is based on the Troncoso & Del Cerro's literacy method. In this section we will provide the details of implementation of the three main components showed in Figure 3.

3.1   System Components

The prototype is composed by three main components:

- **Object recognition tool.** It is a little box that contains an RFID reader and is connected to the computer in order to send the cards to the tablets.
- **Recognizable object set.** It is a group of objects that were redesigned in order to contain an RFID tag that the system can recognize.
- **Tablets.** Tablets or smartphones are used to display the abstract representation of the physical objects. These cards are shown to the children.

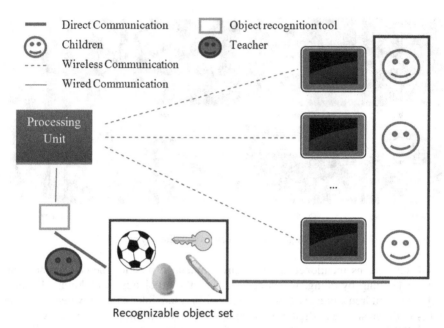

Recognizable object set

Fig. 3. Software Architecture Diagram

The system involves two different users, which are described below.

- **Teacher/Parent/Caregiver.** The main user of the tangible user interfaces and the recognition system. They have to provide the session number to access the processing unit session. They pass objects near the recognition device and the system creates the cards and shows them to the children.
- **Child.** The secondary user of mobile application and physical objects. However they do not interact directly with the processing unit.

3.2   System Workflow

The system's main flow consists of the teacher/parent/caregiver (henceforth teacher) which start the Processing Unit (PU). The PU could be a laptop, a PC or even a server depending on the scale required. The PU hosts the recognition software that determines the object to be presented to the children. It also sends the data to the tablets. The tablets display a card with an image of the object and the word associated with that object. Figure 4 shows an image of a real object presented to the children and a screenshot of the tablet showing the picture and the word. In this case, the label "la bola" refers to the ball in Spanish because the system is being implemented for Spanish speakers.

The tablet application is very simple. It consists of two main screens: login and cards. The login screen requires a session number from the teacher. This session number is given to him/her when the recognition system is executed. This number enables many tablets to be connected to the same work session if that is required, for instance, in a class with several children (several tablets).

Fig. 4. Left: Physical object showed to the children. Right: Tablet displaying the card with the information associated to the object.

The objects (Tangible User Interfaces) were created using a digitalization and additive manufacturing process, i.e., 3D digitalization and 3D printing of the object, which allowed us to create several augmented objects. This process is required in order to embed the RFID tags into the objects maintaining their physical appearance to avoid any cognitive load in the children.

We carry out a performance testing process in order to determine how long it takes from the time when the object is recognized to the time it is displayed on the tablet. For this purpose we used a Wi-Fi network of 36 mbps.

With 12 changes between objects we found that the mean time between the object recognition and the display in the tablet is one second and forty-six milliseconds. Considering that the time frame of an object displayed can vary from one to four minutes, a 2 second delay for image change is not significant.

4   Prototype Evaluation

In order to get a first insight of the prototype and with a final user we carried out an interview with four experts, i.e., special education teachers. The evaluation was conducted in two steps. The first step consisted on executing the prototype functionality using all the components, i.e., Laptop, RFID reader, recognizable objects set and two tablets. We explained the functionality of the system and we asked them about the general impression.

The first part of the evaluation allowed us to understand the issues of the interface (found by the experts) and helped us to improve the user interface.

The second part of the evaluation was a direct interaction of the expert and the system followed by an interview about the user experience. For this purpose we conducted a thinking-aloud test [16].

The interview was recorded and notes were taken during and after the conduction of the test. All the participants agreed that the prototype is useful to enhance the first stages of the literacy process. However, they stressed that the process should be pleasurable and not tedious in order to work.

Figure 5 shows the system being evaluated: when a key (left picture) and a ball (picture on the right) are positioned close to the Recognition Tool the corresponding card is displayed on the tablet.

Fig. 5. Functional System: a key and a ball are recognized by the system and the respective cards are created and sent to the tablets

One of the participants in the evaluation mentioned that the objects could help to create new types of interaction for each child, for instance, they can create stories using the objects.

Teachers also thought that tangible interfaces emphasize the connection between the body and cognition, facilitating thinking through physical actions.

However, they found some problems related with the type of letter and the size of the image. For an introductory phase of reading it is better the font not to be in script. Teachers also state the size of the images and the words should be bigger.

The results of the tests served as feedback for an improved version of the prototype. This preliminary evaluation indicates that the interaction design of our prototype needs to be enhanced and further evaluation in the field is required. Structured experiments are required in order to assess the perceived usefulness and usability of the prototype in real scenarios.

Is important to mention that most of the participants in the evaluation process pointed the fact that the system could be used to help the literacy process in any person, e.g., elders and children without disabilities.

5   Conclusion and Future Work

The results of the prototype evaluation showed that the system can not only assists to teachers but also helps to improve the interaction with children and non-traditional interfaces. It is important to mention that educational inclusion of children with intellectual disabilities works better when the whole community of classmates is involved in same class activities. A technological system for supporting this process is just a tool people can use, i.e., a technological tool can never replace the teacher guide.

We state that, a system with a Tangible User Interface like the one we developed can support teacher and/or parents working with children with intellectual disabilities, especially if the system supports a well-known method –like the Troncoso and Del Cerro literacy method. We want to highlight that our final users are the teacher, i.e., our system supports people who are experts in teaching literacy rather than the children learning it.

Depending on the cognitive deficits, more features can be easily implemented. For instance, the card on the tablet can include a sound or video. In the same way, using their finger children can paint over or follow the written word in the tablet to introduce writing. These new features are scheduled in a future version of the prototype and more evaluations and experiments will be conducted.

References

1. Ferreras, A., Belda, J.-M., Barberà, R., Poveda, R., Urra, M., García, N., Tito, M., Valero, M.: PDA Software Aimed at Improving Workplace Adaptation for People with Cognitive Disabilities. In: Miesenberger, K., Klaus, J., Zagler, W., Karshmer, A. (eds.) ICCHP 2010, Part II. LNCS, vol. 6180, pp. 13–20. Springer, Heidelberg (2010)
2. Philip, K.: HCI beyond the GUI: Design for Haptic, Speech, Olfactory, and Other Nontraditional Interfaces. Morgan Kaufmann Publishers, San Francisco (2008)
3. Al-Wabil, A., Al-Shabanat, H., Al-Sarrani, R., Al-Khonin, M.: Developing a Multimedia Environment to Aid in Vocalization for People on the Autism Spectrum: A User-Centered Design Approach. In: Miesenberger, K., Klaus, J., Zagler, W., Karshmer, A. (eds.) ICCHP 2010, Part II. LNCS, vol. 6180, pp. 33–36. Springer, Heidelberg (2010)
4. Drigas, A.S., Ioannidou, R.-E.: ICTs in Special Education: A Review. In: Lytras, M.D., Ruan, D., Tennyson, R.D., Ordonez De Pablos, P., García Peñalvo, F.J., Rusu, L. (eds.) WSKS 2011. CCIS, vol. 278, pp. 357–364. Springer, Heidelberg (2013)
5. Muró, B., Santana, P., Magaña, M.: Developing reading skills in Children with Down Syndrome through tangible interfaces. In: Proceedings of the 4th Mexican Conference on Human-Computer Interaction, México DF, (2012)
6. Kleiman, J., Pope, M., Blikstein, P.: RoyoBlocks: An exploration in tangible literacy learning. In: Proceedings of the 12th International Conference on Interaction Design and Children, IDC 2013, pp. 543–546 (2013)
7. Kleiman, J., Pope, M., Blikstein, P.: RoyoBlocks: An exploration in tangible literacy learning. In: Proceedings of the 12th International Conference on Interaction Design and Children, IDC 2013, pp. 543–546 (2013)
8. Bentolila, A., Bruno, G.: Learning to read: choosing languages and methods. In: Education for All Global Monitoring Report 2006. UNESCO (2006)
9. Troncoso, M.V., Del Cerro, M.: Síndrome de Down: lectura y escritura. Fundación Iberoamericana Down 21, Santander, Spain (1998)
10. Brotto, A., Pontual, T., Gomes, A., Monteiro, C., Sonnino, R.: e-du box: Educational multimedia with tangible-enhanced interaction. In: Proceedings of the 7th ACM Conference on Designing Interactive Systems, DIS 2008, pp. 139–146 (2008)
11. Tanenbaum, K., Tanenbaum, J., Antle, A., Bizzocchi, J., Seif, M., Hatala, M.: Experiencing the Reading Glove. In: Proceedings of the Fifth International Conference on Tangible, Embedded, and Embodied Interaction, TEI 2011, pp. 137–144 (2011)
12. Wang, D., Zhang, C., Wang, H.: T-Maze: A tangible programming tool for children. In: IDC 2011: Proceedings of the 10th International Conference on Interaction Design and Children, pp. 127–135 (2011)
13. De La Guía, E., Lozano, M., Penichet, V.: Co-StiCap: Sistema Basado en Interfaces de Usuario Distribuidas y Tangibles Para Mejorar las Capacidades Cognitivas en Niños con TDAH. XIV INTERACCIÓN 2013, pp. 61-68 (2013)
14. Schafer, G., Evan, K., Walker, I., Lewis, E., King, S., Soleimani, A., Norris, M., Fumagali, K., Zhao, J., Allport, R., Zheng, X., Gift, R., Padmakumar, A.: Designing the LIT KIT, an interactive, environmental, cyber-physical artifact enhancing children's picture-book reading. In: 12th International Conference on Interaction Design and Children, pp. 281–284 (2013)
15. Stull, A.T., Mayer, R.E.: Learning by doing versus learning by viewing: Three experimental comparisons of learner-generated versus author-provided graphic organizers. Journal of Educational Psychology 99(4), 808–820 (2007)
16. MacKenzie, S.: Human-Computer Interaction: An Empirical Research Perspective. Morgan Kaufmann Publishers Inc., San Francisco (2013)

Online Change Detection for Timely Solicitation of User Interaction

Timothy Patterson[1], Sally McClean[2], Chris Nugent[1], Shuai Zhang[1],
Leo Galway[1], and Ian Cleland[1]

[1] School of Computing and Mathematics,
University of Ulster at Jordanstown, BT37 0QB, UK
{t.patterson,cd.nugent,s.zhang,l.galway,i.cleland}@ulster.ac.uk
[2] School of Computing and Information Engineering,
University of Ulster at Coleraine, BT52 1SA, UK
si.mcclean@ulster.ac.uk

Abstract. The accurate detection of changes has the potential to form a fundamental component of systems which autonomously solicit user interaction based on transitions within an input stream, for example accelerometry data obtained from a mobile device. This solicited interaction may be utilized for diverse scenarios such as responding to changes in a patient's vital signs within a medical domain or requesting activity labels for generating real-world labelled datasets. Within this paper a change detection algorithm is presented which does not require knowledge of the underlying distributions, can run in online scenarios and considers multivariate datastreams. Results are presented demonstrating practicable potential with 99.81% accuracy and 60% precision for real-world accelerometry data.

Keywords: Multivariate change detection, Online change detection, Soliciting user interaction.

1 Introduction

The timely engagement between a system and the end user is a fundamental concept within domains ranging from healthcare, for example responding to changes in a patient's vital signs [1] to machine learning, for example engaging with users after the commencement of a new activity to solicit activity labels [2]. Nevertheless, such engagement may be expensive in terms of user time and, in the event of excessive requests for interaction may degrade the usability and relevance of the system. It is therefore necessary to have a method of change detection which can be utilized to solicit interaction from the user when a transition is detected.

Within [2] we present our previous work in the development of a mobile-based framework for the large-scale gathering and labelling of activity data. Such labels have the potential to provide an invaluable resource to the research community by facilitating the training of supervised algorithms using truly representative data collected in a free-living environment. The developed framework enables the labelling of data via an Android based mobile application and currently

R. Hervás et al. (Eds.): UCAmI 2014, LNCS 8867, pp. 116–123, 2014.
© Springer International Publishing Switzerland 2014

contains two primary components: an activity recognition (AR) module and a labelling prompt module. The AR module is responsible for identifying the user's current action and contains both stationary activities, for example 'standing still' and non-stationary activities, for example 'running'. The AR module detects activities based on 3 second windows with a total of 3 consecutive windows (i.e. 9 seconds of data) being required before an activity is labelled. Upon detecting a transition from an activity to 'standing still' the AR module initiates the label prompting module. This module displays a screen to the user enabling them to click an icon representing the activity they have just transitioned from.

Whilst this approach enables data collection in a relatively free-living scenario there are two fundamental constraints imposed by the overall framework. Firstly, the requirement that a user transitions from an activity to 'standing still' results in potentially informative inter-activity data pertinent to real-world situations being lost. For example, the sequence {stand still - walk - jog - run - jog - walk - stand still} may be considered as a typical series of activities for running. Such inter-activity data could subsequently be utilized for training models which predict, in real-time the activity that a user is transitioning to, thus expediting the AR process by enabling the selection of appropriate classifiers. Secondly, the number of false prompts that a user receives is, to some extent controlled by requiring 3 consecutive 3 second windows containing the same activity. This results in a delay between the user finishing an activity and receiving a prompt. Furthermore, this approach to controlling the number of erroneous prompts results in activities which may have an inherently short duration, for example traversing a short flight of stairs remaining undetected by the AR module.

A popular technique within the literature for detecting changes is the Cumulative Sum Control Chart (CUSUM) which has been utilized in applications such as identifying changes in cardiovascular events [3] and detecting the progression of eye disease [4]. A particular criticism of CUSUM is that it may be inaccurate when identifying sudden shifts that are not from the same distribution [5] which may yield it ineffective when detecting changes based on accelerometry data.

In this paper we present an online multivariate change detection algorithm which may be utilized in a real-time mobile-based activity labelling framework to autonomously solicit user interaction upon detecting a change. We develop the univariate change detection algorithm by Jain and Wang [6] resulting in two main contributions. Firstly, the algorithm in [6] is extended to consider multivariate data streams thus enabling the incorporation of multiple sensors into the change detection process consequently enhancing the overall accuracy of the algorithm. Secondly, we compute the test statistic for *all* positions within a window as opposed to the *most likely point* proposed by Jain and Wang. This has the primary advantage of enabling covariance between sensor observations to be considered in the hypothesis stage.

The remainder of this paper is structured as follows: in Section 2 the Multivariate Change-Detection algorithm is presented. In Section 3 we provide an overview of the experimental setup with subsequent results presented in Section 4. Finally, Conclusions and Future Work are discussed in Section 5.

2   Multivariate Change-Detection Algorithm

Consider a data stream of length q consisting of data points $x_1, x_2, \ldots, x_q$. Each data point x_q is a p element vector where p is the number of sensor observations for each variable. The data stream may contain points from multiple distributions, for example $x_1, x_2, \ldots, x_{k-1}$ may have distribution D_1 whilst $x_k, x_{k+1}, \ldots, x_q$ may have distribution D_2. It is therefore the overall aim of the algorithm to identify the position in the data stream of change points k.

The change-detection algorithm follows an hypothesis-and-verification principle. In the hypothesis step a point is detected within the window under consideration which maximizes the test statistic. In the second stage the hypothesis that a detected change point is significant is verified.

2.1   Hypothesis Generation

In the hypothesis generation stage we pass an analysis window of length n over the datastream assuming that there is a maximum of one change point per window. The movement of the window over the datastream may be either distinct in which case the start of a new window (other than the first) is at position $m + cn + 1$ where m is the padding size and c is the number of previous windows. Alternatively, a sliding window version of the algorithm may be executed with the start position incremented by a predetermined number of data points. For ease of notation we denote the data points within a window as $x_1, x_2, \ldots, x_n$ regardless of their actual position within the data stream. Following Jain and Wang [6] we pad either side of the window with m points such that the analysis window contains data points $x_{1-m}, \ldots, x_{n+m}$ therefore containing a total of $n + 2m$ data points. This padding is necessary to accurately detect change points which occur at the extremities of the window and is particularly crucial when executing a distinct window version of the algorithm.

Within each window we slide an index variable, l, $1 < l \leq n$ subsequently computing summary statistics of the component distributions separated at l. Specifically, we compute the means, $\bar{f}_1(l)$ and $\bar{f}_2(l)$, which contain the mean of observations, in addition to variance-covariance matrices, $S_1(l)$ and $S_2(l)$, which contain the variance of observations in the diagonals and their covariance in the off-diagonals. To ensure that the change detection algorithm can operate in online scenarios we compute $\bar{f}_1(l)$, $\bar{f}_2(l)$ and $S_1(l)$, $S_2(l)$ recursively. Thus as index l increments to position $l + 1$ the summary statistics are calculated as follows:

$$\bar{f}_1(l+1) = \frac{m+l-1}{m+l}\bar{f}_1(l) + \frac{f(x_{l+1})}{m+l}, \tag{1}$$

$$\bar{f}_2(l+1) = \frac{n+m-l+1}{n+m-l}\bar{f}_2(l) - \frac{f(x_{l+1})}{n+m-l}, \tag{2}$$

$$S_1(l+1) = \frac{m+l-1}{m+l}S_1(l) + \frac{1}{m+l-1} \\ \times [x_{l+1} - \bar{f}_1(l+1)]'[x_{l+1} - \bar{f}_1(l+1)], \tag{3}$$

$$\mathbf{S}_2(l+1) = \frac{n+m-l+1}{n+m-l}\mathbf{S}_2(l) - \frac{1}{n+m-l} \quad (4)$$
$$\times [\mathbf{x}_{l+1} - \bar{\mathbf{f}}_2(l+1)]'[\mathbf{x}_{l+1} - \bar{\mathbf{f}}_2(l+1)].$$

Having calculated summary statistics before and after l we proceed to compute the F statistic at position l, F_l as follows [7]:

$$F_l = \frac{n_1 + n_2 - p - 1}{p(n_1 + n_2 - 2)}T^2, \quad (5)$$

where $n_1 = m + l - 1$, $n_2 = n + m - l + 1$, p is the number of variables and T^2 is the Hotelling T-squared statistic calculated as [7],

$$T^2 = (\bar{\mathbf{f}}_1 - \bar{\mathbf{f}}_2)'\left\{\mathbf{S}_p\left(\frac{1}{n_1} + \frac{1}{n_2}\right)\right\}^{-1}(\bar{\mathbf{f}}_1 - \bar{\mathbf{f}}_2), \quad (6)$$

where $\mathbf{S}_p$ is the pooled variance-covariance matrix,

$$\mathbf{S}_p = \frac{(n_1 - 1)\mathbf{S}_1 + (n_2 - 1)\mathbf{S}_2}{n_1 + n_2 - 2}. \quad (7)$$

Under the null hypothesis (i.e. equal distributions) and assuming Gaussian distributions this has an F distribution [7]. We choose the point l which maximizes F_l as the most likely change point within a window and proceed to the hypothesis verification phase.

2.2 Hypothesis Verification

An hypothesis verification stage is executed to prove or disprove the null hypothesis that a significant change did not occur at point l. Firstly, we compute the probability of finding an F value lower than that calculated in Equation 5 resulting in b. The F Cumulative Distribution Function is utilized for this phase with p and $n_1 + n_2 - p$ degrees of freedom. As multiple statistical tests are being simultaneously performed within the window it is necessary to adjust our confidence value, α to reflect the confidence for the entire window and not a single, isolated value. We therefore use a Bonferroni correction [8] to compute a threshold t as:

$$t = \alpha/n. \quad (8)$$

Secondly, we reject the null hypothesis (i.e. a significant change did occur) if,

$$(1 - b) < t, \quad (9)$$

and the position $\mathbf{x}_l$ is subsequently labelled as a change point within the datastream.

When one examines the accelerometry data it can be seen that the actual values at a change point increase or decrease over a range of data points. Thus when executing a sliding window version of the algorithm change points are detected which are adjacent as the datapoints become increasingly indicative of a 'significant' change. We therefore define a further parameter, a which indicates the number of adjacent detected change points required before the algorithm would alert the user to a 'real' change occurring. Furthermore, once a change point satisfying this criteria is detected, sequential adjacent change points are considered as indicative of the same event and would therefore not be dispatched to the user.

3 Experimental Setup

To facilitate the evaluation of change detection algorithms, accelerometry data was captured from a healthy participant wearing two Shimmer wireless sensing platforms [9]. The Shimmers were placed in the middle of the participant's left pectoral and at mid-point between the thigh and knee on the anterior of the participant's right leg. These Shimmer positions enabled anterior-posterior and lateral movements of the subject to be effectively captured [10].

The participant performed multiple tests with each containing two high-level scenarios: 'arrive home' which comprised the subset of activities {ascend stairs, walk, sit down} and 'leave home' which consisted of {stand up, walk, descend stairs} [10]. For the stationary activities 'sit' and 'stand' the participant sat or stood for approximately 30 seconds and then transitioned to the opposite stationary activity. When measuring accelerometry data for non-stationary activities the participant stood for approximately 30 seconds, proceeded to perform the activity for approximately 30 seconds and then transitioned to standing. Throughout activity execution accelerometry data was wirelessly streamed to a receiving computer via the IEEE 802.15.1 Bluetooth communications protocol.

4 Results

Within this section we present results comparing the classification performance of the proposed multivariate change detection algorithm with the univariate approach proposed by Jain and Wang [6]. To enable the evaluation of the univariate approach the magnitude of acceleration was calculated from the x,y and z axes of the captured data and used as input to the univariate algorithm. In order to quantitatively evaluate the algorithms, the start and end data points of each activity for two tests was manually labelled.

We define the positive and negative detection cases as follows: a true positive (TP) is a correctly identified change. When determining true positives a quarter second buffer was included at either side of the manually labelled change point to accommodate subjectivity errors inherent in manual labelling. Thus, a detected change point was considered true if its index in the datastream, $l \in \{z-(f/4)\ldots z+(f/4)\}$ where z is the index in the datastream of the manually labelled change point and f is the sampling frequency in Hz. A further consideration when interpreting true positive results is the level of granularity required by the host application. For example in Figure 1 the graph of accelerometry values with detected change

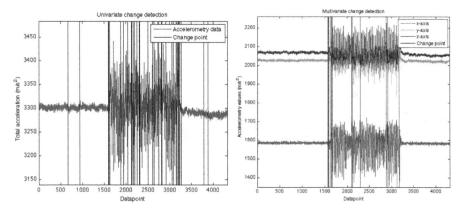

Univariate change detection as proposed Presented multivariate change detection
by Jain and Wang   algorithm

Fig. 1. Example sliding window change detection results for the activity 'stand still - descend stairs - stand still'. The window size was 1 second with confidence $p = 0.025$. The number of neighbours required, a was 1.

points are displayed for the activity 'descend stairs'. There are three possible levels of change for this activity: firstly, there is the transition from standing still to descending stairs; secondly, there are transitions present at each individual step as the subject traverses the stairs; thirdly there are 11 landings present for a total of 102 stairs resulting in the dataset containing multiple transitions between traversing stairs and walking for a short duration (approximately 1 - 4 steps). Bearing in mind the target application of soliciting user interaction after a transition we only consider the primary transitions between high-level activities, for example 'standing still - descend stairs - standing still'. It is useful, however, to note that the level of granularity required can be readily modified by choosing the type of algorithm used, i.e. sliding or distinct, the size of the consideration window and by adjusting the significance level in Equation 8. We define a true negative (TN) as a non-transitional point which is not labelled as a change.

A false positive (FP) is a non-transitional point which is highlighted by the algorithm as a change. In terms of user experience this type of error is likely to be the most detrimental as it will result in them receiving unintuitive requests for interaction. A false negative (FN) occurs when the algorithm fails to detect a change in the user's activity. Bearing in mind our target application this type of error would primarily impact upon the quality of the dataset labels as as the labelling program would not request user interaction.

Due to a disproportionately high number of true negatives in the data, accuracy defined as $\frac{TP+TN}{TP+TN+FP+FN}$ was relatively high ranging from 99.25% to 99.81% for the multivariate approach and 97.92% to 99.22% for the univariate approach. Thus, when evaluating the algorithm we focus on precision defined as $\frac{TP}{TP+FP}$. This is primarily due to our application where unintuitive requests for interaction may degrade user experience.

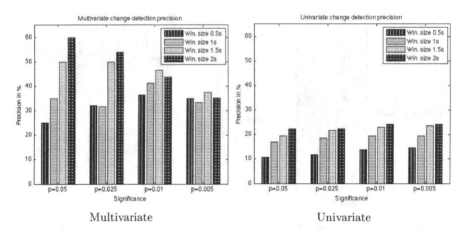

Multivariate   Univariate

Fig. 2. Comparison of change detection precision results for the sliding window version of the algorithm

In Figure 2 the precision of the sliding window version of the algorithm with increments of one data point is presented. The developed multivariate change detection algorithm consistently achieved higher precision than the univariate approach. A maximum precision of 60% was achieved with a window size of two seconds and significance $p = 0.05$. As the required confidence increased the precision decreased for the multivariate approach; this was caused by true change points not satisfying the hypothesis verification stage and therefore being incorrectly labelled as a non-transitional point. The threshold used in the hypothesis verification is directly related to window size (Equation 8). Thus as the window increases in size the threshold decreases resulting in a hypothesized change point requiring a higher F value to reject the null hypothesis. In the multivariate results the accuracy generally increased with window size for $p = 0.05$ and $p = 0.025$. As the confidence increased ($p = 0.01$ and $p = 0.005$) the window size had less impact upon precision with similar results achieved for all window sizes where $p = 0.005$. The minimum precision achieved for the sliding window version of the univariate approach was 11% with a maximum of 25%. The precision of the univariate approach increased with required significance and window size. This was due to a reduced number of false positives caused by a hypothesized change point requiring a higher test statistic value to reject the null hypothesis.

5   Conclusions and Future Work

Within this paper we have presented an approach to change detection which may operate in real-time scenarios, does not require knowledge of the underlying distribution(s) and can incorporate multivariate datastreams. The developed algorithm outperformed the real-time univariate approach by Jain and Wang [6] for both accuracy and precision metrics.

Whilst we have evaluated our approach using real sensor data a key part of future work will be to generate a synthetic dataset thus providing a resource for quantitatively determining the impact of parameter choices. In particular we wish to measure the trade-off between accuracy and computational performance of window size, confidence values and the type of algorithm used. Additionally, bearing in mind the controlled nature of the presented experiments a further part of future work will be to incorporate our multivariate approach to change detection into real-world systems such as mobile-based applications for gathering and labelling activity data. This will enable us to evaluate the algorithm using data collected from multiple individuals within a free-living scenario.

Acknowledgements. The authors acknowledge support from the EPSRC through the MATCH programme (EP/F063822/1 and EP/G012393/1) and to Invest N.I. under R and D grant RD0513844.

References

1. Clifton, D., Wong, D., Clifton, L., Wilson, S., Way, R., Pullinger, R., Tarassenko, L.: A Large-Scale Clinical Validation of an Integrated Monitoring System in the Emergency Department. IEEE Journal of Biomedical and Health Informatics 17(4), 835–842 (2013)
2. Cleland, I., Han, M., Nugent, C., Lee, H., Zhang, S., McClean, S., Lee, S.: Mobile based prompted labeling of large scale activity data. In: Nugent, C., Coronato, A., Bravo, J. (eds.) IWAAL 2013. LNCS, vol. 8277, pp. 9–17. Springer, Heidelberg (2013)
3. Zhang, S., McClean, S., Scotney, B., Galway, L., Nugent, C.: A framework for context-aware online physiological monitoring. In: IEEE International Symposium on Computer-Based Medical Systems, Bristol, UK, pp. 1–6. IEEE (2011)
4. Ledolter, J., Kardon, R.: Detecting the Progression of Eye Disease: CUSUM Charts for Assessing the Visual Field and Retinal Nerve Fiber Layer Thickness. Translational Vision Science & Technology 2(6), 2 (2013)
5. Prajapati, D.R., Mahapatra, P.B.: A new X chart comparable to CUSUM and EWMA charts. International Journal of Productivity and Quality Management 4(1), 103–128 (2009)
6. Jain, A., Wang, Y.-F.: A New Framework for On-Line Change Detection (unpublished), http://citeseerx.ist.pusu.edu/viewdoc/summary?doi=10.1.1.62.5929 (accessed September 2014)
7. Rencher, A.C.: Methods of Multivariate Analysis, 2nd edn. John Wiley & Sons, New York (2002)
8. Bonferroni, C.E.: Il Calcolo delle Assicurazioni su Gruppi di Teste. In: Studii in Onore del Profesor S. O. Carboni Roma (1936)
9. Shimmer. Shimmer 2 Specification and User Manual, http://www.shimmersensing.com/images/uploads/docs/Shimmer_User_Manual_rev2Rk.pdf (accessed September 2014)
10. Zhang, S., Galway, L., McClean, S., Scotney, B., Finlay, D., Nugent, C.D.: Deriving Relationships between Physiological Change and Activities of Daily Living using Wearable Sensors. In: Par, G., Morrow, P. (eds.) S-CUBE 2010. LNICST, vol. 57, pp. 235–250. Springer, Heidelberg (2011)

Virtual Touch Book: A Mixed-Reality Book for Inclusive Education

Juan Mateu[1], María José Lasala Bello[2], and Xavier Alamán[1]

[1] Universidad Autónoma de Madrid (UAM), Madrid, Spain
juan.mateu@estudiante.uam.es, xavier.alaman@uam.es
[2] IES Ernest Lluch, Cunit, Tarragona, Spain
mlasala3@xtec.cat

Abstract. This article presents the Virtual Touch Book, a book with special features that is able to interact with a virtual world. Depending on what page the book is opened, the virtual world contents and behaviour are adapted. An experiment on using this technology was carried out at the IES Ernest Lluch high school, involving students on attention to diversity courses and dealing with the theme "Ancient Greece".

Keywords: virtual worlds, tangible user interfaces, inclusive education.

1   Introduction

Currently, some efforts have been invested in the creation of augmented reality books as learning tools. They are intended to bind or overlay digital contents to a traditional "real" book in order to obtain a significant learning. This section presents the main projects that use virtual books or augmented books for educational purposes.

Billinghurst et al. [1] presents "Magic Book", a book that creates a scene of augmented reality (AR) superimposing virtual models in the pages of a "real" book. Grasset et al. [2] proposes the use of an augmented reality book to tell the story of the first European settlements by providing audio-visual interaction. Clark & Dünser [3] proposes an augmented reality book in which students may carry out creative activities such as drawing and colouring book pages. Then three-dimensional scenes and textured models based on the interactions made by the user are displayed. Digilog Book [4] is an interactive book that explains the cultural heritage of Asia, in which three different dimensions of Asian culture are displayed.

We can see that most of these books are based on superimposing digital contents using techniques of augmented reality (AR). Taking these ideas one step further, in the project described in this article a "mixed reality" book is proposed, which allows linking the conventional content (text and images) of a book with the three-dimensional content that is offered by a virtual world.

2   Description and Implementation of the System

The system presented here is called Virtual Touch Book and is part of the Virtual Touch framework, which is a kit that will allow teachers to develop "mixed reality" educational activities. Other modules of this kit have been presented in [6].

R. Hervás et al. (Eds.): UCAmI 2014, LNCS 8867, pp. 124–127, 2014.
© Springer International Publishing Switzerland 2014

The Virtual Touch Book aims to link the content of a tangible book with three-dimensional contents in a virtual world. Students study the theoretical content using this "real" and tangible book, by reading text and viewing images, to subsequently get involved in a range of practical activities in the virtual world.

The choice for the virtual world platform is OpenSim, which is an open source, cross-platform server that lets you creating different private and controlled virtual spaces. This is very important when dealing with secondary education students: it is necessary to protect them from possible external influences.

The virtual world uses constructions (3D models) that can be imported from modelling tools such as Blender, 3ds Max or SketchUp. For the case study carried out the virtual world has been customized to be an imitation of Ancient Greece, including temples, sculptures, a Greek theatre, an agora, everyday objects, etc...

Within the virtual world there are a series of "bots" that guide students in the steps to be followed at each moment, in order to progress in the activity performed. The virtual world is also connected to a database that stores the questions and answers for each activity and the scores that students are getting.

Regarding the hardware aspects, the "Arduino" microcontroller is used as the hardware platform. Sensors in the tangible book indicate which page the user is looking at, and the Arduino microcontroller sends this information to the Virtual Touch middleware, that process and sends this data to the virtual world, using the Open-Metaverse library [5].

3   Case Study: Applying the System for Inclusive Education at High-School

We have carried out some sessions where we have used the Virtual Touch Book in the IES Ernest Lluch (Cunit). The IES Ernest Lluch is a centre of secondary education that has a high rate of immigration. That has served us well for focusing on inclusive education. This experience has involved 10 students, belonging to two groups. Both groups have an Individualized Plan in its curriculum, in which there is an emphasis on working out social cohesion. Students in the Wellcome course cover all courses of Secondary Education and have different levels of knowledge of Catalan langage (depending on factors such as the time since their arrival to Catalonia and the country of origin).

In the experience they participated half of the Wellcome course students and half of the students in the Open classroom (second course, group F). Keep in mind that diversity courses are oriented to give a very personal attention and therefore the ratio of students per teacher is usually quite small.

The experience has been performed in the same way for both groups. It has involved the teaching unit "The Classical Greece", particularly the section on "Religion and Greek mythology" within the field of Social Sciences. This experience has also allowed students from the Welcome course learning Catalan, because the interaction in the virtual world used Catalan as the working language.

To assess the benefits that could be obtained using the system, with respect to traditional learning methodologies, the group of students from the Open classroom were taught a traditional class on three Greek gods (Zeus, Dionysus and Athena), and then realised an evaluation of the knowledge acquired. Subsequently, the Virtual Touch Book was used to study three different gods (Aphrodite, Artemis and Poseidon), realising a similar evaluation afterwards.

Each page of the book includes information and details on a particular Greek god. Students read the contents and then, according with the god who are studying (and therefore according to the book page that is opened), they must perform a number of tasks in the virtual world relative to that god.

The students begin studying the theoretical content related to a particular god, using the tangible book. Then they use this information to try to find that god in the virtual world. For example, knowing that Poseidon is the god of the sea, and that he is often depicted with a trident, the students should guess where to look for him, and how to recognize him when found. In the Ancient Greek virtual island the students meet a series of conversational bots (avatars created to perform certain pre-programmed actions) that help them in the steps to be followed to resolve the activity. Once the god is found and recognized, the students have to answer a series of questions about the information they have read in the book. If properly answered, they get a syllable of the secret word which allows access to the area of virtual Olympus.

Fig. 1. A student using the Virtual Touch Book

After successfully locating the three gods, the student, with the three obtained syllables, will have to find out the secret word: a prominent Greek philosopher, whose life connects with the main theme of the activity, with the virtual environment and with one of the bots (Pythian, the Oracle of Delphos). Figure 1 shows one of the students working with the Virtual Touch Book.

The first assessment of the students who used this method of learning was very positive with respect to the traditional methods. Firstly, because of the novelty of the approach, and secondly because of the flavour of online game that seems to have this kind of virtual environment. Note that the majority of students who participated had never used a virtual world before, but unwrapped with ease in the movements of the avatar, chat, etc.., just after some basic instructions from the teacher.

After completing the whole process, all students have learned the programmed materials, and both content and procedures were evaluated by objective assessment and self-assessment.

The results of this first experience were encouraging: using the traditional method of giving classes a 60% of the answers were correct, versus a 80% of correct answers when the VirtualTouch Book was used.

4   Conclusions: The Virtual Touch Development Kit

This article has explained in detail the implementation of a "mixed reality" Book and an initial test in an educational setting. The results obtained are promising.

This Virtual Touch Book is part of a bigger system: a development kit. This development kit will allow the implementation of mixed reality applications for educational activities, by any teacher with basic computer skills. We have developed a middleware that allows interacting with the virtual world using tangible artefacts implemented with any of these three technologies. Now the appropriate interfaces will be developed to enable anyone with basic technical knowledge to create applications using the above mixed reality modules within a Lego-like philosophy.

We want to thank the IES Ernest Lluch for all the support during the experience. This project has been supported by the Spanish Research plan (TIN2013-44586-R).

References

1. Bilinghurst, M., Kato, H., Poupyrev, I.: MagicBook: Transitioning between reality and virtuality. In: CHI 2001 Extended Abstracts on Human Factors in Computing Systems, pp. 25–26. ACM, New York (2001)
2. Grasset, R., Duenser, A., Billinghurst, M.: Edutainment with a mixed reality book: A visually augmented illustrative children's book. In: International Conference on Advances in Computer Entertainment Technology (ACE) (2008)
3. Clark, A., Dünser, A.: An Interactive Augmented Reality Coloring Book. In: Proceedings of the IEEE Symposium on 3D User Interfaces (3DUI), pp. 7–10 (2012)
4. Ha, T., Lee, Y., Woo, W.: Digilog book for temple bell tolling experience based on interactive augmented reality, pp. 1–15 (2010)
5. LibOpenMetaverse, http://openmetaverse.org (access Date: June 2014)
6. Mateu, J., Alamán, X.: An experience of using virtual worlds and tangible interfaces for teaching computer science. In: Bravo, J., López-de-Ipiña, D., Moya, F. (eds.) UCAmI 2012. LNCS, vol. 7656, pp. 478–485. Springer, Heidelberg (2012)

Gait Recognition in the Classification of Neurodegenerative Diseases

Eddy Sánchez-Delacruz[1], Francisco Acosta-Escalante[1], Miguel A. Wister[1],
José Adán Hernández-Nolasco[1], Pablo Pancardo[1],
and Juan José Méndez-Castillo[2]

[1] Juarez Autonomous University of Tabasco, Academic Division of Computer,
Cunduacan, Tabasco, Mexico
eddsacx@gmail.com
[2] Specialty Hospital General Dr. Javier Buenfil Osorio, San Francisco de Campeche,
Campeche, Mexico

Abstract. Incorrect disease diagnosis can lead to inappropriate treatment and serious impact on patient health. Neurodegenerative diseases diagnosis is currently based on neurologist observation, but, similarity in symptoms difficult early detection. This diagnosis can be supported by computational techniques such as classification by gait recognition. This has been well established in recent works for common disease like Parkinson, Alzheimer and Huntington, however, the efficiency of these techniques is unsatisfactory and only allow to classify one disease at a time. In this study we establish that meta-classifiers can be applied in diagnosis based on gait recognition for less commons diseases as Diabetic Neuropathy. We improve accuracy for ALS and we obtained the first results for Huntington with binary classification.

Keywords: Gait recognition, classification, neurodegenerative diseases.

1 Introduction

Recent research shows important progress in neurodegenerative diseases classification based on gait recognition [7], [10], [2] and [24], they achieved correct classification rates between 90 and 100 % in the case of Parkinson, 80 and 100 % for amyotrophic lateral sclerosis (ALS), and 50 at 84.17 % in Huntington. However, to our knowledge there are not studies addressing classification of peripheral neurodegenerative diseases such as diabetic neuropathy or other less common as Gillain-Barre.

Gait recognition based on computer algorithms, has given promising results in classification of neurodegenerative diseases. We propose a taxonomy of the techniques used in gait recognition, including electromagnetic waves, we analyze neurodegenerative disease classification percentages to show the gap for improving accuracy, we propose the use of an efficient meta-classifier to obtain competitive results for ALS and we highlight the first results for Huntington disease.

R. Hervás et al. (Eds.): UCAmI 2014, LNCS 8867, pp. 128–135, 2014.
© Springer International Publishing Switzerland 2014

2   Gait Recognition

Gait recognition is an emerging technology that is well justified by the pioneering studies by [17], as shown in the taxonomy in Fig. 1, the recognition may be based on sensors, computer vision (camera), hybrid of these or even electromagnetic waves.

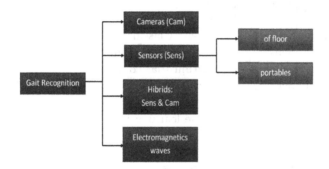

Fig. 1. Taxonomy techniques in gait recognition

Gait recognition has attracted attention as a method to identify people, however this technology is not limited to this purpose but it can be used in health's field to classify neurodegenerative diseases using patterns in gait (biological markers).

3   Gait as an Identifier of Neurodegenerative Diseases: A Neurological Approach

The following studies of neurological area, determine that gait can be used as a biological marker for identifying neurodegenerative diseases:

In [16] authors conducted a study involving 525 men and women over 75 years old. Neurological, psychological and physical evaluations were done to assess the potential of a connection between gait and dementia. The result shows that walking skills is reduced when the mental abilities declines.

Analysis in [20] shows the ability to walk of 1,200 patients from a hospital and compare results with walking ability of healthy people. Tests revealed that a lower stride and a change in gait, were associated with an increase of mental decline known as Mild Cognitive Impairment or Alzheimer fully developed.

In [15] researchers observed walking patterns of more than 1,300 patients. Two or more assessments of mental abilities and walk were performed with each patient over a period of approximately 15 months. The results indicate that mental abilities declines, memory loss and executive function leads to slower stride and stride length reduction.

4   Recent Work

In Table 1 we show previous works for neurodegenerative diseases classification based on gait recognition:

Table 1. Previous work in classification of neurodegenerative diseases

Ref	Disease	Technique	Method	%
[11]	Parkinson	Camera	Analysis of indicators of movement.	100
[4]	Parkinson	Sensors	*AdaBoost* Classifier	97
[13]	Parkinson	Sensors	*LLE* based algorithm	95.57
[5]	Parkinson	Camera	Algorithm that combines *PCA* with *LDA*	95.49
[8]	Huntington	Sensors	Observation	*
[12]	Huntington	Camera	Observation	*
[19]	ALS	Sensors	Machine learning based on *TF Kernel*	93.1
[23]	ALS	Sensors	*PDFs*	82.8
[22]	ALS	Sensors	Least squares support vector machine with *sigmoid kernels*	89.66
[9]	ALS	Sensors	Algorithm to detect stride interval	*
[3]	Alzheimer	Sensors	BSNs	*
[21]	Alzheimer	Sensors	Cox proportional-hazards regression analysis	95
[14]	DLB** y Alzheimer	Sensors	Quantitative gait analysis	*
[7]	Parkinson Huntington ALS	Sensors	Elmans RNN	87.5 88.9 83.3
[10]	Parkinson Huntington ALS	Sensors	Confusion matrix	90 50 50
[2]	Parkinson Huntington ALS	Sensors	Quadratic Bayesian classifier	80 71.429 100
[24]	Parkinson Huntington ALS	Sensors	Classifier of support vector machine	86.43 84.17 93.96

* Not shown because the research was not focused on the classification.
However, included in this study because they are based on gait recognition.
** Dementia with Lewy Bodies.

In the first column article is cited; in the second column contains disease name; in third and fourth columns techniques and methods are presented; finally the last column shows classification rates.

4.1   Analysis

Based on information in Table 1, we established that error threshold can still minimized by calculating arithmetic mean of efficiency percentages in classification (Fig. 2).

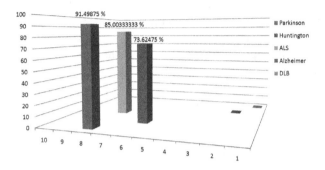

Fig. 2. Arithmetic mean of classification in previous studies

Moreover, it is observed that:

- Studies in [11], [4], [13], [5], [8], [12], [19], [23], [22], [9], [3] and [21] focus on a single disease. Only [8] and [12] focus on Huntington. [3], [21] and [14] focus on Alzheimer.
- Only [14] focus on the DLB disease.
- When classifying a single disease, especially Parkinson, percentages reach 100%.
- Deeper studies for Alzheimer's disease and DLB are needed to improve the percentages of correct classification.
- Studies focus on two and three diseases, reaching acceptable percentage, but not highly accurate [7], [10], [2] and [24].

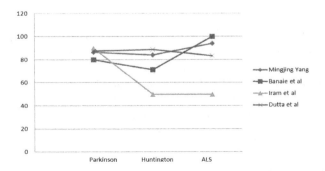

Fig. 3. Comparison studies that focus on three diseases

4.2 Area of Opportunity

We note from previous work the efficiency can be improved by using an adapted algorithm (meta-classifier) in binary classes of neurodegenerative diseases (Fig. 3).

Meta-classifiers have been successfully used to detect breast cancer with an effective rate of correct classification of 95% [6], Spastic Hemiplegia in its early stages with 89.39% of correctly classified instances [1].

As far as we know there is no computational study for a peripheral diseases such as Diabetic Neuropathy. But we suppose that these diseases, like others with movement disorders [16], [20], [15] might be detected with gait recognition.

5 Previous Results

As part of this study we design a discrimination process of binary classes based on meta-classifiers [18]. This process basically contains six phases: 1) creation or selection of databases, 2) subset selection, 3) data formatting to integrate them into a single dataset, 4) sample selection, 5) algorithm selection and 6) validation of classification results (Fig. 4).

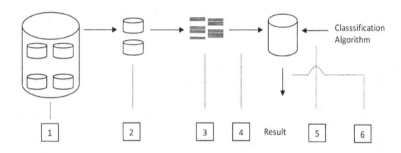

Fig. 4. Discrimination process of binary classes

We use a database of public domain *Gait Dynamics in Neuro-Degenerative Disease Data Base*[1], which contains information on patients with Parkinson's, ALS, Huntington and healthy people (control), attributes are: Elapsed Time (sec), Left Stride Interval (sec), Right Stride Interval (sec), Left Swing Interval (sec), Right Swing Interval (sec), Left Swing Interval (% of stride), Right Swing Interval (% of stride), Left Stance Interval (sec), Right Stance Interval (sec), Left Stance Interval (% of stride), Right Stance Interval (% of stride), Double Support Interval (sec) and Double Support Interval (% of stride). The information was obtained with force sensitive resistors.

---

[1] The database is available at the following link:
http://www.physionet.org/physiobank/database/gaitndd/.

Applying the proposed process, we obtained the results shown in Table 2. Parkinson results are close to better results in previous works by less than 10 percentages points, this is significant because it confirm that using a meta-classifier to a set of three diseases, Parkinson scored the highest percentage.

For ALS we obtain an improvement of 3.0326 % (Table 2), since the state of the art reports a maximum of 93.1 %. We obtain 96.1326 % with two meta-classifiers: *Multiclassclassiffier & RandomCommittee* and *RandomComitee & RandomTree*.

Finally, for Huntington disease we obtained 88,674 % using meta-classifiers *RandomSubSpace & Bagging, Bagging & PART* and *CVParameterSelection & Bagging* given the same accuracy. This is greatest contribution of this work, because about nine out of ten patients with Huntington disease were successfully classified. Results obtained in this work confirms that using meta-classifiers with neurodegenerative diseases data generate competitive rates.

Table 2. Comparison of results: process discrimination with the state of art

Disease	State of art(%)	Proposed process (%)	improvement (- +)
Parkinson	100	90.3581	- 9.6419
ELA	93.1	96.1326	+ 3.0326
Huntington	Not present	88.674	+ 88.674

Results presented in Table 2 were generated using a database with 18,800 records. We ran 955 experiments for each of the diseases, wich means a total of 2,865 tests.

6 Conclusion

We have reviewed the state of the art about classification of neurodegenerative diseases based on gait recognition. The study was done with a set of works addressed until now about on analysis of classification rates achieved and pathologies. We identified some areas of opportunity in the classification of neurodegenerative diseases based on gait recognition.

As an important result we propose the use of an efficient meta-classifier to identify at least two diseases at a time, which we obtain a competitive results for ALS and highlighting the first Huntington disease results.

Acknowledgements. This project is partially funded by CONACyT and the DAIS-UJAT.

References

1. Aguilera, A.I., Cala, L.D., Subero, A.R.: Modelo basado en metaclasificadores para diagnóstico en marcha patológica mediante análisis cinético. Revista Ingeniería UC 17(2), 7–16 (2010)
2. Banaie, M., Pooyan, M., Mikaili, M.: Introduction and application of an automatic gait recognition method to diagnose movement disorders that arose of similar causes. Expert Systems with Applications 38(6), 7359–7363 (2011)
3. Barnes, J., Jafari, R.: Locomotion monitoring using body sensor networks. In: Proceedings of the 1st International Conference on Pervasive Technologies Related to Assistive Environments, p. 47. ACM (2008)
4. Barth, J., Sunkel, M., Bergner, K., Schickhuber, G., Winkler, J., Klucken, J., Eskofier, B.: Combined analysis of sensor data from hand and gait motor function improves automatic recognition of parkinson's disease. In: 2012 Annual International Conference of the IEEE Engineering in Medicine and Biology Society (EMBC), pp. 5122–5125. IEEE (2012)
5. Cho, C.-W., Chao, W.-H., Lin, S.-H., Chen, Y.-Y.: A vision-based analysis system for gait recognition in patients with parkinsons disease. Expert Systems with Applications 36(3), 7033–7039 (2009)
6. de la Cruz, E.S., Alpuín-Jiménez, H., de Jesús Ochoa Domínguez, H., Parra, P.P.: Sdca: System to detect cancerous abnormalities. In: LA-NMR, pp. 115–122 (2011)
7. Dutta, S., Chatterjee, A., Munshi, S.: Hybrid correlation-neural network synergy for gait signal classification. In: Advances in Heuristic Signal Processing and Applications, pp. 263–285. Springer (2013)
8. Grimbergen, Y.M., Knol, M.J., Bloem, B.R., Kremer, B.P.H., Roos, R.A.C., Munneke, M.: Roos, and Marten Munneke. Falls and gait disturbances in huntington's disease. Movement Disorders 23(7), 970–976 (2008)
9. Hausdorff, J.M., Lertratanakul, A., Cudkowicz, M.E., Peterson, A.L., Kaliton, D., Goldberger, A.L.: Dynamic markers of altered gait rhythm in amyotrophic lateral sclerosis. Journal of Applied Physiology 88(6), 2045–2053 (2000)
10. Iram, S., Al-Jumeily, D., Fergus, P., Randles, M., Hussain, A.: Computational Data Analysis for Movement Signals Based on Statistical Pattern Recognition Techniques for Neurodegenerative Diseases. In: Proceedings of the 13th Annual Post Graduate Symposium on the Convergence of Telecommunications, Networking and Broadcasting, PGNet2012 (2012)
11. Khan, T., Westin, J., Dougherty, M.: Motion cue analysis for parkinsonian gait recognition. The Open Biomedical Engineering Journal 7, 1 (2013)
12. Koller, W.C., Trimble, J.: The gait abnormality of huntington's disease. Neurology 35(10), 1450 (1985)
13. Li, S., Wang, J., Wang, X.: A novel gait recognition analysis system based on body sensor networks for patients with parkinson's disease. International Journal of Communication Networks and Distributed Systems 7(3), 262–274 (2011)
14. Merory, J.R., Wittwer, J.E., Rowe, C.C., Webster, K.E.: Quantitative gait analysis in patients with dementia with lewy bodies and alzheimer's disease. Gait & Posture 26(3), 414–419 (2007)
15. Mielke, M.M., Roberts, R.O., Savica, R., Cha, R., Drubach, D.I., Christianson, T., Pankratz, V.S., Geda, Y.E., Machulda, M.M., Ivnik, R.J., et al.: Assessing the temporal relationship between cognition and gait: Slow gait predicts cognitive decline in the Mayo Clinic Study of Aging. The Journals of Gerontology Series A: Biological Sciences and Medical Sciences (2012)

16. Nakamura, T., Meguro, K., Yamazaki, H., Okuzumi, H., Tanaka, A., Horikawa, A., Yamaguchi, K., Katsuyama, N., Nakano, M., Arai, H., et al.: Postural and gait disturbance correlated with decreased frontal cerebral blood flow in Alzheimer disease. Alzheimer Disease and Associated Disorders 11(3), 132 (1997)
17. Nixon, M.S., Tan, T., Chellappa, R.: Human identification based on gait vol. 4. Springer (2005)
18. Sánchez, E., Acosta-Escalante, D., Álvarez-Rodríguez, F.J.: Modelo para discriminación de clases basado en meta-clasificadores. caso: Detección de enfermedades neurodegenerativas. Investigación y Ciencia (2014) (article accepted)
19. Sugavaneswaran, L., Umapathy, K., Krishnan, S.: Discriminative time-frequency kernels for gait analysis for amyotrophic lateral sclerosis. In: 2011 Annual International Conference of the IEEE Engineering in Medicine and Biology Society, EMBC, pp. 2683–2686. IEEE (2011)
20. Theill, N., Martin, M., Schumacher, V., Bridenbaugh, S.A., Kressig, R.W.: Simultaneously Measuring Gait and Cognitive Performance in Cognitively Healthy and Cognitively Impaired Older Adults: The Basel Motor–Cognition Dual-Task Paradigm. Journal of the American Geriatrics Society 59(6), 1012–1018 (2011)
21. Verghese, J., Lipton, R.B., Hall, C.B., Kuslansky, G., Katz, M.J., Buschke, H.: Abnormality of gait as a predictor of non-alzheimer's dementia. New England Journal of Medicine 347(22), 1761–1768 (2002)
22. Wu, Y., Krishnan, S.: Computer-aided analysis of gait rhythm fluctuations in amyotrophic lateral sclerosis. Medical & Biological Engineering & Computing 47(11), 1165–1171 (2009)
23. Wu, Y., Ng, S.C.: A pdf-based classification of gait cadence patterns in patients with amyotrophic lateral sclerosis. In: 2010 Annual International Conference of the IEEE Engineering in Medicine and Biology Society (EMBC), pp. 1304–1307. IEEE (2010)
24. Yang, M., Zheng, H., Wang, H., McClean, S.: Feature selection and construction for the discrimination of neurodegenerative diseases based on gait analysis. In: 3rd International Conference on Pervasive Computing Technologies for Healthcare, PervasiveHealth 2009, pp. 1–7. IEEE (2009)

Adaptive User Interface and User Experience Based Authoring Tool for Recommendation Systems

Jamil Hussain[1], Wajahat Ali Khan[1], Muhammad Afzal[1,] Maqbool Hussain[1],
Byeong Ho Kang[2] and Sungyoung Lee[1,*]

[1] Department of Computer Engineering Kyung Hee University Seocheon-dong,
Giheung-gu, Yongin-si, Gyeonggi-do, Republic of Korea
{jamil,wajahat.alikhan,muhammad.afzal,
maqbool.hussain,sylee}@ oslab.khu.ac.kr
[2] Department of Engineering and Technology, Information and Communication Technology,
University of Tasmania, Australia
byeong.Kang@utas.edu.au

Abstract. User preferences and contextual changes impact the duration of adaptation of user interface (UI) for a particular system, specifically recommendation systems. Static UIs lack reflection of these behavioral changes which lead to bottleneck in the fulfillment of user needs and satisfaction. Therefore, a mechanism to incorporate User Experience (UX) for embedded customization in the UI is required for longer adaptation of the system. We propose an Adaptive UI / UX Authoring Tool that adapts the UI with the help of the information extracted from the UX. UI is provided to the user in recommendation systems based on personal profile and contextual information. Continuous involvement of the user using feedback, web monitoring and gamification to measure his satisfaction and evolution of the personal and contextual information, adapts the UI with the help of UX. UX controls the evolutionary process of the adaptation of the user interfaces and also maintains the personalization aspect. The proposed system guarantees the longer duration of utilization of the services provided by the recommendation systems due to provision of personalized UI.

Keywords: Human Computer Interaction, Adaptive Interface, Personalized UI, User Experience, User Profile Evaluation.

1   Introduction

The key to the success of recommendation systems lies in the functionalities provided in the user interface (UI). The functionalities are reflected by the user needs and contextual information representation in the UI. Even the user needs and contextual information changes with time, therefore the static behavior of the UI results in failure of these recommendation systems. Alexander et al. [1] describe the role of UI in recommendation system as a critical factor in effecting the characteristics such as overall system usability, system acceptance, item rating behavior, selection behavior, trust, willingness to buy, willingness to reuse the recommendation systems, and willingness

---

* Corresponding author.

R. Hervás et al. (Eds.): UCAmI 2014, LNCS 8867, pp. 136–142, 2014.
© Springer International Publishing Switzerland 2014

to promote the system to others [1]. These factors perseverance requires the involve-ment of the user in defining the layout of UI with User Experience (UX).

UX determines the lifeline of the UI by extracting the metrics based on the user in-volvement in the system to measure user satisfaction. Most of the researchers consid-ers UI and UX as same entities but there exists huge difference between them, although they are related to one another. UX metrics define the patterns of interaction between user and the system to measure the effectiveness, efficiency, and satisfaction of the users [2]. This leads to the evolution of behavioral and contextual information in the knowledge bases and finally adaptation of the UI based on these changes. Therefore, a tool is required that manages both UI and UX in adaptive manner for the increase in adaption period of the recommendation systems.

We propose UI/ UX Authoring Tool that caters the UI and UX with the main ob-jective to deal with the adaptive and personalized approach towards building and managing the user interfaces. The proposed system provides Adaptive UI by taking personal profile information, contextual information, and device usage information. Also, user feedback information, user behavior measurement, and user satisfaction measurement with gamification and web monitoring techniques are handled as UX. This eventually leads to the evolution of information in the repositories and personali-zation aspect incorporation in the Adaptive UI.

The rest of the paper is structured as follows: Section 2 describes the existing lite-rature related to the UI and UX. The proposed system methodology is presented in Section 3. Insight into the system is provided in Section 4 with the help of scenario. Finally the system is concluded and future work is described in Section 5.

2   Related Work

UI and UX has been the focus of many researchers as it specifies the lifetime of the system. Literature consists of such work that emphasizes on the importance of UI and UX for the success of the recommendation systems. Nowadays, AUI mostly use the computational approaches such as model-based, bayesian network, and mixed-initiative for adaptation of UI. Jiang et al. [3] proposed an AUI generation framework using web services that use service oriented approach dependent on programming language approach and the rule-based approach. Peissner et al. [4] developed MyUI system that made numerous experiments on user for examining the effectiveness and acceptability of various UI/UX adaptation patterns throughout their interaction. The UI/UX adaptation patterns were executed before adaptation that decreased the costs of adaptation by requesting an explicit user confirmation.

The trend of the UI shifted towards Performance Oriented Interface Design Models and many approaches were proposed based on this technique. Ibrahim et al. [5] consi-dered many factors of UI design that impacts the performance of web applications based on Systematic Literature Review (SLR). They proposed a model that provide guidelines for refining existing web applications in order to utilize used resources in effective manner via its UI.

Wu [6] proposed AUI method of detecting user left and right handed grip of elec-tronic devices and activated the UI accordingly. Dees [7] handled responsive design by automatically adjusting the UI according to screen resolution using media query technique.

In existing UI/UX systems, the UI is not based on context: in which context an application is used and how information is input. In our system along with context, we considered user experience based on many measurement factors such as trust, interaction, reaction, functionality, predictability, and individuality.

3   Methodology

We propose UI/UX Authoring tool to manage the Adaptive UI with the input from the UX in the form of feedback and other metrics as shown in Figure 1. The proposed architecture is divided into two main components: Adaptive User Interface (AUI) and User Experience (UX).

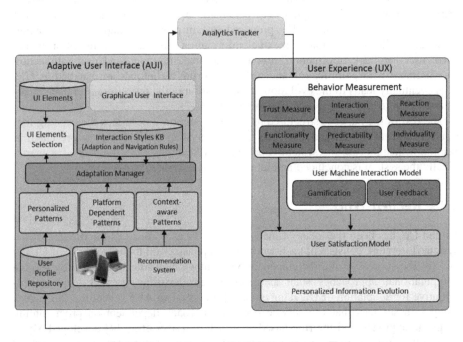

Fig. 1. The architecture of AUI/UX Authoring Tool

3.1   Adaptive User Interface (AUI)

AUI is composed of many subcomponents that obtains user behavior and contextual information for representation in the UI. User information is captured and stored in the User Profile Repository and the contextual information is obtained from the Recommendation System. Also, in addition to these the device information is obtained from the devices that the user uses. User Profile Repository is used for storing the user preferences in his daily life activities. Personalized Patterns are designed, developed, and executed based on the preferences stored in the User Profile Repository. The platform information is fetch by Platform Depend Patterns using style sheet by Media Query. Context aware Patterns obtains the current context about the user from recommendation system.

Adaptation Manager Component behaves as a coordinator between different internal components of the AUI. It takes initial input from the Patterns layer and forwards it to the Interactive Styles KB. Interactive Styles KB stores the adaption and navigation rules that are personalized to specific users. These are used for adaption of the user interface and also navigation between different graphical user interfaces. Interactive Styles KB send back the navigation rules to Adaption Manager, the UI Elements Selection component retrieves the interface elements from UI Elements repository based on patterns for the Graphical User Interface component to build GUI accordingly.

3.2   User Experience (UX)

Behavior Measurement consists of various user experience metrics to evaluate the response of the user. These measurement indicators are used for the evaluation of user response after initially seeing the personalized adaptive user interfaces.

User Machine Interaction Model interacts with the user through questionnaire, and games. The games are best choice to measure preliminary user states in addition to the updating of user profiles with the passage of time. Playing games provides a way to assess many attributes that are related to adaptive interfaces. We used different games such as cards matching, trail making (TM) and others for cognitive and motor test in order to evaluate the user memory, attention, hand precision and processing speed.

User Satisfaction Model process the information obtained from the different measurement indicators for finding out the user satisfaction. A threshold value is set for comparison and degree of adaptation to be carried out in the user interface. Personalized Information Evolution module takes input from the user satisfaction model and forwards the information to the AUI for evolution of the personalized repository.in Figure 2 shows the interaction among components of AUI/UX Authoring Tool.

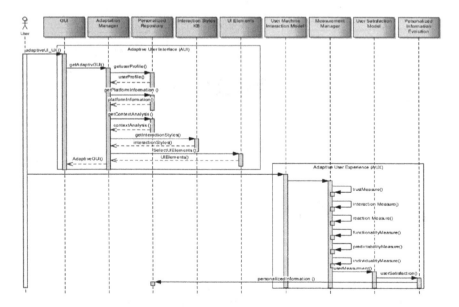

Fig. 2. AUI/UX Authoring Tool Sequence Diagram

4   UI/ UX Authoring Tool Service Scenario

We describe a scenario showing the personalized user interfaces and its adaption with user experience. A diabetes patient scenario is explained for UI/UX Authoring Tool to demonstrate the personalized user interfaces.

Initially, user preferences, platform and context information are extracted by patterns components. In the scenario, the user preferences are watching movies, listening music, playing games, and he is diabetes patient used Samsung S3 smartphone, and currently he is having high glucose level as contextual information obtained from the recommendation system as shown in Figure 3.The Adaption Manager adapt GUI according to patterns such as GUI are adjusted according to Samsung S3 screen and specific UI Elements are selected from the UI Repository based on user preferences and the context. In current context user is having high glucose level, the Adaptation Manger Adapt UI accordingly. The user glucose information is displayed along with diabetes related application and some Games. Initially, GUI are not much interactive, the user experience is lacking and the layout is specific to the theme.

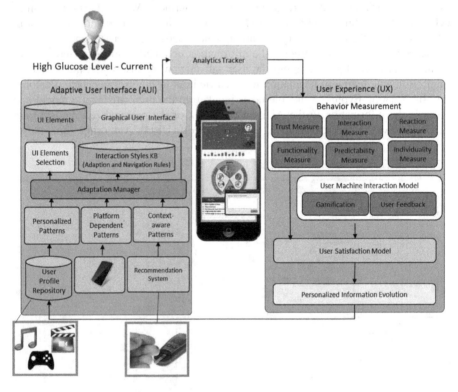

Fig. 3. AUI Workflow Output

Over the time UX module track the user behavior via behavior measurement module using analytics tracker that includes application usage, usability, interaction measure (less number of clicks), reaction measure (complexity), functionality, measure (less features), predictability measure (easy navigation), and individuality measure (color scheme). The user has also played TM game (needed to connect 12 successive nodes correctly and fast) which measures some discrete factors: game completion time, wrong clicks amount that helps in finding some cognitive and motor skills of that user such as attention and processing speed. All information is obtained and provided to the user satisfaction model that calculates the user satisfaction. If the threshold value is achieved then it means that user is satisfied with the current UI and based on the information in the repositories carry on with the personalized interface. Otherwise, as is in the scenario, if threshold is not achieved then user is not satisfied and information needs to be categorized and repositories should be evolved. The entertainment is the preference of the user but entertainment stuff was missing in the previous UI. Also, user has started using Tablet (I-Pad), and color schemes should be changed to purple and blue with more interactive GUI. The entertainment, tablet, and current status of glucose stable information is categorized by the Personalized Information Model. This information is forwarded to the repositories for evolution of the new knowledge. The color schemes, platform information (I-pad), and entertainment information is matched for a particular theme to be selected from the Interactive KB. The final theme is selected and then information is forwarded to the UI Elements Selection module. The UI Elements selection retrieves the UI elements from the UI repository and new adaptive user interface is displayed to the user in shown in Figure 4. The new adaptation is based on the personalized information such as new navigation style with preferred color schemes along with entertainment stuff.

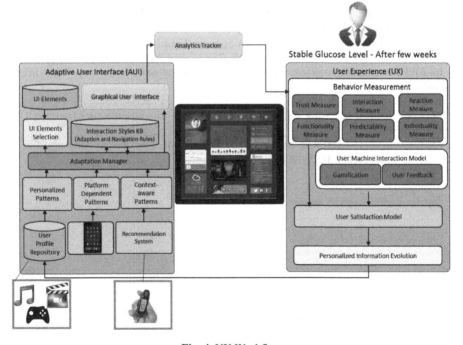

Fig. 4. UX Workflow

5   Summary

In this paper, we proposed AUI/UX Authoring Tool framework for recommendations systems. The framework considered User Experience for adapting the user interface. User experience controls the evolutionary process of the adaptation of the user interfaces and also maintaining the personalization aspect. The AUI will be develop using User Interface Markup Language (UIML) [8] that is based on meta-language which offer an XML based representation for UI.

Acknowledgments. This research was supported by the MSIP (Ministry of Science, ICT & Future Planning), Korea, under the ITRC (Information Technology Research Center) support program supervised by the NIPA (National IT Industry Promotion Agency)" (NIPA-2014-(H0301-14-1003).

References

1. Felfernig, A., Burke, R., Pu, P.: Preface to the special issue on user interfaces for recommender systems. User Modeling and User-Adapted Interaction 22(4), 313–316 (2012)
2. Albert, W., Tullis, T.: Measuring the user experience: Collecting, analyzing, and presenting usability metrics. Newnes (2013)
3. He, J., Yen, I.-L.: Adaptive user interface generation for web services. In: IEEE International Conference on e-Business Engineering, ICEBE 2007. IEEE (2007)
4. Peissner, M., Edlin-White, R.: User Control in Adaptive User Interfaces for Accessibility. In: Kotzé, P., Marsden, G., Lindgaard, G., Wesson, J., Winckler, M. (eds.) INTERACT 2013, Part I. LNCS, vol. 8117, pp. 623–640. Springer, Heidelberg (2013)
5. Ibrahim, R., Razali, R.: A performance-oriented interface design model of web applications. In: 2011 International Conference on Electrical Engineering and Informatics (ICEEI). IEEE (2011)
6. Wu, W.-Y.: Adaptive user interface. U.S. Patent Application 12/334,720
7. Dees, W.: Method of styling a user interface and device with adaptive user interface. US Patent 2002 (2002)
8. Abrams, M., et al.: UIML: An appliance-independent XML user interface language. Computer Networks 31(11), 1695–1708 (1999)

Snow Surface: A Multi-touch Game Using Microsoft PixelSense

Johan Forsling, Sofie Nilsson, Simon Ekström, and Per Grundtman

Luleå University of Technology, Luleå, Sweden

Abstract. This paper presents the design of a simple and entertaining game, developed for the Microsoft PixelSense platform. Snow Surface, was developed in an agile way and the result is an easy and fun game, which proved to take only a few seconds to learn. Snow Surface demonstrates the multi-touch and multi-user features of the PixelSense platform. More graphical effects and animations as well as more going-ons and functionalities in the actual game could improve the user-experience and make the game more fun.

Keywords: Pervasive Computing, Game, Tabletop, PixelSense.

1 Introduction

Samsung SUR40 is a 40 inch display with Microsoft PixelSense technology. It is placed in a horizontal orientation, as a table top on four legs. The design of SUR40 enables multiple users to interact with the display from all directions. The Samsung SUR40 can handle up to 50 fingers touching the display simultaneously. The PixelSense platform [1] is constituted by the hardware Samsung SUR40 with Microsoft PixelSense and the software Microsoft Surface 2.0.

The objective of this paper is to present the main thoughts on the design of the multitouch game. The paper is structured as follows: Section 2 presents some related work. Section 3 presents the main ideas on the design of the game. Section 4 provides a discussion of the design of the game. Section 5 concludes the paper and section 6 presents some ideas on future work for the game.

2 Related Work

There have been a lot of work related to this, where there have been progress on how to increase the user experience on hardware similar to the Samsung SUR40. One interesting paper that relates to this is "Heuristics for the evaluation of tabletop games" [2], which presents 10 heuristics for touch-based games of this scale. The presented heuristics are *Cognitive Workload, Challenge, Reach, Examinability, Adaptability, Interaction, Level of Automation, Collaboration and Communication, Feedback* and *Comfort of the physical setup.*

Another inspirational source for doing this project was "A pervasive Game to Promote Social Offline Interaction" [3], which is a study on how to take computer games to the next level as a social activity by using this sort of interactive technology.

R. Hervás et al. (Eds.): UCAmI 2014, LNCS 8867, pp. 143–146, 2014.
© Springer International Publishing Switzerland 2014

3   Design

The game developed in this project is called Snow Surface. The main idea behind the game was to make it entertaining and also intuitive to learn so that people who are only staying for a few minutes at the table will have a chance to play the game.

3.1   Game Description

Snowflakes with different colors spawns at random locations on the x-axis from the top of the display. The snowflakes will then move downwards with a random speed both horizontally and vertically.

The goal of the game is to tap with a finger on the snowflakes. Players get one point for every snowflake of their color that was tapped on during the game and the player with the highest score at the end wins.

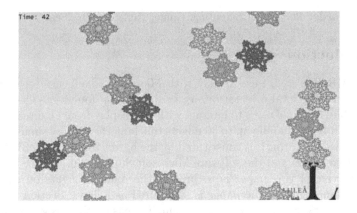

Fig. 1. Picture of the game

4   Discussion

The design of the game described in this article managed to apply a few of the heuristics mentioned in [2], mainly *Cognitive Workload*, *Challenge* and *Feedback*. The heuristics focusing more on player comfort, such as *Adaptability* and *Comfort of the physical setup* was not considered in the same extent, as the design is made for shorter play sessions.

Initially during the design process there was not too much focus on the actual heuristics. The game is mainly designed to be as simple as possible for the user and this minimizes a lot of the usability problems that the heuristics are designed for.

The design contains a usability problem that can be hard to solve, this is the workload when playing the game. How many snowflakes per second should show up? Too many makes the players just tapping the screen frantically, while too few makes the game boring. Various player will have various opinion on how fast they want the game to be. That is why the game presents two difficulty levels, easy and hard. But not even the difficulty levels solve this problem completly.

Compared to the paper on heuristics [2] this paper does not focus on developing new heuristics. Instead it is focusing on designing a new game where the heuristics in the mentioned paper are used as tools for improving the user experience of the game.

The game has been played and tested by a handful of people. They could all understand the rules and goal of the game after a few seconds of interaction with the game.

5   Conclusion

The application demonstrates the multitouch features of the Samsung SUR40 in an entertaining and intuitive manner through a simple multiplayer game. It provides a good basis for further development of the Samsung SUR40 features and can be used as an exhibition object at upper secondary schools to attract new students to the field of multimedia development.

6   Future Work

The game described in this paper only scratched the surface of what is possible with PixelSense. Here is a couple of ideas that came up but did not get realized.

6.1   Aesthetic Upgrades

By adding graphical effects like flickering snowflakes, more advanced animations when a snowflake is clicked upon and a more interesting background, the gaming experience would not seem as flat as its current state.

6.2   Increased Challenge

To enhance the difficulty level, continuously changing flakes were suggested, where at some determined period, the snowflakes turn to an opponents color, forcing the player to step up the focus and time the clicks. Added foe-flakes which would decrement score points when melted could be an addition that would step up the challenge of the game.

6.3   Utilization of All Features

There are features of the Samsung SUR40 that was not used in this game. This includes camera, barcode scanning and the object recognition feature. These features might not be suited for this very project but the potential for interesting games that showcases the Samsung SUR40 is of interest to the group of this project.

References

1. PixelSense Platform,
   http://www.microsoft.com/en-us/pixelsense/default.aspx (Fetched November 19, 2013)
2. Köffel, C., Haller, M.: Heuristics for the evaluation of tabletop games. In: Evaluating User Experiences in Games, Workshop at the 2008 Conference on Human Factors in Computing Systems, CHI 2008, Florence, Italy, April 5-10 (2008)
3. Caon, M., Mugellini, E., Khaled, O.A.: A pervasive game to promote social offline interaction. In: Proceedings of the 2013 ACM Conference on Pervasive and Ubiquitous Computing Adjunct Publication, pp. 1381–1384. ACM (2013)

Evaluation of a Context-Aware Application for Mobile Robot Control Mediated by Physiological Data: The ToBITas Case Study

Borja Gamecho[1], José Guerreiro[2], Ana Priscila Alves[2], André Lourenço[2],
Hugo Plácido da Silva[2], Luis Gardeazabal[1], Julio Abascal[1] and Ana Fred[2]

[1] Egokituz Laboratory, Universtity of the Basque Country, 20018 Donostia, Spain
[2] PIA Group, Instituto de Telecomunicações, 1049-001 Lisboa, Portugal

Abstract. We present the ToBITas mobile Context-Aware application
to control a mobile robot using electromyographic and accelerometric signals acquired from the user's right-hand arm. The signals are acquired
by means of an off-the-shelf low-cost device called BITalino and are processed by an Android smartphone. Our work was developed as a case
study to validate the quality of the mobile applications created with a
rapid-prototyping framework called MobileBIT. We evaluated the application with thirteen participants and the results suggest that participants
were able to adapt to the proposed control mode, completing the task in
a suitable time.

Keywords: context-awareness, mobile computing, physiological signals,
human-computer interaction.

1 Introduction

Over the last few years, the number of wireless devices with embedded sensors
has increased significantly, making Context-Aware mobile applications available
and more appealing to the general public. Following the definition of context
given by Dey 2001 [1], an application is Context-Aware if the interaction between the user and the application is affected by relevant information related to
the entities of that context. Usually these entities are people, objects and the environment where the interaction takes place. The context information is usually
gathered from sensors and processed into meaningful data to generate semantically complex information. Developers choose the relevance of every piece of
information and adapt the application to the context in a proper way. The main
devices for these applications are smartphones and tablets, which make use of
their embedded sensors to gather suitable context information from the user or
the device itself. On the other hand, the success of open-hardware platforms, like
the Arduino, also make possible the proliferation of low-cost devices with a full
range of embedded sensors. As an example of such devices, we have the BITalino board [2], which is particularly interesting due to the fact that it measures

R. Hervás et al. (Eds.): UCAmI 2014, LNCS 8867, pp. 147–154, 2014.
© Springer International Publishing Switzerland 2014

multi-modal physiological data from the users. This expands the sensing capabilities of existing smartphones and leads to a new wave of mobile Context-Aware applications.

As an example of these new applications, we created the ToBITas case study, a mobile Context-Aware application with an extended version of the MobileBIT rapid-prototyping framework [3]. ToBITas is a smartphone application designed to control a mobile robot using the above mentioned BITalino device as the input interface. It is intended for: a) testing the satisfaction and adaptation of users to physiologically-enhanced sensors input methods, in this case, Electromyography (EMG) and Accelerometry (ACC); b) creating an application based on low-cost sensor platforms to extend the smartphone sensing capabilities using a Context-Aware approach; and c) testing the feasibility of the MobileBIT framework to create Context-Aware applications.

2   Related Work

The EMG-based control for computer systems has been a well-studied research topic aimed at replacing traditional input interfaces, namely mouse and keyboard. For instance, in 1998 Rosenberg presented the biofeedback pointer [4], a four-pair electrode-based EMG system to control a two-dimensional pointer with a forearm. Among other applications, this control method is appropriate for mobile environments and to solve accessibility issues. Both approaches were studied in Guerreiro and Jorge (2008) [5], where the authors introduced the EMG as a daily wearable interface and explored different placements for EMG electrodes. Far from the traditional point and click mappings, Constanza et al. (2007) [6] provided a usability study for one and two arms to control multimodal applications while walking. Similarly to our approach, this work detected the movements in the biceps to trigger system events but it has the data processing embedded in the armband microcontroller. ToBITas uses BITalino as the data acquisition device and the smartphone for running the data processing algorithms. This allows us to try different algorithms depending on the application. When it comes to controlling robots, in Rhee et al. (2013) [7] four-channel EMG and three-axis ACC are used to send commands to a humanoid robot. The system detects four arm movements by means of a k-nearest neighbours algorithm, and the robot is activated when the EMG value is over a certain threshold. Our approach follows a simpler configuration of two-channel EMG and one-axis ACC to recognize similar gestures and movements, which is less intrusive for the users.

3   ToBITas

ToBITas has been created as a proof of concept of a Context-Aware application that controls a mobile robotic platform using physiological sensors. The right-hand arm's movements and gestures are the relevant context information from

Table 1. The relationship between the acquired signals, the context information and the system behaviour

Signal	User Movement	Context Information	Robot Command
EMG_1	The user folds his arm	Action_detected: Right_arm_folded	Move Forward
EMG_2	The user closes his hand	Action_detected: Hand_Closed	Open/Close the Claw
		Position_detected: Forearm_up	Move Right
ACC	Tilt the foream	Position_detected: Forearm_down	Move Left
		Position_detected: Forearm_side	Don't Move

the user. There are three types of user movements that will trigger different actions in the robot: i) activating the biceps (e.g. folding the arm), which will make the robot move forward; ii) activating the thenar eminence (e.g. closing the hand), that will alternate between closing and opening the claw; and iii) tilting the forearm to the left or right, making the robot steer in the same direction. Table 1 summarizes this information. We used three devices: a BITalino board, an Android smartphone and a Bot'n roll mobile robot[1]. Targeting the muscles and tilt sensing, we employed the BITalino biosignal platform. It combines EMG and ACC sensors with a wireless communication module that uses Bluetooth technology (Class II v2.0), providing both biosignals acquisition and connectivity to a smartphone. We used the BITalino Board in a configuration that acquires EMG and ACC (z-axis) signals (10 bits @ $fs = 100$ Hz), streaming the raw data to the smartphone via Bluetooth with a baudrate of $115,200$ bps, where all the processing takes place. The EMG electrodes are placed over the muscle fibres of the biceps (EMG 1) and the thenar eminence on the hand (EMG 2), with a distance of approximately 2 cm. The reference electrode is placed on a bone area on the elbow. The ACC sensor is on the BITalino board, which is placed on the right wrist of the user, as shown in Figure 1. For the target device, we used a Bot'n roll mobile robot, which combines a set of physical actuators, namely servo wheels, which allow the robot movements, and a servo claw used to grab objects. It also has a wireless communication module that uses Bluetooth technology (Class II v2.0) with a baudrate of $38,400$ bps. Finally, the smartphone is an LG Optimus F5 with Android 4.1.2, a Dual-Core 1.2 GHz processor and 1 GB RAM. This smartphone runs the Context-Aware application alongside the MobileBIT Framework and acts as the brain of the system. This application includes a user interface and provides calibration, signal processing and management of the communication from/to each platform (BITalino and Bot'n roll). The Android smartphone receives the EMG and ACC data from the BITalino with a sampling rate of 100 Hz. Every 400 ms (40 samples), the signal is processed to obtain a value that is compared with a threshold interval. If it matches the threshold interval, the application sends a command to the Bot'n roll robot, obtaining different responses (see Table 1).

---
[1] http://www.botnroll.com/

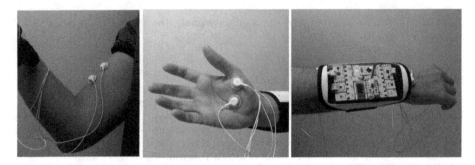

Fig. 1. Electrodes and sensor placement for the right arm. From left to right: EMG 1 (biceps), EMG 2 (thenar eminence), board placement on the wrist with incorporated ACC sensor.

4 Data Processing

The strategy used for the EMG onset detection algorithm consists of two stages: a processing block to filter the signal and extract relevant information and a decision rule block. The purpose of the processing block is to compute the envelope of the EMG signal. The process is based on a sliding window of M=40 samples. It starts by a moving average filter as described by Equation 1, where $x[n]$ is the input signal (EMG), $s[n]$ is the output signal and M is the moving average window size. For a sampling frequency of 100 Hz, the -3 dB cut-off frequency is about 30 Hz and the gain is 20 ms at 0 Hz. The phase shift is 20 ms (two samples), such that

$$s[n] = \frac{1}{M} \sum_{j=0}^{M-1} x[n-j]. \tag{1}$$

Afterwards, signal rectification is performed by computing the absolute value of the sliding window and the DC value $s[n]$ is subtracted, as defined by Eq. (2)

$$z[n] = \left| s[n] - \frac{1}{M} \sum_{j=0}^{M-1} s[n-j] \right|. \tag{2}$$

The processing stage finishes by computing the average value of the sliding window, as described in Equation 3, where M is equal to 40. In the end, we have one resultant value, $y[n]$, for each 40 samples of the raw input signal. An example can be seen in Figure 2 (a)

$$y[n] = \frac{1}{M} \sum_{j=0}^{M-1} z[n-j]. \tag{3}$$

Finally, a simple decision rule is applied to $y[n]$ to determine if there is a muscle contraction when $y[n] > threshold$. Otherwise, the algorithm rejects the $y[n]$ values.

The threshold value is defined during the calibration stage. In this step, the user is asked to contract one muscle at a time. Then, the threshold is calculated and defined manually as 50% of the maximum $y[n]$ value. This value will be used as a baseline value for the system response. The strategy used for ACC movement detection follows the same approach. However, the processing stage consists only of a low-pass filter implemented with a moving average filter, as described by Equation 1. Similarly to the EMG approach, the ACC decision rule is applied to determine the ACC position in each instant and compared with a threshold value interval. The thresholds for the ACC were calculated by the analysis of the values for the processed data and mapping them with the forearm positions. The three positions of the forearm can be seen in Figure 2 (b).

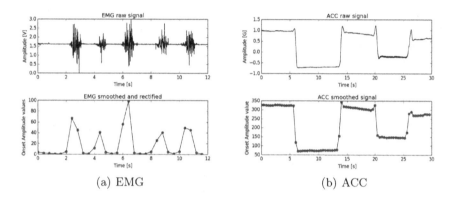

(a) EMG   (b) ACC

Fig. 2. EMG and ACC signals used to evaluate the adopted algorithm. In the top row we show the EMG (left) and ACC (right) raw signals, and in the bottom row we show the signal obtained at the final stage of the adopted algorithm. It is important to highlight how the output of the algorithm we have adopted facilitates the onset detection on the EMG signals.

5   Smartphone Application

To develop the ToBITas mobile application, we adopted the MobileBIT framework. It is intended to facilitate the rapid-prototyping of mobile applications for real-time data acquisition, processing, recording, communication and visualization for the telemedicine and mobile health domains. Further details about the framework can be found in the work of Cânovas et al. (2013) [3].

For ToBITas, four functional blocks were developed: i) a source block to handle the BITalino Bluetooth connection and data acquisition; ii) a functional block with the algorithm described in Section 4; iii) a sink block to interface the smartphone app with relevant context information, like the arm movements;

and iv) a functional block intended to ease the setup of the thresholds for EMG 1 and 2. The Smartphone application just needs to subscribe for context events, and the MobileBIT framework provides this information in real time. Then, the application sends the appropriate message to the Bot'n roll robot.

6 Usability Testing

As previously stated, one of the reasons for the creation of the ToBITas is to test the adaptation of the user to physiologically-enhanced sensor input methods. In addition to this, user satisfaction is also measured. For that purpose we performed an exploratory study evaluating the interaction of the participants with ToBITas completing a simple robot control task. We had two research questions: a) Are the users able to control our system?; and b) Do users feel comfortable with this kind of control? For the former, the times to complete the task were measured for each participant in order to compare the learning effect between participant groups. For the latter, the participants were asked to complete the System Usability Scale (SUS) [8] to obtain insights for user satisfaction.

6.1 Participants

We recruited 13 volunteers (four females) from the surrounding research laboratories of the IST-UL university campus. The participants ranged from 21 to 39 years, and all of them were right-handed. They were divided into three groups by their level of expertise: two of the participants were involved in the design and development of the system (Group C - Experts), while the remaining participants had no prior experience with this system. The two expert participants did not complete the SUS questionnaire to avoid a conflict of interests. Four users reported having some experience with controlling similar systems (Group B - Experienced), and the remaining users had no prior experience with this type of interface (Group A - Novices).

6.2 Procedure

To begin, the demographic background of each user was collected. Subsequently, the BITalino device was set up, and the electrodes were placed as mentioned in Figure 1. Afterwards, the calibration phase was carried out with the help of the researchers, and each user was asked to follow a routine consisting of moving the robot for 1 m to grab a cylindrical object and then releasing it at a given position that was 1 m further from the object.[2] Each participant performed the task three times while the performance was recorded in video and stored together with the log data from the Android application. Finally, the participants completed the SUS questionnaire.

---

[2] http://sipt07.si.ehu.es/bgamecho/ToBITas/Demo_video.mp4 demo video of the task.

6.3   Results and Discussion

All the participants in the experiment were able to finish the proposed task. The time required to complete the task was under 100 s for all participants in Group B and C, while in group A, four participants spent more than 100 s. We saw noticeable differences in the learning effect between each group of participants, as shown in Table 2. For Group C there was no learning effect because those participants had been using ToBITas during its development and were familiar with it. Surprisingly, in the third run, all the participants from both groups A and B spent approximately 55 s to perform the task. This suggests that after two trials, user Group A obtained a similar experience as user Group B.

With regard to the SUS questionnaire, the average score was 73.86%, which is over the 70% required to consider the usability of the system as good. Four of the participants (36%) marked the system with a lower score than 70%, and only one of those scored the system lower than 60%. We noticed that this participant had lower thresholds during the calibration process compared to other participants, which made the system more sensitive to noise. Therefore, on some occasions, it did not follow the participant's demands and expectations. It might have been charged from the noise within the acquisition scenario or had bad electrode placement.

On the other hand, some flaws were detected in the system that must be addressed in future versions. For instance, the tilt movement of the wrist, associated with a right turn by the robot, sometimes also activated the thresholds for the biceps and the thenar eminence muscles. This unintended movement was noticed by some of the participants who started to move their arm more accurately. Others instead followed a strategy of 'only turn to the left' to avoid the undesired movement. New DSP algorithms combining three signals (EMG1, EMG2, ACC) could be tested to fix these issues.

Table 2. Summary of the task performance results for each group of participants measured in seconds. (A: Novice participant, B: Participant with some experience on similar systems controlled by gestures, C: ToBITas developers).

Group	T1 [s]	T2 [s]	T3 [s]	μ [s]	σ [s]
A	140	93	57	96	59
B	104	77	53	78	20
C	25	38	24	29	6
Average	89	70	49	69	16

7   Conclusion

The results of the presented exploratory study show that ToBITas is a functional and usable Context-Aware application, proving that the MobileBIT rapid-prototyping framework is able to provide valid Context-Aware applications.

The input method based on EMG and ACC sensors performed well for the control of a mobile robot. Moreover, since the participants were able to shorten the experience time in every repetition, this seems to indicate that the participants were able to adapt themselves to the system very quickly. Nevertheless, a formal evaluation including increasing number of participants would be needed to reinforce this claim. Another interesting issue for future work is to study how well this application adapts to other input devices with similar characteristics to BITalino and provide an automatic calibration option for the thresholds.

Acknowledgements. EGOKITUZ is funded by the Department of Education, Universities and Research of the Basque Government (grant IT395-10) and belongs to the Basque Advanced Informatics Laboratory (BAILab) supported by the University of the Basque Country UPV/EHU (grant UFI11/45). Borja Gamecho holds a PhD scholarship from the Research Staff Training Programme of the Basque Government. The authors would also like to acknowledge the support of the Portuguese Fundação para a Ciência e Tecnologia (FCT) under the grants PTDC/EEI-SII/2312/2012 and SFRH/BD/65248/2009, as well as the company Bot'n roll for support in use of their platform.

References

1. Dey, A., Abowd, G.D., Salber, D.: A conceptual framework and a toolkit for supporting the rapid prototyping of context-aware applications. Hum.-Comput. Interact. 16(2), 97–166 (2001)
2. Silva, H., Lourenç o, A., Fred, A., Martins, R.: BIT: Biosignal igniter toolkit. Computer Methods and Programs in Biomedicine 115(1), 20–32 (2014)
3. Cânovas, M., Silva, H., Lourenço, A., Canento, F., Fred, A.: MobileBIT: A framework for mobile interaction recording and display. In: Stacey, D., Solé-Casals, J., Fred, A.L.N., Gamboa, H. (eds.) Proc. of the 6th Conference on Health Informatics (HEALTHINF), pp. 366–369. SciTePress (2013)
4. Rosenberg, R.: The biofeedback pointer: EMG control of a two dimensional pointer. In: Digest of Papers of the Second International Symposium on Wearable Computers, Digest of Papers, pp. 162–163 (1998)
5. Guerreiro, T., Jorge, J.: Assessing electromyographic interfaces. JVRB 5 (2008)
6. Costanza, E., Inverso, S.A., Allen, R., Maes, P.: Intimate interfaces in action: Assessing the usability and subtlety of emg-based motionless gestures. In: Proceedings of the SIGCHI Conference on Human Factors in Computing Systems, CHI 2007, pp. 819–828. ACM Press, New York (2007)
7. Rhee, K., You, K., Shin, H.: Intuitive robot control using surface emg and accelerometer signals. International Journal of Electrical, Electronics, Communication, Energy Science and Engineering 7(10), 89–92 (2013)
8. Brooke, J.: SUS: A quick and dirty usability scale. In: Jordan, P.W., Weerdmeester, B., Thomas, A., Mclelland, I.L. (eds.) Usability Evaluation in Industry. Taylor and Francis, London (1996)

Media Sharing across Public Display Networks

Rui José[1], Jorge C.S. Cardoso[2], and Jason Hong[3]

[1] Centro Algoritmi, University of Minho, Guimarães, Portugal
rui@dsi.uminho.pt
[2] CITAR/School of Arts, Portuguese Catholic University, Porto, Portugal
jorgecardoso@ieee.org
[3] Carnegie Mellon University
jasonh@cs.cmu.edu

Abstract. In this work, we consider the scenario of an open display network in which people can post their content to a potentially large set of public displays. This raises the key challenge of how to associate that content with the displays that may provide a more meaningful context for its presentation. The main contribution of this work is a novel understanding of how different properties of the media sharing scenarios may impact their perceived value. We have conceived 24 media sharing scenarios that represent different combinations of three independent variables: content locativeness, the personal nature of content and the scope in which content is being shared. We then invited 100 participants to express their perception of the appropriateness of those scenarios. The results indicate a clear preference for content that is both personal and locative, something that is in strike contrast with the prevailing content on current digital signage networks.

1   Introduction

Current public display systems are not yet a communication medium that can be systematically appropriated by people to publish their own content. However, the emerging principles of Open Display Networks [4], in which large-scale networks of pervasive public displays and associated sensors are open to applications and content from many sources, may create entirely new expectations in regard to the scope of media sharing on public displays. While previous research has already studied many variants of user-generated content for public displays [2][11][8], such research has mainly assumed a publication scenario in which content is posted to a specific display within a clear context of "here and now". However, open display networks create entirely new possibilities for posting user-generated content to a potentially very broad and unknown set of public displays. Unlike the traditional narrowcast model, where content from a single centralized source is distributed to a set of displays, this distribution model entails a many-to-many distribution paradigm in which content from many users can be shown wherever appropriate.

This raises the key challenge of how to redefine appropriateness, beyond the context of "here and now". Like many other forms of communication, including social networking services, media sharing on a public display occurs within the scope

R. Hervás et al. (Eds.): UCAmI 2014, LNCS 8867, pp. 155–162, 2014.
© Springer International Publishing Switzerland 2014

of a wider social context that frames the notion of what might be appropriate to present. When content is posted on a specific display, the context in which it will be shown is implicitly defined by the inherent locativeness of the publication process. Appropriateness is directly linked to the interpretation made by the publisher about the current display setting, and any social negotiation surrounding the shared used of the display is normally implicit in the interaction process itself. However, when considering media sharing across an open-ended set of displays, this association with a specific context is lost. Alternative approaches are thus needed to support the match between content being posted by people anywhere on the network and the displays that may provide a meaningful context for its presentation.

In this study, we aim to understand how user expectations about media sharing across large networks of public displays can be affected by the nature of the content being published and the scope of publication. We assume that users can post media items for presentation across an open network of public displays. Our key research question is to understand how in that context, different properties of the content or different publication scopes may affect the perceived utility of media sharing situations.

2   Related Work

A very broad range of techniques has been studied to enable display systems to accept content originating from users. One of the earlier examples, the Plasma Poster [2], allowed people to submit photos, text, and web pages to a public display using email or a web form. SMS and MMS have also been extensively used as an interaction technique for the spontaneous generation of content. For example, the Joe Blogg project [11] includes a display designed in the form of an interactive artwork where people can send pictures and text messages through MMS or SMS. Hermes [1] explored the use of Bluetooth to enable users to send pictures and other media to a display. The use of Bluetooth names as an interactive feature has been described in [8][5] as an essentially opportunistic alternative that is easily available to enable user-generated content on a broad range of mobile devices.

Despite the many techniques for placing user-generated content on public displays, Huang and Mynatt [7] observed that individuals tend not to be motivated to supply content, or else have difficulty identifying appropriate content. Similarly, Müller et al. [12] describe how public displays may be perceived as a stage in which people will only act if they feel confident about their actions and in full control over the presentation of self.

More general publication practices around large scale networks of public displays have been studied by Friday et al. [6] in a long-term analysis of the e-campus deployment at Lancaster University. Publication practices are also a central topic for Instant Places [9], an open network for public displays that allows people to systematically manage content publication. The system has been deployed across a set of locations at which participants were allowed to create and distribute digital posters for presentation on public displays. Altogether, these findings suggest that at least part of the challenges involved in making user-generated content a reality are not directly related with the interaction process itself. Instead, they seem to be more strongly associated with the motivation, the context and the meaning of the media sharing process.

Location-based Social Networks include location information into their social graph to enable users to see where their friends are, to search location-tagged content within their social graph, and to meet others nearby [10]. The relation between physical co-presence and on-line social friendships has been studied by Cranshaw et al. [3] who have shown that such relation is strongly dependent on the entropy of the locations visited and the number of social ties that a user has in the network. The ways in which different types of interpersonal relationships may be associated with the willingness to share information between people has been studied by Wiese et al. [14]. In this study, we address a specific type of social graph in which the social object is a screen media item and the social connections are primarily aimed at enabling the presentation of that content in socially meaningful contexts. While sharing some of the properties of location-based social networks, particularly the key role of location and presence, a social network for open displays would have to support a new type of social graph that is anchored on places and their role as meaningful contexts for media display.

3   Research Methodology

Our research methodology is anchored on the perceived utility of different scenarios of media sharing across large networks of public displays and how that perception of utility is affected by three independent variables, more specifically: (a) the locativeness of the content being shared, (b) how personal that content is and (c) the scope in which it is being shared. In regard to locativeness, we consider the extent to which content is related to a local scope. We also consider the effect of how personal the content is. Considering the public nature of the displays, our notion of personal does not include any privacy–sensitive content. Instead, we are just considering authorship or the extent to which the content is an expression of identity. Like in most social networks, a media item may have been created by the person herself to express personal views or it may simply have been pulled out from some third-party external source and shared for presentation. Finally, we also consider how different sets of places can provide meaningful contexts for expressing the scope of media sharing. We assume that when posting screen media items to the display network, publishers will be asked to express their view of the respective publication scope, i.e. the set of places where the presentation of that content is seen as appropriate by the publisher.

3.1   Scenario Specification

Since open display networks are not yet a reality that is part of people's everyday lives, we could not base our study on data about existing media sharing practices. We thus devised a study anchored on a set of carefully designed scenarios inspired by common media sharing situations from social media that we re-purposed for the context of open display networks. The goal was to minimize bias on possible content types and also to have scenarios that provided, as much as possible, a familiar frame of reference for participants. We selected a set of popular services with diverse properties in regard to their goals and media sharing practices, more specifically Facebook, Twitter, Pinterest, Craiglist and Causes. For each of these services, we searched for content rankings and identified the types of content that were shared the most. We then pruned the results to exclude content that would clearly not make sense on public displays, either for privacy reasons or because of the nature of the content itself. The result was a selection of 6 media sharing situations that were to be used as seeds for the 24 scenarios in our study. Each situation was described in the form of a short story adapted to fit the specific circumstances of public displays. These stories described the whole context of the media sharing situation, clearly stating, not just the type of content, but also the intentions associated with sharing. The goal was to allow people to identify with the overall media sharing context and motivations. The result of this process is the set of 6 media sharing stories listed in Table 1.

Table 1. The six base stories for the study embedded with different locality and personal properties

ID	Description	Locality	Personal
1	A funny video of a dance	Global	No
2	A Garage sale announcement	Local	Yes
3	Photos of new IPhone launch	Global	No
4	Food at local restaurant	Local	Yes
5	Poster World AIDS Day	Misc	No
6	Missing dog appeal	Local	No

These 6 stories include situations in which the content being shared is potentially relevant on a global scale, e.g. a funny dance video, and other scenarios where the relevance of the content is much more local, e.g. the missing dog. The world AIDS day was not considered for this variable because it was ambiguous in the sense that it was a global campaign with local initiatives that could easily be interpreted both ways. Similarly, the stories also include situations in which content being shared is not at all personal, e.g. the iPhone launch, and situations where content involves a personal form of expression, e.g. sharing a good experience at a local restaurant.

The other independent variable in our study is the media sharing scope. This defines the strategy that people can use to express where it will be more meaningful to show the content that they are sharing on the display network. For this study, we selected 4 types of connections between people and potential places for media sharing: (A) Share in the places most visited by friends [Implicit]; (B) Share in the places marked as favourite [Explicit]; (C) Share in previously visited places [Implicit]; and (D) Share where you are a frequent visitor [Implicit]. Finally, we combined these 4 media distribution strategies with each of the 6 base stories to obtain the final set of 24 media sharing embedded with different treatments of our 3 independent variables.

3.2   Scenario Evaluation

Our experimental setting was thus composed by 24 media sharing scenarios, each corresponding to a different combination of 3 independent variables, more specifically, the locativeness of the content (global or local), the personal nature of content (personal or not), and the distribution strategy used for expressing the media sharing scope (A – D).

The dependent variable is the perceived value that participants associate with each of the media sharing scenarios. To gather this data, we run a survey on Amazon's Mechanical Turk, with workers located at the USA. We divided the 24 scenarios into 4 different evaluation tasks, each consisting of a survey where participants were asked to evaluate how likely was it that they would publish content to a network of public displays in the same way as described in each of the media sharing scenarios. Their answers ranked from 1 (not at all likely) to 5 (very likely). Each task was composed by a subset of 6 of the 24 scenarios, but we selected them in a way that all the 6 base stories (see Table 1) were present on each task. To reduce bias, the order of the scenarios on each task was randomized.

We ran 4 evaluation panels consecutively, over a period of a month. They were all launched at about the same time of the day and their average duration was 6.5 days. The panel size (30) was larger than the number of respondents we eventually selected (25), so that we had some margin to discard recurrences. The larger panel size was also useful for discarding evaluators that did not execute their task in a responsible manner. For identifying these cases, we have followed each scenario evaluation with a verification question to ensure that respondents were paying the appropriate attention to their task. A total of 112 participants answered the 4 evaluation panels. From these, we discarded 8 survey responses done by recurrent evaluators or in which there was evidence of lack of a responsible job. At the end, we randomly discarded 4 others to get the same number of results per scenario and ended up with 100 survey responses by unique participants expressing 600 opinions about the proposed scenarios, and more specifically 25 evaluations on each of our 24 scenarios.

4   Results

The results of this study are grounded on the 100 validated responses obtained from participants. A higher result means that participants perceived the scenario as corresponding to something that they were more likely to do. Overall, the Missing Dog and the Garage Sale scenarios were the 3 scenarios that were consistently rated as being the most likely. However, our analysis is mainly focused on assessing the effects of our study variables on the sub-set of scenarios that correspond to the different treatments of our experience, as represented in Table 2.

Table 2. Means and standard deviations of the responses

Variable	Level	Mean	SD
Locality	Local	3.56	1.32
	Global	2.42	1.30
Personal	Personal	3.40	1.32
	Non-personal	2.98	1.42
Distribution strategy	Dist. A	2.96	1.42
	Dist. B	3.23	1.34
	Dist. C	3.11	1.44
	Dist. D	3.17	1.41

The table shows the mean and standard deviations of the participants' responses for each of those treatments and respective levels. The characteristics that differentiate the treatments are the locality of content (2 levels), the personal nature of the content (2 levels) and the distribution strategy (4 levels).

These same results are also depicted in Figure 1, in the form of boxplots for the various variables and levels. The left and right sides of the boxes represent the first and third quartiles, respectively, and the line inside the box represents the median. Given the nature of our data, with discrete values and all the scenarios having the same minimum (1) and the same maximum (5), we decided to overlay information about the mean value (the dot) and one standard deviation below and above the mean.

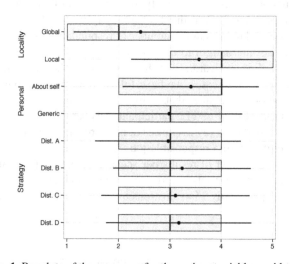

Fig. 1. Boxplots of the responses for the various variables and levels

One of the goals was to identify the effect of the locativeness on the perceived value of the media sharing scenarios. From the 6 base stories, there were 2 (Funny video of a dance in a wedding and Photos from the new IPhone launch) that represented content with potentially global scope and 3 that represented content with local scope (food suggestion at local restaurant, Missing dog and Garage sale). We excluded the World AIDS Day scenario from this analysis because of the ambiguity between local events by the local community and those events being part of a world day. The main result is that participants have clearly favoured content that was local in scope. The scenarios in which content is more locally relevant stand out very clearly in the boxplot as being the ones for which there is a more positive perception of relevance. To verify the statistical significance of these results, we ran a one-way ANOVA test between the two groups (local and global). The results confirm the existence of a statistically significant effect of locality on the perceived value associated with the sharing situation (F1, 498 = 90.54, p < 2e-16).

These results suggest that participants make a very strong association between the locative nature of content and its relevance for publication across public displays.

Our second goal was to identify the effect of the personal nature of content being published to the display network. From the 6 base scenarios, there were 2 scenarios (Garage sale announcement and Food at local restaurant) that were directly about the publisher. The other 4 scenarios (funny video of a dance; Photos from new IPhone launch; Poster on World AIDS Day and Missing dog) represented content that referred to others. This variable follows a behaviour similar to locality. Even though the boxplots for personal content seem less distinct, the median and mean values for personal content are clearly more positive than those for non-personal content. A one-way ANOVA test on the two groups of scenarios (personal and non-personal) confirms that the personal nature of content also has a statistically significant effect on the perceived relevance associated with the sharing situation ($F_{1, 598} = 12.3$, $p = 0.000486$). We thus conclude that participants seem to find more value in the possibility to display information that directly relates to them.

Regarding the ability to express the scope of the publication act, we wanted to observe to what extent people would be sensitive to the 4 distribution strategies embedded in the media sharing situations. The box plots for the distribution strategy show no obvious difference among the various strategies. A one-way ANOVA test on the four groups of scenarios corresponding to the four types of distribution strategies ($F_{3, 596} = 1.052$, $p = 0.369$) indicates that we cannot confirm any statistically significant effect of the distribution strategy on the perceived relevance. Possibly, participants did not have a strong idea about these forms of content distribution or they may simply have failed to make any meaningful distinction between them. All our distribution strategies were to some extent local as they all implied regular physical presence to the places where the displays were located. Therefore, in any of the scenarios, the scope of publication, even if composed by very different sub-sets of displays, was inherently local and seen as appropriate.

Still, the only distribution strategy that was based on an explicitly formed group of displays (those marked as favourite) was the best-ranked one. Even though our results cannot confirm the statistical significance of these findings, they seem to suggest a tendency towards a more explicit control over the set of displays where media is shared.

5   Conclusions

This study has analysed the perceived value of different scenarios of media sharing in open display networks. We have considered the effects of two types of content properties, more specifically, how local and how personal the content is, and also the effect of the social connection of the publisher with the places where content may be shown. The main result is a clear preference for content that is both local and personal. While this may seem at first as an obvious result when we consider the social networking framework, it is in fact in strike contrast to the types of content that can be commonly found in most public displays. This seems to confirm the idea that future open displays networks, where everyone can have some possibility to publish content, are likely be revolve mainly around situated content that is fundamental different from what we have today in current digital signage systems [4]. In our future work, we intend to explore new types of connections between publishers and displays to assess alternatives models to create a meaningful relationship between screen media items and display opportunities.

References

1. Cheverst, K., et al.: Exploring bluetooth based mobile phone interaction with the hermes photo display. In: 7th International Conference on Human Computer Interaction with Mobile Devices Services, MobileHCI 2005, Salzburg, Austria, pp. 47–54 (2005)
2. Churchill, E., et al.: The Plasma Poster Network. Public and Situated Displays Social and Interactional Aspects of Shared Display Technologies, 233–260 (2003)
3. Cranshaw, J., et al.: Bridging the Gap Between Physical Location and Online Social Networks. Human Factors 1968, 119–128 (2010)
4. Davies, N., et al.: Open Display Networks: A Communications Medium for the 21st Century. Computer 45(5), 58–64 (2012)
5. Davies, N., et al.: Using bluetooth device names to support interaction in smart environments. In: International Conference on Mobile Systems Applications and Services, MobiSys 2009, Kraków, Poland, pp. 151–164 (2009)
6. Friday, A., et al.: Reflections on Long-Term Experiments with Public Displays. Computer 45(5), 34–41 (2012)
7. Huang, E.M., Mynatt, E.D.: Shared Displays for Small Communities: Optimizing for Privacy and Relevance. WS Public. Community and Situated Displays (2002)
8. Jose, R., et al.: Instant Places: Using Bluetooth for Situated Interaction in Public Displays. IEEE Pervasive Computing 7(4), 52–57 (2008)
9. José, R., et al.: Pins and Posters: Paradigms for Content Publication on Situated Displays. IEEE Computer Graphics and Applications 33(2), 64–72 (2013)
10. Li, N.L.N., Chen, G.C.G.: Analysis of a Location-Based Social Network. In: 2009 International Conference on Computational Science and Engineering (2009)
11. Martin, K., et al.: Engaging with a situated display via picture messaging. In: CHI 2006 Extended Abstracts on Human Factors in Computing Systems, Montréal, Québec, Canada, pp. 1079–1084 (2006)
12. Müller, J., et al.: Requirements and design space for interactive public displays. In: Proc. of the International Conference on Multimedia, New York, USA, p. 1285 (2010)
13. Scellato, S., et al.: Exploiting place features in link prediction on location-based social networks. In: Proc. of the 17th ACM SIGKDD International Conference on Knowledge Discovery and Data Mining, KDD 2011, New York, USA, p. 1046 (August 2011)
14. Wiese, J., et al.: Are you close with me? Are you nearby? Investigating social groups, closeness, and willingness to share. Human Factors, 197–206 (2011)

They Are Looking… Why Not Interacting? Understanding Interaction around the Public Display of Community Sourced Videos

João Casal and Rui José

Centro Algoritmi, Universidade do Minho, Guimarães, Portugal
{joaocasal,rui}@dsi.uminho.pt

Abstract. In this paper, we study the extent to which the presentation of pedagogical videos on a public display at a communal space of the school is able to promote engagement around those videos. The videos were produced by students from the school itself. Using a mobile application, students could rate, create comments or simply bookmark videos. The evaluation of the platform is made through logs analysis, direct observation and a collective interview with end-users. The results show that even though the videos were able to attract many students to the display, there were not many of them that actually used the application to interact with content. In the final discussion, we explore some of the reasons that may justify this behavior and also the extent to which these videos have managed to foster students' curiosity towards their topics.

1 Introduction

Public displays can play an important role as an enabling technology for Ambient Intelligence, and particularly as an important medium for informal learning. Their ability to break content bubbles and promote serendipitous encounters with pedagogical topics can help to foster curiosity and discussion around those topics. Our work is part of an on-going EU funded research project, called JuxtaLearn, which aims to promote students' curiosity in science and technology through creative film-making, collaborative editing activities and content sharing.

In this work, we aim to study the extent to which the presentation of pedagogical videos on a public display at a communal space of the school is able to promote engagement around those videos. This work follows on a participatory design process where teachers were invited to contribute to the identification of the properties of the display systems that would be deployed [1]. This process has produced an early prototype and also several insights into multiple institutional and ethical concerns associated with this presentation of information in the public space of the school [2]. The involvement of the teachers was also important to bring these key stakeholders into the project, opening the door to a greater appropriation and acceptance of the technology. We also promoted two activities with students that aimed to create videos about a diverse set of pedagogical topics. This way, we were able to use videos that had been created at the school itself, considerably raising the identification of viewers with the exhibited content. The videos were presented on the public display and students could use a mobile application to rate, create comments or simply bookmark them.

R. Hervás et al. (Eds.): UCAmI 2014, LNCS 8867, pp. 163–170, 2014.
© Springer International Publishing Switzerland 2014

Our study aimed to understand the nature of the interactions, both implicit and explicit, generated by the presentation of the videos. To support the evaluation, we used a broad range of qualitative and quantitative techniques, such as logs analysis, direct observation and a collective interview with end-users. The results show that even though the videos were able to attract many students to the display, there were not many of them that actually used the application to interact with content. In the final discussion, we explore some of the reasons that may justify this behavior and also the extent to which these videos have managed to foster the curiosity of students regarding the represented topics.

2   Related Work

Interaction with public displays is mostly expected to occur as part of a public setting where many people may be present, typically carrying out multiple activities and having their own goals and context. Therefore, for interaction to occur, the display must be able to attract and manage people's attention. However, engaging users with interactive public displays is known to be a challenging task. Brignull and Rogers, reported that "a major problem that has been observed with this new form of public interaction is the resistance by the public to participate" [3]. Kukka et al. studied how this barrier to interaction, what they call the 'first click' problem, can be overcome [4]. Previous research has also identified the display blindness effect [5], where people look at the display, but do not see its content. Based on previous experiences that created the expectation that content is not relevant, people just learn to filter it. Müller et al. pointed out that the majority of users only look at the displays if they have the expectation of seeing relevant content [5]. The fear of looking silly while interacting with the display, especially in gestural interfaces, has also been pointed out as another barrier to interaction [3]. Müller et al. also explore the issue of noticing the display interactivity as other barrier for interaction [6].

To better understand these issues, a number of audience behavior frameworks have been proposed to represent the various phases of engagement with public displays and the transitions that occur between those phases. Michelis and Müller describe the Audience Funnel [7] as a framework that focuses on observable audience behavior. This framework is derived on observations from the Magical Mirrors installation, which consists of 4 displays showing a mirror image of the environment in front of them, overlaid with optical effects that react to the gestures of the audience as recognized by a simple motion detection system based on a single camera. The Proxemic Peddler [8] is a prototype public display system that proposes a continuous proxemics interaction framework that takes into account users' identity, distance, and orientation relative to the public display. These multiple audience models have been created for specific purposes, and despite their common patterns they are also highly dependent on particular assumptions about the display setting and usage context. Our work differs in the use of video as the primary media, and in the social context, which may be described as a learning community where most people know each other and in many cases even know the people acting on the videos. Moreover, our methodology of data recovery, categorizing the behavior of mobile users on the ubiquitous environment and attempting to link the in-situ observations with the system logs, also differs from previous work.

3   The Public Display System

The public display used for this study includes a display application that renders the videos published by students and shows some additional information about them. In the space between videos, the audience is informed about which video was shown last and which are to be shown next. The application also displays metadata associated with the videos like title, author, rating and number of votes. Using our mobile application, users can also access this same information on their mobile devices. The mobile application shows a content stream with information about the recently presented videos, giving users easy access to rate, comment or simply access the video on YouTube. The rate feature allows users to classify the videos. The comment feature has the intent of allowing users to let authors know what they think about their creation. The third feature, know more, leads the user to the YouTube page of the video, which allows the personal viewing of the content or access related videos about the same issue. The application on the display frequently shows information about how to download and use the mobile application, incentivizing people to it. In addition to the videos, at regular intervals, the display system also runs other applications that show school information like news or photos of events.

To seed the system with locally relevant videos, we promoted a pedagogical video competition where students created a number of pedagogical videos across different scientific areas. The goal was to overcome the display blindness effect [5] by offering users content that they could more easily identify with and thus perceive as more relevant. To allow users to notice interactivity [6], we created informative digital posters that were being exhibited on the display regularly. The posters have also been posted on the institutional Facebook of the school. In order to raise the interaction with the system, one of the prizes of the video competition was awarded to the most interacted video. This had the goal of fostering the interaction of the participants and also to invite these users to ask their colleagues to interact, promoting a larger adoption of the system. Fig. 1 represents the physical layout of the communal room where the display was located.

The location was selected as the place that would be able to capture students' attention, as this is a space where they hang around during breaks. The room is also a place that most students need to walk through as they go to or return from classes.

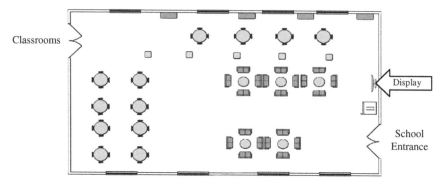

Fig. 1. Public display installation on school students' hall

4   Research Methodology

The research methodology was based on a combination of three techniques: direct observations, analysis of the data recorded by the system and a collective interview to end-users. Direct observations were used to record users' behavior towards the system even before they start using the mobile application. However, to better understand the flow between these two distinct phases of interaction, we made the observations in a way that could later be associated with specific system events generated by that same user on the mobile application. To support this type of registration, we created an electronic form where we could register the observed behaviors along with an automatically generated timestamp. This allowed the researcher to be focused on the audience behavior, while at the same time generating the information that would latter allow these observations to be matched against specific system actions. In total, we conducted 4 hours and 35 minutes of observations in two distinct occasions. The analysis of the system logs was used to complement the direct observation with a concrete indication of the actions performed by users. The final group interview provided important insight on the reasons behind some of the observed behaviors. This interview involved three participants of the 12th grade (one male and two female) and lasted 45 minutes. This session was based on a semi-structured format of an informal conversation guided by key points.

5   Results

Figure 2 summarizes the key patterns of interaction identified during the observations as well as the frequency of occurrence of each.

Interaction with the public display starts with a simple glance, but then it can follow different interaction patterns according to the user context. It is important to mention that, in order to measure attention, the moment users stopped looking at the display were also annotated but, as that is redundant information for the analysis of this graph (because eventually all stop looking), it has not been represented.

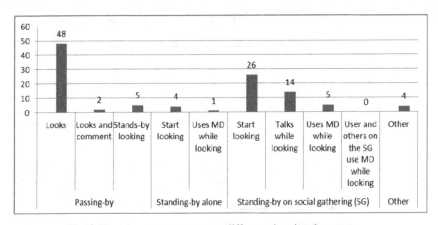

Fig. 2. Engagement events across different situational contexts

We can also verify in Fig. 3 how the observed behaviors were different between the break time, when the room was completely crowded, and class time, when only occasional users were passing-by.

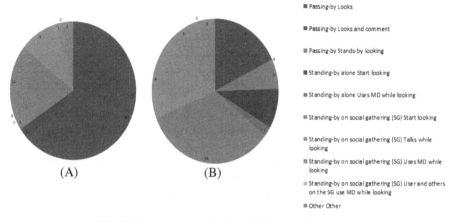

- ■ Passing-by Looks
- ■ Passing-by Looks and comment
- ■ Passing-by Stands-by looking
- ■ Standing-by alone Start looking
- ■ Standing-by alone Uses MD while looking
- ■ Standing-by on social gathering (SG) Start looking
- ■ Standing-by on social gathering (SG) Talks while looking
- ■ Standing-by on social gathering (SG) Uses MD while looking
- ■ Standing-by on social gathering (SG) User and others on the SG use MD while looking
- ■ Other Other

(A)   (B)

Fig. 3. Events observed during: (A) breaks; (B) classes

During the breaks, students are more involved in direct social interaction and not many of them pay attention to the display. However, since the room is crowded, the absolute number of engagement events is higher during these break periods. Table 1 shows that despite the existence of fewer events outside the breaks, they are more likely to be extended interactions, meaning that this is a period of greater availability.

Table 1. Engagement events during breaks and classes

	Break	**Classes**
Number of observed events	54	28
Average time *engaged* with the system	1m 13s	4m57s
Total time *engaged* with the system	1h0m29s	1h54m01s

Regarding the logs recorded on the system, the following results were obtained on approximately a month of use:

- − 20 distinct users signed up (19 of which interacted with videos)
- − 94 interactions with videos were registered;
- − 2 distinct users wanted to know more about videos;
- − In 9 videos, users followed the YouTube link in order to see them again or to watch related videos.

Table 2 lists the interactions per type of production or type of content, giving insights about which are the video performances that foster more curiosity.

Table 2. Number of interactions per type of video performance

Type of production	# of interactions	% of interactions
Students performing	59	62,8
Scenes shot on own city	13	13,8
Content presentation	9	9,6
Based on web resources (ex.: personas talking)	5	5,3
Video tutorial alike	3	3,2
Other (ex.: video contest advertisement)	5	5,3
Total	94	100

The group interview was intended to get a qualitative assessment of the deployment and we will now present the main results of this part of the study:

Current Awareness and Involvement. Every participant had heard about the video contest, knew about the existence of the display and has watched videos on it. However, no participant knew that the display is interactive ("the display don't seem interactive... how do I touch it?").

Motivations for Use. As main motivations for using the ubiquitous system, participants stated that: (1) were curious to see the videos produced by persons they know; (2) motivation to watch or interact depends on the content ("if the video is from my area of interest I will more likely watch it" and "I usually look at the display because I know that my video is being exhibited there").

Interaction Barriers. Students pointed out that: (1) "the display seems just a regular TV... we did not knew we could interact"; (2) "repetition of videos is boring"; (3) "the moment that persons are on that place is for relax not for learning"; (4) "display is too small for the size of the room; (5) "on my previous school existed TVs always displaying stuff and people ignored them"; (6) "I don't have a smartphone, so I cannot interact... however, I'm aware that in my class almost everyone has"; (7) Publicity, too much information, application errors or not understanding how to use are factors of disengagement; (8) "Features like rate are meant to be used once or twice, not to engage users on a system".

Interaction through Personal Mobile Devices. Regarding the interaction mechanism implemented, users stated that: (1) "I was expecting that the display was touch"; (2) "it is a good bet. Nowadays everything can be done through smartphone. But it should allow other form of interaction for the persons that do not have smartphone."; (3) "it is better than touch displays if the features need personal authentication"; (4) "it is worse than touch displays in terms of catching users attention, because if I saw persons touching a display I would go there see what it was"; (5) "has the advantage of allowing multiple interactions simultaneously".

Promotion of Awareness towards Interaction with the System. In order to promote awareness regarding how to interact with the system students suggested to have a physical poster near the display informing that it is interactive ("it is better than posters on the display because this information is always there, not only at some moments").

Video on Interactive Public Displays versus Video on YouTube. This question raised the following points of view: (1) "on YouTube it is possible to see the video without concerns about the rest of the audience"; (2) "it would be interesting to push videos to the public display for viewing with colleagues"; (3) "public displays make students see videos that they would not search for... and they may like it"; (4) "YouTube is meant for individual use and a video application on public displays is interesting for using on a social gathering context".

6   Discussion and Conclusion

A clear finding from these results is the high number of users that pay attention to the display, possibly even commenting about its content with nearby colleagues, but never reach the point of interacting through their mobile devices. In regard to the high interest raised by the videos, the familiarity with the people and the scenes represented in many of those videos seem to have been a fundamental element to create this attention. When passing-by, students would often stop when they recognized a colleague acting on a video.

For the many videos creators, there was also the expectation of seeing their own videos being exhibited. These results seem to confirm that the public presentation of the videos can be a motivating element to the creation of those videos by students and also foster curiosity around those videos. Further research is needed to study the pedagogical relevance of this curiosity towards pedagogical content.

As for the reason why this high attention did not translate into high levels of mobile interaction, we essentially identified that many students never realized that there was this possibility. Despite the intensive communication effort and the video competition prize that was attributed to the video with more interactions, many students never understood they could interact using their mobile phone. This fact, together with students observations like "the display does not seem interactive... how do I touch it?" and "on my previous school existed TVs always displaying stuff and people ignored them" led us to conclude that previous knowledge of users regarding the interaction with public displays affects the adoption of novel forms of interaction. Students were expecting that if the display was interactive it was a touch display, and having that as a fact ignored the disclosed information.

As future work, we will study novel ways to promote interaction associated with the videos that raise curiosity. This essentially means increasing the conversion rate from viewers to users that act on display media.

Acknowledgments. The research leading to these results has received funding from the European Community's Seventh Framework Programme (FP7/2007-2013) under grant agreement no. 317964 JUXTALEARN. We would like to sincerely thank school Escola Secundária de Alberto Sampaio (Portugal) for their collaboration on the technology deployment, on the promotion of the video competition and for the authorization to perform this research on their premises.

References

1. Otero, N., Alissandrakis, A., Müller, M., Milrad, M., Lencastre, J.A., Casal, J., José, R.: Promoting secondary school learners' curiosity towards science through digital public displays. In: Proceedings of International Conference on Making Sense of Converging Media, AcademicMindTrek 2013, pp. 204–210. ACM Press (2013)
2. Lencastre, J.A., Coutinho, C., Casal, J., José, R.: Pedagogical and Organizational Concerns for the Deployment of Interactive Public Displays at Schools. In: Rocha, Á., Correia, A.M., Tan, F., Stroetmann, K. (eds.) New Perspectives in Information Systems and Technologies, Volume 2. AISC, vol. 276, pp. 429–438. Springer, Heidelberg (2014)
3. Brignull, H., Rogers, Y.: Enticing People to Interact with Large Public Displays in Public Spaces. In: International Conference on Human-Computer Interaction, INTERACT 2003, pp. 17–24 (2003)
4. Kukka, H., Oja, H., Kostakos, V., Gonçalves, J., Ojala, T.: What makes you click: Exploring visual signals to entice interaction on public displays. In: Proceedings of the SIGCHI Conference on Human Factors in Computing Systems, CHI 2013. ACM Press, New York (2013)
5. Müller, J., Wilmsmann, D., Exeler, J., Buzeck, M., Schmidt, A., Jay, T., Krüger, A.: Display Blindness: The Effect of Expectations on Attention towards Digital Signage. In: Tokuda, H., Beigl, M., Friday, A., Brush, A.J.B., Tobe, Y. (eds.) Pervasive 2009. LNCS, vol. 5538, pp. 1–8. Springer, Heidelberg (2009)
6. Müller, J., Walter, R., Bailly, G., Nischt, M., Alt, F.: Looking glass: A Field Study on Noticing Interactivity of a Shop Window. In: Proceedings of the 2012 ACM Annual Conference on Human Factors in Computing Systems, CHI 2012, p. 297. ACM Press, New York (2012)
7. Michelis, D., Müller, J.: The Audience Funnel: Observations of Gesture Based Interaction with Multiple Large Displays in a City Center. Int. J. Hum. Comput. Interact. 27, 562 (2011)
8. Wang, M., Boring, S., Greenberg, S.: Proxemic peddler: A public advertising display that captures and preserves the attention of a passerby. In: Proceedings of the 2012 International Symposium on Pervasive Displays, PerDis 2012. ACM Press, New York (2012)

Smart Product Management in Retail Environment Based on Dynamic Pricing and Location Services

Diego Sánchez de Rivera, Carlos López, Ramon Alcarria,
Diego Martín, and Tomás Robles

Technical University of Madrid,
Av. Complutense 30, 28040, Madrid, Spain
{diego.sanchezderiveracordoba,c.lopezgsm}@gmail.com,
{diego.martin.de.andres,ramon.alcarria,tomas.robles}@upm.es

Abstract. Product management and pricing are complex tasks that in many occasions they can be a barrier to offer customers an improved shopping experience. Automatizing this process can help the trade business making easier dynamic services in a retail environment. In this paper, a system of autonomous management is proposed based on current requirements of retail environment. This system is able to acquire different information and integrate dynamic pricing updates based on previous set rules. The authors carried out a basic implementation of the proposed system creating a prototype. This prototype has being used for studying the scalability possibilities the system offers and also test out the compatibility between different subsystems. The requirements of this system have been drawn from proposals made by some Spanish Supermarket managers during execution of the project SMARKET, a project funded by the Ministry of Economy and Competitiveness of Spain.

Keywords: product management, dynamic pricing, location system, prototype.

1 Introduction

In the current economic situation it is a necessary to remain competitive. Business Intelligence and decision support systems will benefit retail companies as factors leading to success, reducing operational costs and improving marketing strategies. Retail companies analyse customer related data trying to define a pattern in consumer behaviour. This trend is accentuated in the era of big data where companies not only capture more information but also use it in a more effective way. Knowing how customers behave and their needs would enable them to offer new products and enhance existing ones. It will also be positive to improve customers´ shopping experience and to increase their perceived value of retail services.

Over the past few years, dynamic pricing has been a strategy of optimising revenue used in various areas and industries, as well as a part of an overall management strategy. First established in the 70s by airline companies, their objective was to respond to emerging and changing patterns of consumer demand. According to the above, we consider it is necessary to investigate business intelligence techniques in retail industry, from electronic labelling of products or dynamic pricing to indoor location

R. Hervás et al. (Eds.): UCAmI 2014, LNCS 8867, pp. 171–178, 2014.
© Springer International Publishing Switzerland 2014

services [1]. The results of this research will be the first step to provide an intelligent decision system for supermarkets. One big challenge is the fact that the amount of data generated by these techniques would have to be automatically.

Novel IoT technologies, enables real data sensing and actuation in complex environments. This infrastructure combined with services based on the Cloud enables the applicability of dynamic pricing systems to retail environment. With the approach proposed in this paper, sensors will track behaviour, monitoring consumer movements, and all the data generated will be processed in real time by complex autonomous systems that will produce an instantaneous response changing product prices. This allows retail companies to base the price of products on different marketing strategies and dynamic pricing algorithms. Furthermore, the result of changing prices based on dynamic pricing techniques will provide information to other systems and processes.

2   Background Technologies and Experiences

Smart product management has been developed to assist marketing strategies with the help of new information technologies. Some works are easily improved by the use of new methods and algorithms in an automated way that leaves the manager the duty of controlling the process [2].

A simple actual example is found on an airline scenario and other transport agencies that take advantage of the contextualized analysis by implementing dynamic pricing systems for their fare creation process [3]. By collecting sensor data and applying mining techniques they are able to offer a personalized client fare. These kinds of techniques are not applied in a retail environment. In order to maximize profits, this will lead to apply combinations of algorithms running against data collections to offer the best price from a distribution table. With these capabilities, the system can observe the clients in order to implement pricing adjustments to achieve an increase in revenues in supermarkets [4].

An important aspect involving new management methods in a retail environment is the real time information needs, allowing clients to make a decision easier. Retail managers are aware of the new display systems that the new technology provides, such as lcd displays, but have excessive spending on electric power, so it is not operational for supermarkets. In this paper we proposed electronic ink technology that is increasing their insight to accomplish new ways to offer information to the end user, with a minimum expenditure of energy [5].

Due to the lack of a simple way to modify the price in a real time situation, that dynamic pricing can't be achieved in a satisfactory manner. Prices can't be adapted to the consumer at the right moment in order to successfully integrate the client in the process of sale. Nevertheless, new indoor location technologies, such as RFID and BLE sensors can be used to provide real time information about customer routes and behaviors when they are buying in supermarkets or stores.

3   Smart Dynamic Pricing for Retail Environment

Adaptation of dynamic pricing concepts to the retail environment required the analysis of the specific requirements of the price management in a supermarket. In this paper we based on the work performed during project SMARKET, which identifies requirements and the most suitable technologies for deploying one smart dynamic pricing system on a retail environment.

Base on such inputs, we can depict the functional structure of a system (the manager-client System) for a retail environment.

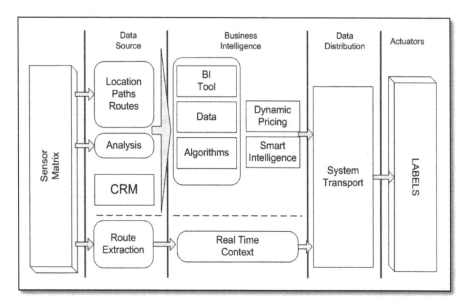

Fig. 1. System Overview

3.1   System Design

The system design is divided in several components (see Fig. 1) contributing to control the whole process of providing information to the general actuators.

At the first stage, the sensors provide the information needed to generate the source data stored in the system "Location Paths & Routes". At this point, the data is unprocessed and waiting to be used in the corresponding analysis to extract the correct parameters and indicators that we will use for the business intelligence at the next step of the process.

Many algorithms are used to process the obtained data. We can subdivide the former analysis in two main ways. The data is stored for a time spaced analysis or it can be used in a real time context for a real time update in retail actuators. This way is used for providing to the customer a better experience in the process of a personalised offer. Supermarkets managers can customize these algorithms to adapt them to their marketing strategies and improve their process in a simple way to obtain more control over their sales chain.

3.2   Smart Sensing and Data Source Environment for Retail

Sensors are the main data providing elements as they can supply important data to analyze this system. These lead a big amount of data of each consumer present in our market.

Real time information consists of locations patterns, routes, times spend on different interest areas and more visited spots. Once the information is gathered it is used for building an interactive map that enables monitoring in a real time context the state of affairs of our retail platform.

Integrating the existing retail CRM with our location information allowing to know exactly which products are the most interesting to the clients and for that reason, these products are more supposed to give better profits, so we may want carry out a selective marketing strategy concerted on that product.

3.3   Business Intelligence for Retail

The business integration with intelligence algorithms has to be extended to multiple inputs in our system. This can make the process of handle this data more complicated as the information data amount increase.

For a successfully business strategy, the process has to take into account some variables concerning logistics. Expiration date of products, transitory issues and seasonal market trends can be differentially to provide a better intelligence in a retail system.

The strategy handle from the salesmen is implied in to the duty of manage how the data is used and taking care of the algorithms rules is also important. Having in mind the customer profile, helped with patterns of behavior collected by our sensors, will develop a better way to understand how clients will react under a certain offer campaign.

The proposed system includes an intelligence model based on input processing and RAM (Reliability, Availability and Maintainability) analysis that takes care of all the inputs we have. To accomplish the main objective, it is important to emphasize the communication between subsystems, maintain a sustainable development, by developing the system modularly.

The Smart intelligence using the existing CRM helps in the process of creation new rules and conditions, based on if () do else if () standards.

Once we have the desired results and the properly real time changes, a coordinated product-label assignment will lead the output results at the proper actuator, resulting in a successfully updated label.

3.4   Data Collection and Information Provision

Technologies applied to locating services has been increasing at last years, this makes the opportunity to choose between different options a challenge. The election in our design has been influenced by our requisites among markets dimensions and system scalability, leaving the RFID Anchors system as the more suitable solution in our environment.

It consists of several "anchors" and a master one connected to a local server in our facilities. The local server filter the information is provided of by different fields such as "trolley ID", "date" or "coordinates" that help us to analyze the data. This takes place over the local server and can be done in a real time task or leaving it for night period if the duty is too heavy. Privacy policy has to be a must, and we take care of this aspect by incorporating loyalty cards to users and linking the trolley to them. A user will be linked to the trolley it is being used at a certain moment.

Information provisions focus on the user's needs to see the price of the products when they are interested in them. The labels can be updates when the strategies found it properly and the customer could be a trigger for an update situation. The labels are wireless controlled and integrate newer technologies such as "Electronic Ink" and "Zigbee".

4   System Implementation and Prototyping

This section presents an implementation case, providing details and explaining the obtained prototyped modules in our test lab. This implementation simplified the main design to a more useful unified architecture as shown in Fig. 2, which allow studying the overall system in a more efficient way.

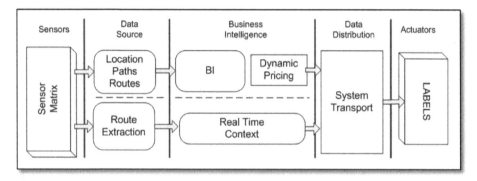

Fig. 2. Simplified scenario

The scenario presented here has been assembled for testing in our facilities, allowing probing the different situations that can come up in a real world setting. The simplified version of the main view does not pretend decrease the ability to generate validate results whereas the main goal is to remove the unnecessary algorithms analysis which can vary depending on the specifics parameters the real scenario have.

4.1   Location Workspace

Chosen a RFID active technology integrated by receivers, formerly called "anchors" and active transmitters or sensors, allow us to monitor real-time location of the customers in the buying process around the retailer environment.

It can be installed up to six "anchors" to cover the whole space, being the maximum surface around 200m^2 although the quantity can be decreased to four if the surroundings are closer to each other. The data acquired by the "master anchor", the only one which has a network connection for data output, is stored in a separated local database, where we can analyze it and mine important parameters such as hotspot places, average time spent or less visited sites.

The data source is used as a real time variable in our dynamic pricing system, for which it has to be analysed in real time and have it ready if a request come up. For a deeper analysis, the load can be held overnight periods and get it available to the retailer the day after.

We have developed a web application allowing us to both watch a real-time situation of the tracked sensors and perform a more in-depth analysis to mine the parameters we have specified before. The main window can be seen in Fig. 3.

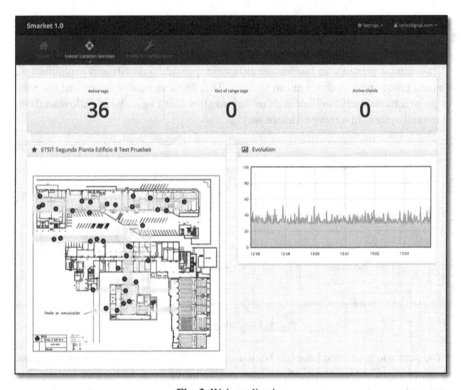

Fig. 3. Web application

4.2 Dynamic Pricing

The control of the system is performed by a specific module which takes care of trigger updates over the price labels. It involves the rule creation process and watch over the different parameters to carry out the price management in the retail outlet.

This module is easily configurable, allowing sellers to set their price change rules and triggers in order to control as many labels are connected to the system. These labels have to be configured so the program knows which product is representing each label. To accomplish it effortless, we take the product information data from the CRM owned by the manager. Dynamic pricing can be referred to several different methods of automatic price variation. We are assuming two ways to achieve it:

Static rules [7] can represent stationary states the retailer wants to provide to their end users, for example a time based offer in which certain products could get a lower price for a limited period of time. These products can be promoted and the public will get more interested about them.

Dynamic rules can develop more active situations over the time they were activated. These rules will need some parameters given in a real time environment to watch the variations and perform the actions configured. Is in this kind of work, when our system is more ambitious, along with the location workspace it becomes a more powerful tool. So, designing a comprehensive set of rules given the available variables such as currently people at place, or a product hotspot in a real time, will lead to a better shopping experience.

4.3   Labelling System

The last step of the system is the delivery of the information updates to the labels themselves. In a regular retail shop, it can be found a large number of labels placed over different shelves, most of them using normal paper and wasting numerous resources along a working period.

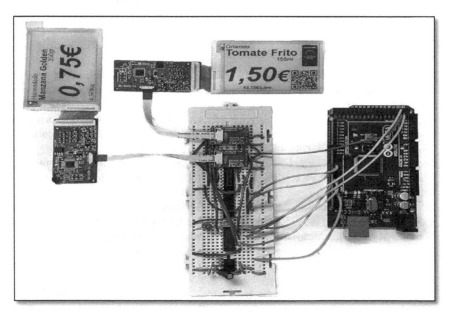

Fig. 4. Labelling Prototype

Fig. 4 shows the prototype in its currently state. It uses an electronic paper based technology to provide the product details and price to the costumers. This ensure to keep giving customers a old like, easy experience while allowing automated pricing process with no breakthrough at midst. Therefore, not only we could show price and information, but it allows showing images and can be personalised to each client.

Arduino is used to get each electronic label controlled by our dynamic pricing software. The prototype is handling two labels at first milestone but is scalable to hundreds of displays, as it uses a common bus to transfer the information among all electronic labels connected.

Main link to the host can be made over a classic USB cable or, as we are testing, wireless communication involving reduced energy consumption protocols like "Zigbee" or "Bluetooth Low Energy" on top of the Arduino communication layer.

5   Conclusion and Future Work

In this paper, a model for price distribution system was presented. We have been able to prove a novel architecture working in a future retail environment based on dynamic pricing and locations services.

Following the SMARKET project, the next few months we will continue testing different methods of integration between location workspace and labeling system, as they can work together to maximize the possibilities the schema offers. Integrating commerce CRM in to our model and analyzing the possibilities it offer, we will figure out how the model we proposed can expand. Building a suitable prototype that can be integrated in a commercial shelf can be a great stage on our research.

References

1. Elmaghraby, W., Keskinocak, P.: Dynamic Pricing in the Presence of Inventory Considerations: Research Overview, Current Practices, and Future Directions. Management Science 49(10) (2003)
2. Li, J.-S., Chen, S.: Real-time dynamic pricing for multiproduct models with time-dependent customer arrival rates. In: 2009 American Control Conference (ACC 2009), St. Louis, MO, USA (2009) ISBN: 978-1-4244-4523-3
3. Guang-Feng, D., Woo-Tsong, L.: Agent-based modeling of supply chain network for adaptive pricing strategy. In: Proceedings of the 2011 IEEE 2nd International Conference on Software Engineering and Service Science, Beijing, China (2011)
4. DiMicco, J.M., Greenwald, A., Maes, P.: Dynamic pricing strategies under a finite time horizon. In: Proceedings of the 3rd ACM Conference on Electronic Commerce (2001)
5. Gonzalez-Miranda, S., Alcarria, R., Robles, T., Morales, A., Gonzalez, I., Montcada, E.: Future Supermarket: Overcoming Food Awareness challenges. In: Seventh International Conference on Innovative Mobile and Internet Services in Ubiquitous Computing, ICDS 2012. Asia Univ., Taichung (2013)
6. Ni, L., Liu, Y., Patil, A.: Landmarc: Indoor location sensing using active RFID. In: 1st IEEE International Conference on Pervasive Computing and Communications, Texas (2003)
7. Martin, D., Alcarria, R., Robles, T., Morales, A.: A Systematic Approach for Service Prosumerization in IoT Scenarios. In: The Seventh International Conference on Innovative Mobile and Internet Services in Ubiquitous Computing, pp. 494–499 (2013), doi:10.1109/IMIS.2013.89

Design and Evaluation of a Smartphone Based Wearable Life-Logging and Social Interaction System

William Burns*, Chris Nugent, Paul McCullagh, and Huiru Zheng

Computer Science Research Institute,
University of Ulster, Jordanstown, UK
burns-w@email.ulster.ac.uk,
{cd.nugent,pj.mccullagh,h.zheng,wp.burns}@ulster.ac.uk

Abstract. In this paper we outline the design, development and evaluation of a smartphone based life-logging and social interaction reminder system intended for use by persons with dementia. By using a smartphone, the wearer's daily activities can be recorded in picture format, along with meta data providing activity levels and location data. In addition to this data, social interactions can also be logged and subsequently identified, using Quick Response (QR) codes. The intervention was evaluated on six healthy participants aged between 24 – 46 years of age who wore the system for 2.5 hours. The qualitative feedback received was that the technology was easy to use and was responsive and accurate at identifying, recording and displaying social interaction data.

Keywords: Smartphone, Life-logging, Dementia, User Interaction, Social Interactions.

1 Introduction

The world's population currently exceeds seven billion people and life expectancy is expected to increase sharply in the next 30 years [1]. With this increased life expectancy, age related impairments, both physical and cognitive are also on the increase [2]. These can range from reduced dexterity, diminished hearing and vision and increased prevalence of chronic diseases. Within the next decade, it is predicted that the number of older persons will outnumber the number of persons aged less than five-years old [3]. As a result, an increasing social and economical burden will be placed on healthcare systems [4].

There are many complications associated with increased prevalence of chronic disease; 75% of older persons have at least one chronic disease with 50% having at least two long term conditions [5]. Of the chronic diseases, dementia, cancer, diabetes, chronic heart disease and stroke are the most common. On a global scale, dementia has an estimated 35 million sufferers [3]. This number is expected to increase within the next 20 years to approximately 65 million people [6].

---

* Corresponding author.

R. Hervás et al. (Eds.): UCAmI 2014, LNCS 8867, pp. 179–186, 2014.
© Springer International Publishing Switzerland 2014

In this paper we present an assistive technology, the R3S (Real-time social Reminder and Reminiscence System), that harnesses mobile and wearable technologies to address the unmet needs specifically relating to personalized information, social contact and perceived safety. This work aims to answer the following research question' "by using technology, is it possible to improve the independence of a person with dementia and enable them to live longer within their own home?".

2   Background and Related Work

Dementia is an 'umbrella' term that describes a number of neurological diseases and conditions that results in reduced cognitive function [7]. There are a number of unmet needs associated with persons with dementia (PwD). These include [8]:

- the need for providing personalized information (e.g. appointments, medication reminders etc.).
- the need for support with regards to the symptoms of dementia. Support to enhance participation and supervision/guidance.
- the need for maintaining social contact and company.
- the need for health monitoring safety.

One of the major components of the proposed system is the use of a life-logging system. Life-logging [9] is the process of recording aspects of one's life using technology. The data collected can comprise pictures, audio, movement and physiological data.

There are a number of commercially available image capturing life-logging devices available. Microsoft have developed the SenseCam [10] which captures an image with a small wearable camera with a fish eye lens. Additional data may be captured using light sensors and accelerometers. All of the images are stored locally on the device's memory card. Doherty et al. used the data recorded from SenseCam to populate a 'SenseCam Browser' that segmented the large dataset recorded into several events within the data [11]. Their software also allowed users to annotate the recorded data.

Memoto is another similar commercially available wearable camera that enables the recording of life-logging data in picture format [12]. It records images every 30 seconds and supplements the data with Global Positioning System (GPS) location information. The recorded data may be analyzed using a smartphone app, which organizes the data into a searchable timeline.

A similar commercial product to the Memoto device is the Autographer [13]. This wearable camera records images and supplementary data for review later on an iOS device. This supplementary data is harnessed from five in-built sensors; accelerometer, magnetometer, PIR (Passive InfraRed), GPS and colour sensors.

By mounting a smartphone onto a helmet, Chennuru et al. captured pictorial life-logging data and supplemented the data with accelerometer data and used language based indexing to organize the data into events [14]. A web based interface was developed to review the recorded data.

The use of life-logging has the potential to address the unmet needs of a PwD, specifically the three needs mentioned above. Data can be retrospectively reviewed to ascertain if a medication was taken, an appointment was made, to whom the wearer interacted with and if they were safe. Nevertheless, this system would be more beneficial to the PwD and indeed their carer, if these lifestyle indicators were monitored in real-time and not retrospectively.

The ability to, in real time, identify social contact is a new area of research. Nevertheless, the AMSSI (Automated Memory Support for Social Interaction) system [15] provides support for recognizing visitors to the user's home i.e. a doctor's visit. The system uses a smartphone and facial recognition to determine the person the wearer is interacting with in addition to monitoring dialogue to determine whether the user requires support. In the event the user requires support the system provides audio feedback to the user. This system is specifically designed to enhance social interaction within the home environment. The benefits of this system are lost if and when the user leaves the home environment. In addition, all potential contacts facial recognition data would need to be captured, analyzed and stored prior or any interaction.

Each of the aforementioned systems has the potential to address individual unmet needs of PwD. The R3S aims to address several of these unmet needs. The difference between these systems and the R3S system are outlined in Table 1.

Table 1. A functionality comparison between the related work and the R^3S ststem

	Life-Logging	Geo Fencing	Social Interaction	Reminiscence	Vitals
SenseCam	☒	☐	☐	☐	☐
Memoto	☒	☐	☐	☒	☐
Autographer	☒	☐	☐	☐	☐
Chennuru *et al.*	☒	☒	☐	☒	☐
CIRCA	☐	☐	☐	☒	☐
AMSSI	☐	☐	☒	☐	☐
R3S	☒	☒	☒	☒	☒

As shown in Table 1, the R3S system offers more functionality suited to addressing the unmet needs of PwD than the other solutions. In the following Section we outline the technological components of the life-logging functionality of the R3S prototype

3   Prototype

The life-logging component of the system, miLifeCam, is comprised of two main technology components, an Android smartphone (ZTE Blade) and Sony Smartwatch wearable display. By using the 3.1 megapixel camera, storage capacity, sensors and wireless communication capabilities of the smartphone a life-logging system was developed. The smartphone can be worn around the wearer's neck and can record an image every 30 seconds along with the location, timestamp and accelerometer data.

In addition to the life-logging data, the system can also identify one of a group of persons wearing a predetermined QR code. This code contains a user ID that the system identifies. When a known individual is identified, R3S records 'who' that person is, their relationship to the wearer and the time of the interaction. The smartphone transmits this information to the smartwatch, which in turn vibrates and displays a picture of the person, their name and relationship to the wearer. Figure 1 shows the overall architecture of the system and how its components interact.

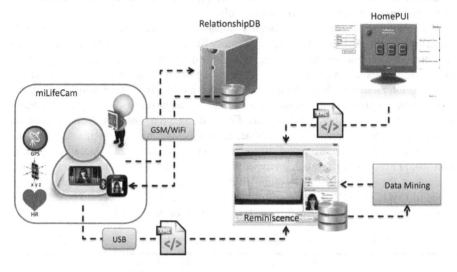

Fig. 1. Architecture of the R3S System detailing the information flow from the wearable life-logger (miLifeCam) to the database (relationshipDB) containg all social contact information. A connection via USB allows the recorded information to be uploaded and displayed on the reminiscence software. The reminiscese software can be personalised in terms of its look and feel by using the HomePUI (Personalised User Interface) tool [16].

A major component of the overall system is the Reminiscence software. This application runs on a desktop PC or laptop and is used to visualize all of the collected life-logging data. In addition to reviewing the data, PwDs and carers can use it as a reminiscence tool and annotate and organize the data into events for future reviewing. Details of the Reminiscence software evaluation is not presented in this paper.

4   Evaluation

The life-logging component of the R3S system (miLifeCam) was evaluated in order to test its general reliability, robustness and accuracy in capturing and recording life-logging data in addition to social interactions. Six healthy participants (3 = Male, 3 = Female) were recruited aged between 24 – 46 years of age. All of the participants in the study had an above average experience with using technology, smartphones in particular.

The participants were asked to wear the smartphone, attached to a lanyard, around their neck in addition to the smartwatch on their wrist (shown in Figure 2 (b)). The participants carried out their normal daily activities and the system recorded approximately 2.5 hours of data for each participant with an average of 313 images being recorded for each participant.

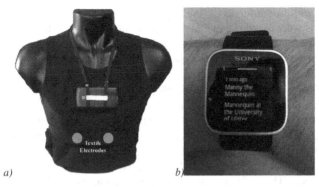

Fig. 2. miLifeCam technology components worn by the participants during the evaluation. a) ZTE Blade smartphone on a lanyard and b) Sony Smartwatch.

Following the recording phase, the participants were asked to review their data using the reminiscence software component (Figure 3). Upon completion of this phase the participants were asked to complete a questionnaire to ascertain the ease of use and effectiveness of the system. In addition to this questionnaire, the participants were asked to score the system using the QUEST (Quebec User Evaluation of Satisfaction with Assistive Technology) questionnaire [17]. The QUEST questionnaire is a 12-item outcome measure that assesses user satisfaction of assistive technologies with two components, Device and Services.

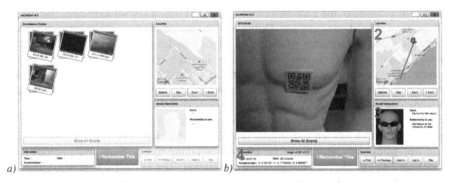

Fig. 3. Screenshots of the reminiscence software developed to review the recorded data from the miLifeCam. This figure shows a) the homescreen with a visual representation of all of the recorded events and b) the recorded data of a selected event (1) with the location of the image on an interactive map (2), social interactions information (3), accelerometer and time/data information (4).

5   Results

In this Section the results of the evaluation of the miLifeCam component of the R³S system are presented. This Section is divided into four Sections each presenting the results of the questionnaires for the *a) miLifeCam & Components, b) Social Interactions, c) QUEST Scores* and *d) Additional Feedback.*

A. miLifeCam and Components

The participants were asked if they liked using the *miLifeCam* and how easy they thought it was to use. Additional questions were asked to ascertain the usability, acceptability and aesthetics of the hardware components (smartphone and smartwatch).

Five of the six participants liked using the *miLifeCam* component, with one answering "Don't Know", in addition, all participants rated the ease of use of the system as either *'Easy'* or *'Very Easy'* to use.

With regards to the smartphone itself, all of the participants belived it to be easy to use with three participants saying the smartphone was 'Big' with a further one saying 'Too Big'. Two participants believed the smartphpen to be 'Heavy' or 'Too Heavy'. Nevertheless, only one participant belived the device to be unconfortable to wear around their neck. The software on the smartphone can be deployed on smaller and lighter Android devices.

Similar questions were asked of the smartwatch, to which on;t one participant thought the smartwatch was 'Big' but all participants believed it to be 'Comfortable' or 'Very Comfortable' to wear. Five of the six participants believed the image clarity of the smartwatch was 'Ok' ($n=4$) or 'Very Clear' ($n=1$). The text displayed on the smartwatch was deemed either 'Ok' ($n=5$) or 'Very Clear' ($n=1$) by all participants.

Due to the nature of the eventual target cohort, namely PwDs, the *miLifeCam* and constituent components were developed in such a way as to require as little interaction as possible, however, to carry out their tasks and services in a passive mode and only presenting information to the user when needed.

B. Social Interactions

During the evaluation, the each participant interacted with a known individual, wearing a QR code, on at least one occasion. During the questionnaires the participants were asked to rate the speed and accuracy of the social interaction detection. Each participant had an average of two interactions with the researcher in order to test the systems identification feature. Five of the six participants were able to identify the interaction on their smartwatch. Regarding the participants rating of the recognition feature participants answered 'Slow' ($n=1$), 'Accurate' ($n=3$) and 'Fast & Accurate' ($n=2$).

As a result, the *miLifeCam* recognition system was able to identify all social interactions with a known individual. Interactions deemed 'fast' and 'accurate' were identified within five seconds of the interaction taking place. 'Slow' interactions took more than five seconds to recognize the interaction. The system was slow to identify the interaction on some occasions but overall performed well and accurately. Not only were the interactions recognized, the real time feedback was sent to the smartwatch and also logged as part of the life-logging service.

C. QUEST Scores

QUEST questionnaires were utilized in order to evaluate how satisfied the users were with the assistive device and the related services they experienced. Figure 4a presents the average score for each participant in relation to their satisfaction with the assistive technology (*miLifeCam*). Figure 4b presents the top satisfaction items selected by the participants on the QUEST scoring sheet.

Items excluded from Figure 4b, because that were not selected by any participant were *Safety*, *Service Delivery*, *Repairs/Servicing*, *Professional Service* and *Follow up service* all of which are options within the QUEST questionnaire.

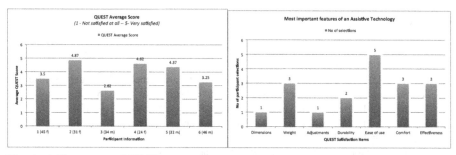

Fig. 4. a) The average QUEST score relating to participant device satisfaction with 1 = Not satisfied at all to 5 = Very Satisfied. The participants ages and gender are also shown and b) Detail of the most important features selected by the six participants as part of the QUEST questionnaire. Other options are available but excluded form the figure because they scored 0

D. Additional Feedback

The participants were able to make any additional comments they thought necessary on the supplied questionnaires. This feedback ranged from reflection on the comfort of the technology devices, such as the smartwatch *"Itched under the strap a little" (Participant 1)* to general thoughts such as *"the system was easy to use and surprisingly easy to forget about" (Participant 6)*.

Several of the participants remarked on the questionnaire that they had forgotten that they were wearing the system. They did not, however, specify if they meant the system as a whole or just the smartphone or watch.

As the system was designed with PwD in mind, once the smartphone and watch were on, the user did not have to do anything with the technology. This came through in the feedback from the participants who commented that they *"...didn't have to do anything" (Participant 6)* and that it was *"Simple and Intuitive" (Participant 3)* and *"...simple to use" (Participant 4)*.

6   Conclusions

In this paper we have presented an evaluation of a wearable life-logging system designed for use by PwD. Not only does this system facilitate the capturing of life-logging data in the form of images and location, but also social interaction with known individuals. We have demonstrated that the miLifeCam system performed well, with all participants finding the system easy to use. The system itself recorded all images within the evaluation timeframe and correctly captured and presented any social interactions.

The system could potentially be used to enable PwD to capture their daily activities in image format in addition to supplementary data such as location and social interactions. It will also enable a real-time prompt of social interactions the PwD may have.

Future work will involve the same evaluation procedure but with a target cohort of users aged 55 years old and above. The use of cognitively intact older people in the evaluation of technologies for PwD has been previously investigated [18] and although not perfect, is beneficial when recruitment of PwD is increasingly difficult. It will also evaluate the system's usability on users who have little or no previous experience with smartphone technologies.

References

[1] CIA World Fact Book, https://www.cia.gov/library/publications/the-world-factbook/geos/xx.html (accessed: July 09, 2013)

[2] Paterson, D.H., Warburton, D.E.: Physical activity and functional limitations in older adults: A systematic review related to Canada's Physical Activity Guidelines. The International Journal of Behavioral Nutrition and Physical Activity 7, 38 (2010)

[3] Kinsell, K., He, W.: An aging world 2008. US Census Bureau, International Population Reports, P95/09-1 (June 2009)

[4] Wallace, J., Mulvenna, M.D., et al.: ICT Interface Design for Ageing People and People with Dementia. In: Supporting People with Dementia Using Pervasive Health Technologies, pp. 165–188. Springer, London (2010)

[5] Office for National Statistics, Ageing. Fastest Increase in the 'Oldest Old', http://www.statistics.gov.uk/cci/nugget.asp?id=949 (accessed: July 09, 2013)

[6] Cost of Care Increases, http://www.guardian.co.uk/society/2011/mar/21/care-old-age-funding (accessed: July 10, 2013)

[7] Armstrong, N., Nugent, C., Moore, G., Finlay, D., Burns, W.: Inactivity Monitoring for People with Alzheimer's Disease Using Smartphone Technology. In: Nikita, K.S., Lin, J.C., Fotiadis, D.I., Arredondo Waldmeyer, M.-T. (eds.) MobiHealth 2011. LNICST, vol. 83, pp. 313–321. Springer, Heidelberg (2012)

[8] Lauriks, S., Reinersmann, A., Van Der Roest, H.G., Meiland, F., Davies, R., Moelaert, F., Mulvenna, M.D., Nugent, C.D., Dröes, R.: Supporting People with Dementia Using Pervasive Health Technologies vol. (2007), pp. 37–61 (2010)

[9] Sellen, A., Whittaker, S.: Beyond total capture: A constructive critique of lifelogging. Communications of the ACM (2010)

[10] Microsoft SenseCam, http://research.microsoft.com/en-us/um/cambridge/projects/sensecam/ (accessed: July 09, 2013)

[11] Doherty, A.R., Moulin, C.J.A., Smeaton, A.F.: Automatically assisting human memory: A SenseCam browser. Memory 19(7), 785–795 (2011)

[12] Memoto, http://memoto.com/ (accessed: July 09, 2013)

[13] Autographer (2013), http://www.autographer.com/#home (accessed: December 19, 2013)

[14] Chennuru, S., Chen, P.-W., Zhu, J., Zhang, J.Y.: Mobile Lifelogger – Recording, Indexing, and Understanding a Mobile User's Life. In: Gris, M., Yang, G. (eds.) MobiCASE 2010. LNICST, vol. 76, pp. 263–281. Springer, Heidelberg (2012)

[15] Bellodi, L., Jasinschi, R.: Dialogue support for memory impaired people. Signal & Information ...(2012)

[16] Burns, W.P., Nugent, C.D., McCullagh, P.J., Zheng, H., Finlay, D.D., Davies, R.J., Donnelly, M.P., Black, N.D.: Personalisation and configuration of assistive technologies. In: Conference Proceedings: IEEE Engineering in Medicine and Biology Society, vol. 2008, pp. 3304–3307 (2008)

[17] Demers, L., Weiss-Lambrou, R., Ska, B.: The Quebec User Evaluation of Satisfaction with Assistive Technology (QUEST 2.0): An overview and recent progress. Technology and Disability 14(3), 101–105 (2002)

[18] Landau, R., Werner, S., Auslander, G.K., Shoval, N., Heinik, J.: What do cognitively intact older people think about the use of electronic tracking devices for people with dementia? A preliminary analysis. International Psychogeriatrics/IPA 22(8), 1301–1309 (2010)

Modular System Development for Flexible Adoption of Ubiquitous Challenges in Energy Management and Control

Daniel Kretz, Tim Neumann, Marek Kretzschmar,
Sebastian Junghans, and Tobias Teich

University of Applied Sciences Zwickau, Dr.-Friedrichs-Ring 2A, 08056 Zwickau, Germany
{daniel.kretz,tim.neumann,sebastian.junghans,
tobias.teich}@fh-zwickau.de

Abstract. Networking and interconnections are key aspects of energy saving ambitions by application of an intelligent and efficient control of technical facilities, automation and building control systems. Industrial companies and enterprises, municipal housing as well as real estate companies but also private persons at home are facing the challenges to reveal potentials for optimization and furthermore massively reduce their energy costs by utilization of innovative technologies in long-term. Therefore, an enormous variety of available technologies, devices, bus systems, and communication protocols is building the base on the one hand but also forms a heterogeneous landscape of ubiquitously available information sources and sinks on the other hand. Consequently, there are special challenges for the development of a flexible software solution for energy management and control. This paper provides a brief insight into our current work and the development of reusable and flexible software components.

Keywords: OSGi, virtualization, ubiquitous information.

1 Introduction

Progressing climate change and limited availability of fossil energy sources are global challenges and hence require innovative technologies and solutions. Nationwide activities, strategy papers, and laws indicate the urgent demand of supply infrastructure upgrades e.g. for the integration of renewable energy sources but also the demand of a long-term engagement. There are several ambitions of the German federal government, e.g. the initialization of a national master plan titled "High-Tech Strategy 2020" in 2006, as well as the "German Renewable Energy Sources Act", to boost renewable energy shares from 35 percent in 2020 up to 80 percent until 2050 [1,2]. In fact, potentials for initiating innovations exist not only on national level. Increasing energy prices are additional challenges for manufacturing companies in their global competition. In fact, it is important to keep affordability of energy costs and to reduce consumption in long-term. Consequently, it is necessary to analyze and control existing

R. Hervás et al. (Eds.): UCAmI 2014, LNCS 8867, pp. 187–190, 2014.
© Springer International Publishing Switzerland 2014

systems holistically to reveal and expose any existing optimization potential by their collaboration. Main objectives are an automatic application of intelligent control mechanisms and optimization for continuously adjusting the overall system including traditional distinct parts. In fact, interconnection and automation is the key of success to achieve an efficient energy consumption and to reduce final costs.

2   Challenges

Today, modern sensors and actors usually provide communication interfaces and technical systems more and more integrate those partly intelligent and communicative devices. Altogether, they provide a ubiquitous information network and penetrate every supply line [3]. As heterogeneous the applications areas are, as heterogeneous are involved devices, measuring instruments and their communication systems. Complex, continuously changing requirements additionally confront the capabilities of components within an intelligent supply network. We require an infrastructure that is able to connect different components of sensors, actors and control devices to realize an intelligent information distribution untainted by any media disruption within a ubiquitous network. On the physical layer we utilize fieldbus and communication standards like RS232, RS458, KNX, CAN and similar. Furthermore, the logical layer provides a plenty of communication protocols like Modbus-TCP, PROFIBUS or CANopen as well as a large variety of proprietary, manufacturer-specific communication solutions [4]. Currently available, market-relevant automation solutions like WAGO-I/O or GIRA home server are optimized for specific applications but they are limited regarding their flexibility, range of services and utilizable sensors and actors. Connecting components of distinct systems usually causes huge efforts. A holistic system view for the integration of comprehensive optimization algorithms requires solutions that are more flexible. Other challenges are given by different involved actors with distinct (and contrary) requirements. Finally, we require a target group dependent, dynamical scaling to provide services and interfaces for different roles.

3   Virtualization Architecture

Essential requirements are flexibility, scalability, maintainability, and especially extensibility for various domains. Single components need to be configurable dependent on demands of the system environment and combinable as much independent from each other as possible. Additionally, we require communication nodes caused by a wide distribution of system parts, especially sensors and actors, as well as the limitation of fieldbus systems regarding range, transmission power, and number of participants. For lower CPU-intensive decision logic, basic data logging tasks and fieldbus-across interaction microcomputers are sufficient. Advantages are their low energy consumption and lower investment costs that are essential for their interconnection in large quantity to allow a ubiquitous information supply. Industrial computers realize more complex calculations and system decisions as well as network aggregation and long-term analysis tasks and forecasts require accordingly dimensioned server systems to process a large amount of data efficiently. Those requirements affected the selection of an operating system and software development runtime of our communication nodes significantly. First, we have selected several Linux derivatives especially for our embedded devices because of lower processor and memory consumption and of course licensing costs in large quantities.

Furthermore, we have selected Java™ runtime for platform independent development and based on Java™ – an Open Services Gateway initiative (OSGi) platform to ensure the development of a modular, scalable, and flexible software solution. Java™ is available for a variety of operating systems and it is scalable from embedded systems, mobile and desktop versions to server and enterprise solutions by specialized editions which finally allow an easy porting [5]. Additionally, the integration of system libraries of manufacturer-specific protocols and hardware-related interfaces is essential but this is supported either by Java™ Native Interface or by Java™ Native Access [6]. The OSGi platform is an open specification for coordinated provisioning and delivery of services on local networks and devices [7]. Great advantages of OSGi are a standardized modularization and clearly defined interfaces. Modules are defined as *bundles* with an independent lifecycle and thus they can be started, stopped, installed or uninstalled during runtime to allow dynamic system changes every time. Although bundles hide internal implementation details, they are self-descriptive including public programming interfaces; they distinguish between versions and define dependencies exactly [8].

Next essential step is to homogenize and integrate the heterogeneous world of indeed similar devices from different manufacturers with partly absolute distinct functionality and incompatible communication via Modbus, KNX, and many more. There is a common risk to adjust developed solutions on manufacturer-specific devices or their specific functionality. Consequently, it is impossible to replace the device in future e.g. by a similar device with different functionality and other communication standards because of a deep refactoring demand. The development of common reusable services e.g. function monitoring or data logging is hampered. Therefore, we have to decouple implemented program logic absolutely from the physical hardware components and communication details. We require a homogeneous interface for hardware communication and a generalized data structure for the description of any system component. Finally, we have extracted basic properties of device categories and mapped them into consistent representations. This is done by hardware-specific adaptors, which are implemented as virtual device instances (Fig. 1). They transform data between communication layers to achieve a homogeneous coupling between hard- and software like device drivers of an operating system do. Device information is mapped or changed via virtual data channels, which are defined by an essential catalogue module. Significant properties that are not supported by specific hardware can be emulated by the adaptor for consistency. In fact, the coupling of different bus systems and mapping of different devices requires individual development of adaptors. At a first glance, this task is sophisticated and an additional effort but this has to be done only once for each device type to transform specific behavior into a common structure. In general, the resulting implementation is highly portable because adaptors only contain specific communication logic and device related routines but no service logic or complex algorithms, which are provided by independent bundles.

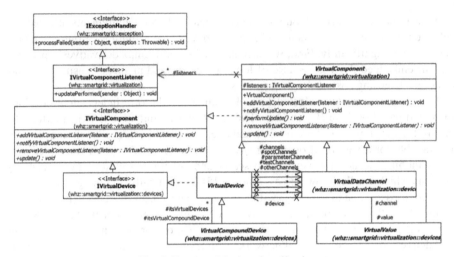

Fig. 1. Extract of device virtualization

4   Conclusion

Based on our core component for device virtualization we have implemented adaptors for different photovoltaic systems, charge stations for electric mobility, smart-meter, weather stations, parking sensors, heating systems, and many more with partially proprietary protocols or incompatible communication standards. Additionally we have adapted the OSGi paradigm and mapped available devices as a service, which leads to highly dynamic system with all advantages of the OSGi service platform. There are basic services for data logging, secure remote communication, user management, and interfaces as well as reporting services.

References

1. Federal Ministry of Education and Research (BMBF): High-Tech Strategy 2020 for Germany, Bonn (2010)
2. Federal Ministry for the Environment, Nature Conversation, and Nuclear Safety (BMU): Renewable Energy Sources Act (2012)
3. Poslad, S.: Ubiquitous Computing: Smart Devices, Environments and Interactions. John Wiley & Sons (2009)
4. Merz, H., Hansemann, T., Hübner, C.: Gebäudeautomation: Kommunikationssysteme mit EIB/KNX, LON und BACnet, 2nd edn. Carl Hanser Verlag GmbH & Co. KG (2009)
5. Hansmann, U., Merk, L., Nicklous, M.S., Stober, T.: Pervasive Computing: The Mobile World. Springer Professional Computing (2003)
6. Ramesh, V., Vasappanavara, A., Vasappanavara, G.: Object-Oriented Programming Using C++ and Java™, India. Pearson Education (2013)
7. OSGi Alliance, OSGi Service Platform Core Specification, Release 4 (2011)
8. McAffer, J., VanderLei, P., Archer, S.: OSGi and Equinox – Creating Highly Modular Java™ Systems. Addison Wesley (2010)

Evolution of RFID Applications in Construction: A Literature Review

Enrique Valero[1], Antonio Adan[1], and Carlos Cerrada[2]

[1] 3D Visual Computing and Robotics Lab, University of Castilla-La Mancha,
Ciudad Real, Spain
valero.rodriguez@gmail.com, antonio.adan@uclm.es
[2] Dept. ISSI, UNED, Madrid, Spain
ccerrada@issi.uned.es

Abstract. Radio Frequency Identification (RFID) technology has been widely used in the field of construction during the last two decades. Basically, RFID facilitates the control on a wide variety of processes in different stages of the lifecycle of a building, from its conception to its inhabitance. The main objective with this paper is to present a review of RFID applications in construction industry, pointing out the existing developments, limitations and gaps. The paper presents the establishment of the RFID technology in four main stages of the lifecycle of a facility: planning/constructive components manufacturing, as-built control and tracking, security and as-is evaluation/maintenance. Conclusions and future advances are presented at the end of the paper.

Keywords: RFID, construction, smart technologies, building.

1 Introduction

One of the most extended and promising wireless non-contact systems is Radio-Frequency Identification (RFID) [1], a technology based on the exchange of information by means of electromagnetic signals. Because of its ability to identify and track objects, RFID is being used for diverse applications: aviation, construction and facility management, health, retailing, logistics or security, among others.

Since the decade of 1990, RFID has been applying in the field of construction. An important number of works has been published and different reviews have been presented. The main objective of this paper is to present a new review that improves the previous reviews in several points:

Organization of the paper. We have taken into account the entire lifecycle of a building, from its conception to maintenance once it is inhabited.

Extending the study framework. We focus not only on the management of materials/resources and the construction site monitoring (as in [20]) but we also tackle the processes before and after the construction procedure.

Current state of art. We have included in our paper the most recent works in this field of research, which are not considered in previous reviews ([6] [20]).

R. Hervás et al. (Eds.): UCAmI 2014, LNCS 8867, pp. 191–199, 2014.
© Springer International Publishing Switzerland 2014

We have organized the paper as follows: in Section 2 we present certain applications of RFID in the initial stages of the constructive process. Section 3 is devoted to showing the monitoring of construction sites and the tracking of resources by means of RFID technologies. In Section 4 some approaches about evaluation and maintenance are presented. Several works, in which radio frequency identification is used to location of users and navigation in interiors are shown in Section 5. Finally, in Section 6 we discuss the different proposals and present the conclusions.

2   RFID Technology in the Initial Stages of the Constructive Process

The environment and working conditions are very different for each constructive process. Therefore, different RFID systems are implemented for different contexts. The storage capacity of the tags and their position in the scene, the type of the device and its operation frequency depend on several parameters such as: the need of changing the tags contents and the privacy of the data, the distance of interrogation, the kind of materials or the portability of the reader [11]. The material of the components in which the tags are adhered could severely interfere with the operation of RFID; hence the importance of evaluating the influence of combining interior materials and RFID tags [28]. As stated in [11], if the tag is mounted on metal, it needs to be mounted around 1 centimeter from the surface. If some tags are placed closer, anti-collision procedures have to be considered. Furthermore, if there are electromagnetic sources working under a frequency similar to that of the system, special considerations should be made. On the other hand, the need for accurate records of an underground infrastructure aims to establish a buried locating system by means of RFID technology [4]. Table 1 illustrates the main objectives of the above mentioned works.

Table 1. Works dealing with initial stages of the constructive process

Initial stages	Material-tags interaction	RFID system selection	Buried systems
[11]	✓	✓	
[28]	✓		
[4]			✓

In 1995, Jaselskis et al. [12] propose to incorporate the RFID technology to delivery, billing and quality control for concrete. The processes of concrete mixing, loading time and delivery location would be monitored and notified to the job site and test lab. More recently, Moon and Yang [22] present a new monitoring system for concrete pouring, storing the data generated during this process and converting them into valuable information for production and quality control.

In order to save time in the construction process, precast components are being more and more used to raise a building. The fabrication of this kind of elements can be inspected and managed by means of RFID. A precast production management system can be developed in order to examine incoming materials and the production and logistic processes [32]. Prefabricated pipe spools are associated to a long supply chain whose monitoring process could be subject to many problems. An RFID application [27] can solve these possible problems by means of the automation of the tracking process.

The above mentioned tasks involve the transportation of materials from the factory to the construction site. Grau, Zeng and Xiao [8] study the shipping and receiving processes of steel constructive components which are transported in a trailer. They have analyzed different kinds of tags, the bed conditions and the truck speed. On the other hand, the mileage of the transportation vehicles is an important factor to consider, aiming to improve the efficiency of these trips and reduce carbon dioxide emissions. This objective can be achieved by means of a radio frequency identification system which reduces the CO_2 emissions from transportation and increases the vehicle loading rate [14].

Different RFID applications for materials manufacturing and transport are compared in Table 2.

Table 2. Different solutions for manufacturing control with RFID

Manufacturing and supply chain	Concrete operations	Precast production management	Pipe spools	Transport and delivery control	CO_2 emissions control
[12]	✓				
[22]	✓			✓	
[32]			✓		✓
[8]					✓
[27]				✓	✓
[14]					✓	✓

3   As-Built Control Using RFID Technologies

Tracking Systems: Materials and Resources. Materials are numerous and commonly scattered in the job site, making truly complex a real-time monitoring of them. In order to track their position in the construction area, structural steel components and precast concrete panels [15] are equipped with RFID tags.

Amounts of components enter to the construction sites, but there also exists an important quantity of residual soils which need to be removed from this area. Aiming to control the correct movement of the waste material, a couple of RFID readers equipped with cameras are installed in the job at the disposal sites and RFID tags are adhered to the windscreen of the trucks[9].

As shown in Table 3, not only the location of materials but also other resources have to be controlled in the construction site. In many occasions, the evaluation of works has to be carried out by a supervisor. However, there are lots of employees moving at the same time in the job site. In order to control the operations executed by workers, they can be equipped with RFID tags [2].

Otherwise, in most of the construction sites and in order to avoid delays, the number of tools exceeds the necessary. However, the addition of RFID tags to the equipment [7] can be a useful strategy to optimize the budget.

The use of heavy equipment in the construction site increases the labour efficiency. However, cranes and excavators are dangerous vehicles which can cause accidents during the building process. In spite of the safety conditions in the job sites, thousands of workers are wounded every year. The development of a personal warning system [2] can alert workers to the dangers of hazard using working area information. Wu et al. [31] have studied and classified the category and frequency of struck-by-falling-object accidents. They present a work for controlling the position of materials and labor force by means of a Zigbee RFID system.

Table 3. Use of RFID tags for resources location

Tracking	Materials	Workers	Equipment
[11]	✓	✓	✓
[15] [9]	✓		
[2]		✓	✓
[7]		✓	
[31]	✓	✓	✓

Table 4. Combination of technologies and RFID for construction site monitoring

Monitoring	Computer Vision	Barcodes	CAD/BIM	AR	GPS	GPRS
[5]	✓	✓				
[21]			✓			
[30]			✓	✓		
[19]					✓	✓

Construction Site Monitoring. The combination of several technologies can automate the construction monitoring systems, helping to measure the progress of every process. Thus, laser scanning and photogrammetry can be used for site representation, RFID and barcodes for collecting actual working hours and modeling for information purposes and updating planned data [5]. The control of the status of materials in the job sites by means of RFID technology is a useful tool to show a 4D CAD model of the building under construction and compare the as-planned model with the as-built one [21]. To visualize the construction progress in real-time, other authors [30] propose the integration of BIM models and Augmented Reality. They suggest the use of an RFID system to track different components.

Table 5. Works focused on the evaluation and maintenance of buildings

Evaluation and maintenance	Drainage systems	Open Buildings	Structural components	Services and FM	Tasks scheduling	Extinguishers/Fire control
[17]	✓					
[3]		✓	✓			
[16]				✓	✓	
[23] [26]						✓

In one of the last publications in this field, Liu et al. present a combination of technologies (RFID, GPS, PDA and GPRS) that monitorizes the watering operations in the construction of earth-rock dams. Trucks are equipped with RFID tags which provide the position of the vehicles [19].

These works, leading to the combination of RFID with other technologies to monitor the construction sites, are compared in Table 4.

4   As-is Evaluation and Maintenance of Buildings

RFID technology has contributed to facilitate and automate the maintenance and evaluation processes in buildings. One of the evaluations carried out during the construction process is the test of the drainage system. The control of drainage systems by means of balls equipped with RFID tags lets us to evaluate in a simultaneous manner several parts of the pipeline, reducing the operation time by 80% and the manpower by 50% [17]. Furthermore, the obtained results can be stored in RFID tags and PDA devices, reducing the human errors.

The lifecycle of a finished building is closely linked to its maintenance, either in new buildings or reconstructed or extended ones [3]. These tasks are related to the periodic inspections of certain elements and their reparation or reposition if it is advisable. The management of the information linked to these works greatly improves with the addition of RFID technologies to the Facility Management field. Thus, the identification of the components to be checked out is carried out in an automatic way, reducing errors and operation time. The information of the status of each component, stored in RFID tags, allows us to monitor the status of equipment in real-time and to manage maintenance sequences [16].

Safety is still an extremely important factor to consider once the building is inhabited. One of the more frequent and feared accidents in buildings are fires. A set of RFID tags can then be used for storing information about the history and the condition of the extinguishers and valves [23]. This information will be also useful for inspections and maintenance labors.

In some occasions, the fire cannot be controlled and the Fire Control Department then acts in order to avoid a serious disaster. In these cases, the automation of the fire rescue procedure can greatly reduce the delays and even save lives. A solution based on RFID which sends rescue drawings and fire control data to a rescue team [26].

Table 5 presents a classification of the works mentioned in this section, taking into consideration their main objectives.

5   Other Applications in Interiors: Location and Navigation

Although the location of an object or a user in an environment by means of RFID technology is an application itself, this operation can be associated to other tasks. Thus, a user equipped with an RFID reader can reach a destination point in a tagged environment [24]. Furthermore, the evaluation of the user position inside a building can be useful to control the lighting of the rooms in an automatic manner [33] or even to interact with certain elements or services equipped with RFID systems.

In certain occasions, the element whose position is calculated is a mobile robot. Placing different tags in an inhabited environment and equipping the robot with two RFID antennas, the relative position of the mobile device can be calculated. If the robot is equipped with a laser scanner, a mapping process of the environment is carried out [13].

Besides the location, RFID technology makes easier the navigation in inhabited interiors. It should be emphasized the navigation of a user in an environment under special conditions (as a fire or under works) or even unknown. In the same manner, blind or visually impaired people may have important troubles to move in unknown or changing environments. An example of a changing environment can be experimented in a grocery store. An RFID system may indicate certain easy navigation rules or even help to find the path to useful destination [18] [10]. In [10], RFID is also combined with QR codes to facilitate the search of products.

6   Discussion and Future Advances

From the conception of a building to its use, either as the only technology or combined with others, the radio frequency identification has contributed to the automation of several works, improving their efficiency and reducing the associate cost. After reviewing the state of art in this framework, there exist several limitations and gaps which bring contractors to choose other available technologies.

Price. Although the price of RFID systems has decreased, different solutions as Near Field Communication (NFC) or barcodes are much cheaper.

Accuracy. Regarding the study of the location of different objects in the scene, the calculation of the position reached with RFID systems is not very accurate.

Interferences. Metals and concrete, very common in the field of construction, can cause some interferences during the information exchange process. In fact, an additional surface must be placed between the tag and the object in many cases. Also reading problems can occur if tags are surrounded by metal.

Standardization. The different legislations existing worldwide about the use of RFID antennas can lead to suppose some difficulties in the trade of tagged components. Currently, the association EPCglobal is involved in the creation of a standard for RFID.

Concerning improvements and future research, different key aspects can be pointed out.

Building renovation. Looking ahead, it is needed to take into account the concept of Open Buildings [3], considering the maintenance of facilities. This idea of renovating buildings instead of constructing new ones is more and more considered nowadays [25].

Building Information Management (BIM). This process, providing physical and functional characteristics of facilities, is going to play a critical role in the transformation of the construction sector. Focused on this field of research, we have presented a system based on the combination of laser scanning and RFID aiming to generate BIM models for inhabited interiors [29].

Acknowledgment. This work has been partially financed by the the Spanish MINECO DPI2013-44776-R, DPI2013-43344-R and CAM RoboCity2030 S2013/ MIT-2748 projects.

References

1. Calis, G., Deora, S., Li, N., Becerik-Gerber, B., Krishnamachari, B.: Assessment of wsn and rfid technologies for real-time occupancy information. In: Proceedings of the 28th Int. Symposium on Automation and Robotics in Construction (2011)
2. Chae, S.: Development of warning system for preventing collision accident on construction site. In: Proceedings of the 26th Int. Symposium on Automation and Robotics in Construction (2009)
3. Cheng, M., Lien, L., Tsai, M., Chen, W.: Open-building maintenance management using rfid technology. In: Proceedings of the 24th Int. Symposium on Automation and Robotics in Construction (2007)
4. Dziadak, K., Kumar, B., Sommerville, J.: Model for the 3d location of buried assets based on rfid technology. Journal of Computing in Civil Engineering 23 (2009)
5. El-Omari, S., Moselhi, O.: Integrating automated data acquisition technologies for progress reporting of construction projects. Automation in Construction 15(3), 292–302 (2011)
6. Ergen, E., Akinci, B.: An overview of approaches for utilizing rfid in construction industry. In: 2007 1st Annual RFID Eurasia, pp. 1–5 (2007)
7. Goodrum, P.M., McLaren, M.A., Durfee, A.: The application of active radio frequency identification technology for tool tracking on construction job sites. Automation in Construction 15(3), 292–302 (2006)
8. Grau, D., Zeng, L., Xiao, Y.: Automatically tracking engineered components through shipping and receiving processes with passive identification technologies. Automation in Construction 28, 36–44 (2012)
9. Huang, R.Y., Tsai, T.Y.: Development of an rfid system for tracking construction residual soil in Taiwan. In: Proceedings of the 28th Int. Symposium on Automation and Robotics in Construction (2011)

10. López-de-Ipiña, D., Lorido, T., López, U.: Indoor navigation and product recognition for blind people assisted shopping. In: Bravo, J., Hervás, R., Villarreal, V. (eds.) IWAAL 2011. LNCS, vol. 6693, pp. 33–40. Springer, Heidelberg (2011)

11. Jaselskis, E.J., El-Misalami, T.: Implementing radio frequency identification in the construction process. Journal of Construction Eng. and Management 129 (2003)

12. Jaselskis, E.J., Anderson, M.R., Jahren, C.T., Rodriguez, Y., Njos, S.: Radio-frequency identification applications in construction industry. Journal of Construction Eng. and Management 121(2) (1995)

13. Joho, D., Plagemann, C., Burgard, W.: Modeling rfid signal strength and tag detection for localization and mapping. In: Proc. IEEE Int. Conf. on Robotics and Automation, pp. 3160–3165 (2009)

14. Kaneko, T., Hamada, K., Kondo, T.: Development of construction logistics system using radio frequency identification. In: Proceedings of the 24th International Symposium on Automation and Robotics in Construction (ISARC 2007) (2007)

15. Kim, C., Ju, Y., Kim, H., Kim, J.: Resource management in civil construction using rfid technologies. In: Proceedings of the 26th International Symposium on Automation and Robotics in Construction (ISARC 2009), pp. 105–108 (2009)

16. Ko, C.H.: Rfid-based building maintenance system. Automation in Construction 18(3), 275–284 (2009)

17. Kondo, T., Uchida, S., Kaneko, T., Hamada, K., Miyaura, S., Okura, M.: Development of rfid-based flow examination system. In: Proceedings of the 23rd Int. Symposium on Automation and Robotics in Construction (2006)

18. Kulyukin, V., Gharpure, C., Nicholson, J.: Robocart: toward robot-assisted navigation of grocery stores by the visually impaired. In: 2005 IEEE/RSJ International Conference on Intelligent Robots and Systems, pp. 2845–2850 (2005)

19. Liu, D., Cui, B., Liu, Y., Zhong, D.: Automatic control and real-time monitoring system for earth-rock dam material truck watering. Automation in Construction 30, 70–80 (2013)

20. Lu, W., Huang, G.Q., Li, H.: Scenarios for applying rfid technology in construction project management. Automation in Construction 20, 101–106 (2011)

21. Montaser, A., Moselhi, O.: Rfid indoor location identification for construction projects. In: Proceedings of the 29th International Symposium on Automation and Robotics in Construction, ISARC 2012, Eindhoven (2012)

22. Moon, S., Yang, B.: Effective monitoring of the concrete pouring operation in an rfid-based environment. Journal of Computing in Civil Engineering 24(1) (2010)

23. Motamedi, A., Hammad, A.: Rfid-assisted lifecycle management of building components using bim data. In: Proceedings of the 26th ISARC (2009)

24. Pradhan, A., Ergen, E., Akinci, B.: Technological assessment of radio frequency identification technology for indoor localization. Journal of Computing in Civil Engineering 23(4) (2009)

25. Sakamoto, S., Kano, N., Igarashi, T., Tomita, H.: Laser positioning system using rfid-tags. In: Proceedings of the 29th International Symposium on Automation and Robotics in Construction, ISARC 2012, Eindhoven (2012)

26. Shiau, Y., Tsai, J., Cheng, S.: Fire control in buildings and the development of rfid applications systems. In: Proceedings of the 24th International Symposium on Automation and Robotics in Construction (ISARC 2007) (2007)

27. Song, J., Haas, C.T., Caldas, C., Ergen, E., Akinci, B.: Automating the task of tracking the delivery and receipt of fabricated pipe spools in industrial projects. Automation in Construction 15(2), 166–177 (2006)

28. Tzeng, C.T., Chang Chiang, Y., Ming Chiang, C., Ming Lai, C.: Combination of radio frequency identification (rfid) and field verification tests of interior decorating materials. Automation in Construction 18(1), 16–23 (2008)
29. Valero, E., Adan, A., Cerrada, C.: Automatic construction of 3d basic-semantic models of inhabited interiors using laser scanners and rfid sensors. Sensors 12(5), 5705–5724 (2012), http://www.mdpi.com/1424-8220/12/5/5705
30. Wang, X., Love, P.E., Kim, M.J., Park, C.S., Sing, C.P., Hou, L.: A conceptual framework for integrating building information modeling with augmented reality. Automation in Construction 34, 37–44 (2013)
31. Wu, W., Yang, H., Li, Q., Chew, D.: An integrated information management model for proactive prevention of struck-by-falling-object accidents on construction sites. Automation in Construction 34, 67–74 (2013)
32. Yin, S.Y., Tserng, H.P., Wang, J., Tsai, S.: Developing a precast production management system using rfid technology. Automation in Construction 18(5), 677–691 (2009)
33. Zhen, Z.N., Jia, Q.S., Song, C., Guan, X.: An indoor localization algorithm for lighting control using rfid. In: IEEE Energy 2030 Conference, pp. 1–6 (2008)

Multi-source Context Data Representation and Distribution in an ICT Tool for Autism Treatment

Federico Cruciani[1], Mark P. Donnelly[2], Leo Galway[2], Francesco Foresti[1],
Cristiano Paggetti[1], and Enrico Vicario[3]

[1] I+ S.r.l. Florence, Italy
[2] University of Ulster, UK
[3] University of Florence, Italy

Abstract. The use of ICT-based pervasive tools within e-health has become more and more commonplace. This has led to the emergence of systems that have to manage idiosyncratic data from multiple sources. In this paper, we present a Context Management Architecture, providing exchange of context data from heterogeneous sources both in real-time, with selective notification of subscribed clients, and off-line, with the use of a RESTful web-service application. The paper also describes a case study whereby the system is applied in support of autism intervention within the EU FP7 funded Michelangelo Project.

Keywords: Pervasive Systems, Data Fusion, Context Aware Systems, Context Data Distribution, Multi-Source Data Representation.

1 Introduction

Following the technology push related to paradigms around *Pervasive Computing*, an increasing range of applications place the focus on *Context Aware Systems* such as those supporting Activities of Daily Living (ADLs) of patients with chronic conditions [1-2] or, as in the case study here presented, to support autism intervention [3-4].

However, the adoption of ICT tools involves the use of multiple sensors with their own data formats, presenting the challenge of building reusable architectures independent from the single application scenario [5-6].

The ability of such systems to adapt their behavior according to changes in the surrounding environment is deeply tied to the level of *perception* of the external environment, i.e. *context information*. Initial definitions of *context* included information on location and identification of users as in [7]. However there is no general heuristic with regard to context definition since data are context information or not depending on their use and interpretation [6]. Nevertheless, abstracting sensor data does not address the issue of efficient management of a very large amount of data that differs also in interpretation, imperfection and time scope. Many solutions address this issue within the scope of *recognition* of phenomena through the use of ontologies, providing within the semantic layer the necessary level of abstraction from data sources [6][8]. Regardless, even though the introduction of ontologies facilitates both interoperability and re-use, the fact that this abstraction is realized in the semantic layer can represent a drawback since ontologies are usually tied to a single application scenario.

R. Hervás et al. (Eds.): UCAmI 2014, LNCS 8867, pp. 200–203, 2014.
© Springer International Publishing Switzerland 2014

In this paper, a Context Management Architecture is presented, which performs integration from multiple heterogeneous data sources while preserving isolation from the ontology used in the semantic layer. Subsequently, a case study is provided that discusses the use of the approach within the EU FP7 funded Michelangelo project [9], which involves use of ICT for autism treatment both in clinic and home scenarios.

2   Context Modeling And Distribution Architecture

The proposed architecture is split in two main layers whose classification is based on Time Scope. We therefore distinguish between real-time management of Context Information, and Aggregation and Dissemination for sporadic information on larger time scales. An event-based approach has been proposed, in which an Event is a representation of quantitative or qualitative variation, as presented in Fig. 1, and only variations of Context Information are logged.

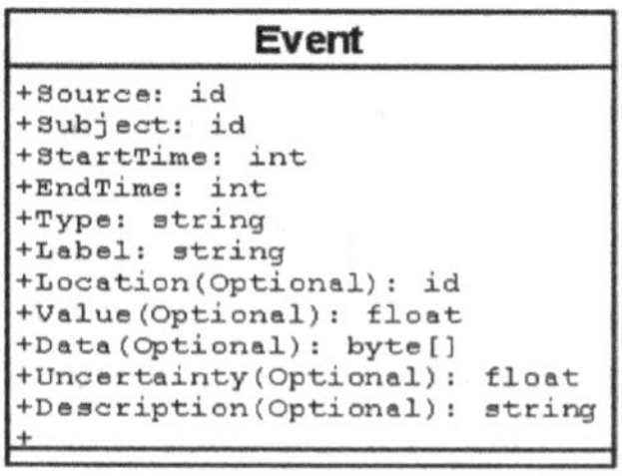

```
                    Event
+Source: id
+Subject: id
+StartTime: int
+EndTime: int
+Type: string
+Label: string
+Location(Optional): id
+Value(Optional): float
+Data(Optional): byte[]
+Uncertainty(Optional): float
+Description(Optional): string
+
```

Fig. 1. Data Structure of an Event: the source identifies the components that generated the Event, Subject provide identification of User. Type and Label are identifier used in the upper semantic layer.

The **Type** and **Label** fields are used for Computational Reflection [10-11] and contain metadata information on the semantic layer of an Event. At this level of perspective the system primarily provides a transport layer, which only the higher semantic layers of the architecture know how to process. Consequently, this approach allows interested parties to filter notifications of context variations on relevant events in a Publish/Subscribe pattern, thereby providing *informed context data distribution* [5], but also preserving isolation from the ontology in use within the upper semantic layer.

As may be observed in Fig. 2, the proposed Context Management Architecture is composed of two primary components: **Real Time Context Broker (RTCB)** and **Context Aggregator**.

The RTCB realizes the connections with the data sources that use an Adapter in order to advertise context variations in the form of Events. Whenever a meaningful change in a signal occurs, an Event is sent to the RTCB via a Web Socket [12]. The RTCB then primarily forwards Events to the Context Aggregator, and to any other subscribed component. Subscribed components can submit their own filter to the RTCB that will be used to filter event notification based on specific values of Type or Label.

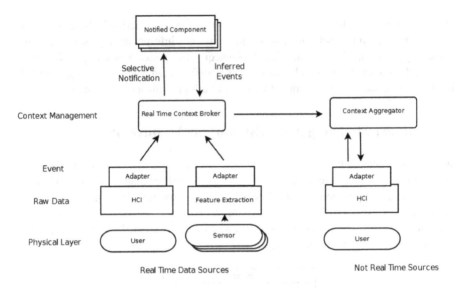

Fig. 2. Context Management Architecture

The Context Aggregator provides a set of REST-based Web Services [13], thereby enabling CRUD (Create Read Update Delete) functions to insert, query or modify Events offline. The offline methods for annotation are stored in form of Events providing a way to retrieve sensor data of interest for analysis through time information. Within the case study of the Michelangelo project, behavioral annotations performed by the clinicians on therapy video footages, allows offline retrieval and analysis of physiological data, in order to check possible correlations between behaviors and measured parameters.

3   Conclusion

Our case study focused on the development of the ICT infrastructure for Context dissemination within a Behavioral Observational platform for autism treatment. This particular scenario requires management of real-time information from physiological sensors, in addition to off-line video-based behavioral annotation. Physiological information sources include the use of both wearable Electrocardiograph (ECG) and Electroencephalograph (EEG) devices, coupled with audiovisual recordings in order to perform off-line behavioral analysis using a video annotation tool [14]. The flexible structure of the architecture permits individual software components to be implemented by the partners of the Michelangelo consortium in a programming language of their choice, thereby minimizing the integration effort. The architecture has being used within a trail phase since March 2014. We expect as next steps to re-use this Context Management Service Layer within other domains, refining and improving its flexibility and facility for adaptation to other ontologies.

Acknowledgements. The research leading to these results has received funding from the European Union - Seventh Framework Programme (FP7/2007-2013) under grant agreement n. 288241. We would like to thank the MICHELANGELO Study Group (S. Bonfiglio, G. Pioggia, K. Maharatna, F. Muratori, A. Giuliano, M. Chetouani and E. Tilmont).

References

1. Cook, D.J., Das, S.K.: How Smart are our Environments? An Updated Look at the State of the Art. Journal Pervasive and Mobile Computing 3(2), 53–73 (2007)
2. Chen, L., Nugent, C.D., Wang, H.: A Knowledge-Driven Approach to Activity Recognition in Smart Homes. IEEE Trans. Knowl. Data Eng. 24(6), 961–974 (2012)
3. Boucenna, S., et al.: Interactive technologies for autistic children: A review. Cognitive Computation (2014)
4. Konstantinidis, E., et al.: Information and communication technologies (ICT) for enhanced education of children with autism spectrum disorders. The Journal on Information Technology in Healthcare 7(5), 284–292 (2009)
5. Bettini, C., et al.: A survey of context modelling and reasoning techniques. Pervasive Mob. Comput. 6(2), 161–180 (2010)
6. Soylu, A., et al.: Context and Adaptivity in Pervasive Computing Environments: Links with Software Engineering and Ontological Engineering. Journal of Software 4(9) (2009)
7. Want, R., et al.: The active badge location system. ACM Transactions on Information Systems (TOIS) 10(1), 91–102 (1992)
8. Bellavista, P., Corradi, A., Montanari, R., Stefanelli, C.: Context-aware middleware for resource management in the wireless internet. IEEE Transactions on Software Engineering 29(12), 1086–1099 (2003)
9. Michelangelo Project, http://www.michelangelo-project.eu
10. Capra, L., Emmerich, W., Mascolo, C.: CARISMA: Context-aware reflective middleware system for mobile applications. IEEE Transactions on Software Engineering 29(10), 929–945 (2003)
11. Chan, A.T.S., Chuang, S.N.: MobiPADS: A reflective middleware for context-aware mobile computing. IEEE Transactions on Software Engineering 29(12), 1072–1085 (2003)
12. Fette, I., Melnikov, A.: The websocket protocol (2011)
13. Fielding, R.: REST Representational State Transfer. PhD. Dissertation, ch. 5 (2000)
14. Cruciani, F., Donnelly, M.P., Nugent, C.D., Parente, G., Paggetti, C., Burns, W.: DANTE: A video based annotation tool for smart environments. In: Par, G., Morrow, P. (eds.) S-CUBE 2010. LNICST, vol. 57, pp. 179–188. Springer, Heidelberg (2011)

Implementing a Platform Agnostic Architecture to Accommodate Heterogeneous Data

Rachel Gawley, Chris Nugent, and Alberto Calzada

School of Computing and Mathematics, University of Ulster, Jordanstown, UK
{re.gawley,cd.nugent,a.calzada}@ulster.ac.uk

Abstract. Many existing smart home solutions focus on one particular environment. With the development of mobile phones and wearable devices, there is the potential to collect data about an individual throughout their daily life as they intersect many different environments. This results in the issue of collecting and processing heterogeneous data from physical environments and individuals. This paper introduces a scalable and easily deployable and maintainable architecture capable of accommodating heterogeneous data and processing the data for consumption across a wide variety of platforms, from mobiles phones and tablets to desktop computers and televisions. A real-world example of the architecture being utilized to monitor the temperature in an office is presented.

Keywords: Software Architecture, Heterogeneous Data, Wireless Sensor Networks.

1 Introduction

The development of personal computers, smart phones, wireless sensor technologies, and GPS has facilitated the development of smart homes. Smart environment technology has applications in the connected health, energy efficiency and home automation domains [1]. These applications all rely on the ability to receive and process data from sensors. There has been significant research focused on connecting physical devices to middleware which will then publish or store the data [2, 3]. Unfortunately, the issue of deployment and connection of sensors is only one half of the problem. There is the issue of creating a scalable, extendable software solution capable of receiving and processing a variety of data types from a smart environment and subsequently displaying the results across a variety of platforms. Many existing solutions focus on one environment, for example, the home, office, car, etc. [4]. Nevertheless, with the proliferation of smart phones and their ability to collect a wide variety of data (GPS, movement, social interactions) there is a wealth of information available about an individual and their life across many environments. The notion of smart environment can be extended from a single setting to potentially encompass all spheres of a user's life. Therefore, any software solution needs to accommodate heterogeneous data from wireless sensors, mobile phones, additional peripheral

R. Hervás et al. (Eds.): UCAmI 2014, LNCS 8867, pp. 204–211, 2014.
© Springer International Publishing Switzerland 2014

devices, social networks and potentially any additional contextual data that can be gleaned about a user, his/her life, and the environments visited. This paper describes a software architecture implementation capable storing and processing heterogeneous data for consumption across a wide variety of platforms with a real-world example.

2 Design

The recent development of commercially available wearable technologies, advances in smart phones, supporting Application Programming Interfaces (APIs), and even the concept of smart home in a box [3], provide stable platforms for relaying data. These physical and middleware solutions can be configured to publish the data to a specified endpoint in an external software solution, directly or via a proxy, for example, desktop computer, mobile devices, etc. One of the simplest and most flexible means of sending data to an online solution is via POST requests [5]. These can be sent from desktop applications, mobile applications, HTML5 applications, etc. The focus of the solution presented in this paper is on receiving end of the POST requests to accommodate the collection of heterogeneous data from a variety of sources. Methods for the subsequent consumption of the data across a variety of platforms (mobile devices, PCs, tablets, televisions, any screen with a web browser) will also be presented.   A scalable and extendable solution capable of accommodating heterogeneous data must satisfy the following design requirements:

— Provide a *standard interface* for queries both to send and receive data.
— Support *generic queries* that request data without knowledge of the data provider, for example, type of sensor, external API, etc.
— Accept *heterogeneous data* from sensors, mobile phones, peripherals, wearable technology, social networks, external APIs, etc.
— Provide a mechanism to *consume data* across a range of devices (platform agnostic), mobile phones, desktop computer, mac, windows, tablets, televisions and any screen with a browser.
— Support an *open ecosystem* that does not confine a user to a specific platform, device range, environment, etc.
— Support *hot swapping* of sensors, device and data sources. These can be replaced with an alternative that does not necessarily need to be the same source type as the previous. No data loss of will be incurred due to this process.
— Interact with existing *legacy data* systems that provide an endpoint for data querying.
— Enable the optional *processing of data* which can be easily extended with new modules.

3   Implementation

The proposed solution addresses the requirements documented in Section 2 by implementing an architecture shown in Fig. 1. The diagram shows the flow of data and internal software structure and design.

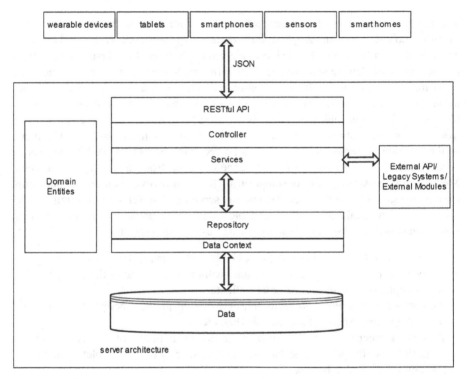

Fig. 1. Software architecture capable storing and processing heterogeneous data for consumption across a wide variety of platforms

The main elements of the solution are as follows:

— *RESTful API* which accepts POST requests from any type of device capable of making such a request. The data is sent in the form of JSON. The data will be sent in its original format. The remote device making the request will know the type of data it is sending and call the appropriate URL/endpoint for that data type.
— *Controller* which is responsible for handling the incoming requests and routing to an appropriate service/action within the system.
— *Services* which are responsible for creating, querying and processing the data. They are separate modules that provide a level of abstraction between the requests and the actual data layer. There are generic for querying different types of data without requiring sensor/input knowledge, for example, light, temperature, steps,

etc. There are specific services for requesting data from an exact type of sensor. By saving the original structured information in the database, both generic and specific data retrieval requests can be made thus increasing the flexibility of the system. The services can also call external legacy systems, APIs, etc. to retrieve data that is not stored within the system.

— *Repository* encapsulates a collection of objects to be returned to a service. Queries built from the service layer are submitted to the repository for satisfaction. This creates an abstraction between domain entities, query request and the actual implementation of the data storage. No knowledge about how the data is stored is required to implement the repository. This provides a clean method of mocking data for automated testing and continuous integration. It also enables the data storage implementation to be changed without any changes to the RESTful API, controllers or services.

— *Data Context* is used to convert data between incompatible types, i.e., domain model and the actual data storage, if necessary.

— *Data layer* is the physical storage of data; this could be in a relational database, files storage, NoSQL, etc. Due to the data context there is no need to interact with the physical storage directly.

— *Domain entities* cross-cut the main layers of the structure. The domain entities model the actual properties and relationships of the data being stored. Then JavaScript Object Notation (JSON) will be structured so that it is deserialized directly into the correct domain entity (object), this will be passed through the system before being stored.

The RESTful API shown in Fig. 1 is the gateway into the remote software system. It also provides a mechanism to request and query the stored data via GET requests. The request mechanism and the consumer client display architectures are shown in Fig. 2. Each different type of device has its own internal data display architecture. This is one of the main concepts behind the proposed solution; each client device has its own structure and data management system, utilizing the native architecture and design features of each platform. The client applications make GET requests for data. The data is returned as JSON which is language independent and contains object information and structure. The JSON data is used to create the model in the client applications. The architectures presented are utilized to create and update a view based on the model data. The consumer clients can make generic requests for example, get light, get temperature, get social data, etc. The requests will contain query string data which be used to constrain the data being returned. The queries can also contain additional request for determining sort order, how many results to return etc. The focus on simply returning data which can form the model facilitates the platform agnostic approach.

For the purposes of this research, the data context is an Object Relational Mapper (ORM) which is provided by .Net Entity Framework. This converts the domain entities into data that can be stored in a relational data (SQL). Storing an accurate representation of the objects in a relational database requires a conversion to be programmed to ensure the properties and relationships are stored accurately. With an

ORM this is not the case, all manipulations are performed on the domain entities (objects) and the ORM will provide a mechanism to convert this into the desired data storage. It reduces the amount of code to be written as it eliminates the need to write the aforementioned data-access code or even understand the underlying data storage structure. A relational database is used in this system for legacy reasons. There are existing systems that utilise relational databases for data storage. This means that only one physical data store is required to support the legacy systems and this new platform. When the legacy systems are switched over to the new platform we can easily switch to a noSQL approach, for example, MongoDB, Couchbase, etc. or a file system storage.

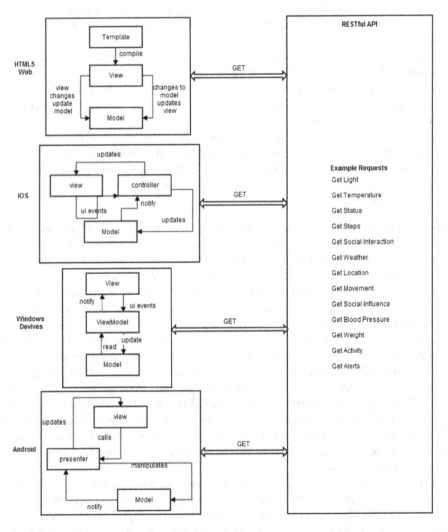

Fig. 2. Consumer client device architectures utilizing the RESTful API to query and request data

4   Room Temperature Monitor Example

To test the complete solution presented in Section 3, an office temperature monitoring application was produced. The solution utilizes Java SunSpot sensors [6] to monitor temperature and light information. A sensor is deployed on every desk and various communal areas throughout the research group offices and labs. A simple Java PC application acts as a broadcaster for all the sensor data; it requests data from the SunSpots and then POSTs it to the remote server shown in Fig. 1 for storage. A snapshot of temperature and light is taken from each sensor every 20 minutes. The frequency of the data requests can be configured in the broadcast application. Client applications for consuming the data are created using the architecture patterns shown in Fig. 2. It was decided that the best view for the data was a visual representation of the room with a colour representation of the temperature. Fig. 3 shows the view in the Android client with the room layout, sensor placement and the resulting temperature interpolation data. Exact sensor data can be viewed by tapping the sensor image.

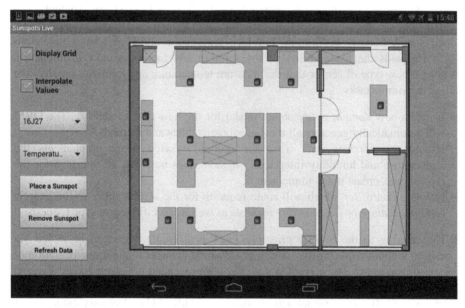

Fig. 3. Visualization of office temperature data on an Android device (Nexus 7)

Each of the clients utilize a generic MVW (Model-View-Whatever) approach which provides a mechanism for the view to update when the model (data) changes. Therefore, adding a new view, for example, a chart system is straightforward and does not require any additional programming of the model or update mechanisms in any of the client applications. By utilizing concrete MVW implementations for each type of client were are able to generate template client applications for each platform which can be utilized for future rapid prototyping of new data consumption applications.

The Client applications call a GET request on the RESTFul API that requests temperature data. The client application does not need to know the type of sensor used other than it is capable of sending temperature data. This facilitates hot swapping of devices and the notion of being an open ecosystem. Any SunSpot could be replaced with another type of sensor that records temperature and sends the data to the server. The client applications do not need to be updated if this happens. A user is not tied into a particular sensor network ecosystem. Similarly, as the data is stored on a remote server and consumed by a variety of client applications, a user is not constrained to a particular client platform for example iOS, Windows, Android. A user can change client platforms at any time and the data will be available.

5   Integrated Data Architecture Vision

The room temperature application was used as a proof of concept of the complete system to confirm that the requirements listed in Section 2 have been satisfied. The system was designed using SOLID programming principles (Single responsibility, Open-closed, Liskov substitution, Interface segregation and Dependency inversion) [7]. This aids the extendibility of the solution and facilitates easy maintenance. Adding a new type of sensor that can measure temperature and humidity requires the following simple tasks:

— Create a new *domain entity* object model for the new type of sensor. The ORM will automatically generate all the data storage tablets and methods.
— Extend the *services* with a sensor specific service which implements the temperature and humidity interfaces. If there does not exist an interface for the type of data, create it and implement it.
— Define a *controller* which will route requests for the sensor either to the generic *GetTemperature* or *GetHumidity* requests as well as specific sensor type requests.

By adhering to the SOLID principles, new sensor/data types can be added via extension without requiring any design or structural changes to the implementation of the existing system. The current system has been extended to accommodate Tynetec PIR, contact and pressure sensors [8], Shimmer accelerometer data [9], Social data from Twitter [10] and personal activity data from FitBit [11]. The easy extension of the solution with these data sources proves that the system can accommodate heterogeneous data from sensors, wearable devices and social networks.

6   Conclusion

There is potential to collect a wide variety of data about an individual throughout their daily life via smart phones, wearable technology and sensors deployed in the environment. The paper presented a solution for collecting and processing heterogeneous data from physical environments and individuals. Methods for consuming the data on potentially any screen were also provided. An example of an office temperature monitoring application was presented as a real-world implementation. The solution was extended to accommodate additional sensors, wearable device data from FitBit and social network data from Twitter. This provides a foundation for a collecting data about an individual and the environments they inhabit rather than focusing on one specific location/situation. The system will continue to be extended with more data sources and methods for processing the data. Future work will concentrate on the identification and development of the client applications in the domains of connected health and ambient intelligence.

References

1. Cook, D.J.: How smart is your home? Science 335, 1579–1581 (2012)
2. Wood, A., Virone, G., Doan, T., Cao, Q.: ALARM-NET: Wireless sensor networks for assisted-living and residential monitoring. University of Virginia, Tech. Rep., pp. 1–14 (2006), doi:10.1109/MNET.2008.4579768m
3. Cook, D.J., Crandall, A.S., Thomas, B.L., Krishnan, N.C.: CASAS: A smart home in a box. Computer 46(7), 62–69 (2013)
4. Cook, D.J., Das, S.K.: How smart are our environments? An updated look at the state of the art. Pervasive and Mobile Computing 3(2), 53–73 (2007)
5. Rodriguez, A.: RESTful Web services: The basics (2008), https://www.ibm.com/developerworks/webservices/library/ws-restful/
6. Java SunSpot, http://www.sunspotworld.com/
7. Martin, R.C.: Clean Code: A Handbook of Agile Software Craftsmanship, vol. 1. Prentice Hall (2008), http://portal.acm.org/citation.cfm?id=1388398
8. Tynetec, http://www.tynetec.co.uk/
9. Shimmer, http://www.shimmersensing.com/
10. Twitter, http://www.twitter.com
11. FitBit, http://www.fitbit.com

Common Data Model in AmI Environments

David Martínez Casas, Sebastián Villarroya Fernández, Moisés Vilar Vidal,
José Manuel Cotos Yáñez, José Ramón Ríos Viqueira, and José Angel Taboada González

COGRADE group, CITIUS, University of Santiago de Compostela, La Coruña, Spain
{david.martinez.casas,sebastian.villarroya,moises.vilar,
manel.cotos,jrr.viqueira,joseangel.taboada}@usc.es

Abstract. Ambient Intelligence environments involve a wide range of different devices typically associated to protocols not compatible with each other. This is probably one of the possible problems to reach the full explosion of the internet of things because of the lack of standards for sensor data exchanging. This paper proposes a solution for the exchange and storage of information developing a generic model to be used with different sources of data. The model is light enough to be used in low-cost and low performance hardware. The paper also describes how the model is used in a scenario supporting different contexts, as industrial devices or environmental data.

Keywords: Internet Of Things, IoT, BACnet, O&M, Data Model.

1 Introduction

In today's world, most of sensors have proprietary software interfaces defined by their manufacturers and used selectively. Each manufacturer brings to market their own solutions. It is true that there are some initiatives [1] to try to unify the way to handle the various devices and services designed but none stands above the rest.

This situation requires significant investment on the part of developers with each new sensor or project involving multiple systems and on the part of the providers of sensors, gateways and portals or services where observations are used. Standardized interfaces for sensors in the Internet of Things (IoT) [2] will permit the proliferation of new high value services with lower overhead of development and wider reach.

In our experience [3] there are some different data type sources: home automation data, environmental data, building management system (BMS) data, health data,... and in each case the data exchange models are quite different: ZWave, BACnet, O&M, ...

Our objective is to develop a common data model for our framework DADIS to the transmission and storage of data in order to generalize all models in a single common data model. To do that a data model is described in the following section and is tested in one scenario with the result that will be discussed in the conclusions.

2 DADIS Common Data Model (DADIS-CDM)

The proposed common data model it has been developed based on OGC Observations and Measurements[1] proposals and is represented in Fig.1. The main components of our data model are explained next.

---

[1] http://www.opengeospatial.org/standards/om

R. Hervás et al. (Eds.): UCAmI 2014, LNCS 8867, pp. 212–215, 2014.
© Springer International Publishing Switzerland 2014

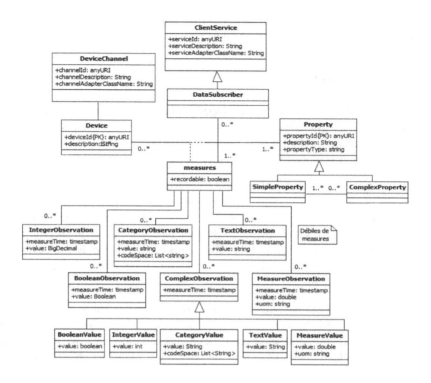

Fig. 1. Proposed common data model

- ClientService. Represents the communication channel towards the applications, fed by the system, both in synchronous or asynchronous manner. This provides, through a set of wrappers, the flexibility to cover a large set of technologies such as HTTP, TCP, XML and JSON.
- DeviceChannel. Represents the communication channel to communicate devices with the system. Takes account of the data communication protocols used by the sensors that send data to the system such as TCP, UDP, HTTP, MQTT and others.
- Device. A device element of the model represents a mechanism that can perform measurements on physical magnitudes, i.e. a sensor.
- Property. A property represents a measure attribute that can be measured by a device and referenced by a name. We consider two types of properties: *SimpleProperty* and *ComplexProperty* (aggregation of simple properties).
- Measure. Association between device and property to take into account a device can measure various properties and a property can be measured by various devices.
- Observation. Represents the value of a property obtained through a measurement process. An observation has a reference to the device that has performed the measurement process, a reference to the measured property, the time instant of the measurement process and the value of the measurement result. Depends on the type of result there are several observation types: *BooleanObservation* (true/false), *CategoryObservation* (option in a group), *IntegerObservation* (dimensionless

integer), *MeasureObservation* (real number with unit of measure), *TextObservation* (free text) and *ComplexObservation* (aggregation of any of the above).

3 Test Scenario

To test our proposed model we've developed a platform in Java programming language running on a Raspberry Pi[2] (low-cost hardware) and using a relational database engine (H2 Database[3]). The objective is testing the monitoring process in a set of university buildings equipped with devices for different contexts:

- A set of 15 buildings equipped with **BACnet** technology that allows us to collect measures of energy consumption, environment, … and perform actions on them.
- A set of **O&M** meteorological stations to collect data from outdoor environment.
- A set of **Zwave** and **XBee** devices to monitor indoor locations in specific points where BACnet is not available. Both, Zwave **and** XBee protocols and devices allow us an indoor mobile monitoring, tuning the sensor network to the different implemented applications.

BACnet [4] is a data communication protocol designed to link together the electronic devices present in buildings, used in an industrial context. BACnet data model is based on the definition of a set of services, objects and properties. We use the read-Property service which allows us to read the properties of BACnet objects and do the following mapping process.

O&M is an international standard for modeling observation events and describing their relations to the target spatial objects under observation, the measured properties & measurement procedure, and the captured data resulting from those events. O&M standard is the basis for our model so it fits naturally.

Z-Wave is a wireless protocol designed for home automation, specifically to remotely control applications in residential and light commercial environments.

Xbee is an open protocol for wireless communications. Since, in this case, we control both sides of the communication we use our common model in JSON format.

```
O&M
    Object_Type: Analog Input
    Instance_Number: 1
    Object_Identifier: Temperature
    Local_Date: March 10, 2014
    Local_Time: 12:30
    Present_value: 22.3
    Units: ºC
```

```
DADIS CDM
    deviceId: AnalogInput:1
    propertyId: Temperature
    measureTime: 12:30 10/03/2014
    value: 22.3
    uom: ºC
```

---

[2] http://www.raspberrypi.org/
[3] http://www.h2database.com/html/main.html

An example of the mapping process to convert data from sensors using BACnet technology is shown in the figure below. The process for O&M, ZWave and XBee is quite similar.

4   Conclusions and Future Work

In this paper we describe a common data model in order to unify the information storage from information related to different contexts: Building Management System, Environmental platforms, health devices... The objective is the sensor data feed in ambient intelligence applications.

We have conducted a series of tests on data linked to various protocols: BACnet, O&M, Z-Wave and XBee and the results have been satisfactory. The common data model is flexible enough to accommodate every of these models without losing information in the process. Running in low-cost hardware with simple databases the platform is capable of manage data from 1000 sources every 30 seconds.

The model can be used in other scenarios where we control both communication sides: wired sensors, wifi, Bluetooth.

The next step would be test the proposed common data model to provide the ability to send commands to devices so that they carry out concrete actions: lighting control, HVAC control, access control, etc.

Acknowledgement. This work has been partially supported by EC under the LIFE12-ENV-ES-001173 project application from Life+ Environment Policy and Governance Programme.

References

1. Atzori, L., Iera, A., Morabito, G.: The internet of things: A survey. Computer Networks 54(15), 2787–2805 (2010)
2. Said, O., Albagory, Y.: Internet of Things. Lap Lambert Academic Publishing (2014) ISBN: 978-3659520853
3. Villarroya, S., Viqueira, J., Cotos, J., Flores, J.: Geodadis: A framework for the development of geographic data acquisition and dissemination servers. Computers & Geosciences 52, 68–76 (2013)
4. BACnet (June 2014),
https://www.ashrae.org/resources-publications/
bookstore/bacnet

Complex Adaptive Socio-Technical Systems Theory View of Ubiquitous Computing Systems Research

Yongming Wang[*], Junzhong Gu, and Zili Zhou

East China Normal University, Shanghai 200241, China
ymwang819@gmail.com, {jzgu,zlzhou}@ica.stc.sh.cn

Abstract. Ubiquitous computing (Ubicomp) researchers have been struggling to realize global ubiquitous computing environment (GUCE). Although Ubicomp systems are studied broadly, there are only a few attempts to study Ubicomp systems based on GUCE especially from theories and high-level abstractions models. To bridge the research gap and provide an appropriate theory and model to underlie Ubicomp systems research, this paper describes the Ubicomp systems from socio-technical systems theory and complex adaptive systems theory perspective. This study gives a set of properties for Ubicomp systems as complex adaptive socio-technical systems which is subsequently used to compare three modeling approaches for Ubicomp systems modeling. Three modeling approaches are system dynamics modeling, discrete-even modeling and agent-based modeling respectively. This explorative and comparative study conclude that understanding Ubicomp systems through the complex adaptive socio-technical system theory and modeling Ubicomp systems through agent-based modeling methodology offer insight into the current complexity of Ubicomp systems.

Keywords: Ubiquitous Computing Systems, Complex Adaptive System, Socio-Technical Systems, System Dynamics Modeling, Discrete-Even Modeling, Agent-based Modeling.

1 Introduction

With the explosive expansion of the Internet of things as the global information infrastructure, coupled with rapid advances in Ubicomp [1] enabling technologies, Ubicomp as a new computing paradigm is emerging. Moreover, with the transition from Ubicomp environments to hyper Ubicomp environments [3], we envision that the future world will possibly be a highly computerized integration environment known as the GUCE which is created upon information environment, physical environment and human social environment. GUCE is mainly characterized by ubiquitous intelligence filled with smart everyday object (named SmartBody in this paper). As basic building

---

[*] Corresponding author.

R. Hervás et al. (Eds.): UCAmI 2014, LNCS 8867, pp. 216–223, 2014.
© Springer International Publishing Switzerland 2014

block of GUCE, SmartBody represents the integration of information environment and physical environment in the building block level.

Although the area of Ubicomp systems are studied broadly throughout the world, there are only a few attempts to study Ubicomp systems based on GUCE, especially from the perspective of theories and high-level abstraction models. As a kind of representative engineered CAS [2], many researchers have indicated that Ubicomp systems complexity is the main obstacle to its understanding and realizing [2]. Therefore, we must have an appropriate theory and model studies to understand and building Ubicomp systems. The similar viewpoint has been emphasized by [3, 4].

As two well-established system theories, socio-technical systems (STS) theory and complex adaptive systems (CAS) theory which is viewed as a new science in the 21 century have been widely used in many disciplines (e.g. economics, social sciences, and biology) to describe and better understand the features, mechanisms and rules of complex phenomena [5]. In general, applying STS theory and CAS theory to other domains may help in better understanding of the mechanisms and features of complex phenomena [6].

The remainder of this article is organized as follows: firstly, Ubicomp systems are described from perspective of socio-technical systems theory and complex adaptive systems theory in sections 2 and sections 3, respectively. After an overview on three modeling approaches in sections 4, these approaches are compared based on described features for complex Ubicomp systems in section 5. Finally, section 6 gives some concluding remarks and some directions for future work.

2   Understanding Ubicomp Systems as STS

STS are systems that involve both complex physical-technical systems and networks of interdependent actors [7]. The key contribution of the socio-technical theory is that the system behavior can be analyzed and improved only by considering both social and technical sub-systems and the interdependencies between them. In other words, the system-level structure and behavior of both social and technical sub-systems give rise to the overall behavior of a socio-technical system. STS theory suggests that systems consist of two parts: a technical system and a social system. The technical system is comprised of equipment and processes; the social system consists of people and tasks.

Ubicomp system can be typically viewed as a STS [4]. It arises from the fact that humans will be embedded in GUCE just as deeply as computational artifacts and as special SmartBody of Ubicomp systems. From one hand, the Ubicomp system is a network of technical elements which are physically inter-connected. On the other hand, in users-centered Ubicomp systems, persons form a social network with cooperative interactions. In addition, natural human-computer interaction between physical elements and humans can influence the decision making process of them. Consequently, the overall performance of Ubicomp systems is the output of behavior of both social and physical networks and the interactions and interdependencies among these networks.

3   Understanding Ubicomp Systems as CAS

To characterize a CAS which was addressed by Holland, several common features have been discussed in the literature. All these features can be generally classified into Micro-level and Macro-level characteristics. Micro-level characteristics are about the internal structure of building blocks [8]. The macro-level characteristics describe how a CAS looks like if we observe and study it at the system level.

3.1   Micro-Level Characteristics of CAS

Numerousness and heterogeneity. A CAS consists of many elements. In addition, these elements normally differ in their characteristic which is frequently called heterogeneity. For instance, an Ubicomp system (e.g., smart hospital system) comprises many different SmartBodys which from different manufacturers.

Local Interactions and Actions. Another key characteristic of CAS is local interactions and actions of the system elements. For instance, in the physical level, the technical entities of an system are interconnected through local area network and spontaneously inter-operate in changing environments. In the social level, interactions are usually in the form of information flows among different persons.

Nestedness. Another characteristic of CAS is that the internal organization of system displays some sort of nestedness associated with some type of hierarchical organization [9]. For example, in a smart city environment, smart homes, smart hospitals and smart marketplaces etc. form a hyper Ubicomp environment, each of these super environments has also several smart rooms and each of these rooms has some internal SmartBodys.

Adaptiveness. Adaptiveness refers to the ability of components of a CAS to change their behavior as a result of interactions with the other components and the surroundings [10]. For example, in smart home, smart air conditioner can adaptability adjusts the indoor temperature according to the different outdoor temperature.

3.2   Macro-Level Characteristics of CAS

Emergence. The system-level behavior in a CAS emerges from the behavior of individual components and their interactions [10]. The overall performance and the robustness of an Ubicomp system to cope with abnormal events are examples of emergent properties.

Self-organization. In CAS, the system-level properties are the result of building block behavior and their interactions. This property is called self-organization. In Ubicomp system, there is no external controller and the overall system behavior emerges from interaction of local autonomous and heterogeneous components.

Co-evolution. The components of a CAS change over time. The physical components learn and adapt to the changing environment and action of other components with time. As a result of all these changes, the system structure change and evolve over time making the GUCE is a highly dynamic and open environment.

Path-dependency. Path-dependency means that current and future states and decisions in a CAS depend on the path of previous states, actions, rather than simply on current conditions of the system. For example, in an Ubicomp system, the decision to discovery and select a specific SmartBody as service provider influences all operational decisions and possible states of the other sub-task in future.

4   Modeling Approaches for CASTS

Three main approaches for modeling CASTS consider different building blocks for describing the system structure and behavior and have some key assumptions about the world. A summary of main characteristics of these approaches is presented in Table 1. Moreover, these modeling approaches have different capabilities to modeling the micro- and macro-level characteristics of Ubicomp systems through complex adaptive socio-technical system theory.

Table 1. Summary of main characteristics of three modeling approaches

SDM	DEM	ABM
System-oriented	Process-oriented	Individual-oriented
Homogenized building blocks	Heterogeneous building blocks	Heterogeneous building blocks
No micro-level building blocks	Object as building block	Agent as building block
Feedback loops	Event occurrence	Decisions and interactions
Stock and Flow	Event and Activity	Agent and Environment
Continuous and discrete	Discrete	Discrete
Experimentation by changing the system structure	Experimentation by changing the system structure	Experimentation by changing the agent rules and system structure
Structure is fixed	Structure is fixed	Structure is not fixed

4.1   System Dynamics Modeling

The SDM [11] was defined as: the study of information feedback characteristics of industrial activity to show how organizational structure, amplification, and time delays interact to influence the success of the enterprise. To capture the complexity of CASTS, Forrester suggested the feedback loop concept and discussed that a CASTS has a multiplicity of interacting feedback loops. Therefore the feedback loop is regarded as the basic building block of a CASTS and the multiple feedback loops is the driver of complex dynamic behavior in a system.

4.2   Discrete Event Modeling

The modeling approach that suggests modeling the real-world systems and processes with distinct events is called DEM [12]. In this modeling approach, the state change of system at any time point is triggered by discrete events. The model evolution is governed by a clock and a chronologically ordered event list. The modeling starts by placing an initial event in the event list, proceeds as an infinite loop that executes the current most imminent event, and ends when an event stops or the list becomes empty. The main advantage of DEM is its capability to model distinctive entities with heterogeneous characteristics.

4.3   Agent-Based Modeling

The ABM is a new kind of modeling approach in which the focus is on representing the individuals in the system which is termed "Agents" and their interaction with each other and their environments [13]. Comparing with two other approaches, ABM is a relatively new. However, some specific features of ABM make it a popular approach for modeling CASTS in different domains. First, it is easy to model heterogeneous building blocks in an open and dynamic system environment. Second, learning, reasoning mechanisms and adaptive behavior can be easily represented in an agent-based model. Finally, agent-based model can be easily extended or reused for other purposes.

5   Comparison of Modeling Approaches

5.1   Capturing Micro-Level Complexity

The SDM, DEM and ABM modeling approaches take fundamentally different perspectives when modeling the micro-level complexity of Ubicomp systems. SDM basically belongs to top-down modeling [14]. In contrast, DEM and ABM are bottom-up modeling.

The top-down modeling approaches in SDM could be problematic for modeling CASTS. Firstly, SDM is unable to model the heterogeneity and numerousness in a CASTS. Instead of working with heterogeneous building blocks with different characteristics, SDM works with an average individual which represent a population of building blocks. In addition, the aggregated view in SDM makes it difficult to model the nestedness and multi-level characteristics of complex Ubicomp systems.

On contrary, the DEM and the ABM have the capability to model micro-level features of CASTS. There are, however, basic differences between these two approaches. Firstly, in DEM the events are the basic building blocks of the model and the occurrence of events is triggered by previous events or timing rules. In ABM, basic building block is agent and all events and activities are triggered by decisions of agents in the system [14]. Moreover, the adaptiveness of building blocks is not usually modeled in a DEM model as entities in the system are considered as passive. Modeling these aspects is solely possible in an ABM.

5.2   Capturing Macro-Level Complexity

The capability of SDM to produce the emergent properties in a CASTS has been questioned by several researchers. The necessary condition for emergent properties in a system is existence of hierarchy of system levels. Since SDM models the behavior of system in an aggregate level, [15] explicitly deny its ability to display the emergence in a CASTS. Similar to SDM, some researchers also argued that in DEM, the macro behavior is modeled by modeler and it is not emerging in the system level [16]. This is in contrast with ABM in which macro behavior is not modeled and it emerges from the micro decisions of the individual agents.

In addition to above arguments, the main drawback of SDM and DEM is in capturing the self-organization characteristics of CASTS. As mentioned before, SDM is not an individual-based modeling in nature. Likewise, DEM models ignore the self-organization as system-level characteristics and the building blocks do not have any intelligence or decision making capability. Consequently, the basically different between ABM and other two approaches is agents, as autonomous decision makers, have certain intelligence and can adaptively alter the way of interactions with other agents and environment [17].

Because of the system structure is assumed fixed in both SDM and DEM approaches, they have also difficulty to capture the evolution of CASTS. In a SDM model, the structure has to be defined before starting the modeling [18]. Similarly, in DEM, the process must be well-defined beforehand [16]. On the contrary, for an ABM the underlying processes are not fixed. Based on its decision making capability and the interactions with other agents and environment, each agent may select a different course of actions and follow a different process. Consequently, the network structure of system is modified dynamically.

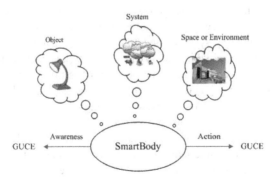

Fig. 1. Modeling everyday objects into SmartBodys

Path-dependency means that the current and future states of CASTS depend on the path of previous states and decisions. This aspect can be captured by all three modeling approaches. The path-dependency in a CASTS, however, has an additional implication which is in transition from current state to the next state of the system, the path of events and states are influential and must be taken into account. With this aspect, there is a basic difference between ABM and two other approaches. Future behavior in a SDM and DEM models only depends on the current state of system. In an ABM, however, individual agents can possess the internal memory of past events which impacts every future decision of that agent and the next state of the system.

Based on the above comparison and discussion, We can be seen, ABM is the exclusive modeling approach which can capture the properties of Ubicomp systems as CASTS. Consequently, modeling everyday objects into agents (named SmartBody) (see Fig. 1) as basic building blocks contribute to realize GUCE and Ubicomp systems. The underlying assumptions in SDM and DEM, however, make it hard to model some of main aspects and consequently, constrain developing a conceptual model for the system.

6   Conclusions

The complexity of Ubicomp systems has become a generally accepted fact, but so far little is known about what to do with this fact. In this paper, we presented a perspective to view Ubicomp systems built upon global ubiquitous computing environment as complex adaptive socio-technical systems. We investigate the question why socio-technical systems theory and CAS theory is reasonable as a theoretical foundation for better understanding Ubicomp systems. By means of comparison and analysis, it was possible to investigate the possibilities of using complex adaptive socio-technical systems theory to describe and understand Ubicomp systems. Most of the characteristic of complex adaptive socio-technical systems theory could also be identified in Ubicomp systems. Based on such evidence, we can conclude that complex adaptive socio-technical systems theory is applicable to understand and describe Ubicomp systems.

Based on the recognition that Ubicomp systems can be treated as complex adaptive socio-technical systems, three main modeling approaches (SDM, DEM and ABM) were compared for Ubicomp systems modeling. The result shows that only ABM can capture the characteristic of Ubicomp systems as complex adaptive socio-technical systems. As mentioned above, the construction of global ubiquitous computing environment and Ubicomp systems are challenging tasks. Through agentification of everyday objects into SmartBody as basic building blocks, we can incrementally construct GUCE based on bottom-up approach and conveniently reuse building blocks in different Ubicomp systems. Moreover, SmartBody can be viewed a carrier of various enabling technologies of Ubicomp and can achieve integration of information environment and physical environment in building block level.

This study can be considered as signaling a new direction to be explored, and offering some avenues for Ubicomp research, rather than as a finished work. In future research, we hope that others working in the field of Ubicomp will be excited to look for opportunities to leverage complex adaptive socio-technical systems theory in

Ubicomp research. For our future work, we plan to study how to realize everyday objects into SmartBodys and build an experimental Ubicomp system or application based on a certain amount of SmartBodys.

Acknowledgments. This research is supported by the Fund of The Shanghai Science and Technology Development Foundation (Grant No. 13430710100). The authors are grateful to the editor and anonymous reviewers for their suggestions in improving the quality of the paper.

References

1. Weiser, M.: The computer for the 21st century. Scientific American 265(3), 94–104 (1991)
2. Haghnevis, M., Askin, R.G.: A Modeling Framework for Engineered Complex Adaptive Systems. IEEE Systems Journal 6(3), 520–530 (2012)
3. Ma, J., Yang, L.T.: Towards a smart world and ubiquitous intelligence: a walkthrough from smart things to smart hyperspaces and UbicKids. International Journal of Pervasive Computing and Communications 1(1), 53–68 (2005)
4. Milner, R.: Ubiquitous computing: shall we understand it? The Computer Journal 49(4), 383–389 (2006)
5. Kuhn, T.: Using Complexity Science to affect a paradigm shift in Information Systems for the 21st century. Journal of Information Technology 21, 211–215 (2006)
6. Grus, L., Crompvoets, J.: Spatial data infrastructures as complex adaptive systems. International Journal of Geographical Information Science 24(3), 439–463 (2010)
7. De Bruijn, H., Herder, P.M.: System and actor perspectives on socio-technical systems. IEEE Transactions on Systems, Man and Cybernetics, Part A: Systems and Humans 39(5), 981–992 (2009)
8. Holland, J.: Hidden Order: How Adaptation Builds Complexity. Perseus Books, Massachusetts (1996)
9. Allen, T.F.H., Starr, T.B.: Hierarchy: Perspectives in Ecological Complexity. University of Chicago Press (1982)
10. Holland, J.H.: Emergence: From chaos to order. Oxford University Press (2000)
11. Forrester, J.W.: Industrial dynamic. Journal of the Operational Research Society 48(10), 1037–1041 (1997)
12. Berrisford, G.: Discrete event modeling. In: OOIS, pp. 340–354. Springer, London (1997)
13. Janssen, M.A.: Agent-based modeling. In: Modeling in Ecological Economics, pp. 155–172 (2005)
14. Heath, S.K., Buss, A.: Cross-paradigm simulation modeling: challenges and successes. In: Proceedings of the Winter Simulation Conference, pp. 2788–2802 (2011)
15. Gilbert, N., Troitzsch, K.: Simulation for the social scientist. McGraw-Hill International (2005)
16. Siebers, P.-O., et al.: Discrete-event simulation is dead, long live agent-based simulation. Journal of Simulation 4(3), 204–210 (2010)
17. Sterman, J.D.: System dynamics: systems thinking and modeling for a complex world. In: Proceedings of the ESD Internal Symposium (2002)

Extending Ambient Intelligence to the Internet of Things: New Challenges for QoC Management

Pierrick Marie[1], Thierry Desprats[1], Sophie Chabridon[2], and Michelle Sibilla[1]

[1] IRIT UMR 5505 Université Paul Sabatier, 31062 Toulouse, France
{Firstname.Name}@irit.fr
[2] Institut Mines-Télécom/Télécom SudParis, CNRS UMR 5157, 91011 Évry, France
Sophie.Chabridon@telecom-sudparis.eu

Abstract. Quality of Context (QoC) awareness is recognized as a key point for the success of context-aware computing solutions. At a time where the Internet of Things, Cloud Computing, and Ambient Intelligence paradigms bring together new opportunities for more complex context computation, the next generation of Multiscale Distributed Context Managers (MDCM) is facing new challenges concerning QoC management. This paper presents how our QoCIM framework can help application developers to manage the whole QoC life-cycle by providing genericity, openness and uniformity. Its usages are illustrated, both at design time and at runtime, in the case of an urban pollution context- and QoC-aware scenario.

Keywords: quality of context, quality criterion, context management, meta-modeling, information model.

1 Introduction

Context-aware applications become more and more common. These applications consume context information extracted from local ambient data, users profiles, heterogeneous and spatially distributed sensors. The behaviour of context-aware applications is strongly affected by the quality of the context information (QoC). QoC-aware applications require a fine and efficient management of the QoC they rely on. QoC is related to any information that describes the quality of context information as defined by [4]. A solution to handle the QoC is to use context managers. Context managers support context information throughout their life cycle. The life cycle of a piece of context information starts when it gets collected by a sensor and ends at its consumption by a context-aware application. A bad quality of context could lead applications to wrong decisions and irrelevant reactions. That is why context managers must take into account QoC at each step of the context information life cycle.

Extending the scope of context managers from local ambient environment to the Internet of Things (IoT) introduces a spatio-temporal decoupling between context producers, such as embedded sensors, and context consumers such as context-aware applications running on mobile devices. Consequently new

R. Hervás et al. (Eds.): UCAmI 2014, LNCS 8867, pp. 224–231, 2014.
© Springer International Publishing Switzerland 2014

challenges arise in order to guarantee the effectiveness and the efficiency of the new generation of context managers, corresponding to Multiscale Distributed Context Managers (MDCM). Such MDCMs must be deployed over various devices or servers, spread across heterogeneous networks or clouds. In addition to the classical key points used for the successful determination of the behaviour of context-aware applications, QoC can contribute to both the effectiveness and efficiency of these kind of context managers.

MDCMs being distributed over the Internet, this implies that there is no more possibility to establish a kind of "one-to-one QoC-based contract" between context producers and consumers, but QoC requirements and QoC guarantees still exist. Context consumers express QoC requirements about the quality they need and symmetrically, context producers express QoC guarantees about their capabilities. According to the expectations of the consumers, MDCMs have to deliver context information with the appropriate QoC. It requires the ability to express filters based on well-defined QoC criteria that may be used within MDCMs to optimize context data routing. Because one of the main functionalities of context managers is to process context information (by aggregation, inference, ...), they also have to manipulate QoC during the execution of these operations. That is why MDCMs should be extensible by enabling the definition and the computation algorithm of any QoC criterion.

This paper presents our QoCIM (Quality of Context Information Model) framework and answers the following questions, highlighted by an urban pollution scenario: (1.) How to take into account the QoC guarantees of producers? (2.) How to apply processes on context and QoC to infer high level information? (3.) How to fulfil the QoC requirements of the context consumers? (4.) How to apply QoC based dissemination to deliver the appropriate context?

The remainder of this paper is structured as follows: Section 2 motivates the use of MDCMs with a fictional scenario inspired from an existing concern: the urban pollution. Related and previous works dealing with context managers and quality of context are presented in Section 3. Section 4 presents the software solution we have built to handle the QoC within MDCMs. Section 5 summarizes our contributions and gives some perspectives.

2   An Urban Pollution Measurement Scenario

This Section proposes a fictional scenario inspired from the citizens' concern on urban pollution and illustrated in Figure 1. A polluted city wants to inform its citizens in real-time about the pollution level in the streets. The purpose is to offer solutions, based on QoC-aware applications, to avoid the most polluted streets when people are walking or riding a bike, for example. To realize it, the city deploys an MDCM to collect as raw data pollution measurements (*e.g.* Carbon Monoxide: 4.6 ppm) and the location of these measurements. Two QoC criteria, the precision defined as "how close together or how repeatable the results from a measurement are" [6] and the freshness defined as "the time that elapses between the determination of context information and its delivery to a

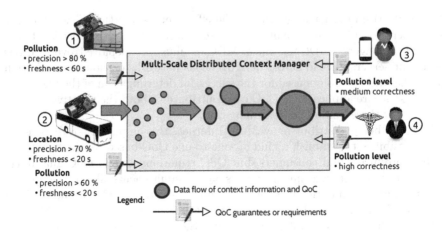

Fig. 1. QoC for the pollution measurement scenario

requester" [4] are also collected by the MDCM as QoC meta-data. The context information, offered by the city services, must be understandable and easy-to-use with a high abstraction level. That is why the raw data are then aggregated by the MDCM to produce a new context information, the pollution level, and a new QoC criterion, the correctness. The pollution level is separately computed for each street with all the available measurements made in the respective street. Inspired from the Air Quality Index[1]the pollution level is divided into six levels: *good, moderate, unhealthy for sensitive groups, unhealthy, very unhealthy and hazardous.* The correctness is defined by [7] as "the probability that an instance of context accurately represents the corresponding real world situation, as assessed by the context source, at the time it was determined" and possesses three values: *low, medium and high. Low* means the pollution level is not reliable while *high* means the pollution level is very reliable. The MDCM also tries to predict the coming pollution level and its correctness a few hours in advance, like the forecast weather system to help citizens prepare their travels.

① The city equips its *bus stations* with sophisticated pollution sensors and an embedded dedicated software. The pollution sensor performs accurate measurements ($\geqslant 80\%$ of precision), but produces measurements, in the worst case, only every 60 seconds. The software is in charge to evaluate the precision of the measurements, and provide the MDCM the pollution as context information and the evaluation of the precision as QoC indicator. The QoC guarantees of the bus stations are therefore: precision $\geqslant 80\%$ and freshness $\leqslant 60$ s.

② *The buses* are also equipped with a pollution sensor and an embedded software. This sensor placed is faster than the sensor placed on the bus station; it produces a measurement, in the worst case, every 20 seconds, but it is less accurate ($\geqslant 50\%$ of precision). The buses still in motion, then a GPS is installed into the buses and computes their location with a medium precision (almost 10

---

[1] Reporting the daily air quality: www.airnow.gov/index.cfm?action=pubs.index

meters). The embedded software supplies the MDCM with the pollution and the location of the bus as context information. The software is also in charge to evaluate and offer to the MDCM the precision of the pollution and the precision of the location as QoC meta-data. The buses are therefore committed to provide their pollution measurements with at least precision $\geqslant 50\%$ and freshness $\leqslant 20$ s. In the same time, they are also committed to provide their location with at least precision $\geqslant 70\%$ and the same freshness.

③ *A general mass-market mobile application* is developed on smart-phones to monitor the location of the users and requests the MDCM to get the pollution level of the streets where the users are. The application notifies them when the pollution is too high and suggests to go in a close and less polluted street if there is one. The application must not indicate wrong informations to users, that is why it needs the pollution level with, at least, a medium correctness. By this way, the notifications of the application do not supply wrong information. This application uses QoC to be more usable and to not display useless information. It also benefits from remote geographical context data that are not available from the ambient space to make relevant recommendations.

④ *A health care application* is provided to asthmatic people. The purpose of this application is to suggest users the best way to avoid the polluted streets. When users walk around the city, the application gets from the MDCM the current and forecast pollution level and suggests the best path to reach their destinations. The application is critical to asthmatic people, that is why the application always requires context information with the maximal correctness. If the MDCM is not able to provide this quality, the application still suggests an alternative paths but warns users about the risks to have an allergy attack and recommends to go in a safe zone until a new relevant path appears. This application operates with geographical and temporal remote context information associated to QoC levels to suggest safe paths and to avoid health troubles.

3 Related and Previous Works

The AWARENESS project [7] identifies three reasons for taking into account the QoC within context managers: (i) "application adaptation" (ii) "middleware efficiency" (iii) "users' privacy enforcement". The authors use five indicators to define QoC and point out the need for a formal methodology for QoC evaluation allowing to share clearly and unequivocally QoC values. They propose that all the parties come to an agreement on QoC before sharing any context information.

The COSMOS project [1] provides mechanisms for the efficient management of QoC. COSMOS is a context manager and handles the QoC provided to applications through contracts. A contract is established between a context-aware application and a context source. The contract defines the QoC level that the context-aware application requires. The COSMOS project does not provide a formal methodology to evaluate QoC as [7] evoked.

Bellavista et al. [3] propose a comparative analysis of context data distribution solutions. The authors propose a generic logical view where they distinguish the context data delivery layer from the context data management layer. The context data delivery layer focuses on disseminating and routing data whereas the context data management layer focuses on the processing and the representation of data. Then, a runtime adaptation support aims to configure and reconfigure the layers. One of the conclusions of [3] states that providing a common definition of the list of criteria used to qualify the context information within the context managers is still an open problem.

Only a few context managers with a QoC management capacity have already been proposed. But, either they still have to fully integrate QoC management [7] or their definition of QoC is not formally specified [1]. One of the objectives of the INCOME project [2] is to fill these gaps by integrating a formal definition of QoC within MDCMs. The purpose of the project is to control the whole life cycle of context information and its associated QoC, from the production to the consumption including the processing. The project intends to manage context information coming from ambient networks, the IoT or clouds.

4   Implementation of the Pollution Scenario with QoCIM

As we proposed in [5], the QoC Information Model (QoCIM) offers a unified solution to model heterogeneous QoC criteria. Figure 2 contains, as a reminder, an overview of QoCIM. QoICM is a meta-model able to support the design and the representation of information about any QoC criterion.

Our approach consists in providing a graphical editor dedicated to graphically produce, at design time, new UML class diagrams of QoC criteria. With the editor, it is possible to edit the criteria by adding new definitions, new descriptions or new values of QoC. The editor also enables to define composite criterion depending on other already defined criteria. For that purpose, we modelled QoCIM as an Ecore model based on the EMF technology[2] and we then developed a graphical editor with the Sirius technology[3].

At programming time, developers of QoC-aware applications choose the required QoC criteria and use the editor to generate the corresponding code. The generated code is able to manage the QoC within context producers or consumers. The link between the value of the QoC and the context information is isolated into an empty method. So, developers just have to complete this method to manage the QoC within the QoC-aware application. In addition, sharing the QoC meta-data with the MDCM is much easier because the QoCIM framework is able to serialize any QoC criterion into XML documents. We developed the module to generate source code with the Acceleo technology[4].

As described in Figure 2, the QoCIM framework operates in four steps. ① *context acquisition* is about QoC guarantees and context acquisition.

---

[2] EMF technology, provided by the Eclipse foundation:
   `www.eclipse.org/modeling/emf`

[3] Sirius project, available on the Eclipse platform: `www.eclipse.org/sirius`

[4] Acceleo project, available on the Eclipse platform: `www.eclipse.org/acceleo`

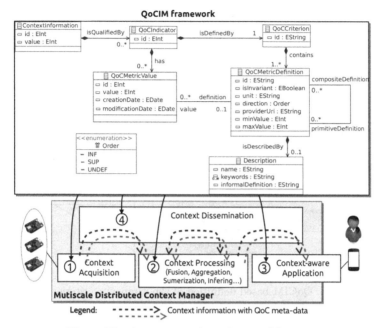

Fig. 2. The four points where QoCIM [5] operates

Communications between context providers and the MDCM are divided in two steps. During the first one, context providers inform the MDCM about their QoC guarantees. In the pollution scenario, the bus stations guarantee their information with a precision of at least 80%. In the second step, context providers publish information with QoC meta-data according to their guarantees.

② *QoC meta-data processing* infers new high informations. Because mobile phones could not process all the measurements made by the sensors, the MDCM provides aggregated information that summarize several raw data. Consequently, the abstraction level of the QoC increases and in our scenario the applications just receive the correctness composite criterion. Figure 3 is the representation of the correctness criterion made with our graphical editor. Combined with the Listing 1.1, it illustrates how the high value of the correctness can be computed within the MDCM. The QoC can also act for the context processing. For example, weighted arithmetic mean aggregates pollution measurements where high coefficient is associated to information with high precision.

③ *context aware applications* express their QoC requirements and consume context information. As for the context acquisition, communications between context consumers and the MDCM are also divided in two steps. During the first one, context consumers negotiate with the MDCM their QoC requirements. In our scenario, the health care application requires context with high correctness. If the MDCM is not able to fulfil the requirements, the application may change them. In the second step, the MDCM delivers to the application the context information with the QoC level it requires.

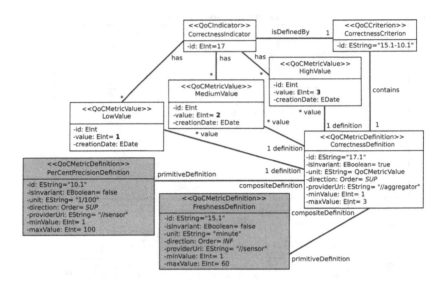

Fig. 3. QoCIM based definition of the composite criterion

```
context CorrectnessDefinition::value(): HighValue
    pre: self.PerCentPrecisionDefinition.QoCMetricValue.value >=
        85 * 100 / self.PrecisionDefinition.maxValue
    pre: self.FreshnessDefinition.QoCMetricValue.value <=
        15 * 100 / self.FreshnessDefinition.maxValue
```

Listing 1.1. Example of OCL consraints used to produce the correctness

④ *context dissemination* is the key feature for providing, in our scenario, the health care application with the suitable context information that it needs. Therefore, the efficiency of the MDCM strongly depends on the QoC-aware routing system used to forward information. Based on the QoC requirements and guarantees expressed by all the entities connected to the MDCM, the routing system dynamically handles, at run time, advertisement and subscription filters. Those filters are composed of many constraints relative to the value of context information or the associated QoC metadata. Following the constraints contained within the filters, the routing system is able to decide whether a context information must be forwarded or not. With the uniformity offered by QoCIM, writing and interpret constraints concerning the QoC metadata is simplified. Indeed, because all the entities share the same QoC model, QoCIM, and our implementation of QoCIM can be serialize as XML documents. Developers of entities just have to write, with a programming language, their expectations about any attributes of QoCIM and then, the routing system is able to analyse the filters and correctly rout the context information. For example, in our scenario, the subscription filter relative to the health care application has constraints to only receive context information with QoC metadata composed of *CorrectnessDefinition*, identified with the attribute *id* equals to 17.1 and *HighValue* identified with the attribute *value* equals to 3.

5   Conclusion and Perspectives

Although several works on QoC modelling and management have been achieved over the past decade, no consensual proposition has emerged. This article illustrates QoCIM, the QoC Information Model we proposed as a generic, expressive and computable QoC information model to be used at any time during the QoC life-cycle management. QoCIM is dedicated to handle any QoC criterion within context managers and context-aware applications. It is able to qualify a piece of context information with different QoC criteria. A same QoC criterion can be reused to qualify different pieces of context information. Sharing the definition of QoC based on the same core concepts, QoCIM offers a common language to express requirements and guarantees for producers and consumers of context. By this way, MDCMs are able to match the needs of these producers and consumers and to evaluate QoC all along the life cycle of context information. The software tool chain we provide facilitates the development of QoC-aware applications. It offers a solution to easily create and use a collection of definitions of QoC criteria derived from QoCIM. Our future works will consist in improving our graphical editor and add the possibility to directly edit QoC guarantees, QoC requirements, and filters used for the dissemination. This will be possible with a Domain Specific Language editor based on QoCIM.

Acknowledgment. This work is part of the French National Research Agency (ANR) project INCOME (ANR-11-INFR-009, 2012-2015).

References

1. Abid, Z., Chabridon, S., Conan, D.: A framework for quality of context management. In: Rothermel, K., Fritsch, D., Blochinger, W., Dürr, F. (eds.) QuaCon 2009. LNCS, vol. 5786, pp. 120–131. Springer, Heidelberg (2009)
2. Arcangeli, J.-P., et al.: INCOME – multi-scale context management for the internet of things. In: Paternò, F., de Ruyter, B., Markopoulos, P., Santoro, C., van Loenen, E., Luyten, K. (eds.) AmI 2012. LNCS, vol. 7683, pp. 338–347. Springer, Heidelberg (2012)
3. Bellavista, P., Corradi, A., Fanelli, M., Foschini, L.: A Survey of Context Data Distribution for Mobile Ubiquitous Systems. ACM Computing Surveys 44(4), 24:1–24:45 (2012)
4. Buchholz, T., Schiffers, M.: Quality of context: What it is and why we need it. In: Proceedings of the 10th Workshop of the OpenView University Association (2003)
5. Marie, P., Desprats, T., Chabridon, S., Sibilla, M.: QoCIM: A meta-model for quality of context. In: Brézillon, P., Blackburn, P., Dapoigny, R. (eds.) CONTEXT 2013. LNCS, vol. 8175, pp. 302–315. Springer, Heidelberg (2013)
6. Neisse, R.: Trust and Privacy Management Support for Context-Aware Service Platforms. Ph.D. thesis, University of Twente, Enschede (2012)
7. Sheikh, K., Wegdam, M., Van Sinderen, M.: Middleware support for quality of context in pervasive context-aware systems. In: Pervasive Computing and Communications Workshops (2007)

Linked Spatial Data for Location-Aware Services

Aimar Rodríguez, Eduardo Castillejo, and Diego López-de-Ipiña

{aimar.rodriguez,eduardo.castillejo,dipina}@deusto.es

Abstract. Geospatial data and location-aware services are becoming more common in the last years. Mobile applications make an extensive use of the built-in GPS devices and platforms on the web offer spatial data through APIs and open datasets. This data has the potential to be used to build rich location based services when merged into a uniform dataset. This paper describes the SORELCOM platform, a GPS-based community where users can share trails and points of interest, which is enriched with knowledge obtained from different sources from the web and is able to offer location aware services.

Keywords: Linked Open Data, Semantic Web, GIS, Geosparql, Location Aware Service.

1 Introduction

Geospatial data is becoming more relevant in our world. Location aware services are on the rise, specially on mobile devices [7]. Smartphone applications take advantage of the built in GPS devices to offer users dynamic services based on location and it has become common for users to spatially tag their social activity. [8]. The increase of interest in spatial data over the web has given birth to platforms like OpenStreetMaps[1], which offer open spatial data.

The Linked Open Data principles [1], at the core of the semantic web, encourage the usage of RDF and SPARQL to represent and query the data. Following these principles, the Open Geospatial Consortium (OGC) has created the GeoSPARQL standard [6] that enables the representation of geographic data and spatial queries using the SPARQL language.

The platform SORELCOM (Social Routes Empowered by Linked Contents and Context Mining) aims to take advantage of these developments. The goal of the project is to merge heterogeneous data from different sources into a uniform semantic model and exploit it to create a rich location aware service.

2 Related Work

GPS communities such as Wikiloc[2] allow users to share their trails and points of interest. In exchange, these sites act as a personal location database and

---

[1] http://openstreetmap.org
[2] http://en.wikiloc.com/

R. Hervás et al. (Eds.): UCAmI 2014, LNCS 8867, pp. 232–235, 2014.
© Springer International Publishing Switzerland 2014

visualizer and are also able to recommend their users appropriate routes based on their location.

Several services around the web offer geographical data; one of the most prominent being OpenStreetMaps (OSM)[3], a collaborative project to create free editable maps [4]. Other examples of such datasets are Geonames[4] and Wikimapia[5].

Currently there is no standard to encode spatial information on the web. While it is true that formats such as GPX exist to interchange spatial features, they only provide a means to encode the geographic information and not any additional data, such as names or descriptions. By following the principles of Linked Open Data and using GeoSPARQL it is possible to integrate the different geographic datasets on the web following a standard.

There is already work being done to bring a spatial dimension to the Semantic Web. The LinkedGeoData[6] project aims to make all the information collected by the OpenStreetMap project available as RDF and to link it with other knowledge bases on the Linked Open Data initiative. In order to represent the spatial features of the stored knowledge this project uses the LinkedGeoData ontology[7].

Geonames has also published its data following the Linked Data patterns. Again, this project uses a custom ontology, the Geonames ontology [8], to encode its data in RDF. However, unlike the LinkedGeoData ontology, this one is concerned only about representing the non spatial features, and uses the wsg84 well known vocabulary for the geographic information.

Several other projects exist which to bring spatial dimension to the semantic web, for example, Strabon a database system for semantic spatial data [5]. All these projects share a common characteristic, they define their own vocabulary for their data model. Due to this, they do not follow standards and do not integrate data from other sources than their own. The goal of this project is to integrate data from different sources, thus, a standard independent of any data model must be used, which is GeoSPARQL.

Location aware computing is increasingly common, specially in mobile computing, where sensors are available. It is very popular among users to tag their activities in a location [8] and many aspects of applications are influenced by the location. The usage of a semantic technologies in conjunction with data from different sources on the web can provide a good foundation for building rich location and context aware services.

3   SORELCOM

The goal of the SORELCOM project is to merge different data sources from the web in a Linked Data model in order to build smart GPS-driven community that

---

[3] http://www.openstreetmap.org/
[4] http://www.geonames.org
[5] http://wikimapia.org
[6] http://www.linkedgeodata.org
[7] http://linkedgeodata.org/ontology/
[8] http://www.geonames.org/ontology/documentation.html

can offer location and context aware services. The architecture of the proposed system is formed by a central server and the web and mobile applications for the end users. A first version of the system already exists, composed solely by the base system (the server) and the web application.

The server contains all the data extracted from different datasets, although currently only OpenStreetMaps and Geonames are used. These data is merged into a common data model following the structure presented in figure ?? . These data is stored on a semantic database capable of GeoSPARQL queries. For the first version only local data, points of interests from Spain, have been included; comprising approximately 350.000 triples.

It is arguable that it would be beneficial to directly use the web services offered by the sites from which information is extracted instead of incorporating it to the database, mainly because of the size of the data. In this case, however, it may be more beneficial to centralize all the information so that it can be transformed into a generic semantic model. One of the benefits is that the data from the different sources will be uniformized into a common format. Besides, it is possible to further enrich the data, by merging features obtained from different sources, for example, a site may contain a classification of a certain point of interest and another one only the description; the merged data model will contain both. In addition to this, by having a single data model it is possible to run inferences over the triples stored in the knowledge base.

Alongside this knowledge repository, a web server, which exposes the contents of the system through an HTTP JSON API, has been implemented using the NodeJS environment. This API provides access to the different information of the system classified in the following resources: **trails, points of interest, geolocated notes** and **users**. The server receives HTTP GET requests, accompanied by some query parameters, when querying for data and POST request accompanied by a JSON body when creating new data. The mentioned resources are accessible through CRUD (Create, Read, Update, Delete) methods, but the API also exposes a limited set of spatial operations.

As most GPS communities, SORELCOM offers the posibility of uploading a trail or point of interest to the database by using a GPX file, since it is the standard way of exchanging GPS data on the web. In addition, a map interface, created with Leaflet[9] is provided. In this map, users can draw trails and mark points of interest, as well as edit their trails in order to correct the errors that sometimes appear due to faults on the recording process.

3.1   Mobile Application

The mobile application develops the concept of Geolocated notes. These notes are small notes, which can be formed by plain text, multimedia or both, are situated in a certain location, last for a limited amount of time and have a visibility aspect associated, for example, public or only for a certain group of users. These notes act as a way of communication between the users of the

---

[9] http://leafletjs.org

platform. A person can leave a note with his smartphone at any moment on his location. When the users which can view it arrive at a nearby location (a radius around the note) they will be notified of the existence of this note and will be able to read it. These notes are posted through the HTTP API.

In addition, a real time service is given through the mobile application. This, the discovery service, will show the user in real time all the nearby points of interest and trails in which he may be interested. As the user moves with his smartphone, notifications will be sent with new features that appear at a certain distance. This service is implemented through a bi-directional real time communication channel between client and server, through the WebSocket technology.

4   Conclusions and Future Work

SORELCOM has created a smarter GPS-driven community, enriched with information obtained from the web. The project is still on development, however, some components are already implemented, such as the web interface and the API. All the information on the system is accessible to anyone, for we want to facilitate the development of applications offering a uniform semantic model for the heterogeneous information found on different sources.

References

1. Bizer, C., Heath, T., Berners-Lee, T.: Linked data-the story so far. International Journal on Semantic Web and Information Systems 5(3), 1–22 (2009)
2. Egenhofer, M.J.: Toward the semantic geospatial web. In: Proceedings of the 10th ACM International Symposium on Advances in Geographic Information Systems, pp. 1–4. ACM (2002)
3. Foster, D.: GPX: the GPS exchange format (retrieved on 2, 2007)
4. Haklay, M., Weber, P.: Openstreetmap: User-generated street maps. IEEE Pervasive Computing 7(4), 12–18 (2008)
5. Kyzirakos, K., Karpathiotakis, M., Koubarakis, M.: Strabon: A semantic geospatial DBMS. In: Cudré-Mauroux, P., et al. (eds.) ISWC 2012, Part I. LNCS, vol. 7649, pp. 295–311. Springer, Heidelberg (2012)
6. Perry, M., Herring, J.: OGC GeoSPARQL-A geographic query language for RDF data. In: OGC Implementation Standard, ref: OGC (2011)
7. de Souza e Silva, A.: Location-aware mobile technologies: Historical, social and spatial approaches. Mobile Media & Communication 1(1), 116–121 (2013)
8. Zickuhr, K.: Three-quarters of smartphone owners use location-based services. In: Pew Internet & American Life Project (2012)

A Wearable Device-Based Personalized Big Data Analysis Model

Shujaat Hussain[1], Byeong Ho Kang[2], and Sungyoung Lee[1]

Department of Computer Engineering, Kyung Hee University, Korea
{shujaat.hussain,sylee}@oslab.khu.ac.kr
Department of Science, Engineering and Technology University of Tasmania,
ABN 30 764 374 782, Australia
byeong.kang@utas.edu.au

Abstract. Wearable devices and the data generated by them gives a unique opportunity to understand the user behavior and predict future needs due to its personal nature. In coming years this data will grow exponentially due to huge popularity of wearable devices. Analysis will become a challenge with the personal data explosion and also to maintain a updated knowledge base. This calls for big data analysis model for wearable devices. We propose a big data analysis model which will update the knowledge base and give users a personalized recommendations based on the analysis of the data. We have designed a personalized adaptive analysis technique for data handling and transformation. This technique also responds to information utilization APIs in a real time manner. We are using mapreduce as our big data technology and ensure that data can be used for long term analysis for different applications in the future.

1 Introduction

In todays world a lot of data is generated by the wearable devices which is not leveraged and processed properly. This data is highly unique due to the personal nature of the wearable device. There is an exponential growth in wearable devices and they collect a lot of data which cannot be processed using conventional techniques. The target data are all the devices revolving around the user which can vary from the smartphones to glasses to wearable clothing. The data gathered from the wearable devices have yet to be properly explored or analyzed to enable the user to make decisions relevant to it.

Nearly 15 million wearable smart devices will be sold this year, amounting to $800 million [1]. All the major sensory data analysis is performed at remote systems, because the capability of a wearable or sensory device is premature to perform analysis on the periodic data. Data storage, their computation limit and multi-tasking compels to use the data at remote servers and then keep the data there at large scale. The same data is used then with new datum to extract hidden trends and states from both historical and their association. There is a lack of techniques and approaches which exploit the sensory data collected by wearable devices and use them for decision making and recommendations.

R. Hervás et al. (Eds.): UCAmI 2014, LNCS 8867, pp. 236–242, 2014.
© Springer International Publishing Switzerland 2014

Also with the constant monitoring by the devices, there is a need for a big data solution which has the ability to analyze the huge amount of data.

Personalized Big data is becoming a reality with wearable computing on the rise. The wearable devices cover but are not limited to medical devices, sensor based wrist wear, headset, glasses, smartphone and clothing. All these devices collect a lot of data through user input and sensors. The next frontier in generating and leveraging data will be wearable computing. They generate data in real time which brings the big data into picture as it is equipped to handle these things. Big data refers to data that grows large in terms of velocity, volume, variety and veracity which mean that conventional techniques and database management tools are not as efficient or effective. The challenge arises from data volume, the speed through which is generated and redundant/noisy data. Big data techniques comprise of new tools which tackle the data deluge through parallelism, redundancy, machine learning and pattern recognition techniques and accommodate massive data analysis through big data infrastructure.

The recent developed devices related to the Human interaction like Googles Glass [2], Pebble [3], Fitbit One [4], heart beat monitor, smartphone, smart shirt etc, show the importance and opens new ways of research and application for IT and media development. Different companies are coming to the market at different angles like wearable as smartphones, pairing with Bluetooth, and applications.

Wearable technologies use sensors that generate sensory data which can be automatically detected, collected, categorized and analyzed. Sensory data can be associated with new datum to learn from the environment. In health care, sensory data from wearable as well as smartphone sensors is used to generate recommendations, monitor physical health activities, generate real-time alerts, and motivate the users for a quick and on time preparation[5]. Sensors are also used at large scale in buildings, institutions, and bridges to monitor their conditions humidity, temperature, heat dissipation and maintenance problems. Sensory data is collected and then based on historical analysis and learning models, alerts are generated to cater pre-cautions, before any damage or collapse [6]. In this paper a system is developed which acquires the data collected by the wearable devices and exploit them according to the user requirements and needs. An adaptive analysis model is created where user can define his requirements and data will be extracted according to those demands and presented in a way to enable the user to make decisions. The data will be stored in Big Data repository which will accommodate the data deluge generated by wearable devices. This will ensure that through this approach, analysis of huge dataset is done. We are using hadoop mapreduce [7][8] as our big data technology. The remainder of the paper is organized as follows. Section 2 briefly reviews related work, section 3 proposes a framework for a big data analysis model for wearable devices. Section 4 describes the experimental setup and section 5 is conclusion and future work.

2   Related Work

One of key differences between wearable devices and conventional devices is that the human and the devices are intertwined with each other which give a huge advantage in contextual situations. Wearable computing is leading towards personalized Big Data and is a basis for new platform. All the sensors in either of the forms are collecting lot of data, low latency analytics and enabling data visualization. The foundation of personalized big data is predictive search and it is entering a new stream. Major big companies like Apple, Google and Samsung are working on predictive search applications [9]. Even the startups and medium level companies are starting to show huge interest as the consumers are highly interested in these gadgets.

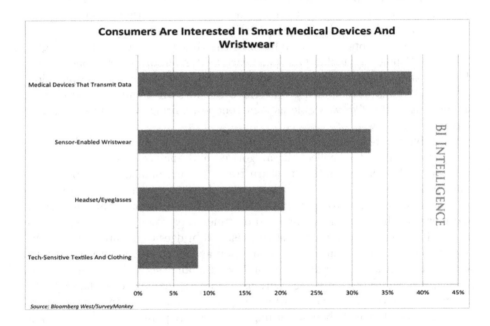

Fig. 1. Key Wearable Devices

Figure 1 [10] above shows the consumer interest in different kind of wearable devices. Medical wearable devices can play a big part in health monitoring and improvement. The most popular wearable device is the wrist wear and the headset/eyeglasses. It has been mentioned in [11] that huge costs is incurred due to underutilized data , so there is a strong need to exploit the data for user personalization. A more data driven approach is needed to properly use the data generated by the wearable devices. It has been emphasized in [12] that knowledge driven approach is also needed for real time continuous activity recognition in a multisensory environment. Data driven decision making can be effectively achieved by big data technology. Data driven decision making is referred as the practice of making decision based on the analysis of data rather than educated guess work and intuition[13]. With this analysis of data one other thing which is of paramount importance is the user's personal approach and providing him with right kind of information. For this there must be customized user based configurations[14].

3   Proposed Framework

Our focus is around the maintenance of the personalized knowledge base of the users and give recommendation based on the data transferred to the big data repository. Usually the main focus is to create a tool that generates personalized knowledge base but today it changes frequently due to different data gathering sources. We extract knowledge from big data and using expert system techniques to create and inquire heuristic knowledge of user and maintain/update this knowledge regularly and incrementally. The proposed system has three main components i.e. the data acquisition and data management, personalized adaptive analysis and personalized adaptive service layer as shown in figure 2. The details are below

3.1   Data Acquisition and Management

Data Acquisition. The data acquisition passes the raw data to data transformation component. The data will be gathered through the android app and then connected to the cloud. The data acquisition takes input from the physical sensors which are attached to different wearable devices like accelerometer, GPS, light etc. The data is passed in an archived from the android application and sent to the data acquisition component.

Data Transformation. The input is the raw data gathered in the data acquisition component. The data transformation layer takes the raw data and partially structure with respect to sensor categorization in a csv or text files. The streaming data is archived so that fast and light communication can be done between the cloud and the wearable device app.

Data Validation. The input is the partial structured data which is passed by the transformation component. The output is to crosscheck the sensor data and remove the redundancies from it. It is then stored in the Hadoop distributed file system. Data validation is done through finding holes in the continuous data timestamps and where the data is not consistent. In this way data will be aligned for training.

3.2   Personalized Adaptive Analysis

The adaptive analysis model will be adaptive and dynamic depending on the user needs and configuration.

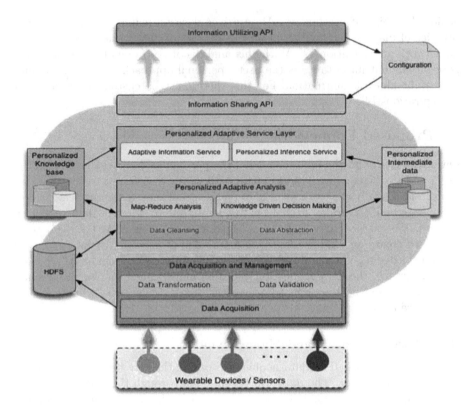

Fig. 2. Proposed Architecture

Data Abstraction. The data abstraction selects user attributes from the configuration file which is processed further. The input of the data is partially structured data that is stored in the HDFS. The data abstraction selects user attributes from the configuration file which is be processed further. The configuration file is populated by the user through the information utilizing API

Data Cleansing. The data cleansing module check the user attributes, their values and structure the schema to store in the personalized intermediate database. The user attributes are passed from data abstraction. The personalized intermediate database is being used to give a real time response to the information utilizing APIs. Querying the HDFS and bringing the relevant data takes a lot of time so an intermediate database is introduced.

Mapreduce Analysis. Hadoop is a cloud computing platform and an open source implementation of MapReduce programming model [8]. In a MapReduce job there are three phases i.e. map, copy and reduce. The structured schema is passed on the mapreduce analysis component as well as the raw logs stored in HDFS. The output is be the historical values of the user attributes and produce training data for the decision making. The mapreduce analysis is an intermediate step to populate the personalized knowledge base. The SQL like queries are used for retrieving the data from the HDFS through Apache PIG[15].

Knowledge Driven Decision Making. This module populate personalized knowledge base through trained parameters which will assist user in decision making. The MapReduce analysis with give the training data to knowledge driven decision making. The output is personalized knowledge base through trained parameters. We are using two machine learning techniques for this framework i.e. nave Bayesian and decision trees.

3.3 Personalized Adaptive Service Layer

Adaptive Information Service. The adaptive information service will use intermediate data to expose user infographics to the user. This will assist user in monitoring his activities in an efficient manner. This information is structured from the raw data acquired and shows statistics in different visualized cues.

Personalized Inference Service. Personalized inference service will use personalized knowledge base to get the facts populated by the knowledge driven decision making and give recommendations to the user. These recommendations will vary from user to user based on the activities and the wearable device.

4 Experimental Setup

We are using two server machines each with 16 GB ram and 8 cores. We installed four virtual machines (VMs) on server 1 and 2 VMs on server two. We are using an android application in the wearable device which archives the data and pass the data through a web service. This data is stored in Hadoop distributed file system. We access the data through Apache Pig scripts. The mapreduce programs are written in java and run on 6 VM hadoop cluster. We populate the intermediate database through these scripts and the adaptive knowledge base through mapreduce programs. There are two types of mapreduce implementation. One is for the analysis and one is the machine learning implementation in which decision making module is trained and tested.

5 Conclusions

Wearable data provides a unique opportunity because the user and the devices have a more intimate connection due to which we can get more relevant and contextual information. The data in the next few years is going to balloon and it is going to be a challenge to analyze and keep an updated knowledge base.

Personalized Big Data is the next wave and associating different data sources will be key to personalization. All of the devices are going to collect a lot of data and present a lot of data in real-time which is an interesting use case for analytics. One of the Key technologies is mapreduce and its open source solution Hadoop. We have proposed a framework to give a real time solution to this problem and at the same time update the knowledge base in a smooth and efficient manner.

Acknowledgments. This research was supported by the MSIP (Ministry of Science, ICT&Future Planning), Korea, under the ITRC(Information Technology Research Center) support program supervised by the NIPA(National IT Industry Promotion Agency) (NIPA-2014-(H0301-13-2001)) This work was supported by the National Research Foundation of Korea (NRF) grant funded by the Korea government (MSIP) (No. 2013-067321).

References

1. wearablesdevcon (2014), http://www.wearablesdevcon.com/article1.aspx
2. Google (2014), http://www.google.com/glass/start/
3. Pebble (2014), http://en.wikipedia.org/wiki/pebble_(watch)
4. Fitbit (2014), http://www.fitbit.com/kr/one
5. Pantelopoulos, A., Bourbakis, N.G.: A survey on wearable sensor-based systems for health monitoring and prognosis. IEEE Transactions on Systems, Man, and Cybernetics, Part C: Applications and Reviews 40, 1–12 (2010)
6. Lorincz, K., Malan, D.J., Fulford-Jones, T.R., Nawoj, A., Clavel, A., Shnayder, V., Mainland, G., Welsh, M., Moulton, S.: Sensor networks for emergency response: challenges and opportunities. IEEE Pervasive Computing 3, 16–23 (2004)
7. Dean, J., Ghemawat, S.: Mapreduce: simplified data processing on large clusters. Communications of the ACM 51, 107–113 (2008)
8. Bhandarkar, M.: Mapreduce programming with apache hadoop. In: 2010 IEEE International Symposium on Parallel & Distributed Processing (IPDPS), p. 1. IEEE (2010)
9. Marrs, M.: (2013), http://www.wordstream.com/blog/ws/2013/06/24/predictive-search
10. Kalakota, R.: (2013), http://practicalanalytics.wordpress.com/2013/08/12/predictive-search-wearable-computing/
11. Chawla, N.V., Davis, D.A.: Bringing big data to personalized healthcare: A patient-centered framework. Journal of General Internal Medicine 28, 660–665 (2013)
12. Chen, L., Nugent, C.D., Wang, H.: A knowledge-driven approach to activity recognition in smart homes. IEEE Transactions on Knowledge and Data Engineering 24, 961–974 (2012)
13. Provost, F., Fawcett, T.: Data science and its relationship to big data and data-driven decision making. Big Data 1, 51–59 (2013)
14. Brule, M.R., et al.: Big data in exploration and production: Real-time adaptive analytics and data-flow architecture. In: SPE Digital Energy Conference, Society of Petroleum Engineers (2013)
15. Olston, C., Reed, B., Srivastava, U., Kumar, R., Tomkins, A.: Pig latin: a not-so-foreign language for data processing. In: Proceedings of the 2008 ACM SIGMOD International Conference on Management of Data, pp. 1099–1110. ACM (2008)

A Web Based Cardiovascular Disease Detection System

Hussam Alshraideh[1], Mwaffaq Otoom[2], Aseel Al-Araida[1],
Haneen Bawaneh[1], and José Bravo[3]

[1] Jordan University of Science and Technology, Jordan
[2] Yarmouk University, Jordan
[3] Castilla-La Mancha University, Spain

Abstract. Nowadays, Cardiovascular Disease (CVD) is one of the most catastrophic and life threatening common health issues. Early detection of CVD is one of the most important solutions to reduce its devastating effects on health. In this paper, an efficient detection algorithm is identified. The algorithm uses patient demographic data as inputs, along with several ECG signal features extracted automatically through signal processing techniques. Cross-validation results show a 98.29% accuracy for the algorithm. The algorithm is also integrated into a web based system that can be used at anytime by patients to check their heart health status. At one end of the system is the ECG sensor attached to the patient's body, while at the other end is the detection algorithm. Communication between the two ends is done through an Android application.

Keywords: Cardiovascular, Classification, Electrocardiography, WEKA.

1   Introduction

Data mining is the process of drawing out useful information from huge datasets. A survey in 2011 showed that consumer analytics ranked the first field where the data mining is applied with 25%, followed by banking and health-care fields by 18.9% and 16.7%, respectively [3]. Studies indicate that bio-informatics is the second most important field of data mining applications [4]. Speculations suggest that data mining is a promising area in engineering applications, medical, and health-care fields.

In this paper, data mining techniques are used in this regard to build an electrocardiogram (ECG) classifier to detect individuals suffering from heart arrhythmias using 18 attributes including personal information, in addition to a number of ECG signal parameters extracted by signal processing techniques.

Recent studies show that Cardiovascular Disease (CVD) is one of the most common health issues these days. World Health Organization (WHO) reveals that 17 million people die from CVD every year [6], where nearly 7.3 million die due to coronary heart disease and 6.2 million due to strokes [7]. For this reason, WHO works on reducing, controlling, and preventing CVD.

R. Hervás et al. (Eds.): UCAmI 2014, LNCS 8867, pp. 243–250, 2014.
© Springer International Publishing Switzerland 2014

Many studies undertake this problem, suggesting a number of actions for reducing this dangerous health problem, where the early diagnosis of CVD is suggested as one of the most important solutions for preventing CVD to be the main reason of death, such that early diagnosis achieves effective treatment by enhancing the therapeutic effectiveness. One of the most important non-invasive methods for detecting different cardiac problems is ECG analysis.

ECG signal is the representation of the electrical activity of the four chambers of the heart it is a series of P wave, QRS complex, and T wave, as shown in Figure 1. P wave is small, positive and round indicating atria depolarization. PR interval begins at the beginning of P wave and ends at the beginning of QRS complex. It represents the time during which a depolarization wave travels from the atria to the ventricles.

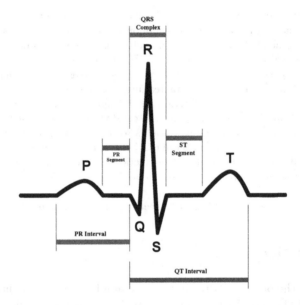

Fig. 1. Normal ECG signal [8]

QRS interval indicates ventricular depolarization and atria repolarization. It contains three deflections: the first negative deflection in this wave is Q wave, R wave is the first positive deflection, and the S wave is the first negative deflection after R wave.

The distance between S wave and the beginning of T wave is ST segment. It represents the time between ventricular depolarization and the beginning of repolarization. The T wave is round and positive it indicates ventricular repolarization. Total ventricular activity is represented by QT interval, and is measured from the beginning of QRS to the end of T wave [9].

When any cardiac abnormality exists, a deviation of ECG signal parameters from their normal values appears. This point is exploited by the researchers where the majority of CVD prediction searches were directed to the analysis of ECG to detect individuals suffering from CVD without any surgical intervention, and in particular to the automated analysis of ECG signal, to reduce the time required for human interpretation of ECG recordings and to increase the accuracy of the results.

The objective of this research is to apply data mining techniques in building a classifier that can detect individuals suffering from heart arrhythmias. CVD classifier was implemented in WEKA [5] using a dataset contains 279 attributes for 452 objects distributed among 12 types of heart arrhythmias. Studying these types of arrhythmias shows that only 18 attributes are sufficient to detect them.

The remaining of the paper is organized as follows. In section 2, a literature review of related issues is provided. A description of the data used for building the model is given in section 3. Model building results are shown in section 4. The developed web-based system architecture is described in section 5. Finally, conclusions and future work recommendations are provided in section 6.

2   Literature Review

Data mining algorithms used in discovering the patterns among ECG signal parameters extracted by signal processing techniques are widely used in the past few decades. Literature review concerning data mining usage in ECG analysis shows that several methods have been varied between using classification and clustering techniques in ECG arrhythmias detection. Majority of those researches were provided by the datasets of MIT-BIH database from Physionet [10], and thus the data mining techniques were combined with signal processing techniques that are used for ECG features' extraction, which is considered the core of classifiers construction.

Artificial Neural Networks (ANNs) are the most common classifiers that are used in cardiac problems detection. In 2011, automated classifier based on Neural Network was proposed by Vishwa et al. [11] using multi channels ECG recordings to distinguish normal from abnormal ECG signals, where it achieved 96.77% [11] . The same accuracy was achieved by Parsad et al. [12]. They improved a classifier using Neural Network to distinguish normal ECG signals from 12 different cardiac arrhythmias. Support Vector Machine (SVM) is also used in this regard. Melgani et al. used SVM to build an arrhythmia detector based on heart beats with 89.72% accuracy [13]. Osowski et al. confirmed the reliability of SVM in building a classifier that could detect 13 types of cardiac arrhythmias in [14]. Furthermore, 93% accuracy was achieved by Nasiri et al. [15] when they improved a classifier for detecting four types of cardiac problems using SVM. Studying the use of clustering techniques in cardiac arrhythmias detection showed that fuzzy clustering was widely used recently, in particular, its integration with Neural Network where this combination achieves almost 99% accuracy [16]. The same combination is used by Ozbay et al. to classify ten types of cardiac problems [17].

3   Data

Cardiac arrhythmia data used in this research was obtained from the website of the University of California at Irvine (UCI) [18]. The dataset contains 279 attributes for 452 instances distributed among 16 types of arrhythmia classes. The dataset was collected in January of 1998. Table 1 shows the 16 types of classes recorded in the dataset and the number of instances for each type. Referring to Table 1, it is noticed that some of the classes have very small number of objects. Such as supraventricular premature contraction that has only two objects, ventricular premature contraction with only three objects, left ventricular hypertrophy with four objects, and only five objects belong to atrial fibrillation. For simplification purposes, those arrhythmias are added to the "others" class. Classes with zero objects were excluded. Below we give a brief description of these types of arrhythmias:

- Normal Sinus Rhythm (NSR): NSR consists of P wave, QRS wave and T wave. A typical normal ECG is shown in Figure 2.

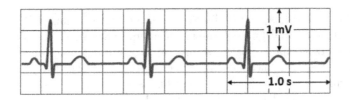

Fig. 2. A typical normal ECG signal [2]

- Sinus Tachycardia: during Tachycardia, the heart beats very rapidly due to the increase in Sinoatrial (SA) node discharge. A noticeable increase in the heart rate is the main indication of Tachycardia.
- Sinus Bradycardia (SB): SB results from slowing the discharge of SA node, reflected as a decrease in the heart rate.
- Bundle Branch Block (BBB): late depolarization of either the left or right ventricles leads to BBB disease, creating a notched QRS complex and a significant widening in QRS interval.
- Myocardial Ischemia and Myocardial Infarction: Myocardial ischemia is a damage in the myocardium layer of the heart because of a partial or a complete blockage of the heart arteries, leading to decreased blood flow and consequently lack in oxygen supply to the heart tissue. It is represented by ST segment elevation or depression. Myocardial infarction is a death in the myocardium layer and represented by abnormal Q wave.
- Atrial Fibrillation (AF): AF is due to the disorganized atrial contractions, where the electrical discharge becomes rapid, erratic and produced from multiple atrial regions. P wave in ECG signal disappears, which represents the electrical activity of the atriums.

- Premature Ventricular Contraction (PVC): it is also known as ventricular premature beat, where the heart beat is initiated by purkinje fiber in the ventricles instead of SA node. The abnormal electrical activity allows PVC to be easily distinguished in the ECG signal. Typical PVC in the ECG signal is shown in Figure 3.

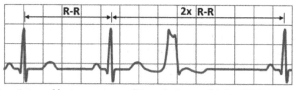

Time interval between normal R peaks is a multiple of R-R interval

Fig. 3. A typical Premature Ventricular Contraction arrhythmia in the ECG signal [2]

Through a careful review of relevant literature, it was found that the considered arrhythmia indicators are: heart rate, QRS interval, P-R interval, P amplitude, Q amplitude, T amplitude, R amplitude, Q width, R width and ST segment elevation and depression. All those attributes are collected in the chosen dataset except the ST segment amplitude, the indicator of myocardial ischemia, and thus, it is expected that the accuracy will be slightly affected by the absence of this attribute. Only attributes mentioned above are taken into consideration in addition to those particular to the patient, including age, gender, weight and height in order to reveal the impact of these demographic variables on the heart status.

4   Results

A cardiac arrhythmia dataset with 18 attributes, 410 objects (42 objects were excluded due to inconsistent data issues) and nine types of classes are used to build a CVD classifier using WEKA software. Five types of classification algorithms available in WEKA, including J48, Jrip, Kstar, ANN, and SVM were used. The SMOTE filter in WEKA was used to generate duplicates of the minority classes. Table 2 shows the achieved accuracy using ten-fold cross-validation testing.

The selected algorithms represent several categories of classification algorithms that are Decision trees, Rule-based classifiers, Bayesian classifiers, Neural Networks and Support Vector Machines. Results show that the linear classifiers (J48, Jrip, and ANN) provide the highest classification accuracy while non-linear classifiers such as SVM has poor performance. NaiveBayes classifier does not provide good classification accuracy since it does not consider dependencies among the attributes.

Table 1. Types of arrhythmias

Class	Number of instances
Normal	245
Ischemic changes	44
Old Anterior Myocardial Infarction	15
Old Inferior Myocardial Infarction	15
Sinus tachycardy	13
Sinus bradycardy	25
Ventricular Premature Contraction	3
Supraventricular Premature Contraction	2
Left bundle branch block	9
Right bundle branch block	50
First degree AtrioVentricular block	0
Second degree AtrioVentricular block	0
Third degree AtrioVentricular block	0
Left ventricule hypertrophy	4
Atrial Fibrillation or Flutter	5
Others	22

Table 2. Accuracy results as obtained throgh 10-fold cross validation

Classifier	Accuracy (%)
J48	98.2923
Jrip	97.9269
NaiveBayes	75.0615
ANN	93.8731
SVM	76.976

5 System Architecture

One main contribution of this work is the integration of the CVD detection algorithm into the cloud, where the infrastructure provided by the cloud is utilized to deal with such timely critical systems. To do so, we developed a system that integrates the ECG sensor with the CVD detection algorithm, the J48, hosted on a remote server using an Android application connected to the web.

The system consists of two main components; client and server. Figure 4 shows the overall structure of our system. The client component is the Android application which can also be programmed as Windows phone application that takes ECG signal wirelessly from the ECG sensor attached to the human body. The sensor was obtained from ABI-med [1]. The Android application receives the ECG signal and saves it as a time series of voltage magnitudes for five minutes. The application then sends the saved data via a web service method, sendECG(), to the server component. The server component hosts our CVD detection algorithm which takes the ECG signal as an input and identifies the class of the CVD, if any. The server then sends the result to the Android application

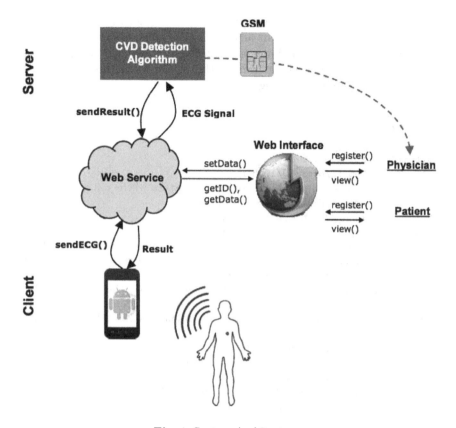

Fig. 4. System Architecture

via a web service method, `sendResult()`. If a CVD was identified, the server also sends an SMS alert to the registered physician, who can also view the ECG history of his patient through a web interface.

6   Conclusion and Future Work

The contribution of this paper is two-fold. First, a CVD classifier was identified by running huge cardiac arrhythmia datasets on several classification algorithms provided by the WEKA software. Using cross-validation, J48 classifier was found to have the best performance in terms of prediction accuracy.

An Android application was developed, as a contribution, to enable patients checking their heart health status at anytime by identifying the different cardiac arrhythmia types. The application connects remotely with the detection algorithm, in this case the J48, via web service methods. Identification results are shared with physicians via web, as well as SMS, and are saved online in the records of the patient.

While J48 has shown very high prediction accuracy, for future work, we plan to extend the work to develop an algorithm that enhances the prediction accuracy more, where more attributes is identified and included. We plan also to use same health status checking framework, developed in this paper, for the Electroencephalography (EEG) signals.

References

1. http://www.abi-med.com/
2. http://www.bem.fi/book/19/19.htm
3. Data Mining Community's Top Resource, "Industries where you applied Analytics/Data Mining in 2011". Website:
   http://www.kdnuggets.com/polls/2011/
   industries-applied-anaytics-data-mining
4. Kumar, D., Bhardwaj, D.: Rise of Data Mining: Current and Future Application Areas. IJCSI International Journal of Computer Science Issues 8 (September 2011)
5. http://www.cs.waikato.ac.nz/ml/weka/
6. Global status report on noncommunicable 20iseases 2010. Geneva, World Health Organization (2011)
7. Global atlas on cardiovascular disease prevention and control. Geneva, World Health Organization (2011)
8. http://gpete-neil.blogspot.com/2011/02/
   simulating-complex-ecg-patterns-with.html
9. Jones, S.A.: ECG Notes Interpretation and Management Guide (2005)
10. PhysioBank Archive Index, Physionet, Cambridge. Website:
    http://www.physionet.org/physiobank/database
11. Vishwa, A., et al.: Classification of arrhythmic ECG data using machine learning techniques, pp. 67–70 (2011)
12. Prasad, G.K., Sahambi, J.S.: Classification of ECG arrhythmias using multi-resolution analysis and neural networks, vol. 1. IEEE (2003)
13. Melgani, F., Bazi, Y.: Classification of electrocardiogram signals with support vector machines and particle swarm optimization, pp. 667–677. IEEE (2008)
14. Osowski, S., Hoai, L.T., Markiewicz, T.: Support vector machine-based expert system for reliable heartbeat recognition, pp. 582–589. IEEE (2004)
15. Nasiri, J.A., Naghibzadeh, M., Sadoghi Yazdi, H., Naghibzadeh, B.: ECG Arrhythmia Classification with Support Vector Machines and Genetic Algorithm, pp. 187–192. IEEE (2009)
16. Ceylan, R., Ozbay, Y., Karlik, B.: A novel approach for classification of ECG arrhythmias: Type-2 fuzzy clustering neural network. Expert Systems with Applications 36(3), 6721–6726 (2009)
17. Ozbay, Y., Ceylan, R., Karlik, B.: A fuzzy clustering neural network architecture for classification of ECG arrhythmias. Computers in Biology and Medicine 36(4), 376–388 (2006)
18. UCI Machine Learning Repository. Website:
    http://archive.ics.uci.edu/ml/datasets/Arrhythmia

A Sensor-Based Method
for Occupational Heat Stress Estimation

Pablo Pancardo[1], Francisco D. Acosta Escalante[1],
José Adán Hernández-Nolasco[1], Miguel A. Wister[1], and Diego López-de-Ipiña[2]

[1] Juarez Autonomous University of Tabasco, Cunduacan, Tabasco, Mexico
[2] DeustoTech, Deusto University, Bilbao, Basque Country, Spain
{pablo.pancardo,francisco.acosta,adan.hernandez,miguel.wister}@ujat.mx,
dipina@deusto.es

Abstract. Occupational Heat Stress (OHS) happens when a worker is physically active in hot environments. OHS can produce a strain on the body which leads to discomfort and eventually to heat illness and even death. Related ISO standards contain methods to estimate OHS and to ensure the safety and health of workers, but, they are subjective, impersonal, performed a posteriori, and even invasive. We hypothesize that a real time automated method is more effective and objective estimating OHS if it fuses data from environmental sensors, unobtrusive physiological body sensors, and takes into account the user profile. We propose a personalized method based on ergonomic calculations to offer a solution. We found that our method allows estimating the personalized effort levels, energy expenditure and drudgery of work for each worker and enables to take informed decisions to control OHS. We think that ISO standards could consider technological advances to propose real-time personalized methods.

Keywords: Personalized method, occupational heat stress, ISO, sensor.

1 Introduction

Heat stress is a health condition for people doing physical efforts in hot environments without enough resting periods. The heat stress level values may go from discomfort until heat stroke, or even death. Standard methods proposed by ISO estimate occupational heat stress based on environment parameters and level of physical activity of workers; metabolic rate estimation; or even invasive physiological measurements of the human body. Proposed methods are generic (based on standard characteristics of people and common trades) and subjective, since they are supported by findings obtained from visual observation or the results from questionnaires answered by workers about their daily activities. Although there are very precise objective methods based on physiological measurements, these studies are based on invasive laboratory tests where workers are performing programmed activities, extracting them from their natural workspace and conditions.

R. Hervás et al. (Eds.): UCAmI 2014, LNCS 8867, pp. 251–258, 2014.
© Springer International Publishing Switzerland 2014

These methods do not allow knowing objectively the heat stress level to which each specific worker is exposed at every moment of their workday. It is necessary to devise a method to automatically monitor the heat stress without requiring human supervision or artificial testing in a laboratory. This method should operate in the workers natural environment whilst they perform their daily work activities. This paper proposes an automated simple method for workers heat stress estimation, customizable to the user profile and intensity of their physical activity and in real-time. It is based on non-intrusive technology, taking into account environment values from the workplace. Thus, the heat stress condition can be known immediately for each specific worker. In our opinion, the proposed method represents a better balance between the social, economic and productive interest of enterprises to ensure the work quality and welfare of their workers. The rest of the paper is organized as follows. In Section 2, the related work is given. Heat stress estimation methods in accordance to ISO are explained in Section 3. In Section 4, the proposed method is presented. The implementation prototype is shown in Section 5. Our conclusions and future works are drawn in Section 6.

2   Related Work

Related works can be divided into two groups. The first one is focused on activities recognition, specific movements detection or energy expenditure estimation. In [1] an accelerometer is used to obtain information that indicates whether all work activities are being performed in the right way. Other studies [2,3], show how to detect unusual movements or postures that could damage the health of workers; in [4] they use a wearable physiological status monitor in order to analyze relationships that might exist between physical stress and productivity. In [5] the goal is the activity classification and energy consumption estimation but based on the number of METs (Metabolic Equivalent Tasks) according to the compendium of activities [6], therefore does not apply to any free activity undertaken. The second group is aimed to estimate heat stress in workers, where most of the works are only based on environmental parameters [7,8], or to predict short-term estimations making use of machine learning [9]. The reviewed studies do not follow our approach. This proposal integrates four essential aspects to more accurately determine the Heath Stress Level (HSL), including: a real-time, data from environmental sensors, physiological measures, and user profile.

3   Standards for Heat Stress

Steps must be taken to ensure that workers are protected from any illness, disease or injury due to their employment activities, as established in the principles of the International Labour Organization (ILO) a specialized agency of the United Nations. ILO estimates that 160 million people are suffering from work-related diseases. That is why ILO recommends the introduction of a preventive safety and health culture, the promotion and development of relevant instruments, and technical assistance; thus contributing to the health and well-being of workers and strengthening the economic competitiveness of companies [10]. Physical risk of heat stress arises when people work in hot environments, performing physical activities with significant efforts. The International Standards Organization (ISO) has standards containing methods to estimate and control OHS. They are used as basis for local standards in many countries and they are applied to estimate the OHS. ISO 7243 standard takes into account environmental parameters (temperature, relative humidity and wind velocity) and workers physical activity level. This includes the easiest method to calculate heat stress and it recommends the percentage of resting time per hour in accordance to obtained values. ISO 7933 uses environmental parameters and worker's metabolic rate estimation, which is convenient because stress is a result of external and internal factors. ISO 9886 considers physiological measurements of the human body to estimate the response to the work. This standard provides greater accuracy because its results are obtained in specialized laboratories. We show in Table 1 some disadvantages for each ISO standard.

Table 1. Related ISO standards disadvantages

Standard	Disadvantages
ISO 7243	Some studies conclude that the application of its results is too cautious. Measurements do not consider variations in the work rate within a work session. Work intensity has to be established as light, moderate or heavy during all the time. Employs only a standard static worker profile.
ISO 7933	It contains two types of methods to estimate the metabolic consumption. For the first type tables are used and in the second, physiological measurements. Both types use values from a standard user (male, 1.8 mts. height, 70 kg. weight, etc.), so that is not a custom method. The measurements are not in real time.
ISO 9886	The method requires several physiological measurements, for example, body temperature is one of the input data where a valid source is one of the following: esophageal, rectal, gastrointestinal, oral, eardrum, the auditory canal and urine. This is very invasive and requires taking measurements in a laboratory.

The ISO standards are independent and are applied commonly in an exclusive way. In order to do something more precise we propose a solution that integrates the benefits of each standard and contributes to compliance. None of the methods proposed by ISO meets the objectives being personalized, in real-time, and unobtrusive. An important step is to know at the moment how much energy a worker has spent as a result of continuous time doing physical efforts.

Technological advances as small accelerometers and devices to measure heart rate make possible an effective real time solution. Some related works have already demonstrated that fusing sensor data is a good option to estimate energy expenditure [11]. In our case it is very convenient because this implies going to an objective effective method. The proposal applies to scenarios that are naturally hot (tropical areas) or artificial (ovens, asphalt work).

4   Heat Stress Method Design

The proposal method to determine the HSL is illustrated in Fig. 1. To asses it, a test device to determine the movement intensity through acceleration, and thus used to classify the effort into light, moderate and exhaustive has been used. The device selected was a Samsung Galaxy S4, Android 4.2.2 (Jelly Bean) Operative System; Octa core chipset; 1.6 GHz Quad + 1.2 GHz Quad CPU; accelerometer, temperature and humidity sensors. The application to estimate physical effort was developed with Java 6.0 language using the ADT tool v22.3.0-887826. We also used a Zephyr Wireless Bluetooth Heart Rate Monitor for Android & Windows Phone 8.

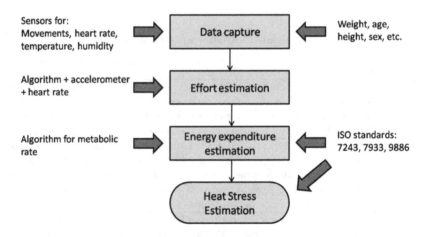

Fig. 1. Proposed automate method

1. **Data Capture**
   In this step environmental parameters (temperature and relative humidity) were captured. ISO 7243 establishes that we should use a Wet Bulb Globe Thermometer (WBGT); however, we used smart phone temperature and humidity sensors because of the portability and easy of data reading. In order to obtain personalized values we introduced subjects characteristics (age, sex, weight, and height) to feed the estimation algorithms. Heart rate was measured after six minutes of resting and after a spring running of 100 meters to obtain the personal minimum and maximum heart rate values.
2. **Physical Effort Estimation**
   Acceleration level and heart rate have a correlation with effort intensity, so, a smart phone was attached to a user arm using a grid. Values from axis

X, Y, Z were saved each 200 milliseconds and each record was labeled as Light, Moderate or Vigorous. If no movements were detected in a moment, the record was labeled as Stable. Sensor data filtering was done using a low-pass technique to attenuate the effect of frequencies from small involuntary movement. We obtained workers drudgery coefficient (light, moderate and vigorous) from heart rate data, in accordance to Frimat criteria [12].

3. **Energy Expenditure Estimation**
   In order to improve the results in the previous step we consider the individual energy expenditure estimation. We first the estimate resting metabolic rate (the quantity of energy expenditure necessary to maintain vital functionality) in accordance to Harris-Benedict equation using sex, age, weight and height. Later we consider effort estimation sampled in step 2. This allowed us to obtain an effective energy expenditure estimation considering effort level in each moment during work day.

4. **Heat Stress Estimation**
   In order to estimate OHS we used -additionally to values obtained in previous steps, an approximation formula WBGTA by the Australian Bureau of Meteorology [13] where freely exposed thermometers are used to measure the temperature of the air.

5   Implementation Prototype

Workload level (Light, Moderate or Vigorous) was calculated from effort level on step 2, from accelerometer values and heart rate, and energy expenditure estimated on step 3. We used Table 2 (from ISO 7243) as a reference to determine when a worker has heat stress.

Table 2. $WBGT_A$ limit temperatures ($^\circ$C) values in accordance to Workload

Work-rest regimen	Workload		
	Light	Moderate	Vigorous
Continuous work	30.0	26.7	25.0
75% work + 25% rest; each hour	30.6	28.0	25.9
50% work + 50% rest; each hour	31.4	29.4	27.9
25% work + 75% rest; each hour	32.2	31.1	30.0

Personal estimation of workload is going to be the difference between standard values from Table 2 and personalized heat stress estimation. For example, two workers with the same environmental conditions doing the same physical activities may differ in workload estimation, conducing to different results in OHS estimation. We show (see Fig. 2) two OHS Android application screenshots with environmental and user personal data. We can see that two workers with the same environment and activities conditions have different results (workload) of OHS.

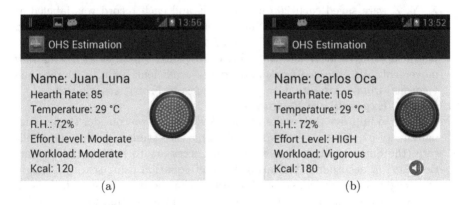

Fig. 2. a) User working without OHS; b) User working with OHS

On the left hand side of Fig. 3 how sensors were ported by a user is illustrated. On the right hand side, a graph of the intensities of efforts during the measurement period is shown.

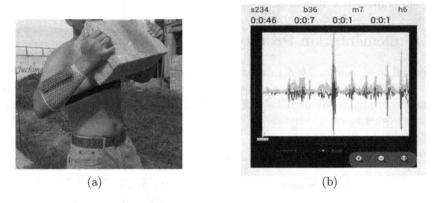

Fig. 3. a) User working; b) Record activity

Apart from measuring HSL the devised solution also includes reactivity features, since it alerts the user when HSL is over passed and the worker supervisor in case the recommended HSL is exceeded for a period ignoring the systems recommendations. We have made a basic evaluation of the overall system, but a complete evaluation is in course.

6   Conclusions and Future Works

As we established in our hypothesis, an automated method for estimating heat stress is more effective and less invasive than ISO methods, if it uses unobtrusive sensor technology to capture in real time: user profile, environmental parameters and effort intensity. We found that our simple method can offer to users a clear vision to interpret energy expenditure and arduousness index in order to estimate occupational heat stress. The advantages of sensor technology for activity recognition and to estimate energy expenditure in workplaces have been validated by some authors [5,14]. Our method has important advantages. For instance, it is easy to implement and employs personalized real time measures instead of tables values created from a standard person. An important limitation of this project is that we do not consider scenarios where workers have to carry heavy objects or to climb stairs, which increases physical effort. In fact, for the moment it is oriented to jobs where workers employ hands to work. Another limitation is about how to capture special considerations (sick or pregnant workers) into method. Our target population is common adults, therefore, people with special characteristics like obese or with high muscle mass are not considered. This study highlights the importance that ISO standards could include technological devices to build personalized methods. The present study demonstrates that our proposed Heat Stress Estimation grounded on sensor data fusion represents an opportunity to estimate occupational heat stress more effectively, in real-time and in a personalized manner, when compared to ISO standards. Our lab-based experiments have shown that our method is effective to give users enough data to take decisions about establishing a work-resting time program in accordance to heat stress estimation or drudgery of work. Our solution is a good example about how off-the-shelf mobile, personal health and sport monitoring devices sensibly combined can give place to a new generation of non-intrusive effective mechanisms to monitor health variables, in this case heat stress level. It is a good example on how context-awareness, personal sensing and mobile computing can enable Ambient Assisted Working. Further work will consider recent wristband that are less obtrusive than chest band and contain sensors as skin temperature and sweating rate that would offers new opportunities. It would be interesting to log data during time to analyze correlations with future ailments or diseases. Even, to build a health issues prevention system .

References

1. Koskimaki, H., Huikari, V.: Activity recognition using a wrist-worn inertial measurement unit: A case study for industrial assembly lines. In: MED 2009 (2009)
2. Migliaccio, G., Teizer, J., Cheng, T., Gatti, U.: Automatic Identification of Unsafe Bending Behavior of Construction Workers Using Real-Time Location Sensing and Physiological Status Monitoring. In: Proceedings of Construction Research Congress 2012, pp. 633–642 (2012)
3. Senyurek, L., Hocaoglu, K., Sezer, B., Urhan, O.: Monitoring workers through wearable transceivers for improving work safety. In: 2011 IEEE 7th Int. Symp. Intell. Signal Processing, pp. 1–3 (2011)
4. Gatti, U., Migliaccio, G., Bogus, S., Schneider, S.: Using Wearable Physiological Status Monitors for Analyzing the Physical Strain-Productivity Relationship for Construction Tasks. Bridges 10 (2014)
5. Cho, J., Kim, J., Kim, T.: Smart Phone-based Human Activity Classification and Energy Expenditure Generation in Building Environments, Seoul, Korea (2012)

6. Ainsworth, B.E., Haskell, W.L., Whitt, M.C., Irwin, M.L.: Compendium of Physical Activities: an update of activity codes and MET intensities. Medicine & Science in Sports & Exercise (2000)
7. Callejon-Ferre, A.: Improving the climate safety of workers in Almería-type greenhouses in Spain by predicting the periods when they are most likely to suffer thermal stress. Applied Ergonomy (2011)
8. Marucci, A., Pagniello, B., Monarca, D., Colantoni, A., Biondi, P., Cecchini, M., et al.: The heat stress for workers during vegetable grafting in greenhouses. In: International Conference RAGUSA SHWA 2012, pp. 321–328 (2008, 2012)
9. Rednic, R., Kemp, J., Gaura, E., Brusey, J.: Networked Body Sensing: Enabling real-time decisions in health and defence applications. In: ICACSIS 2011 (2011)
10. Reinert, D., Flaspöler, E., Hauke, A.: Identification of emerging occupational safety and health risks. Safety Science Monitoring 3 (2007)
11. Curone, D., Secco, E.L., Tognetti, A., Magenes, G.: An Activity Classifier based on Heart Rate and Accelerometer Data Fusion. International Journal of Bioelectromagnetism 15(1), 7–12 (2013)
12. Frimat, P., Amphoux, M., Chamoux, A.: Interprétation et measure de la fréquence cardiaque. Revue de Médicine du Travail XV(4), 147–165 (1988)
13. American College of Sports Medicine. Prevention of thermal injuries during distance running - Position Stand. The Medical Journal of Australia 141(12-13), 876–879 (1984)
14. Tao, C., Miglaccio, G., Teizer, J., Gatti, U.: Data Fusion of Real-Time Location Sensing and Physiological Status Monitoring for Ergonomics Analysis of Construction Workers. Journal of Computing in Civil Engineering 27(3), 320–335 (2013)

Self-adaptive Service Deployment in Context-Aware Systems

Gabriel Guerrero-Contreras, José Luis Garrido,
Carlos Rodríguez-Domínguez, and Sara Balderas-Díaz

University of Granada
Software Engineering Department, E.T.S.I.I.T.
C/ Periodista Daniel Saucedo Aranda s/n, Granada, Spain
{gjguerrero,jgarrido,carlosrodriguez}@ugr.es, sarabd@correo.ugr.es

Abstract. Ubiquitous environments present a dynamic network topology which implies frequent context changes which can affect the availability of the services deployed in the system. In order to obtain the full potential that this kind of environments can provide to assist human beings, this challenge must be faced. Service replication models in combination with self-adaptive capabilities may help to improve service availability and strengthen the system. In this work, it is presented a conceptual model to support a run-time service deployment taking into consideration relevant context information, such as resource availability, network topology and service requirements.

Keywords: Context-awareness, self-adaptation, ubiquitous environments, Service Oriented Architecture (SOA).

1 Introduction

Context-awareness provides the basis to design software systems sufficiently independent to adapt to changes that occur in their context, in order to maintain or even improve the quality of user experience, without his/her explicit intervention. Providing self-adaptive capabilities to a software system is crucial in ubiquitous environments, which are characterized, among other issues, by the existence of frequent changes in the execution context.

Among the approaches to successfully address the design of software in dynamic environments, service oriented architecture and middleware technologies based on event-driven architectures can be highlighted. However, they are not sufficient to completely support a dynamic environment. For example, there are different scenarios where security forces apply protocols of action intended to support victim identification. The Mobile Forensic Workspace [6] is a support system that allow exchange information with nearby devices in order to support data sharing between forensic experts. In some scenarios, common network infrastructures may not be available, and the users that compose the working group are moving around the scene. This implies unstable connections (disconnections

R. Hervás et al. (Eds.): UCAmI 2014, LNCS 8867, pp. 259–262, 2014.
© Springer International Publishing Switzerland 2014

and network partitions) which affects to the availability of the services, compromising the consistency of the information [4] and making collaboration between the users more difficult. Consequently, complementary techniques and methods to such approaches focused on self-adaptation must be adopted at architectural software design.

Self-adaptation is a wide field of research, and several parts of the system can be affected. For instance, [8] is focused on adapting the internal functioning of the service in order to improve its performance and efficiency, and in [7] adaptable communication middleware services are provided. In this paper, a conceptual model to support the service deployment in context-awareness environments is introduced. This model allows to provide a solution to enhance the availability of the services, with an efficient resources consumption.

The rest of this paper is structured as follows. Section 2 presents related work which have tried to address the dynamic features of these environments; Section 3 proposes a conceptual model to support the service deployment in context-awareness environments; and finally, conclusions and future work are summarized in Section 4.

2   Related Work

Some research works have addressed the self-adaptive deployment and replication of services in environments with a dynamic topology. In [3,1] the devices that will host a service replica (host devices) are selected on the basis of their hardware capabilities, without taking account the topology of the network. In [5] the host device is chosen by its position within the topology, however, it is a static node and dynamic features are not considered. In [1], service replicas will be created when too many requests are made to a service from an external group. While in [2] the replica will be created when a node predicts a partition, and this node irrespective of its capabilities, will host the service replica.

Usually, regardless of specific issues, these are ad-hoc solutions developed for specific scenarios and therefore they are based on an implicit context model. This makes difficult the reutilization of the solutions, and thus they are difficult to apply in other scenarios which will present different requirements. The contribution of this paper is to provide a general foundation to address the dynamic deployment of service replicas by taking into consideration relevant context information, such as node resources, network topology and service requirement.

3   A Model for Self-adaptive Service Deployment

In this section, a conceptual model for the service deployment in context-aware systems is presented (Figure 1). The diagram shows the managed context information related with the dynamic replication of services in context-aware environments. Although there are crosscutting information that affects in a similar way all services deployed in the system, such as the device's battery, there are other information that affect in a greater or lesser measure the deployment of services according to their requirements. Therefore, the services must specify their requirements independently. This would allow the system to distribute the workload among the network's nodes, providing the appropriate deployment of the services on the nodes according to their requirements.

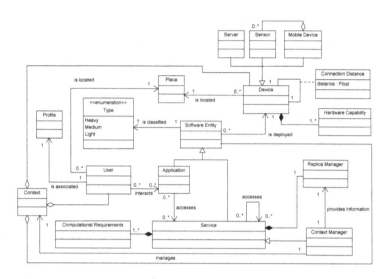

Fig. 1. A conceptual model for service development in context-aware systems

In addition to the hardware capabilities there is additional context information to be taken into account: number of clients, dependencies between services and number of service replicas. This information is supplemented with the connection distance between device pairs (customer/server distance) and in which devices are the software entities allocated. Moreover, the services may be classified as light, medium or heavy, indicating the cost of their replication. Similarly, an application can be also classified into light, medium or heavy, this will provide information about the traffic generated in the communication with the service. User's location and his/her profile may also help to anticipate the deployment of a service. In this way, if the system detects a specific user in a room, the system could place a service replica in a computing device located near to the user.

In an asynchronous model system, the Replica Manager (RM) is responsible for the synchronization of the operations performed on the different service replicas. In the proposed conceptual model, additionally, the RM encapsulates the adaptation logic regarding the deployment of this replica. To this end, the different replica managers should carry out, in a distributed manner, a coordination process in order to provide the most suitable solution regarding to the deployment of the service replicas. When a context change is detected, the RM should communicate with the Context Manager (CM) service in order to check if it is necessary to modify the deployment of the replica. If so, the RM will search for the device most suitable to deploy the replica.

4   Conclusions and Future Work

The proposed model takes into consideration an efficient resource consumption, different networking topology and service requirements, in order to provide a suitable deployment to a specific context situation. Moreover, it considers cross-cutting context features to deploy service replicas and the requirements of the service to provide efficient and flexible technological solutions. As for future work, a complete implementation of the approach will be developed, in order to perform a deep study about the different configuration parameters and to compare the behaviour and the performance to other approaches.

Acknowledgment. This research has been partially supported by the Spanish Ministry of Economy and Competitiveness with European Regional Development Funds (FEDER) under the research project TIN2012-38600.

References

1. Ahmed, A., Yasumoto, K., Shibata, N., Kitani, T.: Hdar: Highly distributed adaptive service replication for manets. IEICE Transactions on Information and Systems 94(1), 91–103 (2011)
2. Derhab, A., Badache, N., Bouabdallah, A.: A partition prediction algorithm for service replication in mobile ad hoc networks. In: Second Annual Conference on Wireless On-demand Network Systems and Services, WONS 2005, pp. 236–245. IEEE (2005)
3. Dustdar, S., Juszczyk, L.: Dynamic replication and synchronization of web services for high availability in mobile ad-hoc networks. Service Oriented Computing and Applications 1(1), 19–33 (2007)
4. Guerrero-Contreras, G., Garrido, J.L., Rodríguez-Domínguez, C., Noguera, M., Benghazi, K.: Designing a service platform for sharing internet resources in MANETs. In: Canal, C., Villari, M. (eds.) ESOCC 2013. CCIS, vol. 393, pp. 331–345. Springer, Heidelberg (2013)
5. Mihailovic, A., Kousaridas, A., Jaron, A., Pangalos, P., Alonistioti, N., Aghvami, H.A.: Self-management for access points coverage optimization and mobility agents configuration in future access networks. Wireless Personal Communications 72(1), 343–374 (2013)
6. Rodríguez-Domínguez, C., Benghazi, K., Garrido, J.L., Garach, A.V.: Designing a communication platform for ubiquitous systems: The case study of a mobile forensic workspace. In: New Trends in Interaction, Virtual Reality and Modeling, pp. 97–111. Springer (2013)
7. Rodríguez-Domínguez, C., Benghazi, K., Noguera, M., Garrido, J.L., Rodríguez, M.L., Ruiz-López, T.: A communication model to integrate the request-response and the publish-subscribe paradigms into ubiquitous systems. Sensors 12(6), 7648–7668 (2012)
8. Ruiz-López, T., Rodríguez-Domínguez, C., Ochoa, S., Garrido, J.L.: Mdubi: A model-driven approach to the development of self-adaptive services for ubiquitous systems. Sensors, 1–25 (in press, 2014)

Patient and Medications Tracking by Means of RFID Technology at the Public Ambulatory Hospital of A Coruña

María Martínez Perez[1,2], Jose Ramon Vizoso Hermida[1], Isabel Martín Herranz[1], Guillermo Vázquez Gonzalez[1], and Carlos Dafonte Vazquez[2]

[1] Xerencia de Xestión Integrada de A Coruña, A Coruña, Spain
Maria.Martinez.Perez@sergas.es
[2] University of A Coruña, A Coruña, Spain

Abstract. RFID is nowadays a leading topic of considerable public interest at different levels. Indeed, it is a challenge to implement RFID (Radio Frequency Identification) systems successfully so that they become an integrating part of existing processes in the healthcare environment, rather than being relegated to the status of mere pilot projects. It is therefore very interesting to improve patient safety by using RFID technology to trace patients and medications, and to identify the binomial patient/medications administered at the ambulatory hospital during the process of prescription-validation-preparation/dosage-dispensing-administration of drugs to the patient.

Keywords: adverse events, RFID, traceability, ambulatory hospital.

1   Introduction

Patient safety in the health care process is a key point in the quality of care received by the patient during his or her stay at the hospital. Building a safe clinical practice includes the simultaneous achievement of several objectives: to identify which diagnostic and therapeutic clinical procedures are safe and effective; to ensure that they are applied to those who need them, and to perform them correctly and without errors [1]. The main purpose of such a system is to minimize the occurrence of so-called adverse events [2][3]: any accident or incident collected in the patient's medical history that has or could have caused harm to the patient, mainly linked to the care conditions.

2   Application Scenario

The public ambulatory hospital of A Coruña is characterised by the high turnover of patients whose prescribed medications have long-term pre-established guidelines (21 days, monthly...). All medications included have special features in the process of prescription, preparation and/or administration, such as medications that are

R. Hervás et al. (Eds.): UCAmI 2014, LNCS 8867, pp. 263–267, 2014.
© Springer International Publishing Switzerland 2014

prescribed for serious pathologies (neurological, cardiovascular, of a locomotor device, chronic, rare), etc. The normal routine of the ambulatory hospital determines that when a patient arrives he or she must meet several conditions before being administered medication: they must have their prescribed medication, they must have been given medication previously, and there must have been clinical testing with favourable results.   Once a patient reaches that point, the Pharmacy Department is asked to prepare the medications. What would happen if, when the medication arrives, the patient has left? Or if the drug is lost? Or if there is no notification when the medicine reaches the ambulatory hospital?

When the Pharmacy Service sends the medication, it cannot easily and safely include on one single label very desirable information, such as the patient, composition, time of production, the responsible pharmacist, the time it was sent, who prepared it, stability, special conditions of usage, previous medication, infusion rate, the batch and expiry of each of the components and batch and expiry of the final product, etc.   At the moment when the nursing staff have to administer a drug to the patient, it would be of great benefit to have a practical guide to the conditions of use of these drugs, stored in a tag (the aforementioned characteristics), as well as the most important data about the patient development along with the medication to be administered or others.

3   Development

The aim of the analysis phase is to obtain documentation of the process of prescription-validation-preparation/dosing-dispensing-administration of drugs to patients at the ambulatory hospital. The sub-processes that have been modelled are those described below:

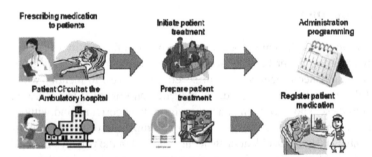

Fig. 1. Prescription-validation-preparation/dosing-dispensing-administration of drugs to patients

- Prescribing medication to patients: the doctor is responsible for diagnosing the pathology and specifying the name of the medication, its dosage, etc.
- Initiate patient treatment: before administering certain medications to the patient, it is necessary to request its authorisation from the responsible committee at the hospital.

- Administration programming: the doctor programmes when the drug will be given to the patient.
- Programming the activity of Intravenous Mixtures Section of the Pharmacy Service: after having received the doctor's programming, this section periodically validates prescriptions and organises the work of the Pharmacy Service nursing staff in charge of preparing intravenous mixtures.
- Patient Circuit at the Ambulatory hospital: when the patient arrives at the ambulatory hospital, he or she has a flexible course, yet one that is defined beforehand, from the entry until the discharge from the hospital.
- Prepare patient treatment: If necessary, when the patient arrives at the ambulatory hospital, the doctor checks that the state of health is adequate to administer the medication and if so, gives the order of preparing the drug to the pharmacy department. Otherwise, when the patient's admittance into the ambulatory hospital is detected, the request is sent automatically.
- Register patient medication: When the nursing staff prepares to administer medication to the patient, it must check that this will be done unmistakably and under the appropriate administering conditions (dose, expiry date, rate of infusion, etc...)

After finishing the modelling, critical points are visibly detected; at this point it is appropriate to implement RFID technology in order to undertake measures of improvement [4]. It has been concluded, together with clinical experts, that it is essential to obtain the traceability of medicines from their production until being administered to the patient at the ambulatory hospital. This includes increasing the information available on the label that identifies the medication as well as achieving thorough checks on the transport of the drug from its leaving the pharmacy department until its being delivered to the nursing staff at the ambulatory hospital. Moreover, it is essential to obtain the traceability of the patients from their arrival at the ambulatory hospital until their departure. This way, it is controlled, without any error, that patients have arrived at the hospital, that the doctor is evaluating their health state, that they are in the rest area, or that they are finally receiving the drug prescribed by the doctor. Not to mention the importance of unmistakably identifying each one of the patients throughout their stay at the hospital. In order to achieve the tracking of patients and medications, it is necessary to implement the RFID systems indicated below:

1. RFID system for the production of medicine in the Pharmacy Service

- HW components: passive RFID and NFC tag for the labelling of drugs to be administered, RFID and NFC (Near Field Communication) readers for associating the UID (Unique Identifier) of the RFID, and NFC devices with the data relating to the drug in the database designed for the system.
- SW components: application responsible for associating the UID of the passive RFID and NFC tags with the medication data available on the system's database.

2. RFID System for tracking medications during transportation to the Ambulatory hospital

- HW components: access points, exciters, active WIFI RFID tag to track the cart which transports the medicine and passive tag which identifies the medicine.
- SW components: software responsible for storing the time of the medication leaving for the ambulatory hospital. Application responsible for storing the time of each of the medicines passing through the established checkpoints.

3. RFID system for the traceability of patients at the ambulatory hospital

- HW components: access points, exciters, active Wi-Fi tag to locate and identify the patient during their stay at the ambulatory hospital
- SW components: localisation engine that calculates the position of the patient and alerts in the case of the undue arrival or departure of the patient at the hospital. Application for setting the value of the configurable parameters of the tags (retransmission frequency, number of channels for transmitting the RFID device, etc.)

4. RFID System for the traceability of medications at the ambulatory hospital

- HW components hw: tray format RFID device located at the delivery point of medications to the nursing staff at the ambulatory hospital
- SW components: software responsible for storing the delivery time of the medication to the nursing staff at the ambulatory hospital

5. RFID System for administering the medication to the patient at the ambulatory hospital

- HW components: Mobile phone for the nursing staff, patient active Wi-Fi tag.
- SW components: application which allows the nursing staff to unmistakably verify that they are about to administer the correct medication to the patient and under the appropriate administering conditions.

4   Conclusions

This work shows the technical viability of RFID in a sanitary environment: obtaining the traceability of medications, patients, and the binomial patients/prescribed drug increases patient safety by minimizing the appearance of adverse events. RFID integration is expensive but more than justified when considering the high risk of the medications involved in the project and the significant increase in patient safety when administering drugs at the ambulatory hospital of A Coruña. Finally, it is important to notice that the selected RFID components allow for the correct functioning of the system at the ambulatory hospital at A Coruña and that this work therefore goes beyond a mere pilot project; it could actually be integrated into the daily clinical practice of the hospital.

References

[1] Leape, L.L., Berwick, D.M., Bates, D.W.: What Practices Will Most Improve Safety? Evidence-Based Medicine Meets Patient Safety. JAMA 228, 501–507 (2002)

[2] Aranaz Andrés, J.M., Aibar Remón, C., Vitaller Burillo, J., Ruiz López, P.: Estudio Nacional sobre los Efectos Adversos ligados a la Hospitalización. In: ENEAS 2005. Ministerio de Sanidad y Consumo, Madrid (2006)

[3] Kohn, L.T., Corrigan, J.M., Donaldson, M.S.: To err is human: Building a safer health system. Institute of Medicine National Academy Press, Washington, D.C. (1999)

[4] Yazici, H.J.: An exploratory analysis of hospital perspectives on real time information requirements and perceived benefits of RFID technology for future adoption. International Journal of Information Management 34, 603–621 (2014)

Towards a Hand-Based Gestural Language for Smart-Home Control Using Hand Shapes and Dynamic Hand Movements

Hassan Saidinejad, Fabio Veronese, Sara Comai, and Fabio Salice

DEIB - Politecnico di Milano - Polo Regionale di Como
Via Ponzio 34/5, 22100, Milan, Italy
name.surname@polimi.it

Abstract. The application of gestural application can vary a lot: from a simple pointing mechanism to a visual sign language. Application of gestural interaction as a sign language with a proper formalism to interact with the technology has not been studied much. In this work, we present our Kinect-based gesture recognition system that is able to recognize personalized hand shapes and dynamic hand movements. We then describe how we created a "language" for smart-home control based on a specific syntax over sequences of hand shapes and hand movements.

Keywords: Gestural interaction, sign language, smart home control.

1   Introduction

"Kendon's Continuum" (coined by David McNeil [1]) refers to the categorization of gestures on the following continuum: *gesticulation, speech-framed gesture, pantomime, emblems, sign language*. Gesticulations are unconscious hand and arm movements. Speech-framed gestures are speech accompanied with a linguistic role. In pantomime, information is conveyed only through body movements and facial expression. Emblems are conventional symbols like *thumbs up*. Finally, sign language has all the characteristics of a language. Sign language is a language with words produced and perceived visually exploiting hands, arms, head, body, and facial expressions [2].

Gesture-based interaction offers another modality to interface with technological artefacts. The complexity of the gestural interaction in its various applications can vary from a simple pointing mechanism to a visual sign language. This usage spectrum for different applications can be mapped to the "Kendon's Continuum": research in multimodal gesture/speech interaction corresponds to *gesticulations* and *speech-framed gestures*. *Pantomime* can be related to interaction through dynamic body movements. *Emblems* can be associated to hand shapes that symbolically convey some information. Finally, *sign language* can be related to a gestural interaction with technological artefacts that is based on a well-defined syntax and word creation mechanism. Application of gestural interaction as an HCI-specific sign language with a proper formalism is not well

R. Hervás et al. (Eds.): UCAmI 2014, LNCS 8867, pp. 268–271, 2014.
© Springer International Publishing Switzerland 2014

studied. In this work, we explain the gesture "language" for smart home control, the syntax of the smart-home control messages, and the implementation of the smart-home control application.

Research on gestural interaction has developed various guidelines for gesture interaction design. Nielsen et al. [3] proposed a user-centered approach to choose appropriate gestures. Wachs et al. [4] list a set of requirements that target both the gesture recognition system (e.g., detection accuracy) and the gestural interaction design (e.g., learnability). Richness of vocabulary and complexity of communication has also been a concern. Epps et al. [5] stated that using hand shapes can expand the interaction vocabulary for table-top gestures. We think that the increasing number of available functionalities in a smart home could push the gestural interaction towards the sign language extreme of the "Kendon's Continuum" for an efficient communication with the smart home.

2   Towards the Smart Home Gestural Language

For smart-home control commands a simple model is considered which consists of four elements: place, action, object, and action parameters; for example, dim (action) the ceiling light 2 (object) in the kitchen (place) to 50% (parameter). In case one or more constituents of a smart-home control command is missing, the command is considered as implicit that necessitates the *disambiguation process*.

Component Disambiguation Process It is the process of transforming an implicit command to an explicit command and is defined on three dimensions:

- **Context-based Disambiguation**: Context information could be exploited to disambiguate a non-explicit command. For instance, using a location-aware system it is possible to complete a command with missing place.
- **Logical Context Disambiguation**: Disambiguation could be done with respect to the logical relation between the specified components of the command. That is, specification of one of the components of the command could logically constraint the choices for implicit components.
- **Default-based Disambiguation**: This type of disambiguation is simply based on predefined default preferences of the user.

A simple priority-based conflict resolution was opted for the conflicts of context-based and default-based disambiguations (giving priority to the latter).

Command Creation Static hand poses and dynamic hand movements are the basic building blocks of the language. Σ denotes the alphabet of the language:

$$\Sigma_p = \{p_1, p_2, ..., p_n\}, \Sigma_d = \{d_1, d_2, ..., d_m\}, \Sigma_{special} = \{w, x, c, t\} \subset \Sigma_p$$

where Σ_p represents the set of hand poses (e.g., victory sign), Σ_d represents the set of dynamic hand movements, and $\Sigma_{special}$ are some special syntactic poses. w and c are related to dynamic hand movements. Intentional dynamic hand

Table 1. Actions for Z-Wave Network Devices

Action	Action Parameter	Device(s)
Turn On	-	Appliance Switch, Light
Turn Off	-	Appliance Switch, Light
Dim-Shade	percentage(%)	Light,Shade
Open	-	Door Lock, Water Valve
Close	-	Door Lock, Water Valve

movements need to be distinguished from normal hand movements. w indicates the start of a dynamic hand movement and c is used for confirmation at the end of a dynamic hand movement. So, the smallest meaningful dynamic hand movement message chunk looks like this: wd_ic. Finally, x indicates the cancellation of the message. Words are made by arbitrarily combining hand pose and dynamic hand movement chunks. So, words are defined as follows:

$$(p_1|p_2|...|p_n|wd_1c|wd_2c|...|wd_mc)^+$$

For example, $W = p_1p_2wd_5c$, denotes the word W which is composed of the concatenation of three chunks, namely p_1, p_2 (hand pose chunks), and wd_5c (hand movement chunk). Each command component (place, action, object, and action parameters) is represented by a word: $s \in (W|\epsilon)^4t$ where s is a command, W is a word, and t is the message termination signal. In case of a fully explicit command the structure of an SHTM s looks like this: $s = WWWWt$.

Smart-Home Control Application. Our lab environment is equipped with Z-Wave domotic devices. Table 1 summarises some of the smart home control actions. The vocabulary of the smart-home application is depicted in Figure 1. This vocabulary has been designed by the authors. 5 words are defined for the actions; 6 words are defined to represent objects (Z-Wave devices); and 6 words are defined for action parameters. Special symbols correspond to hand poses in $\Sigma_{special}$. We have created 17 words in total. The average length of the words in our vocabulary is close to 3 (min=1,max=5).

3   Discussion on Word Creation

An effective communication system strives for expressiveness and conciseness. On the other hand, limited capabilities of the human mind ask for less cognitive load. Deutscher [6] argues that three elements account for the dynamism of the language: economy, expressiveness, and analogy. Inspired by his work, we suggest some guidelines for word creation: (1) *Economy - Create Small Words*: the smaller a word is the less is the effort to communicate it. This is essential especially for a sign language using hand gestures; (2) *Expressiveness - Allow for Overhead*: the gesture word for door lock object (see Figure 1) is of length of 5 (max). However, it is quite expressive when decomposed: initial hand pose (closed door with the fist), dynamic middle part (inserting the key), and the last hand pose (open door); and (3) *Analogy - Make Order*: order and repeating patterns can decrease the cognitive burden in the process of message creation.

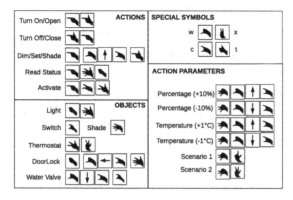

Fig. 1. The vocabulary of the smart-home application

4   Conclusion

Using gestures for a sign language gives rise to many challenges. A deeper understanding of sign languages is needed to understand how the syntax and grammar of a sign language is different from a speech-based language. This could result in devising more appropriate grammars for an HCI sign language. Word creation is another challenging task. In this work, we were limited to some hand shapes and simple dynamic hand movements. A hand gesture recognition system with capabilities comparable to human visual perception faculty can pave the way for more complex gestural words and structures. Finally, user studies are needed to evaluate such gestural interfaces. We are planning to conduct a user study to evaluate our gestural language for smart home control.

References

1. McNeill, D.: Hand and mind: What gestures reveal about thought. University of Chicago Press (1992)
2. Liddell, S.K.: Grammar, gesture, and meaning in American Sign Language. Cambridge University Press (2003)
3. Nielsen, M., Störring, M., Moeslund, T.B., Granum, E.: A procedure for developing intuitive and ergonomic gesture interfaces for HCI. In: Camurri, A., Volpe, G. (eds.) GW 2003. LNCS (LNAI), vol. 2915, pp. 409–420. Springer, Heidelberg (2004)
4. Wachs, J.P., Kölsch, M., Stern, H., Edan, Y.: Vision-based hand-gesture applications. Communications of the ACM 54(2), 60–71 (2011)
5. Epps, J., Lichman, S., Wu, M.: A study of hand shape use in tabletop gesture interaction. In: CHI 2006 Extended Abstracts on Human Factors in Computing Systems, pp. 748–753. ACM (2006)
6. Deutscher, G.: The unfolding of language. Random House (2010)

Using Wavelet Transform
to Disaggregate Electrical Power Consumption
into the Major End-Uses

Francisco-Javier Ferrández-Pastor[1], Juan-Manuel García-Chamizo,
Mario Nieto-Hidalgo, Vicente Romacho-Agud, and Francisco Flórez-Revuelta[2]

[1] Dept. of Computing Technology, University of Alicante, P.O. Box 90
03080 Alicante, Spain
[2] Faculty of Science, Engineering and Computing, Kingston University,
Kingston upon Thames, UK

Abstract. This paper proposes an innovative method based on wavelet
transform (WT) to decompose the global power consumption in elemen-
tal loads corresponding to each appliance. The aim is to identify the
main entities that are responsible of total electricity consumption. The
research demonstrates that the WT could be used to identify simpler
electrical consumption patterns as a part of total consumption curve.
Real power measurements has been used in this work. The results obtained have shown the accuracy to decompose consumption curves using
WT. This work could be used to develop new energy management services that will improve ambient intelligence.

Keywords: Disaggregated energy, wavelet transform, electrical consumption, NILM.

1 Introduction

Advances on monitoring and controlling of energy consumption improve development of energy management systems and smart grids to be used at home,
industry and any complex installation. Know how each appliance contributes to
total consumption is used to optimize scheduling, avoid waste and automatize
some tasks. In the reverse way, the power consumption curve can be decomposed in its constituents or individual appliances or entities that are working
simultaneously. Some techniques as wavelet-transform, statistical analysis and
other ones could be used to that end. Figure 1 shows the consumption of each
major appliance (different color) riding over the other ones to conform the global
consumption curve I(t). This could be expressed as:

$$I(t) = i_1(t) + i_2(t) + ... + i_n(t) \tag{1}$$

being I, the electrical current of the appliance j, and n the number of appliances.
WT has been used to analyze electrical signals [1]. It works obtaining series
of non-stationary functions [21]. In this paper, adapted wavelets are used to

R. Hervás et al. (Eds.): UCAmI 2014, LNCS 8867, pp. 272–279, 2014.
© Springer International Publishing Switzerland 2014

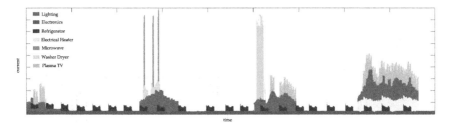

Fig. 1. Aggregated electrical consumption

decompose power consumtion. Related works and concepts about WT analysis are revised, followed by a proposal to obtain consumption patterns. Finally, the experiments made at housing, demonstrate the capabilities of this method to identify consumption pattern of the appliances.

2   State of Knowledge about Analysis of Power Consumption

There are two main approaches to decompose total electricity consumption: Intrusive Load Monitoring (ILM) and Non-Intrusive Load Monitoring (NILM). Traditional load monitoring techniques are considered intrusive because the consumption of each appliance is measured separately [5,11]. The NILM concept, proposed in [9], consist of analyzing the global power consumption to infer the appliances being used. It is the commonly used method today. A review on NILM approaches is presented in [10], that point out NILM could provide meaningful feedback when used in available commercial devices.

An evaluation of the realistic potential and limitations of NILM techniques is presented in [17]. Recent works have developed new non-intrusive techniques for load monitoring. [20] provides a comprehensive overview of NILM systems and methods to decompose the measured power consumption. Wavelet analysis has been widely applied in signal analysis, image processing, numerical analysis, etc. [8]. Its capabilities to study the signal taking into account time and frequency simultaneously has been used to extract information by mean of convolution with an adapted wavelet. A new method to process radar signal by using WT techniques to recognize patterns is proposed in [12]. The experimental results demonstrate that it is effective and radar signal could be processed in real time. WT has been used to obtain characteristics in medical electrocardiographic signal [6]. Applications of WT in electrical systems are analysis of electrical power [4], power quality information [2], fault detection and location [13] and signal processing [7]. A NILM proposal using WT is the analysis of transient features on the power signatures [3]. Recent research show the usefulness of multi-modal approach using data from separate environmental sensors (light, sound, etc.) [1,15].

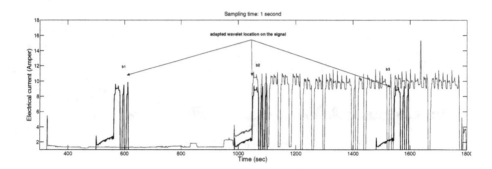

Fig. 2. Pattern detection with adapted wavelet. A wavelet $\Psi_{a,b}(t)$ of fixed dilation at three distinct locations on the signal. A large positive value of coefficients is returned in location b2.

3   Electrical Signal Characterization Using Wavelet

The Wavelet Transform $W_\Psi S$ of a signal $S(t)$ is defined as the sum along time of the signal multiplied by scaled and shifted versions of the wavelet function Ψ. It is given by:

$$W_\Psi S(a, b) = \int_{-\infty}^{+\infty} S(t)\Psi_{a,b}\, dt \qquad (2)$$

$$\Psi_{a,b}(t) = \frac{1}{\sqrt{a}}\Psi^*\left(\frac{t-b}{a}\right) \qquad (3)$$

where * denotes complex conjugation, $\Psi_{a,b}(t)$ is a window function called the mother wavelet, a is a scale factor and b is a translation. Here $\Psi\left(\frac{t-b}{a}\right)$ is a shifted and scaled version of a mother wavelet, which is used as a base for wavelet decomposition of the input signal.

Electrical current signal is captured in realtime by a sensor and used as electrical variable (figure 2). Acquisition of the current signal is simple and its value integrates the behaviour of each appliance. The process of capturing every signature is a monitored procedure: the variations of the electrical current (rms) are measured when a device is connected, when its state is stable and when it is disconnected. In this paper, a Pattern Detection with Adapted Wavelets approach is used. Patterns and their values in the scale-position (frequency-time) can then be identified in electrical power signals. Figure 2 shows an example where the adapted wavelet (pattern of a signal) is fixed at different locations to detect if it exists in the captured signal. Diferent energy coefficients are obtained when the wavelet transform with a specific pattern is applied to the electrical signal in different locations.

Adapted signals can be created as new wavelet patterns [19,14,16]. In order to build a new wavelet pattern, a signal form f_i (appliance signal obtained in supervised phase) is necessary. Each new wavelet Ψ_i is obtained by approximating

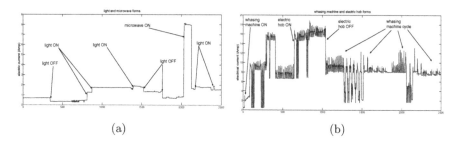

(a)   (b)

Fig. 3. Process of forms detection in supervised phase (a) Lights switched on-off and microwave (b) Electric oven and washing machine

each form f_i using conversion functions. The usefulness of this construction is demonstrated when it is applied to a detection problem [12,18]. This task consists on employing the adapted wavelet to identify the patterns stemming from the basic form on an aggregate signal.

4   System Details

The proposed approach consists of two phases, supervised and monitoring phase.

Supervised Phase. The events that produce electrical connection and disconnection of appliances (lighting, microwave, television, etc.) are classified as adapted wavelets. When profiling the appliances to build the knowledge base, the users make controlled connections and disconnections that generate specific signatures for the various power consumption modes for each appliance or device. The system records the instants in which the appliance is switched on/off and the stable state after the connection (Figure 3). This work considers some of the most usual devices at home: fridge f_1, microwave f_2, washing machine f_3, electric oven f_4, plasma TV f_5, lights f_6, air conditioner f_7 (Figure 4). First,

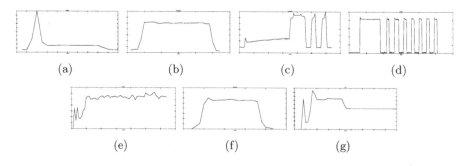

Fig. 4. Adapted wavelets ψ_i captured in the supervised phase (a) Fridge (b) Microwave (c) Washing machine (d) Electric oven (e) Plasma TV (f) Light (g) Air conditioned

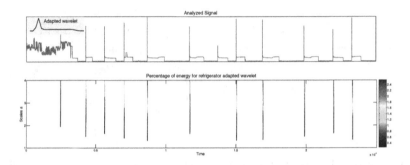

Fig. 5. Example of Energy E_Ψ obtained by WT between electrical signal and fridge adapted wavelet

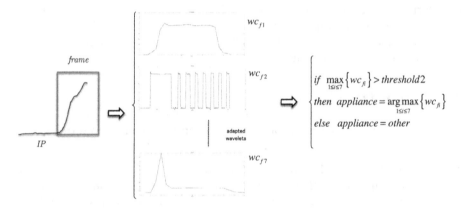

Fig. 6. Monitoring phase: WT between frame captured and each wavelet adapted form

following a supervised human-guided process, the signals associated with the activation of each of the main appliances are recorded. Then, a wavelet representing each of the signals Ψ_i is obtained. Finally, a wavelet pattern of each form is made. The main feature used are the Energy E_{Ψ_i} obtained with the coefficients of the wavelet transform. Ψ_i is an adapted wavelet function for each pattern f_i. The wavelet transform is computed on the original signal using adapted wavelet functions Ψ_i.

Monitoring Phase. The aggregate curve of electrical consumption (captured during a monitoring process) is processed applying a wavelet transform using adapted wavelet functions Ψ_i. Actual and recorded data are used to identify power events (connection/disconnection of appliances). Once an event is detected a frame of the power signal captured is analysed using wavelet transform treatment and pattern recognition techniques. The frame is processed with pattern-adapted wavelets Ψ_i, recorded in supervised phase. WT are sensitive to the choice of the initial point from which the signal is analysed. To overcome

---

Algorithm 1. Calculation of the initial point (IP) of an event

---

if $|\Delta I_k| = |I_{t_k} - \frac{1}{n} \sum_{j=1}^{n} I_{t_{k-j}}| > threshold$ **and** $sign(\Delta I_k) = sign(\Delta I_{k+1})$ **then**

$\quad IP = I_{t_k}$

if $sign(\Delta I_k) > 0$ **then**

$\quad$ appliance is ON

else

$\quad$ appliance is OFF

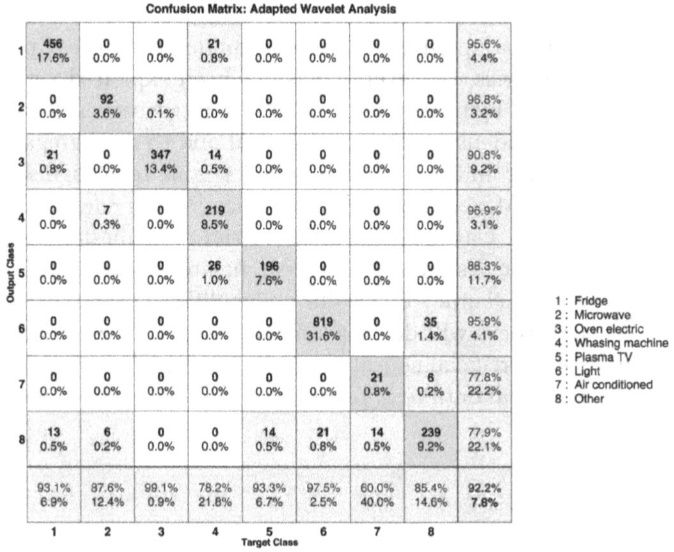

Confusion Matrix: Adapted Wavelet Analysis

	1	2	3	4	5	6	7	8	
1	456 / 17.6%	0 / 0.0%	0 / 0.0%	21 / 0.8%	0 / 0.0%	0 / 0.0%	0 / 0.0%	0 / 0.0%	95.6% / 4.4%
2	0 / 0.0%	92 / 3.6%	3 / 0.1%	0 / 0.0%	0 / 0.0%	0 / 0.0%	0 / 0.0%	0 / 0.0%	96.8% / 3.2%
3	21 / 0.8%	0 / 0.0%	347 / 13.4%	14 / 0.5%	0 / 0.0%	0 / 0.0%	0 / 0.0%	0 / 0.0%	90.8% / 9.2%
4	0 / 0.0%	7 / 0.3%	0 / 0.0%	219 / 8.5%	0 / 0.0%	0 / 0.0%	0 / 0.0%	0 / 0.0%	96.9% / 3.1%
5	0 / 0.0%	0 / 0.0%	0 / 0.0%	26 / 1.0%	196 / 7.6%	0 / 0.0%	0 / 0.0%	0 / 0.0%	88.3% / 11.7%
6	0 / 0.0%	0 / 0.0%	0 / 0.0%	0 / 0.0%	0 / 0.0%	819 / 31.6%	0 / 0.0%	35 / 1.4%	95.9% / 4.1%
7	0 / 0.0%	0 / 0.0%	0 / 0.0%	0 / 0.0%	0 / 0.0%	0 / 0.0%	21 / 0.8%	6 / 0.2%	77.8% / 22.2%
8	13 / 0.5%	6 / 0.2%	0 / 0.0%	0 / 0.0%	14 / 0.5%	21 / 0.8%	14 / 0.5%	239 / 9.2%	77.9% / 22.1%
	93.1% / 6.9%	87.6% / 12.4%	99.1% / 0.9%	78.2% / 21.8%	93.3% / 6.7%	97.5% / 2.5%	60.0% / 40.0%	85.4% / 14.6%	92.2% / 7.8%

Output Class (vertical axis) / Target Class (horizontal axis)

1 : Fridge
2 : Microwave
3 : Oven electric
4 : Whasing machine
5 : Plasma TV
6 : Light
7 : Air conditioned
8 : Other

Fig. 7. Case of use: Confusion matrix obtained

this problem and to determine the initial point (IP) the instant t_k when the event begins is established in Algorithm 1; where I_{t_k} is the electrical current at $t = t_k$. Given a set of adapted waveletes Ψ_i the goal is to obtain energy E_{Ψ_i} of each of them. Figure 5 shows a scalogram where the wavelet transform is filtered through an adapted wavelet for fridge appliance $E_{\Psi_{fridge}}$. The coefficients obtained from the wavelet analysis provide a close approximation to the original signal and therefore may be used to identify this appliance. Figure 6 shows the monitoring phase.

Use Case. This method has been tested in a real environment. An energy meter was installed in a house where the aggregate and individual consumption of different devices have been captured in a supervised phase along 7 days (sampling times: $1Hz$ and size of the frame: 8 samples/points). Appliances identified are associated to devices that connect when the event occurs. A set of seven signal forms ($f_{1..7}$) has been taken (Figure 4). These forms are the appliances captured in the supervised phase, for each form an adapted wavelet ($\psi_{i..7}$) is built. Wavelet Transform for each adapted wavelet $\psi_{i..7}$ is calculated when an event is detected. A vector of energy coefficients: $[wc_{f1}, wc_{f2}, wc_{f3}, wc_{f4}, wc_{f5}, wc_{f6}, wc_{f7}]$ is obtained. The $argmax\{wc_{f_i}\}$ provides the detected form f_i. An absolute maximum in wavelet transform coefficients of E_{Ψ_i} indicates the type of appliance. Figure 7 shows the confusion matrix of 7 days tested in the house.

5   Conclusion

Wavelet transform with adapted signals is a technique with great potential for power consumption analysis. However, it has not been exploited yet. This work shows that data captured by power meters, in a non-intrusive way, can be treated with wavelet analysis to identify activity electrical and to disaggregate the total electricity into the major end-uses. This method is able to recognise behaviour of people and may be used to develop of new services and in energy management services and smart grids. Can be used in industrial or domestic scenarios in a simple way with low cost systems. In the near future, additional datasets will be collected to test the accuracy of results under different combinations of use of appliances. Future works will develop unsupervised systems with WT using different classifiers (e.g. artificial neural networks, genetic or statistical methods) and other kind of electrical data (e.g. transient signal, active and reactive power or power factor)

References

1. Berges, M., Soibelman, L., Matthews, H.: Leveraging data from environmental sensors to enhace electrical load disaggregation algorithms. In: Tizani, W. (ed.) Proceedings of the International Conference on Computing in Civil and Building Engineering (2012)
2. Brito, N., Souza, B., Pires, F.: Daubechies wavelets in quality of electrical power. In: Proceedings of the 8th International Conference on Harmonics and Quality of Power, vol. 1, pp. 511–515 (1998)
3. Chang, H.: Non-intrusive demand monitoring and load identification for energy management systems based on transient non-intrusive demand monitoring and load identification for energy management systems based on transient non-intrusive demand monitoring and load identification for energy management systems based on transient feature analyses. Energies 5, 4569–4589 (2012)
4. Chul-Hwan, K., Aggarwal, R.: Wavelet transforms in power systems. i. General introduction to the wavelet transforms. Power Engineering Journal 14(2), 81–87 (2000)
5. Farinaccio, L., Zmeureanu, R.: Using a pattern recognition approach to disaggregate the total electricity consumption in a house into the major end-uses. Energy and Buildings 30(3), 245–259 (1999)
6. Figueiredo, M., Almeida, A., Ribeiro, B.: Home electrical signal disaggregation for non-intrusive load monitoring (nilm) systems. Neurocomputing 96, 66–73 (2012)

7. Haibo, H., Shijie, C., Youbing, Z., Nguimbis, J.: Home network power-line communication signal processing based on wavelet packet analysis. IEEE Transactions on Power Delivery 20(3), 1879–1885 (2005)
8. Hariharan, G., Kannan, K.: Review of wavelet methods for the solution of reaction diffusion problems in science and engineering. Applied Mathematical Modelling 38(3), 799–813 (2014)
9. Hart, G.: Non-intrusive appliance load monitoring. Proceedings of the IEEE 80(12), 1870–1891 (1992)
10. Jiang, L., Jiaming, L., Suhuai, L., Jin, J., West, S.: Literature review of power disaggregation. In: Proceedings of 2011 International Conference on Modelling, Identification and Control (ICMIC), pp. 38–42 (2011)
11. Kolter, J.Z., Johnson, M.J.: Redd: A public data set for energy disaggregation research. In: Workshop on Data Mining Applications in Sustainability (SIGKDD), San Diego, CA (2011)
12. Li, C., Zhang, C.: The pattern recognition of radar signal by self-adapted wavelet. In: 2007 International Symposium on Microwave, Antenna, Propagation and EMC Technologies for Wireless Communications, pp. 1199–1203 (2007)
13. Liang, J., Elangovan, S., Devotta, J.: A wavelet multiresolution analysis approach to fault detection and classification in transmission lines. International Journal of Electrical Power and Energy Systems 20(5), 327–332 (1998)
14. Mesa, H.: Adapted Wavelets for Pattern Detection. In: Sanfeliu, A., Cortés, M.L. (eds.) CIARP 2005. LNCS, vol. 3773, pp. 933–944. Springer, Heidelberg (2005)
15. Parson, O., Ghosh, S., Weal, M., Rogers, A.: Using hidden markov models for iterative non-intrusive appliance monitoring. In: Neural Information Processing Systems Workshop on Machine Learning for Sustainability (2011)
16. Ravier, P., Amblard, P.O.: Combining an adapted wavelet analysis with 4th-order statistics for transient detection. Signal Processing 70(2), 115–128 (1998)
17. Sharp, T.: Non-intrusive load monitoring systems: Considerations for use and potential applications. ACEE Summer Study on Energy Efficiency in Buildings 2, 241–247 (1994)
18. Shen, D., Ip, H.: Discriminative wavelet shape descriptors for recognition of 2-d patterns. Pattern Recognition 32(2), 151–165 (1999)
19. Theodoridis, S., Koutroumbas, K.: Pattern Recognition. Elsevier (2002)
20. Zoha, A., Gluhak, A., Imran, M.A., Rajasegarar, S.: Non-intrusive load monitoring approaches for disaggregated energy sensing: A survey. Sensors 12(12), 16838–16866 (2012)

A Novel Approach for the Population and Adaptation of Ontology-Based User Profiles

Kerry-Louise Skillen[1], Chris D. Nugent[1], Mark P. Donnelly[1], Liming Luke Chen[2], William Burns[1], and Ivar Solheim[3]

[1] School of Computing and Mathematics, University of Ulster, UK
{k.skillen,cd.nugent,mp.donnelly,wp.burns}@ulster.ac.uk
[2] School of Computer Science, De Montfort University, UK
liming.chen@dmu.ac.uk
[3] Norwegian Computing Center, Norway
ivar.solheim@nr.no

Abstract. User personalisation within context-aware applications has become increasingly prevalent in recent years. The use of ontologies enriched with semantics has enabled the creation of highly relevant user profiles, which have been used to facilitate the personalisation of assistive services. Existing work highlights the challenge of aiding non-expert users to intuitively manage their own profiles. This paper details a new approach to help enable the automatic creation, population and adaptation of ontology-based user profiles. Primarily, the research aims to create and enrich ontological profiles over time, for the purposes of user personalisation. The approach has been realised through the development of an intuitive desktop application, which has been evaluated through a series of experiments.

Keywords: User profile, ontology, usage mining, adaptation, clustering, data analysis, data mining, context, semantic web.

1 Introduction

User profile representation has become an increasingly prevalent area of research in recent years. Spanning across multiple domains of knowledge, researchers have encouraged the use of ontologies as a means to solve problems of data interoperability and more recently, to enable personalisation via user-based models [1]. User profile modelling involves the creation of a data structure, which holds various characteristics about a user [2]. One of the key challenges associated with ontological engineering is the complexity involved in the ontology creation process, in particular for non-expert users. There have been several tools developed to create and edit ontologies. While such editors provide visualised interfaces and collaborative environments, they are primarily aimed towards developers with in-depth ontological engineering expertise, leading to a lack of support for end users [3]. Previous work has addressed the simplification of creating ontology instances [4], the creation of simple templates for ontology population [3] and the challenge of automatic adaptation of semantic

R. Hervás et al. (Eds.): UCAmI 2014, LNCS 8867, pp. 280–287, 2014.
© Springer International Publishing Switzerland 2014

rules to various contexts [5]; however, little work involves the simple automation of ontological user profiles via the mining of real usage data and the adaptation of these over time. In particular, adaptation of user profiles is a key research focus. A significant growth in demand for user-based applications has occurred, sparking research into the areas of user modelling and context-aware personalisation. Upon defining a user profile for a target application domain, it is possible to learn behaviour habits over time and therefore infer new knowledge for the purposes of providing personalised assistance to that user [1]. Some of the key challenges that exist involve the learning curve associated with the use of semantic representation and the complexity of the ontological engineering process involved.

This paper focuses on the easy creation and population of user profiles within ontology models, via the mining of real-user data. This data consists of usage collected by an external EU funded project MobileSage [6], and our own collected datasets. Section 2 discusses related work within the area of user profile representation while Section 3 describes the overall application framework, focusing on the key enabling technologies and components that support the proposed approach. Section 4 provides a detailed description of how the process of generating ontology-based user profiles is automated. Section 5 details the implementation process, including experimental setups and user evaluations. Section 6 provides some conclusions for this study.

2   Related Work

Various tools are available that allow users to create their own user profiles. These include widely used ontology editors such as Protégé [7], SWOOP [8], or Ontolingua [9]. A comprehensive overview of some of the key editors can be found in [10]. They also enable users to format the models via ontology representation languages (e.g. OWL, XML or RDF(s) [11]). While these tools exist, they are primarily aimed at experts within the field of ontological reasoning; making them difficult to learn for the non-expert users. Other existing work aims to ease the effort of learning such languages, by building simplified visual editors such as TODE [12] or OntoGen [13]. OntoGen is a visual editor that uses text-based mining techniques to reduce the complexity of ontology editing for all types of user. Related works within this domain do not put focus on the user-friendly generation of user profile content using mined data. One study of note is the research conducted under the MobileSage project. This research involved the analysis of usage data of Help-on-Demand (HoD) services to focus on user interface and content adaptation for the personalisation of assistive services to older individuals [14]. The novelty of this work is on the approach used to create and amend these profiles, and further adapt them over time to facilitate enhanced personalisation of context-aware applications. Specifically, the approach uses data mining techniques to automate the process of producing ontology based user profiles that contain information that is personalised. As a result, we present an application framework that describes the components involved in the process of automating the creation of ontology-based user profiles. This framework builds on that proposed by MobileSage in [14] by eliminating the manual process of creating the profiles.

3   The Approach

To achieve an automated user profile, this work has adopted a hybrid approach. Firstly, (1) the use of user data to generate ontology-based user profiles, and (2) the development of a desktop application to aid non-experts in representing such profiles.

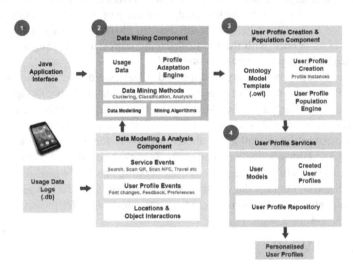

Fig. 1. Overall control flow of the key components within the application framework

Component (1), as shown in Figure 1, is the *Application*. The application is desktop-based and provides a user-friendly interface for the user to load an ontology model, and also select and mine the usage log, to automatically create and populate a profile based. The *Data Mining Component* (2) is comprised of several sub-components. These include usage log data, a profile adaptation engine and a series of mining methods/algorithms used by the application. In the current study, the usage data has been collected under evaluations coordinated within the MobileSage Project, where real-end users tested the functionalities of a HoD application and the overall usage was recorded. Once the usage data is effectively mined for any user patterns, this data is used to initiate the *User Profile Creation and Population Component* (3). This component contains the loaded template ontology model, which is pre-loaded with general user concepts. Upon creating the new user profile, the next stage is to populate this profile with specific user-related information. This information is generated based on the mining conducted within component (2). It is within *the User Profile Population Engine* that the mined data is pre-processed and mapped to specific user concepts within the ontology model. Component (4) consists of the *User Profile Services*. This component involves the management and storage of the ontology model and the newly created user profiles. Once a new user profile is created, an instance is stored and the pre-loaded ontology template is updated to allow the mined data to be inserted into it. The *User Profile Services* component holds the models and profiles within a simple profile repository. The novelty with this approach lies in the method used to effectively extract user data from usage datasets and how the application provides an intuitive interface to any level of user to manage their own user profiles over time.

A. Usage Mining & Pattern Discovery

To populate a user profile with user information, a sufficient dataset is required to enable the extraction of usage patterns. In this work, we analysed over 25 database logs (1 database representing 1 person), with an average of 60 – 70 records of usage data. Using one of the sample datasets collected, the *Data Mining Component* acts as a key enabling technology to support the approach used, and extracts user information relating to: *user locations, personal and device preferences, personal information and application settings.* Using the *k*Means-clustering algorithm [15], the mining component runs through all locations stored and presents a centroid in the form of a central location. The final centroids are used to determine the user's most frequent locations and this contextual information can help enable personalised services or events to link to specific user locations. We analysed the data and discovered specific patterns via the use of logical rules to determine user preferences over time. In this work, we make use of classical logic rules (*C-Rules*) that are expressed using the logical proposition of *'IF.... THEN.'* Figure 2 presents an example of a rule-based mining algorithm used to update the user profile with user-specific attributes. This can be extended further to incorporate the user location to determine the user's preferences at different service locations.

> *GET all usage log data (.db) AND all eventDetails "User_Profile_Feedback"*
> *FOR each "userInput"*
> *ADD value of "userInput" to array*
>   *COUNT highest value of feedback modes in array*
>   *IF result of highest feedback count == "Video" OR "Audio" OR "FText" OR "Text"*
>   *SET media feedback property to highest value*
> *CREATE new object property axiom for UserProfile_x*
> *UPDATE UserProfile_x with hasPreferredMediaContentType == "Video" OR "Audio" OR "FText"*

Fig. 2. An example rule-based algorithm, created to show how the usage log is mined for user preferences

4   Profile Creation and Adaptation

The user profile is a key enabler of user personalisation, as information such as preferences may change over time, meaning the profile needs to adapt accordingly.

A. Creation of the User Profile

As shown in Figure 3, the application interface contains a series of sequential steps. The user is initially required to load in a template ontology model. This template file will contain standard user concepts such as *'Preferences'*, or *'Activity.'* The OWL-API can also be used to create the model initially via the use of the OWL ontology manager. This model template can be created via Java and several class concepts can be declared and loaded in. The application loads the files and transforms simple mined data into ontological concepts written in the Web Ontology Language (OWL). The next step is to load the required usage data log, which contains a database of un-processed data relating to: *user location co-ordinates, service usage, activities, Internet connectivity, device interactions, and preferences changes.* The next step is to check if a user profile concept already exists within the ontology model, and if found it is then extracted. The OWL-API is then used to manipulate the concept by creating a class assertion (a modification to an existing axiom). Upon creating this new assertion, a new instance of that class is also created.

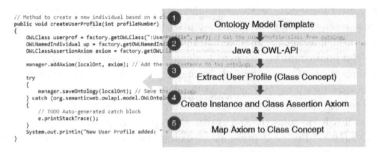

Fig. 3. The automated creation and population processes involving five key steps

B. Population of the User Profile

An ontology model can be described as a series of linked concepts, which contain relationships between the upper-level concepts and their instances. The process of populating these profiles involves the insertion of both the concept and relation instances into an existing ontology model, via the method of instance mapping. A concept (or class) instance can be described as the specific realisation of an object. For example, a *'Preferences'* class concept in an ontology may contain several related instance objects such as *'Media Preferences'* or *'Screen Preferences.'* A challenge that exists within existing research is the handling of redundant data [4]. Within ontology models, redundant data could take the form of duplicate instances of a class or duplicate properties relating to a specific instance. For example, if a userprofile_4 already exists within an ontology model, another userprofile_4 should not be created as this could lead to inconsistency within the model. The application iterates through a process of elimination by identifying any duplicate instances. If a userprofile_1 exists, the next profile that will be created will be userprofile_2. If the same user tries to create two profiles, an error will occur. One of the key components involved in the population of the user profile is the *Concept/Instance Extraction Component.* This is responsible for the rendering of specific ontology concepts or instances from data extracted from the usage logs. This component operates by creating a number of assertions. The *OWLObjectPropertyAssertion* is used by the OWL-API to add new properties to instances within the ontology model. The user profile, also referred to as an *OWLNamedIndividual*, is selected and various assertions are made to this instance.

C. User Profile Learning and Adaptation

Specific personalised user information is extracted from mined usage data sets, for the purposes of building semantically enriched user profiles. This approach is presented using a specific domain of context-aware HoD services within pervasive environments; however, it can be easily applied to a variety of domains. Whilst automating the process of creating the user profile aids users in enhancing personalised services, it is important to realise that this information is dynamic, and may change over time and therefore the profile must be able to adapt to these changes accordingly. To address such a challenge, the application can learn user profile behaviours and enrich the content to match these changes. Continuous mining of real-time data enables the enrichment of the profile as new patterns are discovered, modifying the existing ontology model. It is likely that over time, a user will change their usage patterns as they become familiar with the services provided. In addition to the user profile we introduce the concept of ontology-based 'contextual' profiles. These context profiles are linked to the user profile class in the model via the *hasContextProfile* object property. These profiles would contain information relating to specific user locations, object interactions at these locations and services requested at specific times/dates. The context profiles contain information that is specific to certain events, at various time periods. For example, the user may request that the volume level of any output media is very high when using a busy ticket machine in central London, but may then change their preferences to have a lower volume when at a quieter station.

5   Implementation and Proof-of-Concept Evaluation

The application was created using the *OWL-API* (within Eclipse) and provides a user-friendly interface (as shown in Figure 4) to enable users to create and populate their own profiles, based on usage data, for use in ontology models. The application does not allow a user to create a user profile without any existing usage data to work from. If no database is loaded, there is no data to mine, and the application checks if this file exists before proceeding. If no file exists, the mining process will not be carried out. The application was built based on a specific scenario, focusing on automating the process of creating and updating user profiles for HoD applications. The data that is mined was collected from user usage data over time (via the use of the MobileSage HoD application). This data was then used as a basis to populate the user profiles, but any data could be used.

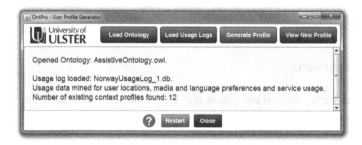

Fig. 4. The main interface screen of the user application

The usage log data was derived both from the HoD user evaluation trials set up by the MobileSage project and our own collected datasets. The usage data was stored within a SQLite database where the contents were sorted prior to the file being used by the application. For this work, we used a user ontology model that we have previously created for various user-based scenarios. This template was created within Protégé and stores simple user-related concepts. Upon loading the application, the user is presented with one clickable option to select and load an existing ontology model (*.owl* file) through a file explorer menu. Upon selecting an Ontology to load, the application then runs through several mining methods when the user clicks the "Generate Profile" option. Once the data has been mined, the patterns extracted and the new profile created, the user can view this newly generated profile via the "View New Profile" option. When selecting to generate a new user profile, the application checks how many profiles currently exist within the ontology model, and a new profile is added after these (through the creation of an instance in the form *UserProfile_x*).

In order to initially test both the accuracy and end-to-end functionality of the developed application, a proof of concept evaluation was undertaken. This was undertaken by a researcher within the Smart Environments Research Group (SERG) [1], at the University of Ulster, UK. The initial tests involved deploying a sample HoD application (initially piloted by MobileSage) onto a smartphone and collecting a sufficient dataset over the course of one week. The researcher was given a sample persona to benchmark the tests against, an Android-enabled smartphone, 6 NFC tags encoded with media feedback types and a scenario to adhere to. Over the 5 days, the researcher carried the smartphone during their normal daily activities. It was required at certain times to use the HoD application over the course of each day. After the usage data was collected, it was then analysed on a desktop computer within SERG and used as a basis for mining and pattern extraction to enable the creation of an ontology-based profile. The initial results show that the usage data collected enabled an accurate representation of the profile. The data collected proved to have a high accuracy rating. For example, the researcher was told to set their font-size on their smart-phone to large, but also set their media feedback preference (while using the HoD application) to 'Audio'. This data was recorded on the phone and when analysed and mined using our application, the results showed that the researcher's persona was partially sighted. Comparing the automated profile with the initial false profile set up, the data was successfully mined to discover this and therefore this information could then be stored and used in their own Ontology-based user profiles. Further evaluations will be carried out in due course, to successfully gather a larger, more comprehensive dataset to be fed into the system.

6   Conclusions

In this paper we introduced an approach to enable the automatic creation, population and adaptation of ontological user profiles, via the development of a desktop

---

application. We analysed the use of usage data to enable the extraction of user patterns, which were then used as a basis for creating the individual user profiles. The application has been realised and implemented, providing an intuitive GUI for users. The approach was initially evaluated within SERG where real usage data was collected over a period of time with a researcher working with a smart-phone application. Future work will involve a full-scale user evaluation to be conducted later in the year.

References

1. Eyharabide, V., Amandi, A.: Ontology-based user profile learning. Appl. Intell. 36, 857–869 (2012)
2. Skillen, K.-L., Chen, L., Nugent, C.D., Donnelly, M.P., Burns, W., Solheim, I.: Ontological user profile modeling for context-aware application personalization. In: Bravo, J., López-de-Ipiña, D., Moya, F. (eds.) UCAmI 2012. LNCS, vol. 7656, pp. 261–268. Springer, Heidelberg (2012)
3. Jupp, S., Horridge, M., Iannone, L., Klein, J., Owen, S., Schanstra, J., Wolstencroft, K., Stevens, R.: Populous: A tool for building OWL ontologies from templates. BMC Bioinformatics 13, S5 (2012)
4. Petasis, G., Karkaletsis, V., Paliouras, G., Krithara, A., Zavitsanos, E.: Ontology population and enrichment: State of the art. In: Paliouras, G., Spyropoulos, C.D., Tsatsaronis, G. (eds.) Multimedia Information Extraction. LNCS (LNAI), vol. 6050, pp. 134–166. Springer, Heidelberg (2011)
5. Kumar, V., Fensel, A., Fröhlich, P.: Context Based Adaptation of Semantic Rules in Smart Buildings. In: Proceedings of International Conference on Information Integration and Web-based Applications & Services, IIWAS 2013, pp. 719–728 (2013)
6. MobileSage – Situated Adaptive Guidance for the Mobile Elderly (October 5, 2013), http://mobilesage.eu/
7. Noy, N.F., Sintek, M., Decker, S., Crubézy, M., Fergerson, R.W., Musen, M.A.: Creating semantic web contents with protege-2000. IEEE Intelligent Systems 16, 60–71 (2001)
8. Kalyanpur, A., Parsia, B., Sirin, E., Grau, B.C., Hendler, J.: Swoop: A web ontology editing browser. Web Semantics: Science, Services and Agents on the World Wide Web 4, 144–153 (2006)
9. Farquhar, A., Fikes, R., Rice, J.: The ontolingua server: A tool for collaborative ontology construction. International Journal of Human-Computer Studies 46, 707–727 (1997)
10. Singh, A., Anand, P.: State of Art in Ontology Development Tools. International Journal of Advances in Computer Science and Technology 2 (2013)
11. Hitzler, P., Krötzsch, M., Parsia, B., Patel-Schneider, P.F., Rudolph, S.: OWL 2 web ontology language primer. W3C Recommendation 27, 1–123 (2009)
12. Islam, N., Siddiqui, M.S., Shaikh, Z.A.: TODE: A dot net based tool for ontology development and editing. In: 2010 2nd International Conference on Computer Engineering and Technology (ICCET), pp. V6-229–V6-233 (2010)
13. Fortuna, B., Grobelnik, M., Mladenic, D.: OntoGen: Semi-Automatic Ontology Editor. In: Smith, M.J., Salvendy, G. (eds.) Human Interface, Part II, HCII 2007. LNCS, vol. 4558, pp. 309–318. Springer, Heidelberg (2007)
14. Burns, W., Chen, L., Nugent, C.D., Donnelly, M.P., Skillen, K.L., Solheim, I.: Mining usage data for adaptive personalisation of smartphone based help-on-demand services. In: The 6th International Conference on Pervasive Technologies Related to Assistive Environments (PETRA), Rhodes Island, Greece (2013)
15. Jain, A.K.: Data clustering: 50 years beyond K-means. Pattern Recog. Lett. 31, 651–666 (2010)

Architecture of a Mobile App Recommender System for People with Special Needs

María Isabel Torres-Carazo, María José Rodríguez-Fórtiz, María Visitación Hurtado, José Samos, and Vanesa Espín

ETSIIT, Dpto. Lenguajes y Sistemas Informáticos, University of Granada, Granada, Spain
{Misabeltorres,vespin.martin}@gmail.com,
{mjfortiz,mhurtado,jsamos}@ugr.es

Abstract. International initiatives promote the development of software applications and technologies which are suitable for people with disabilities or special needs. Although there are currently various apps to assist, facilitate and support different kinds of activities for these users, app repository search mechanisms are rigidly categorized and do not take into account the disabled user's profile or context when recommending the most suitable apps available. The aim of this paper is to define an architecture of a new platform supporting an ontology-based recommender system on the features of the apps available in app stores.

Keywords: Apps, Repository, Searching, Architecture, Ontology, Recommender System, People with Disabilities.

1 Introduction

New technologies are increasingly prevalent in our daily lives and mobile devices now enable information to be accessed by considering user profiles and ubiquity. As a result, disabled people are able to access the information by themselves in the same way as other users.

The advance of assistive technologies such as screen readers and voice input has possibly already demolished barriers, enabling users with special needs the same access as anyone [1]. However, many mobile devices or applications are not always easy to use and possible access barriers might even result in a digital gap to the exclusion of the disabled.

In order to solve this problem, various companies and organizations are working on the development of more accessible mobile devices and apps. However, most potential users are unaware of them or do not know how these can fit their requirements and needs.

Our research into the functionality of app repositories (Google Play, iTunes Store and Windows Store) identified that relevant information for disabled users was often hidden in the description section, was missing or was mentioned on another web page. The complexity, lack of clarity and the small print of app descriptions made searches particularly difficult for the disabled user. Almost every app repository provides

R. Hervás et al. (Eds.): UCAmI 2014, LNCS 8867, pp. 288–291, 2014.
© Springer International Publishing Switzerland 2014

classification in certain categories such as games or books. They also enable a search to be made based on age, price, relevance or keywords. None of the stores takes into account the user's profile or other context information (with the exception of the user's location in one app store) when the application search is performed. For this reason, the proposal of this paper is to define an architecture that includes a new app called m-RECACC, which is based on a semantic-based recommender system grounded on various app features, user profile and context.

The remainder of the paper is organized as follows: Section 2 describes the proposed architecture and Section 3 provides a summary of our conclusions and future lines of research.

2   Architecture of the App Recommender System

2.1   Purpose of the System

The process of recommending apps to users requires an app domain expert to study and classify apps in repositories according to different criteria. This expert also categorizes different levels and types of disability and the contextual information that can be considered and categorized. The result of this process is the knowledge base used by the m-RECACC app.

At the core of our proposal is the special m-RECACC application. This is installed and configured by the users with disabilities or their assistants. Configuration of m-RECACC involves the creation of a specific profile (personal details and disabilities) for each device user. The recommender system considers this profile and the knowledge base when recommending the most suitable apps available. The user can then either decide to install the recommended app or not.

2.2   Architectural Components

In view of all the factors involved in the search and recommendation processes, we propose the system architecture shown in Figure 1.

Application Environment: This environment is represented by the apps located in the app repositories, such as, for example, Apple Store, Google Play or Windows Store.

User Environment: In the same way as [3], recommender systems can use context by means of mobile device services or sensors.

Server Application Knowledge Base: This knowledge base contains a data store and an editor to manage it. The data store includes the user profile, context and app features. These are stored as ontologies in order to provide classifications with a sematic meaning and a more detailed taxonomy. In the case of the user profile, an ontology based on the AEGIS ontology [4]. The knowledge base also consists of the relationships and rules relating the information of the ontologies. We have also conducted an exhaustive study into various app repositories such as iTunes Store and Google Play. Focusing only on visual impairment, we have compiled and classified about 80 apps. The characteristics that have been considered for the classification of these apps include category, language, operating system, price, voice synthesis, vibration, sounds and colours. In terms of user environment, the system records information about the user's location, noise level, brightness, timestamp or any data provided by mobile devices or obtained using body or environmental sensors.

The knowledge base manager can use the data store editor to perform modifications. The main advantage of the use of the knowledge base lies in its independence in terms of the m-RECACC app: a change made to the knowledge base does not necessitate a modification to the mobile app.

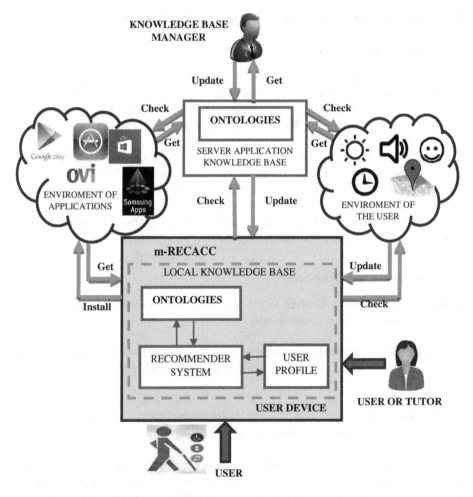

Fig. 1. System Architecture

Mobile Search and Recommendation Application: The users should first install the m-RECACC app on their device. In order to improve efficiency, a local copy of the knowledge base is stored on the device. m- RECACC app includes the user profile and the recommender system. The user profile is configured by the user's tutor and contains all the features relating to each specific device user. The system is therefore able to obtain the most suitable individual recommendation for each user.

The recommender system considers the information gathered by means of ontologies about the user profile, their context and the app features. It provides filtering strategies based on semantic reasoning techniques that discover relevant relationships between the users' preferences, context and items to be recommended.

3   Conclusions and Future Lines of Research

Traditional app store browsers are unable to refine individual searches to user needs or context, and classification of app searches is limited to certain prefixed parameters. Furthermore, app descriptions do not normally indicate whether an app might be suitable or useful for a person with special needs.

In this paper, we have proposed an architecture that includes a recommender system using a knowledge base which is formalized by means of ontologies. A recommendation strategy for suggesting the most suitable apps to disabled users has been designed on account of user profile, context information, apps features and user interests.

By way of future work, the recommender system will be completed with filtering strategies based on semantic reasoning techniques and the mobile app included in the architecture will be implemented.

Acknowledgements. The authors would like to thank the CEI-BioTic Campus of International Excellence of the University of Granada that supported the project related with this research "Stimulation software applications for early intervention in partially sighted and blind children through the use of mobile touchscreen devices".

References

1. Shaomei, L., Adamic, L.: Visually impaired users on an online social network. In: Proceedings of the SIGCHI Conference on Human Factors in Computing Systems, pp. 3133–3142 (2014)
2. Resnick, P., Varian, H.: Recommender Systems. Communications of the ACM 40(3), 56–58 (1997)
3. Bing, F., Shaoyi, L., Kaiquan, X., Hao, C., Chen, Z., Huaping, C.: A novel mobile recommender system for indoor shopping. Expert Systems with Applications 39(15), 11992–12000 (2012)
4. AEGIS Project, http://www.aegis-project.eu/

Semantics Based Intelligent Search in Large Digital Repositories Using Hadoop MapReduce

Muhammad Idris[1], Shujaat Hussain[1], Taqdir Ali[1], Byeong Ho Kang[2], and Sungyoung Lee[1]

[1] Department of Computer Engineering, Kyung Hee University, Korea
{idris,shujaat.hussain,taqdir.ali,sylee}@oslab.khu.ac.kr
[2] Dept. of Science, Engineering and Technology UoT, Australia
byeong.kang@utas.edu.au

Abstract. Information contained in large digital repositories consisting of billions of documents represented in various formats make it difficult to retrieve the desired information. It is necessary to develop techniques that are accurate and fast enough to retrieve the desired information from hay stack of online digital repositories. On one hand, Keyword based systems and techniques have high recall and performance, however, they have low precision. On the other hand, semantics based systems have high precision and good recall, however, their performance decreases with data growth. Therefore, to improve precision and performance, we propose semantics based searching framework using Hadoop MapReduce to process the data at large scale. We apply semantic techniques to extract required information from digital documents and MapReduce programming model to apply these techniques. Application of semantic techniques using MapReduce distributed model will result in high precision and good performance of user query result.

1 Introduction

Online digital repositories are increasing in size and varieties amounting to terabytes and petabytes of data[1]. The data growth in digital documents is even more than approximation of Moore's law. Performing search on large scale digital documents using traditional search engines is tiresome, slow and monotonous. The existing and established searching techniques use word-counting[2], and document indexing[3] to accomplish their job. Existing semantics systems performance decreases with the increase of information in large repositories. Numerous digital repositories such as IEEE[4], ACM[5] and MEDLINE[6] processed through distributed solutions available for traditional keywords and indexing techniques in[2][3], however, there is lack of a distributed system that process large information with its semantics and tagging efficiently. Conventional systems and techniques such as in [7][8][9][10] focus on processing data semantically to increase the accuracy of intended user query, however, its performance decreases because of its sequential and procedural nature. Searching data at large scale (big data) has been discussed by many researchers, many systems and techniques have been proposed

R. Hervás et al. (Eds.): UCAmI 2014, LNCS 8867, pp. 292–295, 2014.
© Springer International Publishing Switzerland 2014

using traditional sequential and distributed frameworks. MapReduce(MR) has also been adopted by many large organizations for analytics such as in Google[11], Facebook[12] and XML processing[13], e-mails processing respectively. All these systems use Hadoop-MR, while no such system exists that adopts and considers semantics based searching of digital data using MR. In this paper, we propose Hadoop-MR[14] based parallel and distributed search technique in digital repositories with semantics as discussed in[7] to gain the accuracy and performance. Accuracy is achieved through adaption of semantic searching and performance through implementing in separate *map* and *reduce* phases as shown in Figure 1. Due to its distributed and independent nature of processing, the proposed framework outperforms existing semantics based processing systems.

2   Proposed Framework

In this section, we describe architecture of a searching engine on digital documents using MR. The detailed architecture is shown in Figure 1 and here we discuss individual components, their work and results. We assume that the data has already been crawled in HDFS and the data is in the heterogeneous formats. Results returned by the proposed framework will be stored back to HDFS which can then be searched intelligently and easily. Our proposed framework consists of 3 modules based on MR three phases: *map partition*, and *reduce* modules. Each module has other sub components.

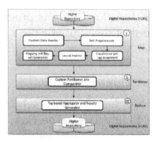

Fig. 1. Architecture of Semantic Based Search in Large Repositories

2.1   Map Module

Map module shown in Figure 1 (I) shows sub-components that extract the meta data from documents semantically which is described as follows.

Custom Data Reader/Pre-processor: Since Hadoop divides input data into data chunks with default size of 64MB and data is in heterogeneous formats. Therefore, firstly we read a whole single file as input to mapper to avoid the data of a single file being distributed across multiple mappers. This helps in exact identification, indexing of the document, word, and tagging relationship. Finally, the document is parsed for slang removal. As the professional documents related to research and academia often does not contain slang, however, here it will remove the words that do not play an important role in the context identification such as *is, am, are, they, these, those, and other many such type of words*. It will focus on the key words and vocabularies that can be used in the context identification such as sections of the document and tagging the word to the section according to their importance.

Classification and Tag Assignment/Lexical Analysis: Each digital document consists of many sections e.g. research documents contains sections: title, abstract, introduction, and conclusion. It identifies each part of document and tag the words that appear under this section. It classifies text into different section based on weight of it appearing in each section. Terms are extracted and categorized as single terms and compound terms. For compound terms, it will use the stop words mechanism while single terms are directly identified. After identification, it will perform lexical analysis using Parts Of Speech(POS) technique. POS is performed with the help of thesaurus and stemming is performed to correctly identify the concept words. A term may be occurring multiple times, therefore, we include term clustering based on the document and their frequency.

Mapping and (k,v) Pair Generation: In this sub-component, results of previous are processed to *map* each word to its section, and index the section and word both to the document. Since in MR, the *map* output must be in (key, val) pairs, therefore, data is processed to generate the pairs with words as *key* and the rest of the semantic data as its *value*. (Key, val) pair generation helps in partitioner and reducer step to perform clustering and indexing of documents.

2.2   Partitioner Module

This module has the only sub-component i.e. *partitioner and comparator* as shown in Figure 1(II). The (key, val) pairs generated by the *map* module are processed by partitioner module to shuffle the data between nodes in the cluster. Shuffling is performed based on keys (concept words). Words with same semantics are forwarded to a single reducer for further aggregation and final output generation. The partitioner component is customized to avoid data skew, in case, if skew occurs, it distributes the data to other available reducers.

2.3   Aggregator and Results Generator

Figure 1(III) shows the final component in the architecture and the data forwarded by the previous modules is collected and aggregated by *reduce* module based on their keys. As their keys represent the concept, therefore, a concept occurring in each document is aggregated with all its semantics and ranked based on its frequency and importance of the section of document. The ranking helps in returning results to a query easily. each concept is also indexed to a document it belongs to. The results of reducer are in (key, val) format and stored directly into the Hadoop repository. Once all steps are performed, data in HDFS will be ready for querying and searching. The searching of results are of two kinds: a) online search, b) offline search. In online, the query will be directly processed by this framework and the results will be returned to the user. In offline, the data is preprocessed and the query result is directly returned from the data in HDFS.

3 Discussion and Conclusion

In this paper, we presented an architecture for semantics searching over large repositories using Hadoop-MR. MR programming model is used to perform computation and process the data in parallel over cluster of commodity hardware. Semantic techniques are used to attain focus on the correct terms identification. The proposed architecture combines distributed processing with semantics based processing to provide an in-depth search with high performance over large datasets. Currently, our focus is to develop semantics based intelligent search engine using Hadoop-MR to achieve high performance and recall. In future, we intend to extend our architecture to other data formats to extend its applications.

Acknowledgments. This work was supported by the Industrial Strategic Technology Development Program (10035348, Development of a Cognitive Planning and Learning Model for Mobile Platforms) funded by the Ministry of Knowledge Economy, Korea.

References

1. Manyika, J., Chui, M., Brown, B., Bughin, J., Dobbs, R., Roxburgh, C., Byers, A.H.: Big data: The next frontier for innovation, competition and productivity
2. Pennebaker, J.W., Francis, M.E., Booth, R.J.: Linguistic inquiry and word count: Liwc 2001, vol. 71, p. 2001. Lawrence Erlbaum Associates, Mahway (2001)
3. Moffat, A., Zobel, J.: Self-indexing inverted files for fast text retrieval. ACM Transactions on Information Systems (TOIS) 14, 349–379 (1996)
4. IEEE-org: IEEE digital library, http://ieeexplore.ieee.org/xplore/home.jsp
5. ACM-Org: ACM digital library, http://dl.acm.org/
6. National Library of Medicine.: Medline, http://www.nlm.nih.gov/bsd/pmresources.html
7. Khattaka, A.: Context-aware search in dynamic repositories of digital documents
8. Bonino, D., Corno, F., Farinetti, L., Bosca, A.: Ontology driven semantic search. WSEAS Transaction on Information Science and Application 1, 1597–1605 (2004)
9. Rodríguez, E.A.: Determining semantic similarity among entity classes from different ontologies. IEEE Transactions on Knowledge and Data Engineering
10. Laclavík, M., Šeleng, M., Hluchý, L.: Towards large scale semantic annotation built on mapReduce architecture. In: Bubak, M., van Albada, G.D., Dongarra, J., Sloot, P.M.A. (eds.) ICCS 2008, Part III. LNCS, vol. 5103, pp. 331–338. Springer, Heidelberg (2008)
11. Ghemawat, S., Gobioff, H., Leung, S.T.: The google file system. ACM SIGOPS Operating Systems Review 37, 29–43 (2003)
12. Borthakur, D.: Facebook has the worlds largest hadoop cluster
13. Yuan, P., Sha, C., Wang, X., Yang, B., Zhou, A., Yang, S.: XML structural similarity search using mapReduce. In: Chen, L., Tang, C., Yang, J., Gao, Y. (eds.) WAIM 2010. LNCS, vol. 6184, pp. 169–181. Springer, Heidelberg (2010)
14. Dean, J., Ghemawat, S.: Mapreduce: Simplified data processing on large clusters. Communications of the ACM 51, 107–113 (2008)

MLM-Based Automated Query Generation
for CDSS Evidence Support

Muhammad Afzal[1], Maqbool Hussain[2], Taqdir Ali[3], Wajahat Ali Khan[4],
Sungyoung Lee[5], and Byeong Ho Kang[6]

[1-5] Dept. of Computer Engineering, Kyung Hee University, Korea
[6] Dept. of Engineering and Technology, ICT, University of Tasmania, Australia
{muhammad.afzal,maqbool.hussain,taqdir.ali,
wajahat.alikhan,sylee}@oslab.khu.ac.kr,
Byeong.Kang@utas.edu.au

Abstract. Clinical decision support system (CDSS) is fast becoming a requirement in diverse medical domains to assist physicians in clinical decisions. Physicians look at the research evidences for satisfaction in CDSS assisted clinical
decisions and also to keep their knowledge up-to-date. Research evidences are
available in the form of studies, summaries, and other formats published in
credible journals, books and reviews as online sources. The most important and
critical part to get the evidences in a better way is the search query generation
and its optimization. A query that is characterized by domain context and clinical workflow, and optimized for the target search engine in order to generate
right and relevant results. In most cases, the search queries are generated manually, which require a lot of physicians' time to get the right information. Other follow automated way of generating queries from electronic medical records,
which make it difficult to associate evidences to the clinical decisions. The role
of the source from where the queries are created is highly important. We are
presenting the work of query generation from Medical Logic Modules (MLMs)
as a main source of query contents. We create different query set from the concepts used in MLMs expended with domain ontology derived from SNOMED
CT. The results are compiled with respect to coverage using classified training
set of over 380 research articles. The proposed work is demonstrated to physicians and their feedback upon time saving as well as presentation of information in the context was highly positive.

Keywords: CDSS, Query Generation, Query Expansion, Evidence Support.

1 Introduction

Over the last few decades, the ever-increasing output of scientific publications has
introduced new requirements for professionals, e.g., physicians, who have to locate
the exact papers that they need for their clinical research work amongst a huge number of publications [1]. Only MEDLINE/PubMed Baseline yearly citations totals from
2014 are 22,376,811 reported on in statistical reports on MEDLINE/PubMed Baseline
data by U.S. National Library of Medicine [2]. The research paper searched by the

R. Hervás et al. (Eds.): UCAmI 2014, LNCS 8867, pp. 296–299, 2014.
© Springer International Publishing Switzerland 2014

physicians are mainly based on the input queries. The contextual enriched and pertinent queries results in better output as compared to ad hoc queries.

In most cases, the search queries are generated manually, which require a lot of physicians' time to get the right information. Other follow semi-automated and automated ways of generating queries from electronic medical records or electronic health records [1, 5, 6, 7, 8], which make it difficult to associate evidences to the clinical decisions. The role of the source from where the queries are created is highly important. There is lack of associating clinical decision, made by clinical decision support system (CDSS) with research articles as evidence in order to get satisfaction over the system decisions and keep up-to-date with research literature. An approach is required that can automatically generate contextual queries able to find right and relevant evidences to support the clinical decisions made by CDSS.

We are presenting the work of query generation from Medical Logic Modules (MLMs) [3] as a main source of query contents. MLM is Arden Syntax encoded representation containing sufficient knowledge to make a single decision. The system generate the queries with two different strategies; MLM only queries, MLM-Domain Ontology combined queries. Within these two strategies, we identify several variations to formulate query and test results against each method. Each query returned results in variation and relevancy is checked with research articles in training set.

2   Methodology

This work is undertaken as a part of a Smart CDSS system [9]. Smart CDSS consists of three major components with several subcomponents. The three components are; knowledge authoring, knowledge base, and research evidence support. *Knowledge authoring component* provides the environment for physicians to create their clinical knowledge in the form of knowledge rules. The knowledge rules are created using domain ontology derived from SNOMED CT. It has the verification and compilation subcomponents for verifying and compiling the rules [10]. *Knowledge base* maintains the knowledge rules in the form of Medical Logic Module (MLM). MLM encapsulates knowledge as software module that triggers an action based on data event generated at healthcare system [3]. Initially the MLM was intended to have single logic that act on single set of data and result in single set of actions. However, now it can support to invoke other MLMs that result in chaining of actions with its own logic and set of data elements. Each MLM contains slots which are logically grouped into three required categories and one optional category; maintenance, library, knowledge and resources (optional).

For query generation, we are utilizing the "knowledge" category of MLM that contains slots to specify intention of what MLM does. Its sub-slot includes data slot (define terms used in MLM), evoke slot (specify context of MLM evocation), logic slot (the actual condition to be tested on terms) and the action slot (specify the action that should be taken in case condition is true). The third part i.e. *research evidence support* provides the mechanism to incorporate relevant articles as evidences for the decisions of CDSS [11, 12]. There are two models of this mechanism; push model and pull model. In push model, the evidence incorporation is automatic without any involvement of human while in pull model, semi-automatic approach is applied with human participation. In this paper, the focus is push model where we are generating the queries from MLMs of knowledge base components automatically. The process of generating query automatically to search evidences from online sources involves three important steps as shown in Fig. 1.

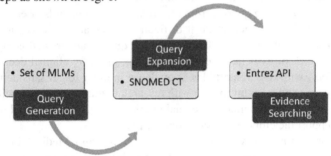

Fig. 1. Query generation, expansion, and evidence searching model

Query Generation utilizes the actuated MLMs that participated in clinical decision and build the query from the terms embodied in logic part of the MLMs. *Query Expansion* expands the terms with standard vocabulary of SNOMED CT for the purpose to increase the relevant results coverage. *Evidence Searching* utilizes Entrez Programming Utilities (eUtils), a stable interface into the Entrez query and database system at the National Center for Biotechnology Information (NCBI) used by PubMed search engine [4].

The system has been developed for head and neck cancer domain and tested different patient cases by generating both simple and expanded queries. The average recall score of simple queries was 75% while for expanded queries it was 95%. It proves that expansion of query terms plays an important role to consider for better results.

3   Conclusion

Evidence support is among the important parts of any contemporary CDSS system. It not only increases the satisfaction level of users including physicians, nurses and clinical researchers rather also provides a coherent way to keep the knowledge base up-to-date. In the form of MEDLINE we have access to more than 21 million reviewed research articles in medical domain. The most critical obstacle is the coherent integration of research evidence with the decisions of CDSS system. We presented query generation model containing three primary steps: query generation, query expansion and evidence searching. The results are evaluated with the help of training set having classification of 380 research articles for different anatomical sites of head and neck cancer. The results proved that expanded query provides better coverage as compared to simple non-expanded query. The automation of evidence searching has reduced much of the physicians' time spent on designing manual queries.

Acknowledgement . This work was supported by the Industrial Strategic Technology Development Program (10035348, Development of a Cognitive Planning and Learning Model for Mobile Platforms) funded by the Ministry of Knowledge Economy(MKE, Korea).

References

[1] Perez-Rey, D., et al.: CDAPubMed: A browser extension to retrieve EHR-based biomedical literature. BMC Medical Informatics and Decision Making 12(1), 29 (2012)

[2] Statistical Reports on MEDLINE/PubMed Baseline Data, http://www.nlm.nih.gov/bsd/licensee/baselinestats.html (accessed on January 25, 2014)

[3] Ohno-Machado, L., et al.: The GuideLine Interchange Format A Model for Representing Guidelines. Journal of the American Medical Informatics Association 5, 357–372 (1998)

[4] Sayers, E., Wheeler, D.: Building Customized Data Pipelines Using the Entrez Programming Utilities (eUtils) (2004)

[5] Cimino, J.J.: An integrated approach to computer-based decision support at the point of care. Transactions of the American Clinical and Climatological Association 118, 273 (2007)

[6] Perez-Rey, D., et al.: CDAPubMed: A browser extension to retrieve EHR-based biomedical literature. BMC Medical Informatics and Decision Making 12(1), 29 (2012)

[7] Chuang, S.-L., Chien, L.-F.: Automatic query taxonomy generation for information retrieval applications. Online Information Review 27(4), 243–255 (2003)

[8] Kim, Y.S., Kang, B.-H.: Search query generation with MCRDR document classification knowledge. In: Gangemi, A., Euzenat, J. (eds.) EKAW 2008. LNCS (LNAI), vol. 5268, pp. 292–301. Springer, Heidelberg (2008)

[9] Hussain, M., Khan, W.A., Afzal, M., Lee, S.: Smart CDSS for Smart Homes. In: Donnelly, M., Paggetti, C., Nugent, C., Mokhtari, M. (eds.) ICOST 2012. LNCS, vol. 7251, pp. 266–269. Springer, Heidelberg (2012)

[10] Ali, T., Hussain, M., Khan, W.A., Afzal, M., Lee, S.: Authoring Tool: Acquiring sharable knowledge for Smart CDSS. In: 35th IEEE Annual International Conference of the Engineering in Medicine and Biology (EMBC 2013), July 3-7 (2013)

[11] Afzal, M., Hussain, M., Khan, W.A., Ali, T., Lee, S., Ahmad, H.F.: Meaningful Integration of Online Knowledge Resources with Clinical Decision Support System. In: Biswas, J., Kobayashi, H., Wong, L., Abdulrazak, B., Mokhtari, M., et al. (eds.) ICOST 2013. LNCS, vol. 7910, pp. 280–285. Springer, Heidelberg (2013)

[12] Afzal, M., Hussain, M., Khan, W.A., Ali, T., Lee, S., Kang, B.H.: KnowledgeButton: An Evidence Adaptive Tool for CDSS and Clinical Research. In: International Symposium on INnovations in Intelligent SysTems and Applications (INISTA 2014), June 23-25 (2014)

Mobility Pattern Based Misbehavior Detection to Avoid Collision in Vehicular Adhoc Networks

Mohammad Abdur Razzaque, Fuad A. Ghaleb, and Anazida Zainal

Faculty of Computing
University Technology Malaysia
JB, Malaysia

Abstract. Vehicular Ad-hoc Network (VANET) can improve road safety through collision avoidance. False or bogus information is a real threat in VANET's safety applications. Vehicles or drivers may react to false information and cause serious problems. In VANETs drivers' behavioral tendencies can be reflected in the mobility patterns of the vehicles. Monitoring mobility patterns of the vehicles within their transmission range helps them in earlier detection of the correctness of the received message. This paper presents a misbehavior detection scheme (MDS) and corresponding framework based on the mobility patterns analysis of the vehicles in the vicinity of concerned vehicles. Initial simulation results demonstrate the potential of the proposed MDS and framework in message's correctness detection, hence its corresponding applications in collision avoidance.

1 Introduction

Vehicles can issue false alerts either unintentionally due to internal failure and faulty nodes, or intentionally for selfish reasons. Malicious nodes might have intention to cause collision and may also attempt to gather sensitive information about other nodes [4,2,3]. So, it is important to detect the misbehaving vehicles and false information sent by them. Hence, integration of entity centric (responsible for misbehaving vehicles) and data centric (responsible for false message) in a single MDS will be useful. Most existing works [4,2,3] are data centric or entity centric MDS and they do not exploit mobility pattern of the vehicles. This paper presents a mobility pattern based MDS and corresponding framework for VANETs. It employs a hybrid mechanism of both data-centric and entity-centric to cover wide range of misbehaviors. It depends on the shared location and time information periodically sent among the vehicles.

2 Overview of the Proposed MDS and the Framework

Design and implementation process of the MDS and framework includes: (i) selecting the considered VANET model, (ii) MDS setup, and (iii) design of the MDS components. It also includes the detection algorithms. Considered VANET

R. Hervás et al. (Eds.): UCAmI 2014, LNCS 8867, pp. 300–303, 2014.
© Springer International Publishing Switzerland 2014

model allows both Vehicle to RSU-Road Side Unit (V2R) and Vehicle to Vehicle (V2V) communications. At least two RSUs are needed, one in each end of the highway. Front RSU is responsible for initializing vehicles to be engaged in the highway VANET. The second/last RSU is responsible in reporting the misbehaving vehicles.

Offline MDS setup initializes a vehicle to highway system, vehicle sends request to the RSU asking to join to the highway's VANET. First RSU verifies the vehicle's security related issues and then sends the road map to the vehicle. In online operation two types of messages are considered in the MDS: alert messages and beacons. Alert messages are used to broadcast event or warning. Beacons carry out locations and time information. Beacons help to build the Location Anonymous Messages (LAM) and Location Time Table (LTT) [1].

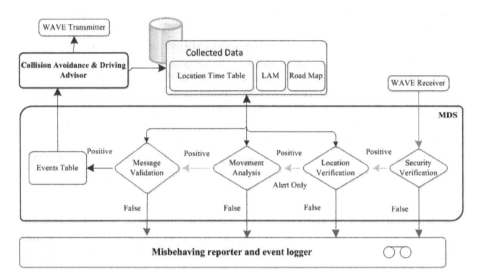

Fig. 1. The Proposed MDS Framework

2.1   The Proposed MDS Design

As shown in Figure 1, the proposed MDS consists of several modules such as security verification module, position verification module, movement analysis module, and plausibility detection module. These modules are responsible of misbehavior detection. Once vehicles receive beacons or alert messages through its receiver, the received information is checked in each module. Failure on one module aborts the operations and report into misbehavior logger for auditing. If the alert is true, it will be registered in the event logger. The Collision Avoidance and Driving Advisor (CADA) unit of the framework reports the true alert to the driver.

CADA notify the drivers about abnormal situations. For example, if a vehicle received a accident alert, then the driver should react to avoid piling up on the event location. To avoid the accidents or being in critical situations, vehicle need to keep proper distance between its location and the preceding vehicle. If the driver violates this distance and not comply with speed regulation, the MDS reports the vehicle to the RSU and then to the law enforcement parties. In doing so, a vehicle will try to maintain safe distance from others, which leads to decrease any potential collision.

3 Simulation Results

In this section we present the simulation results of the proposed MDS in terms of detecting the correctness of the message. Considering the importance of PCN alert in VANETs, we have used it to test the false message detection capability of the proposed scheme and framework. Numbers of other alert messages are similar to it and MDS treats these alerts in the same way. So, the PCN alert scenario is enough to validate the system operations. Information used in this simulation are: (i) vehicles count = 80, (ii) speed 60-120 km/h (iii) length of tested distance 6 km and (iv) minimum stopping distance 40-140 m. Figure 2 shows the response of vehicles in case of a true and false PCN alerts. It is clear from Figure 2 (a) that the mobility pattern of the vehicles in the alert position is different (red marked). The changes in the mobility pattern represent the response to the alert, means true alert. On the other hand, Figure 2 (b) shows that no vehicle in the vicinity has responded to the claimed alert because they did not see any problem according their current views of the road. It seems very normal pattern, hence no vehicle responded to the false alert. Thus the proposed MDS can exploit mobility patterns to detect PCN's or any alert messages' correctness and guide the drivers to behave accordingly and avoid collision. As shown in Figure 3 (a), CADA helps the drivers to keep safe distance from others and react safely in compared to VANET without CADA Figure 3 (b).

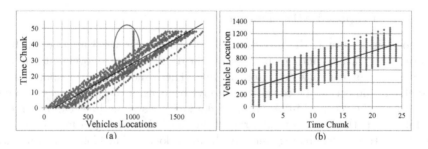

Fig. 2. The Mobility Pattern (a) in True alert and (b) in False alert

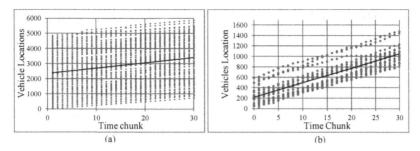

Fig. 3. The Mobility Pattern (a) with the CADA and (b) without the CADA

4   Conclusion

The proposed MDS depends on the shared location and time information periodically sent among the vehicles. By analyzing the collected locations and times, vehicles using this MDS can independently differentiate between normal and abnormal behavior, and hence can detect misbehaving nodes and their bogus claim or messages. This correct message detection ultimately helps CADA to act properly in case of possible collision. CADA also helps vehicles to keep safer distance from others to avoid chance of collision.

A number of issues remain for future works. We need to conduct additional simulations with extended parameters (e.g. larger area of movement, dynamic speed). Also, we need to analyze the MDS for security and privacy solutions to penalize the misbehaving nodes.

Acknowledgement. Authors would like to thank Universiti Teknologi Malaysia and Ministry of Higher Education, Malaysia for sponsoring this research under vote numbers: 4F205.

References

1. Ghaleb, F.A., Razzaque, M., Isnin, I.F.: Security and privacy enhancement in vanets using mobility pattern. In: 2013 Fifth International Conference on Ubiquitous and Future Networks (ICUFN), pp. 184–189. IEEE (2013)
2. Ghosh, M., Varghese, A., Gupta, A., Kherani, A., Muthaiah, S.: Detecting misbehaviors in vanet with integrated root-cause analysis. Ad Hoc Networks 8(7), 778–790 (2010)
3. Ruj, S., Cavenaghi, M.A., Huang, Z., Nayak, A., Stojmenovic, I.: On data-centric misbehavior detection in vanets. In: 2011 IEEE Vehicular Technology Conference (VTC Fall), pp. 1–5. IEEE (2011)
4. Sun, J., Fang, Y.: Defense against misbehavior in anonymous vehicular ad hoc networks. Ad Hoc Networks 7(8), 1515–1525 (2009)

Towards a CVL Process to Develop Agents for the IoT

Inmaculada Ayala, Mercedes Amor, and Lidia Fuentes

Universidad de Málaga, Departamento de Lenguajes y Ciencias de la Computación
Campus de Teatinos s/n, 29071 Málaga, Spain
{ayala,pinilla,lff}@lcc.uma.es

Abstract. One of the most important challenges of this decade is the Internet of Things (IoT) or the integration of devices from the real world in the Internet. IoT systems are usually composed of heterogenous and interconnected lightweight devices that support applications that are subject to change in their external environment and in the functioning of these devices. The management of the variability of these changes, autonomously, is a challenge in the development of these systems. Agents are a good option to develop IoT systems due to their distributed nature, context-awareness and self-adaptation. Our goal is to enhance the development of IoT applications using agents and advanced software techniques like Variability Modeling. Specifically, we propose to use Self-StarMAS agents and CVL. In this contribution, we propose a CVL process for the development of Self-StarMAS agents.

Keywords: Agents, CVL, IoT, Variability modeling.

1 Introduction

One of the most important challenges of this decade is the Internet of Things (IoT) or the integration of devices from the real world in the Internet [2]. IoT systems are usually composed of heterogenous and interconnected devices such as different types of sensors, cameras or mobile phones, just to mention a few. These devices support applications such as Ambient Assisted Living (AAL) or Smart Cities that are subject to dynamic changes in their environment, inside the devices that comprise the system (e.g. resource scarcity) or in the global network that comprises the IoT application (e.g. failure of one of the nodes). One of the challenges in the development of the IoT is to effectively manage the variability and the complexity of these changes, autonomously.

The distributed nature of IoT systems, the autonomy, the context-awareness and the self-adaptation properties make software agents a good choice for the development of autonomous IoT applications. Our goal is to enhance the development process of self-managed IoT systems using software agents and advanced software engineering techniques. This allows an effective reconfiguration of these heterogenous and distributed devices and manages the evolution and reuse of their components. In order to successfully tackle the reuse, bearing in mind the

R. Hervás et al. (Eds.): UCAmI 2014, LNCS 8867, pp. 304–311, 2014.
© Springer International Publishing Switzerland 2014

inherent variability of IoT systems, we propose to use Variability Modeling [7]. Variability Modeling tries to efficiently describe more than one variant of a system. It is often associated with Software Product Lines [11] and its objective is to create and manage many variants of a product, also known as mass customization. Specifically, we propose to use Self-StarMAS [4] agents and the Common Variability Language [12].

Self-StarMAS is a family of Aspect-Oriented agents with self-management capabilities, which is based on the Malaca agent architecture [1]. We have chosen this agent technology because its agents can be embedded in typical devices of the IoT, like sensors, and can communicate through different agent platforms (APs) and network technologies. Moreover, its self-management capability can manage variability at runtime [5]. Using Self-StarMAs agents we can develop the IoT application as a community of cooperating self-managed agents. For its part, CVL is a domain-independent language for specifying and resolving variability. This language is a proposed standard of the Object Management Group (OMG) and it has been applied to application domains, similar to the IoT [10,8]. CVL provides our development process with appropriate reuse mechanisms to develop a family of Self-StarMAS agents in the IoT, paying particular attention to the inherent variability of these systems. In this contribution, we present a CVL process for the development of Self-StarMAS agents in the IoT.

This paper is organized as follows, Section 2 presents Self-StarMAS agents. Section 3 overviews CVL. Section 4 presents our main contribution the CVL process for Self-StarMAS agents. Section 5 explains the background in related work; and the paper closes with the conclusion and a discussion of future work.

2   Self-StarMAS Agents

Self-StarMAS is a FIPA[1] compliant agent system, which adapts and extends standard agent technologies to help in the development of IoT applications. In this system we can distinguish two parts: Self-StarMAS [5], a set of cooperating agents developed for lightweight devices; and the AP where agents are deployed, which is the middleware that provides a set of (FIPA-compliant) services for those Self-StarMAS agents running in several lightweight devices (i.e. the AP).

The different versions of Self-StarMAS agents are embedded in Android devices, Sun SPOTs [14] and Libellium waspmotes [15]. They have self-management capabilities, adapted to the resources of devices where agents are embedded [5]. Self-StarMAS agents for Android devices consider goal-oriented and reactive reasoning engines. Self-StarMAS agents can be executed on top of different APs and can use different transport protocols, by simply plugging in the correct distribution aspect. For instance, by using the Jade-Leap plug-in, these agents can communicate with other agents registered in this AP. However, current APs for lightweight devices are not entirely capable of managing both device and transport protocol heterogeneity, and have strong limitations to ensure communication interoperability in IoT systems. The Sol AP [3] has been created to

---

[1] The Foundation for Intelligent Physical Agents, http://www.fipa.org/

cope with these limitations. The work of Self-StarMAS with Jade-Leap and Sol has been validated in previous works [6,5,3] showing good results with regard to memory occupation, message latency and resource consumption.

FIPA-based agents require a set of services from the FIPA AP that are related to the transportation of messages between agents, and with the discovering of agents and services. Sol is a FIPA-compliant AP particularly suitable for developing applications for IoT environments. This AP acts as an agent-based middleware that provides a set of services for the agents and behaves as a gateway to support communication heterogeneity.

The main features of this AP are the support for communication of agents in heterogeneous devices, coping with heterogeneous transport protocols (WiFi, Bluetooth and ZigBee) and group communications often required by pervasive systems. Additionally, Sol has remote nodes (Sol Clients), which communicate with the node in which Sol is running. The development of these clients has been necessary for the implementation of applications distributed over wide areas. Sol clients support devices with low-range communication technology such as mobile phones that use Bluetooth, Sun SPOTs and Libellium waspmotes. These clients can run in desktop computers and in Meshlium multi-protocol routers [16].

In summary, the combined use of Self-StarMAS and Sol provide the necessary means for developing IoT applications. Self-StarMAS agents can take advantage of the Sol AP, to communicate through different transport protocols and send multicast messages to a group of related agents. With this approach, the functionality of the IoT applications is decomposed in a set of Self-StarMAS cooperating agents that use the Sol AP for location and communication between agents.

3   Common Variability Language: Overview

CVL is a domain-independent language for specifying and resolving variability over any instance of any language defined using a MOF-based metamodel (e.g. UML or a Domain Specific Language (DSL) defined in Ecore) [12]. The instance of the MOF-based metamodel is referred to as the *base model* and CVL allows us to specify its *variability model* (see Fig. 1).

The *variability model* is a specification in CVL of the base model variabilities and has two parts. The first part is defined over the *base model* and marks its variation points. There are different types of variation points that can indicate the *existence* of an element in a MOF-model, the *substitution* of a single object or an entire model fragment for another, the *value assignment* of a particular slot of the model or a domain specific variability associated with objects, where the semantics of this domain specific variability is specified explicitly using a transformation language such as ATL [13]. This type of variation point is called a *Opaque* variation point. Additionally, variation points can be grouped in *Configurable Units*.

The second part of the *variability model* defines the relationships between the variation points of the base model using a hierarchical structure called a variability specification (VSpec) tree. A VSpec tree is composed of VSpecs that indicate choices in the MOF-model. The sub-tree under a VSpec means that the resolution of this VSpec imposes certain constraints on the resolutions of the VSpec in its sub-tree, these constraints will be explained in the following section within the VSpec tree of our MAS. Additionally, it is possible to specify explicit constraints. VSpecs are abstracts and they do not define which base model elements are involved nor how they are affected. The effect on the base model is specified by *binding variation points*, which refer to the base model, and this provides the linkage between the base model and the VSpec tree.

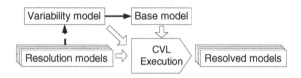

Fig. 1. Common variability language as specified in [12]

Variability Modeling is regarded as the enabling technology for delivering a wide variety of software systems of high quality in a fast, consistent and comprehensive way. In software development processes, CVL is used as shown in Fig. 1. Once the *variability model* and the *base model* have been defined, a set of VSpecs are selected from the VSpec tree, this selection of VSpec is referred to as the *resolution model*. Then the CVL is executed and it obtains the *resolved model*, a product model, fully described in the MOF-based metamodel, which is a variation of the *base model* according to the choices that have been made in the *resolution model*.

4   CVL Development Process for Self-StarMAS Agents

As stated in the introduction, our goal is to develop an appropriate reuse mechanism to develop a family of systems in the IoT, paying particular attention to the inherent variability of IoT systems. To do this, we propose to use Self-StarMAS agents and a development process based on CVL (see Fig. 1). The first step for in our CVL process is to define the *variability model* over the *base model* of the Self-StarMAS agents.

The VSpec tree of our CVL process (see Fig. 2) has three types of VSpec: *choice* like *SelfManagement*, which represents a yes/no decision; *variability classifier* (VClassifier) like *Agent[1..*]* whose resolution means creating instances and then providing per-instance resolution for the VSpec in its sub-tree; and *composite VSpec* (CVSpec) like *Handheld* whose resolution requires resolving the VSpecs inside it.

The root concept of the tree is *MultiAgentSystem* that implies the resolution of the VClassifer *Agent[1..*]*. For each of the resolutions of *Agent*, the *Device Type* and the *Agent platform* where the agent is deployed (solid lines). Optionally, the agent has a *Reasoning Engine* and *SelfManagement* capabilities (dashed lines). The *Reasoning Engine* has an explicit constraint, *Handheld IMPLIES Reasoning Engine*, which makes the choice of a *Reasoning Engine* mandatory, when the CVSpec *Handheld* is chosen. The VSpec *Device Type* has a *group multiplicity* 1...1, which means that only *Handheld* or *Sensor mote* can be selected. This is also applied to *Reasoning Engine* with *Goal-Oriented* and *Reactive*. In the case of *Agent platform*, one or more of the members of the group composed by *Sol, Jade-Leap* and *Blue* can be selected. If *Sol* is chosen, then *Sol Client* can be optionally resolved to true. On the other hand, *Sol Client* is mandatory if *Sensor mote* is chosen. Finally, *Sol Client* has a group multiplicity with *Bluetooth* and *ZigBee*.

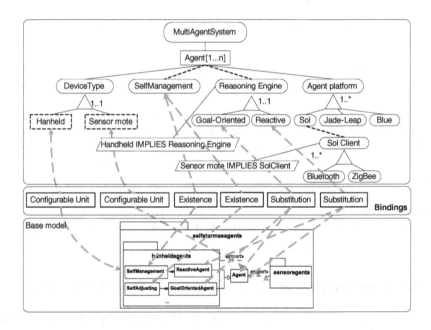

Fig. 2. Variability model and base model of Self-StarMAS CVL development process

The base model of the Self-StarMAS agents (see bottom of Fig. 2) reflects the agents described in Section 2. It comprises an agent class which is extended by *ReactiveAgent* and the *GoalOrientedAgent* from the package *handheldagents*, and other classes inside the package *sensoragents*. There are 6 bindings between the VSpec tree and the base model, two of them are Configurable Units and they will be explained in the following paragraphs, the other two are both *Existence* and mean that the selection of the VSpec (e.g. *Goal-Oriented*) implies the selection of the Variation point in the resolved model (*GoalOrientedAgent*) and finally, the last two are both *Substitution*, which means that one element of the base model (e.g. *Agent*) will be substituted by another (*ReactiveAgent*).

Given the Variability Model and the Base model, the next step is to select the features from the VSpec tree, taking into account the explicit constraints in the Resolution model and generating a Resolved model. Due to limitations of space, this paper focus on the CVSpec *Sensor Mote* (see Fig. 3) and its corresponding Configurable Unit. As stated in Section 2, Self-StarMAS agents can be embedded in Sun SPOT sensor motes and in Waspmote, the CVSpec illustrates the different choices for the configuration of these agents. The Configurable Unit contains binding between the CVSpec and the base model. In the resolution model we choose a *Waspmote*, with an *Gases Sensor Board*, an *Expansion Board* (it is mandatory due to restrictions in this CVSpec) and a *Wireless Interface ZigBee*.

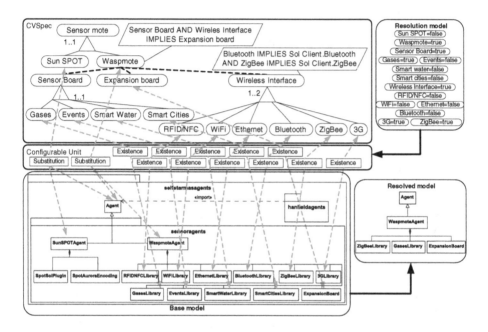

Fig. 3. CVL process for Self-StarMAS

5   Related Work

Variability Modeling and Software Product Lines (SPL) have been widely used in different application domains. Agents and SPL have been previously integrated in many different works [9,19,17,18], the integration of both technologies, together, is known as MAS-PL (Multi-Agent System Product Lines). The work presented in [9], proposes a modification of the GAIA methodology that uses SPL to analyze and design MAS. The proposed methodology achieves a reduction of 48% in times for developing and documentation compared to the original GAIA methodology. MaCMAS [19] is an Agent Oriented Software Engineering methodology to develop families of MAS using SPL. This approach considers self-management properties as an important part of the SPL. In [18], a software development process is proposed for MAS-PLs. This contribution provides mechanisms for documenting the variability of agents and obtaining the trace of the features of the selected agents in the different configurations of the agent during the derivation of products process. Finally, the work presented in [17], presents an empirical study that shows the advantages of using SPL in MAS with regard to the enhancement in the modularization of the agents and the stability of the resultant products. The publications presented here are recent and support the use of Variability Modeling to enhance the development of MAS, however none of them address the special features of IoT systems, like the heterogeneity or the self-management properties, except [19]. The latter approach focuses on the modeling of the self-management properties in robotic agents at the application level and does not consider the variability present in the devices where the agents are deployed.

6   Conclusion

In this paper we have presented a CVL process for the development of MAS in the IoT. The contribution of this approach is a mechanism that promotes the reuse of agent features to develop IoT systems based on agents. We have proposed the variability model of Self-StarMAS which is particularly good for the development of these kinds of systems.

This initial approach is the first step towards enhancing the development of self-management systems for the IoT, using software agents. Our goal is to perform the reconfiguration of heterogenous and interconnected devices and the evolution of the system, even at runtime, using agents and the advanced software engineering techniques that variability modeling allows. In order to achieve this goal we plan to automatize the process of generating the configuration of the agents by applying Model Driven Development (MDD) carefully considering the requirements of IoT devices. Additionally, the use of agents allows a fully decentralized solution for the IoT to be implemented, which them behaves as an autonomous system because of the addition of the self-management properties. As for future work, we plan to detail self-management properties in the VSpec tree of Self-StarMAS agents taking into account the scarcity of resources in sensors and mobile devices, and the monitoring capabilities that are so necessary in self-management solutions. Additionally, we plan to combine this CVL process with the MDD process of Self-StarMAS agents [6].

Acknowledgements. This work is supported by the projects P09-TIC-5231, P12-TIC1814, TIN2012-34840 and INTER-TRUST FP7-317731, by the International Campus of Excellence Andalucía TECH and by the University of Málaga.

References

1. Amor, M., Fuentes, L.: Malaca: A component and aspect-oriented agent architecture. Information and Software Technology 51(6), 1052–1065 (2009)
2. Atzori, L., Iera, A., Morabito, G.: The internet of things: A survey. Computer Networks 54(15), 2787–2805 (2010)
3. Ayala, I., Amor, M., Fuentes, L.: An agent platform for self-configuring agents in the internet of things. In: Proceedings of ITMAS 2012, Valencia, Spain, June 5, pp. 65–78. Universidad Politècnica de València (2012)
4. Ayala, I., Amor, M., Fuentes, L.: Self-management of ambient intelligence systems: A pure agent-based approach. In: Proceedings of the AAMAS 2012, vol. 3, pp. 1427–1428. IFAAMAS (2012)
5. Ayala, I., Amor, M., Fuentes, L.: Self-configuring agents for ambient assisted living applications. Personal and Ubiquitous Computing 17(6), 1159–1169 (2013)
6. Ayala, I., Amor, M., Fuentes, L.: A model driven engineering process of platform neutral agents for ambient intelligence devices. Autonomous Agents and Multi-Agent Systems 28(2), 214–255 (2014)
7. Bayer, J., Gerard, S., Haugen, A., Mansell, J., Müller-Pedersen, B., Oldevik, J., Tessier, P., Thibault, J.P., Widen, T.: Consolidated product line variability modeling. In: Software Product Lines, pp. 195–241. Springer, Heidelberg (2006)
8. Cetina Englada, C.: Applying Software Product Lines to Build Autonomic Pervasive Systems. Ph.D. thesis, Universitat Politècnica de València (2010)
9. Dehlinger, J., Lutz, R.R.: Gaia-pl: A product line engineering approach for efficiently designing multiagent systems. ACM Trans. Softw. Eng. Methodol. 20(4), 17:1–17:27 (2011)
10. Gamez, N., Fuentes, L., Troya, J.: Self-adaptation of mobile systems with dynamic software product lines. IEEE Software 99(PrePrints), 1 (2014)
11. van Gurp, J., Bosch, J., Svahnberg, M.: On the notion of variability in software product lines. In: Proceedings of Working IEEE/IFIP Conference on Software Architecture, pp. 45–54 (2001)
12. Haugen, O.: Common variability language. Tech. Rep. ad/2012-08-05. Object Management Group (August 2012)
13. Jouault, F., Allilaire, F., Bézivin, J., Kurtev, I., Valduriez, P.: Atl: A qvt-like transformation language. In: Companion to the 21st ACM SIGPLAN Symposium on OOPSLA, pp. 719–720. ACM (2006)
14. Labs, O.: Sun spot world. Program the world! http://www.sunspotworld.com/ (March 2014)
15. Libellium Comunicaciones Distribuidas S.L.: Waspmote technical guide (2012)
16. Libellium Comunicaciones Distribuidas S.L.: Mehslium technical guide (2014)
17. Nunes, C., Kulesza, U., Sant'Anna, C., Nunes, I., Garcia, A., Lucena, C.: Comparing stability of implementation techniques for multi-agent system product lines. In: Proceedings of CSMR 2009, pp. 229–232 (March 2009)
18. Nunes, I., de Lucena, C.J., Kulesza, U., Nunes, C.: On the development of multi-agent systems product lines: A domain engineering process. In: Gomez-Sanz, J.J. (ed.) AOSE 2009. LNCS, vol. 6038, pp. 125–139. Springer, Heidelberg (2011)
19. Peña, J., Rouff, C.A., Hinchey, M., Ruiz-Cortés, A.: Modeling nasa swarm-based systems: Using agent-oriented software engineering and formal methods. Software & Systems Modeling 10(1), 55–62 (2011)

Using the Spatial RIMER+ Approach to Estimate Negative Self-rated Health and Its Causes across Northern Ireland

Alberto Calzada[1], Jun Liu[1], Chris Nugent[1], Hui Wang[1], and Luis Martinez[2]

[1] School of Computing and Mathematics, University of Ulster, Jordanstown, UK
[2] Department of Computer Science, University of Jaen, Spain
{a.calzada,j.liu,cd.nugent,h.wang}@ulster.ac.uk,
luis.martinez@ujaen.es

Abstract. Self-rated health is a commonly-used survey technique that helps collecting information about the public health in an area. It is widely recognized that self-rated health has a strong correlation with key public-health variables such as deprivation, poverty, fear of crime or mortality. Therefore, it is a useful tool when assessing the public health situation of a neighborhood or town. This paper utilizes a recently-developed decision framework, named, Spatial RIMER+, to model a decision problem using real data where self-rated health is unknown in certain areas of Northern Ireland and needs to be estimated. The results retrieved in the study demonstrate the high accuracy of the methodology as well as its the flexibility and applicability to model a wide range of spatial decision scenarios.

Keywords: Self-Rated Health, Spatial Decision Support Rule-Based Systems Knowledge-based approach, Knowledge representation.

1 Introduction

Self-assessed health rates are usually considered as key measures and powerful surveying techniques, since they can be used to identify other negative issues affecting a neighborhood or town namely mortality, deprivation, fear of crime or poverty, among others [1-4]. In this regard, they can be utilized by authorities in many decision support situations related to public health, budget allocation and general policy-making, among others. Therefore, this self-assessed general health status could be considered as an alternative measure to help identifying vulnerable areas that require some type of action to improve their current situation. However, as self-rated health is usually collected just through questionnaires delivered to the public at a regular basis (such as censuses), it is likely that this information is not always up-to-date and/or available on time, for example to make decisions such as budget allocation or policy making, which involve the current public health situation. These cases can be considered as decision support scenarios, in which although some information might be available, it is difficult to generate a timely and accurate prediction or make the right decision.

R. Hervás et al. (Eds.): UCAmI 2014, LNCS 8867, pp. 312–319, 2014.
© Springer International Publishing Switzerland 2014

This research considers that the location of different elements involved in a decision support scenario, such as attributes, actors or information, may be of vital importance in real-case situations, which are commonly associated to certain geographical areas. In this regard, Spatial RIMER+ [5] has been recently presented as a decision model able to acknowledge different elements of real-case environments as well as different uncertainties related to them. In Spatial RIMER+, the geographic location of these elements is not only used for representation and visualization purposes, but it is also considered as an integral part of the decision-making process, taking advantage of cutting-edge spatial analysis methodologies [6]. Therefore, Spatial RIMER+ can be considered as a spatial decision support methodology [7], that takes advantage of the latest developments in both spatial analysis and decision support research areas. The case studies presented in this paper are focused on detailing how Spatial RIMER+ can be used to estimate how the population of different areas across Northern Ireland self-rates their health. Using real data obtained from the Northern Ireland Statistics and Research Agency (NISRA), a possible decision scenario is considered.

The remaining of this paper is structured as follows: Section 2 briefly details the Spatial RIMER+ method and Section 3 introduces the case studies performed in this research and presents a decision scenario that could benefit from Spatial RIMER+. Finally, Section 4 concludes this paper.

2   Spatial RIMER+ Approach

The Spatial RIMER+ approach [5] was developed in order to recognize the spatial dimension of real-case decision problems, where many elements are geographically referenced. Spatial RIMER+ was developed as an extension of the Extended Belief Rule-Based Inference Methodology using the Evidential Reasoning approach (RIMER+) [8]. In RIMER+, knowledge is represented by means of Extended Belief Rule-Bases (E-BRBs), designed to meet the need of handling uncertain and heterogeneous information. To achieve so, E-BRBs incorporate belief degrees embedded in all the antecedents and consequent terms of a rule, to capture nonlinear causal relationships as well as uncertainty. Thanks to these belief degree distributions, the direct input transformation is achieved by using the linguistic terms of the antecedent or consequent attribute, which can be defined as one of the following cases: (1) matching function methods using fuzzy membership functions; (2) rule-based or utility transformation methods; or (3) subjective valuation methods, for attributes of qualitative nature. By using one of these 3 options, every input can be directly transformed as a belief distribution form, with no loss of information during the process. Consider the following example of an extended belief rule:

IF "Crime" is {(High, 0.7), (Low, 0.3)} AND "Education" is {(Satisfactory, 0.6),   (1)
(Poor, 0.3)} THEN "Deprivation" is {(High, 0.6), (Low, 0.4)}

The "Education" antecedent has a belief degree of 60% for the "Satisfactory" term and 30% for the "Poor" one, leaving undefined the remaining 10%. This undefined part represents the incompleteness degree of the antecedent.

E-BRBs are normally used to integrate in the decision process some key elements of real-world decision problems, like vagueness (with linguistic terms), uncertainty (with beliefs), information incompleteness (partially known beliefs in antecedents and/or consequents) and nonlinear relationships between indicators (with IF-THEN rules; between its antecedents and the consequent). They also provide a flexible way to incorporate hybrid input information (both quantitative and qualitative) as well as mechanisms to weight and model the importance of some rules and/or attributes above others [8]. All these aspects of E-BRBs become essential when trying to deliver useful support in complex real-world problems. For further technical details about RIMER+ and its E-BRBs please refer to [8].

It is important to note that RIMER+ also provides a straightforward rule generation scheme [8], which allows a direct generation of an extended belief rule for each piece of information available. Therefore, in order to model a real-case decision scenario to estimate the deprivation in an area of study, one rule with the same attributes than (1) would be generated for each data instance located at a difference position. In this regard, a dataset with N observations spread around the study area would produce N extended belief rules with the same attributes than (1), but with different values (belief degrees). Such set of rules would represent the spatial variations of the dataset across the study area, and can be used to estimate unknown values and produce decision support outcomes, as it is detailed in the case study presented in this paper. Using the location of a data instance from which each extended belief rule was generated; Spatial RIMER+ upgrades the RIMER+ framework by including this spatial information in the decision-making algorithm and automatically processes it.

In order to acknowledge this spatial information in the decision-making process, a connection at a technical level between the decision support software implementing the RIMER+ method, named RIMER+ Tool and a Geographic Information System (GIS), named gvSIG [9] had to be established [5, 10]. Then, at a methodological level, Spatial RIMER+ follows the mainstream pattern of spatial analysis research and practice, also known as Tobler's First Law of Geography: "Everything is related to everything else, but near things are more related than further ones" [6]. Once an input geographically referenced in the study area is assigned into the Spatial RIMER+ system, Tobler's idea can be modeled by applying high weights to extended belief rules located near the input, and low weights to other rules located further away. To achieve this, the following Gaussian kernel function that assigns a geographic weight to each extended belief rule is applied:

$$w_k^g(R_k, X) = e^{-0.5\left(d(R_k,X)/h\right)^2} \qquad (2)$$

where w_k^g is the geographic weight of the kth extended belief rule (R_k) relative to the location of the input X. The function d returns the distance, in the GIS map units between the rule R_k and the input X, and h is a value known as the bandwidth [5 - 7]. Each w_k^g assigned to its corresponding extended belief rule will indicate the spatial relevance of that rule in relation to X. Therefore, in the upgraded spatial version of the RIMER+ model, each w_k^g will be taken into account in the rule activation process. In other words, the spatial element is included in the E-BRB as an extra rule antecedent, whose relative weight is assessed within (2) using a distance function (d). Finally, the rule geographic weight is combined with the rule activation weight, which measures the similarity between X and R_k, (see [8] for more details) in the following way:

$$w_k^* = w_k \cdot w_k^g \qquad (3)$$

The combined activation weight (w_k^*) reflects the data similarity between inputs and the kth rule (with w_k – see [8] for further details about how this similarity is calculated) and also includes the spatial relevance of the kth rule in relation to X (using w_k^g). By considering this, both data and spatial information are integrated into the decision model using a single equation. Therefore, the computational cost of adding spatial information on the decision model is barely noticed. After calculating w_k^* for all the extended belief rules, they can be aggregated using the Evidential Reasoning (ER) algorithm, as it is normally done with w_k in the RIMER+ approach [8].

3   Case Study

The scenario presented in this research aims at illustrating the value of the Spatial RIMER+ in solving real-case decision scenarios related to public health issues. The situation proposed for this analysis is based on the estimation of self-assessed general health provided by the residents of different areas of Northern Ireland as part of the census carried out in 2011. More concretely, this study aims at estimating the percentage of population that consider their health to be *bad* or *very bad* in order to analyze in which areas this negative assessment is generalized and what are the causes of it. This was modeled as an attribute to be estimated, named BAD_HEALTH.

Table 1. Attributes used to estimate self-assessed health in Northern Ireland

Attribute and Description
BAD_HEALTH: Percentage of population that consider their health as *bad* or *very bad*.
MARITAL: Percentage of population whose marital status is: Single, Married, Separated, Divorced and Widowed.
ED_LEVEL: Percentage of population with: No Qualifications and qualifications at levels 1, 2, 3 and 4.
RETIRED: Rate of population in retirement.
CARS: Percentage of households with: No access to any car or van and access to *one*, *two*, *three* and *four or more* vehicles.
TRANS_WORK: Percentage of residents that travel to work by: driving, taxi and on foot.
HBC: Rate of Housing Benefit Claimants (HBC) as a share of the total population in the area
OCCUPANT: Rate of population that own their household and rate of population that rent from *Northern Ireland Housing Executive* or from *a housing association or charitable trust*.
JAC: Percentage of Jobseeker Allowance Claimants (JAC) as a share of the total of population.
EC_PROF: Rate of population that are: working full-time, unemployed and who have never worked before.
ALL_UNEMP: Percentage of households in which all adults are currently unemployed.
DLAR: Rate of population receiving Disability Living Allowance (DLAR).
LIM_LTD: Percentage of population with a long-term limiting disability.
INAC_LTD: Rate of population that are economically inactive due to a long-term disability.
HH_LTD: Rate of households in which one or more persons have a long-term disability.

In order to estimate the BAD_HEALTH attribute, a number of dependent attributes were considered. The attributes listed in Table 1 were defined as Utility functions [8], organized in a hierarchy where the attribute to be predicted (BAD_HEALTH) is located on top and the nodes at lower levels are used to estimate the values of their parent nodes. Figure 1 illustrates the hierarchy used in the case studies presented in this paper:

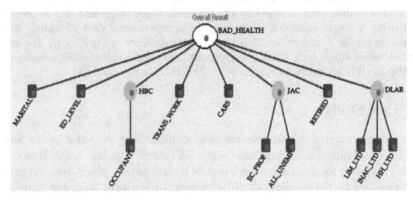

Fig. 1. Hierarchy of the health self-assessment decision problem. Adapted from the Geo-RIMER+ software.

In Figure 1, input attributes (leaf nodes) are depicted as nodes colored in darker grey tones, while intermediate nodes are represented in light grey colors and the root node (BAD_HEALTH) is located at the top of the hierarchy colored in white. As it can be observed from Figure 1, the BAD_HEALTH attribute is estimated based on its 8 son attributes in the hierarchy. However, in the case where there is no information available for some of them, defined as intermediate nodes (HBC, JAC and DLAR), they could be estimated using their own son attributes. For example, if the value for the HBC attribute is unknown in a certain location, the OCCUPANT attribute could be utilized to estimate it. The HBC attribute can be also considered as a milestone or partial goal within the decision problem. That is, the hierarchical representation allows assessing which aspects of the problem affect the overall output the most. In the case of this study, having some attributes grouped within three intermediate nodes maybe be useful to: (1) organize different aspects of the decision problem and (2) discover the reasons why the population of a certain area consider their general health to be bad or very bad (if it is due to poor housing, poor economic activity or a high rate of people with long-term disabilities, among others). From a policy-making perspective, estimating values for these three intermediate nodes when they are unknown can also be of great utility in order to allocate budget for benefits and allowances to support population suffering from these issues. All the studies presented in this research suppose that information is not available for the HBC, JAC and DLAR attributes, so these intermediate nodes are also estimated in order to obtain a prediction for the BAD_HEALTH attribute.

The data utilized in this study was collected from the Northern Ireland Statistics and Research Agency (NISRA), which regularly publishes data regarding many aspects of Northern Ireland. In addition, this information can be represented in a GIS system thanks to the map products provided by the Ordnance Survey (OSNI) or the Land and Property Services (LPS). These maps are reproduced under the Northern Ireland Mapping Agreement (NIMA) reference MOU 203, which applies to non-commercial research produced within the University of Ulster. The dataset used in the study included in this research consists of 582 observations that describe Northern Ireland at Electoral Ward level.

Using this data, a possible decision support scenario was evaluated, based on the estimation of unknown areas, where information of neighboring areas is utilized to deem unknown values of public's self-rated health in certain regions. The following subsection describes and presents the results obtained after the Spatial RIMER+ method was used to solve this situation.

3.1   Estimating Unknown Observations

Public health policies and budget allocations usually need to be studied for the entire of Northern Ireland before a decision is taken. Therefore, information to support such decision making processes needs to be available for every region. This study supposes that self-rated health information is not available for certain areas, for example because a region was unable to provide the required information on time for some reason. In such case, estimations for the areas belonging to that region would need to be provided to policy makers in order to deliver their decisions accurately and on time. In this study, it is supposed that the *North Coast and Glens* region could not provide this information. Figure 2 represents the missing areas that would need to be estimated within Northern Ireland:

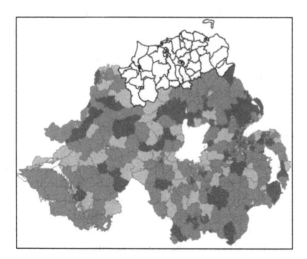

Fig. 2. The North Coast and Glens LGD did not provide information about health self-assessment of its 68 areas, depicted in white with bold boundaries. Map source: LPS.

If the information for the input attributes of the hierarchy represented in Fig. 1 is available, the self-assessed health and the other intermediate attributes could be estimated for the missing areas. In this context, the remaining information that is known for the rest of Northern Ireland can be considered as a training dataset used to generate extended belief rules for the intermediate and root nodes of the hierarchy. Then, the input information available for the *North Coast and Glens* areas can be assigned to the system to obtain an output. If the real data of the predicted observations is available, it can be compared with the estimated values, as it is the case of these studies, in which for the 68 areas estimated the Mean Absolute Error (MAE) was just 1.53%. Figure 3 illustrates the absolute error obtained for each observation:

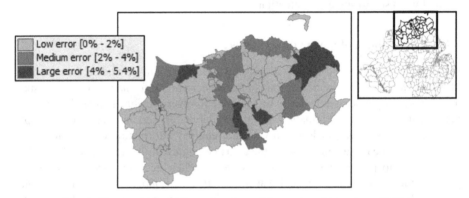

Low error [0% - 2%]
Medium error [2% - 4%]
Large error [4% - 5.4%]

Fig. 3. Absolute Error in the estimations of the system. Map source: LPS.

As it can be observed in Figure 3, in most observations the absolute error of the predicted observation against the real data is less than 2%, and in just 5 observations the error is greater than 4%. Note that in order to obtain these estimations for the BAD_HEALTH attribute, the HBC, JAC and DLAR intermediate attributes had to be also estimated using their nodes sons. That is, these estimations were the base to predict the self-rated health (BAD_HEALTH).

4   Conclusion

Self-rated health can be considered as a crucial measure that can help identifying risk factors and therefore take the right actions to enhance the current public health situation of an area. This research proposed to use Spatial RIMER+ as a decision framework that could help modeling a decision scenario that aims to estimate self-assessed health where it is needed in order to for example develop policies and allocate budget. Spatial RIMER+ uses the information available from several attributes, expert knowledge and the spatial relationships between data samples to estimate the values of unknown areas. Spatial RIMER+'s decision model is based on organizing attributes in a hierarchy, so the causes of a poor self-rated health can be analyzed in depth. Since the real values of the 2011 Northern Irish census are publicly available, they could be compared against the results delivered by Spatial RIMER+, which considered as highly satisfactory due to the low absolute error between the original and predicted data.

Further research includes assessing Spatial RIMER+ in more complex public health decision scenarios as well as developing different applications such as downscaling or prediction over time, among others.

References

1. Ziersch, A.: Neighbourhood 'Social Infrastructure' for Health: The Role of Social Capital, Fear of Crime and Area Reputation. In: Nriagu, J.O. (ed.) Encyclopaedia of Environmental Health, pp. 72–78. Elsevier, Burlington (2011)
2. Subramanyam, M., Kawachi, I., Berkman, L., Subramanian, S.V.: Relative deprivation in income and self-rated health in the United States. Social Science & Medicine 69(3), 327–334 (2009)
3. Van Jaarsveld, C.H., Miles, A., Wardle, J.: Pathways from deprivation to health differed between individual and neighborhood-based indices. Journal of Clinical Epidemiology 60(7), 712–719 (2007)
4. Benyamini, Y.: Why does self-rated health predict mortality? An update on current knowledge and a research agenda for psychologists. Psychology & Health 26(11), 1407–1413 (2011)
5. Calzada, A., Liu, J., Wang, H., Kashyap, A.: A Novel Spatial Belief Rule-Based Intelligent Decision Support System. In: IEEE International Conference on Systems, Man and Cybernetics (IEEE SMC 2013), Manchester, UK, October 13-16, pp. 639–644 (2013)
6. Lloyd, C.D.: Local Models for Spatial Analysis, 2nd edn. CRC Press, Taylor and Francis Group (2011)
7. Sugumaran, R., De Groote, J.P.: Spatial Decision Support Systems: Principles and Practices. CRC Press (2010)
8. Liu, J., Martinez, L., Calzada, A., Wang, H.: A novel belief rule base representation, generation and its inference methodology. Knowledge-Based Systems 53, 129–141 (2013a)
9. gvSIG Project (2010), http://www.gvsig.org/web/home/
10. Calzada, A., Liu, J., Wang, H., Kashyap, A.: A GIS-based Spatial Decision Support Tool Based on Extended Belief Rule-Based Inference Methodology. In: Intl. Workshop on Knowledge Discovery, Management and Decision Support, EUREKA 2013 (2013)

A Leader Election Service for Crash-Recovery and Omission Environments

Christian Fernández-Campusano, Roberto Cortiñas, and Mikel Larrea

Computer Architecture and Technology Department
University of the Basque Country UPV/EHU
Paseo Manuel de Lardizabal 1, 20018 San Sebastián, Spain
{christianrobert.fernandez,roberto.cortinas,mikel.larrea}@ehu.es

Abstract. Leader election is a key service for many dependable ubiquitous systems. It eases the consistent management of replicas in current highly available computing scenarios. This paper presents our work on the design of a leader election service for crash-recovery and omission environments, in order to support fault-tolerant agreement protocols, e.g., Paxos.

1 Motivation

Ubiquitous computing scenarios are composed of a high number of heterogeneous nodes (servers, personal computers, hand-held devices...) that interact seamlessly, exchanging information according to distributed protocols. Since nodes have different degrees of availability and reliability, in order to tolerate failures and achieve good scalability, many systems rely on replication, offering a dependable service. A key aspect of the management of a replicated system is to maintain its consistency, in a transparent manner and despite failures. In this regard, it has been shown that a totally ordered multicast communication guarantees the consistency of replicated systems [1].

The consensus problem [12] is at the heart of many agreement problems in fault-tolerant distributed computing, including total order multicast. Roughly speaking, in consensus processes propose an initial value and have to decide on one of the proposed values. This apparently simple problem has been shown to be unsolvable deterministically in asynchronous systems where at least one process may crash [7]. A way of circumventing this impossibility consists in equipping the system with an unreliable failure detector [3]. Note that such a system is no longer purely asynchronous, since it has been strengthened with a failure detector, which encapsulates the synchrony required to solve consensus. Also, consensus protocols relying on an unreliable failure detector are by nature indulgent [8], i.e., they always preserve safety (no two processes decide differently) and guarantee termination as soon as the failure detector converges, something that is assumed to happen eventually.

One of the best known consensus protocols is Paxos [9], which relies on an eventual leader election service, also known as the Omega failure detector [2].

R. Hervás et al. (Eds.): UCAmI 2014, LNCS 8867, pp. 320–323, 2014.
© Springer International Publishing Switzerland 2014

Recently, we have shown that Paxos outperforms other consensus protocols that are not leader based such as the well-known rotating coordinator based Chandra-Toueg consensus protocol [6]. That work compared two architectures for solving Secure Multiparty Computation [13], a security problem that can be reduced to solving consensus in omission environments by using a tamper-proof smartcard based platform named TrustedPals [4]. The failure detector used for both architectures was an eventually perfect one adapted to the omission failure model, that we transformed into the leader service required by Paxos. Thus, the "cost" of the leader election service was higher than strictly needed. Alternatively, in this work we focus on the design of a more efficient specific leader election service, which tolerates the crash-recovery of any process as well as omission failures.

2   System Model

We consider a system model composed of a finite and totally ordered set of processes that communicate only by sending and receiving messages. Every pair of processes is connected by two unidirectional communication links, one in each direction. Communication links are reliable, and cannot create or alter messages.

Concerning timeliness, we assume that the system is partially synchronous, i.e., there exist upper bounds on processing time and on message communication delay, although those bounds are NOT known a priori by processes [5].

Processes can fail by crashing. Crashes are not permanent, i.e., crashed processes can recover. In every execution of the system, we have the following three disjoint subsets: (1) eventually up, i.e., processes that eventually remain up forever (including those that never crash, also named always up), (2) eventually down, i.e., processes that eventually remain crashed forever, and (3) unstable, i.e., processes that crash and recover an infinite number of times.

Processes can also fail by omission at sending and/or receiving messages. Omissions can be selective, i.e., with respect to a given process, or general. Also, omissions can be transient or permanent. Observe for example that a permanent send and receive omission failure is indistinguishable from a (permanent) crash.

Indulgent consensus protocols require a *majority of correct processes*. Hence, we will assume a majority of eventually up and non omissive processes in the system, namely the correct *core*. Actually, we could have weakened the previous assumption by considering that a majority of eventually up processes can communicate (directly or indirectly) without omissions. This would require a systematic forwarding of messages in order to cope with omissions. Also, we do not assume the existence of any always up process. On the other hand, eventually down and unstable processes are considered incorrect, and can suffer any kind and number of omissions.

Finally, in this work we assume that processes have access to stable storage that maintains its content despite crashes. This way processes can upon recovery resume their execution from the point where it stopped upon crash, provided the state was duly stored in stable storage. Note also that stable storage can be used by a process to count how many times it has crashed and recovered [11].

3   Leader Election Definitions and Protocol

Chandra, Hadzilacos and Toueg defined in [2] the Omega failure detector class for crash environments. The output of Omega at a process p is a single process q that p currently considers to be correct (it is said that p trusts q). The Omega failure detector class satisfies the following property: there is a time after which every correct process always trusts the same correct process. From this, it is said that Omega provides an eventual leader election service. The importance of Omega comes from the fact that it has been shown to be the weakest failure detector allowing to solve the consensus problem with a majority of correct processes [2].

Observe that the previous definition, made for the crash failure model, does not say anything about incorrect processes (in particular, unstable processes), which are allowed to disagree at any time with correct processes, which can affect negatively an attempt to solve consensus due to the existence of several leaders (the termination of leader based consensus relies on the eventual existence of a unique alive leader). It is thus interesting that eventually all the processes that are up (either correct or unstable) and can communicate with the core (either directly or indirectly), agree on a common and correct leader process. The following definition for Omega in the crash–recovery failure model with stable storage has been proposed in [10]: there is a time after which every process that is up, either correct or unstable, always trusts the same correct process.

The previous reasoning only applies to alive processes that can communicate with the correct core. Clearly, processes that, due to continuous crash-recovery or permanent omissions, become disconnected/partitioned from the core cannot be forced to agree on the correct leader.

Finally, an implementation of Omega can be communication-efficient, defined as follows [10]: there is a time after which only one process (the elected leader) sends messages forever. Observe that this definition implies that unstable processes eventually stop sending messages. Note also that in order to satisfy this property we require the elected leader to *directly* communicate without omissions with the rest of alive processes. Otherwise, i.e., if we weaken the communication assumption, message forwarding is required (formally, in this case eventually only the elected leader would send *new* messages forever, that would be forwarded by the rest of processes in order to reach all the processes in the system).

We are currently designing and proving the correctness of a new leader election protocol, adapting the communication-efficient Omega algorithm for crash-recovery with stable storage proposed in [10] in order to cope also with omission failures. For that, we are using sequence numbers combined with the use of stable storage. This way, eventually all the alive processes will permanently trust the eventually up process that has crashed and recovered a minimum number of times. Unstable processes that can communicate with the core will finally write in their stable storage the identity of this leader, and will subsequently read this identity from stable storage upon recovery. Note that this is not needed for correct processes belonging to the core, since they will eventually remain up forever and thus will communicate timely with the leader. As future work, we plan to implement our leader election protocol in order to analyze experimentally its performance. Also, we aim at designing an alternative leader election protocol where processes do not have access to stable storage (possibly assuming the existence of an always up process), comparing the two solutions both analytically and empirically. As the ultimate and ambitious goal, we are interested in determining the weakest system assumptions for implementing a communication-efficient leader election service.

Acknowledgments. Research supported by the Spanish Research Council, under grant TIN2013-41123-P, the Basque Government, under grant IT395-10, and the University of the Basque Country UPV/EHU, under grant UFI11/45.

References

1. Birman, K.P., Joseph, T.A.: Reliable communication in the presence of failures. ACM Trans. Comput. Syst. 5(1), 47–76 (1987)
2. Chandra, T.D., Hadzilacos, V., Toueg, S.: The weakest failure detector for solving consensus. Journal of the ACM 43(4), 685–722 (1996)
3. Chandra, T.D., Toueg, S.: Unreliable failure detectors for reliable distributed systems. Journal of the ACM 43(2), 225–267 (1996)
4. Cortiñas, R., Freiling, F.C., Ghajar-Azadanlou, M., Lafuente, A., Larrea, M., Penso, L.D., Soraluze, I.: Secure failure detection and consensus in trustedpals. IEEE Trans. Dependable Sec. Comput. 9(4), 610–625 (2012)
5. Dwork, C., Lynch, N.A., Stockmeyer, L.J.: Consensus in the presence of partial synchrony. J. ACM 35(2), 288–323 (1988)
6. Fernández-Campusano, C., Cortiñas, R., Larrea, M.: Boosting dependable ubiquitous computing: A case study. In: Urzaiz, G., Ochoa, S.F., Bravo, J., Chen, L.L., Oliveira, J. (eds.) UCAmI 2013. LNCS, vol. 8276, pp. 42–45. Springer, Heidelberg (2013)
7. Fischer, M.J., Lynch, N.A., Paterson, M.: Impossibility of distributed consensus with one faulty process. J. ACM 32(2), 374–382 (1985)
8. Guerraoui, R., Raynal, M.: The information structure of indulgent consensus. IEEE Trans. Computers 53(4), 453–466 (2004)
9. Lamport, L.: The part-time parliament. ACM Trans. Comput. Syst. 16(2), 133–169 (1998)
10. Larrea, M., Martín, C., Soraluze, I.: Communication-efficient leader election in crash-recovery systems. Journal of Systems and Software 84(12), 2186–2195 (2011)
11. Martín, C., Larrea, M., Jiménez, E.: Implementing the omega failure detector in the crash-recovery failure model. J. Comput. Syst. Sci. 75(3), 178–189 (2009)
12. Pease, M.C., Shostak, R.E., Lamport, L.: Reaching agreement in the presence of faults. J. ACM 27(2), 228–234 (1980)
13. Yao, A.C.C.: Protocols for secure computations (extended abstract). In: FOCS, pp. 160–164. IEEE Computer Society (1982)

Decision Making Environment
Based on Prosumer Services for Tracing Drugs
in a Hospital Pharmacy Department

Diego Martín, Ramón Alcarria, Álvaro Sánchez-Picot*, and Tomás Robles

Technical University of Madrid,
Av. Complutense 30, 28040 Madrid, Spain
{diego.martin.de.andres,ramon.alcarria,tomas.robles}@upm.es
alvaro.spicot@gmail.com

Abstract. Systems adaptation and functionality addition could pose great efforts and high costs if done by expert developers, especially when it comes to ambient intelligence environments. In this paper it is presented an ambient intelligence environment for decision making in the pharmacy department of Gregorio Marañón Hospital of Madrid, composed of a drug traceability infrastructure (Drug TraIN) and a ubiquitous application for enabling the pharmacy staff to create and execute Decision Making Services for Prosumer Pharmacy (DM-SePP). The authors carried out a case study where 16 people from pharmacy staff were involved in services creation showing that they are very satisfied with the application, evaluating it as relevant. Furthermore, the authors have analyzed the effort required to create services by pharmacy staff contrasting it with the one required by expert developers, showing that the effort is lower when using a prosumer environment.

Keywords: prosumer, case study, decision maker, ECA rules, drug traceability, hospital pharmacy, RFID.

1   Introduction

Nowadays the user participation is a new trend where some especial users often called prosumers [1], formed by the combination of the words *producers* and *consumers*. They were originally producers and consumers of content but recently are emerging a new kind of prosumers: the "service prosumers" [2] who would like to add new functionality to their tools, platforms and ambient environments (AmI). However, the development of applications for ambient intelligence environments usually involves complex systems and high experienced developers, which incurs in high efforts and costs. If a layer for creating services by prosumers on an ambient intelligence environment is offered, then it will enable the prosumers to add new functionalities to the environment, satisfying their new requirements and saving efforts and costs.

---

* Corresponding author.

R. Hervás et al. (Eds.): UCAmI 2014, LNCS 8867, pp. 324–332, 2014.
© Springer International Publishing Switzerland 2014

In this paper we present an ambient intelligence environment for tracing drugs in the pharmacy department of Gregorio Marañón Hospital of Madrid, a project funded by the Ministry of Economy and Competitiveness of Spain. The main contributions of this intelligence ambient project are: a drug infrastructure (Drug TraIN) for tracing drugs at pharmacy department based on RFID and a Manager for Decision Making Services for Prosumer Pharmacy (DM-SePP), a platform to enable the pharmacy staff to create and execute services over Drug TraIN.

The authors carried out a case study, where 16 people from the pharmacy staff was involved, in order to validate the solution proposed analyzing the prosumers´ satisfaction with the environment and the effort needed to create a DM-SePP, contrasting it with the effort required by expert developers from a software development organization.

2   Related Work

There are studies researching the prosumer philosophy and the provision of applications for the creation of prosumer services [3] or holistic frameworks [4]. These tools offer different creation strategies such as [2] natural languages and, semi-automatic solutions requiring more effort from the users [5]. In this research work we have analyzed more closely those that provide graphical interfaces for ubiquitous systems because that characteristic helps the definition of the services. The Mashup tools Marmite and Yahoo Pipes combine existing Web contents and services from multiple websites and process, filter and direct the information to different sinks, such as databases, map services and web pages. Some web applications such as Zapier or IFTTT enable the creation of services by prosumers that interact with other web services such as Twitter, Facebook, etc. but do not offer an interface to interact with a particular system.

In our approach we combine the benefits of the mashup tools and the adaptation of the ECA (Event, Condition, Action) rules concept [6].

There are a few studies analyzing the user satisfaction with prosumer environments and also there are a few references to researches considering the effort required to create prosumer services using an ambient intelligence environment.

3   Prosumer Services for Managing a Hospital Pharmacy Department

In this section we describe the deployment of an ambient intelligence environment composed of two main elements: **Drug TraIN** (Drug Traceability Infrastructure), a system for drug traceability in the pharmacy department of Gregorio Marañón Hospital based on RFID technology. **DM-SePPs** (Decision-Making Services for Prosumer Pharmacy) a data model for describing services that works over **Drug TraIN**, and finally, **DM-SePP Manager**, a tool for managing (creating and provisioning).

3.1   Drug TraIN (Drug Traceability Infrastructure)

Drug TraIN is an ambient intelligence environment deployed at the hospital pharmacy department of Gregorio Marañón of Madrid through a research project funded by the Spanish Ministry of Economy called UNICA ID. The deployment was performed by an SME, partner of the UNICA ID project.

Drug TraIN is composed of a drug registration and delivery stand, a RFID arch for tracing the drugs at the main entrance of the pharmacy and a repository that stores the events of the RFID reader and writers

At the drug registration and delivery stand, the pharmacy staff registers the drugs that will be stored in the pharmacy; sticking a label generated by a RFID label printer. The staff can also deliver the drugs to a patient using a handheld RFID reader or a handheld barcode scanner. Fig. 1 shows the deployment of this stand.

At the main entrance of the pharmacy four UHF antennas were disposed forming an RFID arch (as seen in Fig. 2). The RFID arch is able to track the entry and exit of drugs as a single element as well as a set of them.

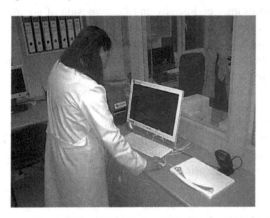

Fig. 1. Drug registration and delivery stand   **Fig. 2.** RFID arch

All RFID readers and writers generate EPCIS (Electronic Product Code Information Service) events when they read or write an RFID tag from a drug and the system stores those events in a repository. The system also informs to DM-SePPs about these events.

3.2   DM-SePPs Manager

DM-SePP Manager is an ambient intelligent tool for decision making and provisioning of prosumer services in a hospital pharmacy department. This tool is a full graphical tool based on cloud capabilities and executable on any device with a web browser. It is able to manage DM-SePPs data model describing services that can run over Drug TraIN helping the pharmacy staff to trace drugs in order to create special functionality added to the Drug TraIN without hiring a specialized development team for developing that new functionality.

DM-SePP Manager has two different operating environments: service creation and service provision environments; both are programmed using HTML5, CSS3 and JavaScript. The service creation environment helps prosumers to create DM-SePPs through a graphical environment (see fig. 3). The service provision environment consists of an execution engine of DM-SePPs where users can start, pause or stop services created previously; the engine listens to the events produced by Drug TraIN and compares them with the events of the running DM-SePPs and, if they match, the engine executes the action defined in the service.

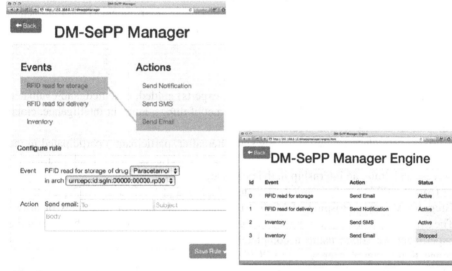

Fig. 3. DM-SePP Manager – creation view   **Fig. 4.** DM-SePP Manager - Engine view

The DM-SePP are based on ECA (event, condition, action) rules, but in previous research [2] we showed that the "condition" element presented modelling problems for prosumers, so in this research work this element was removed. This composition paradigm describes service composition by providing two related components: **Event (E)**, as an occurrence triggering the action execution and **action (A)**, describing the realization of a certain action when the event occurs.

The components of type Event connect with the traceability event generation and query system through an EPCIS Query Interface Repository, installed in the hospital environment, which provides the framework with information about the medicines crossing some RFID arcs (name of the drug, registration time, expiration date, etc.). The implemented Actions consist of the selection of different communication channels for drug notifications (email, sms, and web notifications).

4   Experimental Validation

This research work was guided by the next research questions:

a) Which is the subjective satisfaction of pharmacy staff using the environment proposed in this paper?

b) What is the effort required to create services using a prosumer environment compared to develop the same functionality by a software development organization?

A case study was designed in order to analyze and respond those research questions. The case study was divided in three phases where 16 people from the hospital pharmacy department of Gregorio Marañón of Madrid used the DM-SePP Manager to create real services for solving software requirements at the pharmacy. The researchers had little control of the people using the prosumer environment. This approach is appropriate to replicate the experiment in similar contexts.

4.1   Context

The authors of this research work (hereafter, experts) guided, executed, and evaluated the case study, whose research areas are internet of things, ambient intelligence, cloud computing, knowledge management, etc.

Sixteen people from the pharmacy staff (hereafter, participants) participated in the experimentation having more than five years' experience in hospital pharmacies process and doing an internship in the pharmacy.

Drug TraIN is a very committed system deployed at the Pharmacy Department at Gregorio Marañón Hospital of Madrid that has a daily flow of thousands of drugs. The system cannot be interrupted and cannot be exposed to errors; for this reason the experiment was done using a completely identical and cloned system but without connection to the pharmacy. The EPCIS events have been reproduced from the repository of Drug TraIN, the experts selected one month of EPCIS records from the pharmacy meaning more than 10.000 EPCIS events.

The participants, using DM-SePPs, created three services in order to solve three typical problems proposed by the pharmacy chief.

4.2   Planning

The case study plan was divided in three phases:

-Training phase: Participants received some training with the prosumer philosophy, the DM-SePPs, its elements, how to configure it and use the tool. Training sessions consisted of a one-hour lecture at the beginning of the experimental validation given by one of the experts. And also the experts resolved any doubt from the participants during the experiment's execution.

-Service Creation phase: This phase was divided in two parts in order to be operative, the participants are actual employees of the pharmacy so it was not possible to execute the experiment at the same time with all the participants. Therefore, there were 10 participants at the first part and 6 more participants at the second one. The main objective of this phase was that the participants had to create three services each

one solving standard problems from the hospital pharmacy; proposed by the chief of the pharmacy. The participants used DM-SePP Manager to model the services.

-Evaluation phase: In this phase the experts evaluated 48 DM-SePPs created during experimentation and also analyzed 16 surveys in which the participants were asked about the prosumer philosophy and the use of DM-SePPs Manager.

4.3   Data Collection

The information collected to address the first research question (*Which is the subjective satisfaction of pharmacy staff using the environment proposed in this paper?*) was obtained from a survey where the participants were asked about some satisfaction indicators of DM-SePP Manager, DM-SePPs and their elements.

The information collected to address the second research question (What is the effort required to create services using a prosumer environment compared to develop the same functionality by a software development organization?) were the following:

-The effort to build the DM-SePPs by participants. The experts extracted from the log files the time needed to build each service.

-The estimated effort required to create the services by a software development organization. These estimations were made by a group of four experts from the software development organization that developed and deployed Drug TraIN.

5   Results

This section analyses the results obtained. The results will be shown trying to response two research questions proposed in this research work.

Subjective Satisfaction of Pharmacy Staff with the Environment Proposed
This section presents an analysis of the satisfaction perceived by 16 participants of the experiment. The participants were asked about three satisfaction aspects: satisfaction, relevance, and frustration using the system, in a Likert scale from 0 to 5.

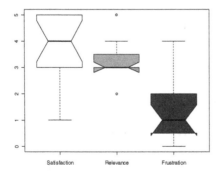

Fig. 5. Satisfaction evaluation

Fig. 5 shows that the overall evaluation of the participants for satisfaction was positive, with an average of 3.69, although the values are quite scattered meaning that some participants were unsatisfied. However the relevance also had fairly high scores, but in this case the dispersion was lower. This means that the perceived relevance of the system is very high, indicating that participants require such prosumer systems, but satisfaction had scattered values because the DM-SePPs Manager is a prototype and still have look and feel problems.

Values for frustration confirm the idea proposed above, overall frustration has been quite low with an average of 1.44; in addition participants who rated the system as unsatisfactory also rated it as frustrating. That hypothesis was confirmed by a correlation test between the variables measuring satisfaction and frustration, the results were positive indicated by an inverse correlation ($r = -0.69$) between these variables and a strong significance ($\rho < 0.005$). It can be said that prosumer systems, that enable users to create services are very important and necessary, but it is also very important to develop useful and functional applications, and it is necessary to be very careful with the "look and feel" in order to not thwart the future prosumers.

Effort Required to Create Services Using a Prosumer Environment Compared with the Develop of Same Functionality by a Software Development Organization

A study of the effort required to build services using DM-SePPs Manager was carried out and was compared with estimations made by four expert developers associated to the project from the partners who developed and deployed Drug TraIN, so they were familiar with the system.

A brief summary of the effort required to build or develop services is presented in Table 1. The results show that using a prosumer platform for creating services incurs less effort than creating them by expert developers. A Mann-Whitney U test was performed in order to confirm the hypothesis; the results were positive and within the expected significance, $\rho < 0.001$.

Table 1. Summary of the effort spent in building or developing the services (Measured in minutes)

	Prosumers		Developers	
	Median	SD	Median	SD
Time to build three DM-SePPs	18	6.09	200	102.47

6   Discussion and Future Work

This research work presents a development and deployment made in the pharmacy department of Gregorio Marañón Hospital of Madrid carried out through a research project funded by the Ministry of Economy of Spain. The system is divided into two main subsystems: Drug TraIN, an infrastructure for tracing drugs at the pharmacy based on RFID technology and DM-SePP Manager, a prosumer platform designed to create and provisioning services in the pharmacy.

A case study has been carried out with the participation of the pharmacy staff (16 people), which were involved in the creation of three services to solve prototypical problems for drug traceability in the pharmacy, proposed by the pharmacy chief. All the participants had the same experience at the pharmacy and the same experience with mobile technologies.

The research work was designed in order to answer two research questions that guided this work and also will guide this section:

Subjective Satisfaction of Pharmacy Staff with the Environment Proposed. The results obtained shown that prosumer platforms are very relevant in order to create simple services to increase the functionality and to help prosumers to solve specific problems. The problems that can be solved with the prosumer platform are conditioned by the functionality provided by the platform, but it will be increased in the future. The subjective perception of the relevance was high among participants as well as the satisfaction with the use of the application. Although there were a few participants who rated the application as unsatisfactory; these same participants also rated it as frustrating. The reason for these results is that the application is in beta stage and still contains errors that affected participant judgment. Therefore, it is necessary to continue the development and improvement of the application as it is highly valued as relevant by the participants.

Effort Required to Create Services Using a Prosumer Environment Compared with the Develop of Same Functionality by a Software Development Organization
The results demonstrate that the effort required to create services using a prosumer environment is lower than developing the functionality by a software development organization. Despite this, it is necessary to take into account some other considerations such as: the quality of the services, the time spent to train the prosumers compared with the time spent to develop the prosumer platform, the functionality of the services created by prosumers or by expert developers

These issues are very interesting and very important to answer. Thus, the authors of this research work are conducting a new research in order to answer these questions where more participants from the pharmacy department of Gregorio Marañón will be involved.

Acknowledgement. This work was supported by the projects UNICA ID (TSI-020302-2010-39) and CALISTA (TEC2012-32457). The authors thank all the projects partners especially to Dr. Ana Herranz-Alonso and all the staff of Gregorio Marañón Hospital of Madrid.

References

1. Drossos, N., Mavrommati, I., Kameas, A.: Towards ubiquitous computing applications composed from functionally autonomous hybrid artifacts. In: Streitz, N., Kameas, A., Mavrommati, I. (eds.) The Disappearing Computer. LNCS, vol. 4500, pp. 161–181. Springer, Heidelberg (2007)

2. Martin, D., Alcarria, R., Robles, T., Morales, A.: A Systematic Approach for Service Prosumerization in IoT Scenarios. In: The Seventh International Conference on Innovative Mobile and Internet Services in Ubiquitous Computing, IMIS 2013, July 3-5, pp. 494–499 (2013), doi:10.1109/IMIS.2013.89
3. Morales, A., Alcarria, R., Martín, D., Robles, T.: Enhancing evacuation plans with a situation awareness system based on end-user knowledge provision. Sensors (2014), doi: 10.3390/s140611153
4. Serrano, E., Poveda, G., Garijo, M.: Towards a Holistic Framework for the Evaluation of Emergency Plans in Indoor Environments. Sensors, 4513–4535 (2014)
5. Martin, D., García Guzmán, J., Urbano, J., Amescua, A.: Modelling Software Development Practices using Reusable Project Patterns: A Case Study. Journal of Software: Evolution and Process 26(3), 339–349 (2014), doi:10.1002/smr.1587
6. Martín, D., López-de-Ipiña, D., Alzua-Sorzabal, A., Lamsfus, C., Torres-Manzanera, E.: A Methodology and a Web Platform for the Collaborative Development of Context-Aware Systems. Sensors 13, 6032–6053 (2013)

Visual Privacy by Context:
A Level-Based Visualisation Scheme

José Ramón Padilla-López[1], Alexandros Andre Chaaraoui[1],
and Francisco Flórez-Revuelta[2]

[1] Department of Computer Technology, University of Alicante,
P.O. Box 99, 03080 Alicante, Spain
{jpadilla,alexandros}@dtic.ua.es
[2] Faculty of Science, Engineering and Computing, Kingston University,
Penrhyn Road, KT1 2EE, Kingston upon Thames, UK
F.Florez@kingston.ac.uk

Abstract. In a near future, a greater number of individuals in long-term care will live alone. New solutions are needed in order to provide them support and increase their autonomy at home. Intelligent monitoring systems based on computer vision may provide a solution. However, privacy related issues must be solved beforehand. In this paper, we propose a level-based visualisation scheme to give users control about their privacy in those cases in which another person is watching the video. These visualisation levels are dynamically selected according to the context by displaying modified images in which sensitive areas are protected.

Keywords: privacy, context, intelligent monitoring, ambient-assisted living.

1 Introduction

Video-based applications are being used more and more frequently in Ambient-Assisted Living (AAL). Computer vision techniques allow to monitor an environment and report on visual information, which is generally the most direct and natural way of describing the world. These advances have given video cameras the ability of 'seeing', thereby becoming smart cameras. They are used for several applications, from tasks such as object recognition and tracking to recognition of actions and activities of daily living, or even human behaviour analysis during a long period of time [1]. These new abilities enable the development of novel AAL services for people in need of care, *e.g.* a home accidents detection. Although video cameras allow to obtain a huge amount of environmental data in a non-intrusive and straightforward way, their usage in private spaces brings up ethical concerns related to the privacy of their inhabitants. Smart cameras in private spaces threatens privacy protection [5]. Hence, it seems unreasonable to use cameras there. Indeed, the usage of consumer electronics products like Google Glass currently raise suspicion due to people being recorded without

R. Hervás et al. (Eds.): UCAmI 2014, LNCS 8867, pp. 333–336, 2014.
© Springer International Publishing Switzerland 2014

consent. Therefore, there are some privacy issues that need to be solved in advance before using smart cameras in private spaces. In this paper, a level-based visualisation scheme that aims to solve some privacy issues is presented.

2   Privacy Protection

Although there are several stages in which privacy protection may be involved, this paper is focused on the visualisation stage, *i.e.* the visualisation of the video by a human viewer. This work is a continuation of another one presented in [4]. In that work, we introduced a paradigm for people monitoring that considers privacy from early stages on. In the present work, we have reviewed the privacy requirements and the privacy issue has been addressed following a privacy-by-context approach.

In contrast to works where privacy is protected by using blurring or pixelating effects to modify an image [3], this contribution is more similar to [2], where several ways of displaying an object (*i.e.* visual abstractions) are proposed according to the closeness between objects and viewers. Similarly, in our work privacy is protected by means of a set of visualisation models that provide a given level of protection. But the use of a specific model is determined by the context. In other words, visualisation models establish the way in which non-protected video images are modified before being displayed in order to conceal sensitive information of the subject. As the the correspondence between a given instance of the context and the visualisation level must be performed by the assisted person in advance, our privacy-by-context approach empowers people to adapt privacy to their preferences.

The context has to provide enough information so as people can decide by whom, how and when they are watched. Different privacy protection needs of an individual have been considered (identity, appearance, location, and ongoing activity or event) in order to decide which variables are part of the context. This leads us to propose a context made up of the following variables: i) the observer, ii) identity of the person (to retrieve the privacy profile), iii) closeness between person and observer (*e.g.* relative, doctor or acquaintance), iv) appearance (dressed?), v) location (*e.g.* kitchen), and vi) ongoing activity or detected event (*e.g.* cooking, watching TV, fall). By using these variables, an individual can describe a situation and choose the corresponding visualisation level for this situation (see Table 1).

3   Implementation

A software prototype for our visualisation scheme has been developed considering eight visualisation models (see Fig. 1). The silhouette of the person is considered as the sensitive area, thereby these models focus on protecting identity and appearance. The implemented visualisation models use some visual effects to conceal the person, replace the individual with something different, or even make the person disappear completely. Next, we describe each model:

Table 1. An example of the privacy levels (see Sect. 3) selected by John according to the context

#	Observer	Rest of the context	Visualisation Level
1	My daughter Mary (caregiver, relative)	dressed, living room, watching TV	Raw Image
2	My daughter Mary (caregiver, relative)	undressed, shower, fall	Highly protected (Silhouette)
3	Alice (my doctor, friend)	dressed, living room, watching TV	No image

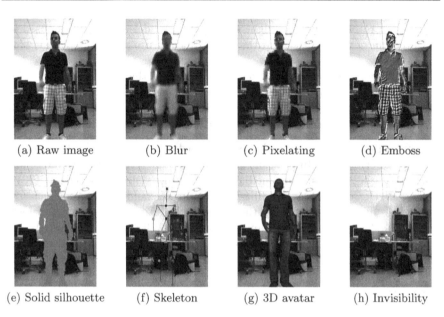

(a) Raw image   (b) Blur   (c) Pixelating   (d) Emboss

(e) Solid silhouette   (f) Skeleton   (g) 3D avatar   (h) Invisibility

Fig. 1. Visualisation models included in our implementation

(a) **Raw image**. It does not modify the raw image, so no protection is provided. In some cases, it could be useful to assess the gravity of a detected event.

(b) **Blur**. The silhouete is smoothed. Although a balance between privacy and awareness is not provided, it can partially protect the appearance.

(c) **Pixelating**. It reduces the image resolution. As in blur, it can partially protect the appearance.

(d) **Emboss**. This model removes colour information of the image (corresponding to skin, hair, etc.) but it preserves the structure of the textures.

(e) **Solid silhouette**. Information about colour and structure of textures is removed. Height and shape allow identification. Nudity is partially protected.

(f) **Skeleton**. A virtual skeleton that mimics the movements is used. Colour and shape are fully removed (nudity protection), but posture is preserved.

(g) **3D avatar**. A 3D avatar that mimics the movements is used. Appearance information is completely removed, preventing direct identification.
(h) **Invisibility**. The person is completely removed from the image. Interaction with the environment can be seen (e.g. objects) but not the person.

4 Conclusion

In this paper, we have presented a privacy scheme that uses visualisation levels for privacy preserving. The selection of the appropriate level is handled by the assisted person according to the context made up of six variables. By using this, the individual can decide how to be visualised in any situation. We have also developed a prototype that has eight visualisation models. These are focused on the protection of the identity and the appearance of the person, and they work in real time.

As future work, it would be interesting to compare the different visualisation models as well as develop new ones. Also, other image regions should be considered as sensitive areas so as to prevent indirect identification. Further research will be carried out in order to recognise identity and appearance to enhance the context.

Acknowledgements. This work has been partially supported by the Spanish Ministry of Science and Innovation under project 'Detección temprana de síndromes de fragilidad y demencia mediante análisis visual de la marcha' (TIN2013-47152-C3-2-R). José Ramón Padilla-López and Alexandros Andre Chaaraoui acknowledge financial support by the Conselleria d'Educació, Formació i Ocupació of the Generalitat Valenciana (fellowships ACIF/2012/064 and ACIF/2011/160 respectively). The funders had no role in study design, data collection and analysis, decision to publish, or preparation of the manuscript.

References

1. Chaaraoui, A.A., Climent-Pérez, P., Flórez-Revuelta, F.: A review on vision techniques applied to human behaviour analysis for ambient-assisted living. Expert Systems with Applications 39(12), 10873–10888 (2012)
2. Chinomi, K., Nitta, N., Ito, Y., Babaguchi, N.: PriSurv: Privacy Protected Video Surveillance System Using Adaptive Visual Abstraction. In: Satoh, S., Nack, F., Etoh, M. (eds.) MMM 2008. LNCS, vol. 4903, pp. 144–154. Springer, Heidelberg (2008)
3. Frome, A., Cheung, G., Abdulkader, A., Zennaro, M., Bo, W., Bissacco, A., Adam, H., Neven, H., Vincent, L.: Large-scale privacy protection in google street view. In: 2009 IEEE 12th International Conference on Computer Vision, pp. 2373–2380 (September 2009)
4. Padilla-López, J.R., Flórez-Revuelta, F., Monekosso, D.N., Remagnino, P.: The "Good" Brother: Monitoring People Activity in Private Spaces. In: Omatu, S., Paz Santana, J.F., González, S.R., Molina, J.M., Bernardos, A.M., Rodríguez, J.M.C. (eds.) Distributed Computing and Artificial Intelligence. AISC, vol. 151, pp. 49–56. Springer, Heidelberg (2012)
5. Senior, A., Pankanti, S.: Privacy protection and face recognition. In: Li, S.Z., Jain, A.K. (eds.) Handbook of Face Recognition, pp. 671–691. Springer, London (2011)

Evaluation of "Fair Trade" Metaphor as a Control Privacy Method for Pervasive Environments

Esquivel Salas Abraham, Pablo Alfonso Haya, and Xavier Alamán

Escuela Politécnica Superior, Universidad Autónoma de Madrid,
C. Francisco Tomás y Valiente. 11, 28049 Madrid, Spain
abraham.esquivel@gmail.com, {pablo.haya,xavier.alaman}uam.es
http://amilab.ii.uam.es/

Abstract. This paper presents a proof of concepts from which the metaphor of "Fair Trade" is validated as an alternative to manage the private information of users. Our privacy solution deals with user's privacy as a tradable good for obtaining environment's services. Thus, users gain access to more valuable services as they share more personal information. This strategy, combined with optimistic access control and transactions registries mechamisms, enhances users' confidence in the system while encouraging them to share their information, with the consequent benefit for the community. The study results are promising considering the user responses regarding the usefulness, ease of use, information classification and perception of control with the mechanisms proposed by the metaphor.

Keywords: Fair Trade Metaphor, Privacy Management, Ambient Intelligence.

1   Introduction

Ambient Intelligence is a promising research area that opens attractive perspective for improving human-computer interaction. Since AmI Systems require knowing user's private information, privacy issues are especially relevant and subject of an active discussion [1, 2, 3]. Several technological methods have been used by organizations to address privacy [4, 5] as result of the mix between computer security and cryptography fields [6]. In this sense, a major step in leveraging AmI comes from overcoming their legal [7], ethical and psychological issues [8].

Privacy is a dynamic phenomenon [9, 10], therefore, we can say that privacy management is a permanent negotiation where the private and public boundaries are constantly changing in response to the circumstances. Furthermore, we pose that a particular privacy configuration depends on the user sharing a service, and the service itself. In consequence, depending on the users and services involved, user's privacy needs will change.

A first approximation to establish those limits can be to manually configure privacy, assigning the desired level to each source of information. The key problem relays on the degree of privacy desired for a source of information depends not only on the

R. Hervás et al. (Eds.): UCAmI 2014, LNCS 8867, pp. 337–344, 2014.
© Springer International Publishing Switzerland 2014

user and the source, but also on the context. To configure a priori each possible arising situation for every source of information can be an overwhelming task that justifies the use of automatic management solutions. The success of such automatic management solutions depends directly on the trust the user place on them. This trust depends on the following requirements: a) The model must be simple enough to be understood by a non-technical user, and b) The user must be able to modify the automatic configuration at any moment. In developing our framework we focused particularly on the importance of usability. Especially in this case, confidence and trust are synonyms of usability.

This paper presents a proof of concept to validate our framework, which is called "Fair Trade" metaphor (for more detail, see [11]). Our framework is a managing privacy proposal for environments where the violation is not intentional, but a product of interaction between users, and those with an Active Environment.

2   Taxonomy of Personal Information

Information is probably the most important element of privacy. In fact, privacy can be summarized as protecting information loosely enough to permit interaction but sufficiently tight to preserve confidentiality. According to the nature of the user's personal data, we classify information in two categories: long-term information and short-term information. The former comprises information with a low changing rate -e.g. telephone number, address, social security number- The latter, on the other hand, contains information of changing nature -e.g. identity, location, activity. These two types of information have their own strengths and weakness. Thus, since static information is probably valid in the future, a single unwanted access will endanger the information in the long term. Consequently we can categorize this information as especially sensible in a time line. On the contrary, dynamic information may change with time, for what it could seem less sensible, on the other hand, is precisely this kind of information what really describes a person's way of living -e.g. where you are, doing what and with who. Therefore, even not especially sensible in a time line, this kind of information is more directly related to what we understand by privacy than the previous one.

Long term data are insensible to context changes, meaning that once the value is revealed to an unwanted receiver, the data is compromised forever. In this case, the main concern must be who has rights to access the information while when, where, or how is accessed are not relevant. Accordingly, the privacy mechanism associated to long-term personal data is based on a restrictive approach, in which the user must specify which individuals can access each piece of long-term information.

Contrary to long term information, we consider only three types of short- term information: identity, location and activity. Even though identity can be considered -as it is in fact- as long-term information, it must be also kept within the short-term ones due to the indexing function it bears. Thus, without identity, nor location neither activity has any sense.

Short-term information is classified according to two discrete axes: privacy level and personal data. The accuracy of the information varies with the privacy level. This accuracy is characterized by different degrees of granularity of each variable. Although different scales and values can be considered, our three levels approach is motivated by simplicity of use, in other words, remain simple enough to be comprehensible by non-technical user. The three privacy levels are:

— Restricted: In this level a non-disclosure of information is achieved.
— Diffuse: Personal data can be retrieved with some level of distortion. Thus, for each variable, an intermediate value is established hinting at the real one without revealing it.
— Open: The information is revealed without any modification. Hence, the community receives the information as accurate as possible.

3   "Fair Trade" Metaphor

Our proposal relies on the following assumption:

"Users will accept to harm their privacy if, on return, they receive valuable services and they are able to track the flows of their disclosed information."

Our information management protocol is among those referred to as "fair trade politics", in other words, a user can see another user's context variable (identity, location, activity, time) -with the degree of privacy established by the owner- if he harms his privacy equally. This model comprises only what we called dynamic information for what opening or closing the static one to some, none or all others is up to the information's owner through manually configuring so.

For example, following the previous approach, if a user defines his privacy level as Diffuse, his personal data will be shown after being filtered but he would only be able to retrieve filtered information from others in the best case, even from those with an Open privacy level. At the end, the amount of shared information grows information needs, making context-aware services more useful and valuable.

Different mechanisms are used to support our privacy control system. An optimistic access control allows free access to information, with strict registration of whom, what and when accedes to it. This registration acts as a dissuasive mean to prevent abuses within the system.

Templates, combined with default configurations, help users in controlling their privacy and modifying it when necessary. The goal is to promote user's interest in protecting his/her static information in a practical and simple way. Thus, if a user wants to show his/her telephone number he/she will explicitly specify, through a template, to which user or group of users must be shown. Contrary to dynamic information, templates for static information use a restrictive configuration.

Optimistic access control provides a logging service to maintain informed users about who accesses their information and in what degree. This mechanism provide a way to detect inappropriate, suspicious or abusive conducts (for instance, to detect a user consulting activity and location of others excessively in the course of the day). The punitive measures can consist in applying in a restrictive privacy to that specific user, expelling him/her from users' group of confidence and in consequence, limit the quality of services he/she many receive, Additionally, a voting system could be applied in which those conforming the community maintain a list of unpleasant users to which deny services in the environment.

4   Context, Purposes and Characteristics of Study

To validate our hypothesis we developed a context-aware privacy-sensitive instant messenger with which to evaluate how feasible is the "Fair Trade" metaphor as a privacy control mechanism. The prototype runs on top of the infrastructure deployed in the Universidad Autónoma de Madrid [12] and Instituto Tecnológico Superior Zacatecas Norte, a working version is been used daily by the researcher staff of our group. We are working on making an evaluation on a broad variety of end-users, in order to determine whether the number of different privacy levels has to be grown or not and if user's black lists should be public.

The goal of our study is to evaluate the possibility of encouraging users to share their private information promoting the use of contextual services by the community. The instant messenger was developed under "Fair Trade" metaphor, and was used as a means of communication between habitants of two real active environments.

The proposed methodology is as follows:

— A previous interview to the candidates, and pre-questionnaires
— Installation of Instant Messaging Client
— Use on a daily basis (two weeks approximately).
— Second interview (feedback effects) and post-questionnaires
— Recoveries of the transaction log file for review.

The interview consists of three sections. The first one contains some questions, which attempt to determine the perception of privacy by the user, classifying different kind of information according to his/her importance. The second one, determine preferred privacy control mechanisms available for the system in order to alert when someone accesses to his/her private information.

A call for participation was launched to computer science students of Instituto Tecnológico Superior Zacatecas Norte, related to the experiment called "privacy perception in Active Environments". Applicants must have a computer, internet connection, availability for installation and use of an instant messaging application. Twenty one students were selected, all frequent users (daily use) of IM applications (except two who reported using it at least a couple of times a week), with ages ranging from 19 to 24 years old, 14 were men and 7 women.

The initial interview evaluated the perception of user privacy. It was important to get the user's opinion regarding:

— The factors involved in establishing the level of privacy and the order of importance, in a given situation.

— Information considered sensitive (importance of being disclosed to third parties), and utility (advantage to know certain information from a third party).
— Privacy control (control mechanisms, receivers, granularity, optimistic/pessimistic policy).
— Feedback (system alert notifying you that someone has accessed to your private information).

The second interview was applied as a means of feedback in order to evaluate the ease of use, learning and satisfaction of the IM application, but mainly to know the perception of the usefulness of the proposed privacy management.

4.1   Instant Messaging Client

Since sensing technologies might not be available in every place, the IM client allows configuring manually an alternative version of the location and activity values. Nevertheless, information obtained directly from sensors will always be preferred to information stated manually, in order to avoid conscious chatting from malicious users. In AmiChat short-term information is defined in terms of location and activity and the three privacy levels defined in section 2 are incorporated to the IM:

— Restricted. Privacy has the highest level of closeness. Personal information remains secret; as a consequence the user loses IM quality of service. When the user connects to the IM his/her identity will be shown as "anonymous", as they will be all their buddies' identity too, regardless their privacy configuration. Albeit this lack of context information (identity, activity and location) the IM service remains active so the user can send and receive messages even though he does not know to whom or from whom.
— Diffuse. In this privacy level, information is retrieved with certain granularity. User's real identity is replaced with an alias. As a consequence, the user will only view the alias of his/her buddies with diffuse or open privacy levels. The activity to be shown is selected, as in many commercial IMs, from a list with three different options: "Write me!!", "Away" and "Don't disturb". Regarding location, the result value is obtained from environment sensors after being filtered by the privacy middleware. Location information is gathered from two different kind of sensors. On one hand, working spaces such offices and laboratories are outfitted with RFID readers. Users getting in and out of environment should pass their RFID cards. Events on change locations are notified to the IM server. Additionally, a spatial model provides a hierarchy of environments including relationships between them, such inclusion or adjacency. On the other hand, IM monitors the user's personal computer status by means of a resident program that informs if the user is connected or is away. The previous spatial model also represents inclusion relationship between resources and environments. Thus, if a user is using her PC, IM can infer where she is.
— Open. Personal information is completely open; hence the user is able to see others' information with the highest possible resolution: the one defined by

the information owner. The identity shown is the real one and the location and activity values are directly inferred from sensors (e.g. "At the computer abraxas, but not working" or "At room lab b403"). Thus, personal information is traded for quality of service.

5   Results

Regarding the perceived usefulness (measured on a scale where 1 is not useful, 5 is very useful) of "Fair Trade" metaphor for privacy control in the instant messaging application, the results showed that: a) Is useful (4.4), b) It provides control over the activities of my life (3.4) and c) Meets my needs (4.1).

The responses (where 1 is very hard, 5 is easy) in terms of ease of use, showed that: a)It is easy to use (4.5), b) it is flexible (4.3), c) I can use successfully anytime (3.8).

Learnability of metaphor in the IM application, users responded (measured on a scale where 1 mean disagree, 5 strongly agree) that it is very easy (4.6). The satisfaction degree (where 1 means not satisfy me, I am satisfied 5), derived from the following questions: a) I am satisfied with the application (4.09), b) I recommend to a friend (4.14), c) It was a pleasant experience to use (4.19). The most important part of the second interview is in the perception of privacy control, where the following results were obtained (1 means disagree, 5 strongly agree): a) It was clear the difference between short term and long term personal information (4.57), b) The privacy mechanism allowed his identity, location and activity remained at a safe level of disclosure (4.71), c) The application goes according to the active environment services (4.2), d) Short term privacy preferences, were reliable despite of who was with me when using the application (4.33), e) Privacy preferences change according to the time of day when a user uses the application (3.57), f) You had control of their location at any time (4.57), g)You had control of their telephone number at any time (4.47), h) You had control of their activity (what you were doing): working, resting, busy, etc. (4.57), i) You had control of their identity at any time (4.57).

The Factors according to user responses are relevant to determining its level of privacy in a given situation, are (beginning by the most important to the less):1)where the information is stored, 2) The situation, 3) Content, the meaning of the information, 4) Receiver, 5)Role that it plays in the situation-parent, child, boss, employee, teacher, 6) Retention, how long it takes until the information is removed, 7) Information use by the receptor, 8) Who is with the receiver, 9) Who is there with the owner of the information, 10) Location of the information's owner, 11) Location of the information's receiver, 12) Hour of the day in which information is consulted.

Regarding the sensitivity of the information (importance to be disclosed to a third party), the results (beginning by the most important to the less) are: Phone number, identity of people around me, location - where I am, name and last name, company where you work, address, main email account, occupation, date of birth, what am I doing. The privacy preferences also depend on cultural and social aspects. Some states in México have a high incidence of crimes such as extortion and kidnapping, which can be seen in the value of certain information such as the phone number and identity.

Concerning the control mechanisms for managing privacy, three proposals were provided a) Manually (privacy would be setting a priori for each situation), b) Trained (for each access information in a different situation, the privacy level would be asked, and it will be stored for future use), and c) automatically (the system decides the level based on profiles or behavior patterns). The result was that in long term personal information such as identity, address, phone number there is a trend towards manual administration. On the other hand, the location information (where I am) or what I'm doing, which is considered short term personal information, on the second interview, the user motivation was changed from manual to an trained or automatic configuration.

In the results can appreciate that the user prefer make changes, depending on the situation, at the level detail of his/her short term information, as in the case of location, activities the user is performing and occupation.

6   Discussion and Conclusions

The finding provides support to the theoretical framework of this study, and indicates that as a result of the interviews we can conclude that users find useful the classification of information (short/long term information). Regarding short term information, the user prefers to maintain strict control (restrictive configuration) through manual administration, over the disclosure of his information.

One goal of this study was to classify information according to its importance. According to our results, the long term information value and its classification is directly dependent on cultural and social aspects.

With regard to the short-term information, the study shows that variables like identity, location and activity are appropriate to publicize the dynamic context of a user.

Given the variety of situations that may arise in the context of an active environment, the users prefer a short-term information management through trained or automatic control mechanisms (based on templates, combined with default configurations), controlling the exposure information degree (granularity), even to a receivers group.

After using the application and the second interview, users were willing to use an optimistic politic for the treatment of short-term information if, on return, they receive valuable services and they are able to track the flows of their disclosed information.

Interesting results was obtained from development of applications based on Fair Trade mechanisms, where users exchange their personal data in a symmetric way and users are both, consumers and producers of personal information.

As future work, it would be necessary to implement punitive measures to punish optimistic access control abusers, as a blacklist. The develop of new applications under the "Fair Trade" metaphor, sharing the blacklist to denying services to abusers until the community revoked punishment.

Acknowledgements. This work has been funded by the Spanish Ministerio de Ciencia e Innovación through the e-Integra project (TIN2013-44586-R).

References

1. Muhtadi, J., Campbell, R.H., Kapadia, A., Mickunas, D., Yi, S.: Routing Through the Mist: Privacy Preserving Communication in Ubiquitous Computing Environments. In: 22nd International Conference on Distributed Computing Systems (22nd ICDCS 2002), pp. 74–83. IEEE, Vienna (2002)
2. Bellotti, V., Sellen, A.: Design for Privacy in Ubiquitous Computing Environments. In: Proceedings of The Third European Conference on Computer Supported Cooperative Work (ECSCW 1993), p. 75. Kluwer Academic Publishers, Milan (1993)
3. Satyanarayanan, M.: Privacy: The Achilles Heel of Pervasive Computing. IEEE Distributed Systems Online 3(4) (2003)
4. Shen, Y., Pearson, S.: Privacy enhancing technologies: A review. Technical report HPL-2011-113, HP Labs (2011)
5. Wang, Y., Kobsa, A.: Privacy-Enhancing Technologies. In: Handbook of Research on Social and Organizational Liabilities in Information Security. IGI Global Snippet (2008)
6. Danezis, G., Gürses, S.: A critical review of 10 years of privacy technology. In: Proceedings of Surveillance Cultures: A Global Surveillance Society?, UK (2010)
7. Solove, D.: A taxonomy of privacy. University of Pennsylvania Law Review 154(3), 477 (2006)
8. Stone, A.: The Dark Side of Pervasive Computing. IEEE Pervasive Computing 1(2), 4–8 (2003)
9. Palen, L., Dourish, P.: Unpacking "privacy" for a networked world. In: Proceedings of the 2003 Conference on Human Factors in Computing Systems, pp. 129–136. ACM Press, Ft. Lauderdale (2003)
10. Langheinrich, M.: Privacy in Ubiquitous Computing. In: Krumm, J. (ed.) Ubiquitous Computing Fundamentals, pp. 95–160. CRC Press (2009)
11. Esquivel, A., Haya, P.A., García-Herranz, M., Alamán, X.: Managing Pervasive Environment Privacy Using the "Fair Trade" Metaphor. In: Meersman, R., Tari, Z. (eds.) OTM-Ws 2007, Part II. LNCS, vol. 4806, pp. 804–813. Springer, Heidelberg (2007)
12. Haya, P.A., Montoro, G., Alamán, X.: A Prototype of a Context-Based Architecture for Intelligent Home Environments. In: Meersman, R. (ed.) CoopIS/DOA/ODBASE 2004. LNCS, vol. 3290, pp. 477–491. Springer, Heidelberg (2004)

RecordMe: A Smartphone Application for Experimental Collections of Large Amount of Data Respecting Volunteer's Privacy

David Blachon[1,2], François Portet[1], Laurent Besacier[1], and Stéphan Tassart[2]

[1] Laboratoire d'Informatique de Grenoble
Grenoble 1/Grenoble INP/CNRS UMR 5217, 38041 Grenoble, France
{david.blachon,francois.portet,laurent.besacier}@imag.fr
[2] STMicroelectronics, 75669 Paris, France
stephan.tassart@st.com

Abstract. Since the spread of smartphones, researchers now have opportunities to collect more ecological data. However, despite the many advantages of existing databases (e.g., clean data, direct comparison), they may not suit all criteria for a particular experiment, resulting in an unavoidable tradeoff between the gain they provide and the lack of some labels or data sources. In this paper, we introduce RecordMe, an Android application ready to use for the research community. RecordMe allows to continuously record many different sensors and sources and provides a basic GUI for quick and easy settings. Also, a mark up interface is embedded for experiments that need it. Because of the high sensitivity of some data, RecordMe includes features for protecting volunteers' privacy and securing their data. RecordMe has already been successfully tested on different smartphones for 3 data collections.

Keywords: Mobile and sensor data acquisition, Context Sensing technology, Databases for data mining, Non-intrusive smart technology.

1 Introduction

The recent spread of smartphones and tablets has opened many opportunities for the research community. Leveraging smartphones many resources, standard development frameworks, and the many potential volunteers, new sensing ways have emerged such as participatory sensing [1]. Another hot topic is the use of personal data collected through smartphones for tasks such activity recognition or context recognition [2]. In any of these cases, researchers must collect data to build systems and evaluate them.

Early studies have performed such sensing for collecting personal data such as Reality Mining [3], a campaign for collecting data through a particular smartphone provided to around 90 participants. More recently, Kiukkonen et al [4] collected data of almost 200 volunteers over several months. Both campaigns provided useful databases (although they relied on a single brand of smartphones), containing volunteers' location, social interaction clues or accelerometer

R. Hervás et al. (Eds.): UCAmI 2014, LNCS 8867, pp. 345–348, 2014.
© Springer International Publishing Switzerland 2014

readings [4]. Existing databases offer many advantages such as handling tools, annotated data, provided evaluation methodology, easy and direct benchmarking.

However, such databases may not fit all the criteria, especially when it comes to use for a task a database that was acquired for another task. Hence, researchers have to trade research objectives off for the gain of time and money of using such databases. Moreover, existing databases are rarely provided with the tools that were used for their acquisition, which makes difficult to reproduce such acquisitions. In fact, to the best of our knowledge, no tool is available for the research community to collect personal data on smartphones.

In this paper, we introduce RECORDME, an Android application designed for the research community so as to collect data through volunteers' smartphones. RECORDME can continuously record data through around 20 different sources embedded on smartphones. A basic GUI allows an easy and quick use and can be configured. A mark up view is included in the GUI to allow volunteers to fill in personal annotations when experiments require it. Finally, because of the high sensitity of some collected data, built-in features allow to protect volunteers' privacy and secure data. In Section 2, RECORDME is introduced while Section 3 reports first statistics and feedbacks of its use for data collections.

2   RECORDME: A Collecting Application for the Research Community

2.1   Design

RECORDME can record almost 20 different data sources at a time, both continuous or event-based, and provide either raw data or processed ones. Table 1 summarizes recorded sensors and processings if any.

This core feature is wrapped up with a basic GUI that allows volunteers a total control of the recording (see Figure 1). Indeed, she/he can select the sources to record, start and stop them at any time, and a notification informs her in real time about the status of the recording. If required, data transmission can be performed through a button on the main view that will start a wifi connection and transmit data through Secure Copy Protocol (SCP) to a predefined server.

Table 1. Summary of sensed sources

Type	Sensors	Data
Continuous	Accelerometer, Barometer, Ambient light, Magnetometer, Gyroscope	Raw 3-axis readings
Continuous	Audio	DFT coefficients magnitudes
Event	Proximity sensor, Headset, Battery Screen State, Communication Logs (Call, SMS, Data, Bluetooth, Wifi)	Status transitions (e.g., on/off) Service status (e.g., in service) Comm. status (e.g., ringing)
Event	Communication logs, application use	Hash function on character strings (ids, MAC addresses, app names)
Event	GPS, Wifi	Translation of coordinates

Because some experiments might require volunteers to report some notes or mark up, the GUI provides a view for such purpose. The markup template can be configured to provide predefined fields to fill in so as to make annotation quick and easy. However, volunteers can switch to text free areas for writing down their own annotations.

2.2 Privacy and Security

For ensuring privacy care and security of the data, RECORDME embeds built-in features. For instance, data older than 48 hours are deleted on a regular basis. Also, audio sensing is stopped when volunteers pass a call.

Specific processing are applied to sensitive data. Location coordinates from GPS or Wifi hotspots are translated then stored on the device so that it is not straightforward for non-experimenters to use them. For audio, RECORDME does not save raw signal but features computed on the fly. Coefficients magnitude of the Discrete Fourier Transform (DFT) are computed on 50% overlapping buffers of approximately 25 ms. Then, consecutive vectors are averaged on a window of approximately 200 ms. These settings guarantee that the raw signal cannot be reconstructed.

Also, character strings such as phone numbers from incoming calls or SMS, MAC addresses of nearby Bluetooth or Wifi devices, or cell tower ids are processed since they are sensitive. Since only correlation between the occurrence of those elements with other flows of information and with markups are of interest, a non reversible transformation by hash function is applied to protect privacy. A hash function associates a unique identifier to every input so that the distribution and correlation of the occurences are unchanged.

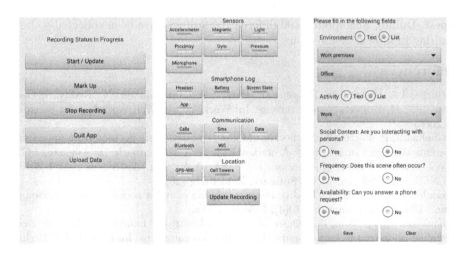

Fig. 1. Screenshots of RECORDME : from left to right, Home view (a), Source Selection view (b), and Markup view (c)

3 Conclusion

Three experiments have been run with RECORDME and are rich in feedbacks. First one is that RECORDME was stable on most tested smartphones. Only one smartphone had an original behaviour that consisted in stopping sensing when its screen turned off. We found that it was likely to be accountable for the constructor. Our workaround was the installation of a screen locker that kept the screen on then allowed a continuous recording. We also received volunteers' feedbacks about their experience with the application, especially that the marking up process was not convenient. Indeed, one collection campaign required volunteers to mark up just after the end of an activity. Some volunteers reported that they sometimes forgot: either they provided a delayed mark up or they just skipped it. Workarounds could be to ask volunteers to follow predefined scenarios or to orally record annotations.

Depending on experiments to perform and countries legislation, RECORDME can provide different security levels to protect volunteers' data. For instance, for an experiment that studies urban volunteers' motions and requires GPS coordinates collection, levels of security can be configured so that GPS coordinates are secured when stored on smartphones (by applying a translation for instance). Then, when transferred to the experimenters, coordinates are anonymized. Further processing of the coordinates is still possible by temporarily reversing the security processing (providing that volunteers agreed), yet the coordinates would remain anonymized. One of the data collections that used RECORDME performed in such a way and registered the protocol to the CNIL[1].

So far, RECORDME has already been successfully installed and tested on more than 10 different smartphones from different brands (Acer, Google, Motorola, Samsung, Sony, Wiko) and Android OS versions 2.3 and 4.0. The three different data collections total almost 30 volunteers, located in different areas of France (mainly Grenoble, a South-Eastern town) and around the world (Budapest, Dublin, Singapour). 100 different recordings have been collected so far, resulting in a total of 430 hours.

References

1. Burke, J.A., Estrin, D., Hansen, M., Parker, A., Ramanathan, N., Reddy, S., Srivastava, M.B.: Participatory sensing. In: World Sensor Web Workshop (at Sensys) (2006)
2. Chahuara, P., Portet, F., Vacher, M.: Making context aware decision from uncertain information in a smart home: A markov logic network approach. In: Augusto, J.C., Wichert, R., Collier, R., Keyson, D., Salah, A.A., Tan, A.-H. (eds.) AmI 2013. LNCS, vol. 8309, pp. 78–93. Springer, Heidelberg (2013)
3. Eagle, N., Pentland, A.: Reality mining: Sensing complex social systems. Personal and Ubiquitous Computing 10(4), 255–268 (2006)
4. Kiukkonen, N., Blom, J., Dousse, O., Gatica-Perez, D., Laurila, J.: Towards rich mobile phone datasets: Lausanne data collection campaign. In: Proc. ICPS, Berlin (2010)

---

[1] Please visit its website for more details http://www.cnil.fr/english/. Our file reference is 0750532.

Distributed Power Management System with Dynamic Load Management Based on Multi-agent System for Smart Grid

Rafael Jesús Valdivieso-Sarabia, Francisco Javier Ferrández-Pastor, Juan Manuel García-Chamizo, and Mario Nieto-Hidalgo

Department of Computer Technology, University of Alicante, Carretera San Vicente del Raspeig s/n, 03690, Alicante, Spain {rvaldivieso,fjferran,juanma,mnieto}@dtic.ua.es

Abstract. Power management in city electrical network has some challenges like to enhance renewable power supply, optimize distribution or network's integrity. Usually, conventional parameters are considered like costs and power constraints but load management is ignored to reduce environmental impact that energy generation produces as well as other aspects are ignored too. To address these limitations, a proposal based on a multi-agent system, which is developed in JADE framework, is introduced. The demand satisfaction is conditioned to the available power by mean of strategies oriented to control consuming spikes and to satisfy the future power demand as long as possible. Electrical network of a medium-size city is simulated to show the complex equilibrium that must be made to attend energy requests coming from a set of consuming centres. This study case let us confirm the feasibility of the power supply solution based on load management, in this context.

Keywords: power management, multi-agent system, simulation, smart grid.

1 Introduction

The use of renewable power supplies is growing as a consequence of exhaustion of raw material and environmental impact of traditional energy sources. Smart grids allow to schedule the power distribution and to integrate renewable power plants based on wind, sun, biomass, etc. Power management and control systems are relevant in many real-life applications and contexts like smart grids, off-grid houses, vehicles, industry, computers and embedded or wearable computing. The challenging problem of power management systems is aimed by the target of optimizing distribution but, at the same time, reducing environmental pollution through improving the use of renewable energy sources, reducing the economic cost and satisfying networks power constraints [1].

Traditional solutions consist of centralized systems because they were focused on power constraints but paying no more attention to the new culture of sustainability. Actual societies and their power systems are complex networks, so centralized

R. Hervás et al. (Eds.): UCAmI 2014, LNCS 8867, pp. 349–356, 2014.
© Springer International Publishing Switzerland 2014

approaches require powerful computing resources, since optimal distribution presents temporal cost which depends on the number of nodes. Distributed solutions seem to be more appropriated to the smart grid paradigm and the use of load management techniques allow to reduce the power consumption that is not necessarily required. Smart grid management systems are based on planning algorithms which minimize economical cost, satisfying requirements like stability and voltage regulation. The main algorithm families which satisfies the electrical constraints are unit commitment algorithms (UCA) and optimal power flow (OPF). UCA is focused on current stability and OPF is focused on voltage control using constraints that represents the transmission mode [2]. The potential value of multi-agent systems (MAS) technology to the power industry is described in [3], which discusses why MAS are appropriate to power engineering applications.

Merdan et al. [4] introduces a system for monitoring, diagnosis and coordination of distributed generation and consumption based on MAS. The control is based on keeping the voltage within a range. It presents a MAS architecture based on 2 layers of agents. The first layer, called Management Layer is responsible for managing the network stability, supporting interface with users through a Supervisory Control and Data Acquisition (SCADA). The second layer, called Execution Layer represents the network topology, facilitating communication between agents and allows interactions between them. The architecture of agents depend on the type of device you want to represent. Its capabilities to represent complex networks depends on the use of substation agents, which are software that interfaces different networks. It does not support load management in order to reduce consumption.

Lagorse et al. [5] proposes a management system for distributed energy sources. The proposal is focused on a photovoltaic generator, chemical batteries, supercapacitors and a grid connection. Power distribution is achieved through a witness which decides which is the responsible agent for carrying on the control. As the witness is passed from one agent to other, the distribution of computational load is done by ensuring that all actors are involved. In this case, loads are not controlled by any agent, because is the end user who has to do it. This approach is passive because the load management is done by the user, so the system is not able to reduce energy consumption autonomously.

Zeng et al. [6] introduces a MAS for distributed hybrid generation system which models wind turbine, photovoltaic array, battery, and grid connection. The most of related proposals are context-aware, so they are designed and developed according to the particular features of the system to handle. This means that management strategies are defined in a particular way for each case, usually characterized by a lack of dynamism in changes or impacts on the environment. Moreover, power distribution proposals do not consider directly recent collateral parameters like environmental impact of power sources. Those which try to improve the use of renewable power sources do not use load management techniques in order to match power demand with available power. There are load management techniques used in electronic devices such as dynamic power management (DPM) [7, 8] which modify the behaviour of components to reduce the overall power consumption.

This proposal introduces a distributed power management system based on load management techniques, designed and developed with MAS paradigm. The multi-agent power management system is suitable for the electrical network of a city, in order to manage energy generated by distributed heterogeneous power sources into several consumption centres. The management strategies are based on interactions among agents for getting the proper power distribution, improving the use of renewable energy sources and using load management policies. Load management allows to cut power consumption down to balance the overall consumption, when it is required. The MAS is developed for Java Agent Development Framework (JADE) [9]. The power demand and supply is simulated for a city which can be powered by renewable energy sources. The power distribution is discussed in order to determine the feasibility of power management strategies.

2   Agent-Based Model of Distributed Power Management System

Agent-based models are powerful enough for represent complex, dynamic and adaptive systems [10]. Intelligent agents are able to negotiate and interact with other agents and react to environmental changes modifying its behaviour [11].

According to our aim of getting a distributed power management system, we have made some conceptual simplifications: considering an electrical system like a set of heterogeneous power sources, transmission lines, batteries storage and consumption centres; and ignoring the energy lost due to Joule effect in transmission lines because it is not relevant for determining the feasibility of load management.

There are three kinds of agents that are able to handle energy: Source Agents (SA) which represent power suppliers that provide electricity to the whole system; Transponder Agents (TA) which models storage mediums like batteries or transmission lines; and Consumer Agents (CA) which represents power consumption centres. Each kind of agent is defined by a set of attributes that allows the particularization of a real device. SA agents are defined by the role of energy producer (Prod) and CA agents are defined by the role of energy consumer (Con) whereas TA agents are defined by both of them. The agent-based model is described in further details in [12, 13].

2.1   Agent's Interaction

The agent-based model topology matches with network topology [10]. The topology determines the interaction among agents and each interaction shows which kind of agent is allowed to request actions to other agents. There are two types of interaction which are based on FIPA contract-net iterative protocol: power request and load management request. CA agents are able to communicate with TA and SA to request power. TA and SA interacts with CA and TA to request for a reduction of power consumption.

2.2   Distributed Power Management

The power management is fully distributed because it is achieved through the interaction among agents. It is described briefly in [12]. The general aim of power management is to supply power from SA to CA improving the use of renewable energy sources and reduce power consumption when there is not enough power for the whole system. Each agent is able to take its own decisions, although it has to negotiate with other agents in order to achieve its goals. These negotiations are made by interactions for power request and load management.

Each agent can discover which agents are linked to him, so it is able to request for an action to other agent or to carry on an action triggered by a request from a third agent. The management task starts when an agent with Con role, CA or TA, needs power, so it initiates the power request interaction protocol. This power request is sent to the linked agents with Prod role, SA or TA. Each Prod agent, who has received a power request answers with the available power that is able to supply a time interval. When Con agent receives all the answers of the Prod agents, it initiates a local decision process to determine which Prod agents are the proper candidates to meet the goals. The local decision making of each agent is modelled by an objective function. This function takes into account the particular features of each Prod agent (environmental impact, economic cost, reliability) for ordering the answers from best to worst. This function gives priority to Prod agents, which have the lowest value of environmental impact, considering reliability and economic cost. Each attribute has a particular weight that is adjusted for each agent. So, when the Con agent chooses the bests agents, it requests to proportional quantity of required power in order. This interaction can be iterated until the Con agent does not need more power or all Prod agents reject the power requests.

The next step is to send a message to linked Prod to inform that the power request interactions are finished. When a Prod agent receives the finishing message of all the linked Con agents, then it makes a decision to request for reduce consumption to the linked Con or to send a no action message to indicate that the power management is finished. If the Prod agent decides to reduce power consumption, then it initiates a load management interaction protocol sending a reduce power request to all the Con agents that are buying power from the previous step. There are several policies in order to develop the load management. These policies changes the number of agents requested to reduce power consumption and the power that each one should reduce. So, there are three policies: low-high, high-low, med-med. The first one request to a low number of agents to reduce the maximum power that are able. The second one request to a high number of agents to reduce the minimum power that are able. The last one is balanced between the number of agents requested and the power requested to reduce.

After, load management interactions are finished the power distribution for this period is done, so the management can be scheduled for the next period of time.

2.3   User Experience and Load Management

When a Con agent receives a request for reduce the power consumption, it replies with the power that can be saved modifying its behaviour or disabling any functionality which requires so much energy. So, all the functionalities of each Con agent must be classified into critical and non-critical according to the end user. This task is relevant because it determines the amount of power that can be saved without decrease the end user comfort. The end user is who has to select the load management policies and the functionalities of each agent that can be disabled.

This proposal allows to encourage the energy saved by end users, e.g. electrical companies could apply a discount in the bill according to the power reduced in a particular period of time. This solution can prevent power peaks demand in certain time and it allows to reduce the energy imported from other countries.

3   Distributed Power Management Applied into a Smart Grid

The city considered for this study case has a population of 222,422 inhabitants and power can be supplied by 5 distribution substations identified as F1, F2, F3, F4 and F5. According to the end users, distribution substations represent the city power sources, which provide energy and are connected to the national electrical grid. Although, the maximum power of each one is limited by the electrical transmission line constraints, we assume that are able to supply the power required, although they present a high environmental impact. Moreover, there are two electrical gas oil generators, F6 and F7, which present a high environmental impact and provide energy exclusively to each city's hospital. In addition, 3 renewable energy sources F8, F9 and F10 are considered for make more complex and richer the study. They present a low environmental impact. F8 represents a thermosolar power plant with a maximum power of 24GWh/year, it presents a cost of 0.28€/kW. F9 models a photovoltaic power plant that is able to supply a maximum power of 2.2 GWh/year, it has a cost of 0.38€/kW. Finally, F10 represents a wind farm with a maximum power of 38.5 GWh/year, it has a cost of 0.08 €/kW.

The overall power consumption of the city is around 807.2 GWh/year. Consumptions centres can be discretized in function of their particular use of energy, so we consider 9 heterogeneous consumption centres CA1 to CA9: street lighting, hospital A, hospital B, industrial area A, industrial area B, residential area, shopping mall, sport zone and University Campus. The power required by each one is calculated assuming a linear distribution time from the city overall power consumption and the data provided by [14]. Each one is characterized by the aggregation of functionalities that they perform, the power required by each functionality and whether it is possible to turn it off for reducing the overall power consumption according to end user criteria. CA1 is able to disable a function which requires 1500 kW. CA2 can disable 2 functions which require 80 and 61 kW respectively. CA3 can disable 2 functions which require 52 and 30 kW. CA7 can save 1347kW and 500kW more. CA8 can save 728kW and 200 kW more. And CA9 can save 2138kW and 700 kW.

Physical connections allow transport energy from power suppliers to power consumers. According to our simulation purpose, we assume the following physical connections among them. Each consumption centre can be powered by F1, F2, F3, F4 and F5. C2 can be powered by F6. Likewise, F7 is able to provide power to C3. Regarding to renewable power sources: F8 can provide power to C7, C8 or C9; F9 is able to supply power to C2 and C3; and F10 can supply power to C1, C7 and C9.

3.1   Results of Power Management Distribution

The MAS has been modelled and developed for JADE in order to evaluate the whole system behaviour. The power supply and demand patterns are simulated for 24 hours. Power management strategies are triggered at each hour like the Spanish daily electricity market operating rules. Power generation of sources FA8, FA9 and FA10 has been calculated using following assumptions: solar radiation of a summer day; wind speed of the city geographical location [14]. An electric failure has been introduced in FA1, FA2, FA3, FA4 and FA5 from 7:00AM up to 9:00AM for illustrate the overall behaviour during this period.

Generation information of the most relevant power sources FA1-5 (a), FA8 (b), FA9 (c) and FA10 (d) is shown in figure 1. The information is related: to the available power (blue line) that each one is able to supply; the global power supplied (red line); and the local power supplied to their linked CAj agents. It shows that renewable energy sources (FA8, FA9 and FA10) present higher priority than FA1-5. All the renewable power is supplied except FA10, which it does no supply all the power during 3 hours.

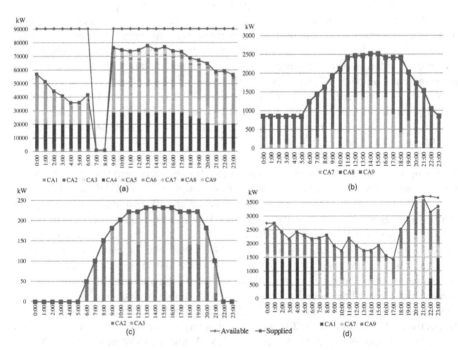

Fig. 1. Power supplied (red line) and available (blue line) by FAi to CAj. (a) Power supplied by FA1-5 to CA1-9. (b) Power supplied by FA8 to CA7-9. (c) Power supplied by FA9 to CA2-3. (d) Power supplied by FA10 to CA1, CA7 and CA9.

Power consumption information of the most relevant consumption centres CA1 (a), CA2 (b), CA8(c) and CA9 (d) is introduced in figure 2. It shows for each one: the power required (blue line); the power supplied (red line); which are the providers (positive columns); and the power saved as a consequence of load management actions (negative values). The difference between the power required and supplied is because of the power saved for disabling non critical functionalities, if it is available. Failure of power supply between 7:00 and 9:00 of FA1-5 is partially solved by the available energy from renewable power sources. The total energy saved thanks to load management of all consumer agents is around 13649 kW/h.

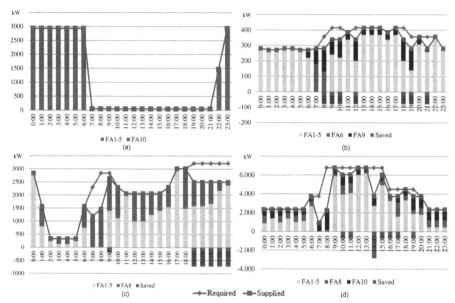

Fig. 2. Power supplied to (blue line), required by (red line) and saved by (negative values) CAi, which is supplied by FAj. (a) Power supplied to CA1 by FA1-5 and FA10. (b) Power supplied to CA2 by FA1-5, FA6 and FA9. (c) Power supplied to CA8 by FA1-5 and FA8. (d) Power supplied to CA9 by FA1-5, FA8 and FA10.

4   Conclusions

A Multi-agent system has been proposed that manages power distribution through load management in a city. It is developed using the JADE agent development framework. The proposed distributed management strategy is aimed to improve the use of renewable energy sources and it works to ensure supply. A simplified version of the electric network of a city with renewable energy sources is introduced for simulating the power demand and supply. Our proposal has been tested on it.

The obtained results of power distribution suggest that the power management system reacts to dynamic changes in the electrical network, accurately. Our load management policy allows to satisfy demand coming from consumer centres depending on the capacity of power generation without decrease substantially the end user comfort. Consumption could be attended dynamically using criteria focused on minimize power. This work represents a chance for electric companies to develop an incentive system to motivate customers to reduce their consumption.

The future work is focused on improve the power source decision function taking into account more accurate parameters and to validate it in real contexts i.e. an isolated house powered by several renewable energy sources.

Acknowledgments. This work was partially supported by University of Alicante, Unión Fenosa and Caja de Ahorros del Mediterráneo under a research grant.

References

1. Carrasco, J.M., Franquelo, L.G., Bialasiewicz, J.T., Galvan, E., Guisado, R.C.P., Prats, M.A.M., Leon, J.I., Moreno-Alfonso, N.: Power-Electronic Systems for the Grid Integration of Renewable Energy Sources: A Survey. IEEE Transactions on Industrial Electronics 53, 1002–1016 (2006)
2. Bevrani, H., Hiyama, T., Mitani, Y.: Power system dynamic stability and voltage regulation enhancement using an optimal gain vector. Control Engineering Practice 16, 1109–1119 (2008)
3. McArthur, S.D.J., Davidson, E.M., Catterson, V.M., Dimeas, A.L., Hatziargyriou, N.D., Ponci, F., Funabashi, T.: Multi-Agent Systems for Power Engineering Applications 2014; Part I: Concepts, Approaches, and Technical Challenges. IEEE Transactions on Power Systems 22, 1743–1752 (2007)
4. Merdan, M., Prostejovsky, A., Hegny, I., Lepuschitz, W., Andren, F., Strasser, T.: Power Distribution Control Using Multi-Agent Systems. In: Sen Gupta, G., Bailey, D., Demidenko, S., Carnegie, D. (eds.) Recent Advances in Robotics and Automation. SCI, vol. 480, pp. 323–333. Springer, Heidelberg (2013)
5. Lagorse, J., Paire, D., Miraoui, A.: A multi-agent system for energy management of distributed power sources. Renewable Energy 35, 174–182 (2010)
6. Zeng, J., Liu, J.F., Ngan, H.W., Wu, J.: A multi-agent solution to energy management of distributed hybrid renewable energy generated system. In: IET Conference Publications, vol. 2009, pp. 112 (2009)
7. Dargie, W.: Dynamic Power Management in Wireless Sensor Networks: State-of-the-Art. IEEE Sensors Journal 12, 1518–1528 (2012)
8. Li, D., Wu, J.: Scheduling on Heterogeneous DVFS Multiprocessor Platforms. In: Energy-aware Scheduling on Multiprocessor Platforms, pp. 41–52. Springer, New York (2013)
9. Bellifemine, F., Poggi, A., Rimassa, G.: Developing multi-agent systems with a FIPA-compliant agent framework. Softw. Pract. Exper. 31, 103–128 (2001)
10. Macal, C.M., North, M.J.: Tutorial on agent-based modelling and simulation. Journal of Simulation 4, 151–162 (2010)
11. Wooldridge, M.: Intelligent Agents. In: Multiagent Systems: A Modern Approach to Distributed Modern Approach to Artificial Intelligence, pp. 27–78. The MIT Press (1999)
12. Valdivieso-Sarabia, R.J., Garcia-Chamizo, J.M.: Power Management Strategies based on Multi-Agent Systems for Portable Devices Equipped with Renewable Power Sources: Laptop Case Study. In: Sustainable ICTs and Management Systems for Green Computing, pp. 283–302. IGI Global (2012)
13. Valdivieso-Sarabia, R.J., Ferrandez-Pastor, F.J., Garcia-Chamizo, J.M.: Distributed Optimization of Finite Resource Planning for Asincronous and Non-linear Systems: Application to Power Management. In: Demazeau, Y., Müller, J.P., Rodríguez, J.M.C., Pérez, J.B. (eds.) Advances on PAAMS. Advances in Intelligent Systems and Computing, vol. 155, pp. 211–216. Springer, Heidelberg (2012)
14. IDAE: Informe anual de consumos energéticos. Año 2009. Instituto para la Diversificación y Ahorro de Energía, IDAE (2009)

Towards an Evaluation of a Metadata Standard for Generative Virtual Museums

Daniel Sacher[1], Benjamin Weyers[2], Daniel Biella[1], and Wolfram Luther[1]

[1] Computer and Cognitive Science (INKO) and Center for Information and Media Services (CIM), University of Duisburg-Essen, Germany
{daniel.sacher,daniel.biella,wolfram.luther}@uni-due.de
[2] Virtual Reality Group, RWTH Aachen University, Germany
weyers@vr.rwth-aachen.de

Abstract. A methodology for evaluating the ViMCOX metadata format for designing virtual museums is discussed. Two evaluation approaches are presented, addressing (1) design aspects of virtual museums, the completeness of the metadata from the visitor's point of view as well as measuring the acceptance of virtual museums and (2) a qualitative survey in collaboration with museum experts to identify metadata requirements and feature sets for curator tool implementations.

Keywords: Virtual Museum, 3D Museum, Evaluation, Virtual Museum Feature Set Survey, Curator Survey, ViMEDEAS, ViMCOX, Replicave.

1 Introduction

In recent publications [1–5], we presented the curator software suite Virtual Museum Exhibition Designer using an Enhanced ARCO Standard (ViMEDEAS). ViMEDEAS combines authoring tools, frameworks and a metadata scheme–for the hierarchical description of virtual museums–to cover the entire design process of planning, creation, archiving, dissemination and presentation. The metadata scheme Virtual Museum and Cultural Object Exchange Format (ViMCOX) is a presentation format for exhibition catalogs and fully walkable 3D virtual museums. It supports interactive exhibition content, outdoor areas and spatial exhibition design including illumination concepts as well as free and guided virtual museum tours. ViMCOX is based on international metadata standards and uses LIDO as an interchange and harvesting format for cultural objects. The key idea is to have a common modeling language capable of structuring and presenting virtual 3D museums, and outlives rapidly changing technological trends.

Different research fields have been addressed by ViMEDEAS: metadata modeling and interoperability [1, 5], design of virtual museum exhibitions in terms of (semi-) automatic generative approaches or manual design [1, 2, 4] or the development of curator software and authoring tools [3, 4]. This paper describes the evaluation approach of the ViMCOX based on an extended version of the Virtual Leopold Fleischhacker Museum [6]. Various evaluation and assessment approaches which are applicable for ViMEDEAS are discussed beforehand.

R. Hervás et al. (Eds.): UCAmI 2014, LNCS 8867, pp. 357–364, 2014.
© Springer International Publishing Switzerland 2014

2   Evaluation Approaches

In general, evaluation aspects can be considered from the vantage points of different user groups involved in the development and use of virtual museums with focus on their individual needs. In addition, software engineering and respectively data modeling, handling as well as the completeness and interoperability of the metadata format ViMCOX are relevant facets during the evaluation process. To assess the interoperability to other metadata formats, a crosswalk between LIDO and VIMCOX is sufficient, since LIDO mappings to other relevant digital heritage metadata formats are already defined [7]. Discussions with curators demonstrated that there are no generally accepted requirements for curator tool implementations (2D/3D or grabber) and desired features will vary depending on collection types, exhibition space architecture, and the application scenarios of virtual museums cannot be generalized. ViMCOX was designed to allow flexible use and development of authoring tools and graphic libraries [1], thus, focus is not the evaluation of specific implementations. Most evaluation approaches found in the literature are standalone developments and have focus on software quality, usability or the comparison of perceived user experience in virtual museums. The assessment of the generative approach [2] and ViMCOX' feature set can be elaborated by comparing the user experience perceived in different museum exhibitions comprising the same content on display: real museum exhibitions, equivalent reconstructions, (semi-) automatically generated museums with and without post-processing as well as exhibition designs created by art history experts.

Another interesting aspect of (generative) virtual museums is to let users curate their own exhibitions based on open data collections, for example to get children involved. In [8] a comparison of real and virtual exhibition visits was elaborated by measuring the user experience, affection and knowledge acquisition with a prior visit of a 3D reconstruction of a permanent exhibition. The feasibility of reconstructing real exhibition rooms using ViMCOX was presented in [5], where a room of the Museum of Contemporary Art (MAC, Santiago de Chile) was digitized. Due to the geographic distance and destruction provoked by an earthquake we suspended the evaluation process to a further longer stay in Santiago de Chile. Another approach for evaluating a virtual museum metadata format was elaborated by the Augmented Representation of Cultural Objects (ARCO) project. The evaluation [9] of the ARCO metadata schema elements using domain experts is in fact applicable for ViMCOX. But ViMCOX uses a generic concept for storing digital resources [1]. ViMCOX maintains a minimal set of resource discovery and rights management metadata and provides pointer to richer museum documentation. Digital resources can be integrated using multiple resource representations and ViMCOX keeps track of the rights of the original work of art, the digital surrogates including divergent rights if applicable. For the purpose of presentation in the 3D scene, ViMCOX facilitates the enrichment of digital resources with additional descriptions, metadata and supplementary material. Thus, an evaluation of the completeness on metadata level using domain experts is not expedient.

In [10], the authors developed a user experience evaluation questionnaire applicable to virtual museums with focus on utility, learnability, efficiency and stimulation. This approach was approved during the Archeovirtual fair by evaluating 24 virtual museums applications and more than 300 participants. The questionnaire is a result of the VMUST project general research findings for evaluating various virtual museums [11]. We adapt this questionnaire to gather feedback on the design aspects of virtual museums, the completeness of ViMCOX feature set from the visitor's point of view as well as measuring the acceptance of virtual museums.

To identify relevant, time-consuming and supportable curator tasks and to determine requirements and feature sets for curator software implementations, virtual museum metadata and the presentation of virtual museums, a second survey gathers qualitative information from different museum institutions about the diversity of exhibition design processes and practices.

3   Virtual Museum Feature Set Survey

As basis for the evaluation serves the Virtual Leopold Fleischhacker Museum [6]. The virtual museum depicts the life and work of the German-Jewish sculptor and artist Leopold Fleischhacker and comprises 14 thematic areas, 13 exhibition rooms and one outdoor area in the form of an Ashkenazi cemetery. The museum features multilingual metadata, descriptions and assets (DE, EN, FR), interactive guided tours, and approximately 30 minutes of German voice recordings. The virtual museum has by design no interactive exhibits, thus, the comparison of learning behavior of adults and children cannot be elaborated, as described in [8], where children prefer creative (role) play and adults prefer simulations and interactive references. Nevertheless, the Virtual Leopold Fleischhacker Museum illustrates all stylistic devices of ViMCOX except interactive exhibition content, levels and complex floor plans or room structures respectively. The virtual museum is scheduled for a traveling exhibition in form of an interactive 3D kiosk system that can be operated using touch screen input.

The survey will be carried out without using technical instruments nor system based support for capturing user's behavior in terms of navigation, visitation or duration profiles or eye-tracking techniques. The questionnaire is separated into 4 sections to gather (1) demographic data as well as the visitor's initial stimulation for real museums, (2) collect feedback on free navigation and interactive tours, (3) comparison of both use cases and stimulation. Section (4) of the survey is designed as interview with pointed questions to identify design flaws, missing concepts or features, improvement suggestions, comparison to real museum visits, subjective increase of knowledge, general acceptance of virtual museums as well as the visual fidelity/quality which is of course biased due to kiosk system resolution. The duration of the survey is scheduled for 60 minutes, where each use case occupies 15 minutes. The interviewer will document the behavior and visitor's remarks and measures the time for the completion of the tasks assigned in the use cases.

The first section of the survey gathers general demographic data: age, gender, occupation, information and communication technology (ICT) knowledge–internet usage, general 3D/VR/Gaming experience and computer usage frequency–as well as museum experience and visitation frequency. User groups are covered based on demographic data only, without establishing a user group specific questionnaire. In addition the questionnaire collects data about (previous/initial) experiences with computer aided learning and virtual museums. Further user biased factors to measure acceptance of virtual museums are the user's interest in and attitude towards art, museums and museology.

Each use case has an extended questionnaire (utility, learnability and efficiency) extracted from [10] and additional pointed questions (Likert scale) about specific features of the virtual museum designed to aid in utility and learnability. A subsequent questionnaire compares the experience perceived during the free exploration and the interactive guided tours.

Use Case 1. Observes free navigation throughout the exhibition rooms and the outdoor area. The use case predetermines important exhibition areas and art works that should be visited by the user as well as interesting offerings of the virtual space to gather feedback on architectural design, visual quality, movement freedom, supplementary material and general interaction with the virtual museum.

Use Case 2. Focuses on guidance in terms of navigation and content mediation to determine if users prefer preset content in "context" (which is of course limited by tour design and content) to be compared to studies of Werner Schweibenz addressing the information need and behavior of virtual museum visitors [12]. This scenario uses a pre-selected set of tours and necessitates the visitor to visit and view the same content as in the first use case.

The extended stimulation questionnaire of [10] is designed as follow-up to determine general feedback, experience, re-use, recommendation, acceptance of the visit as well as the growth of interest in museums and art in general.

The survey ends with an interview. The interview questions gather feedback on important impressions and experiences, which expectations of virtual museums were met, which features were particularly good or bad, how do the participants prepare themselves for real museum visits, comparison to a real museum visits, advantages and disadvantages of virtual museums and general interest-growth.

4   Curator Survey

General requirements for and implementations of curator software can be found in the literature [13, 14]. A 3D curator software with advice from museum staff of a single institution was developed in [15]. Standards, metadata formats, thesauri, language specific and multimedia related content in use by European institutions is presented in [16]. These findings in addition to discussions with curators, represent not a holistic view on museum staff requirements and all application scenarios of virtual museum, thus, it is likely that individual and presumably lightweight (software) solutions and metadata for the generation of virtual museums are required. The following survey will be partitioned into 6 parts to reflect the actual need for curator software and identifies application scenarios for virtual museums. The questionnaire addresses the following topics: the creation process, planning and realization; employment of external companies; frequency of new and changing exhibitions; utilities used during exhibition design; and which facility characteristics and architectural difficulties curators have to face during the design process. In addition, application scenarios and features of virtual museums as well as requirements and biased features for curator tool implementations are elaborated. The survey concludes with an optional section to determine the metadata formats and collection management software in use and gathers previous digitization efforts and experiences.

Exhibition/Spatial Characteristics: The first section of the survey addresses exhibition area related questions: how many thematic areas, rooms, floors, buildings are available and if the institutions make use of outdoor areas. Which architectural features, obstacles and shapes do their exhibition areas have and how are exhibition areas connected by means of elevators, staircases, ramps or outdoor areas for example a inner courtyard. Further questions determine how exhibition rooms or areas are separated, for example using partition walls and in which manner exhibition items are mounted to these structures and which shape and geometric recesses. Lighting related questions collect information about light installations, to determine the use of colored light and purpose of light sources, for example to guide visitors or to emphasize exhibits. Which exhibition types does the participating institution have: temporary-, permanent-, special-, travelling/touring-exhibitions and how is the temporal and spatial allocation onto the exhibition areas per annum. This section also covers interactive exhibits, guides or other multimedia installations as well as multilingual offerings that are not covered in [16], such as information signs, catalogs/flyer, tours and online offerings.

Planning and Realization: The second part addresses the planning and development of exhibitions. How often are new exhibitions planned, realized or modified and how many exhibitions are developed and hosted in parallel. Which specifications are made by artists, sponsors or lenders such as illumination, fond, typography, framing or distances and gaps between exhibits? Which software and additional equipment such as drawings/sketches, 2D floorplans or (curator) software are utilized during the design process. Are existing designs of previously hosted exhibitions re-used and are exhibitions designed in dialog with project partners or are external designs used? Followed by statements of processes which are time-consuming, automatable and which task need assistance/support. Do the participation institutions employ external companies to outsource the planning, realization or the creation of content and materials or if all tasks are realized in-house. Which challenges, obstacles and unique features do the institutions face during the development? Another interesting topic covered, is the archiving of exhibition designs and how are these documented for the exchange with other institutions.

Virtual Museums: The third part of the questionnaire thematizes virtual museums and narrows down possible use cases. Which virtual museums are desired, ranging from fictional exhibitions whether manually created or computer generated; replication of institutional exhibition areas, buildings or outdoor areas; or the reconstruction of heritage sites? Which exhibit related information should be retrievable in the virtual museum, such as free text descriptions, documentation or supplementary materials? Which interaction patterns are desired, such as interactive experiments, animated exhibits, de-construction or reconstruction of exhibits or geometric modifications. Are there any use cases where sound effects or animated lights are required? Should virtual museums provide tracking functionality, for example logging of visited exhibits and dwelling time, pathes covered or the possibility to capture visitor's feedback? Which application fields of virtual museums and curator software are suitable for the participation institution: planning and archiving of real exhibitions, creation of virtual museum presentations for the internet, virtual museum as information system to support visitors on-site, preparation and reflection of visits, let visitors curate own exhibition based on the institutional collection and/or exhibition areas?

Curator Software: This section identifies requirements and is based on feature sets of curator software prototypes developed in diploma theses at the University of Duisburg-Essen and research findings presented in [15] as well as collaborations with curators. The feature sets provided are categorized into object positioning; addition of temporary structures, navigation aids; tour planning; linking and sorting of exhibition areas, connection and integration of metadata and databases, printing functionality for the creation of exhibition plans (with or without dimensions) or art catalogs; 3D preview; exhibition templates (3D models, generic or templates); which parts of the building should be digitized: indoor and outdoor views of the building and/or outdoor areas. A further question elaborates which features in a curator software are desired, features are numbered and the selection is designed as a Likert scale to provide a weighted bias. A follow-up question determines desired software packages and participants should provide a combination of item numbers for the following software package themes: planning, archiving, realization and if possible provide own use cases. To close this section a free text input filed is offered to collect additional features which were not enlisted.

Metadata and Digitization: The last section addresses general questions to determine collection related characteristics: exhibition types, digitization processes, metadata and exchange formats, databases and collection management systems in use. Questions related to the digitization process collect how many objects and exhibition environments have been digitized and which formats, technologies, techniques were used.

5   Preliminary Results

The virtual museum feature set survey was elaborated using a portable system, since the kiosk system is not on public display yet. Thus, the survey is a user test rather than a visitor test within a real usage scenario, which is a point of criticism [10, 17]. In addition, we interviewed a heterogeneous observation group to gather feedback from ICT, VR and art history experts; average museum users; computer affine users, as well as computer novice. VR experts are researchers from the Virtual Reality Group of the RWTH Aachen University and art history experts are from the Salomon Ludwig Steinheim-Institut. Preliminary results in form of the interviewers' observations are described in the following paragraph, we interviewed 35 participants. The majority of users only navigate using the provided interactive map, located at every entrance, to access other exhibition areas rather than using the doors. In larger exhibition areas, users tend to loose orientation and it is in general cumbersome to navigate back to the interactive map which required in the majority of cases a 180° rotation. Most users are missing a layout or exhibit plan especially for orientation purpose in the outdoor area or in general to get an overview of exhibition items. Thus, the majority of users are demanding a interactive map accessible via the UI. While the collision detection for assets was deactivated, users got stuck on 3D exhibits for example the tombstones in the outdoor area. The design of the tour UI was not intuitive for the majority of users, they tend to access information via the exhibits rather than using the corresponding pictograph in the UI. In addition, the tour interface should support interrupting and resuming of tours. Motion patterns as in real museums were observable, users will pursue the first movement direction they embark, which is rather random due to the touch screen. Tutorials are not remembered, users need to interact with the system first to learn the use. Two inexperienced users also required advise from the interviewer. Content wise, not all stylistic devices of our metadata and 3D framework and the concepts of virtual museums were used. Many users demand more contextual information especially for tour content selection, material-tech descriptions, general explanations and related materials of objects, places and actors. But the curator design specifications excluded external resources and linked material.

Preliminary results of the curator survey are that individual requirements and a demand for lightweight tools exist, it is therefore necessary to have a common and flexible modeling language, such as ViMCOX, to support individual authoring tool implementations. Loosely coupled (meta)data integration is required due to varying metadata formats and different access to the collection management and in some cases objects are not part of the institutional database. Curators prefer simplistic user friendly tools, for example 2D positioning on floor plans with 3D preview supporting different navigation modes and avatar sizes (children, wheelchair users). Generic objects (vitrines, partition walls), object placeholder and re-useable room templates are useful during the design process. Grouping of and composite exhibits, scales and dimensions as wells as the annotation of objects and rooms (safety clearance, payload) should be adhered. Virtual museums and curator tools may be predominantly used for design and planning only and are not accessible for the general public, which also excludes interaction patterns and relaxes the demand for visual quality in these cases.

Furthermore, mobile grabbing software would be a huge benefit for digitizing and archiving procedures, especially for art galleries.

References

1. Sacher, D., Biella, D., Luther, W.: Towards a versatile metadata exchange format for digital museum collections. In: Proc. of the 2013 Digital Heritage International Congress, pp. 129–136 (2013)
2. Sacher, D., Biella, D., Luther, W.: A Generative Approach to Virtual Museums. In: WEBIST, pp. 274–279. SciTePress (2013)
3. Biella, D., Luther, W., Baloian, N.: Virtual Museum Exhibition Designer Using Enhanced ARCO Standard. In: XXIX Int. Conf. of the Chilean Computer Science Society (SCCC), pp. 226–235 (2010)
4. Biella, D., Luther, W., Sacher, D.: Schema Migration Into A Web-based Framework for Generating Virtual Museums and Laboratories. In: 18th Int. Conf. on Virtual Systems and Multimedia (VSMM), pp. 307–314 (2012)
5. Biella, D., Luther, W., Baloian, N.: Beyond the ARCO standard. In: 16th Int. Conf. on Virtual Systems and Multimedia (VSMM), pp. 184–191 (2010)
6. Sacher, D., Brocke, M., Heitmann, M., Kaufhold, B., Luther, W., Biella, D.: The Virtual Leopold Fleischhacker Museum. In: Museums and the Web: Proc. (2013)
7. Ronzino, P., Amico, N., Niccoluccin, F.: Assessment and comparison of metadata schemas for architectural heritage. In: Proc. of CIPA (2011)
8. D'Alba, A., Jones, G.: Analyzing participants' perceptions, attitudes, and knowledge outcomes in an art museum tour, after using a 3dimensional virtual museum. In: Proc. of Society for Information Technology & Teacher Education International Conference (2013)
9. Sylaiou, S., Economou, M., Karoulis, A., White, M.: The Evaluation of ARCO: A Lesson in Curatorial Competence and Intuition with New Technology. Comput. Entertain. 6(2), 23:1–23:18 (2008)
10. Gockel, B., Graf, H., Pagano, A., Pescarin, S., Eriksson, J.: VMUXE. In: Marcus, A. (ed.) DUXU/HCII 2013, Part I. LNCS, vol. 8012, pp. 262–272. Springer, Heidelberg (2013)
11. Pescarin, S., Pagano, A., Wallergård, M., Hupperetz, W., Ray, C.: Evaluating virtual museums: Archeovirtual case study. Archaeology in the Digital Era, 74 (2012)
12. Schweibenz, W.: Who are the Visitors of the Virtual Museum and What are they Interested in? i-com, 7(2), 11–17 (2008)
13. Dachselt, R.: Eine deklarative Komponentenarchitektur und Interaktionsbausteine für dreidimensionale multimediale Anwendungen. Der Andere Verlag (2004)
14. Chittaro, L., Ieronutti, L., Ranon, R.: VEX-CMS: A tool to design virtual exhibitions and walkthroughs that integrates automatic camera control capabilities. In: Taylor, R., Boulanger, P., Krüger, A., Olivier, P. (eds.) SG 2010. LNCS, vol. 6133, pp. 103–114. Springer, Heidelberg (2010)
15. Gomes, J., Carmo, M., Claudio, A.: Creating and Assembling Virtual Exhibitions from Existing X3D Models (2011),
http://docs.di.fc.ul.pt/handle/10455/6748
16. McKenna, G., De Loof, C.: ATHENA D3.1 Report on existing standards applied by European museums (2010), http://www.athenaeurope.org/getFile.php?id=396
17. Pescarin, S., Wallergird, M., Hupperetz, W., Pagano, A., Ray, C.: Archeovirtual 2011: An evaluation approach to virtual museums. In: 8th Int. Conf. on Virtual Systems and Multimedia (VSMM), pp. 25–32 (2012)

SmartCity: Public Transportation Network Planning Based on Cloud Services, Crowd Sourcing and Spatial Decision Support Theory

Jonathan Frez[1], Nelson Baloian[2], and Gusravo Zurita[3]

[1] School of Informatics & Telecommunications Engineering,
Universidad Diego Portales, Santiago, Chile
[2] Department of Computer Science, University of Chile, Beauchef 851, Santiago, Chile
[3] Information Systems and Managment Department. Universidad de Chile,
Diagonal Paraquay 257, CP 8330015 Santiago, Chile
jonathan.frez@gmail.com, nbaloian@dcc.uchile.cl,
gzurita@fen.uchile.cl

Abstract. Cities are growing and the number people using smartphone's and tablets it also increasing. There are many applications that collects data from users and its context. Some of these applications are producing complete and useful databases that can be used to support some cites problems. In particular spatial planning problems like transportation network planning. In this work we presented a method to use existing crowdsourcing data and cloudservices to support a transportation network decision making process. The method is based the Dempster-Shafer Theory to combine the different sources information and to model transportation demand.

Keywords: mobile data, probabilistic scenarios, Dempster-Shafer theory, transportation network, crowdsourcing, cloudservices.

1 Introduction

Cities are constantly growing as they requirements. The cities decision making problems are becoming more complex, and better methods to evaluate solutions alternatives are needed in order to support this growing [1].

Several of the decision problems are related to spatial context. A typical spatial problem is to define a place or area to support an specific requirement or service. For example, where to build a new street, set a residential or industrial area, place parks, commercial areas, hospitals. Furthermore, cities are constantly changing, are they have dynamic problems, for example in public transportation services. The transportations routes can be dynamically defined in order to respond to dynamic requirement and restrictions. Some of the decisions related to this problem are where to place a bus station, define a route, define multiple routes, or even a full transportation network.

R. Hervás et al. (Eds.): UCAmI 2014, LNCS 8867, pp. 365–371, 2014.
© Springer International Publishing Switzerland 2014

According to [2], a "Smart City" is city that monitors and integrates data and information of its critical infrastructures, including roads, bridges, tunnels, rails, subways, airports, seaports in order to better optimize its resources, and maximizing services to its citizens.

At same time, citizens are using information technologies (IT) to consume and provide data that can be used to support the decision making process of several of the new and old requirement of cities.. Some of the (IT) used by citizens can be are supported by Cloud Computing Services providing Software as a Service (SaaS). The software as a Service model of Cloud Computing, are often accessed by citizens as mobile applications and web interfaces [3]. Some of the SaaS services with spatial data properties are for example Google Maps, OpenStreetMaps and WAZE. These services provides geo-localized data in a graphical way, they are free, and they share a singular characteristic: They use Crowdsourcing data to provide data.

In this paper, we used the services provided by Google Maps, OpenStreetMaps and Waze, to develop a Spatial Decision Support System (SDSS) for transportation network planning. Specifically the Origin-Destination (OD) evaluation. In order to deal with uncertain and incomplete data sources we propose to evaluate de OD using a DSS theory called Dempster Schaffer Theory[4]. This Theory is designed to model decisions based on uncertain and incomplete data, by modelling "how much" a hypotheses can be supported by data.

2   Related Work

According to [5], a "Smart City" is intended as an urban environment which, supported by pervasive IT systems, is able to offer advanced and innovative services to citizens in order to improve the overall quality of their life.

In [6], a user-friendly web-based spatial decision support system (wSDSS) aimed at generating optimized vehicle routes for multiple vehicle routing problems that involve serving the demand located along arcs of a transportation network is presented. The wSDSS incorporates Google Maps™ (cartography and network data), a database, a heuristic and an ant-colony meta-heuristic developed by the authors to generate routes and detailed individual vehicle route maps. It accommodates realistic system specifics, such as vehicle capacity and shift time constraints, as well as network constraints such as one-way streets and prohibited turns. The wSDSS can be used for "what-if" analysis related to possible changes to input parameters such as vehicle capacity, maximum driving shift time, seasonal variations of demand, network modifications, and imposed arc orientations. The system was tested for urban trash collection in Coimbra, Portugal.

An important crowdsourcing database is the OpenStreetMap project [7]. Worldwide, several volunteers are currently contributing information to this "free" geodatabase. In some cases this databases exceeds proprietary ones by a 27% [8], and for some authors [9] it is even more complete that Google maps or Bing maps. OpenStreetmap information has been proposed to support traffic related decisions by develop traffic simulations [10], or solutions to achieve a new web based trip optimization tool [11]. It has been also used to support transportation network planning [12]. Furthermore, due to the recent interest in spatially aware systems for pedestrian routing and city exploration; plus the proliferation of smartphones with GPS receivers among the general public, but at the same time due to their problems of noisy and inaccuracy, in [13] it is described a spoken-dialogue prototype for pedestrian navigation in Stockholm by using various grounding strategies and based on OpenStreetMaps. Similarly, Jacob et al. [14], present a web-based, multi-lingual, campus guidance system with emphasis on pedestrian navigation aimed at providing support for delegates attending International Conferences at the National University of Ireland Maynooth campus. They develop a system based on OpenStreetMap for generate shortest pedestrian paths using both outdoor pavements and indoor corridors between various buildings and points of interests.

A well-known and popular crowdsourcing geodatabase is being generated by Waze. Waze is mobile GPS application that allows to measure and report different traffic conditions and events. For examples it automatically detects traffic jams, users can report accidents, objects in the road, weather effects on the roads, and other kind of alerts. In the literature we did not find a decision support systems using Waze data, the main reason could be because it is hard to obtain. However, we found traffic condition analysis systems [15] based on real time data obtained from Waze.com using a WebCrawler, and a accidents data mining analysis proposal [16] based on the same real time data from the web page of Waze.com. In this work the data is obtained using the same technique, we developed a WebCrawler to reconstruct an historical database based on the published data on waze.com.

The literature regarding spatial decision support systems we are focused on the trend to use belief functions [17], in particular Dempster-Shafer Theory. The Dempster-Shafer theory was developed in 1967 by Dempster and extended by Shafer. It proposes to use sets of hypotheses regarding a variable (e.g. the temperature values in X are always between t1 and t2) associated with a probability of being correct. Using Belief functions we can provide a "hypotheses support value" called belief. The belief can be assigned to a certain geographical area that accomplish a hypotheses set.

3   The OD Route Problem

Regional transportation networks are composed transportation lines, railways, highway, and different transportation are designed to cooperate and complement an urban scale transportation solution [18]. The planning of the paths or routes of the new or existing transportation methods are usually based on existing basic data, of transportation network, volume predictions and the distribution in the network, [19].

When a decision maker chooses a route, the travel time and time reliability are important factors under demand and supply uncertainty. According to [20], modern urban road transportation design is to optimize the system performance, make the traveler arrive in destination conveniently and quickly. Furthermore, when designing an urban route for a new transportation service, the choices must consider the behavior and reliability of transportation network. Another important factor is the OD traffic demand [21]. The OD describe the quantity of traffic demand between a particularly OD during a time period.

A public transportation system is a complex network. In Santiago de Chile city it is composed by bus stations, bus routes, subway stations, and subway routes, shared taxy stations and shared taxy routes. Each OD are composed by a start station and an ending station. A single OD can have multiple sub-OD in a single route. The design of a public transportation system is a complex task that requires to analyze the public demand for transportation, the traffic demands of the alternative routes for each OD, and the reliability of the OD. In order to define an OD route base on uncertain demand information, we propose to adapt a concept named Belief Maps [17]. This concept is based on the Dempster-Shafer Theory. A Belief Maps allows to evaluate a geographical area generating a suitability evaluation about a set of hypotheses that support a solutions proposal. For example, Figure 1 shows the belief degree of find people in each evaluated area. The hypotheses that supports this map can be "People goes to commercial areas", or "People can be in industrial areas or schools".

Fig. 1. Belief Map Example, Where people can be

4   Determining the OD Route

Using Belief Maps we propose a new concept called Belief Routes (BR). A BR can be used to evaluate demand hypotheses of an OD. A Belief Route is composed by 3 basic elements: *A set of hypotheses that defines a possible transportation demand of an OD*; *The Origin and Destination*; *The "polyline" or path of the route.* Using this definition of Belief Route, the decision maker can compare different paths evaluating the demand requirements in each OD. Furthermore, the decision maker can also adjust the Origin or Destiny. Another important factor in the OD evaluation is the transportation and reliability time. In order to support both indicator we propose to combine the traffic information from Waze creating a belief value based on historical data. We call the result of this combination as Belief Congestion Route (BCR).

In order to explain the use of the BR and BCR in the decision making processes we are going to use a basic example: A single OD with 2 alternative paths. In Figures 2 and 3, two different alternatives are show (A and B respectively). In this example route A is shorten than B, and the travel time is also shorter according to Google Directions API.

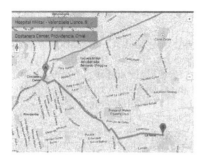

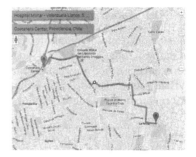

Fig. 2. Route A   **Fig. 3.**   Route B

In figures 4 and 5, the transportation demand is represented by a BR, according the OpenStreetMap and the proposed hypothesis, route B as more demand than route A.

Fig. 4.   Belief route A   **Fig. 5.** Belief route B

In figures 6 and 7 the BCR of each route are shown. According to the Waze information of both paths, the route A as more belief of having congestions or traffic jams witch implies less reliability.

Fig. 6. Congestion route A   **Fig. 7.** Congestion route B

From the example we can note that route B has less congestion and more demand that route A. However route A is shorter and the desition will depend of what kind of OD the decision maker is looking for. In order to support the decision, the visual evaluation of the BR and BCR is not enough. An evaluation metrics framework is needed and it will be part of the future work.

4.1   Description of the Application

The developed prototype allows to define an OD pair and it automatically provides the shortest route using the Google Route Service. It also provide a hypotheses specification method for transportation demand modelling and it generates two types of visualization: The demand Belief route and the Congestion route (see Fig 8). The platform provide Average Belief of the generated 3D visualization.

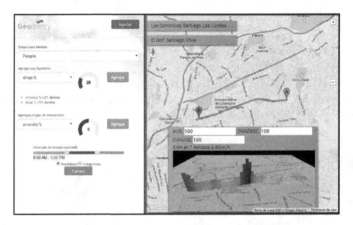

Fig. 8. Evaluation of an OD using the developed application

The application allows to set a transportation demand hypotheses set compatible with the Dempster-Shaffer Theory. It also allows to include some model restrictions, for example: avoid schools. After the hypotheses are included, the application allows to choose the type of 3d map will be generated: BR or BCR.

5   Conclusions

In this work we presented a method to use existing crowdsourcing data to support a transportation network decision making process. The method uses the Dempster-Shafer Theory to provide a framework to model transportation demand based on the OpenStreetMap Data. The method also provide a simple way of use the Waze application data to provide a congestion probability value to each segment of a route.

In this work we propose that the use of croudsourcing data to build the transportation demand metric and the congestion probability it is possible to support a transportation network decision making process.

References

1. Heilig, G.K.: World urbanization prospects the 2011 revision. United Nations, Department of Economic and Social Affairs (DESA), Population Division, Population Estimates and Projections Section, New York (2012)
2. Harrison, C., et al.: Foundations for smarter cities. IBM Journal of Research and Development 54(4), 1–16 (2010)

3. Chourabi, H., et al.: Understanding smart cities: An integrative framework. In: 2012 45th Hawaii International Conference on System Science (HICSS). IEEE (2012)
4. Shafer, G.: A mathematical theory of evidence, vol. 1. Princeton university Press, Princeton (1976)
5. Piro, G., et al.: Information centric services in Smart Cities. Journal of Systems and Software 88, 169–188 (2014)
6. Santos, L., Coutinho-Rodrigues, J., Antunes, C.H.: A web spatial decision support system for vehicle routing using Google Maps. Decision Support Systems 51(1), 1–9 (2011)
7. Haklay, M., Weber, P.: Openstreetmap: User-generated street maps. IEEE Pervasive Computing 7(4), 12–18 (2008)
8. Neis, P., Zielstra, D., Zipf, A.: The street network evolution of crowdsourced maps: OpenStreetMap in Germany 2007–2011. Future Internet 4(1), 1–21 (2011)
9. Ciepłuch, B., et al.: Comparison of the accuracy of OpenStreetMap for Ireland with Google Maps and Bing Maps. In: Proceedings of the Ninth International Symposium on Spatial Accuracy Assessment in Natural Resuorces and Enviromental Sciences, July 20-23. University of Leicester (2010)
10. Zilske, M., Neumann, A., Nagel, K.: OpenStreetMap for traffic simulation. In: Proceedings of the 1st European State of the Map–OpenStreetMap Conference (2011)
11. Klug, M.: CS Transport-Optimisation–A Solution for Web-based Trip Optimization Basing on OpenStreetMap. In: 19th ITS World Congress (2012)
12. Joubert, J.W., Van Heerden, Q.: Large-scale multimodal transport modelling. Part 1: Demand generation (2013)
13. Boye, J., et al.: Walk this way: Spatial grounding for city exploration. In: Natural Interaction with Robots, Knowbots and Smartphones, pp. 59–67. Springer, Heidelberg (2014)
14. Jacob, R., Zheng, J., Ciepłuch, B.z., Mooney, P., Winstanley, A.C.: Campus guidance system for international conferences based on OpenStreetMap. In: Carswell, J.D., Fotheringham, A.S., McArdle, G. (eds.) W2GIS 2009. LNCS, vol. 5886, pp. 187–198. Springer, Heidelberg (2009)
15. Silva, T.H., de Melo, P.O.S.V., Viana, A.C., Almeida, J.M., Salles, J., Loureiro, A.A.F.: Traffic Condition is More than Colored Lines on a Map: Characterization of Waze Alerts. In: Jatowt, A., et al. (eds.) SocInfo 2013. LNCS, vol. 8238, pp. 309–318. Springer, Heidelberg (2013)
16. Fire, M., et al.: Data mining opportunities in geosocial networks for improving road safety. In: 2012 IEEE 27th Convention of Electrical & Electronics Engineers in Israel (IEEEI). IEEE (2012)
17. Frez, J., et al.: Dealing with Incomplete and Uncertain Context Data in Geographic Information Systems. In: IEEE (ed.) Computer Supported Cooperative Work in Design (CSCWD), pp. 129–134. IEEE, Hsinchu (2014)
18. Yang, L., Wan, B.: A Multimodal Composite Transportation Network Model and Topological Relationship Building Algorithm. In: International Conference on Environmental Science and Information Application Technology, ESIAT 2009. IEEE (2009)
19. Liu, S., et al.: Modeling and simulation on multi-mode transportation network. In: 2010 International Conference on Computer Application and System Modeling (ICCASM). IEEE (2010)
20. Xu, L., Gao, Z.: Bi-objective urban road transportation discrete network design problem under demand and supply uncertainty. In: IEEE International Conference on Automation and Logistics, ICAL 2008. IEEE (2008)
21. Castillo, E., et al.: The observability problem in traffic models: algebraic and topological methods. IEEE Transactions on Intelligent Transportation Systems 9(2), 275–287 (2008)

User Interface Design for Test and Diagnosis Software in Automotive Production Environments

Nikolaj Borisov[1], Annette Kluge[1], Wolfram Luther[1], and Benjamin Weyers[2]

[1] University of Duisburg-Essen, Forsthausweg 2,
47057 Duisburg, Germany
{nikolaj.borisov,annette.kluge}@uni-due.de,
luther@inf.uni-due.de
[2] RWTH Aachen University, Seffenter Weg 23,
52074 Aachen, Germany
weyers@vr.rwth-aachen.de

Abstract. In this paper, we present a first approach to a new test and diagnosis user interface (TDUI) as an application scenario for ambient intelligent systems in production environments, which represents one specific domain for urban areas. This method is based on a first evaluation study in 2012, identifying relevant requirements for the development of such TDUIs. It is planned to be implemented based on a formally defined Interaction Logic Layer (ILL), which connects the physical user interface layout with the test system. It allows the user to easily control and adapt the test and diagnosis application, to display and convey information characterizing the process state. Finally, this approach makes the TDUI implementation highly flexible and adaptive regarding the individual user and the requirements of the production environment.

1   Introduction

Automotive companies are always in search of new technologies and concepts to improve their production processes by increasing product quality, reducing costs, and enhancing job satisfaction and thus directly influence the development and form of urban areas [1]. For the initiation and testing of the electrical installation in particular, in the last five to ten years, new testing and diagnosis processes, as well as technical installations have been developed. For instance, the portable RCU control unit is used as a wireless terminal in the DSA test system family (www.dsa.de).

Still, these installations focus mainly on achieving a highly standardized test task rather than offering usable tools and devices for the worker in charge of undertaking final testing or searching for untypical electronic component faults or system errors in cars segregated from the production line. Visual inspections and manual operations on components in the cockpit or checks outside of the car are necessary where electronic control devices or sensors alone are not able to test these functions. Therefore, the test environment sends a request to a worker for a button to be pressed or a typical driving action to be performed manually and acknowledges the correct performance or documents a malfunction of the component or functionality being tested.

R. Hervás et al. (Eds.): UCAmI 2014, LNCS 8867, pp. 372–375, 2014.
© Springer International Publishing Switzerland 2014

Until now, there has been no involvement of the worker in the development process of devices implementing the communication between the worker, the testing system, and the car. This has resulted in unusable physical devices and in errors, wrong or omitted actions, and, finally, in more time being spent by the worker than necessary on finishing a car, as we have documented in initial studies [2] in a German automotive company.

We agree with the authors of [3] that UI design, especially in safety-critical processes, should meet various categories of requirements, i.e., task conformance, support of mandatory or multiple control strategies, provision of unambiguous feedback in response to user actions, and reporting on actual process states such that the user can predict subsequent process states in accordance with his/her mental process model. Adequacy of interaction elements, flexibility in partitioning the task among multiple actors, using multimodal fault toleration and error avoidance dialogues with forward and backward error recovery are further needs. Typical key issues coming from cognitive science are enhanced situation awareness, reduced mental workload, increased efficiency, and help in choosing operator's modality and experience.

Inspired by recent work on page layout, design spaces [4], style guides and UI guidelines resources, we propose work in progress towards a new approach for modeling adaptive user interfaces (UI) for a future TDUI to reduce errors in interaction and increase the ubiquitousness of these devices by enhancing the process and task logic and the communication between workers, car, and test system. Finally, this effort aims at the creation of an intelligent ambient system for production environments as one specific domain in urban areas.

2   Context and Method

Current computer science research is focusing new methodologies to create adaptive human computer interfaces that can be reconfigured on the fly to offer the best possible support for users' and tasks' requirements. One of the challenges in this context is to find an equilibrium between competence, interests, and satisfaction on the user side while meeting requirements concerning reachability of goals, safety, reliability, privacy, and ergonomics on the communication side. Reconfiguration and customization of multimodal, distributed, mobile I/O interfaces allow for new forms of activities that are spatially and temporally decoupled from specific places, to offer various levels of task and role delegation to computer-based work places, and users receiving different degrees of computer support. To respond to these requests, a temporary delegation of functions to other persons offers more degrees of freedom in organizing working hours and enables individuals to switch between different tasks.

A human-computer dialog based on a reconfigurable interface with flexible interaction logic (modeling the behavior of the user interface) and varying tasks is a precondition to realizing this new scenario and enables individuals to assume or delegate their responsibilities, to form ad hoc work groups, to assign work among those involved according to their availability or abilities while respecting safety, reliability, and quality issues. This multidisciplinary approach, which includes psychological and sociological aspects of awareness and job satisfaction in the design, reconfiguration, and evaluation of human-computer interfaces, seeks to develop a powerful framework, UIEditor [5], with various components to design, reconfigure, and render visual UIs. To gather the necessary information, workers are interviewed directly when carrying out their job [1]. The result of our study will be a user-interface modeling process that, on one hand, creates UIs in a usable form for the car initiation and customization process in the automotive industry and supports a modeling approach for ambient systems in production environments, on the other.

3   UI Design for Testing and Diagnosis – First Results

This section presents initial results from a part of our exploratory study in the field, obtained by interviewing 36 workers during their work including a questionnaire of 19 questions to be answered on a 5 point Likert scale. The workers are performing car functionality testing on the production line with an experience between a few week and 40 years.

Initial Insights: We reviewed current control and diagnosis software and detected several weaknesses and mistakes in the UI design. Often this software is produced on demand by third party companies without adequate requirements concerning UI design and usability. As a consequence, producers are more or less free to realize concepts that have not been developed and evaluated with user feedback. Input and output UI elements are randomly placed on the screen, messages use cryptic abbreviations instead of clear pictograms or symbols, information channels provide a lot of state messages in rapid succession displayed in small fonts by default, rendering them unreadable. As a result, they can be frequently overlooked. Certain steps may need the user's acknowledgement, while others do not. No clear deliberate taxonomy is used. Time between subsequent steps cannot be influenced by the user, progress in the process is not displayed, and no back function (for the correction of previous input or for any other reason) is implemented. Hand terminals in use are not versatile; various functions like barcode reading, protocol printing and text input are suboptimal; existing interface devices are relatively heavy and prevent the worker from moving around the object being inspected and from having both hands free for manipulation.

Methodology: Reconfigurable modeled UIs based on design spaces is one possible approach, which tackles the above-introduced problems on the basis of the formal modeling of user interfaces. Using these kinds of techniques enables a simple and effective adaption of the UI, which can be adapted to the changing roles of workers, who may be experts, novices, or group leaders. The interaction logic is described via a new formal modeling language called FILL that is accompanied by the modeling, simulation, and reconfiguration framework UIEditor [5]. With this approach, a UI is modeled in a two-layer structure, where the first layer is a physical layer and models the outward appearance of the UI, and the second layer is the interaction logic and implements the behavior of the UI as a set of data processing routines. These processes convert input actions executed by the user into data, which can be processed by the system to be controlled. Furthermore, data generated by the system is processed by the interaction logic and finally presented to the user on the physical representation of the output device.

Interaction logic as modeled with FILL is transformed into reference nets, which are a special type of Petri nets. Reference nets provide suitable features, such as complex data types as tokens, the ability to describe references between various net instances and Java code, as well as timing and so forth. Further options are the modeling of hierarchical structures in the interaction logic layer, which allows the adaption to various roles in testing and diagnosis scenarios, and the modeling of multimodal interaction between workers and software systems. Changes in the design or in the constellation of roles in the testing processes can be formally realized and then simulated with a new interface design by using graph-transformation systems.

Because it increases usability, enhancing the framework UIEditor with new multiuser, multimodal dialogue analysis components for the flexible-use case environment of this contribution renders communication between workers, the testing system, and the cars more flexible and thus more versatile and ubiquitous.

Conclusion: Evaluating the collected comments of a sample of workers has enabled us to identify several important points. The most important issue is to design a new handy and versatile mobile interface which provides the same facilities as before with a structured design separating reading, information displays, and input elements to acknowledge process steps or to go forward and backward. Various kinds of hardware devices will be discussed in this context, such as handheld input devices, heads up displays, or even devices that project a UI design on the worker's sleeve that allows him to input key press events on an immaterial interface. The worker is assisted during the entire diagnosis task or guided through each task with hints and graded guidance in performing each step. This is partly done by inbuilt car sensors that intangibly track and detect the worker's position and recognize specific actions. It would be interesting to work out options for alternative ways to communicate or to accomplish the task step by step while modifying the order in which tasks are performed or the way the system's requests are responded to, based on the worker's experience. A further option is to allow the presentation of adaptive information in textual or pictorial form. Beginners like more feedback and encouragement than skilled users. Finally, we will propose a new functional UI design for the car startup software.

References

1. Borisov, N., Kluge, A., Luther, W., Weyers, B.: Integrated production workers into user Interface Design for Diagnosis Devices in Automotive Production Environments: Field experiences and lessons learned. In: Stephanidis, C. (ed.) Poster, Part II, HCII 2013. CCIS, vol. 374, pp. 469–473. Springer, Heidelberg (2013)
2. Schwarz, F.: Entwicklung und Einsatz innovativer HMI-Software zur Diagnose elektronischer Steuergeräte in der Automobilindustrie, PhD Dissertation U Passau (2008)
3. Galliers, J., Minocha, S., Sutcliffe, A.G.: A Causal Model of Human Error for Safety Critical User Interface Design. In: Special Issue on Interface Issues and Designs for Safety-Critical Interactive Systems of the ACM Transactions on Computer-Human Interaction
4. Ballagas, R., Rohs, M., Sheridan, J., Borchers, J.: The Design Space of Ubiquitous Mobile Input. In: Lumsden, J. (ed.) Handbook of Research on User Interface Design and Evaluation for Mobile Technologies. IGI Global, Hershey (2008)
5. Weyers, B.: Reconfiguration of User Interface Models for Monitoring and Control of Human-Computer Systems. PhD Dissertation, University of Duisburg-Essen, 2011, Dr. Hut Verlag (2012)

The Role of Assistive Technologies
for Older Adults in Urban Areas

Anna Kötteritzsch[1] and Benjamin Weyers[2]

[1] Universität der Bundeswehr, Werner-Heisenberg-Weg 39, 85577 Neubiberg, Germany
anna@koetteritzsch.net
[2] RWTH Aachen University, Seffenter Weg 23, 52074 Aachen, Germany
weyers@vr.rwth-aachen.de

Abstract. Research in the field of Ambient Assisted Living (AAL) introduces
assistive technologies in various contexts, e.g., medical applications for clinics,
or activities in home environments. Assistive technologies have the potential to
help prevent isolation and lack of social support arising from a growing number
of older adults living in single person households in urban areas. In order to examine the role of such technologies and identify challenges and potentials of
systems and services, we investigated existing literature of the past decade.
Whereas many contributions support the individual user or social connection,
only few integrate location-based information or urban structures. Future research is confronted with a multitude of challenges, e.g. considering network
technologies, market uptake or adaptation, and potentials, e.g. the support or establishing of social neighborhood structures. This literature review contributes
in achieving an overview of the state of the art and research areas that will draw
an increasing focus according to demographic change.

1 Introduction

The rapidly changing population in urban areas and larger distances between family
members and friends result in an increased isolation of older adults living in single-
person households. Likewise, demographic change implicates a higher percentage of
older adults with age-related impairments and a growing gap in healthcare services.
With the aim of creating better living conditions for this population group, research in
the field of Ambient Assisted Living (AAL) introduces assistive technologies, which
address older adults, nursing staff, and family members in various contexts. These
contexts are specified by care facilities, medical applications in hospitals and rehabilitation clinics, as well as everyday-life activities in home environments. AAL systems
therefore implement intelligent algorithms to process gathered sensor data and generate information supporting care givers or older adults to organize their daily life [1].
To maintain physical and cognitive abilities and thereby reduce future care needs,
specific AAL systems concentrate on the prevention and intervention of age-related
impairments. Many systems also consider social components for their implementation. However, assistive technologies differ in their possible effect on social structures

R. Hervás et al. (Eds.): UCAmI 2014, LNCS 8867, pp. 376–383, 2014.
© Springer International Publishing Switzerland 2014

in urban environments. When embedded into urban areas, many challenges and research questions arise from the development of assistive technologies for older adults.

This work presents a literature review to identify the impact of AAL systems on older adults living in urban areas. In section 2, we present prevention and intervention systems, classified into categories in terms of supporting older adults. Based on the results, we point out what challenges research faces when creating technologies for older adults in urban areas and show the potential of considering the location and related social structures in developing tomorrow's assistive systems (section 3).

2   Assistive Technologies for Older Adults

A growing number of people living alone with a lack of social contacts effects economic and social systems in urban areas [2]. Hence, authorities need to adjust and facilities and existing structures for community interaction and urban planning [3]. Different measures of participation may individually influence these aspects, ranging from assistive technologies for individual support to local community services. We examined the user involvement to differentiate the impact of a technology on older adults in urban areas. We identified three levels of measurements to involve older adults in local social structures by means of an existing infrastructure.

The first level is dedicated to *single-user applications*. These applications indirectly affect urban areas by maintaining autonomy through encouraging physical and cognitive activity of the dedicated older adults. These applications enable them to participate in social life and reduce expenses for care by supporting prevention and intervention of impairments through analyzing individual behavior and providing services and functions for older adults, families, and care personnel.

Co-located or virtual multi-user applications as well as *single-user application for community* interaction represent a second level. These applications indirectly influence urban structures by enhancing or facilitating social interaction in (inter-) generational contexts. This level includes technologies that provide spaces or facilitate opportunities to share experiences or enrich social structures.

A third level of technologies directly influences urban areas by *reacting to information gathered in the relevant area and in its population*. The goal of approaches on this level is to enable and support the connection of people with similar areas of interest or people living in the same district. Location-based services or social networks use algorithms for the analysis of personal information, as well as match-making algorithms to connect people with similar interests or problems living in the same area. These approaches use existing structures in urban environments for supporting older adults or develop technologies to foster the acceptance and usage of those structures.

2.1   Search, Selection and Analysis of Literature

In order to discuss the role of AAL technologies in urban areas, we investigated existing literature from 2004 to 2014. Contributions were extracted from four databases: ACM Digital Library, IEEE Xplore Digital Library, DBLP Computer Science Bibliography, and SpringerLink based on the appearance of the keywords "assisted living", "eldery", "senior", "older adult", "aging", or "intergenerational" in headline or abstract. We also filtered the proceedings of IWAAL, UCAmI, PETRA, ASSETS,

CHI, CSCW, as well as the AAL Forum, AAL Congress, and the German Conference on Human-Computer Interaction (MuC). Only end-user applications designed for and studies evaluating the use of systems for older adults were considered. Middleware systems connecting different services and design studies were not included. After eliminating duplications, 639 relevant systems were extracted out of 856 scientific contributions. When analyzing the systems, they differed in certain aspects that could be grouped into the following categories: 0. Level of support (some systems are assigned to more than one support level), 1. Type of contribution, 2. Application context, 3. Focused user group, 4. Information required, 5. Technologies for tracking information, 6. System adaptation, and 7. Status of the presented application. Furthermore, objectives, measurements, user interaction mechanisms and evaluation methods were examined. In the following, the overall results of the literature review are presented. Due to the high number of contributions, we listed one approach representing the work within its field for each relevant topic.

2.2   Level 1 - Support of Individual Users

Table 1 lists approaches that support individual users. 562 contributions were assigned to this category, their focus ranging from the support of physical or cognitive activities [4], everyday life tasks in private [5, 6] or work environment [7], help to cope with impairments [8, 9] and care support. Most approaches focus on accident management by monitoring healthcare status [10], analyzing activities [11], or predicting behavior. Technologies used to gather information include sensor networks (including pressure, motion, and radio frequency sensors), video camera tracking, RFID and NFC tracking, as well as logging of system usage. Monitoring systems focus on care personnel as their main user group, however, some approaches put the older adult into control by allowing the adaption of monitoring conditions. Another major scope in the analyzed contributions is digitally supported cognitive or physical therapy. The majority of rehabilitation systems support user based content adaptation in order to provide suitable training for older adults with varying needs. Playful concepts are often used in therapy systems, aiming at an increased motivation. Task support systems are also used for individual support. Based on information on the location or time, they provide reminders, structure activities, and give instructions on how to perform certain activities. While most of the contributions present prototypes (529), a few products for individual support were already introduced to the market (13), and some propositions have not yet exceeded a conceptual phase (18). Evaluations of system efficiency have been conducted for most of the systems, while actual (long-term) effects on the user were not included. By enabling older adults to participate in social living activities, these technologies influence urban living structures.

2.3   Level 2 - Support of Community Interaction

124 of the analyzed approaches focus on co-located or virtual multi-user applications and single-user applications for community interaction. These systems or studies aim at enhancing or facilitating social interaction by providing shared spaces for exchanging information with peers and relatives [12, 13], or tools for mediated synchronous interaction, e.g., video communication [14]. They foster co-located activities through providing

challenging or cooperative multi-user interaction [15, 16]. Different approaches supporting community interaction are listed in table 2. Technologies could be grouped into three
major contexts according to the used measurements. While few approaches support multi-user co-located or computer mediated activities, a major part of systems focus on asynchronous media and information sharing, and some aim at awareness or social presence
enhancement. Most technologies are in a prototypical (114), or conceptual status (7). One
service and two healthcare portals on the market were presented. Furthermore, most of
the systems were evaluated considering social presence. Technologies on this level have
an indirect impact on urban structures, because they enable interaction over distances and
influence social behavior in (inter-) generational contexts.

Table 1. Examples of technologies supporting individual users, classified by type (**SY**stem,
SErvice, **ST**udy), context (**NAV**igation support, **MON**itoring, **REH**abilitation, **PLA**yful
interaction, **PHY**sical activity, **TAS**k support, **MOB**ility cupport, **SOC**ial interaction, language
TRAnslation, **SHA**red content, virtual **PRE**sence, **LEA**rning environment, Social Network
System, **VID**eo communication, social **SUP**port, **ACT**ivity support, **MAT**chmaking,
INFormation system), user (Older Adults, Care Personnel, CareGivers, InterGenerational,
HElpers and services), information (**LOC**ation of user, **MOV**ement information, User **IN**tention,
ACTivities performed by user, **HEA**lth data, **SIT**uation information), tracking (Wireless Sensor
Network, **CAM**era-based tracking, Sensor-Based Tracking, **CON**nection logging, Global
Positioning System, **MAN**ual insertion), adaptation (User-Based, **ROU**te adaptation, **INT**erface
adaptation, **CoNT**ent adaptation), and status (**PR**ototype, product in **MA**rket, **CO**ncept)

Ref.	Type	Context	User	Information	Tracking	Adaption	Status
[4]	SY	REH, PLA	OA	UIN	MAN	UB, CNT	PR
[5]	SE	TAS	OA	HEA	N/A	N/A	MA
[6]	SY	TAS	OA	LOC, MOV	GPS, SBT	UB, CNT	CO
[7]	SY	TAS, PLA	OA	N/A	N/A	N/A	PR
[8]	SY	NAV	OA	LOC, MOV	WSN, CAM	CNT	PR
[9]	SY	MOB	OA	LOC, UIN	GPS, MAN	CNT	PR
[10]	SY	MON	CP	LOC, HEA, MOV	WSN, CAM	N/A	PR
[11]	SY	MON	OA	HEA, UIN	SBT, MAN	UB	PR

2.4   Level 3 - Support of Local Community Structures

The contributions listed in table 3 represent different approaches supporting local
communities and structures within urban areas. 24 applications could be assigned to
this level of support, represented by the results listed in table 3. Despite of the small
number of results, the presented approaches show a wide variation of measurements.
Technologies focus on the accessibility [22], as well as localization and mapping [23,
24] of services and technologies for older adults. Furthermore, they connect peer
groups [25], match user objectives, encourage location-based meetings [28], and
connect people in need with assistive services [27]. Thereby, they create new local

community structures. Interaction measures reach from playful approaches, to location-based user ratings. All technologies allow for at least content adaption, based on the user location. Research projects developed prototypes (19) or concepts (3), whereas socio-technological support services have been successfully implemented into local communities [29]. User groups supported include older adults, care personnel, voluntary helpers, service facilities, and peer groups. The approaches have been evaluated in terms of contributing to social structures, or are derived from qualitative and quantitative research. By supporting mobility and the uptake of existing structures, systems on this level directly influence urban areas and the people living in them.

Table 2. Examples of technologies supporting community interaction (see table 1 categories)

Ref.	Type	Context	User	Information	Tracking	Adaption	Status
[12]	SY	SOC, SHA	OA, IG	N/A	N/A	N/A	PR
[13]	SY	SNS	OA	UIN	MAN	UB, CNT	PR
[14]	SY	PRE, VID	OA	ACT	CAM, MAN	CNT	PR
[15]	SY	SOC, PLA	OA, IG	UIN, ACT	MAN	CNT	PR
[16]	SY	PHY, PLA, SOC	OA	ACT	SBT	UB	PR
[17]	SY	SOC, PLA, LEA	OA, IG	UIN, ACT	MAN, CON	N/A	PR
[18]	SY	TRA	OA	N/A	SBT	UB	PR
[19]	SY	MON	CG	LOC, MOV	CAM	N/A	PR

Table 3. Examples of technologies supporting community interaction (see table 1 categories)

Ref.	Type	Context	User	Information	Tracking	Adaption	Status
[20]	SY	SUP	OA, HE	LOC	GPS	INT	PR
[21]	SY	MON	OA, CP	ACT, LOC	CON	ROU	PR
[22]	SY	SOC, SHA	OA	LOC, MOV	GPS	CNT	PR
[23]	SY	SOC, PLA	OA	LOC	MAN	CNT	PR
[24]	SY	ACT, SOC, MAT	OA	LOC, SIT	GPS	CNT	PR
[25]	SY	NAV, SUP	OA, HE	LOC, SIT	SBT	CNT, UB	PR
[26]	SY	SNS, SOC, ACT	OA	LOC, ACT	MAN	CNT	CO
[27]	SE	SOC, LEA	OA	N/A	N/A	N/A	MA

3   Assisting Older Adults in Urban Areas

Given the existing literature on assistive technologies for older adults, future research is confronted with a multitude of potentials and challenges when developing such systems for urban environments. Cities are confronted with an increasing number of older adults and rapidly changing social and environmental factors. These trends direct researchers towards seizing opportunities to support social interaction and making use of existing information and services. However, spatial conditions must be considered when adapting research prototypes to realistic settings. Many technologies presented in section 2 do not take boundaries into account that occur when they are operated in between buildings and heterogeneous network systems. Advanced (wireless) network and sensor technologies, as well as the integration and interchange of multiple solutions should be considered to avoid connection losses and technology failures. An increasing number of projects focus on developing middleware solutions for assistive technologies that systematically gather data and allow for interoperability of different services. Nevertheless, a majority of analyzed contributions do not integrate connection requirements but develop encapsulated systems. Standardized interfaces and data security measures must be composed to transfer technologies into real user groups and contexts. Additionally, it is important to consider heterogeneous abilities and allow for adaptation. In the reviewed literature, many projects develop technologies according to physical or cognitive impairments of older adults. Adaptive systems have the potential to provide suitable interfaces and content for older individuals with varying abilities and preferences, when they implement adequate tracking and analysis.

Another major challenge of future assistive technologies for older adults is the market uptake of research results. Although many research projects create suitable technologies for supporting individual capabilities and fostering social interaction, only few technologies are actually introduced to the market. One of the barriers mentioned in the previously discussed literature is the technology skepticism and the lacking acceptance within the user group of older adults. However, with changing technology literacy of older adults and close living spaces of young and old, future older adults are characterized by curiosity and interest towards developments.

Nevertheless, with a growing number of older adults in urban areas the need for connecting various generations of people to sustain social support increased. Thus, these demographic changes do not only lead to challenges for AAL, but offer a great potential for the development of supportive technologies. Suitable assistive systems contribute in connecting neighborhood communities and creating spaces for intergenerational exchange. The support of these structures promise great potentials in terms of coping with care issues and isolation. An increasing number of older adults in urban areas also brings together people with similar interests or problems as well as many retirees willing to contribute to social structures and looking for shared activities. Therefore, community services need to be adapted to older adults helping in the society. Considering these structures, the demand of technologies for social matchmaking will potentially grow. Only little of the presented literature takes these structures into account, e.g., systems which connect older adults with voluntary helpers. AAL systems can potentially prevent isolation and enhance mobility that arise from changing urban structures. Furthermore, when spatial and social environments as well as individual needs are ade-

quately considered, future research can meet the challenges mentioned above and benefit from the opportunities within local communities.

4   Conclusion

Within this contribution we classified existing literature of the last decade focusing on
assistive technologies for older adults. We examined many technologies that have an
impact on older adults living in urban areas by directly or indirectly influencing the
utilization of urban structures. By means of sorting these technologies into different
categories, potentials and challenges for future research technologies for older adults
in urban areas could be identified. Moreover, this literature review contributes in
achieving an overview of technologies that have been developed. Future work in the
area of AAL will face upcoming challenges but also high potentials that emerge from
a growing target group living in urban areas when focusing on local communities.

References

1. Fischer, O., Wittpahl, V.: Realisierungsmöglichkeiten und Limitierungen eines preiswerten
   AAL-Assistenz-Systems mittels Smart Devices. In: Wohnen–Pflege–Teilhabe– "leben
   durch Technik" (2014)
2. Kumata, A., Tsuda, Y., Suzuki, H., Ra, E., Morishita, T.: Advanced community model using daily life information transmitter for supporting welfare workers and senior citizens
   living alone in a welfare society. In: 8th International Conference on Ubiquitous Robots
   and Ambient Intelligence (URAI), pp. 414–417. IEEE (2011)
3. Langdon, P., Clarkson, J.: Designing inclusive futures. Springer (2008)
4. Kötteritzsch, A., Schmitz, C., Lemân, F.: Spaß vergisst man nicht: Motivierung zur De-
   menzintervention. In: MuC 2013 Workshop Proceedings, pp. 375–381 (2013)
5. Avila, N., Sampogna, C.: e-Health – Ambient Assisted Living and Personal Health Systems. In: Springer Handbook of Medical Technology, pp. 1217–1246. Springer, Heidelberg (2011)
6. Daxhammer, J., Pichen, J., Plonka, J., Löffler, D.: Smart Lens-Augmented Reality als All-
   tagshelfer. In: MuC 2013 Visions (2013)
7. Korn, O.: Industrial playgrounds: how gamification helps to enrich work for elderly or impaired persons in production. In: Proceedings of the 4th ACM SIGCHI Symposium on Engineering Interactive Computing Systems, pp. 313–316. ACM (2012)
8. Abascal, J., Bonail, B., Casas, R., Marco, Á., Sevillano, J.L., Cascado, D.: Towards an intelligent and supportive environment for people with physical or cognitive restrictions. In:
   Proceedings of the 2nd International Conference on PErvasive Technologies Related to
   Assistive Environments, p. 10. ACM (2009)
9. Carmien, S., Dawe, M., Fischer, G., Gorman, A., Kintsch, A., Sullivan Jr., J.F.: Socio-
   technical environments supporting people with cognitive disabilities using public transportation. ACM TOCHI 12(2), 233–262 (2005)
10. Amoretti, M., Copelli, S., Wientapper, F., Furfari, F., Lenzi, S., Chessa, S.: Sensor data fu-
    sion for activity monitoring in the PERSONA ambient assisted living project. Journal of
    Ambient Intelligence and Humanized Computing 4(1), 67–84 (2013)
11. Kanis, M., Robben, S., Hagen, J., Bimmerman, A., Wagelaar, N., Kröse, B.: Sensor monitor-
    ing in the home: giving voice to elderly people. In: Proceedings of the 7th International Confe-
    rence on Pervasive Computing Technologies for Healthcare, pp. 97–100. ICST (2013)

12. Apted, T., Kay, J., Quigley, A.: Tabletop sharing of digital photographs for the elderly. In: Proceedings of the SIGCHI Conference on Human Factors in Computing Systems, pp. 781–790. ACM (2006)
13. Burkhard, M., Nutsi, A., Koch, M.: Einsatz von Spaß und Humor zur Förderung sozialer Aktivität. In: Mensch & Computer Workshopband, pp. 369–374 (2013)
14. Fuchsberger, V., Sellner, W., Moser, C., Tscheligi, M.: Benefits and hurdles for older adults in intergenerational online interactions. In: Miesenberger, K., Karshmer, A., Penaz, P., Zagler, W. (eds.) ICCHP 2012, Part I. LNCS, vol. 7382, pp. 697–704. Springer, Heidelberg (2012)
15. Herrmanny, K., Budweg, S., Klauser, M., Kötteritzsch, A.: Gameinsam – A playful application fostering distributed family interaction on TV. In: EuroITV Proceedings, pp. 21–22 (2012)
16. Gerling, K.M., Schulte, F.P., Masuch, M.: Designing and evaluating digital games for frail elderly persons. In: Proceedings of the 8th International Conference on Advances in Computer Entertainment Technology, p. 62. ACM (2011)
17. Robier, J., Majcen, K., Prattes, T., Stoisser, M.: Jung und Alt Gemeinsam spielend lernen. In: Mensch & Computer 2013-Workshopband (2013)
18. Anastasiou, D.: Speech-to-speech translation in an assisted living lab. In: Proceedings of the 4th International Conference on PErvasive Technologies Related to Assistive Environments, p. 60. ACM (2011)
19. Nait Aicha, A., Englebienne, G., Kröse, B.: How lonely is your grandma?: detecting the visits to assisted living elderly from wireless sensor network data. In: Proceedings of the 2013 ACM Conference on Pervasive and Ubiquitous Computing Adjunct Publication, pp. 1285–1294. ACM (2013)
20. Baumann, K., Klein, P., Mrsic Carl, A., Bender, D.: Gamification in the inDAgo HelpMe application. In: Mensch & Computer 2014-Tagungsband (2014)
21. Abad, J.-A., Gorricho, J.-L.: A Device Search Strategy Based on Connections History for Patient Monitoring. In: Omatu, S., Rocha, M.P., Bravo, J., Fernández, F., Corchado, E., Bustillo, A., Corchado, J.M. (eds.) IWANN 2009, Part II. LNCS, vol. 5518, pp. 831–838. Springer, Heidelberg (2009)
22. Bentley, F., Basapur, S.: StoryPlace. Me: The path from studying elder communication to a public location-based video service. In: CHI 2012 Extended Abstracts on Human Factors in Computing Systems, pp. 777–792. ACM (2012)
23. Birn, T., Holzmann, C., Stech, W.: MobileQuiz: A Serious Game for Enhancing the Physical and Cognitive Abilities of Older Adults. In: Stephanidis, C., Antona, M. (eds.) UAHCI/HCII 2014, Part III. LNCS, vol. 8515, pp. 3–14. Springer, Heidelberg (2014)
24. He, S., Jiang, L., Li, Z., Zhang, X.: Commucity: A social network system for the non-resident elderly in big cities in China. In: Proceedings of the Second International Symposium of Chinese CHI, pp. 97–102. ACM (2014)
25. Burns, W., Chen, L., Nugent, C., Donnelly, M., Skillen, K.L., Solheim, I.: Mining usage data for Adaptive Personalisation of Smartphone based Help-on-Demand services. In: Proceedings of the 6th International Conference on PErvasive Technologies Related to Assistive Environments, p. 39. ACM (2013)
26. Fan, C., Forlizzi, J., Dey, A.: Considerations for technology that support physical activity by older adults. In: Proceedings of the 14th International ACM SIGACCESS Conference on Computers and Accessibility, pp. 33–40. ACM (2012)
27. Forbes, P., Gibson, L., Hanson, V.L., Gregor, P., Newell, A.: Dundee user centre: A space where older people and technology meet. In: Proceedings of the 11th International ACM SIGACCESS Conference on Computers and Accessibility, pp. 231–232. ACM (2009)

Smart Museums –
Exploiting Generative Virtual Museums

Daniel Sacher[1], Benjamin Weyers[2], Daniel Biella[1], and Wolfram Luther[1]

[1] Computer and Cognitive Science (INKO) and Center for Information and Media
Services (CIM), University of Duisburg-Essen, Germany
{daniel.sacher,daniel.biella,wolfram.luther}@uni-due.de
[2] Virtual Reality Group, RWTH Aachen University, Germany
weyers@vr.rwth-aachen.de

Abstract. This paper describes a metadata-based tour recommendation approach for on-site museum and outdoor visits. Recommendations
are calculated utilizing spatial exhibit distribution, museum layout, user
and navigation profiles, additional constraints as well as art work descriptors. We propose a service-oriented architecture for generating 3D
virtual museums as well as a WebSocket layer to process sensor data
during the museum visit.

Keywords: Virtual Museum, 3D Museum, Smart Museum, ViMEDEAS,
ViMCOX, Replicave.

1 Introduction

The development of smart museum systems that adapt to user models for providing personalized content is a complex task. The adaptive features of virtual
3D museums comprise of their architectural design, the arrangement of exhibits,
the supplementation of suitable educational materials (sometimes multilingual),
and navigation aids or user-to-object interaction modes of varying complexity
[1]. In some cases, the exhibition environment has to be created dynamically and
the software needs to monitor the user's behavior to create adaptive tours, which
detect user preferences during the visit. In recent publications, we addressed the
standardization for the modeling of virtual museums including the dynamically
generation of the exhibition environments using cross-collection content [2, 3].
Based on these works, this paper discusses a real open-air museum scenario,
which is supported by techniques from virtual 3D museums and metadata standards. The main contribution is a model of a domain specific implementation
for exploring museums as artifact of urban areas. Main focus will be the tour
planning and creation, which involves movement profiles gathered through GPS-
based devices and other sensors, questions and answers tagged interactively by
visitors, recommendations of exhibits and submitted tours, as well as the exhibition item metadata. The discussion of the tour planning and creation system
will be motivated from a set of requirements. We will present our framework

R. Hervás et al. (Eds.): UCAmI 2014, LNCS 8867, pp. 384–387, 2014.
© Springer International Publishing Switzerland 2014

ViMEDEAS for the modeling of virtual museums which offers all relevant implementations for metadata modeling and tour specification [2–6]. Finally, we will identify components for future work implementations and a concept for a user study to evaluate the system.

2 Scenarios

In terms of smart museums, two application scenarios can be identified: (1) mobile experience and guidance on-site using handhelds for example when visiting museums or cultural site as described by the smart museum project [7] and (2) the virtual museum for domestic use, e.g., to reflect and prepare visits as iterative process including scenario (1) or as standalone visit. A virtual 3D museums will support the user's visit in both scenarios by presenting high fidelity resources, metadata, and supplementary material. Scenario (1) can be categorized into indoor and outdoor experiences, where different location detection methods can be applied, for example using (manual) alpha-numeric input, image-based information, QR codes, RF technology, or other sensory data such as GPS. The virtual museum visit (2) uses spatial/algorithmic approaches to detect the user's location and behavior such as preferences for art, navigation, interaction patterns, movement profile, and a logging of the viewing/browsing history. For the second scenario, we exclude the automatic generation of exhibition spaces using query results from key word searches as described in [2], because this would represent a completely new exhibition. Nevertheless, plain keyword searches, which directly link to viewpoints or suggesting paths can be considered in our scenarios. Furthermore, we dispense with the ability to directly access exhibition areas or items via the teleporter metaphor as well as the re-arrangement of exhibition areas.

In both scenarios, our approach seeks to support the navigation and to provide tour suggestions. The key idea is to combine the structural and exhibit related information of ViMCOX (a metadata format for virtual museums, discussed in more detail below in Section 3) with user profiles (demographic data, ratings, interests, browsing history) to (re-)calculate probably interesting exhibition items and routes during a visit or to let the visitor select generated/recommended tours. A similar approach for generating personalized museum tours based on user profiles, semantically enriched museum collections, and semantic web technologies is presented in [8], where visitors can prepare individual real museum tours using content filtering or using recommended tour sets. In this scenario, handheld tour guides help them to navigate within the real museum using 2D floor plans.

3 ViMCOX Model

The ViMCOX metadata format provides the semantic structure of exhibitions and complete museums, which includes the hierarchical description of buildings, levels, rooms, and outdoor areas. It therefore includes information about navigation paths expressed as connectivity graphs and information about connectors such as stairways, elevators, and other metaphorical 3D representations [2, 5]. This information represents the basic data for tour planning and recommendation, as it defines the spatial structure of the museum and possible paths. Resource information such as the exhibit type (2D, 3D, multimedia, interactive), keywords, size/dimension (passepartout, scale, frame), linked camera positions, positioning as well as the relation to other pieces of art can be derived from the ViMCOX metadata. Furthermore, ViMCOX is based on LIDO, thus, thesauri and vocabulary can be used for the purpose of normalization. In case of outdoor areas [5], ViMCOX merges the visualization (3D landscape model, vegetation) and additional semantics expressed in ViMCOX metadata. For example, the modeling of additional paths, such as roads or passages, described as 3D point sets as well as the specification of exhibition areas and landmarks as navigation aid can be realized. Related objects and supplementary materials can be linked directly to exhibits by curators and other basic exhibit context information are available via ViMCOX object metadata as well as pointer to richer museum documentation [2]. Tour planning in ViMCOX can be elaborated utilizing TourML [2] by referencing external user generated tour content (XML) or tours created by curators that are defined in situ. Tours can be described in an abstract manner as a set of assets in a certain order represented as graph. The compilation is influenced by various constraints, parameters and combinations: such as the user profile and preferences, museum layout, durations, user's selections or includes and excludes respectively, content filtering, similarity as well as item ratings. In terms of rating, we would like to use a passive and active measurement, where passive (system-driven) rating corresponds to proximity and duration of a stay, browsing of metadata and supplementary material of a resource or the detection of the preferences for certain metadata representations. Recommendations in synergy with movement profiles form sensor data and other user profiles is also an interesting aspect for outdoor and indoor tour suggestions. In addition, active (user-driven) rating corresponds to preferences for art and the user's demographic data specified in the user's profile, the user's ratings of tours, areas, or resources as well as questionnaires or the sharing of objects in a Web 2.0 scenario.

The selection of art works can be elaborated on basis of content/category filtering or using cosine similarity for artworks. The spatial neighborhood of exhibition areas and their connectivity for outdoor areas is already specified in metadata but can be enriched using additional movement profiles. For indoor scenarios, the connectivity graphs, room dimensions, and connector positions can be utilize to calculate various paths. In some cases partition walls are used to organize rooms and should be included for collision free path calculation and distance measurement. Distance measurement within exhibition areas can be elaborated, as described above, using the exhibit positions, dimensions, or scale and their assignments to room structures, such as, (partition-)walls, floors or ceiling.

4   Future Work

As described in [3], the Replicave framework allows the generation of virtual museums for the rendering platforms X3D and X3Dom. X3Dom runs on mobile platforms and can utilize modern web technologies. We are proposing a service-oriented architecture including a server to host the user profiles and WebServices (SOAP, RESTful) for 3D and tour content creation using ViMCOX. On handheld systems, we propose an X3Dom render layer to display virtual museums on mobile platforms including a sensor layer to gather sensor data and to update the virtual museum representation. The X3Dom rendering layer can receive updates from the sensor layer via a REST API (PULL) for full state updates or via WebSockets (PUSH) for live updates such as position, orientation, and other user interactions. The 3D WebService architecture can also be utilized to store different 3D reconstructions of real museums which are accessible via perma-links. Furthermore, we need to evaluate our metadata-based (category filter) tour recommendation approach in comparison to an ontology-based approach where art history experts can model more granular relations and where ViMCOX is only used for the purpose of presentation. To assess our approach of using 3D virtual museums on-site, we will create a user centered case study using a reconstructed cemetery located in the German Rhine-Ruhr area and additional GPS sensor and user's movement data to recommend routes. The reconstruction comprises two reconstructed tombstone fields including 10 reconstructed tombstones crafted by the German-Jewish sculptor Leopold Fleischhacker.

References

1. Lepouras, G., Vassilakis, C.: Adaptive virtual reality museums on the web (2004), http://www.uoc.edu/humfil/articles/eng/pujol0304/pujol0304.pdf (accessed January 31, 2013)
2. Sacher, D., Biella, D., Luther, W.: Towards a versatile metadata exchange format for digital museum collections. In: Proceedings of the 2013 Digital Heritage International Congress (Digital Heritage), pp. 129–136 (2013)
3. Sacher, D., Biella, D., Luther, W.: A Generative Approach to Virtual Museums. In: Krempels, K.-H., Stocker, A. (eds.) WEBIST, pp. 274–279. SciTePress (2013)
4. Biella, D., Luther, W., Baloian, N.: Virtual Museum Exhibition Designer Using Enhanced ARCO Standard. In: XXIX International Conference of the Chilean Computer Science Society (SCCC), pp. 226–235 (November 2010)
5. Biella, D., Luther, W., Sacher, D.: Schema Migration Into A Web-based Framework for Generating Virtual Museums and Laboratories. In: 18th International Conference on Virtual Systems and Multimedia (VSMM), pp. 307–314 (2012)
6. Biella, D., Luther, W., Baloian, N.: Beyond the ARCO standard. In: 16th International Conference on Virtual Systems and Multimedia (VSMM), pp. 184–191 (October 2010)
7. Smartmuseum, SMARTMUSEUM Cultural Heritage Knowledge Exchange Platform (2009), http://www.smartmuseum.eu/
8. Aroyo, L., Stash, N., Wang, Y., Gorgels, P., Rutledge, L.: CHIP demonstrator: Semantics-driven recommendations and museum tour generation. In: Aberer, K., et al. (eds.) ASWC/ISWC 2007. LNCS, vol. 4825, pp. 879–886. Springer, Heidelberg (2007)

Monitoring Physical Activities Using Smartphones

Pablo Romo[1], Sergio F. Ochoa[1], Nelson Baloian[1], Ignacio Casas[2], and José Bravo[3]

[1] Computer Science Department, University of Chile
Av. Blanco Encalada 2120, 3rd Floor, Santiago, Chile
{promo,sochoa,nbaloian}@dcc.uchile.cl
[2] Computer Science Department, Pontifical Catholic University of Chile
Av. V. Mackenna 4860, Santiago, Chile
icasas@ing.puc.cl
[3] Castilla-La Mancha University
Ciudad Real, Spain
jose.bravo@uclm.es

Abstract. It is well-known that physical activities contribute to keep the people healthy. However, the modern life style impacts negatively on the amount of physical activity that we do during the day. Many times the people do not perform enough exercise because they are not aware of the amount of physical activity that they have done. In order to make the persons aware of this aspect of his life, this article presents a mobile application that monitors the amount of exercise they do every day and it informs properly to the user. The system, named AMOPA, allows caregivers or doctors monitoring particular patients, to access this information remotely in order to support the person being monitored. The system was evaluated using laboratory tests, and the results indicate a good performance and accuracy in the detection of the people physical activities. Moreover, the monitored process has a low impact on the energy consumption of the devices used to capture and process the information.

Keywords: Monitoring of physical activities, healthcare, model lifestyle, urban population.

1   Introduction

The modern life style has brought us comfort, safety and fast-access services according to our needs and interests. However, this impacts negatively on the amount of physical activity that we do every day, and consequently, on our physical and mental condition. This situation is emphasized in urban areas, where the comfort and services for the people tends to be more available, affordable and easy to access [1].

The indicators in most countries around the world show high and growing rates of sedentarism in urban populations. Particularly in Chile we can see that 70% of the people do not perform physical activity, and 90% of them can be considered as sedentary [2].

Usually the people are not aware of the amount of physical activity that they do and have to do during the day. This limitation makes that many people, who can and want

R. Hervás et al. (Eds.): UCAmI 2014, LNCS 8867, pp. 388–395, 2014.
© Springer International Publishing Switzerland 2014

take some action for reducing their sedentarism, cannot do it because they are not aware of this situation. This lack of awareness represents is an important restriction to face this syndrome, and thus to reduce its consequences on the people health.

There are also other cases, in which people (usually older adults) have to do physical exercises daily, because of medical prescription, as a way to improve their health conditions. Although a person decides to do it, addressing this challenge would require perseverance, commitment and usually external support. Today, there are many commercial systems that allow a person to monitor how much exercise he has done during the day, but just few of them are usable for elderly people. Moreover, people in charge of providing external support do not count on an easy way to know when the monitored person (e.g., an older adult) has done his daily physical activities, and thus determine if they have to take some action or not to help reach such a goal.

This article presents a mobile application named AMOPA (Application for Monitoring Physical Activity), which has been designed to support older adults and the people providing external help (e.g. caregivers or relatives of an older adult). The application runs on a smartphone, and it uses its peripherals to determine the amount of physical activity performed by its user. Such information is delivered properly to the monitored persons and also to monitoring people. Thus, the system makes them aware about the amount to physical activity that has been done. The users can access to an historical record of their physical activity to see the evolution in the time. This service is also available for monitoring people.

Next section presents the related work. Section 3 describes the architecture of the monitoring systems and its main components. Section 4 shows the main user interfaces of the system and services provided through them. Section 5 presents and discusses the preliminary results. Section 6 shows the conclusions and future work.

2   Related Work

Several solutions have been proposed to monitor the physical activities of the people, which are typically focused on gathering information to support particular health treatments. For instance, Guo [3] developed a mobile solution that records the number of steps done by a person and the number calories spent on it. The application also delivers voice messages to the monitored person encourage him to perform physical activity when needed. This application was particularly designed to support patients with mental disorders, and it does not allow the participation of monitoring people.

Oner et al. [4] propose a mobile application that runs on a smartphone and monitors the balance of a person while waking. The application intends to determine, in an early stage, the risk of falls in elderly people, and eventually to deliver notifications to caregivers or medical personnel that monitor the elderly.

Shin et al. [5] developed an algorithm to recognize physical activities also using mobile devices. Their algorithm tries to reduce the energy consumption using an external device attached to a smartphone. Energy consumption is always a major concern of the mobile software applications [6], and few of them really consider this design aspect.

3   Architecture of the System

The application for monitoring physical activity (AMOPA) uses a client-server architecture, but the relationship between client and server is loosely-coupled. This means that each component works independently of the other, but particular services are provided when both components are available at the same time.

The client component considers both, a local and a remote monitoring application. The first one runs in the smartphone of the people being monitored, and it works in background most the time. This component is used to gather information about the physical activity performed by the user and to provide him awareness about it. Such information is also stored in the server during pre-established periods.

The remote monitoring application retrieves the information stored in the server and informs to external users about the physical activity performed by the person monitored by them. This information can be retrieved on-demand and it considers both, new and historical data.

The server acts as a (loosely-coupled) intermediary between these two client applications and the collected data. Figure 1 shows the system architecture, which considers the previously mentioned components.

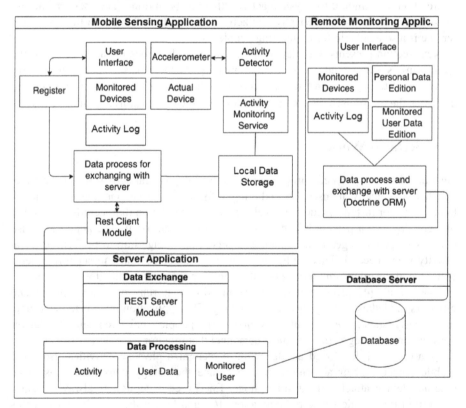

Fig. 1. Architecture of AMOPA

During the system design we considered two different strategies for determining the amount of physical activity performed by a person. The first strategy was based on counting steps, and the second one was focused on determining the intensity of the physical activity per time unit. Both strategies use the accelerometer to capture the basic information used to calculate the indicators. We decided do not use the GPS for supporting these monitoring activities, as a way to keep the energy consumption of the mobile applications under control. Clearly, if these applications consume much energy, jeopardizes the usefulness of the proposed system.

Following this goal, the data captured by the mobile sensing application is sent to the server every one hour, whenever people are monitoring to the local user. In other case the data is sent once per day.

3.1   First Measurement Strategy

As mentioned before, the first approach considered steps counting. After analyzing various third-party services we realized that most of them imposed restrictions to the system implementation, and they did not provide accurate information. Therefore, we decided to implement a pedometer, which considers the number of steps done by a person, and also his velocity, to determine an indicator that represents the amount of calories spent by the user. The identification of steps is done by comparing the last movement of the user, with the next one. The accuracy of this comparison depends on the place in which the smartphone is placed. For instance, if the device is in a belt case, the step recognition is much more accurate than if it is in the pocket.

3.2   Second Measurement Strategy

Recent studies indicate that walking 30 minutes per day has important long term benefits for health condition of the people. Every walking activity must involve at least 10 minutes for being considered useful for the people health. Therefore, the mobile application must determine if the walking periods of a person contribute or not to improve his health condition.

Using the accelerometer, the application determines the intensity and duration of the people activities. These activities are then classified by intensity using the Dynamic Time Warping algorithm [7]. This algorithm uses pre-loaded values for each user, which are gathered during a setting process of the application. Then, considering the activity duration and intensity we can determine if the activity should be computed or not by the system.

4   Implemented System

Next sections show the user interface of both monitoring client applications, and also the services that they provide to the users.

4.1   Local Monitoring System

As mentioned before, this component runs in the smartphone of the monitored person. The main services provided by this module are: registration, self-monitoring,

monitoring of other people (remote monitoring), history of physical activity, and check the list of monitored devices. Fig. 2 presents the main the user interfaces.

When the person creates a user account into the application, he has to choose if he will use the system for self-monitoring or monitoring to other people (Fig. 2.a and 2.b). Depending on that decision the application presents different services to the user.

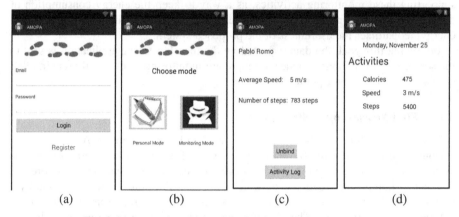

(a)   (b)   (c)   (d)

Fig. 2. Main user interfaces of the local monitoring component

Once completed the registration process, the smartphone starts to record the physical activity using a service that runs in background. The recorded information is periodically sent to the server. If the user decides turn off his telephone, the application will be automatically opened the next time that the device is turned on. Therefore, the user does not longer need to trigger the monitoring process.

When the user checks the physical activity that he has done during the day, the user interface shows him the average speed and the number of steps done during the walking activities (Fig. 2.c). Through such an interface the user can access his historical record (activity log) and ask for a particular day. In that case the application shows him a summary of the calories burned during the day, the number of steps and the average velocity of the user during the physical activity periods (Fig. 2.d).

4.2   Remote Monitoring Application

This Web information system allows users to monitor the physical activities of other users. Figure 3 shows the main user interface of the activity log, which is accessed by choosing a particular day and monitored device. The results are shown in a simple way to ease its readability.

5   Preliminary Results

This section presents the results of the three tests performed to the system. The first two tests are focused on determining the system accuracy during the data gathering process (i.e. while collecting the physical activity of the user). The last test identifies the energy consumption of the system and compares it with other proposals.

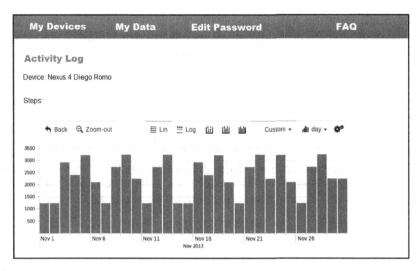

Fig. 3. View of the activity log

5.1   Accuracy of the Pedometer

A test was done not only to the implemented pedometer, but also to other implementations. The test involved to walk ten steps using the smartphone in the pocket of the user's pant, which is probably the worst place (in terms of sensing capability) to locate the smartphone. During the test the user had to walk to three different speeds. This was monitored by an assistant who was in charge of ensuring that the samples were comparable. This activity was repeated five times for each velocity; Fig. 4 shows the average error rates in the step detection.

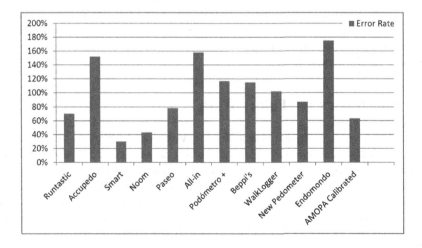

Fig. 4. Error rate using the pedometer

The results show that AMOPA has a 60% of error. Although this value is high, it is lower than most of the other implementations that were evaluated. This rate falls to 5% if the device is located in a belt case, which is clearly appropriate to monitor physical activity.

5.2   Accuracy Using the Intensity Approach

This test involved a person walking during 20 minutes to a constant velocity. Three different velocities were used in this test: low (0.6 m/s), medium (1 m/s) and high (1.4 m/s). Table 1 shows the accuracy of the system detecting the intensity of the people movements. These results show a high accuracy in the detection of the movement intensity; therefore it can also be used to determine the physical activity of the people.

Table 1. Pedometer accuracy

Test	Accuracy
Test 1	97%
Test 2	94%
Test 3	99%

Table 2. Energy consumption

Experiment	Accelerometer	AMOPA	Total Energy Consumption
Test 1	8%	4%	12%
Test 2	6%	5%	11%
Test 3	5%	2%	7%

5.3   Energy Consumption

In order to determine the energy consumption of the system, we used three different devices. The test considered devices with full charge used by the same user during the same time period. Once the AMOPA system is triggered, the application monitored the person activity during six hour. After that period we checked the amount of energy consumption by device, considering both the application and the accelerometer. Table 2 shows the obtained results. There we can see that the total consumption is around 10% after six hours, which does not produce an important impact on the device autonomy.

6   Conclusions and Future Work

This article presents a software system that allows people, particularly older adults, to monitor their physical activities. This information can also be accessed remotely and on-demand by caregivers, doctors or monitoring people. The system implemented two complimentary mechanisms for detecting the physical activity of the monitored person; i.e. a pedometer and an indicator of the intensity of the user's movements. Considering both mechanisms the system records and informs the physical activity performed by the user.

The accuracy of these mechanisms is quite good to make suitable estimations, and the energy consumption of the system is also acceptable for monitoring activities.

The users participating in the preliminary evaluations found the system usable and useful. However, additional and formal test needs to be conducted in this sense to see the real impact of this proposal.

Acknowledgments. This work has been supported by Fondecyt (Chile), Grant N° 1120207; FONDEF, Grant: D10i1286; and by the UBIHEALTH project, FP7-PEOPLE-2012-IRSES, European Commission, Grant: 316337.

References

1. Bernstein, M.S., Morabia, A., Sloutskis, D.: Definition and prevalence of sedentarism in an urban population. American J. Public Health 89(6), 862–867 (1999)
2. Chilean National Institute of Sports, National Study on Sports and Healthy Habits on People over 18 Years Old (in Spanish) (2010), http://www.ind.cl/estudios-e-investigacion/investigaciones/Documents/2012/encuesta_nacional_habitos.pdf
3. Guo, Q.: Android Health-Care App: Multi-function Step Counter. Master Thesis, Mid Sweden University, Faculty of Science, Technology and Media, Department of Information Technology and Media (2012)
4. Oner, M., Pulcifer-Stump, J., Seeling, P., Kaya, T.: Towards the Run and Walk Activity Classification through Step Detection: An Android Application. In: Proceedings of the 34th Annual International Conference of the Engineering in Medicine and Biology Society, pp. 1980–1983 (2012)
5. Shin, J., Shin, D., Shin, D., Her, S., Kim, S., Lee, M.: Human Movement Detection Algorithm Using 3-Axis Accelerometer Sensor Based on Low-Power Management Scheme for Mobile Health Care System. In: Bellavista, P., Chang, R.-S., Chao, H.-C., Lin, S.-F., Sloot, P.M.A. (eds.) GPC 2010. LNCS, vol. 6104, pp. 81–90. Springer, Heidelberg (2010)
6. Ferreira, D., Dey, A.K., Kostakos, V.: Understanding Human-Smartphone Concerns: A Study of Battery Life. In: Lyons, K., Hightower, J., Huang, E.M. (eds.) Pervasive 2011. LNCS, vol. 6696, pp. 19–33. Springer, Heidelberg (2011)
7. Muller, M.: Dynamic Time Warping. In: Information Retrieval for Music and Motion, ch. 4, pp. 69–84. Springer (2007)

Co-creation as the Key to a Public, Thriving, Inclusive and Meaningful EU IoT

Rob van Kranenburg[1], Nathalie Stembert[2], M. Victoria Moreno[3],
Antonio F. Skarmeta[3], Carmen López[4], Ignacio Elicegui[4], and Luis Sánchez[4]

[1] University of Liepaja, Latvia
[2] Rotterdam University of Applied Sciences, The Netherlands
[3] University of Murcia, Spain
[4] University of Cantabria, Spain

Abstract. Contrary to the general approach of creating Internet of Things (IoT) services from a business perspective, the SOCIOTAL project addresses the design of citizen centered IoT solutions. For this, it is required to create new IoT solutions from the citizens' point of view and for the immediate benefit of the citizens without necessarily involving city or commercial service providers. A co-creation approach towards definition of user scenarios is adopted by the EU project SOCIOTAL, resulting in a series of workshops with groups of citizens in two cities, where the issues they face and how IoT could help and improve the citizen quality of life were discussed. The drivers and barriers for IoT as well as the results of these workshops are presented in this paper, among which we highlight the main requirements for defining effective user-centric services.

Keywords: Internet of Things, Smart cities, User-centric services.

1 Introduction

One hundred years ago England and Germany went to war. At CEBIT, David Cameron said: "Take British ingenuity in software, services and design, add German excellence in engineering and industrial manufacturing and together we can lead in this new revolution", as the UK and Germany could find themselves on the forefront of a new "industrial revolution" with the Internet of Things (IoT)" [1] as a huge transformative development - a way of boosting productivity, of keeping us healthier, making transport more efficient, reducing energy needs, tackling climate change" [3]. The next step is building a EU platform that aligns today's technological realities with the decision-making systems that are complexity friendly.

The EU project SOCIOTAL [2] proposes to establish an IoT eco-system that puts trust, user control and transparency at its heart in order to gain the confidence of everyday users and citizens. The project will encourage the citizen's immersion in the IoT by providing socially aware tools and mechanisms that simplify complexity and lower the barriers that the IoT must still face.

In the initial period of the project, we focus on the definition and analysis of potential scenarios and use cases. A co-creation approach towards definition of

R. Hervás et al. (Eds.): UCAmI 2014, LNCS 8867, pp. 396–403, 2014.
© Springer International Publishing Switzerland 2014

user scenarios was adopted. A series of workshops with groups of citizens were organized in Santander (Spain) and Novi Sad (Serbia). These workshops were called as *co-creation workshops* [9]. In this paper we present the methodology and the results of the co-creation workshops, and argue that early co-creation with end users in the building of use-cases assists in prioritizing requirements that are aligned with the current drivers of IoT.

The co-creation workshops were realized with the research teams at Santander and Novi Sad, delegates from City Councils, a group of developers from the SO-CIOTAL IoT Meetup group, a specific target-group of end-users in a particular SOCIOTAL use-case (janitors) and a group of citizens with no expert knowledge. The groups correspond to four main stakeholders in IoT that need to work together. Within each of these groups we investigate how IoT can facilitate and assist the categories of collaboration: vertical collaboration (individual citizens collaborating with solution promoters. Example: Fix my street); vertical and horizontal collaboration (individual citizens collaborating with solution promoters and then, collaborating among them in a p2p way. Example: Carpooling.); and, horizontal collaboration (p-2-p collaboration among citizens. Example: Circle of care and Collaborative housing).

In the next 2 years SOCIOTAL will build tools to create cohesion in all three categories, study the types of collaboration within each category and create links and bridges between the three categories in order to create a network-effect.

The rest of the paper is organized as follows: Section 2 puts the proposal in context by reviewing recent related activities. Section 3 describes the drivers and barriers that can encourage or brake the citizen's approach to the IoT. Section 4 details how SOCIOTAL is approaching the IoT design from the co-creation and the experience from the sessions carried out in Santander and Novi Sad. Finally, Section 5 concludes the paper with a set of final remarks and presenting future lines.

2   Related Work

The IoT is not a new concept of technological breakthrough. Over the past 50 years the notion of smartness in machines, objects and the environment was iterated in pervasive computing, ambient intelligence and in research programmes, which targeted a broad population, and attempted to create novel interaction paradigms for interacting with information.

The need for non-technical research as the developments got closer to everyday lives of citizens was acknowledged in the 1996 EU Call for Proposals of the i3: Intelligent Information Interfaces, an Esprit Long-Term Research initiative. Its aim was to develop new human centered interfaces for interacting with information, aimed at the future broad population. This approach was also the starting point and rationale for the EU-funded proactive initiative The Disappearing Computer a cluster of 17 projects by interdisciplinary research groups. The third research iteration of this approach was Convivio (2003-2005), a thematic network of researchers and practitioners from many backgrounds (computer science, human sciences, design, business) developing a broad discipline of human-centered design of digital systems for everyday life.

Living Memory was part of i3. Its purpose was to provide members of a "selected community who live and work in a particular locality or neighbourhood with a means to capture, share and explore their collective memory with the aim to interpret and preserve the richness and complexity of local culture" [13]. The subyacent idea was that active involvement of community members throughout the entire research trajectory would ensure the development of relevant and meaningful interfaces for content creation, communication and preservation that prove to be usable and attractive for the community members. This project built an interactive table to be used in the neighborhood and be placed in community centres, bus stops and other local meeting spaces.

3   Drivers and Barriers for IoT

3.1   Drivers

All current computing and IoT paradigms place connectivity and content-centric networking centrally as an ecology of devices, protocols, services and networks, such as RFID, active sensors, biometrically-related smart camera data, 2D and 3D bar codes and 6LoWPAN (IPv6 over Low power Wireless Personal Area Networks) or ZigBee. At the core of this ecology there is a seamless flow between user centric data flow such as BAN/PAN (Body/Personal Area Network) and community data flow such as LAN/WAN (Local/Wide Area Network).

M2M vendors currently cannot interface their sensor capabilities beyond an optimizing function. No one is asking for an Internet of Things. Citizens have no idea about what they can expect and why they should hand over their washing machines to a local grid to ensure energy efficiency. Yet we can observe four trends that point towards a growing acceptance of the drivers that are fuelling the connectivity of IoT:

1. A growing desire to be involved in decision making that should be supported. Citizens "feel that they have very little influence on decision-making and that their own involvement in politics will have little effect on the way the country is run, the desire to actually be involved in decision-making, both locally (43%) and nationally (38%) continues to outpace their personal sense of efficacy and influence" [12].
2. Waste and efficiency arguments. With a projected global population surpassing 9 billion people by 2050, an uncertain and changing climate future, and up to 50% of food lost between production and consumption, our agricultural systems that generate food, fiber, feed, and biofuels need to be smarter and more efficient.
3. Sharing is the new buying, and IoT is facilitating this trend: In the US over 80 million people are sharing goods, 23 million in the UK and 10 million in Canade. These figures come from research from Jeremiah Owyang who claims that sharing is the new buying [11].
4. Big Data and IoT facilitates better decision-making. In their book [10], Chip and Dan Heath describe a decision-making process they called multi-tracking

considering several options simultaneously. The more we can automate the processing and presentation of more decision-making options, the less we have to deal with any of those options becoming conflated with the ego of an individual decision-maker. Big data analytics, therefore, can enable businesses of all sizes to make better decisions in less time with bigger data and smaller egos.

A successful IoT means the best possible feedback on our physical and mental health, the best possible deals based on real-time monitoring for resource allocation, the best possible decision-making based on real-time data and information from open sources, and the best possible alignments of our local providers with the global potential of wider communities. But in order to get towards this positive vision of a successful IoT we posit that stakeholder coordination is critical. It is necessary to have a toolset of co-creational methods between the engineers and the domain experts, the engineers and the application designers, the engineers and the policy experts from local up to transnational (UN, EU, ICANN, and M2M) and logistics standard bodies, and more importantly between all of these groups and ordinary citizens, end-users, who will determine by their real and everyday actions if they trust such a connected environment or not.

The role of the co-creation toolset is to support others to take decisions and show them all the structural power dependencies in that process, to make things transparent and to make the decision process itself visible. It is therefore vital that co-creation is involved in the initial creation of the use cases, their scope and particular scenarios.

3.2 Barriers

The proliferation of IoT ecosystems is radically affecting the ways in which people manage their lives: at work, at home, and socially.

Two substantive dimensions of IoT technologies are: the privacy requirements of users and the security requirements of users and systems. Security and privacy requirements of IoT systems are particularly important because of their potential to both enable and constrain the use of these new technologies that are set to the hallmark of the modern digital, interconnected world. As IoT systems are used increasingly to manage personal information, threats to personal privacy and security are also increasing. A key difficulty however, is that these threats themselves are changing, and indeed change from one context to another, requiring systems to adapt and communicate with their users in order to ensure that these users, their personal information, and any other assets that they value are protected. Nevertheless, users find it difficult to articulate their security and privacy requirements, particularly in the new situations in which they find themselves using new technologies. And in any case, the security and privacy requirements that arise in one situation are rarely the same as those that arise in another.

On the other hand, the success of user-centric services based on IoT technologies depends primarily on people participating and sharing the information flows generated by smart objects around them and in their possession (for instance, their smart phones). Enabling such participation and sharing requires a number of technical challenges to be addressed, such as lowering the technological barrier of user participation by making solutions simple, easy to use and affordable. More importantly, however, willingness on the part of people to participate in these systems is required. This willingness is predominantly dependant on the perception of people: the perceived trust and confidence in IoT and the perceived value that the IoT generate for them. In other words, the greater the trust of users in the IoT, the greater their confidence in the system and the more willing they will be to participate. Thus, at first glance, it is necessary to understand the willingness of people to have intelligent systems at their service, since, although these systems are intelligent, they are under the complete control of users.

In SOCIOTAL we propose to study the security and privacy of IoT systems in a holistic way: developing techniques to model and represent security and privacy problems, engaging with potential user communities to better understand security and privacy concerns, and delivering usable tools that fulfil user needs and facilitate user interaction with IoT systems in order to manage security and privacy concerns and make optimum decisions taking into account users requirements.

4   Engaging Communities to the IoT Development

With the goal of jointly designing IoT developments with end users to cover their needs, two co-creation workshops have been already carried out in the SOCIOTAL project.

4.1   Co-creation Workshop in Santander

The purpose of the co-creation workshop is to carry out the design process together with the end users in order to uncover their needs, to find the positive and negative points of connectivity in the scenarios and to build interfaces to the devices/sensors that will be deployed; in short to make IoT beneficial for the end user. The process serves a double purpose; to get the needs of the users in a structured way, and to make them more aware of the sensors and what they are doing. One of the main goals of these workshops was to build awareness among the SOCIOTAL partners that are preparing use cases that it is possible to receive structured input from end users as early as the initial brainstorming phase. If the use case was already defined, the idea was to find a productive way of engaging end users targeted in the use case to assist and co-define the prioritization of activities within the use case.

The process follows different steps: choose cards with everyday situations, set a use case analyzing how IoT could help in these situations, visualized the use case over the table in terms of location, objects, intelligence (sensors and network), data flow, interface input/output and actors involved, and finally evaluate it in terms of incentives, barriers, devices and willingness to use these devices for the purpose of the use case.

At the end of the workshop an enthusiastic discussion about the benefits of the co-creation workshop emerged, and some conclusions about the process are presented below.

– **Accomplishments:**
  • A set of different situations where IoT could add value were selected to start the discussion.
  • An entirely new and feasible use case was developed and analyzed through all different steps mentioned above.
  • Insights in the interaction of the target users with the IoT network were gained through role playing of the use cases.
  • The workshop led to a number of requirements for the old and new use cases.
  • It helped SOCIOTAL researchers to prioritize requirements above others (based on the needs of the target group).
– **Recommendations for the workshops with the target group:**
  • Fostering discussions is basic to elicit valuable feedback from the end users.
  • Time has to be managed carefully, one use case per workshop is the maximum to have fruitful results.
  • Participants have to be selected according to their level of technical expertise.
  • Collaboration between the SOCIOTAL researchers and the target group is important to guide the participants (the process can be still too technical), yet also to let the SOCIOTAL researchers engage with the target group to uncover their needs.

The main lesson learnt from this workshop was that the process could help rank the necessities, the must and should haves, of end-users in the current use-cases as it will draw good and structured feedback from real users.

4.2 Co-creation Workshop in Novi Sad

As the previous one, the purpose of this co-creation workshop [9] is to uncover the needs of the end users during the design process. The workshop started with a total of seven participants, among which a number of SOCIOTAL researchers were present. During the session three other participants walked in and out to observe and contribute to different parts of the workshop. At the time of wrapping the workshop up an enthusiastic discussion emerged with the conclusions presented below.

– **Accomplishments:**
  • Time management went well, the workshop took exactly 2,5 hours.
  • The participants shifted and moved through the different workshop steps very smoothly while discussing.
  • Seven candidate use cases were identified.

- From these use cases, three were described in terms of barriers and incentives to participate and one use case was selected collectively.
- The selected use case was visualized in terms of location, objects, intelligence (sensors and network), data flow, interface input/output and actors involved.
- The use case was evaluated in terms of devices and willingness to use these devices for the purpose of the use case.
- Insights in the interaction of the target users with the IoT network were gained through role playing of the use cases.
- The workshop led to a number of requirements, but also covered a number of possibilities to incorporate a number of business models for the new use case.

– **Recommendations for the workshops with the target group:**
  - The workshop with the target group ideally is recorded on video. This ensures that all valuable data are captured, but also that two facilitators are free to moderate, facilitate and make pictures of the workshop.
  - The data can be analyzed according to the method of "statement card analysis".
  - To start the workshop with the interaction cards, in order to get insights in the aspects that are important for the target group and to discover new use cases.
  - Seven participants is the largest number of people one group can host, ideally a group consist of 5-6 participants. If there are multiple facilitators, multiple groups can participate in the workshop at the same time.
  - The setting of the workshop should be set-up before the workshop. A table where all participants can gather around and reach the workshop materials is essential.

5   Conclusions

This paper has presented the co-creation as a mean to bring the IoT closer to the citizens and make them participants in the construction of their real needs, as well as, from the point of view of the researcher, a way to extract or discard requirements and features from the final user that improve the performance of the solutions developed.

We have summarized the motivations that are driving the projects developing the upcoming IoT to move from the business to the citizen perspective, presenting the drivers and barriers that are found while bridging this gap.

Among other activities that the SOCIOTAL project proposes to make the citizen unit-holder of the IoT, we have presented how the project has employed co-creation (methodology, accomplishments and recommendations for future workshops) at Santander and Novi Sad in order to create, define and obtain direct feedback from the citizens to prioritize and build all together use cases which cover their real needs.

In this sense, during the next 2 years, the SOCIOTAL project will continue carrying out more workshops concurrently to the development of the different use cases, enabling accurate and early feedback.

Additionally, the project will focus its efforts in other activities to bring IoT to the citizens and developers such as the IoT Meet-up groups set up in Santander [4], Novi Sad [5], Ghent [6], Grenoble [7] and Guildford [8], with more than 350 members already.

Acknowledgments. This work has been sponsored by European Commission through the FP7-SOCIOTAL-609112 EU Project.

References

1. Atzori, L., Iera, A., Morabito, G.: The internet of things: A survey. Computer Networks 54(15), 2787–2805 (2010)
2. SOCIOTAL project, http://sociotal.eu
3. Internet of things to get £45m funding boost. BBC News Business (March 9, 2014), http://www.bbc.com/news/business-26504696
4. Internet of Things Meetup Santander: http://www.meetup.com/IoT-Santander/
5. Internet of Things Meetup Novi Sad:
   http://www.meetup.com/This-group-is-part-of-the-sociotal-eu-project/
6. Internet of Things Meetup Ghent:
   http://www.meetup.com/Internet-of-Things-Ghent/
7. Internet of Things Meetup Grenoble:
   http://www.meetup.com/Internet-of-Things-Grenoble/
8. Internet of Things Meetup Guildford:
   http://www.meetup.com/Internet-of-Things-Guildford/
9. Stembert, N.: CoCreate the Internet of Things, http://cocreatetheiot.com
10. Heath. C, Heath, D.: Decisive: How to Make Better Choices in Life and Work. Crown Publishing Group (2013)
11. Owyang, J.: Sharing is the new buying,
    http://www.slideshare.net/jeremiah_owyang/sharingnewbuying
12. Handsard Society. Audit of Political Engagement 11, The 2014 report:
    http://www.hansardsociety.org.uk/research/
    public-attitudes/audit-of-political-engagement/
13. Living Memory project:
    http://web.media.mit.edu/~federico/living-memory/english/central.html
14. Ethic Inside: http://www.ethicsinside.eu
15. Kyffin, S.: Lessons learnt from LIVING MEMORY @ 1:3 - listening to and developing technology for ordinary people (2003),
    http://www.i3net.org/ser_pub/services/
    magazine/february2003/i3originals.pdf

An Inertial-Based Person Tracking and Vital Data Acquiring for Low-Cost Patient Monitoring Systems

Thitipun Chobtrong*, Markus Haid, Mustafa Kamil, and Ersan Guenes

Completence Center for Applied Sensor Systems
Darmstadt University of Applied Sciences, Darmstadt, Germany
thitipun.chobtrong@h-da.de

Abstract. The project presented in this paper, has been developed by the cooperation between Competence Center for Applied Sensor Systems (ccass) at Darmstadt University of Applied Sciences, and Fraunhofer Institute for Production and Automation Engineering (Fraunhofer IPA) in Stuttgart. The target of this project is to innovate and develop an inertial-based tracking device for a low-cost patient monitoring system and tracking applications. This developed device is integrated with an inertial sensor system that enables it to measure the kinematic characteristics of a patient who wears this device. The initial-based device is able to detect emergency situation, such as falls, and simultaneously acquiring vital data for health-monitoring. When an emergency situation is detected, the integrated system sends a warning signal, the current position and vital-information of the patient wearing the device to their caretakers or nurses. This monitoring system is economically attractive for mass production, because it is compact, light-weight and low-cost. Moreover, this device can be used for a wide range of innovative applications in the industrial, medical and security sector.

1 Introduction

Nowadays, a system which is able to acquire vital data and track a person in the same device has never been launched in medical equipment industry, even though there are many research projects in fields of telemedicine, assisted living and e-health. The target of the majority of developed health devices is only to monitor personal vital data. For instance, the "BioHarness combi-chest-sensor" (from Velamed Science in Motion) is successfully developed for acquiring electrocardiography (ECG) data, skin temperature, respiratory rate and the level of activity of a user. Therefore, the health condition of the user is continuously observed for an emergency situation. However, if an emergency situation occurs, the current position of the patient is very important for rescuers. Because the patient has to be treated immediately, the rescuers need to find the patient as soon as possible. Accordingly, the main objective of this study is to develop a system that combines vital data acquisition and position-tracking of a patient.

---

* Corresponding author.

R. Hervás et al. (Eds.): UCAmI 2014, LNCS 8867, pp. 404–407, 2014.
© Springer International Publishing Switzerland 2014

2   Concepts

The objective of this presented project is to develop a sensor system for reliably detecting emergency situation, i.e. falling-down, and continuously acquiring patient's vital data. Additionally, this system is able to track the position of the user for reducing time to find the patient. Because the focus of this project is to keep cost of the device to a minimum, a low-cost inertial sensor system is applied for this application.

The inertial sensor system has two main components, a three-axis accelerometer and a three-axis gyroscope. The inertial sensor system measures the acceleration and angular-velocity of an object in six degrees of freedom [1]. The system is able to detect falling-down movement by using algorithms developed and optimized in Matlab. Furthermore, this sensor system can classify the movement of a user, i.e. walking. For the user's comfort, the housing of this sensor system is ergonomic and worn around the user's chest at solar plexus position. To observe diaphragmatic excursion, the solar plexus is the best position to acquire the patients respiratory rate.

3   Realization and Fall Detection

A LabVIEW application, based on object-oriented programming, is developed to realize a concept of the system. Therefore, this application is extendable and supports other plug-ins making it possible to add further functions to the system, e.g. acquiring the blood pressure of a patient, and calculating energy expenditure [2].

To discriminate between falls and the activities of daily living (ADL), the discriminant algorithm based on Bayesian decision theory has been implemented for this system as described in [3]. Unlike the fall detection algorithm using threshold-based algorithm in [4], the posture will be categorized as a fall when a free-fall point is detected and the magnitudes of the acceleration signals and the turn-rate signals is classified as FALL class.

The free-fall point Φ is detected when the current magnitude of the acceleration signals is less than a free-fall threshold ϕ as Eq. 1 where m_a is the acceleration magnitude and a_i is the current acceleration signal in i-axis. The magnitude of the acceleration signals rapidly decrease while falling down. However, the free-fall point is sometime detected in some postures, e.g. walking.

$$\Phi = \begin{cases} 0 & \text{if } m_a \geq \phi \\ 1 & \text{if } m_a < \phi \end{cases}, \text{where } m_a = \sqrt{a_x^2 + a_y^2 + a_z^2} \qquad (1)$$

Heuristically, the FALL class and NO-FALL class can be classified by using the maximum magnitudes of acceleration signals and turn-rate signals. These maximum magnitudes are determined by finding the maximum magnitudes of the signals in each 500 millisecond time interval. Both of the maximum magnitudes of acceleration signals and turn-rate signals are used as the feature of the Bayesian decision.

The advantages of Bayesian decision theory are that the model is parametric and be able to be adapted for more classes as mentioned in [5]. Because, the NO-FALL class will be studied for classify specific classes in the future work, the Bayesian decision method is more suitable for this application than other two-categories classification techniques, i.e. N-nearest point [6].

4   Experiments

To test the performance of the fall-detection algorithm, the experiments have been done by using five participants. There were eight test cases as shown in Table 1. In each test case, the tests were repeated five times per participant. The IMU100 was worn by the participants for acquiring the data during each test, and it sent the acquired data to a posture recognition application to classify the participants' movement. This posture recognition application is developed with LabVIEW, and implemented the fall-detection algorithm for detecting falls.

5   Results

As shown in Table 2, the fall-detection algorithm successfully detected all falls. Moreover, there is no false detection occurred in these experiments.

The tests TB1, TB2, TB3 and TB4 are scenarios that a patient falls down on the floor in variant levels. While the patient wearing the IMU100 was falling down, the free-fall detection algorithm successfully detected this movement. Furthermore, the impact from hitting floor produced significantly strong magnitudes of the signals from the accelerometers and the gyroscopes in the IMU. Therefore, the classifier algorithm was able to successfully classify these tests as FALL class.

On the other hand, the test TB5, TB6, TB7 and TB8 produced relatively small signal magnitudes. These magnitudes are significantly smaller than the magnitudes produced by the movement in FALL class, because there was no strong impact during the tests.

Table 1. Test description

Test name	Description
TB1	Suddenly falling down on carpet
TB2	Suddenly falling down on hard floor
TB3	Kneeling and falingl down on hard floor
TB4	Kneeling and slightly falling down on hard floor
TB5	Going to sit on a chair
TB6	Walking down a stair
TB7	Fast walking down a stair
TB8	Driving a car on the road that have a bump, a ballast and curbstone

Table 2. Test results

Test	TB1	TB2	TB3	TB4	TB5	TB6	TB7	TB8
Number of tests	50	50	50	50	50	50	50	50
Detected as FALL	50	50	50	50	0	0	0	0
Detected as NO-FALL	0	0	0	0	50	50	50	50
False detection	0	0	0	0	0	0	0	0

6   Conclusion and Further Development

Since the presented monitoring system is low-cost and compactly designed, it is economically attractive to be manufactured in mass production. All of the previously described advantages and system features offer a wide range of innovations in industrial and medical applications. These possible applications can be divided into three main segments: Home & Health Care, Outdoor & Activity and Industrial.

For next improvement , this inertial sensor system will be added with new plug-ins for other applications, such as monitoring vital data for first responders-like fire-fighters or paramedics, and also transfer data via Bluetooth Low Energy. However, the focus of this study is still developing low-cost sensor systems that are suitable for mass production in the future.

References

1. Titterto, D.H., Weston, J.L.: Strapdown inertial navigation technology. The Institution of Electrical Engineers and the American Institute of Aeronautics and Astronautics (2004)
2. Bouten, C.V., Westerterp, K.R., Verduin, M., Janssen, J.D.: Assesment of energy expenditure for physical activity using a triaxisal acceleromenter. Journal of the American College of Sport Medicine (1994)
3. Duda, R.O., Hart, P.E., Strk, D.G.: Pattern Classification. Wiley (2001)
4. Bourke, A.K., Lyons, G.M.: A threshold-based fall-detection algorithm using bi-axial gyroscope sensor. Ph.D. dissertation. University of Limerick. Limerick. Ireland (2006)
5. Chobtrong, T., Haid, M., Guenes, E., Muenter, M., Kamil, M.: Bolt-identification using an IMU with Bayesian Decision Theory. In: Collaborative European Research Conference 2012 Darmstadt (2012)
6. Langley, P., Iba, W., Thomas, K.: An analysis of Bayesian classifiers. In: The Tenth National Conference of Artificial Intelligence (1992)
7. Mathie, M.J., Coster, A.C.F., Lovell, N.H., Celler, B.G.: Detection of daily physical activities using a triaxial accelerometer. Medical and Biological Engineering and Computing 41 (2003)

Privacy-Preserving Security Framework for a Social-Aware Internet of Things

Jorge Bernal Bernabe, Jose Luis Hernández,
M. Victoria Moreno, and Antonio F. Skarmeta Gomez

University of Murcia, Department of Information and Communications Engineering
Campus de Espinardo, 30100 Murcia, Spain
{jorgebernal,jluis.hernandez,mvmoreno,skarmeta}@um.es

Abstract. As smart objects are getting part of our personal space, the new associated services must tackle both, the inherent requirements of IoT and the needs of citizens using such services. Security, trust and privacy concerns are the cornerstone requirements of a social Internet of Things, where users want to share and obtain information in a huge opportunistic environment of connected devices and services. The paper presents an IoT security framework, being devised in the scope of SOCIOTAL EU project, which is based on the Architecture Reference Model (ARM) of IoT-A EU project. The framework extends the traditional ARM putting strong emphasis on security, trust and privacy concerns in order to cope with more opportunistic and secure sharing models required in a social-aware IoT scenarios, where users can set up dynamically communities and bubbles of devices and users.

Keywords: Internet of Things, Security, privacy, Identity Management.

1 Introduction

The Internet of Things (IoT) integrates a large number of technologies and envisions a variety of things or objects around us that, through unique addressing schemes and standard communication protocols, are able to interact with each others and cooperate with their neighbors to reach common goals[2]. This emerging trend, along with the global deployment of mobile devices, such as smartphones or tablets, are redefining the way people exchange information and communicate with their surrounding environment, transforming cities into *smart cities*. These incipient ecosystems are expected to be composed by sensors, smart devices and appliances that can be remotely monitored and accessed by users or cloud services, resulting in a new generation of intelligent and ubiquitous environments [8].

In this context, security and privacy are going to be the key needs in the deployments of new applications, since citizens will only accept such deployments, if they can really trust on the devices and applications. Thus, IoT environments need to rely on user-centric IoT infrastructures, which make use of adapted and integrated mechanisms of security, trust and privacy. In this regard, the IoT-A[4]

R. Hervás et al. (Eds.): UCAmI 2014, LNCS 8867, pp. 408–415, 2014.
© Springer International Publishing Switzerland 2014

project defines an Architectural Reference Model (ARM) for IoT systems in order to promote common understanding at high abstraction level. It describes the essential building blocks for building compliant IoT architectures including a traditional design of the security functional group of components. Additional architectures were proposed by other remarkable efforts at European level, such as BUTLER [1] or FI-WARE [7] based on the specific set of requirements from particular application domains.

This paper presents the SOCIOTAL EU project[1] framework, which is based on the ARM of IoT-A, where personal devices connected to the Internet offer valuable tools for content generation, publishing and data sharing in a reliable, secure and private way. The framework extends the traditional ARM security group putting strong emphasis on security, trust and privacy concerns in order to cope with more opportunistic and secure sharing models required in a social-aware IoT scenarios, where users can set up dynamically communities and bubbles composed of devices and users. Namely, the framework extends ARM with a Context Manager, as transversal component which enables the rest of the components in the framework to cope with the pervasive and ubiquitous nature of IoT. In addition, the framework includes a privacy-preserving identity management system that endow users with means to achieve anonymity, data minimization and unlinkability based on anonymous credential systems. Furthermore, the security framework introduces a Group Manager component to deal with more flexible secure sharing models within bubbles of users and or SmartObjects.

The rest of the paper is organized as follows: section 2 provides a general overview of concepts of identities in IoT as well as some notions to privacy-preserving Identity Management Systems. Then, Section 3 describes different kinds of social IoT relationships, which lead to the establishment of dynamic communities and bubbles. Section 4 describes the privacy-preserving security framework to cope with the aforementioned enhanced functionalities. Finally, Section 5 concludes the paper with a set of final remarks and presenting future lines.

2   IoT Identities

IoT represents the next evolutionary step of the digital era, where privacy of individuals is seriously threatened since their personal data can be disclosed without their awareness or consent. Individuals should be able to control which of their personal data is being gathered, under which circumstances as well as who is collecting such information. Privacy-enhancing technologies help to deal with this problem providing means to achieve anonymity, data minimization, unlinkability as well as other techniques to provide confidentiality and integrity of sensitive data.

To this aim, the usage of Partial Identities as identity-preserving mechanism, allows users to define a subset of the personal attributes, from their real identity,

---

[1] http://sociotal.eu

in order to identify them in a given context. The idea is to avoid using the whole credential (e.g. the user X.509 certificate) when using a service since probably only a small set of attributes of the credential are really needed. Thus, the IoT Identity Management system should be able to manage one or more partial identities of a user and determine which particular personal data is disclosed in which context. Users can take advantage of the usage of partial identities to authenticate against IoT services in order to access them securely while disclosing, at the same time, the minimum amount of personal data. Anonymous credential systems allow user to send cryptographic proofs, instead of the whole credential, stating that she is in possession of certain attributes or claims. Although some remarkable efforts such as SWIFT2 or Primelife3 European projects have been undertaken regarding privacy-preserving identity management systems, IoT ecosystems require new identity management solutions to cope with new challenges due to inherent nature and requirements of IoT, where the identities of a huge amount of heterogeneous smart objects need to be managed. Current proposed solutions need to be adapted to the envisioned scenarios allowing more flexible sharing models, as well as volatile and dynamic associations between entities, while privacy is still preserved, keeping data minimization and unlikability as main concern.

In this sense, concepts such as IoT identity imprinting or IoT identity delegation are being considered in order to cope with the requirements of novel privacy-preserving identity management approaches for IoT. Identity imprinting can be defined as the process to stamp a partial identity to a specific smart object depending on contextual conditions. Therefore, in this case, the owner of it can act as Issuer for the issuance of credential and partial identities for the objects he manages. The way in which smart objects can obtain temporal partial identities can be achieved by defining imprinting policies. These policies could be evaluated in order to get a partial identity for a specific transaction. Identity delegation can be used to manage the identity of devices or smart objects acting on behalf of their owners (e.g. a smartphone). In this way, identity delegation makes reference to the fact that objects can use owner's partial identities to act on behalf of her. As previously mentioned for imprinting, delegation could be tackled by credentials being issued and signed by owners. This credential would contain a specific field to indicate the partial identity of the delegator or owner.

3   IoT Communities and Bubbles

Although some classification of the relations among smart objects have been already proposed in IoT [3], the proposed approach is mainly driven by the utility which is derived by the considered relation and the function of the involved objects. In the scenarios of SOCIOTAL project, where privacy is of paramount importance, relationships among devices and users and the way in which different objects are grouped should be also driven by the nature of the involved objects. Thus, we have identified five main kinds of relationships:

- Personal object relationship: between objects belonging to a same owner. Among these objects the accessibility to their data and services is open.
- Co-location object relationship: among objects that are placed in close locations but without needing to be placed always in the same places, i.e. among objects whose distance in a certain moment is lower than one predefined.
- Common Interest relationship: this kind of relationship is established between users or smart objects that share the same or similar target goal like provide a common IoT application.
- Social object relationship: this relationship refers to those kind of interactions between smart object performed sporadically or continuously because of the social relations among their owners.
- Parental object relationship: is defined among similar objects, built in the same period by the same manufacturer (the role of family is played by the production batch).

Relations are never static but can exist and change depending on time and space. Relationship among users and smart objects drives the way communities and bubbles are defined and set up. A **Community** can be defined as a set of users and or smart objects that are in contact because of certain kind of relationship. Communities are registered somewhere centralized and can be deployed either locally for the objects belonging to the community or for instance in the Cloud. The community requires an administrator in charge of perform basic operation on users and manage the community.

On the other hand, a **Personal Bubble** is a set of smart objects that are in contact because they belong to the same owner. In the Personal bubble the smart objects complies with the same security/privacy policies. Additionally, to consider others devices as member to your personal bubble as long as other owners allows that.

An **Opportunistic Bubble** is a dynamic data sharing group that is not registered as community or bubble anywhere. The Opportunistic Bubble is privacy preserving bubble comprised of a set of members that could be unknown each other. An SmartObject or user is implicitly part of an opportunistic bubble just as consequence of satisfying a particular set of identity features given by the fact of possessing specific attributes in its credentials or comply with a special predicates in the attributes.

4   Privacy-Preserving IoT Security Framework

The proposed security framework is based on the security functional group of IoT-A Architecture Reference Model (ARM) [4]. Nonetheless, given the dynamic and distributed nature of IoT, there are scenarios which require more secure and dynamic data sharing models where information can be shared with a group of entities (bubbles or communities). Thus, our IoT security framework, in addition to the IoT-A proposal, puts special attention to privacy preserving, contextual management as well as the security when sharing data within IoT Communities and Bubbles. To this aim, the framework defines innovative security and privacy mechanisms, including two new security components: the Group Manager and the Context Manager. Figure 4 shows the main components of the security framework with the main interactions among them.

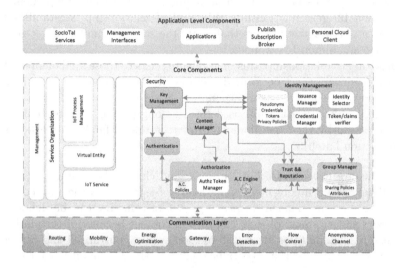

Fig. 1. Security IoT framework based on ARM

4.1   Authentication and Authorization

The Authentication component enables authenticating users and SmartObjects based on the provided credentials. It allows binding a real identity to a subject. As a result of the authentication process, an assertion is generated to be used afterwards in the authorization process, to declare that a specific subject was authenticated successfully. In this sense, SAML protocol [2] is used in our framework to handle the authentication tokens.

Traditional authentication mechanisms based on for instance login-password or electronic IDs have been addressed and solved even in the emerging IoT paradigm. Our framework addresses also more sophisticated ways of performing authentication by ensuring, at the same time, privacy and minimal disclosure of attributes. Thus, this kind of alternative privacy-preserving way of authentication is handled in the framework by the Identity Management Component.

Access Control component is responsible for making authorization decisions based on access control policies. Thus, the policies specify which particular actions that subjects (SmartObject or user) or groups (communities of bubbles) are allowed to perform over a target resource (e.g. IoT Service) under certain conditions. In this regard, the framework makes use of XACML [3] to define au-

---

[2] SAML: http://docs.oasis-open.org/security/saml/v2.0
[3] XACML: http://docs.oasis-open.org/xacml/3.0

thorization policies. Additionally, for constrained devices our framework is able to perform capability-based access control based on the mechanism presented in [6]. It describes authorization tokens specified in JSON and ECC optimizations which are used by constrained devices to access IoT services.

4.2 Identity Management

The Identity Management component is responsible for managing the identities of the SmartObjects and users. The component is able to take into account privacy concerns to manage credentials either from users or SmartObjects, in a privacy-preserving way. It is able to endow subjects with mechanisms to ensure anonymity, which is done mainly issuing pseudonyms and proof of credentials to minimal personal data disclosure. The Identity management is able to trace back pseudonyms to root or actual identities. The IdM is able to verify anonymous credential and then, in case the identity is proved, the IdM interacts with the authentication component which is the one that actually delivers authentication assertion to be used during a transaction.

The Credential Manager module of the Identity Management system is responsible for managing and storing the credentials, which are used by subjects to request information from an IoT services. The module when installed in the consumer or subject side, interfaces with another Verifier entity (the IoT service) allowing such subjects to present their credentials or proof of credentials, during the presentation process. These credentials can be obtained from an independent entity acting as Issuer of credentials. Thus, the Issuance Manager is in charge of interact with the Issuer (i.e. the Credential Authority), in order to obtain the proper credentials. The credential can be use afterwards to derive proofs of identity to be presented to a Verifier (e.g. IoT Service provider) in order to prove the identity condition while disclosing the minimum amount of private information.

The Token/Claims Verifier module aims to validate the identity proofs which are used by subjects when trying to access to an IoT service. The Identity Manager is endowed with a cryptographic engine sub-module responsible for low level cryptographic operations. It relies on cryptographic external libraries like U-Prove or Idemix to carry out the issuance and proof operations required by the anonymous credential system. It also handles pseudonyms, non-device bound secrets and system parameters. The information provided by the Context Manager component is used by the Identity Selector module to handle the usage of particular partial identities under a specific context. Such context information may come from other SmartObjects or sensors deployed in the vicinity or within the same commuity or bubble.

4.3 Group Manager

The Group Manager component enables sharing information, in a secure and private way, with those groups of entities (communities or bubbles) which satisfies certain particular set of identity attributes values. These particular sets of attributes are represented by attribute sharing policies which are influenced by context information where the data sharing is being performed. This component manages opportunistic bubbles using of Attribute based encryption mechanism, namely the CP-ABE scheme [5]. With this scheme, data to be shared within the bubble or community is encrypted under a policy of attributes, while keys of participants are associated with sets of attributes. Only those target users which satisfies particular identity attributes (those given in the policy) possess the cypher keys to decrypt the data. In this way, a data producer can exert full control over how the information is disseminated to other entities, while a consumer's identity can be intuitively reflected by a certain private key.

4.4   KEM

The key Exchange and Management (KEM) component assists peers involved in a communication in the process of establish a security context, like setting up tunnels for a security communication. It involves cryptographic key exchange and provide interoperability between the peers in order to reach an agreement regarding the security functions to use for the communication. Our framework focuses on the part of the KEM component which deal with the keys management in the privacy preserving Identity Management System as well as the Group Manager by means of the CP-ABE cyphering scheme.

4.5   Context Manager

The Context Manager component is one of the key components in the framework. It defines and maintains the context that is continuously being generated and detected by different context enablers. A user may be part of different bubbles and the participation to one or the others can be dynamic and adapted to the user context. The Context Manager hides details about information gathering mechanisms that are adopted by the context enablers, like Indoor Localization enabler to obtain device positions in buldings. The Context Manager can be queried by the Group Manager in order the latter to share, securely and in a private way, data between opportunistic bubbles, according to the context.

4.6   Trust and Reputation

The Trust and Reputation component enables to establish a reliable IoT environment where users can interact with IoT services and other SmartObjects in a trusted way. It allows other security components of the framework to take security and privacy decisions according to the quantified trust scores. Consumers are given means to choose to interact with IoT Services that satisfies certain trust scores. Trust scores are also used to manage and share data in bubbles as well as to evaluate the degree of social interaction between users involved in a bubble. The component interacts with the Context Manager in order to obtain behavioral information about users, SmartObjects, IoT services and bubbles and compute the trustworthiness of a given entity.

5   Conclusions

This paper has presented a security framework based on the Architecture Reference Model (ARM) of IoT-A that extends the traditional ARM security functional group, putting strong emphasis on security and privacy concerns in order to cope with more opportunistic and secure sharing models required in a social-aware IoT scenarios. The framework extends ARM with a Context Manager, as transversal component that enables the rest of the components in the framework to cope with the pervasive and ubiquitous nature of IoT. Besides, the framework includes a privacy-preserving identity management system that endow users with means to achieve anonymity, data minimization and unlinkability. Moreover, the security framework introduces a Group Manager component to deal with more flexible secure data sharing models within bubbles of users or SmartObjects. As future work we envisage to deploy and test the security framework in the IoT scenarios defined in the scope of SOCIOTAL project.

Acknowledgments. This work has been sponsored by European Commission through the FP7-SOCIOTAL-609112 EU Project, and the Spanish Seneca Foundation by means of the Excellence Researching Group Program (04552/GERM/06) and the FPI program (grant 15493/FPI/10).

References

1. Butler fp7 eu project. deliverable 3.2: Integrated system architecture and initial pervasive butler proof of concept (2013)
2. Atzori, L., Iera, A., Morabito, G.: The internet of things: A survey. Elsevier Computer Networks 54(15), 2787–2805 (2010)
3. Atzori, L., Iera, A., Morabito, G., Nitti, M.: The social internet of things (siot)– when social networks meet the internet of things: Concept, architecture and network characterization. Computer Networks (2012)
4. Bassi, A., Bauer, M., Fiedler, M., Kramp, T., van Kranenburg, R., Lange, S., Meissner, S.: Enabling things to talk (2013)
5. Bethencourt, J., Sahai, A., Waters, B.: Ciphertext-policy attribute-based encryption. In: IEEE Symposium on Security and Privacy, SP 2007, pp. 321–334. IEEE (2007)
6. Hernández-Ramos, J.L., Jara, A.J., Marín, L., Skarmeta, A.F.: Dcapbac: Embedding authorization logic into smart things through ecc optimizations. International Journal of Computer Mathematics, 1–22 (2014)
7. Sotiriadis, S., Petrakis, E.G., Covaci, S., Zampognaro, P., Georga, E., Thuemmler, C.: An architecture for designing future internet (fi) applications in sensitive domains. In: 2013 IEEE 13th International Conference on Bioinformatics and Bioengineering (BIBE), pp. 1–6. IEEE (2013)
8. Weiser, M.: The computer for the 21st century. Scientific American 265(3), 94–104 (1991)

Big Data and IoT for Chronic Patients Monitoring

Diego Gachet Páez, Fernando Aparicio, Manuel de Buenaga, and Juan R. Ascanio[1]

Universidad Europea de Madrid, 28670 Villaviciosa de Odón, Spain
[1] Encore Solutions. C /Albalá 5, 28037 Madrid, Spain
{gachet,fernando.aparicio,buenaga}@uem.es,
juan.ascanio@encore.es

Abstract. Recent data of the European Union reveals that the main chronic pathologies are the Cardiovascular Disease (CVD), the main cause of death in Europe, and respiratory diseases, specially the Chronic Obstructive Pulmonary Disease (COPD). Each year CVD causes over 4 million deaths in Europe alone and over 1.9 million deaths in the European Union (EU). According to the WHO (World Health Organization), in 2030 COPD will be the third leading cause of death, and the first cause of sanitary costs in Europe, due to the profiles of the expenses in health sector and the long time expenses by age groups and their important associate morbidity. New medical applications based on remote monitoring can help treat those chronic diseases but significantly will increase the volume of health information to manage, including data from medical and biological sensors, being then necessary to process this huge volume of data using techniques from Big Data. In this paper we propose one potential solution for creating those new services, based on Big Data processing and IoT concepts.

Keywords: internet of things, cloud computing, elderly, sensors.

1 Introduction

Nowadays current health care systems are characterized by a number of drawbacks inherent in the system that prevent greater effectiveness in service. Some include for example *reactivity*, i.e. only apply if patients are in a critical status, preventive diagnosis practically does not exist, or no budget is available for this, and are limited to awareness campaigns, *discontinued in care*, i.e. the public or private health systems only monitoring patients for moments, having a large separation in time between them. The health systems only *focus on major dependent or very sick patients,* and patients have to travel to medical centers for tests or medical consultation, also the *consultation and emergency* services are saturated, often for pathologies that do not require more than a simple health check. It involves huge costs in both public administration and families and the highest percentage of costs is due to a minority of patients.

Modern e-health services based on the use of Information and Communication Technologies could help to avoid those problems in health systems and transforming

R. Hervás et al. (Eds.): UCAmI 2014, LNCS 8867, pp. 416–423, 2014.
© Springer International Publishing Switzerland 2014

the sanitary system in *preventive*, i.e. remote patients monitoring can help us to detect changes in their illness tendency and generating alarms according to it for use by caregivers or medical personnel before reaching a critical situation. *Proactive*, i.e. it is possible to have full control about patient situation in any moment anywhere, *participative* or in other words all health care and social ecosystems (patients, social workers, family members and physicians) would participate in the future improvements of the system. *Global*, i.e. it is possible to apply this concept to all types of patients, independently of their state of illness, and we could reduce the costs related with medical consultation and patient monitoring and consequent treatments, in addition to allow patients to go to medical consultations only when necessary and improving the ratio cost/patient, allowing better distribution of costs among different patient types.

Taking into account that situation, it becomes extremely important to develop tools and services that enable new personalized healthcare services[1] for both elderly dependants and chronics, using extensively information and communication technologies, with this approach we will be sure about the present and future sustainability of the public health services. These new services should be focused to be part of a comprehensive health service for elder and chronic people in relation to their overall health.

2   Related Work

The aging population and the increase of people with chronic diseases is a scenario that poses significant challenges in how to design and deliver services to this population. There is already evidence and experience that help us rethinking what key issues should be taken into account to design a sensible health model oriented to this new paradigm. The clinical care approach for chronic and dependent patients by itself is important but limited; a multidimensional approach is required, where different elements must be enablers of the change as for example the ICT.

Some recent home-based solutions for chronic patient monitoring are focused on using sensors as blood pressure or pulsioximeters, connecting them to a concentrator or gateway and then transmitted to some repository, broadband communications infrastructure can provide additional support for developing this approach. Indeed, this infrastructure is able of supporting advanced solutions based on tele-visits, remote assistance, and crossed consults to different e-Health repositories by expert's team.

Nowadays, the use of wireless devices to monitor patients is achieving a maturity level, going farther than traditional SMS or alert signals, including web-based solutions for evaluating information coming from sensors, also including some wearable sensors for use with chronic heart patients as well sportsmen for determining their physiological response to exercise. The functionalities are focused towards assistive functionalities. The increasing market of tele-monitoring solutions requires the development not only of e-Health services but the design and adaptation of business models centered on mobile monitoring covering both indoor and outdoor. Approximately since 2010 there are proposals for incorporating some services offered by the cloud architecture into the health monitoring systems. For example, in Rolim[2] the authors describe an architecture in which the sensor information is sent to the cloud via a network devices, allowing integration of processing capabilities and ubiquitous access to the data offered by the cloud. The main difficulties that we can observe in these systems to be put into production are related to the heterogeneity, reliability and security of the data transmitted by the network components. Companies like Corventis, LORD MicroStrain or AT4Wireless or are already engaged in the development of services and / or biomedical devices related to telemedicine and chronic remote patient monitoring. Moreover, although the Big Data concept and techniques [16] are being used in fields as for example Smart Cities, it is not widely used in the biomedical field and specifically in the field of telemedicine or patient monitoring for the use and integration of data from biosensors.

Despite some modern solutions, in general, current data mining techniques which involve patients monitoring and data protection in the medical domain are in an alarming early state.

3   Proposed Architecture for Indoor/Outdoor Chronic Patient Monitoring

The proposed technological architecture for chronic patient monitoring and dependant persons care, both outdoors and indoor as well as its associated services is presented in Figure 1.

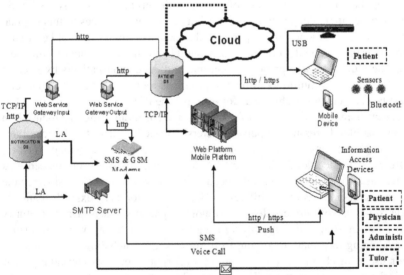

Fig. 1. Proposed Architecture for indoor /outdoor chronic patients monitoring

Main parts of this architecture has been developed in the context of Virtual Cloud Carer (VCC)[3][8] project although some modules are still being developed, the architecture consists of the following main elements:

- A smart mobile device being used by chronics patients and dependent which in turn accepts the data from vital sign sensors and sends this information via the mobile network 3G/HDSPA or Internet. The architecture also permits the use of a smart phone as a dedicated mobile device for intermediary data processing. A rule generation system for activation of alarms to be sent to the chronic patient's caregivers or nursing or medical personnel. In fact this is the core of the system in order to produce early diagnose and new e-health services.
- Interoperability and messaging platform for the delivery of information to all involved actors in the system, using the latest technological advances in communication (SMS, mail, voice automated systems and PUSH technology).
- A website platform that allows both social workers and family caregivers, consult the associated patient information from both a desktop computer and/or from mobile devices.
- A module for finding health-related information; in this case the user can make use of a Web interface for searching using natural language medical terms related to their health status, his module gets information from various sources such as MedlinePlus or FreeBase [4].

4   Smart Mobile Device and Sensors

The design of a mobile device to capture vital signs from sensors, should take into account the diversity of technologies and different communication protocols available today for interaction with the sensors and the Internet. At present time we are doing tests with a Bluetooth pulseoximeter and wired electrodes for detecting cardio respiratory diseases; the device allows taking sensor data with a configurable sampling frequency, filtering, storing and sending this information to the Internet, the prototype is based on a PIC 18F87J60, figure 2 shows the main components corresponding to a GPS unit, GSM unit, PIC microcontroller, Bluetooth module and power supply.

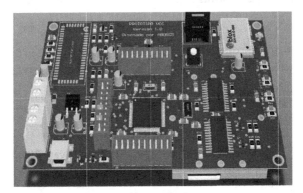

Fig. 2. 3D model for Smart mobile device

5   Using Big Data Techniques for Biosignals Data Storage and Processing

The data capture system has as main objective the acquisition and transmission of patient's vital sign monitoring to the system for process them. This system is composed of two subsystems: a system of "in-house" monitoring, which allows monitoring of a patient while he/she is in his home or in controlled places and the "outdoor" system monitoring that is in charge of patient monitoring while he is out of home or out of controlled places such hospitals or clinics.

As we explained before, the system has several sensor devices such as a pulse oximeter, electrocardiogram sensor, accelerometer, body temperature sensor, etc. all of them are connected to our microcontroller based smart device, is this device which handles the sensor data using polling and then transfer it to the mobile phone via Bluetooth. Although it is possible to transmit directly the data to the Internet using the smart device, for the first tests we use an Android mobile phone with 3G connection, to transmit data to a server on the Internet using a synchronization mechanism.

Due to large amount of data to be generated, the current general models based on common databases (mostly relational) are not sufficient, it's not that they are not required, they are simply not enough, if it is necessary to use Big Data technologies for store and process this information. The number of collected data per second depends on the slower pulse oximeter sensor, so in our case we can collect about 100 samples per second. Data is stored on the phone using files whose records have a format that corresponds to a tuple of three elements (sensor_id, time_stamp, value). Each record occupies 10 bytes of memory. When the file size is 500 KB it is closed and another file for continuing to save the most recent data is created. The file name consists of the user's ID and extension that determines the order of the file.

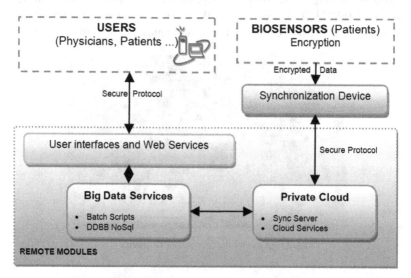

Fig. 3. Data Storage and Processing Modules

In order to process data in the cloud, instead of directly transmit it from mobile phone to the internet, we used a synchronization mechanism using the BitTorrent Sync protocol [5], this is a proprietary peer-to-peer file synchronization tool available for most popular Operating Systems. It can sync files between several devices on a local network, or between remote devices over the Internet via secure, distributed P2P technology. The data files saved in the mobile phone are synchronized on the server so that a private cloud is created; this scheme permits us to process data almost in real time. Figure 3 shows principals components of the Data Storage and Processing modules. On the server side and due the large amount of data to be processed, we have decided not to use the classical SQL relational databases, instead we decided to use NoSQL databases [6], after comparing the performance of some of them we have decided to use RIAK database [7] which is a distributed, scalable, open source key/value non relational database.

In Riak there is a simpler data model in which an "Object" is the largest and smallest data element. When performing any fetch or update operation in Riak, the entire Object must be retrieved or modified, there are no partial updates or fetches. Objects are the only unit of data storage in Riak. Normally, objects have only one metadata - value pair, but when there is more than one, the object is said to have "siblings". Others important components in RIAK are buckets and keys, buckets are used to define a virtual key space and provide the ability to define isolated non default configuration, buckets might be compared to tables in relational databases. Keys in Riak are simply binary values (or strings) used to identify Objects. In our case we are modeling our data in Riak creating a bucket for users, where the key value is an identifier and the value is an object containing the user data (first name, last name, etc) and list of sensors attached to him, at the other hand, exists also a devices (sensors) bucket containing a key formed by the user id and device id and as value an object containing the necessary data to identify the last data transmitted by one sensor.

The tuple (username, device, lastDataKey) identifies all buckets in which all data from each sensor -or group of sensors- are stored. With the pair (username, device) we identify each bucket and with lastDataKey we can identify the last record of this bucket. Using the last record all information of one sensor (or group of sensors) can be recursively recover using the value previousDataKey stored in each bucket. This schema is shown in Figure 4.

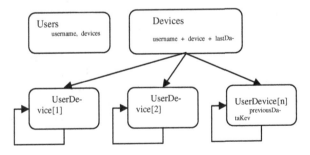

Fig. 4. Buckets in RIAK

With this organization is possible to query the data in order to obtain information about all sensor values in a concrete time interval, the last values taken by a sensor etc.

6   Conclusions and Future Work

We are convinced that new e-Health services could help to transform the sanitary system in preventive, proactive, global and participative, maintaining a full control about patient's situation and a reasonably cost[10][11]. During the last stages of the research we will running two case studies (scenarios) to demonstrate the functionality of the developed architecture, a scenario has to deal with home tele-monitoring based on more known sensors as blood pressure equipment, pulsioximetres, temperature and motion sensors, etc. while another scenario will consist of a day care centre for elder people, who in turn can carry the mobile device or mobile phone with vital signs sensors, the data will be stores in a cloud infrastructure and processed using Big Data techniques for doing early diagnose and providing new e-health services based on data analysis, these scenarios will permit participation of users that can validate developed technology.

Acknowledgements. The Virtual Cloud Carer Project has been developed by the European University of Madrid, and the companies Cubenube and Encore that is the project coordinator; VCC has been partially funded by the Spanish Ministry of Industry, Tourism and Trade TSI-020100-2011-83 through Avanza2 R&D framework. Some modules of the proposed architecture are still being developed with funds granted by the Spanish Ministry of Science and Innovation under project iPHealth (TIN-2013-47153-C3-1).

References

1. WHO global report. Preventing chronic diseases: a vital investment, World Health Organization (2005)
2. Rolim, C.O., Koch, F.L., Westphall, C.B., Werner, J., Fracalossi, A., Salvador, G.S.: A Cloud Computing Solution for Patient's Data Collection in Health Care Institutions. In: Second International Conference on eHealth, Telemedicine, and Social Medicine, ETelEMED 2010, pp. 95–99 (2010)
3. Páez, D.G., Aparicio, F., Ascanio, J.R., Beaterio, A.: Innovative Health Services Using Cloud Computing and Internet of Things. In: Bravo, J., López-de-Ipiña, D., Moya, F. (eds.) UCAmI 2012. LNCS, vol. 7656, pp. 415–421. Springer, Heidelberg (2012)
4. Bollacker, K., Evans, C., Paritosh, P., Sturge, T., Taylor, J.: Freebase: a collaboratively created graph database for structuring human knowledge. In: Proc. ACM SIGMOD International Conference on Management of Data, pp. 1247–1250. ACM, New York (2008)
5. BitTorrent Sync.,
   http://www.bittorrent.com/intl/es/sync/technology
6. NoSql Databases, http://nosql-database.org/

7. Riak Database, http://basho.com/riak/
8. Gachet, D., Aparicio, F., Buenaga, M., Padrón, V.: Personalized Health Care System with Virtual Reality Rehabilitation and Appropriate Information for Seniors. Sensors 12(5), 5502–5516 (2012) ISSN 1424-8220
9. López-Fernández, H., Reboiro-Jato, M., Glez-Peña, D., Aparicio, F., Gachet, D., Buenaga, M., Fdez-Riverola, F.: BioAnnote: A software platform for annotating biomedical documents with application in medical learning environments. Computer Methods and Programs in Biomedicine (2013)
10. Lounis, A., Hadjidj, A., Bouabdallah, A., Challal, Y.: Secure and Scalable Cloud-Based Architecture for e-Health Wireless Sensor Networks. In: 2012 21st International Conference on Computer Communications and Networks (ICCCN), pp. 1–7 (2012)
11. Nkosi, M.T., Mekuria, F.: Cloud Computing for Enhanced Mobile Health Applications. In: 2010 IEEE Second International Conference on Cloud Computing Technology and Science, pp. 629–633 (2010)
12. Redondi, A., Chirico, M., Borsani, L., Cesana, M., Tagliasacchi, M.: An integrated system based on wireless sensor networks for patient monitoring, localization and tracking. Ad Hoc Networks 11(1), 39–53 (2013)
13. Shiraz, M., Gani, A., Khokhar, R., Buyya, R.: A Review on Distributed Application Processing Frameworks in Smart Mobile Devices for Mobile Cloud Computing. IEEE Communications Surveys Tutorials PP(99), 1–20 (2012)
14. Simanta, S., Lewis, G.A., Morris, E., Ha, K., Satyanarayanan, M.: A Reference Architecture for Mobile Code Offload in Hostile Environments. In: 2012 Joint Working IEEE/IFIP Conference on Software Architecture (WICSA) and European Conference on Software Architecture (ECSA), pp. 282–286 (2012)
15. Steele, R., Lo, A.: Telehealth and ubiquitous computing for bandwidth-constrained rural and remote areas. Personal and Ubiquitous Computing 17(3), 533–543 (2013)
16. Kim, G.-H., Trimi, S., Chung, J.-H.: Big-data applications in the government sector. Commun. ACM 57(3), 78–85 (2014)

Geographic Service Discovery
for the Internet of Things

Martin Bauer and Salvatore Longo

NEC Laboratories Europe,
Kurfürsten-Anlage 36,
69115 Heidelberg, Germany
{martin.bauer,salvatore.longo}@neclab.eu

Abstract. In the Internet of Things vision, physical things become part of the Internet and, . as a result, the Internet extends into the physical world. Applications start to be aware of the users' environment and users can have mediated interactions with the physical world through the Internet of Things. Within the physical world, the spatial structure, which can be described by geographical coordinates, is relevant for finding services. Thus geographic service discovery becomes a core part of an Internet of Things infrastructure. The key problem to solve is how to efficiently extract the set of services whose geographic service area overlaps with the geographic scope of the request from the potentially huge number of services in the Internet of Things.

In this paper, we investigate the use of spatial indexes for the efficient discovery of services within an area specified by geographic coordinates. An experimental evaluation based on a prototype implementation demonstrates the feasibility of the approach by measuring the performance with respect to the request throughput under varying parameter settings and configurations.

Keywords: Internet of Things, service discovery, spatial index, geographic area, throughput evaluation.

1 Introduction

Today more and more products are being equipped with sensors and actuators, and many of these are connected to the Internet. In the Internet of Things (IoT) vision, these sensors and actuators become part of an IoT infrastructure that is accssible to a variety of applications, typically through IoT services hosted in the cloud. This enables a new class of opportunistic IoT applications that are not configured or hard-wired for specific IoT services; they need to discover relevant ones, e.g. in the current physical environment of a user, making discovery a key functionality for an IoT infrastructure, as identified in the functional view of the Architectural Reference Model (IoT ARM) [1].[1]

---

[1] The IoT ARM was developed in the European Project IoT-A [2].

R. Hervás et al. (Eds.): UCAmI 2014, LNCS 8867, pp. 424–431, 2014.
© Springer International Publishing Switzerland 2014

With the number of connected IoT devices growing into the billions – e.g. Cisco forecasts 50 billion devices connected by 2020 [3] – the discovery functionality needs to be highly scalable. To achieve the required scalability, a distributed discovery approach is needed since the throughput of a single node in the cloud is always limited. The number of nodes involved in each discovery operation should be limited as well, as this may become the bottleneck for aggregation.

Geographic loaction based on geographic coordinates is a slective criterion for the distribution, i.e. one node is responsible for a certain geographic area. Geographic coordinates are easy to determine, e.g. by using GPS or selecting a location on a map and also highly selective, e.g. there may be millions of services providing air quality information, but only a few are related to the location of interest. Within a single node, efficient access can be achieved by using a spatial index structure. Some spatial index structures like quadtrees [4] or kd-trees are used for indexing point locations, whereas R-trees [5] and its variants can also be used for indexing area locations, which we need for indexing service areas.

In this paper, we propose a cloud-based distributed service discovery for the Internet of Things, based on geographic scopes. Geographic Information Systems (GIS) have been using spatial data infrastructures with catalogues for geographical information [6]. These are utilized for storing and accessing large amounts of relatively static geographic information like roads or buildings, but not for the discovery of services. On the other hand, there have been proposals for ontology-based service discovery using symbolic locations [7]. The focus of our approach is on using geographic scopes based on geographic coordinates. The core contribution is on measuring key performance aspects for evaluating the practical feasibility of such an approach – something we have not been able to find elsewhere.

Section 2 gives an overview of the geographic service discovery architecture and the functionalities provided. Section 3 presents the evaluation of our prototype. We first look at the performance of a single node and then we analyze the distributed case with a single provider, allowing a perfect geographic partitioning, where each node is responsible for a distinct geographic area and the multi-provider case with overlapping geographic service areas. Finally, we provide a conclusion and an outlook on future work in Section 4.

2 Approach

The core idea of geographic discovery is to find information related to a geographic area. The geographic area is given as a *geographic scope*. In addition the information to be discovered needs to be specified. The result of a geographic discovery request is all the information whose geographic location matches the geographic scope. Geographic location can be given as a point location or an area location. For example, a point location may be suitable for determining the location of small objects, whereas services may have larger service areas, e.g. the area covered by a video camera.

2.1 Functionality

Overall, the approach follows the service-oriented architecture (SOA) paradigm [8]. In a typical interaction, a client queries the geographic discovery for service descriptions (represented in RDF/XML), providing a service specification, which specifies what services are of interest to the client, and a geographic scope, that describes the geographic area for which the services are requested. The geographic scope is then matched against the geographic service areas, filtering the service descriptions according to the service specifications. The fitting service descriptions are returned to the client. Subsequently the client may call one or more of the services using the information provided.

To serve the different needs of applications, we see the requirement to support synchronous one-time discovery requests, as well as requests for continuous asynchronous notifications informing about changes.

In addition, management operations for inserting, updating and deleting service descriptions with the respective service areas are needed in order to update index structures. For the purpose of this paper we only evaluate synchronous discovery requests (with rectangles specified by the coordinates of two diagonal vertices as scopes).

2.2 Architecture

In the following subsections, we first describe the internal architecture of a single geographic index server and then we describe the distributed architecture that we proposed to achieve the required scalability as well as the envisioned multi-provider approach.

Geographic Index Server. The geographic index server implements the discovery and management operations described above, using a REST-like binding. The internal subcomponents are the discovery indexer based on the spatial index and the object information index. The discovery indexer part implements the logic core of the geographic index server using an in-memory spatial index, based on an R-Tree [5], indexing the geographic information, or a persistent spatial index implementation, which internally also uses an R-Tree index. The in-memory object information index is used for storing other information associated to the services like the output of a service or the service type. We decided to use the standard R-Tree data structure because we need a spatial index structure that can handle rectangular geographic areas, as we are indexing service areas.

Distributed Architecture. Due to the large number of IoT services and the required throughput to serve the expected number of application requests, a single geographic index server will not be sufficient. Therefore, we propose a distributed hierarchical architecture as shown in Figure 1. We introduce catalogue servers that do not store the service areas of IoT services, but rather the service areas of geographic index servers. So for the discovery of IoT services first the top-level catalogue server is contacted, which then uses the geographic scope to identify the (small) set of geographic index servers that have overlapping service areas. The request is then forwarded to this subset and the results are aggregated.

In principle, a hierarchy of catalogue servers can be used as indicated in Figure 1, since catalogue servers can transparently be used instead of geographic index servers.

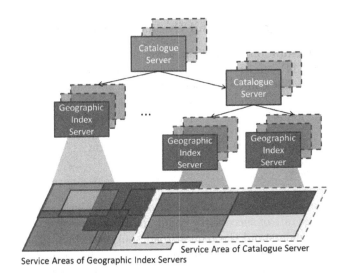

Service Area of Catalogue Server

Service Areas of Geographic Index Servers

Fig. 1. Distributed geo-discovery architecture

If the distributed geo-discovery infrastructure is operated by a single operator, the geographic areas served by geographic index servers can be partitioned as shown on the right bottom part of Figure 1, which would be useful with respect to limiting the number of servers that have to be contacted for executing a certain request. For the Internet of Things, we consider a scenario with multiple operators more likely. These operators may also want to keep their core information to themselves for both business and privacy reasons. As a result, there may be multiple geographic index servers responsible for a certain area as shown in the left bottom part of Figure 1. In Section 3 we provide an initial comparison of the two cases to get an idea what performance penalty has to be paid in the multi-operator case with overlapping service areas.

3   Evaluation

In this section, we investigate the performance and scalability of our geographic discovery approach. First we describe the testbed configuration together with the evaluation methodology. The main operation evaluated is the service discovery based on geographic scopes. We show how our approach performs with respect to throughput in different settings. For a single geographic index server, the parameters we vary are the number of service descriptions stored, the number of requests executed, the available network bandwidth, the size of the result set, and the use of persistent and in-memory spatial index implementations. Finally, we evaluate a distributed setting with partitioned as well as overlapping geographic areas.

3.1   Testbed Configuration and Evaluation Methodology

Our testbed configuration has a client-server structure, where the client establishes several HTTP connections to the server on which the geographic index server is running. The connection between server and client is a point to point 100Mbit LAN connection. The server on which the geographic index server was running has the following configuration:

- CPU: Intel(R) Core(TM) i5-2400 CPU @ 3.10GHz
- OS: Ubuntu Server 12.10
- MemTotal: 8GB

The overall evaluation is focused on a throughput analysis where the throughput is the average rate of successfully communicated and executed requests. The main goal is to understand the request load supported by a geographic server running on a single node. For this reason we look at the throughput of the *discover* operation and how different network bandwidths affect this. Two tools were used for performing the measurements: ab (Apache Benchmark) [9] and Netem [10]. The first is an open source Apache tool for benchmarking HTTP servers and the second is a tool for emulating different network bandwidths.

3.2   Experimental Result

We first investigated how a single geographic index server performs and later on we evaluated the distributed approach. Before the real tests we analyzed which parameters could influence the performance, and we identified the following parameters:

- the number of inserted service descriptions
- the available network bandwidth
- the response body size

The tests were selected based on the identified relevant parameters.

Single Geographic Index Server Evaluation. First we analyzed how the geographic discovery performs for the discover operation taking into account the network layer. For this evaluation we performed several discovery requests (100, 1,000, 10,000, 100,000), with a fixed response body size (making sure that only

5 locators, that is the url where the service description is stored, were returned per each request, encapsulated in an XML message with response body size of 1578 bytes). The achieved average throughput was around 2,000 requests/second. The performed tests have demonstrated that the number of inserted service descriptions has little if any influence on the discovery throughput.

The tests performed on the internal index structure show that no matter if there are 500 or 100,000 services inserted in the geographic index server, the geographic discovery operation is only marginally affected. Therefore, all following tests are based on a geographic index server pre-populated with 10,000 services.

The next step was to analyze how the available network bandwidth limits the geographic discovery throughput using different network configurations. For changing the network configuration, we used the netem [10] tool with the following ethernet configurations: 1Mb, 10Mb and 100Mb uplink/downlink.

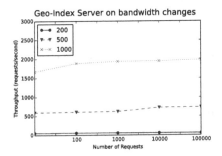

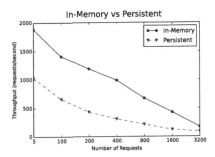

Fig. 2. Geographic discovery evaluation on changing network bandwidth

Fig. 3. Throughput comparison between in-memory and persistent implementation

As shown in Figure 2, there is a strong relation between the bandwidth size and the throughput. With a 10Mbit bandwidth, the maximum throughput achieved was about 700 requests/second but in case of 100Mbit we got around 2,000 requests/seconds. The bandwidth limits the information transfer rate and this directly affects the discovery throughput, indicating that the limiting factor is the size of the response messages and not the index lookup.

The next step was to compare the current implementation of the geographic discovery, based on an in-memory spatial index, with a persistent implementation that is using postGIS for the spatial indexing. Figure 3 shows the comparison. It is evident that the in-memory approach is more efficient in terms of throughput compared to the persistent one. In addition to that, it is interesting to see how the throughput decreases with increasing response body size (i.e. number of discovered services). As also shown in Figure 3, if the response body size is small, i.e. 5 stored services, the throughput is about 2,000 requests/second but in case of 3,200 services the performance drops to less than 200 requests/second. This demonstrates how the available network bandwidth and the number of discovered services can significantly influence the overall performance.

Catalogue Approach Evaluation. The evaluation of a single geographic index server was the basis for understanding how a distributed geographic discovery architecture, described in Section 2, could perform. We evaluate the catalogue approach focusing more on which benefits it introduces and which price we need to pay in terms of throughput.

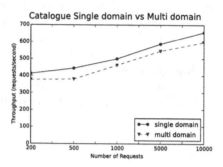

Fig. 4. Catalogue server throughput evaluation: single vs. multi-domain

The evaluation of the distributed approach with one catalogue server took into consideration the single and multi-domain approaches. In the first case there is a single operator that will serve a particular geographic area that could be partitioned as shown on the right side of the tree in Figure 1. In this case each geographic index server could be assigned to a specific area without any overlaps. In the case of the multi-domain approach the overlap between areas cannot be prevented as shown on the left side of the tree in Figure 1. The tests were performed using the same testbed configuration with one catalogue and four geographic index servers running on the server. Results are shown in the Figure 4. Compared to the single geographic index server evaluation, the overall performance decreased and this seems reasonable because we introduced an additional layer between the test client and the geographic index server. The maximum catalogue throughput achieved in this environment was about 650 requests per second for the single domain approach. The penalty is almost 2/3 of the achieved throughput on a single server (2,000 requests/seconds). The performance comparison shows that the penalty for having overlapping service areas is visible, but limited as shown in Figure 4.

4   Conclusion

As can be seen from the evaluation, the available network bandwidth plays an important role for the overall performance of the geographic discovery infrastructure. This shows that a high selectivity of the request, i.e. limiting the result set early in the process is important. Using geographic scopes already provides relatively high selectivity as compared to other parts of the service description.

In addition, the network bandwidth should be taken into account when choosing the representation of the information, e.g. a plain RDF/XML-based representation is relatively verbose and thus has a negative impact on the throughput. A distributed setting with a single catalogue server has a lower performance, because the catalogue server has to wait for and aggregate responses from the geographic index servers. The good point is that it is comparatively cheap to replicate catalogue servers as the set of geographic index servers is expected to be relatively stable compared to the set of IoT services, so the overhead of keeping replicas synchronized is low. Based on the measurements we took, we believe that it will be possible to build a scalable geographic discovery infrastructure for the Internet of Things. As a next step, we plan to analyze a large scale IoT scenario with respect to the discovery request load it generates and evaluate what geographic discovery infrastructure configuration is needed to support such a load and whether such a configuration seems viable from a business perspective.

Acknowledgment. This paper describes work undertaken in the context of the projects *Internet of Things Architecture (IoT-A)* and *MobiNet.*. IoT-A and MobiNet are Large Scale Collaborative Projects supported by the European 7th Framework Programme under the contract numbers 257521 and 318485 respectively.

References

1. Bassi, A., Bauer, M., Fiedler, M., Kramp, T., van Kranenburg, R., Lange, S., Meissner, S. (eds.): Enabling Things to Talk: Designing IoT solutions with the IoT Architectural Reference Model. Springer, Heidelberg (2013)
2. IoT-A European Project, http://www.iot-a.eu
3. Cisco IoT Forecast, http://share.cisco.com/internet-of-things.html
4. Finkel, R., Bentley, J.: Quad trees a data structure for retrieval on composite keys. Acta Informatica 4(1), 1–9 (1974)
5. Guttman, A.: R-trees: a dynamic index structure for spatial searching. In: Proceedings of the 1984 ACM SIGMOD International Conference on Management of Data, SIGMOD 1984, pp. 47–57. ACM, New York (1984)
6. Groot, R., McLaughlin, J.: Geospatial data infrastructure - Concepts, cases, and good practice. Oxford University Press (2000)
7. Lutz, M.: Ontology-based descriptions for semantic discovery and composition of geoprocessing services. Geoinformatica 11(1), 1–36 (2007)
8. Papazoglou, M.P., Traverso, P., Dustdar, S., Leymann, F.: Service-oriented computing: State of the art and research challenges. Computer 40(11), 38–45 (2007)
9. Apache Benchmark Tool, http://httpd.apache.org/docs/2.2/programs/ab.html
10. Netem, Network Emulator Tool, http://www.linuxfoundation.org/collaborate/workgroups/networking/netem

Towards Scalable DNS-Based Service Discovery for the Internet of Things

Badis Djamaa and Mark Richardson

Cranfield University, Shrivenham, SN6 8LA, UK
{b.djamaa,m.a.richaradson}@cranfield.ac.uk

Abstract. The Internet of Things promises to integrate Constrained-Node Networks (CNNs) with the Internet in a standard interoperable manner. To achieve this, automated, efficient and standardised discovery of things and their services is required. We developed EADP: an efficient, extensible and adaptable discovery protocol for CNNs. In this paper, we study the challenges of adopting DNS-based Service Discovery (DNS-SD) as a service description for EADP. We implemented DNS-SD for EADP in Contiki OS and evaluated it in Cooja. Results show the capacities of such an approach to transparently bridge between CNNs and the Internet. However, many DNS-SD related issues have been identified and need to be addressed to achieve interoperable discovery of things.

Keywords: Internet of Things, Service Discovery, DNS-SD, Contiki OS.

1 Introduction

Automated, efficient and standardised discovery of services hosted by Constrained-Node Networks (CNN) such as wireless sensor networks is a critical requirement to realise the Internet of Things. For this, well-established description technologies should be adapted for CNNs [1]. This avoids maintenance and interoperability problems related with new descriptions. One such effort is DNS-based Service Discovery (DNS-SD) which re-uses DNS records for service discovery. To advertise and lookup services, DNS-SD is coupled with multicast DNS (mDNS) and/or unicast DNS. We present a coupling of DNS-SD with our EADP protocol [2] to overcome mDNS limitations in CNNs. This presents a first step into allowing a seamless integration of CNNs running EADP/DNS-SD with local networks running mDNS/DNS-SD and with global Internet services using DNS/DNS-SD.

2 Related Work

DNS-SD defines conventional usage of DNS records to facilitate the discovery of network services. It specifies how a particular service instance can be described and accessed using PTR, SRV, TXT and A/AAAA records. The role of each record along

R. Hervás et al. (Eds.): UCAmI 2014, LNCS 8867, pp. 432–435, 2014.
© Springer International Publishing Switzerland 2014

with an example of a light service are represented in Table 1. Clients lookup a service by requesting the PTR records. The result is a set of matching *Service Instance Names* of the format *<Instance>.<Service>.<Domain>*.When a client chooses a specific *Service Instance Name*, it asks for its SRV and TXT records. SRV record gives the port number and host name where the service resides, while additional information is convoyed via the TXT record in a *key-value pair* format. From a CNN perspective, this multi-step process is very resource consuming. To avoid this, DNS-SD recommends including additional records, believed to be subsequently requested, in the *additional* section of a response. While some related works [3] recommend to disable this feature for CNNs, others [4] use it as the basis for optimisations. We revisit this in section 4 and provide some recommendations.

Table 1. a DNS-SD description of a light service over CoAP (Constrained Application Protocol)

Record	Role	Example
PTR	Assigns service instances to a service	_coap._udp IN PTR light1._coap._udp
SRV	gives the host and port of an instance	light1._coap._udp IN SRV 0 0 5683 node1.local.
TXT	user defined text	IN TXT path=/light/27
AAAA	maps a hostname to an IPv6 address	node1.local. IN AAAA fdfd::1234

To enable DNS-SD in ad hoc environments, mDNS is generally used. As mDNS is not designed for CNNs, we developed EADP. EADP provides high discovery rates and fast discovery times with low resource consumption. To assure these qualities, EADP adopts a fully-distributed push-pull approach delivering three main components: a user agent responsible for discovering services via multicast; a service agent responsible for registering and advertising services' information; and a state maintenance mechanism responsible for managing local directories and reacting to network dynamics. EADP replies are delivered via unicast.

3   Towards Scalable DNS-SD with EADP

To assure scalability, EADP proposes a trickle-inspired algorithm which advertises a service only when an inconsistency *(new or update)* appears. When the network is consistent, the algorithm keeps quiet. Advertised services are cached by intermediate nodes which can respond to queries on behalf of others. In addition to the benefits presented in [2], this mechanism allows optimizing, compressing and enhancing advertised DNS-SD messages while being backward compatible with existing DNS-SD deployments. To assure backward compatibility, EADP/DNS-SD adopts standardized DNS-SD messages for its requests and replies. To reduce traffic, EADP/DNS-SD advertisements are optimized, advertised and cached throughout the network (redundant information, e.g. in Table 1, is not sent). This reduces the distance traveled by verbose requests and replies. In addition, EADP responses are sent via unicast which is less costly in CNNs compared to multicast. Note that if a node does not understand an EADP/DNS-SD advertisement, it simply and silently drops it.

Following this specification, non-constrained nodes running mDNS and CNN nodes running EADP can query each-others services and get replies back in a standard manner. Non-constrained node services can be announced in the CNN and get advertised and cached using EADP/DNS-SD. However, CNN services will be only announced and cached inside CNNs. This does not affect the user experience as the multi-hop CNN is the most time consuming. Thus, clients inside the CNN querying for non-constrained services can get them quickly as they are already cached, while non-constrained clients can get CNN services quickly from neighboring CNN nodes caching them. This integration is a first step into achieving interoperable worldwide discovery of things solutions.

4   Results and Discussions

We implemented EADP/DNS-SD in Contiki OS and evaluated it on a 6-hop line topology of sky motes in Cooja. One node acts as a provider providing two instances (light1 and temp) of a service (_coap._udp). A client, placed at different distances from the provider, issues a lookup every 15 seconds by sending a PTR query for _coap._udp. After getting the list of available instances, it chooses one and submits a query for its SRV record followed by another for TXT records and finally an AAAA query to resolve the provider's hostname. We measure the discovery time of a lookup as the time from sending the PTR query until receiving the AAAA record. We measure the radio duty cycle as indicator of communication energy. Finally we report the discovery success rate as the ratio between sent requests and successfully resolved ones. To put results in context, we compared EADP/DNS-SD with its version when disabling the advertising component (EADPd/DNS-SD). Parameters and results are depicted in Table 2 and Fig. 1.

As can be seen from Fig. 1 (a), the average discovery time increased with distance. EADPd keeps it increasing as result of the multi-step discovery process spanning long distances; EADP keeps the time relatively constant at a low value which provides a stable user experience regardless of the service location. In addition, Fig. 1 (b) shows that the discovery success rate decreases with increasing distance. When compared with EADPd, EADP increased the success rate. This is explained by the fact of reducing the distances traveled by queries and responses, which minimizes the risk of losses. Finally, Fig. 1 (c) shows a good saving in energy for EADP. This is achieved thanks to advertising compact messages which minimize distances travelled by verbose requests and replies. This last figure may change with frequent network *churn* which triggers more advertisements; however, because of advertisements' compact format, we argue that a good saving in energy can be registered. Finally, to further enhance the performance, we recommend using the *additional* section of a SRV response to include the TXT and AAAA. In addition to minimizing the number of requests and responses, this allows using DNS name compression techniques. However, this is not recommended with PTR records as the PTR query may result in many replies for the user to choose from.

Table 2. Simulation parameters

Parameter	Value
Simulation parameters	Time = 360s, range = 50 m, #nodes = 7, medium = UDGM
Trickle	Imin = 10s, Imax = 80s, k=1
Low-layer protocols	RPL / 6LoWPAN / CSMA / ContikiMAC (16Hz check rate)

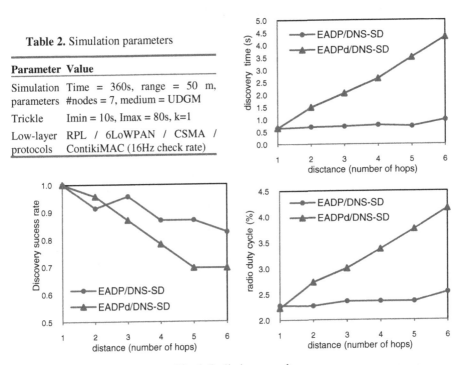

Fig. 1. Preliminary results

5   Conclusion and Future Works

We presented a proof-of-concept integration of EADP/DNS-SD. Results show that this can minimize discovery time and consumed energy while increasing success rate. Besides enhancing EADP, we plan to implement the above recommendations along with enhancing the performance at the radio duty cycling layer which imposes delays on DNS-SD bursts. Thus while unicast, used in replies, benefits from burst forwarding, multicast, used in requests and advertisements, lacks it. We are working to provide this feature for multicast. Finally, we are investigating mechanisms, such as the recent IETF query filtering draft, to optimize the queries.

References

[1] Tschofenig, H., Arkko, J.: Report from the smart object workshop. RFC 6574, IETF (2012), http://tools.ietf.org/html/rfc6574
[2] Djamaa, B., Richardson, M., Aouf, N., Walters, B.: Towards efficient distributed service discovery in low-power and lossy networks. Springer Wireless Networks Journal (2014), doi:10.1007/s11276-014-0749-3
[3] Jara, A.J., Martinez-Julia, P., Skarmeta, A.: Light-Weight Multicast DNS and DNS-SD (lmDNS-SD): IPv6-Based Resource and Service Discovery for the Web of Things. In: International Workshop on Extending Seamlessly to the Internet of Things (2012)
[4] Klauck, R., Kirsche, M.: Enhanced DNS message compression - Optimizing mDNS/DNS-SD for the use in 6LoWPANs. In: IEEE International Conference on Pervasive Computing and Communications Workshops, pp. 596–601 (2013)

Unified Platform for M2M Telco Providers

Mário Antunes, João Paulo Barraca, Diogo Gomes,
Paulo Oliveira, and Rui L. Aguiar

Instituto de Telecomunicações, Universidade de Aveiro, Aveiro, Portual
{mario.antunes,paulonascimento}@av.it.pt, {jpbarraca,dgomes,ruilaa}@ua.pt

Abstract. Although many environments are powered by M2M solutions, users do not have a simple way to gather their collective knowledge and program devices' behaviour. Also, Telco providers still lack proper components for enabling integrated services over their networks. We present the final architecture of the APOLLO project, which delivers a enhanced M2M platform encompassing sensors, management and applications platform for a major Telco provider. APOLLO builds on top of ETSI M2M specifications and rich service execution environments providing easy orchestration of services to end-users.

Keywords: IoT, IoS, Service Orchestration, Telco, M2M.

1 Introduction

Millions of sensors collect data about equipment status, environmental conditions, process execution, and human activities, presenting huge opportunities to the development of both smart environments and increasingly efficient business processes.

The ETSI M2M standard [1] is now mature enough to provide solutions for such massive sensing and acting scenarios, and is now being supplemented by the worldwide OneM2M initiative [2]. Although both ETSI M2M and OneM2M provide components and interfaces for low-level communication and management of devices, as well as integration with Telco infrastructures, they do not address the needs for processing and visualisation capabilities for this IoT. As a complement to these approaches, we propose a novel M2M platform that merges the Internet of Things (IoT) with the Internet of Services (IoS), providing the necessary components to create a useful platform for service creation in this environment.

The APOLLO platform combines the ETSI M2M low level communication and management components, with a higher-level data manipulation layer that follows a SOA approach. It provides several services to analyse, process and manipulate sensory data, data routing to multiple tenants, and advanced machine learning processes. Furthermore, it gives users a GUI to design M2M workflows

---

[1] http://www.etsi.org/technologies-clusters/technologies/m2m
[2] http://www.onem2m.org/

R. Hervás et al. (Eds.): UCAmI 2014, LNCS 8867, pp. 436–443, 2014.
© Springer International Publishing Switzerland 2014

that can be instantiated by the platform. As validation, after being tested in two different scenarios, our solution is now being deployed as the reference M2M platform for a major European Telco provider.

The remainder of the paper is organised as follows. The most relevant M2M platforms are discussed in Section 2. In Section 3 we present the conceptual architecture of the APOLLO architecture, and its different domains. The evaluation use cases are described in Section 4. Finally, the conclusions and the future work are presented in Section 5.

2   Related Work

M2M applications and services have been proposed following mostly vertical or limited approaches. This has hindered interoperability and the realisation of a unified M2M platform, able to address multiple use cases.

Sensor Andrew [7] aims to create a multi purpose sensing network. Its primary goal is to have a living laboratory where applications can be rapidly prototyped. The platform enforces the re-utilisation of technology and components, but falls short when compared with modern software approaches as it lacks methods to do preliminary processing of sensory information coming from the gateways, as well as standardised and scalable data store methods for analysing the information collected, hindering future evolution.

SensorAct [3] is a middleware that supports applications performing operations on sensors and actuators, e.g. query current and historical data or trigger notifications. Nevertheless, it fails to provide a strong Application Layer, therefore is not suitable for supporting processing tasks. Furthermore, it does not allow external entities to interact with the devices.

SenseCampus [9] aims to connect places and entities in the physical world with objects in the cyber-space. This coupling creates an ubiquitous service that not only promotes the distribution of information among the various users, but also gives support to activities that take place in the environment.

BuildingDepot [1] provides an extensible and distributed system, enabling storage, access control, and management of information. It's architecture focus on three components: Data Service (*DataS*) stores information generated by sensors together with meta-data that identifies the context and the appropriate sensor; Directory Service links institutions with *DataS*, and stores meta-data from child *DataS* to allow searching; User Service stores information on users and groups from a particular institution.

Both SenseCampus and BuildingDepot provide Web access to sensory data, but do not provide any flexible mechanism to process, analyse or transform it. Both projects communicate with the sensors through a non-standard protocol, limiting the addition of third party sensors. Also, they lack a proper management and operational platform with the capability to integrate and audit device operation.

The industry is perhaps even more active than academia in addressing this issue. Xively[3] is an Web based IoT solution, providing management capabilities for device provisioning, and creation of communication pipes. Sen.se [4] is a platform that enables collection, processing and actuation of sensory information. The platform enables users to integrate existing applications based on flows of information. They provide specialised back-ends to disseminate information, but only provide basic data manipulation services. Both solutions lack integration with pre-existing management infrastructures.

Telco operators are interested in providing M2M platforms to their clients, and have building their own M2M portfolio [6]. However, Telco solutions mostly focus in the provision of SIM cards and of basic services around managed connectivity. While useful, these services do not present an environment that fully leverages the existing communication and management capabilities of Telco infrastructures, as well as the user base and communication coverage, a requirement obvious for a Telco approach to M2M provision.

3   The APOLLO Platform

In this work we develop a novel IoT/IoS architecture that covers aspects related to network, device management, services and applications overcoming the shortcomings of the solutions before identified. The APOLLO platform aims to enable integration of a wide range of smart devices, both sensing and acting, which are handled by a single, unified platform. Linked to this infrastructure is the existing Telco cellular infrastructure, fully integrated. APOLLO aims is to allow multiple tenants to deploy their services with agility and reduced time to market.

The platform abides to ETSI M2M and can be divided in three major domains: Sensor, Network, and Service (see Fig. 1). These domains closely related with IoT/IoS, enabling the Telco operator to act as the vital glue holding both concepts together, and presenting an offer with added value to clients.

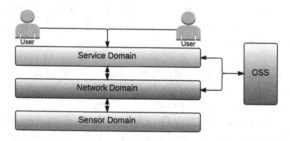

Fig. 1. Architecture of the APOLLO platform

In the following subsections the several domains are discussed with greater detail.

---

[3] https://xively.com/

[4] http://open.sen.se/

3.1   Sensor Domain

The Sensor Domain (SD) is composed by sensors, actuators, and gateways, that enable integration of physical environments into the management platform. These devices can range from micro-controllers used in low power sensing scenarios, to appliances, cell phones, and other device with M2M capabilities.

Amongst other functions this domain is responsible for enabling smart devices to communicate with the remaining M2M network, abstracting the communication with sensors, and managing the communication facilities at each M2M enabled site through its gateway. Particular scenarios may use different (non ETSI aligned) devices. Still, values are sensed and reported to the upper layers, following strict rules, and using lightweight protocols (see bellow).

APOLLO takes advantage of the ETSI M2M specifications to support seamless integration between heterogeneous sensors and the services present in the upper domains, and supported by a Telco OSS platform. At the level of the Sensor Domain, this reflects in the adoption of a strict architecture for gateways and sensors.

The SD (see Fig. 2) is mostly organised around Service Capability Layers (SCLs). Each SCL is a smart sensor or gateway device, fully supporting the management capabilities of the APOLLO framework. An M2M platform cannot restrict the sensors it supports, as different scenarios and applications will impose very specific operational specifications. Therefore, the APOLLO platform considers the existence of both Smart Sensors, and Legacy Sensors. The first support the full Device SCL (DSCL) architecture and communicate through means of the Gateway SCL (GSCL). The later are not capable of supporting a DSCL component and instead use specialised protocols. Moreover, these sensors can be directly connected to the M2M components or to other broker. When considering hybrid or migration scenarios, where an already existing install base is present, it is common to assume that other brokers may be present.

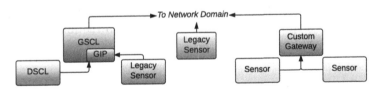

Fig. 2. Components of the Sensor Domain

We considered that sensors can communicate through standard M2M methods, such as CoAP [8], but also enabled support for other communication solutions in the platform, ranging from proprietary RF signals, to higher level telemetry protocols. Still, the actual payload of each sensor in APOLLO was standardised using JSON [4]. For custom sensors that didn't produced JSON documents, adaptation components had the role of creating documents with the correct schema.

3.2 Network Domain

The Network Domain (ND) consists of the device and network management components, hosted by a Telco operator platform. Under the ETSI approach, this reflects the Network Service Capability Layer (NSCL), which in our case is integrated with the existing Operation Support Systems (OSS). The main function of these components is to serve as aggregation points for devices to connect and disseminate information. A relevant aspect is that tenant information must be mapped from the higher layers into the ND. This effectively enables the NSCL to enforce unified access control and accounting, as well as auditing and extended debugging, due to the integration with the Telco OSS (see Fig. 3).

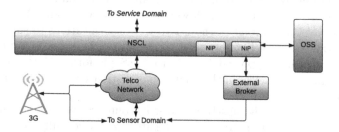

Fig. 3. Components of the Network Domain

Components can be shared amongst Telco operators/providers as well as by clients with legacy M2M infrastructures. In this case, the NSCL considers the existence of external brokers, which can be directly integrated, or communicate through Network Interworking Proxies (NIP).

As part of an enhanced M2M platform, components of the network domain are also responsible for the management and auditing of devices, providing programmatic interfaces that facilitate device provisioning and debugging. M2M device management is vital as it provides the means for integration of devices, which are heterogeneous by nature and can belong to a multitude of tenants. OMA-DM[5] is our base line for Operations Administration and Management (OAM) support, and can map into each device accordingly to the inherent individual characteristics.

3.3 Service Domain

At the Service Domain there is little notion of the device characteristics, and only data objects are exchanged between service endpoints. The components in this domain connect to the Telco OSS and to the NSCL component of the Network Domain, and exchange service information in order to compose a rich SOA environment. It was envisioned that multiple tenants could make use of the M2M platform, while keeping low latency and tenant isolation. Fig. 4 depicts the general architecture of the Service Domain and its most relevant components.

---

[5] http://openmobilealliance.org/about-oma/work-program/device-management/

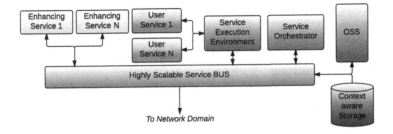

Fig. 4. Components of the Service Domain

This domain is based on the concept of a Highly Scalable Service Bus (HSSB). An internal component of the bus acts as a Network Application (NA) and registers the currently active topics with the NSCL. Therefore, all information relevant for services and users that reaches the NSCL is injected into the service bus as documents. Usually each context-aware platform defines a context representation that suits their specific needs. This breaks compatibility between platforms and limits the quantity of context information that can be used in M2M applications. To minimize this issue we developed a context storage solution that is agnostic to the context representation and provides advanced search capabilities that overcome the lack of structure [2].

Due to scalability reasons, we consider the service bus actually to be composed by several instances, subscribed to different groups of devices, and with some level of routing between them. From our perspective, as we also consider the existence of multiple NSCLs, the platform can easily be scaled horizontally by adding more instances that deal with a subset of the topics published by sensors. Each HSSB contains multiple Enhancing Services (EN), providing additional functionality over the documents that are published to the HSSB. As an example, an EN can take the temperature, humidity and wind from a Weather Station and enrich the document with the indication that there is a risk of frostbite to plants. Some other ENs can provide richer documents to authorised services-on demand, and effectively play the role of development accelerators and product enhancers, created by Telco providers, to facilitate service development and deployment to their clients.

The platform allows for tenants to develop and deploy services (User Services) directly into it, benefiting from being closer to the data (lower latency). Tenants may deploy two kinds of services: developed on their own following basic web services guidelines and API's, or orchestrated through the supplied graphical user interface. Both service kinds are deployed in the Service Execution Environment (SEE) and made available to all other services through Web Services.

4   Evaluation Use Cases

The APOLLO platform was instantiated into multiple scenarios for testing, of which we highlight two: Precision Agriculture focusing in low latency sensing and actuation; and Road condition assessment focusing in massive number of events in a Smart City.

4.1   Smart Agriculture

In the Smart Agriculture scenario we equipped a local agriculture school (ESAC in Coimbra) greenhouse with APOLLO smart sensors and actuators. Sensors where based on low power μC, battery/solar powered, capable of monitoring parameters from soil, water, air and radiation. Sensor operation relied on a variable duty cycle, adapted to the power left in their Li-Ion batteries. This was required in order to maintain the network operational in days with reduced solar intensity. Communication between sensors and the gateway used ZigBee radios with mesh capabilities and the CoAP protocol. The GSCL component reported information through a 3G network. Several Gateway Applications closely interacted with the sensors creating richer information, or enabling low latency direct actuation. In our case, farmers were interested in detecting leaks and avoiding frostbite. Moreover, the flow based service creation interface allowed the definition and analysis of workflows controlling several aspects of the greenhouses. The platform handled about 1 million of events per month, all handled in real time as actuation could be required.

4.2   Road Surface Monitoring and Pavement Analysis

We targeted also a scenario for road condition assessment through pothole detection, recurring to crowd sourcing, massive data collection, using off-the-shelf mobile devices and machine learning techniques. An Android App was created and made available to citizens who would place their monitoring phones in the dashboard of their cars.

Each monitoring phone would monitor the location, speed, and 3 axis acceleration with a frequency of 15Hz. The system assesses the road surface condition of several vehicles (use case similar to [5]). Sensors would report information every 5 hours using their 3G connection, or immediately if a Wifi connection was available. Data flows to an intermediate gateway, and then is dispatched to the NSCL. Finally, information is stored in several databases for the purpose of benchmarking and analysis.

The documents generated by the vehicles are filtered in order to detect high peaks in the Z (vertical) axis. After we leveraged our cluster based storage for detecting anomalies based on high Z peaks events, and a machine learning approach for determining anomalies based on a reference road segment. As a result we obtained 82% in determining potholes under realistic conditions. We had no control over the vehicle, driving style, vehicle condition, or cell phone location. We processed 10 Million reports per month for the duration of the pilot, which enabled us to build a detailed map covering the entire Aveiro region, and even part of the Center region of Portugal.

5   Conclusions

We have presented the architecture of the APOLLO platform. It combines ETSI M2M low level communication and management components with higher-level data manipulation that follows a SOA approach. The platforms allows users to develop innovative M2M services that can be deployed on it. As validation our solution was implemented to be the reference M2M platform for a major Telco provider.

Acknowledgements. This work has been partially funded by the Portuguese AdI QREN under grant agreements No. 2011/021580 (APOLLO) and CENTRO-07-ST24-FEDER-002031 (CLOUD THINKING).

References

1. Agarwal, Y., Gupta, R., Komaki, D., Weng, T.: Buildingdepot: An extensible and distributed architecture for building data storage, access and sharing. In: Proceedings of the Fourth ACM Workshop on BuildSys, pp. 64–71 (2012)
2. Antunes, M., Gomes, D., Aguiar, R.: Context storage for m2m scenarios. In: Proceeding of IEEE International Conference on Communications, Selected Areas in Communications Symposium (ICC 2014 SAC) (2014)
3. Arjunan, P., Batra, N., Choi, H., Singh, A., Singh, P., Srivastava, M.B.: Sensoract: A privacy and security aware federated middleware for building management. In: Proceedings of the Fourth ACM Workshop on BuildSys, pp. 80–87 (2012)
4. Bray, T.: The JavaScript Object Notation (JSON) Data Interchange Format. RFC 7159 (Proposed Standard) (March 2014), http://www.ietf.org/rfc/rfc7159.txt
5. Eriksson, J., Girod, L., Hull, B., Newton, R., Madden, S., Balakrishnan, H.: The pothole patrol: Using a mobile sensor network for road surface monitoring. In: Proceedings of the 6th International Conference on MobiSys, pp. 29–39 (2008)
6. Nkumbwa, R.: Emerging next generation communication technology: Unveiling the ubiquitous society. In: 2010 International Conference on Education and Management Technology (ICEMT), pp. 1–5 (November 2010)
7. Rowe, A., Berges, M.E., Bhatia, G., Goldman, E., Rajkumar, R., Garrett, J.H., Moura, J.M.F., Soibelman, L.: Sensor andrew: Large-scale campus-wide sensing and actuation. IBM Journal of Research and Development 55(1.2), 6:1–6:14 (2011)
8. Shelby, Z., Hartke, K., Bormann, C.: The Constrained Application Protocol (CoAP). RFC 7252 (Proposed Standard) (June 2014), http://www.ietf.org/rfc/rfc7252.txt
9. Tokuda, H., Nakazawa, J.: Sensecampus: Sensor enabled cyber-physical coupling for ubiquitous services. Journal of Information Processing 20(1), 45–53 (2012)

ARIIMA: A Real IoT Implementation of a Machine-Learning Architecture for Reducing Energy Consumption

Daniela Ventura[1], Diego Casado-Mansilla[2], Juan López-de-Armentia[2],
Pablo Garaizar[2], Diego López-de-Ipiña[2], and Vincenzo Catania[1]

[1] University of Catania, Catania, Italy
{daniela.ventura,vincenzo.catania}@dieei.unict.it
[2] Deusto Institute of Technology - DeustoTech, University of Deusto, Bilbao, Spain
{dcasado,juan.lopezdearmentia,garaizar,dipina}@deusto.es

Abstract. As the inclusion of more devices and appliances within the IoT ecosystem increases, methodologies for lowering their energy consumption impact are appearing. On this field, we contribute with the implementation of a RESTful infrastructure that gives support to Internet-connected appliances to reduce their energy waste in an intelligent fashion. Our work is focused on coffee machines located in common spaces where people usually do not care on saving energy, e.g. the workplace. The proposed approach lets these kind of appliances report their usage patterns and to process their data in the Cloud through ARIMA predictive models. The aim such prediction is that the appliances get back their next-week usage forecast in order to operate autonomously as efficient as possible. The underlying distributed architecture design and implementation rationale is discussed in this paper, together with the strategy followed to get an accurate prediction matching with the real data retrieved by four coffee machines.

Keywords: IoT, RESTful Infrastructure, Machine Learning, ARIMA Models, Eco-aware Everyday Things, Energy Efficiency, Coffee-Maker.

1 Introduction

The potential of the IoT to drive a sustainable everyday life is more than probable. This fact is easily evidenced through its current application domains such as agriculture, energy saving at home or in industrial settings and the pollution and traffic control within the cities. One example of such potential is the Google's Nest Thermostat, perhaps the most famous IoT gadget during 2014. Their designers disclosed that it can become carbon neutral in a period of just eight weeks after its first usage. Carbon neutrality refers to the greenhouse gases that were created by manufacturing and distributing the device are offset by the energy savings one obtains from using it[1].

---

[1] https://nest.com/blog/2014/04/22/todays-earth-day-tomorrow-should-be-too/

R. Hervás et al. (Eds.): UCAmI 2014, LNCS 8867, pp. 444–451, 2014.
© Springer International Publishing Switzerland 2014

However, it is still controversial how other myriads of IoT devices (everyday consumer appliances, fitness trackers or kitchen appliances) can be also labeled as green devices along their life-cycle: from manufacturing to disposal[2]. These new devices are designed to replace old-fashioned ones. Therefore, their inclusion will rise to an augment of electronic waste that probably will end in the landfill.

This paper describes the implementation of an approach that addresses this latter IoT challenge. Our proposal lies in two pillars: First, it is focused on embedding intelligence through open hardware electronics within everyday appliances of shared use (e.g. beamers, coffee-makers, printers, screens, portable fans, kettles, etc.). Our aim is transforming these electronic devices into Internet-connected eco-aware everyday things rather than replacing them by new ones. As a proof of concept, in the presented work we have focused on electronic coffee machines located in four different work-laboratories. The second pillar, it is to design and implement a RESTful infrastructure that enables to these eco-aware appliances to reduce their energy waste. It is devised to intelligently process in the back-end the most efficient operation mode at any time for each shared device and to give back such information to them, i.e. the appliances are able to operate autonomously in an eco-friendly manner.

We have named this architecture ARIIMA (the capital letters of the six former words in the paper title) as an analogy with the predictive model used to forecast the appliance's usage, ARIMA model. The presented paper makes a reality the theoretical design reported in a previous authors article [7] by implementing it.

2   Background

In the literature we have found several IoT architectures (e.g. LinkSmart Project [1], RestThing [2], S3OiA [3], Gao et al. [4], Wang [5] and Weiss et al. [6]). Their main features are: *1)* ability to integrate heterogeneous devices (even constrained [1]); *2)* REST-based architectures [2,3,4]; *3)* easy to merge with Cloud-services [5]; *4)* simple services and applications composition [1,2,3] and *5)* standardized formats to store the data [4]. Among the works reviewed, the architecture proposed by Wang [5] is the only one similar to ARIIMA in its application domain, i.e. energy efficiency. In that article the author focused on making a campus more energy efficient. He used Zigbee and RFID readers to control the laboratories' temperature and their occupation. The aim was to switch on or off the air conditioner efficiently by means of real time temperature measures. The architecture that we propose borrows some of the ideas of the works surveyed to create a RESTful platform with JSON as the established data format to exchange information. Our proposal is not restricted to a local domain like [6], i.e. in ARIIMA the Internet-connected devices can update their data from everywhere, therefore intermediate gateways are not needed. One of the main differences of our approach compared with the others, is the addition of an energy forecasting web-service based on the energy consumption reported by the same devices in the past. Another important outcome of our approach lies in its own implementation.

---

[2] http://www.wired.com/2014/06/green-iot/

Several architecture proposals that has been reviewed lack of a real development only presenting a conceptual design. Comparing ARIIMA with Wang's architecture, we can emphasize our completely open hardware/software solution[3] and its wide range of application. Thus, the presented architecture can be extrapolated to any context of appliances' automation towards energy efficiency.

3   Design Rationale

In a early author's work [7], we already studied the electric coffee machines' functionality. We distinguished the two typical operation modes of these appliances and we disclosed their associated power consumption: *1)* `On-Off` mode, consisting in repetition of actions "switch on", "waiting for the coffee machine to heat", "prepare the coffee" and immediately "switch off"; *2)* `Standby` mode, in which the appliance is permanently ready to be used and no long warming time is needed when one wants to prepare a coffee. Our major contribution was to theoretically demonstrate that depending of the number of people that use the appliance in each hour (note that it is not the same the usage of a couple in their private setting as the usage of many workers in a workplace), it is convenient to introduce a new appliance's operating mode in order to save energy. Thus, one that adjusts the coffee-machine's operation depending of the usage it is subjected to. In rush hours (3 coffees or more per hour) the coffee-maker should remain on (`Standby` mode), while periods of lower use it has to be switched off (`On-off` mode). In order to predict the appliance's utilization, time-series forecasting was applied, specifically ARIMA models. This methodology assumes that past patterns (number of coffee intakes per hour) will similarly occur in the future, and therefore are predictable. In the next sections, the implementation of the overall architecture that holds the theoretical idea presented in [7] is disclosed.

4   Implementation

Our ARIIMA proposal tries to overcome two problems: the lack of Internet connection in old-fashioned devices and their energy inefficiency. Thus, it transforms non-sustainable appliances into more eco-friendly Internet-connected smart ones. To enable Internet access to the coffee machines, we have attached to them a microcontroler which features Ethernet interface and that is compatible with Arduino MEGA (`iBoard Pro`). To overcome the energy efficiency issue, we have managed the forecasting of coffee machines' usage directly on a RESTful server. This architecture delegates the computing intensive coffee consumption forecasting process to a Cloud-based service, thus reducing the microcontrollers' processing as much as possible. The RESTful server provides REST APIs to receive energy data from appliances and to generate the weekly forecast associated to each sustainable coffee machine. According to RESTful principles, it exposes stateless services that can be observed in Table 1.

For a better understanding of the interaction among the ARIIMA's components, we have divided the logic in two subsections: Data storing and forecasting.

---

[3] https://github.com/dieguich/linked_data_coffee-maker/tree/UNO/ARIIMA

Table 1. The three different Cloud-based services offered by the ecoserver

URI	HTTP Method	Description
/ecoserver/	POST	request to save new energy consumption events
/ecoserver/predictions/	GET	get the prediction for all coffee-makers
/ecoserver/predictions/[*deviceID*]	GET	get the prediction of the coffee-maker with parameter [*deviceID*]

4.1 Data Storing of Energy Consumption Events

It is necessary to keep track of the timestamps of every coffee intake to predict the working mode that the coffee machine should hold in each hour-slot along the working day. Each `iBoard Pro` features a RTC clock which is synced within a one second precision once a day by means of a pool of NTP servers depending of the country where the appliance is located. The retrieved time is stored within the RTC clock that has its own battery. If the NTP servers are not reacheable or the mains goes down, the Arduino board can always remains in synchronization by using its local time.

These data have to be stored to be used later for time series analysis. Taking into account that an Arduino board is a resource constrained device with reduced memory storage resources (Arduino MEGA have 4 Kb of EEPROM memory), it is not suitable to store large amounts of data. Therefore, we have designed the architecture shown in Figure 1 to manage the data storing of consumed coffees.

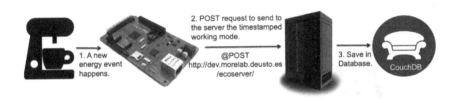

Fig. 1. ARIIMA architecture used for data storing of energy consumption events

Whenever a new energy event is detected, the Arduino board captures some information like its timestamp, the energy value consumed in Wh, the state in which the machine is set, and so forth (an example of the complete JSON object in which these data are structured can be observed in Listing 1). Then, the microcontroler sends the JSON to the ecoserver via a POST request. Finally, the server carries out the storing of the JSON object as a document inside a CouchDB NoSQL database. CouchDB is itself an HTTP server acepting CRUD operations over JSON documents.

Listing 1. Sample of a JSON energy event sent by Lab1's coffee-maker

```
{
    "deviceID": "Lab1",
    "device_type": "COFFEE-MAKER",
    "datetime": "2014-03-05T10:23:41Z",
    "time_secs": 43215,
    "consumption_type": "MAKING_COFFEE",
    "consumption_time_in_secs": 34,
    "energy_consumption_kWh": 16.8
}
```

4.2   Forecast of Coffee Machine's Next-Week Usage

The data collection process described in the previous subsection is used to predict the appliance's operating mode for the working days of the next-week (from Monday to Friday). The computational phase is done by a Cloud-based web service and it is performed weekly (on Sundays). The sorted data-flow related with the time-series prediction can be observed in the Figure 2.

The first task is to search for the number of coffees consumed in each of the hour-slots along the previous 23 working days (about 1 month of data). These data are used to infer the operating mode that the appliance should perform in each hour-slot for each working day on the new week. The information returned by the CouchDB database has to be transformed by the server in a dataset processable by an R script. To perform this conversion, every working-day is divided into slots of 12 hours (from 7am to 7pm) and the total amount of coffees made in each hour is calculated. Using this vector as input parameter, the ARIMA forecasting is executed (second step in Figure 2). The outcome prediction gives the number of coffees that are expected to be consumed in 5 days ahead for each hour slot. The prediction is furthermore valuated in different confidence bounds (80% and 95%). We have tested the different forecasting intervals and

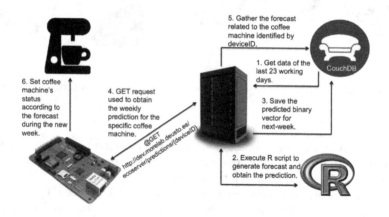

Fig. 2. ARIIMA architecture used to forecasting the coffee machine's next-week usage

we selected 80% confident value as the more accurate. Its selection is discussed in the next Section. Since the Arduino board needs to know the operation mode to assume for each hour-slot, the forecast is translated to a binary vector. For this aim, we logically evaluated whether each predicted number of coffee intakes exceeds the threshold of three coffees. In that case we set the correspondent time slot to 1 (work in `Standby mode`), or contrary set it to 0 (work in `On-Off mode`). This binary vector is saved as JSON object inside the database with the format showed in Listing 2.

Listing 2. Predicted 60 bits of binary data. Each bunch of 12 bit corresponds to each working-day (7am-7pm) of the new week.

```
{
    "deviceID": "Lab1",
    "prediction": "0011100001100111000011..."
}
```

In the 4th step of the Figure 2, each smart coffee-maker gathers weekly its prediction through a HTTP GET request sending its *deviceID*. When the server receives the request, it queries the database filtering by the *deviceID* received getting a JSON object (see Listing 2). The server sends the prediction vector back to the microcontroler and the Arduino board saves it in its EEPROM memory. In this way, everyday of the new week, it reads the sequence of 12 bits corresponding to that working day. In each hour-slot it applies the forecast automatically by using a relay leveraged within each device's On-Off button.

5 Evaluation and Results

To select the prediction which is closer to the real data, we compared the 5 days-ahead forecasted values with the real data observed during the forecasted period. The "training set" used to compute the prediction refers to 23 days from 21st May 2014 to 20th June 2014. Therefore, the empirical data are the next five working days (from 23rd June 2014 to 27th June 2014).

The ARIMA forecast issued by the R script give us different confident intervals (80% and 95%) for the exact number of coffees that are predicted in each slot, a.k.a. point forecast. Hence, we measured the binary closeness between the real data, and four different predicted data: *1)* point forecasted values; *2)* the values corresponding to the upper bound with 80% rate of confident; *3)* those corresponding to the upper bound with 95% rate of confident; and *4)* the mean between the point forecasted values and the values corresponding to their upper bound with 95% rate of confident.

The prediction's vectors that we compared are those already transformed to binary data like the presented in Listing 2. Therefore, we reviewed a survey of binary distances and similarities [8] to select, among 76 methods proposed there, Hamming, Jaccard and Sokal-Michener (also called Simple Matching) as candidate distances. The Hamming distance gives us the exact number of binary mismatching, while Jaccard and Simple Matching give equal weight for matches and non-matches as expressed in[4]. To ease the selection of the most accurate measure, we distinguished two type of prediction's errors: *1)* heavy (false negative); and *2)* light (false positive). The former refers to the mismatching that occurs when the real coffee machine's operating mode was `Standby` but the value predicted was to set `On-Off` mode; The latter alludes to the error occurred when the real coffee machine's operating mode was `On-Off` but the value predicted was to set `Standby` mode. The energy wasted related to heavy errors is greater than light errors.

The closeness of the four different predictions intervals using each of the proposed distance-measures for four coffee machines are shown in Table 2.

Table 2. Distances calculated for 4 different coffee machines placed in four laboratories. Hamming distance gives an scalar measure (**h**, refers to heavy errors and l to light ones), while Jaccard and SM give their closeness value normalized between 0 and 1.

Coffee Maker	Distances	P.Forecast	80%	90%	Mean
Lab1	Hamming	10 (**h**:10, 1:0)	21 (**h**:3, 1:18)	37 (**h**:1, 1:36)	16 (**h**:7, 1:9)
	S.Matching	0,16	0,35	0,61	0,26
	Jaccard	1,0	0,75	0,80	0,84
Lab2	Hamming	6 (**h**:6, 1:0)	5 (**h**:5, 1:0)	27 (**h**:0, 1:27)	6 (**h**:6, 1:0)
	S.Matching	0,1	0,08	0,45	0,1
	Jaccard	1,0	0,83	0,88	1,0
Lab3	Hamming	6 (**h**:5, 1:1)	11 (**h**:0, 1:11)	34 (**h**:0, 1:34)	8 (**h**:1, 1:7)
	S.Matching	0,1	0,18	0,56	0,13
	Jaccard	0,6	0,55	0,79	0,5
Lab4	Hamming	7 (**h**:6, 1:1)	7 **h**:5, 1:2)	7 (**h**:5, 1:2)	7 (**h**:5, 1:2)
	S.Matching	0,11	0,11	0,11	0,11
	Jaccard	1,0	0,87	0,89	0,87

The analysis of the results shows that for Lab2 and Lab4's coffee machines the prediction closest to the real data is provided by the upper bound with 80% rate of confidence for all the evaluated distances. Lab1's coffee-maker shows that the 80% confidence bound is the most accurate when applying the Jaccard coefficient while using Simple Matching and Hamming distances is more accurate the point forecast. The point forecast presents a higher number of heavy errors than 80% (10 vs. 3). Thus, the amount of waste energy using the point forecast is greater. For Lab3, the average seems to be the most accurate prediction, however, the upper bound with 80% rate of confidence presents closer results in every distance evaluated. In base of these considerations, we have decided to use always the upper bound with 80% of confidence level whenever we want to calculate the forecast of coffee machine's next-week usage for any coffee-maker.

---

[4] http://tinyurl.com/murubf3

The Jaccard coefficient is selected as the more suitable for our scatter dataset since this distance does not take into account the number of zero-matching.

6 Conclusions

The approach presented in this article has two targets. First, it aims to reduce the ecological impact that would cause the replacement of every old-fashioned consumer appliance by new Internet-connected ones. Our proposal is to embed an electronic adaptor within everyday appliances so they can become sustainable-IoT devices avoiding the replacement, and therefore the grow of electronic waste. Second, we provide a Cloud-based infrastructure that enables the eco-aware appliances to approximate their energy consumption to their optimal efficiency. This paper has described the REST-based architecture implementation and it has opened the path to demonstrate how the eco-aware devices (in this paper, a set of capsule-based coffee machines) could reduce their ecological impact towards carbon neutrality by means of ARIMA-based predictive models computed in the Cloud. Our ongoing work is to measure the energy consumption related with the EcoAdaptor and the Cloud based infrastructure to find out whether it can be offset with the saving attributed to the approach presented (15% per week, i.e. around 140 Wh per week as was proved in [7]). The whole ARIIMA infrastructure is currently deployed in our own servers, we plan to install it within any Cloud-platform such as Amazon EC2 or Google Cloud Platform. With this future enhancement, our solution can scale, be sustainable and reliable as the IoT requires.

References

1. The LinkSmart Project (August 2014), http://www.hydramiddleware.eu/
2. Qin, W., et al.: RestThing: A Restful Web service infrastructure for mash-up physical and Web resources. In: Proc. of EUC 2011, pp. 197–204 (2011)
3. Vega-Barbas, M., Casado-Mansilla, D., et al.: Smart Spaces and Smart Objects Interoperability Architecture (S3OiA). In: Proc. of IMIS 2012, pp. 725–730 (2012)
4. Gao, L., Zhang, C., et al.: RESTful Web of Things API in sharing sensor data. In: Proc. of ICITST 2011, pp. 1–4 (2011)
5. Wang, H.-I.: Constructing the Green Campus within the Internet of Things Architecture. Journal of Distributed Sensor Networks, 1–8 (2014)
6. Weiss, M., Guinard, D.: Increasing Energy Awareness Through Web-enabled Power Outlets. In: MUM 2010, pp. 20–30 (2010)
7. López-de-Armentia, J., Casado-Mansilla, D., López-de-Ipiña, D.: Reducing energy waste through eco-aware every-day things. Journal of MIS 10(1) (2014)
8. Seung-Seok, C., et al.: A Survey of Binary Similarity and Distance Measures. Journal of Systemics, Cybernetics and Informatics 8(1) (2010)

Ambient Intelligence Services Personalization via Social Choice Theory

Emilio Serrano, Pablo Moncada, Mercedes Garijo, and Carlos A. Iglesias

Technical University of Madrid, Madrid, Spain
{eserrano,pmoncada,mga,cif}@dit.upm.es

Abstract. There are a great number of situations in *Ambient Intelligence* systems which involve users trying to access shared resources such as: music, TVs, decoration, gym machines, air conditioning, etcetera. The use of *Social Choice* theory can be employed in these situations to reach consensus while the social welfare is maximized. This paper proposes a multi-agent system to automate these agreements, points out the main challenges in using this system, and quantifies the benefits of its use in a specific case study by an agent-based social simulation.

Keywords: Service customization and personalization, Social Choice, Ambient Intelligence, Agent-based Social Simulation, Agreement technologies, Multiagent systems.

1 Introduction

Ambient Intelligence (AmI) systems need to be aware of the users preferences, intentions, and needs [1] to offer different services whose main goal is to augment their live quality. Some examples of use of AmI are: to design office spaces that smoothly move information between displays, walls, and tables; or, learning to customize lighting and temperature based on learned resident preferences [1]. These services raise an important question: what happen when resources are shared and there are conflicts between users' preferences?. There are cases where there is an obvious answer. For example, regarding temperature, an arithmetic mean among users' preferences seems reasonable. Nevertheless, there are a large number of scenarios where this is not an option such as deciding a TV channel or a lift background music. As a result, AmI services have to reach consensus trying to maximize users' satisfaction.

Although this issue is not usually addressed in AmI specialized literature, fortunately, *agreement technologies* (ATs) [2] have studied it in depth. ATs deal with technologies for practical application of knowledge in order to reach agreements automatically. ATs have covered a large variety of negotiation aspects such as: multi-issue negotiations, concurrent negotiations, strategy-proof mechanisms, argumentation, auctions, voting, etcetera [3]. In this scope, the use of *social choice* theory, which is concerned with the evaluation of alternative methods of collective decision-making [4], appears as a straightforward solution because its primary goal is to make a group decision.

R. Hervás et al. (Eds.): UCAmI 2014, LNCS 8867, pp. 452–459, 2014.
© Springer International Publishing Switzerland 2014

However, social choice has mainly focused on theoretical works which deal with political elections [5]. Therefore, there are a number of dilemmas to be solved in this scope: what are the benefits of using a voting system in an intelligent environment?; what are the most suitable voting systems?; and, what differences does this case present when compared to political elections?. To the best of authors' knowledge, this paper and another authors' contribution [6] are the first works which propose the use of social choice to improve the access to shared services in AmI environments and which quantify its benefits. The experimental results are given in the scope of an intelligent hotel where users can share TV screens in the hall.

The paper is organized as follows. After revising the background in section 2, section 3 studies a general agreement service for AmI environments. Then section 4 presents the experiments conducted and the results obtained. The paper concludes in section 5.

2 Background

The most relevant research streams in *agreement technologies* include:

- *Auction theory*: it analyses protocols and agents' strategies in auctions. Auctions are usually used in systems where the auctioneer wants to sell an item and get the highest possible payment.
- *Negotiation or Bargaining Theory*: the agreement is modelled as a sequential game where agents alternate in making offers according to an underlying protocol.
- *Contracting theory*: a very well-know protocol in this domain is the contract net protocol [7] which allows a contractor agent to contract one or more participant agents to undertake some task.
- *Social Choice Theory*: combining individual preferences, interests, or welfares to reach a collective decision or social welfare in some sense [4].

Among these streams, the authors consider the use of social choice as the most suitable option for resolving conflicts in AmI. The main reason is that it is focused on maximizing social welfare. Furthermore, there are a number of scenarios where users have a peer to peer relationship and, besides expressing their personal preferences, there is nothing else to be said in a negotiation. In contrast, the bargaining theory is also a feasible option for some scenarios, e.g. if agents' preferences may change by argumentation.

As explained by Procaccia [5], *social choice theory* has seen few applications to date. The reason given by the author is that political elections, which are perhaps the most prominent social decision making mechanisms, are very difficult to change. Social choice research has been mainly theoretical, being the work by Arrow et al. [4] its maximum exponent. This research line focuses on verifying that a voting system satisfies certain mathematical properties such as the majority criterion; i.e. if one candidate is preferred by a majority (more than 50%) of voters, then that candidate must win. As seen in the introduction, when

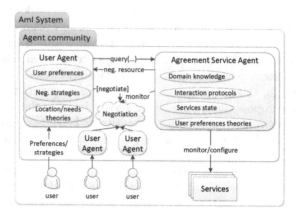

Fig. 1. A general multi-agent based agreement service for intelligent environments

social choice is used to resolve to conflicts in shared resources into AmI environments these theoretical studies do not respond to a series of questions of great interest such as how much satisfaction should developers expect after including these techniques. To answer these questions, it is necessary a simulation-based experimental research.

Aseere et al. [8] present one of the few works which: (1) combines social choice with an practical application distinct from political elections; and which (2) gives experimental results to quantify the benefits obtained. These authors propose a multi-agent system based on an iterative voting protocol where student agents could vote to decide which courses the university would be running.

3   A Multi-agent System Combining Social Choice and Ambient Intelligence

The generic agreement service for shared resources in intelligent environments is assumed to be a *multi-agent system* [9] for several reasons: (1) the agent theory has covered a great variety of negotiation aspects [3] and, therefore, these systems are very appropriate for an agreement service; and, (2) this paradigm has been widely used for the development of AmI given the *Agent-based Ubiquitous Computing* [10] (although it does not fully cover AmI [11]).

Figure 1 summarizes this multi-agent system. Basically, there are a number of users which can use one of several shared resources in the environment and an agent community which aims to maximize the satisfaction of users.

Each user has assigned an agent, *user agent* (UA), which negotiates on her behalf. The basic elements needed for this are: (1) the preferences of the user with regard to a service, which allow the UA to obtain what the user wants; and (2) the agreement strategies (or negotiation strategies), which allow the UA to make the best out of her participation [12]. Assuming these two basic elements, there are several possible final AmI systems which fit this design. In the most complex case, the user agent has to detect this information. Regarding indoor location, there are a number of works which deal with this problem by using wireless technologies such as Global Positioning System (GPS) [13], Radio Frequency IDentification (RFID), wireless local area network (WLAN), mobile cellular network, wireless mesh networks [14], bluetooth, etcetera [15]. Identifying the different users and their locations is very challenging, but the problem is even more complicated if the user does not give her service preferences. Assuming that the configuration given for the service is the preferred by the user and conducting learning algorithms is feasible [16]. On the other hand, if this service is shared, users may not like the parameters given. Therefore, sentiment analysis and detecting emotions through face recognition techniques would be necessary in this case.

The second agent included in this generic system is the *Agreement Service Agent* (ASA). The ASA provides UAs with the necessary information to negotiate. Firstly, the ASA contains Domain knowledge of services which can be as simple as a list of services with their possible configurations (music themes or TV programs currently available) or an ontology establishing different relations among these configurations. Secondly, the ASA gives the agreement protocols, specified in high-level agent communication languages (ACLs, e.g. FIPA-ACL [17]), which allows UAs to interact independently of the technology employed in their development. These agreement protocols are the negotiation rules, the rules governing the negotiation which have to be shared among negotiating agents regardless of their agreement strategies [12]. Thirdly, the ASA also monitors the negotiations carried out by the UAs and stores the service state (current configuration, current users, etcetera). Finally, the ASA may use the information obtained by monitoring negotiations to elaborate theories about users preferences which can be employed to give a better service [18]. For example, these theories could be used to advance the results of a negotiation or to suggest one of several services according to the preferences similarity among the current users of the service and the incoming user. Note that the ASA is a smart agent according to Nwana classification [19] because its autonomy, cooperation and learning; whereas UAs, assuming that the needs and location learning are not included, are collaborative agents.

4   Experimental Results

To hint at the potential of the system described above, this section presents an agent-based social simulation to quantify the benefits of using social choice in a well-known scenario. This scenario presents a hotel floor where there is a shared hall with three large television screens that can be used by different clients or users. Figure 2 shows the floor and the shared services marked in circles. Users have *user agents* (UAs) which know their preferences for the shared service and their location. When more than one client accesses a shared resource simultaneously, UAs contact an *agreement service agent* (ASA) to try to reach

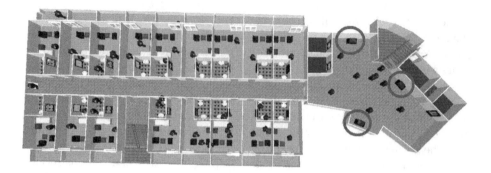

Fig. 2. Hotel floor to evaluate system proposed

an agreement by some social choice method. This ASA can suggest another service to the UA based on past interactions performed by the latter agent. Once a consensus is reached among different UAs, the ASA selects the chosen configuration. The voting is repeated again when new clients join the group or a client that accesses the resource leaves it.

The experiments are conducted during 2000 time steps and repeated 100 times with different users populations. The voting systems considered are: Range voting, plurality voting, cumulative voting, Borda voting and approval voting [4]. The basic metrics to quantify the suitability of a voting system is the *accumulated satisfaction* (*as*, satisfaction of the population from the beginning of the experimen) and the *maximum time without wanted configuration* (mwc, the worst user's wait for something she wants). The experiments show the arithmetic mean of these metrics for the 100 different populations. Inasmuch as the *"time step"* unit is employed to discuss the time dimension, the specific machine where the simulations have been conducted is irrelevant.

The results for different voting methods are shown in figure 3. Regarding the accumulated satisfaction (*as*), the range voting offers the best performance: 69%. On the other hand, the worst result is with a basis policy included in the experiments: the first user in accessing the resource decides the configuration (the second one decides when this leaves, and so on). This gives an accumulated satisfaction of 57%. Therefore, in this case, voting methods can increase satisfaction by 12%.

One interesting difference between the social choice application considered in this paper and the hegemonic case contemplated in social choice literature, political elections, is that, even giving random preferences, there are significant differences in satisfaction. In political elections and a number of cases, random preferences cause uniform results whatever is decided with whatever method used because there are always plenty of voters happy with the election result. As shown in the experiments, this does not happen when different subsets of users vote when they want to use a shared service.

In addition to the two extreme cases discussed above, the Borda method gets 67%, Approval 65%, Cumulative voting 61%, and Plurality 60%. Therefore,

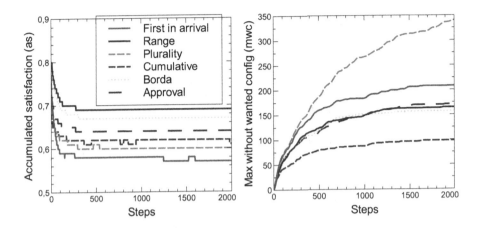

Fig. 3. Experimental results, different voting methods without pre-selection techniques

although range voting gets 4% more satisfaction, Approval voting could be employed due to its better usability, i.e. it is easier for users to decide whether a configuration is approved or not than marking each option.

5 Conclusion and Future Works

This paper hints at the potential of considering social choice techniques automated by multi-agent systems in intelligent environments. For the case study considered, the results show that the use of range voting achieves 12% more *as* than the basis method which consists of allowing the first user in accessing the resource to decide the configuration. The approval voting, which presents a better usability than range voting, gets 8% more *as*. However, if the service owner is more interested in avoiding long waits, cumulative voting gives the best *mwc*: 98.1 time steps. Although this result is less than half the time required with the basis method, the worst result according to this metric is given by the most commonly used voting method, the plurality method (304.2 t.s.).

Concerning the future works, there are a number of considerations which would improve the system presented. Firstly, the inclusion of location and need theories in the user agent model. Secondly, the consideration of tactical voting and the effect that different populations with different strategies can cause in different voting systems. Finally, there are a large number of voting systems which could be considered besides those included. Another future line is the application of social choice to emergency management to enhance aspects such as coordination [20] and situation-aware systems [21].

Acknowledgments. This research work is supported by the Spanish Ministry of Economy and Competitiveness under the R&D project CALISTA (TEC2012-32457).

References

1. Cook, D.J., Augusto, J.C., Jakkula, V.R.: Ambient intelligence: Technologies, applications, and opportunities. Pervasive and Mobile Computing 5(4), 277–298 (2009)
2. Jennings, N.R.: Agreement technologies. In: van Leeuwen, J., Italiano, G.F., van der Hoek, W., Meinel, C., Sack, H., Plášil, F. (eds.) SOFSEM 2007. LNCS, vol. 4362, pp. 111–113. Springer, Heidelberg (2007)
3. Ito, T., Hattori, H., Zhang, M., Matsuo, T.: Rational, Robust, and Secure Negotiations in Multi-Agent Systems. SCI, vol. 89. Springer, Heidelberg (2008)
4. Arrow, K.J., Sen, A.K., Suzumura, K. (eds.): Handbook of Social Choice and Welfare, 1st edn., vol. 2. Elsevier (2011)
5. Procaccia, A.D.: How is voting theory really useful in multiagent systems? http://www.cs.cmu.edu/~arielpro/papers/vote4mas.pdf
6. Serrano, E., Moncada, P., Garijo, M., Iglesias, C.A.: Evaluating social choice techniques into intelligent environments by agent based social simulation. Information Sciences 286, 102–124 (2014)
7. Smith, R.G.: The Contract Net Protocol: High-Level Communication and Control in a Distributed Problem Solver. IEEE Transactions on Computers C-29, 1104–1113 (1980)
8. Aseere, A.M., Gerding, E.H., Millard, D.E.: A voting-based agent system for course selection in e-learning. In: Proceedings of the 2010 IEEE/WIC/ACM International Conference on Web Intelligence and Intelligent Agent Technology, WI-IAT 2010, vol. 02, pp. 303–310. IEEE Computer Society, Washington, DC (2010)
9. Woolridge, M., Wooldridge, M.J.: Introduction to Multiagent Systems. John Wiley & Sons, Inc., New York (2001)
10. Mangina, E., Carbo, J., Molina, J.: Agent-Based Ubiquitous Computing. Atlantis Ambient and Pervasive Intelligence. We Publish Books (2010)
11. Nakashima, H., Aghajan, H., Augusto, J.C.: Handbook of Ambient Intelligence and Smart Environments, 1st edn. Springer Publishing Company, Incorporated (2009)
12. Benyoucef, M., Keller, R.K.: An evaluation of formalisms for negotiations in E-commerce. In: Kropf, P.G., Babin, G., Plaice, J., Unger, H. (eds.) DCW 2000. LNCS, vol. 1830, pp. 45–54. Springer, Heidelberg (2000)
13. Alcarria, R., Robles, T., Morales, A., López-de Ipiña, D., Aguilera, U.: Enabling flexible and continuous capability invocation in mobile prosumer environments. Sensors 12(7), 8930–8954 (2012)
14. Chung, J., Gonzalez, G., Armuelles, I., Robles, T., Alcarria, R., Morales, A.: Experiences and challenges in deploying openflow over real wireless mesh networks. IEEE Latin America Transactions (Revista IEEE America Latina) 11(3), 955–961 (2013)
15. Liu, H.L.H., Darabi, H., Banerjee, P., Liu, J.L.J.: Survey of wireless indoor positioning techniques and systems (2007)
16. San Martín, L.A., Peláez, V.M., González, R., Campos, A., Lobato, V.: Environmental user-preference learning for smart homes: An autonomous approach. J. Ambient Intell. Smart Environ. 2(3), 327–342 (2010)
17. Fip, A.: FIPA ACL Message Structure Specification (SC00061G). FIPA TC Communication (December 2002)
18. Serrano, E., Rovatsos, M., Botía, J.A.: Data mining agent conversations: A qualitative approach to multiagent systems analysis. Information Sciences 230, 132–146 (2013)

19. Nwana, H.S.: Software agents: An overview. Knowledge Engineering Review 11, 205–244 (1996)
20. Alcarria, R., Robles, T., Morales, A., Cedeño, E.: Resolving coordination challenges in distributed mobile service executions. International Journal of Web and Grid Services 10(2), 168–191 (2014)
21. Morales, A., Alcarria, R., Martin, D., Robles, T.: Enhancing evacuation plans with a situation awareness system based on end-user knowledge provision. Sensors 14(6), 11153–11178 (2014)

Creating and Validating Emergency Management Services by Social Simulation and Semantic Web Technologies

Geovanny Poveda, Emilio Serrano, and Mercedes Garijo

Technical University of Madrid, Madrid 28040, Spain
{gpoveda,eserrano,mga}@dit.upm.es

Abstract. One of the most promising fields for Ambient Intelligence (AmI) is the implementation of intelligent emergency plans. By using AmI, it is possible to improve the collaboration and coordination strategy of response efforts in emergency situations. Despite AmI systems are generally evaluated by using Living labs, it is desirable to use simulations in the emergency case. Simulations have allowed emergency committees and emergency experts to improve the performance and efficiency of many emergency plans while decreasing the limitations of regular drills and AmI restrictions. However, despite their wide range of benefits, simulations are currently facing many problems. Among those, simulations are performed in an ad-hoc model and are usually "closed". To improve this situation, this paper proposes using semantic web technologies as a powerful tool to reuse, extend, and combine different simulation components.

Keywords: Service creation strategies, Emergency plans, Ambient Intelligence, Ambient Intelligence Simulation, Agent-based Social Simulation.

1 Introduction

Ambient intelligence (AmI) is an emerging discipline in information technology in which people are empowered through a digital environment that primarily consists of sensors and devices connected through a network [1]. AmI offers a digital environment in which it is possible to support the cooperation of devices, services and people [2]. One of the most promising fields for AmI is implementation of intelligence emergency plans. By using AmI it is possible to improve the collaboration and coordination strategy of response efforts in emergency situations.

One of the most common ways to evaluate AmI systems is by using living labs (LL). LL refer an approach for representing a user-centric methodology for sensing, prototyping, validating and refining complex solutions in evolving real life contexts [3]. The benefits of using LL to validate emergency plans are highly valued. LL use an infrastructure that enables people to simulate the real environment of physical spaces such as houses or buildings with multiple IT

R. Hervás et al. (Eds.): UCAmI 2014, LNCS 8867, pp. 460–467, 2014.
© Springer International Publishing Switzerland 2014

devices connected and distributed across a network. However, in this approach some features are modelled without including a complete characterization of people and spaces. Living labs face some restrictions such as: (1) control the variables and parameters related to emergency, (2) control the time constant of the emergency.

Over the last years Agent Based Social Simulation (ABSS) have been used by many emergency experts and emergency committees. Currently, ABSS are usually "closed" and for specific services, i.e., they cannot be parameterized to adapt them to other cases beyond the studied case. Moreover, the experiments are not reproducible, i.e., the information given about how the authors have built the simulations is insufficient to repeat them. Many simulation models are often accompanied by underlying assumptions that are unknown to the researchers or cannot be explicitly characterized for a particular model.

It is necessary to provide a solution for the ad-hoc emergency modelling issue and subjective interpretations for improving the emergency plan strategies by including more realistic egress plans in the emergency simulations. Ontologies are useful across the simulation modelling and for knowledge sharing [4]. In order to provide ontology driven simulations and improve the aforementioned short-comings, we propose a mechanism based on Semantic Web Technologies. More specifically, a model where users can build emergency scenarios based on contextual information and semantic relationships. Our model has been defined as a subsystem on top of the semantic architecture framework proposal by Serrano et al. [1]. In particular, we have followed the methodology for the evaluation of emergency plans and we have adapted the vision presented in such work by implementing a module to support the creation and validation of emergency simulations.

This paper is organized as follows. Section 2 presents an overview of the most common frameworks used for validating emergency plans. The overview includes a description for ABBS frameworks and emergency domain simulator framework. Section 3 introduces the proposed architecture by describing the most important components. Next, section 4 introduces the implementation of a semantic module used to validate the proposed architecture. Finally, section 5 summarizes the results and points out the possible future research directions.

2   Background

This section describes some of the most important frameworks used for validating emergency plans by using the simulation approach. We have included two main categories: (1) ABBS frameworks and (2) emergency domain simulator frameworks.

2.1   Agent-Based Social Simulation Frameworks

An interesting wiki [5] on platform comparisons presents the large number of frameworks available for general ABSS. This wiki currently lists 81 frameworks

462   G. Poveda, E. Serrano, and M. Garijo

with information that is important for the purpose of this paper, such as the license. To the best of the authors' knowledge, none of these simulators gives abstract mechanisms for simulating emergency plans. In general, the most popular ABSS frameworks, such as NetLogo, MASON and Repast, do not offer tools to build a realistic environment model with the capacity to perform emergency-plan evaluations. Nevertheless, these platforms can supply interesting support for developing more abstract resources.

2.2 Emergency Simulation Frameworks

Currently there are several domain-specific frameworks to address the emergency simulation approach for indoor environments. Some interesting works such as [6], [7], [8], [9], [10] and [11] have shown the importance of studying emergency plans based on simulation approach. However, currently, their design and validation process need to consider new tools, components and platforms for reducing the development effort and facilitate the deployment of realistic simulations.

Some of them need to support knowledge sharing and reuse mechanisms. In [6], the authors propose an interesting approach for supporting the egress in crowd simulations. However, its architecture is based on an ad-hoc approach in which actions are performed by restricted subjects from a multi agent world. There is not AmI features that allow designers to create participatory simulations and augmented experiments for the crowd actions. In [8], the authors propose an interesting approach for supporting the emergency egress process. However, every function around the egress situation does not include user profile characterizations. In [7], the authors propose an interesting architecture for emergency response simulation which includes human, environment and validation features. However, it does not include mechanisms to formalize the emergency knowledge. There is not ontology modelling.

In [1], the authors have proposed a methodology for developing and using a holistic framework based on an ontological approach. The architecture shows a novel and useful approach for generating and validating emergency plans. The architecture has been designed by using a service-oriented approach in which a set of components are defined for offering a set of functionalities as emergency services. In this framework, ontologies are used to formalize the emergency knowledge domain and provide a common understanding that allows users to support the reasoning process and integration service.

3   Proposed Architecture

In an attempt to narrow down the aforementioned shortcomings, we have designed a semantic emergency model and we have implemented a semantic utility in order to validate the stated model. The semantic utility has been created for supporting the emergency simulation development process on a simulator framework named EscapeSim [12]. The proposed architecture is presented in Fig 1. The design phase of our architecture includes a modelling domain knowledge

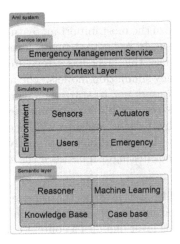

Fig. 1. Proposed Architecture

process, which is based on ontology called EinSim. This ontology aims to clip all the phases of simulation emergency process together. EinSim Ontology schema has been designed to maintain the integrity with semantic trends and standards to keep the ontology simple and put impact on its usability and easy to appliance to encourage other developers. For a detailed technical information about the EinSim Ontology schema please refer to ontology website [13].

3.1 Components

The presented is used as a basis for the the implementation of agents in the emergency simulation model. The proposed architecture allows users to design, create and validate emergency simulations and emergency services. The architecture has three layers: (1) semantic checking and discovery components at the bottom; (2) a simulation layer; and, (3) a component for deploying emergency management services.

Semantic Checking and Discovery Components Layer. The base layer is composed of set of elements that enable users to use semantic reasoning features for checking model consistency, checking model relations and augmented inferences in the case of AmI services. The core element of this layer is a reasoner, which act as an intermediate entity between the domain knowledge and a machine learning component. Inference feature is provided by using a discovery mechanism which allows systems to infer relations on the knowledge base and "facts" on a case-based component. One important feature of this layer is the decoupling level, which able designers and developers to use the semantic checking and inference component without the need to instance the simulation component. Thus, it is possible that external platforms or AmI services can use those features without simulation features.

464   G. Poveda, E. Serrano, and M. Garijo

Simulation Layer. This layer is composed of set of the elements that enable designers to represent some of the most important features and conditions related to the emergency simulation. In order to define a standard for the definition of emergency simulation models, this layer has a repository in which are specified a common-base of emergency simulation models. The aim of this repository is to define a frame that allows users not to start the emergency simulation process from scratch. This layer is responsible for offering the API functions from the frameworks simulators. This layer is replaced with the reality in the final AmI system deployed. When the the context layer is properly designed, the emergency management system does not distinguish between the simulation and the reality.

Service Component. The last layer is the service emergency management component, which is responsible for exposing reasoning capabilities and simulation features functions. This layer includes a context component, whose function is to identify the context of the external request and provide specific services according it. Services have been designed to be consumed by using the RESTFUL architecture. This approach takes advantage of some principles of multi agent system paradigm and semantic web by providing a unique resource for every entity of the simulation model and for every node of the reasoning layer.

4   Implementation

As mentioned above, we have created a semantic utility for evaluating and validating the proposed architecture. We have designed a Java component which provides an auto-assisted design wizard utility for building emergency simulation scenarios by applying reasoning capabilities for checking model consistency and checking model relations. The Java component is composed of two modules: (1) *a simulation control module*, which is responsible for controlling the verification and validation process on simulation and (2) *an adaptation module*, which is responsible for checking the consistence of the simulation models. Another function of adaptation model is to generate the mappings between ontological concepts and objects from simulator framework. In order to facilitate the simulation design process, a model repository beans have been created. It is basically a component in which the common-base elements of the simulation process are stored.

Simulation workflow start by using the models stored on the repository: (1) user model, (2) environment model and (3) catastrophe model. When users instance the simulation control, it provides a function that enables users to be assisted for defining the features related to every model. Thus, designers and developers can create models according to the features that they need to use from the model beans. As a part of the simulation verification process, a function is deployed for checking the restrictions and inconsistency on the emergency simulation models. There is a function responsible for checking the relations and dependence between the simulation models. This function instances a reasoning mechanism in order to advise users for a possible mistakes, dependencies and suggestions. Thus, every time users choose elements from the model beans, a reasoning mechanism is enabled for checking the relations and restrictions. Proposed simulation workflow has followed some recommendations of managing distributed process proposed by Alcarria et al [14] and Chung et al [15].

Fig 2 gives an example of OWL class with restrictions. This OWL class is included in the public ontology given in this paper [13] and can be linked by the interested reader. Class restrictions are analyzed automatically by a semantic reasoner, such as Jena, when building a disaster model with the JavaBeans repository. For example, given the restriction started in line 5, instances of this OWL class (called individuals in OWL) have to include an object property called *hasPhysicalPlace*. This properties relate instances of two OWL classes. Thus, if there is not an environment model previously defined in the simulation, the reasoner does not allow the developer to define a specific disaster as an individual (or instance) of the OWL class described. After defining the property hasPhysicalPlace, the reasoner may be used to check that the property is in the correct domain and range according to the ontology definition and the specific developer instantiation. Specificity, this property [13] belongs to the *EnvironmentModel* domain and its range is *PhysicalPlaces*. As seen, the use of an ontology and a semantic reasoner enables developer to follow a methodological order on the model definitions.

```
1
2   <owl:Class rdf:about="&geosim2;Disaster">
3       <rdfs:label xml:lang="en">Disaster</rdfs:label>
4       <rdfs:subClassOf rdf:resource="&geosim2;Model"/>
5       <rdfs:subClassOf>
6           <owl:Restriction>
7               <owl:onProperty rdf:resource="&geosim2;
                    hasPhysicalPlace"/>
8               <owl:minCardinality rdf:datatype="&xsd;
                    nonNegativeInteger">1</owl:minCardinality>
9           </owl:Restriction>
10      </rdfs:subClassOf>
11      <rdfs:isDefinedBy rdf:datatype="&xsd;string">http://minsky
            .gsi.dit.upm.es/~gpoveda/geosim/0.1.3/ns.owl#</
            rdfs:isDefinedBy>
12      <rdfs:comment xml:lang="en">Description of a disaster
            modelled with EinSim ontology</rdfs:comment>
13  </owl:Class>
```

Fig. 2. OWL Restriction

Once restrictions and relations are checked, the simulation control module (explained at the beginning of this section) generates the simulation model (see simulation layer in Fig 1). This model is a file that contains the descriptions and relations about the users, environments and catastrophe models by means of RDF triples. RDF statements are generated by applying a set of rules that execute a mapping process between the values specified by user on the wizard utility and the ontological model. The next step inside the simulation workflow is to check if the simulation model is consistent with the ontology EinSim [13]. Basically, this activity involves analyzing every subject and predicate of the RDF relations. The aforementioned process is conducted automatically using the reasoner (Jena API in our case). Once the emergency simulation consistency is verified, the adaptation module (explained at the beginning of this section) uses a mapping process to perform the transformation of the ontological classes instances (defined RDF) into objects (Plain Old Java Object). Finally, simulation is running according to the EscapeSim [12] framework features.

Currently, UbikSim[1], a general AmI simulator, has been extended to implement different modules of the framework proposed in the EscapeSim [12] library.

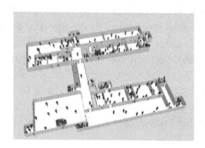

Fig. 3. Simulation scenario in EscapeSim

5   Conclusion and Future Works

In this paper, we have presented an architecture for designing and validating emergency plans by using a novel semantic-based approach. This approach is based on an ontological domain knowledge that provides reasoning capabilities for checking models and discovery relations features. By applying this approach, the experience on the development and design process is enhanced by allowing: (1) to be assisted step by step with the construction of emergency simulation; (2) to extend and reuse simulation models concepts (user, environment and emergency) by using portable RDF emergency simulation resources; and, (3) to extend and reuse simulation components previously implemented which could be automatically suggested by semantic web technologies.

The paper gives an ontology for this purposes [13] and a partial implementation of the framework [12]. Although the complete implementation is a future work, the open and free source of EscapeSim already allows the interested user to create new environments (walls and rooms may be drawn, and then, the user can drag and drop other elements, such as sensors, users or furniture) and creating new user profiles with different emergency plans, Fig 3 shows an example of emergency simulation scenario on EscapeSim. A video is available on-line[2].

---

[1]   https://github.com/emilioserra/UbikSim/wiki.

[2]   http://goo.gl/IsALQz.

Acknowledgments. This research work is supported by the Spanish Ministry of Economy and Competitiveness under the R&D project CALISTA (TEC2012-32457).

References

1. Serrano, E., Poveda, G., Garijo, M.: Towards a holistic framework for the evaluation of emergency plans in indoor environments. Sensors 14(3), 4513–4535 (2014)
2. Alcarria, R., Robles, T., Morales, A., Diego, Aguilera, U.: Enabling flexible and continuous capability invocation in mobile prosumer environments. Sensors 12(7), 8930–8954 (2012)
3. Eriksson, M.: State-of-the-art and good practice in the field of living labs (2006)
4. Morales, A., Alcarria, R., Martin, D., Robles, T.: Enhancing evacuation plans with a situation awareness system based on end-user knowledge provision. Sensors 14(6), 11153–11178 (2014)
5. ABSS frameworks list, http://en.wikipedia.org/wiki/ABM_Software_Comparison
6. Lozano, M., Morillo, P., Lewis, D., Reiners, D., Cruz-Neira, C.: A distributed framework for scalable large-scale crowd simulation. In: Shumaker, R. (ed.) Virtual Reality, HCII 2007. LNCS, vol. 4563, pp. 111–121. Springer, Heidelberg (2007)
7. Jain, S., Mclean, C.R.: An architecture for integrated modeling and simulation for emergency response
8. Zoumpoulaki, A., Avradinis, N., Vosinakis, S.: A multi-agent simulation framework for emergency evacuations incorporating personality and emotions. In: Konstantopoulos, S., Perantonis, S., Karkaletsis, V., Spyropoulos, C.D., Vouros, G. (eds.) SETN 2010. LNCS (LNAI), vol. 6040, pp. 423–428. Springer, Heidelberg (2010)
9. Yotsukura, S., Takahashi, T.: Framework of an emergency management system using different rescue simulators. Advanced Robotics 23(9), 1233–1246 (2009)
10. Araujo, R., Rocha, R., Campos, M., Boukerche, A.: Creating emergency management training simulations through ontologies integration. In: 11th IEEE International Conference on Computational Science and Engineering Workshops, CSE-WORKSHOPS 2008, pp. 373–378 (July 2008)
11. Pan, X., Han, C., Law, K.H., Claude Latombe, J.: A computational framework to simulate human and social behaviors for egress analysis
12. Garijo, M., Poveda, G., Serrano, E.: EscapeSim website, https://github.com/gsi-upm/EscapeSim
13. Garijo, M., Poveda, G., Serrano, E.: EinSim website, http://minsky.gsi.dit.upm.es/~gpoveda/einsim/
14. Alcarria, R., Robles, T., Morales, A., Cedeno, E.: Resolving coordination challenges in distributed mobile service executions. International Journal of Web and Grid Services 10(2), 168–191 (2014)
15. Chung, J., Gonzalez, G., Armuelles, I., Robles, T., Alcarria, R., Morales, A.: Experiences and challenges in deploying OpenFlow over real wireless mesh networks. IEEE Latin America Transactions (Revista IEEE America Latina) 11(3), 955–961 (2013)

Smart Dynamic Pricing Based on ECA Rules and Electronic Ink Labeling for Retail

Diego Sánchez de Rivera, Álvaro Sánchez-Picot,
Ramón Alcarria, Diego Martín de Andrés, and Tomás Robles

Dept. de Ingeniería de Sistemas Telemáticos,
Technical University of Madrid, Spain
{diego.sanchezderiveracordoba,alvaro.spicot}@gmail.com,
{ramon.alcarria,diego.martin.de.andres,tomas.robles}@upm.es

Abstract. Product pricing requires complex task to offer customers real time information and current price values at the point of sale. Information technologies can solve the problems associated to the generation and distribution systems of the product information. In this paper, a system for autonomous price management and distribution is presented. Using ECA rules and electronic ink technologies, a simple administration task is required to configure the global system. The result is a composite of a software application module and a hardware distribution prototype working together to provide price updates in a market environment. The requirements of this system have been drawn from proposals made by some Spanish Supermarket managers during execution of the project SMARKET, a project funded by the Ministry of Economy and Competitiveness of Spain.

Keywords: management, dynamic, pricing, ECA rules, system, prototype.

1 Introduction

Over the past few years, dynamic pricing has been a strategy of optimising revenue used in various areas and industries, as well as a part of an overall management strategy. First established by airline companies, their objective was to respond to emerging and changing patterns of consumer demand. These strategies attempt to incentive the customer to buy in a way that they feel a better shopping experience. Expanding new ways of selling to other business areas which until now, it can't be done, either by the lack of resources or material complications it could lead would be a new impulse to this type of trading. New technologies can make posible novel selling techniques previously only feasible on bigger industries with a high profile of business and revenue [1].

Electronic ink as seen in his functional aspect fits perfectly in this new ecosystem. Providing unattended displays and labels we won't worry about old problems like wasting paper every time a price needs a change or a new product become offered.

According to the above, we think it is necessary to research a new way of processing sells and price establishments to provide to the big or small commerce tools they

R. Hervás et al. (Eds.): UCAmI 2014, LNCS 8867, pp. 468–475, 2014.
© Springer International Publishing Switzerland 2014

can use to take advantage of this new ways of information. With the help of new technology systems, retail companies will see the benefits of automated processing. It eases the dynamic price labour and working together with intuitive software, managers will be able to provide all necessary information to the system to work in an autonomous way. The software process, guide the price changes with no external help, taking down the costs and improving revenues [2].

Using algorithms, prices could vary in a more suitable way, attracting more interest in a certain time, getting more customers and following marketing strategies. Retail managers may implement new ways of vending, implementing new stock control methods and providing information to the systems.

The rest of this paper is structured as follows: we start in section 2 with an analysis of related work and introducing the technologies used here. In section 3 we introduce the concept of ECA rules and its relation to the system. In section 4 we present our architectural proposal of the system. Section 5 is dedicated to the software internals and section 6 we develop the necessary infrastructure. Conclusions and future work will be discussed on section 7.

2   Related Work

Smart dynamic pricing can benefit from being able to include in the business rule processing, algorithms designed to make better use of all involved variables. Mathematical procedures designed to maximize profits deriving the optimal price for each sale and production and stock levels offer the ability to produce a valuable tool for markets managers in the price establishment's tasks [3]. This may lead to take the most appropriate sale strategy at certain times, with the ability to change parameters on the fly if the expected revenues are not obtained.

These decisions can have a complex operation for the user who is not used to these aspects, or that non-technical user should know. Therefore, the use of ECA rules adapted to these decisions and the use of protocols established before in a defined marketing strategy will make it easy for the end user configurations of these techniques based on events [4].

The traditional information systems require manual labor in the process of information exchange. The events in which information needs to be updated are set by the agents involved in the sale process and often this information has to be changed manually at the point of sale. New specialized technologies supporting information are helpful in this process [5]. Facilitating the task of updating information by reusing these infrastructures avoid a waste of material and time in these procedures.

Automated algorithms were used into intelligence environments to provide best choices and improve the user satisfaction along the system count on enough information of the clients. Agent based social simulations helps create a proper notion of the customer desire and roles [6].

3   ECA Rules for Retail Management

3.1   Backgrounds and Definitions

ECA refers to the Event condition action, being a shortcut to the structure of active rules in event driven systems. The fundamental construct of ECA are relative rules of the form **On** *Event* **If** *Condition* **Do** *Action.*

Each rule consists of three parts:

The Event
It specifies the signal that triggers the invocation of the rule. The events can be received by system inputs from the external environment. The type of an event can be based on a time basis or triggering by a changed input value, also real time events also can be implemented as inputs.

The Condition
It is a logical test that, if evaluates to true, causes the action to be triggered. In some scenarios, a false evaluated condition will conduct a different action. Complex operators can be added to the condition defining complicated tests to be executed to obtain a result.

The Action
It consists of updates or proceedings which have to be performed to complete the rule. Actions that are triggered by reactive rules may also be complex

An ECA rule determines what actions are performed if a certain triggering event occurs and a certain state condition holds. This can be seen as the new algorithm generation in new commerce environment. Managers create different rules for each behavior they want in his markets.

The simplicity of an event- condition- action schema leads us to provide an easy tool directed to non technical users for a product prices control. A typical use case can be the normal price variations in a temporary stock of products, in which a dedicated ECA rule performs the action of varying the price automatically, saving time and resources.

In the next section we focus on the main use cases our system can be helpful.

3.2   Application Scenarios of Dynamic Pricing

For the simplicity of our software prototype, we focus the self-acting capacity on two mainly settings. A "happy hour" time period and external variables of control.

Happy Hour
This appellation refers to a marketing campaign based on discount a fixed percent of the price for a limited time period, getting increase encouragement of the clients to buy a selected product.

As it is a simple marketing strategy, in practice it is difficult to effectively perform real time changes on the prices of the chosen products. The use of an ECA rule and a real time price changing system, take out all the ravels of the proceedings.

External Variables
As we discussed on section 2, product expiration date is an important factor of the product lifecycle. As the expired products can't get sold, it is crucial to trade up them before that date. New pricing systems can pull the users for a quick dispose if the price changes according to expire dates. ECA rules again are useful for letting the manager operate price algorithms.

4   Solution and Architectural Design

In this section we propose a system design to provide the necessary tools for an autonomous dynamic price system. The system overview can be seen over the next figure.

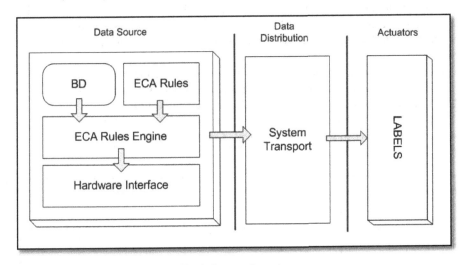

Fig. 1. System Overview

The system is divided in several components (see Fig. 1) contributing to provide information to the actuators.

4.1   Data Source

First phase of the diagram centers on the data collection and processing to generate the price changes actions. The software gathers data both from the product database and the ECA rules inserted by the market manager. Databases provide essential information such as regular prices and expiration which the ECA rules use to induce the price updates. Once the actions are triggered, the hardware interface delivers the information to display through the system transport to the labels.

This package is the main component of the dynamic management software installed in a dedicated computer on the required location. It is connected to the actuators over an exclusive link to the actuators, relaying the communication in a eligible transfer technology.

4.2   Data Distribution and Actuators

Data distribution relay the transfer of information between the source to the actuators, and it is responsible of manage the multiple labels connected to. It has to discern between all actuators and display the information only in the desired label. We will discuss our hardware solution in chapter 6.

5   System Development Based on ECA Rules

In this section we explain the software solution that we have developed to offer a relative simple interface to manage ECA rules and its implications to the generation of the proper triggers for a price change. The software will present a graphic interface in which the qualified personal has to model the rules they want to apply in the labels connected.

Proposed software was design to comply with the principles of Software as a Service (SaaS) architectures. Therefore, the main capabilities we have considered in this design are distributed architecture and event-driven architecture.

Human agents and software agents can, consequently, interact with this architecture creating events in a live environment. Conditions are evaluated continually to provide real time actions to the actuators.

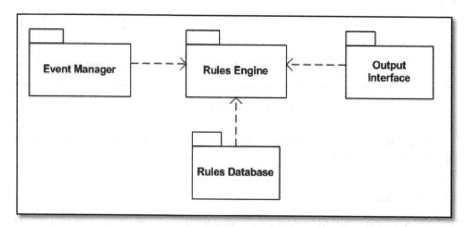

Fig. 2. Component view

System interface consists in two differentiated sections: a static information sender and a real time events configuration. This second section hosts the ECA rule engine for the dynamic price functionality.

Fig.2 shows the relationships between all major components in the software module. The main engine which controls all incomings events is the rule manager, as it is responsible of the condition evaluations to generate the triggers.

Once an event reaches the system, the rule engine checks its database to perform corresponding ECA validations and send the information over the output interface. Events can be received from several ways. In this prototype we are focusing on time based and user inputs events. A time based event will be generated when a certain amount of time has passed, causing the rules engine to check for new incoming changes of the information.

6   Development of a Provision Infrastructure Based on e-ink Displays

We present here a novel data distribution system to provide the required tools for a working dynamic price scenario. In Fig. 3, a diagram shows the necessary components needed in the labeling system.

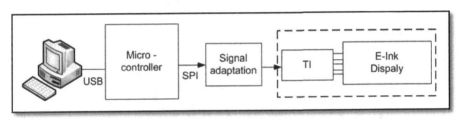

Fig. 3. Modules diagram

6.1   Micro-Controller

A computer based controller is needed to provide some intelligent actions to the labeling system. This component is responsible of discern between all installed displays and send the adequate information to the desired one. Furthermore, it supplies the pc interface to the software agent and this connection can be made wireless if the controller is capable of it. In our prototype we chose an Arduino Mega with an USB interface to the manage program.

Arduino SPI interface is used to communicate with the connected displays, by using a common bus and a selection signal we are capable of select the final display in which the information will show up. SPI consists in a bidirectional connection, using two signals wires, one clock and one chip-select wire in order to pick out the desired receptor in a shared bus.

A battery can be used to power the micro-controlled, as the amount of energy used by the system is kept down at idle times and only used when a new display change is received.

6.2   Signal Adaptation

For a correct work of the signals between micro-controller and e-ink displays, a selection and adaptation module has to be placed. Arduino digital outputs are 5 volts [v] powered, while display input ports are 3v. A level-shifter is needed in order to connect them to the main controller.

In addition, we also use the signal adaptation module to unlink the e-ink displays whenever there is no information being transmitted, decreasing the power impact of the energy source.

6.3   E-ink Display

Labels have been designed to show essential information to market customers, they use a e-ink technology providing a paper like look and minor power consumption. Manufacturer "Pervasive Displays Inc." supply 2,7" displays which we use in the pretotype.

An e-ink label is composed of an e-ink display and a "Timing Controller" module, which allows us to link up the displays using a SPI interface

Next figure shows the working prototype.

Fig. 4. Data distribution & Labelling Prototype

7   Conclusion and Future Work

In this paper dynamic price generation software and a provision infrastructure for markets was presented. ECA rules in addition to price production algorithms facilitate the configuration of the system to non-technical users. A novel infrastructure based on e-ink displays helps the automatic price change duty in order to allow real time price information to the customers.

Some scenarios were tested in a controlled environment, using a wired connection to provide the information to the data distribution system we proved the correct operation of the complete schema.

Following to this first accomplishment, further tests are planned to improve the functionalities of the software and enhance the interface connection to the distribution module.

The use of wireless protocols instead of a USB link will lead to a proper autonomous work. Ability to use different algorithms for each type of products and allow introducing thereof in a real time environment will enable a more satisfactory use of the proposed system.

References

1. Bianchi, C., Bivona, E.: Opportunities and pitfalls related to e-commerce strategies in small–medium firms: A system dynamics approach. Syst. Dyn. Rev. 18, 403–429 (2002), doi:10.1002/sdr.256
2. Robles, T., Alcarria, R., Morales, A., Martín, D.: Supporting variability dependencies for rule-based service compositions in prosumer environments. International Journal of Web and Grid Services 10(2/3) (2014)
3. Gaimon, C.: Simultaneous and dynamic price, production, inventory and capacity decisions. European Journal of Operational Research 35(3), 426–441 (1988)
4. Heimrich, T., Specht, G.: Enhancing ECA Rules for Distributed Active Database Systems. In: Chaudhri, A.B., Jeckle, M., Rahm, E., Unland, R. (eds.) Web Databases and Web Services 2002. LNCS, vol. 2593, pp. 199–205. Springer, Heidelberg (2003)
5. Gonzalez-Miranda, S., Alcarria, R., Robles, T., Morales, A., Gonzalez, I., Montcada, E.: Future Supermarket: overcoming Food Awareness challenges. In: Seventh International Conference on Innovative Mobile and Internet Services in Ubiquitous Computing, ICDS 2012. Asia Univ., Taichung (2013)
6. Serrano, E., Moncada, P., Garijo, M., Iglesias, C.A.: Evaluating social choice techniques into intelligent environments by agent based social simulation. Information Sciences 286, 102–124 (2014)

Personalisation of Intelligent Homecare Services Adapted to Children with Motor Impairments

Miguel Ángel Valero[1,2], Maria Lindén[2], Juan Ramón Velasco[3], and Mats Björkman[2]

[1] Dep. of Telematic and Electronic Enginering, Universidad Politécnica de Madrid, Spain
mavalero@diatel.upm.es
[2] School of Innovation, Design & Engineering, Mälardalen University, Västerås, Sweden
{maria.linden,mats.bjorkman}@mdh.se
[3] Departamento de Automática, Universidad de Alcalá, Spain
juanramon.velasco@uah.es

Abstract. Ambient Intelligence could support innovative application domains like motor impairments´ detection at the home environment. This research aims to prevent neurodevelopmental disorders through the natural interaction of the children with embedded intelligence daily life objects, like home furniture and toys. Designed system uses an interoperable platform to provide two intelligent interrelated home healthcare services: monitoring of children´s abilities and completion of early stimulation activities. A set of sensors, which are embedded within the rooms, toys and furniture, allows private data gathering about the child´s interaction with the environment. This information feeds a reasoning subsystem, which encloses an ontology of neurodevelopment items, and adapts the service to the age and acquisition of expected abilities. Next, the platform proposes customized stimulation services by taking advantage of the existing facilities at the child´s environment. The result integrates Embedded Sensor Systems for Health at Mälardalen University with UPM Smart Home, for adapted services delivery.

Keywords: Adapted services, children, disabilities, home embedded sensors.

1 Introduction and State of the Art

Ubiquitous Computing and Ambient Intelligence (AmI) bring forwards innovative opportunities to provide key health services at the Point of Care [1]. The availability of smart monitoring solutions at home can provide medical doctors, physiotherapists and carers with reliable data about people´s health status when required. This facility could trigger secondary and tertiary prevention activities to reduce disease related complications for children with musculoskeletal impairment, as stated by the World Health Organization and the World Bank [2]. This paper details EDUCERE, a set of child adaptable smart care services that use AmI paradigm for early attention of motor impairments in children who are often not diagnosed or treated by health care entities.

The Council of Children With Disabilities of the American Academy of Pediatrics pointed out in 2006 the possibility to identify infants with developmental disorders at

R. Hervás et al. (Eds.): UCAmI 2014, LNCS 8867, pp. 476–479, 2014.
© Springer International Publishing Switzerland 2014

the home scenario [3]. Thus, the personalised analysis of children's interaction with the daily life objects, such as toys or home furniture, could help to find out potential disorders on their neurodevelopment in a natural way. This new smart environment for the child needs data acquisition from embedded intelligence sensor systems in order to provide an adaptable reasoning subsystem with real time data that supports decision taking according to scientific knowledge about the children´s evolution. The service must take into account that usability, reliability and privacy of such systems are critical to guarantee a natural and safe interaction of the child, and this requires a user-centred development approach [4].

Embedded Sensor Systems can support the use of smart-objects based interaction to acquire and process physiological and environmental parameters at home. Example of interesting parameters to monitor is motion parameters, as activity levels and deviations from normal behavior, position, acceleration, and motion patterns for daily interaction. Multiple innovations demonstrate the feasibility to manage the interaction with the environment of people with movement disorders for homecare [5, 6].

The aim of this research paper is to show the design and integration of EDUCERE adaptable home healthcare services, which use the potential of embedding sensors in toys and pieces of furniture, in order to carry out smart prevention and early attention of motor impairments by monitoring and stimulating children´s physical activities.

2   System Design for Adaptive Home Healthcare Services

This research requested to design a set of children centred adaptable home healthcare services that rely on the personalisation capabilities of the system according to the expected human interaction procedures. Thus, the system functionality was defined by starting from the user characterization at the home environment. Further to the modelling of users´ needs or wants, published by Skillen et al. in 2012 [7], the system should have scientific knowledge about the children's neurodevelopment and motor impairments. Orlin et al. validated the age and Gross Motor Function Classification System (GMFCS) to test the participation of children with physical disabilities in home and community activities [8]. In this way, the service could monitor children´s interaction at the home through their participation, defined as 'involvement in life situations' by the International Classification of Functioning, Disability and Health.

UML 2.0 communication diagrams facilitated the modelling of the interactions of the embedded intelligence daily life objects (home´s furniture and toys) with the child, the family and healthcare staff. Thus, involved experts got a clearer view of the system by describing its static structure and behaviour. Fig 1. shows the interaction process between the child (C), the ambient sensors (AS), the local reasoner (R), the health professionals (P), the smart toys (S) and the furniture (F). E.g.: AS detect the presence of C and report R which initiates S; S records how C plays with it and AS record other interactions between C and F; R gets data from S and AS and reports P who is able to readapt the behaviour of S related to some development items (i).

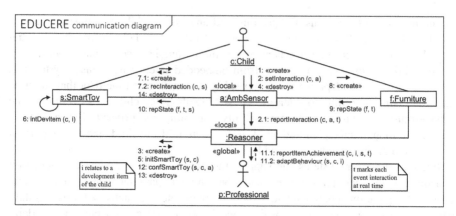

Fig. 1. Child-centred adaptable system and service behaviour

3   Service Integration and Testing

The service testing requires integrating devices and Embedded Sensor Systems for Health, developed at Mälardalen University, with the customisable reasoning platform deployed at UPM Smart Home. This living lab provides a real bedroom, living room, kitchen and bathroom to test the child´s interaction with daily life objects. Full system can provide feedback from available motion sensors, connected home appliances and three prototyped smart toys, which are natural for children to play with: a carpet, a teddy bear and a ball. The home gateway is in charge of suggesting stimulation tasks by activating lights and sounds though open X.10 commercial devices.

The smart toys are connected to the local reasoning subsystem that manages the data acquired by embedded sensors. The absence of neurodevelopment ontologies led to develop one from scratch starting from scientific knowledge about children´s growth. Thus, the subsystem takes into account the children´s development items to adapt its follow-up services to their specific age and acquired abilities. In this way, the solution supports personalized intelligent health services at home that utilize ad hoc smart toys and ambient sensors to infer potential disorders, suggest stimulation activities and securely provide health care experts with valuable real time feedback.

EDUCERE defines three categories to group the children according to their lower and upper limbs skills acquisition: a) zero to one, b) one to three and c) three to six years old. The smart carpet addresses to group a) whose aim is to use motion and pressure sensors to test how the children start to move, lay on the carpet and crawl. Next, the smart teddy bear allows to identifying and stimulating the use of upper limbs at group b) by using touch and pressure detectors. Finally, the smart ball can support in category c) the follow-up of advanced lower and upper limb activities and its interaction with the home environment. The experiments will be carried out with 10 children per group who assist to a nursing school and a school for children with specific needs. Two groups of experts (teacher, physiotherapist and psychologist) will analyze how the children interact with the smart toys, the benefits of acquiring this real time data, and the ability of the system to adapt its behavior to the child´s needs.

4   Conclusions

This system goes one-step forward on existing AmI works as it takes into account the development skills of children with motor impairments to create daily life based markers that push home health services by acquiring data from the so-called "Smart Toys". The integration at the UPM Smart Home of the Embedded Sensor Systems for Health of Mälardalen University, paves the way to make research about the feasibility to take advantage of daily life objects, like home´s furniture and toys enriched with sensing capabilities, to monitor the skills´ acquisitions of children with disabilities.

Acknowledgments. Authors would like to thank the State Programme for Research, Development and Innovation, oriented to Societal Challenges, of the Spanish Ministry for Economy and Competitiveness that supported the results of this paper through EDUCERE project (TIN2013-47803-C2-1-R) and the Swedish Knowledge Foundation for supporting the research profile ESS-H and International guest professor.

References

1. Lindén, M., Björkman, M.: Embedded Sensor Systems for Health – Providing the Tools in Future Healthcare. In: Proc. of pHealth 2014 (11th International Conference on Wearable Micro and Nano Technologies for Personalized Health), Vienna, Austria, pp. 11–13 (2014)
2. World Health Organization, World Bank: World report on disability, Geneva, p. 8 (2011), http://www.who.int/disabilities/world_report/2011/en/index.html
3. Council on Children With Disabilities, Section on Developmental Behavioral Pediatrics, Bright Futures Steering Committee, and Medical Home Initiatives for Children With Special Needs Project Advisory Committee: Identifying infants and young children with developmental disorders in the medical home. Pediatrics 118, 405–415 (2006)
4. De Rouc, S., Jacobs, A., Leys, M.: A methodology for shifting the focus of e-health support design onto user needs: a case in the homecare field. International Journal of Medical Informatics 77(9), 589–601 (2008)
5. Lindén, M., Åkerberg, A.: Innovations to control the environment for persons with movement disorders: Support in home care. Recent Patents on Biomedical Engineering 6(2), 109–126 (2013)
6. Chen, L., Hoey, J., Nugent, C.D., Cook, D.J., Yu, Z.: Sensor-based Activity Recognition. IEEE Transactions on Systems, Man, and Cybernetics, Part C: Applications and Reviews 42(6), 790–808 (2012)
7. Skillen, K.-L., Chen, L., Nugent, C.D., Donnelly, M.P., Burns, W., Solheim, I.: Ontological User Profile Modeling for Context-Aware Application Personalization. In: Bravo, J., López-de-Ipiña, D., Moya, F. (eds.) UCAmI 2012. LNCS, vol. 7656, pp. 261–268. Springer, Heidelberg (2012)
8. Orlin, M.N., Palisano, R.J., Chiarello, L.A., Kang, L.-J., Polansky, M., Almasri, N., Maggs, J.: Participation in home, extracurricular, and community activities among children and young people with cerebral palsy. Developmental Medicine & Child Neurology 52, 160–166 (2010)

End-User Service Distribution
for Efficient Inter-Domain Execution

Ramon Alcarria, Diego Martín, Tomás Robles, and Alvaro Sánchez-Picot

Technical University of Madrid, Spain
{ramon.alcarria,diego.martin.de.andres,tomas.robles}@upm.es,
alvaro.spicot@gmail.com

Abstract. The problem of service distribution has been considered in the fields of task delegation, grid computing and cross-organizational interoperability. This paper proposes a process model transformation technique based on activity aggregation to efficiently distribute services between different actors involved in its execution. We propose a workflow decomposition method based on SPQR fragments and the definition of a service distribution method based on a cost model. This cost model considers not only the transmission of information between activities for data and control scopes but also the cost of activity execution in different domains. Finally we validate our method by providing a tool that introduces the distribution information into the workflow, applying our distribution method in a use case and describing the transformation process to distributed BPEL code.

Keywords: service distribution, cost model, process model transformation, SPQR-tree decomposition.

1 Introduction

Service distribution enables an efficient execution of services, located in various domains. Workflow execution models must decouple the complexity of business process implementations from the fragmentation and distribution tasks, hiding some implementation details of the business process from certain participants.

Fig. 1 shows a business process of a service described in BPMN (Business Process Modeling Notation) language, in which activities are linked in the control plane (with arrow connectors) and in the data plane (with dotted connectors). The service is fragmented into two domains, through the *Pool1* and *Pool2* swimlanes, defined in the BPMN specification.

The aim of our work is to achieve efficient decomposition into domains of a user-defined service, considering a cost model that measures the difficulty of separating any pair of activities in two different domains. We base on business process transformations, which define views to facilitate process changes (process adaptation and reuse, arrival or removal of new and existing stakeholders), abstracting from the complete workflow.

R. Hervás et al. (Eds.): UCAmI 2014, LNCS 8867, pp. 480–487, 2014.
© Springer International Publishing Switzerland 2014

Section 2 describes the concepts of service distribution and Section 3 defines the SPQR-tree decomposition technique. Section 4 describes the workflow distribution method based on the business process model abstraction technique. Finally, Section 5 describes a proof of concept based on a use case and Section 6 some conclusions.

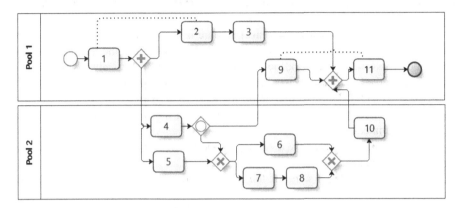

Fig. 1. BPMN service example

2   Service Distribution, Related Work and Definitions

Fig. 1 shows a business process of a service described in BPMN (Business Process Modeling Notation) language, in which activities are linked in the control plane (with arrow connectors) and in the data plane (with dotted connectors). The service is fragmented into two domains, through the Pool1 and Pool2 swimlanes, defined in the BPMN specification. The rest of the paper considers services as workflows and treat service distribution in the field of activity distribution, workflow graphs and workflow fragmentation.

Service distribution into different domains shown in Fig. 1 is justified because the participant in *Pool 2* does not have to know the inner aspect of the process that is running the participant *Pool 1*. Thus, privacy in information and processes is ensured. There may be high-coupling between activities from different swimlanes, both in the data plane and in the control plane. This implies a large exchange of data between the terminals to execute a distributed service and a lack of efficiency from the point of view of communication between terminals. We also plan to reach a distribution of activities as efficient as possible from the point of view of the exchanged data between them.

The soundness property [1] allows the correct workflow fragmentation and subsequent transformation. A process model is structurally sound (structurally correct) if there is exactly one process entry, one process exit and each activity is on a path from the process entry to the exit.

We define a k-connected graph when there is no set of k-1 elements, each a vertex or an edge, whose removal disconnects G.

The SPQR-tree decomposition is defined as a hierarchical decomposition of a bi-connected graph (meaning that if any vertex were to be removed, the graph will remain connected), aimed to identify its triconnected fragments. The modular technique of SPQR-tree decomposition provides more granularity in fragments than using a technique based on the decomposition into SESE (Single Entry edge and Single Exit edge) fragments [2,3].

We define an F fragment as canonical if there is no activity contained in F which may constitute a fragment with activities outside F. This leads to the theorem stated in [4]: A decomposition of a workflow in their canonical fragments always results in a single tree. In the SPQR model we distinguish 4 types of fragments:

S-type fragment: Contains a maximum sequence of activities.

P-type fragment: Contains a parallel split from the input to the output of the fragment, with number of branches ≥ 2.

Q-type fragment: Formed by a single connector. Because of its simplicity it will not be considered in the diagrams.

R-type fragment: When none of the above applies. R-type fragments are triconnected fragments.

A formal definition of a SPQR-tree can be found in [5]. A process model fragment obtained after SPQR-tree decomposition of a structurally sound process model is sound if the split and join semantics of the gateway nodes doesn't present structural conflicts such as deadlocks or parallel cycles. In this paper we work with sound workflows and fragments.

Fig. 2 (left) shows a SPQR decomposition of the workflow in Fig. 3.

3   Decomposing Workflow Graphs into Fragments

The fragmentation process divides the workflow into SPQR fragments with the idea that applying transformation techniques and algorithms over fragments is less complex that considering the complete workflow. The fragmentation processes are often used to check the workflow soundness [1], to prevent structural conflicts such as deadlocks or parallel cycles [6] and also to transform unstructured workflows in semi-structured or structured, for example in order to make BPMN to BPEL (Business Process Execution Language) conversion [7,8].

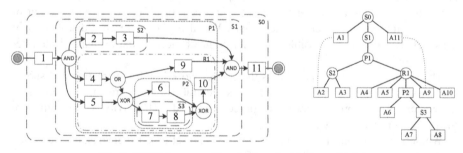

Fig. 2. SPQR decomposition (left) and related tree (right)

Fig. 2 shows a fragmentation of the workflow presented in Fig. 1. The specific process that fragments a workflow into SPQR fragments is out of the scope of this paper and is well explained in the literature [5].

We define two types of relations between canonical SPQR fragments: parent-child and predecessor-successor. These SPQR fragments can be organized into a hierarchy according to their relations. Although some authors consider appropriate to reflect just the parent-child relation [2], in our model we are considering data dependencies among activities as well.

Fig. 2 (right) shows the SPQR-tree decomposition of the structure presented in the left part of the figure. The first level of the tree contains the root node, which represents the complete workflow. From this node the parent-child relation between fragments is represented vertically and the predecessor-successor relation is represented horizontally. Dependencies between activities are represented as solid lines (relationship in the control plane) and dashed lines (relationship between data-sets in the data plane) between nodes.

We can see how the S2 fragment and the A2 activity have a parent-child relationship and are represented at different levels in the SPQR-tree. The relationship in the data plane between A1 and A2 activities is defined with a dashed line at different levels of the tree.

In the control plane the predecessor-successor relation is not included in the SPQR-tree but, in some cases, such as in the case of activities belonging to S and P fragments, this relation can be discovered, as two siblings belonging to an S fragment always follow a predecessor-successor relation (A2 and A3) whereas two sibling nodes belonging to a P fragment are always executed in parallel. In this way, we can determine that there is control relationship between A3 (end node of a branch of P, which completes S1) and A11 (next brother after S1).

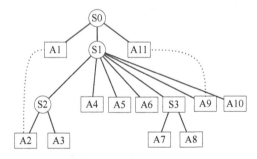

Fig. 3. SESE decomposition of example service

This fragmentation technique allows more granularity to obtain the tree of nodes than other techniques, such as those based on SESE fragments [2]. A decomposition into SESE fragments for the example service would show only the fragments in red of Fig. 2 (left) and would generate the tree of Fig. 3, which contains much less information (for example the relation between A3 and A11 activities, previously mentioned, cannot be expressed).

4   Transformation for Efficient Workflow Distribution

The defined workflow transformation process uses the *aggregation* process transformation technique to aggregate fragments in the SPQR-tree. This section defines the transformation operation, our workflow distribution method and the associated cost model.

4.1   Abstraction Technique for Model Transformation

Business process model abstraction (BPMA) has been proposed recently [2] as a technique to generate process models from a root model, preserving the overall process logic and leaving out insignificant process details in order to retain information relevant for a particular purpose. This technique is based on the abstraction process, which reduces the amount of information about a concept in order to conceptually isolate it and thus understand it better.

The application of the BPMA technique consists of the transformation of the root model to a new model, preserving the relations between original and abstracted models regarding meaning and order preservation.

It is a challenge to determine what portion of knowledge of a business process is meaningful and subject to be preserved and what other characteristics or properties are less important and will be changed or filtered in the transformed model. In the abstraction approach we rely solely on aggregation of activities, whereas other works also develop elimination techniques [9]. We use the aggregation technique instead of the elimination technique because it allows us to retain properties of the abstracted activities such as the costs of execution and communications to be used in our cost model.

We define the aggregation function as an activity transformation function $aggr(a_1, a_2) \rightarrow a'$ in which a set of activities a_1 and a_2 are transformed to an activity a'. We consider that a_1 is aggregated over the activity a_2. The number of activities will be reduced in the number of times the *aggr* function is invoked.

4.2   Cost Model

The defined cost model provides the necessary information so that the distribution of activities is as efficient as possible. Attributes such as completion time, throughput performance or hardware capacity are commonly used to calculate execution costs in workflows. Services, in our scenario, do not consider fast execution as a priority feature, but rather both the processing and communication costs.

Our model associates a normalized value [0..1] to each edge connecting a pair of activities, which represents the communication cost, and other value [0..1] in the activity itself, which represents the execution cost.

The cost function $distribCost(a_1, a_2)$ returns a normalized real number when a pair of activities is given as input to perform an aggregate function. This number indicates the degree of difficulty or unlikeness to aggregate two activities.

4.3   Workflow Distribution Method

Fig. 4 represents the defined workflow distribution method in a workflow diagram. We start from a business process annotated with cost information and the activities that belong to a particular domain. This activities are called fixed activities are the workflow distribution with be around them.

The *modelTransformation* function is the main function of the distribution method. It uses the activity aggregation technique in order to aggregate activities to fixed activities so that at the end we have all the activities in distributed domains. This function invokes the *selectCandidate* function, which returns a set of one or more candidates to be aggregated to fixed activities. The $aggr(c, a_f)$ function performs the aggregation of a candidate to a fixed activity.

The *selectCandidate* function iterates from all fixed activity neighbors and calculates the distribution cost of each pair of activities. Once the distribution cost d is calculated, activities with highest distribution cost are returned as candidates to be aggregated.

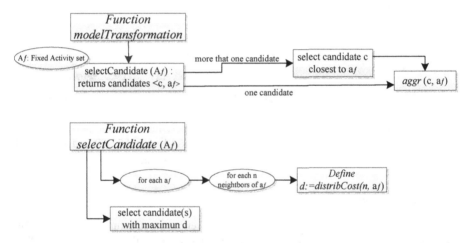

Fig. 4. Diagram of workflow distribution method

5   Distribution Method Application and BPEL Transformation

In this section we validate our defined model and method through a case study example. We have customized the Bizagi tool by creating a special activity we call fixed activity. We define *DomainID* to indicate the domain in which the activity must be executed and *SeparationCost* defines the cost model for all connectors.

5.1   Service Distribution

Using the Bizagi tool shown in Fig. 5, a document is generated in XPDL (XML Process Definition Language) and we parse the document using JDOM in order to generate a process graph with the jbpt[1] (Business Process Technologies 4 Java) tool, version 0.2.77. We use the information contained in the Activity and Transition nodes, as the information about fixed activities (DomainID) and cost of transitions (SeparationCost) is included on the label ExtendedAttributes from the XPDL document.

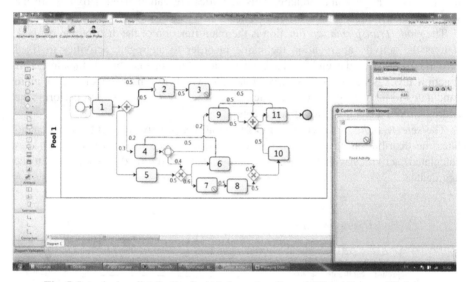

Fig. 5. Introducing distribution input information through Bizagi Process Modeler

The final result of the distribution is seen in Fig. 1, in which the service is presented with two pools, corresponding to the activities A1, A2, A3, A9 and A11 (pool of domain 1) and A4, A5, A6, A7, A8 and A10 (pool of domain 2).

5.2   Transformation to BPEL

BPEL translations are quite complex due to differences in structure between BPMN and BPEL. Since acyclic unstructured models that are directly supported by BPEL [10], R fragments are converted to flow/sequence/if BPEL fragments. The behavior of the distribution method by which preference is given to the aggregation of activities within the same fragment is justified by the subsequent association of BPEL constructs. For example, communication between nodes that belong to the same sequence (S fragment) has not a high cost while the cost of a *receive* includes the cost of data handling and the cost of correlation for every subsequent receive [11].

Sometimes, due to the processing cost related to an activity, the defined distribution method extracts it from its belonging fragment, which adds complexity to the transformation of the workflow graph to BPEL code. This occurs to the A9 activity, which is extracted from R fragment that contained it. Therefore, to perform a BPEL conversion we have to add a *send+receive* clause between the OR gate and the activity A9.

---

[1] http://code.google.com/p/jbpt/

6   Conclusion

This paper addresses the need for workflow distribution among participants to involve them in service design and distribution. Focusing in efficient distribution, we use process model transformation techniques, particularly the aggregation process (inherited from business process modeling abstraction), to distribute workflow activities depending on distribution cost model. This cost model considers the cost of transmission between activities, both at the control and in the data planes and also the cost of executing an activity in a given domain.

The main contribution of our work is to apply a decomposition based on SPQR-trees and develop a distribution method that depends on information about the activities fixed by the user in a specific domain. Our contribution provides a more efficient activity distribution than other works, due to the level of granularity provided by the SPQR fragmentation compared to other solutions based on SESE fragments.

References

1. van der Aalst, W.M.P., Hirnschall, A., Verbeek, H.M.W.: An Alternative Way to Analyze Workflow Graphs. In: Pidduck, A.B., Mylopoulos, J., Woo, C.C., Ozsu, M.T. (eds.) CAiSE 2002. LNCS, vol. 2348, pp. 535–552. Springer, Heidelberg (2002)
2. Polyvyanyy, A., Smirnov, S., Weske, M.: On Application of Structural Decomposition for Process Model Abstraction. In: Proceedings of the 2nd International Conference on Business Process and Services Computing, Leipzig (2009)
3. Vanhatalo, J., Völzer, H., Leymann, F.: Faster and More Focused Control-Flow Analysis for Business Process Models Through SESE Decomposition. In: Krämer, B.J., Lin, K.-J., Narasimhan, P. (eds.) ICSOC 2007. LNCS, vol. 4749, pp. 43–55. Springer, Heidelberg (2007)
4. Vanhatalo, J., Völzer, H., Koehler, J.: The refined process structure tree. Data & Knowledge Engineering 68(9), 793–818 (2009)
5. Battista, G.D., Tamassia, R.: On-line maintenance of triconnected components with SPQR-trees. Algorithmica 15(4), 302–318 (1996)
6. Hauser, R.F., Friess, M., Kuster, J.M., Vanhatalo, J.: An Incremental Approach to the Analysis and Transformation of Workflows Using Region Trees. IEEE Transactions on Systems, Man, and Cybernetics, Part C: Applications and Reviews 38(3), 347–359 (2008)
7. Ouyang, C., Dumas, M., ter Hofstede, A.H.M., van der Aalst, W.M.P.: Pattern-based translation of BPMN process models to BPEL web services. International Journal of Web Services Research (JWSR) 5(1), 42–62 (2007)
8. Recker, J.C., Mendling, J.: On the translation between BPMN and BPEL: Conceptual mismatch between process modeling languages. In: The 18th International Conference on Advanced Information Systems Engineering. Proceedings of Workshops and Doctoral Consortium, pp. 521–532 (2006)
9. Smirnov, S., Reijers, H.A., Weske, M., Nugteren, T.: Business process model abstraction: A definition, catalog, and survey. Distrib. Parallel Databases 30(1), 63–99 (2012)
10. Garcia Banuelos, L.: Translating BPMN models to BPEL code. GraBaTs (2009)
11. Nanda, M.G., Chandra, S., Sarkar, V.: Decentralizing execution of composite web services. In: Proceedings of the 19th Annual ACM SIGPLAN Conference on Object-oriented Programming, Systems, Languages, and Applications, pp. 170–187 (2004)

A Four-Leaf Clover Shape Methodology
for Prosumer Service Developments

Diego Martín, Ramon Alcarria, Alvaro Sánchez-Picot,
Tomás Robles, and Diego Sánchez de Rivera

Technical University of Madrid, Spain
{diego.martin.de.andres,ramon.alcarria,tomas.robles}@upm.es,
{alvaro.spicot,diego.sanchezderiveracordoba}@gmail.com

Abstract. Software development in software development organizations is a complex process and may require knowledge management techniques. If the development is oriented to the creation of a prosumer platform for managing ambient intelligence scenarios, the development could be even more complex. In this paper we present a prosumer model based on our experiences developing prosumer platforms for ambient intelligence scenarios. The model we proposed is composed of a set of six roles (users, service consumers, prosumers, advanced prosumers, platform developers and domain experts), a lifecycle for the prosumer services with eight different states and a methodology where four of the mentioned roles cooperate to develop a service provisioning platform and to propose new add-ons to improve the platform functionality in order to create services in a concrete ambient intelligence scenario.

Keywords: prosumer, mashup development, mobile service provision, prosumerization methodology.

1   Introduction

User participation and end-user development are new tendencies nowadays. A special kind of users called prosumers [1] (by the combination of the words producers and consumers) must be studied from the point of view of software development, as well as software *prosumerization* as a process of adapting software to be used by prosumers. The evolution of this especial users was mentioned by the FIA [2] (Future Internet Assembly) stressing the importance of considering them in the process of platform development and service provisioning.

We define service prosumerization as the process to allow end-users to create services with the same functionality as those created by traditional creation techniques. Service prosumerization requires the definition of a platform able to accept the participation of the users; creating, sharing and extending new functionalities. Thus, the functionality provided by prosumer services depends on the operations allowed by the design tools included into the platform. Design tools for service prosumerization have some special requirements that are not solved with current development models, such as the different kinds of roles that participate in this process, the service lifecycle and

R. Hervás et al. (Eds.): UCAmI 2014, LNCS 8867, pp. 488–495, 2014.
© Springer International Publishing Switzerland 2014

the design of a methodology that includes those new roles. These requirements are essential to provide users with tailored service creation and provision tools and are suitable for ambient intelligence platforms.

Some special requirements rise up from the design of platforms where that kind of roles are involved; these requirements are not totally solved with the actual development methodologies [3]. These requirements are essential to provide users with tailored service creation and provision tools. Apart from our previous work [1] [4], there are studies that explicitly take into account the new prosumer role but only as customer involvement in the business process [5]. Nor is there much information about the prosumerization of an existing platform and be benefited of the end-user participation and development.

In this paper we present six kinds of roles that can actively participate in the development of a platform; users, service consumers, prosumers, advanced prosumers, developers and domain experts. We also present a new service lifecycle where the possible states of a service are defined. Finally, we present an approach of a methodology for developing prosumer platforms, taking into account all the roles and stakeholders, using the services as knowledge objects [6] [7].

2   Prosumer Model, Background and Methodological Approach

The word prosumer perfectly describes millions of users in the revolution of Web 2.0, since they are more and more involved into uploading information to the network and, at the same time, they are consumers of the same one, creating what so called virtual communities. The success of these communities shows that there is a great interest in the prosumer model. For example, there are communities oriented to a prosumer market such as Ebay, others that give value to virtual objects (Second Life) and others that enable publication and consumption of multimedia content (Youtube).

These communities are based on traditional services, managed in a centralized way. This is possible because of their generic nature, and a reduced number of exploitation models. In particular, service definition, pricing, authentication, authorization, and accounting are performed exclusively by a specific service provider, in some cases an operator. Provisioning of a large variety of micro services, probably customizable by users, would require a dramatic increase of management resources. This incredible management effort coming from the provisioning of microservices for a global customer community by a single (or a small set of) service provider(s) can be evaded by delegating microservice management functions to the service provider. New business ideas are emerging for these scenarios, such as tradable microservices, which allow to be handed from one actor to another by a transfer of ownership accompanied by some monetary exchange.

This section summarizes our developments of prosumer platforms for service provisioning in ambient intelligence scenarios such as GISAI-Pharma [8], SASEP [9], holistic frameworks [10] or Goal-Oriented frameworks [11]. Section 2.1 presents a set of six roles observed during the development of the mentioned platform, Section 2.2 shows the service lifecycle composed of eight different states, and, finally, Section

2.3 proposes a methodological approach for developing, creating and improving a service prosumer platform in an ambient intelligence scenario.

2.1   Roles in Prosumer Platforms

During the developing of several platforms for service provisioning and end-user development; we have devised the following six roles, presented in Fig. 1.

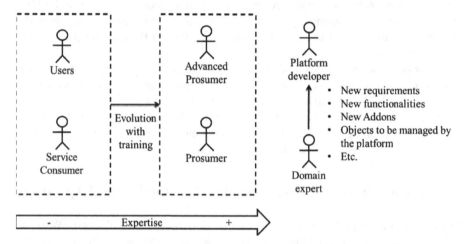

Fig. 1. Roles in prosumer platform development

Users: those who use the platform in a traditional way without exploiting the benefits of the prosumer philosophy. They only use the platform at superficial level; they don't search for services published and developed by prosumers. They also are the more passive users, and for this reason it should be taken actions to empower these users in the utilization and development of prosumer services. The best way to motivate these users is through training sessions, workshops given by other colleagues from its organization that are considered prosumers.

Service consumers: they are users who use services developed by other prosumers but currently are unable to develop their own services. They do not become prosumers but are able to consume services. They are more active than users, but they need to be also empowered with the utilization of a prosumer platform. We propose the same action (training) to motivate these users with the utilization of services.

Prosumers: they are users able to produce and consume services; the consumed services may come from its own developing as well as from the development of others; but they produce services for its own consumption. Prosumers are different from the two previous kinds of users because their producing intentions and they are different from the platform developers due to their better engagement with the platform domain.

Advanced prosumers: those prosumers who, in addition to create their own services, give enough quality to their services to share them to other prosumers. At this level we can propose the idea to monetize the work done by this prosumers. In addition, these users are able to devise new platform requirements as well as new modules, operations and add-ons; proposing them to the platform developers. These actors are very valuable for the development of the platform because they are able to generate new requirements that will improve the platform.

Platform developers: they are experienced designers and programmers who implement the platform as required by the domain specialists and the needs from the advanced prosumers. These actors are expert developers with extensive experience in application analysis, design, development and deployment, but they do not have enough knowledge about the business domain.

Domain experts: They have an extensive knowledge of the business domain where the platform was developed and they can be prosumers or not. They propose functional requirements to platform developers; they also propose new features and new objects to manage the platform. They have an executive vision of the platform and can help proposing more strategic long-term functionalities.

2.2   Lifecycle of Prosumer Services

Prosumer services can be considered as knowledge objects [12] because they enclose the knowledge required to execute functionality in a prosumer platform. As knowledge objects, prosumer services include elements that describe **how** to apply the services, **when** to apply the services, and the **resulting context** of using this pattern.

Services as knowledge objects have several states depending on their maturity, development, use, etc. In this research work we present a lifecycle composed of eight states (Fig. 2 a).

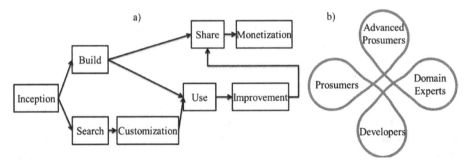

Fig. 2. a) lifecycle of prosumer services, b) methodological approach for platform development

Inception: Every service comes from an idea; a problem to be solved by the platform using its operations, functionalities, and objects that it can control etc. Services that can be created are limited by these functionalities; thus at this point it is determined which services can be created and which not. Of those who can create can proceed to the next phase: "Service Building". Advanced prosumers or domain experts can propose new operations, functionalities and new elements to be controlled by the platform; collecting new requirements for the platform developers.

Build: The service starts to exist in the prosumers' hand. They interact with the platform to create the service devised at "Service inception" state; they can create the services from scratch, from other service previously created or a service template; using the functionalities, operations and objects controlled by the platform. For service sharing the prosumer should annotate it with information describing for which problems it could be used.

Share: At this state, the prosumer can decide to share the created services, making it available for other users. For this to be possible, the service must have been used and tested, demonstrating sufficient quality. Thus, users who share services are advanced prosumers.

Monetization: When services have sufficient quality and have been tested by the prosumer who created it and those who not, the creator may think to get a benefit from sharing it; because it will solve a major problem to many prosumers and they will be willing to pay for them.

Search: A service must be shared in order to be found by another prosumer. This is the first stage that a prosumer must perform before creating a new service. It is preferable to use and customize a service already created instead of creating one from scratch because an already created service should have better quality. The platform may offer a system to find these shared services, using different query elements such as textual queries, graphical queries, queries as examples, etc.

Customization: Typically shared services do not solve exactly the problem of the prosumers who retrieve it. At this stage the prosumers must make the necessary changes to the retrieved service, using the platform. In addition, the modified services can be republished. This cannot be considered an improvement because it solves a different problem from the original.

Use: When a service is created, retrieved or customized it is ready to be executed. The platform must offer a system to control, execute and monitor the different services running on the platform with two different views. The first is the prosumers' view where they can take control of their own services. The second one is the developers' view where all the services are monitored in order to control all the system if an error occurs.

Improvement: Generally, all developments need debugging and improvement. Besides, if these developments are made by people who are not expert developers, this process should be more important to obtain sufficient quality. For this reason, the prosumer platform must enable the simulation of the execution of services. Through this simulation environment, prosumers learn to improve the quality of their services.

2.3   Methodological Approach

In this section we propose a methodological approach for developing, maintaining, improving and populating with services a prosumer platform for service provisioning. The methodology will be presented from the point of view of four of the six roles described above; thus it will have a four-leaf clover shape (Fig. 2 b). These four roles are: prosumers, advanced prosumers, platform developers and domain experts. The other two roles (users and service consumers) have not been taken into account for two main reasons: the first reason is because the platform is designed to be used by those 4 users (prosumers, advanced prosumers, etc.); and the second one because the users and service consumers have to evolve into prosumers to develop their full potential.

A platform for service provisioning would be a small or medium-sized development focused on quality, test-driven, with continuous integration. For these reasons and from our experience, we recommend the use of agile methodologies such as XP [13], Kanban [14], Scrum [15], Agile RUP [16], etc. In this particular case we recommend the use of Scrum as we believe the most useful in this kind of developments and their use is widespread. We do not recommend the use of traditional methodologies for the development of this kind of platforms which are too heavy and the end-users (prosumers) are not integrated into the development process.

Developers

Platform provisioning: Developers are responsible for the execution of the platform development process through the requirements raised up from the stakeholders such as domain experts, users, managers, etc. Platform development should be done following the classic steps proposed by the applied methodology, usually: requirements acquisition, analysis, design, implementation and testing. The most important thing is to know from whom the requirements are originated; so in user-driven developments is essential to listen to prosumers and advanced prosumers and, of course, to domain experts.

Add-ons development: When the platform is developed it is necessary to maintain it by the suggestions coming from the prosumers and domain experts. They will suggest new add-ons and features to build better and more powerful prosumer services. They will also propose new elements to be controlled by the platform.

Prosumers

Training: Users must receive specific training on the use of the prosumer platform in order to evolve into a role with more participation with the platform. This activity must be done in closeness to the developers but the prosumers and advanced prosumers can also help with these training sessions. This activity must be highly collaborative among all platform users and developers; must be practical and enjoyable using real examples or simulations. This is the best way to improve the services within the platform.

Service devise: At this stage prosumers find a problem they would like to solve. They can try to search for a service that solves the problem with little customization. If they don't find any service, they have to decide whether it is resolvable using the elements offered by the platform. If they can solve the problem they can start the next step: building. If not, they can propose new functionalities to the developers.

Building: Prosumers use the platform to build services on their own without the help of developers but they may consult with other prosumers. The developer objectives are: developing the platform, solving technical problems with the platform and developing new features.

Evaluation: It is necessary to evaluate created services because this is one of the ways to know if a service meets its requirements. Measuring several indicators shows if services are well build and can be published or whether the platform needs new add-ons.

Advanced Prosumers

Improvement: There are two kinds of service improvements: the functionality improvement and the information improvement.

Prosumers develop their own particular services thinking in solving their own particular problem; but services can solve more general problems if they are extended, creating a template or pattern of a service that can be published and even sold to other users. The advanced prosumer can use the platform service simulator to test the improvements and check whether the service can be published and monetized.

The information improvement consists of improving the service's knowledge elements that describe it. The platform uses those knowledge elements to index and search the information; so the better descriptions are the better search is performed.

Sell: When a service has sufficient quality the advanced prosumer may think about publishing the service and getting benefits selling it to another prosumer.

Domain Experts

Platform requirements: Domain experts are the main source of requirements for developing the platform at the beginning of the project when the platform is only an idea and also when the platform is deployed.

Functionality devise: The platform manages prosumer services in ambient intelligence scenarios. Those scenarios are always changing: new objects to control and new operations applicable to the objects. Therefore new needs will appear on the scenario and the platform must solve them. Domain experts are the perfect way to discover these changes.

New Add-ons proposal: As seen above, domain experts will discover new functionalities but they can also propose new elements to be managed by the platform since the elements of an ambient intelligence scenario may change; and the platform must be adapted to these changes as well. Once again, domain experts will be able to change (remove, add or replace) these new elements in the platform.

3   Conclusions

Platforms for managing ambient intelligence scenarios are a reliable solution and will gradually become more widely used. But the development and maintenance of these platforms can be a very complex process that could pose high efforts and great costs due to the number of the roles and the high interaction among them. This increased complexity may cause the project to fail. This is why in this paper we have proposed a new set of roles to be considered, a service lifecycle considering services as knowledge objects [7] used in these platforms and a methodological approach to develop and maintain a prosumer platform for ambient intelligence scenarios. These proposals are the result of our experiences in developing such platforms. As future works we propose to conduct a research experimentation to prove that the use of these three elements (roles, service lifecycle and methodological approach) proposed in this paper really offers improvements over using other classical (agile or not) methodologies.

References

1. Martín, D., Alcarria, R., Robles, T., Morales, A.: A Systematic Approach for Service Prosumerization in IoT Scenarios. In: Int. Conf. on Innovative Mobile and Internet Services in Ubiquitous Computing (IMIS), pp. 494–499 (2013)
2. Future Internet Assembly Research Roadmap v2.0. Available at the European Future Internet Portal, http://www.future-internet.eu (retrieved: May 14, 2014)
3. Carrera, A., Iglesias, C.A., Garijo, M.: Beast methodology: An agile testing methodology for multi-agent systems based on behaviour driven development. Information Systems Frontiers 16(2), 169–182 (2014)
4. Alcarria, R., Robles, T., Morales, A., González-Miranda, S.: New Service Development Method for Prosumer Environments. In: Proc. of the Sixth International Conference on Digital Society, Valencia, Spain, pp. 86–91 (2012)
5. Ohfuji, T., Noda, T.: Quality function deployment: Integrating customer requirements into product design. In: Akao, Y. (ed.). Productivity Press, New York (2004)
6. Martin, D., García Guzmán, J., Urbano, J., Amescua, A.: Modelling Software Development Practices using Reusable Project Patterns: A Case Study. Journal of Software: Evolution and Process 26(3), 339–349 (2014)
7. Martín, D., García Guzmán, J., Urbano, J., Lloréns, J.: Patterns as Objects to Manage Knowledge in Software Development Organizations. Knowledge Management, Research & Practice 10(3), 252–274 (2012)
8. Alcarria, R., Martín de Andrés, D., Robles, T., Morales, A.: A case study for validating a prosumer framework in drug traceability scenarios. In: Urzaiz, G., Ochoa, S.F., Bravo, J., Chen, L.L., Oliveira, J. (eds.) UCAmI 2013. LNCS, vol. 8276, pp. 311–318. Springer, Heidelberg (2013)
9. Morales, A., Alcarria, R., Martín, D., Robles, T.: Enhancing evacuation plans with a situation awareness system based on end-user knowledge provision. Sensors 14(6), 11153–11178 (2014)
10. Serrano, E., Poveda, G., Garijo, M.: Towards a Holistic Framework for the Evaluation of Emergency Plans in Indoor Environments. Sensors 14(3), 4513–4535 (2014)
11. Fernández-Villamor, J.I., Iglesias, C.A., Garijo, M.: A Framework for Goal-Oriented Discovery of Resources in the RESTful Architecture. IEEE Transactions on Systems, Man, and Cybernetics 44(6), 796–803 (2014)
12. Merrill, M.D.: Knowledge objects and mental models. In: International Workshop on Advanced Learning Technologies (IWALT), pp. 244–246 (2000)
13. Beck, K.: Extreme programming explained. Ed. Addison-Wesley Professional (2001)
14. Shingō, S.: A Study of the Toyota Production System from an Industrial Engineering Viewpoint, p. 228. Productivity Press(1989) ISBN 0915299178
15. Schwaber, K., Beedle, M.: Agile Software Development with Scrum. Pearson Education (2008)
16. Ambler, S.W., Nalbone, J., Vizdos, M.: Enterprise unified process. Prentice Hall Press (2005) ISBN:0131914510

Services Collaboration Supported by a B2B Platform in Retail Environment

Álvaro Sánchez-Picot, Tomás Robles, Ramón Alcarria, and Diego Martín

Technical University of Madrid,
Av. Complutense 30, 28040 Madrid, Spain
alvaro.spicot@gmail.com,
{tomas.robles,ramon.alcarria,diego.martin.de.andres}@upm.es

Abstract. The collaboration between services enables the communication between business entities in an efficient way. In order to achieve the uniformity between the provision and consumption of information we use platforms that can place different actors in the same context and that take advantage of the business architect figure, that defines the business logic implemented through the business process. In this paper it is described a platform that enables business collaboration to the exchange of product information in a retail environment. The proposed system is based on a B2B cloud based platform that provides support for the business logic and the collaboration among business partners. We validate this system through the implementation of some applications that enable farmers, food transportation companies and supermarkets to share information.

Keywords: Future Internet, generic enabler, business process, business architect.

1 Introduction

Traditionally, shopping sites have been focused primarily on providing customers with an environment that eases the access to products based on marketing techniques in the form of: fidelity cards, design of aisles, shelves layout, proper replenishment, stock management and etcetera. Nonetheless, with the advent of new shopping trends by customers willing to buy only products that match their particular ideological preferences, those shopping sites are facing the need of a revamp process to supersede those old-fashioned techniques where product categorization and information displayed on products are static and lacking of interactivity as they are no longer suitable to support the shopping process and satisfy customers demands. This revamp process takes place within the search for competitiveness in supermarkets [1] and can be achieved by harnessing the power and seamless integration of current service paradigms: Future Internet and Service collaboration.

B2B integration automates business processes shared with traditional business partners. The goal of B2B platforms is automation of the complete commerce process that involves a range of business processes (and sometimes documents), which

R. Hervás et al. (Eds.): UCAmI 2014, LNCS 8867, pp. 496–502, 2014.
© Springer International Publishing Switzerland 2014

include not just the buyer or seller of the goods or services, but also banks and third party logistics companies.

B2B has been used in retail for decades in retailers' buying and distribution systems. With maturity of the technology and the environments, more and more retail firms have deployed B2B to enhance their operation efficiency and effectiveness.

A B2B platform offers many services, but they work in general purpose solutions, not specifically tuned for any scenario. In this paper we explain how a B2B core platform that can be configured by a business architect in order to support one specific "business logic" is suitable for supporting requirements of the retail environment.

The B2B platform is deployed on the cloud, and can be thus configured and used from any Internet equipment. It is also optimized for its use in mobile devices what enables the user a great mobility.

The structure of the paper is as follows. Section 2 reviews related works with B2B platforms and retail and supermarkets environments. Section 3 explains the business collaboration process using new features presented in the Future Internet. Section 4 describes the platform created and explains the details of how the collaboration between entities works. Section 5 shows how the platform has been developed and the elements necessary to deploy it. Section 6 validates the platform explaining some applications that make use of it. Finally section 7 talks about the conclusions of this project and possible future works.

2   Related Work

Much has been said about the necessity for business to collaborate between them and about the different approaches taken to create a platform that enables this collaboration between different entities [2][3]. Some languages exist that make this task easier such as Business Process Execution Language (BPEL), Web Services Choreography Description Language (WS-CDL) or XML Process Definition Language (XPDL). This languages enable the creation and execution of workflows based on certain Business Process Modeling and some enable the user to create its own workflows [4].

In relation to the retail environment, much works needs to be done to use the new technologies to offer more and clearer information to the user [1]. Today the user expects more information in his hands so he can clearly analyze all options and buy the one he thinks is better. Supermarkets are slowly evolving in order to satisfy the customers and are adapting new technologies in their stores offering a more vivid experience for the user. Some examples of these technologies are the use of interactive displays to let the users explore the information of the product they want to sell [5] and the use of user authentication via the smartphone so the supermarket can keep an updated user profile with credit card info so he can easily make a transaction [6].

3   Business Collaboration, a Future Internet Approach

The Future Internet (FI) tries to expand the functionalities of the actual Internet, enabling developers to easily reuse certain modules used for specific tasks. These modules are called Generic Enablers (GE) and facilitate tasks common in most projects such as managing users and its credentials, storing data in databases, managing data backups or adding a security layer in the application [7]. There is a lot of different private software that solves those previously mentioned problems, but one of the ideas in the FI is to create an open source and universal solution for, these and more to come, problems with the benefits that implies that everyone is using the same modules.

This project uses some of those GE and expands its functionality to enable business collaboration and creates a platform that anybody could use to offer its own information and benefit from other's entity data, ideally generating a global B2B collaboration platform for the retail environment. In this way everything related to the retail environment would be standardized and everybody could access the public data in this platform and use it to its own benefit generating new applications that exploit the platform and offering some new data to that platform.

This platform could be easily expanded to other areas creating specialized platforms that share the information within its entities. Most of the work to create other platforms is already done enabling the data exchange, data storage, user management and much more functionalities. Also new functionalities added to one platform could be easily exported to the others.

4   A FI-Based Solution for Service Collaboration

In this chapter it is explained how the platform works, what are its components and how they interact. Initially we describe how a business architect, defining the role, loads the business models in the platform and how the models include some rules in order to process the data properly defining some boundaries. Should those boundaries be exceeded an Expert System will be informed and it will respond with some actions to execute.

4.1   Loading in the Platform the Scenery Model

The main role in the platform is the Business Architect that is the one whose task is to configure the platform with all the parameters necessary for a retail environment and also to extend it with future needs. He also has to load and later manage the models uploaded to the platform that define the message interaction. The whole structure of the platform and the different entities can be observed in Figure 1.

We can identify 3 main components in the structure. First there is the Management Information System (MIS) that provides the data that comes into the platform and has been initially configured with some parameters with the messages structure to send the information and communicate with the Core Platform. One example of a MIS is a sensor network in a farm that from time to time recollects data and sends it for a later evaluation.

In the middle we have the Core Platform that allows Business Collaboration through messages, communicating both the MIS and the application logic. It also contains certain rules that are applied to the data received from the MIS and checks if they are within the predefined boundaries.

Finally applications connect to the platform in order to receive information from

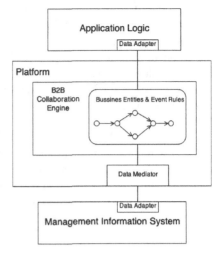

Fig. 1. Platform Structure

one or more MIS and they also contain the logic necessary to process that information and actuate should something have gone wrong.

4.2 Business Process Design and Data Flow

The main idea of the platform is to enable different entities communicate easily allowing data flow and automated process that manages this information and can analyze the data and find problems applying some predefined rules.

The whole communication process in the business platform and how the data flows through the Core Platform and the interaction of different agents with this information can be seen in figure 2.

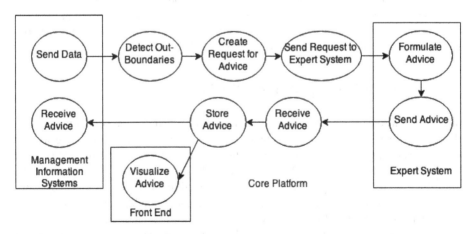

Fig. 2. Data flow

We can identify four different entities in the flow. The first one is the Management Information Systems that is where the information originating from the sensors, or any other data it is processing, is evaluated. Should some of the information indicate some problem, MIS also expects an advice from the Expert System in order to try to solve the problem following the instructions included in the advice.

Another entity is the Expert System that processes requests coming from the MIS and following some internal rules it generates some instructions in order to solve the problem requested.

Another entity is the Core Platform that is a data bus that communicates the MIS and the Expert System and can store the advices generated.

The final entity is the Front End that enables a user to visualize the information stored in the platform. It can be accessed from anywhere with an Internet connection as the interface is optimized both for desktop and mobile devices.

The data flow starts with the Management Information Systems sending new data. If that data is not inside some previously defined boundaries, an advice is created and forwarded to the Expert System. Otherwise, if the data is between those boundaries nothing happens as everything is expected to be working properly.

The advice is created using a previously defined structure that includes the data sent by the MIS as

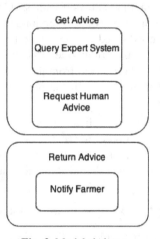

Fig. 3. Model skeleton

seen in Figure 3. This advice can ask both for the help of an expert system or for a human advice. Once the Request for Advice arrives at the Expert System it processes the advice and formulates a new advice that will contain the necessary steps to follow given the data received. The Expert System sends the advice to the Core Platform that will then proceed to store it so that it can be later accessed and visualized in the Platform Front End. After that the advice is sent to the MIS that once received will continue processing the information in the advice.

5   Platform Development and Deployment

The Core Platform has been developed mainly in Java using some collaboration tools that greatly facilitates the development and the collaboration of a lot of people such as code repositories, in order to store the different versions and keep a history with all the changes made in the code. The interface of the applications that make use of the platform are created using HTML5 and other related technologies so that they work both in a desktop environment and in a mobile one and are independent of the operating system. The servers of these applications use various technologies such as NodeJs and Java and serve the interface to the client, communicate with the platform and apply certain logic with the data received and sent. The messages interchanged through the platform are xml files with a structure predefined by the Business Architect and the models uploaded to the platform.

The deployment of the platform is in servers in the cloud, expecting a high uptime due to having backup machines, should the main ones have problems. Also data backups are created periodically and a generic enabler manages the platform users and another one takes care of the security. During maintenance machines can be easily put down and new one can be turn on due to everything being working with virtual machines. And if more resources are required new virtual machines are created to support the main ones and balance the load. Similarly if some machines are not required they are turned off in order to save resources.

The client requires no special software in their devices as all the information is accessed through the browser, anyhow, special applications can be created for platform specific access such as in Android or iOS if they are considered necessary in order to improve the customer experience.

6   Validation

The scenario presented in this paper has been validated creating some applications that make use of the platform functionalities. One of those applications is the Product Information App that enables users in a supermarket to scan a product barcode and obtain all the information related to that product in its lifecycle from the farmer to the supermarket including the supply chain. It also shows information related to the product itself such as for example calories, fats and sugars.

These applications make extensive use of the platform requesting information from the different systems and gathering the responses in order to present them to the user. It also gives feedback to the other entities in the supply chain, enabling the user to rate the product and optionally making some comments about it. This information is sent through the platform and the corresponding entity receives the information that then can act gathering more information about the product or sending messages to other entities in the supply chain.

7   Conclusions and Future Work

Business to business collaboration is evolving towards offering a more specific solution designed to solve a specific problem. Automated process are required to monitor the data and solve most of the tasks, but human intervention is still required and should be quickly informed about a specific problem with access to as much information as possible.

The more interactions there are in this kind of platforms, the more beneficial it is to all its entities. In the future we seek a standardized B2B platform that offers all the basic tools and easily enables the creation of new ones as new problems arise. The easier the platform the more users adopt it, allowing more information exchange. This is the objective of the Future Internet, to offer universal and open source tools for everybody to easily use and collaborate.

Acknowledgement. This work was supported by the projects FIspace (E13 0925-405) and CALISTA (TEC2012-32457).

References

1. Gonzalez-Miranda, S., Alcarria, R., Robles, T., Morales, A., Gonzalez, I., Montcada, E.: Future Supermarket: Overcoming Food Awareness Challenges, Madrid, Spain, pp. 483–488 (2013)
2. Morales, A., Robles, T., Alcarria, R., Cedeño, E.: On the Support of Scientific Workflows over Pub/Sub Brokers, Madrid, Spain, pp. 10954–10980 (2013)
3. McAfee, A.P.: Enterprise 2.0: The dawn of emergent collaboration, pp. 21–28. MIT (2006)
4. Martin, D., Alcarria, R., Robles, T., Morales, A.: A Systematic Approach for Service Prosumerization in IoT Scenarios, Madrid, Spain, pp. 494–499 (2013)
5. Strohbach, M., Martin, M.: Toward a Platform for Pervasive Display Applications in Retail Environments, Heidelberg, Germany, pp. 19–27 (2011)
6. Urien, P., Piramuthu, S.: Framework and authentication protocols for smartphone, NFC, and RFID in retail transactions, Paris, France, pp. 77–82 (2013)
7. Moltchanov, B., Rodriguez, O.: Generic enablers concept and two implementations for European Future Internet test-bed, Turin, Italy, pp. 304–308 (2014)

Feature Based Similarity Measure

Shreeya Sengupta, Hui Wang, William Blackburn, and Piyush Ojha

School of Computing and Mathematics,
University of Ulster, Jordanstown BT370QB, UK
sengupta-s@email.ulster.ac.uk, {h.wang,wt.blackburn,pc.ojha}@ulster.ac.uk

Abstract. This paper proposes a feature based similarity measure. The proposed measure calculates the likeness between two time series based on the number of common features between the series. This approach is different from the commonly used approach of estimating likeness based on the distance or similarity between two series. The approaches based on the distance or similarity between two series often interpret the series either as a numeric series or a text series. This however, may not always be desirable. Interpreting some series, such as video from a 'human vision' perspective is favourable over interpreting them as simple numeric or text series. The feature based measure proposed in this paper attempts to interpret video series from a human viewpoint. It considers objects and their relative spatial and temporal positions while estimating likeness between two video time series. It also attempts to handle spatial and temporal variabilities, which abound in videos by extracting spatio-temporal invariant features. This paper introduces the measure and presents some very initial evaluation of the proposed measure. Initial results are encouraging and shows a future research possibility.

Keywords: similarity measures, video activity recognition, SIFT features.

1 Introduction

Similarity measures are algorithms that measure the degree of likeness between two given time series based either on the distance between them or by the similarity between them. This degree of likeness plays a crucial role in the classification of a time series. A series is often classified to the class whose members have maximum likeness with the series. Some of the widely used similarity measures in the classification literature are Euclidean (EUC) [1], dynamic time warping (DTW) [4], longest common subsequence (LCS) [2] and all common subsequence (ACS)[7]. While EUC and DTW are distance based measures, LCS and ACS are similarity based measures. Distance based measures are often applied on numeric time series and similarity based measures are applied on text time series. So, any time series (financial, medical, video, audio) irrespective of their field is considered either as a numeric series or as a text series. However, interpreting any series

R. Hervás et al. (Eds.): UCAmI 2014, LNCS 8867, pp. 503–510, 2014.
© Springer International Publishing Switzerland 2014

as either a numeric or a text series may not always be desirable. For example, in a video activity time series following situations may arise:

- Same activity video may be shot at varying scale due to the distance of the subject from the camera.
- Same activity may be performed at different time (nighttime or daytime).
- The time taken to perform an activity may vary from subject to subject.
- The video may have several subjects instead of one and activities of each of them need to be recognised. For example, CCTV footages of a railway station or an airport or a bus station offer a scenario where several subjects are involved.

The above situations give rise to several challenges that needs to be addressed while computing the likeness between two activity time series. Space and time variabilities, also known as spatial and temporal variabilities arise due to the first three situations; while in the last situation occlusion is a challenge. Thus, there is a need for an algorithm which can measure the degree of likeness by overcoming these challenges. Further, such a measure is favourable which computes likeness between videos by considering the objects in them, the relative spatial and temporal positions of the objects, the foreground and the background of the videos. In other words, it compares two videos from the perspective of a 'human vision'. This paper proposes a new similarity measure which attempts to calculate the likeness between two activity video series from the viewpoint of a 'human vision'. The next section (Section 2) introduces the measure in detail.

2   Feature Based Similarity Measure

The feature based similarity measure is described in Algorithm 1. Algorithm 1 takes as input two videos: a test video $vt(x, y, t_i)$ and a training video $vtr(x, y, t_j)$. Both the videos have a certain number of frames $f_{t_i}(x, y)$ and $f_{t_j}(x, y)$. For each frame in both the videos, keypoints and SIFT features are computed. Further, the number of common keypoints between the two videos $(K_{vt,vtr})$ is computed by taking a cumulative sum of the number of common keypoints $(K_{f_{t_i}, f_{t_j}})$ between each pair of frames (f_{t_i}, f_{t_j}). In the pair of frames considered one frame is from video $vt(x, y, t_i)$ and other is from $vtr(x, y, t_j)$. The main idea of Algorithm 1 is that similar videos may have more keypoints in common than dissimilar videos.

3   Similar Work

The similarity measure proposed in this paper has similarities to the region based image similarity proposed in [6]. In the measure proposed in [6], first, for a pair of test image and training image (referred to as reference image by Shashikanth and Kulkarni), keypoints and SIFT descriptors were computed. Then, the keypoints that were common to both the images were computed and a SIFT score between them was calculated by SIFT matching. Further, the test and the reference

Algorithm 1. Feature Based Similarity Measure

Input: A test video $vt(x, y, t_i)$ with $f_{t_i}(x, y)$ frames where $i = \{1, 2, \cdots, q\}$
A training video $vtr(x, y, t_j)$ with $f_{t_j}(x, y)$ frames where $j = \{1, 2, \cdots, p\}$

Output: $K_{vt,vtr}$

For each frame in $vt(x, y, t_i)$ and $vtr(x, y, t_j)$ compute keypoints $K_{vt} = \{\kappa_{f_{i_i}}\}$ and $K_{vtr} = \{\kappa_{f_{t_j}}\}$ and SIFT features $\Delta_{vt} = \{\delta_{f_{t_i}}\}$ and $\Delta_{vtr} = \{\delta_{f_{t_j}}\}$ respectively.

while $i \neq q$ and $j \neq p$ **do**
    For a pair of frames $(f_{t_i}(x, y), f_{t_j}(x, y))$, calculate the number of keypoints $K_{f_{t_i}, f_{t_j}}$
    present in both the frames
end while

Add all the $K_{f_{t_i}, f_{t_j}}$ to obtain the total number of common keypoints $K_{vt,vtr}$ between $vt(x, y, t_i)$ and $vtr(x, y, t_j)$

---

images were segmented and the belongingness of the keypoints to the segmented regions were determined by region based segmentation. The SIFT score for the matched keypoints and the belongingness of the keypoints were then provided as inputs to a fuzzy based matching system. The fuzzy system, based on some defined fuzzy rules, calculated the similarity between the test and the reference images. Shashikanth and Kulkarni termed this measure as "region similarity".

The algorithm proposed in this paper (Algorithm 1) introduces a preliminary method, simpler than region similarity measure, to estimate similarity between test and training videos using SIFT features. Without the use of segmentation and fuzzy logic, Algorithm 1 estimates a measure of similarity by simply counting the number of common keypoints between test and reference videos. Figure 1 compares the derivation of region based similarity and feature based similarity measure.

As can be seen in Fig. 1, the figure on the left represents the steps for computing region based similarity and the figure on the right represents feature based similarity of this paper. The measure of similarity in region based similarity depends on the score of a common keypoint and the belongingness of a keypoint to a region. The score and belongingness of a keypoint is used as inputs to a fuzzy matching system which makes the final decision on similarity. For feature based similarity, the similarity depends only on the number of common keypoints between the two input videos. The main motivation for the feature based similarity measure was to design a measure based only on spatio-temporal features, so that the likeness between two videos is obtained based on the likeness of their features (objects, foreground, background). This approach to calculate likeness is more in line with human perception of likeness (similarity).

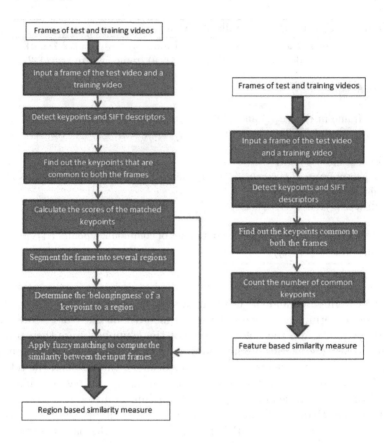

Fig. 1. Comparison of region based similarity measure and feature based similarity measure

Initial experiments were conducted to evaluate the effectiveness of the proposed feature based similarity measure. The proposed measure was applied to video activity recognition. The recognition strategy, initial experimental results and possible future works are explained in the upcoming sections.

4   Recognition Strategy Using Algorithm 1

Figure 2 shows the recognition strategy employed to recognise activities from video data using feature based similarity measure.

In Fig. 2, vt is a test video and $vtr1, vtr2, vtr3$ are the training videos. The test and the training videos are given as input to the SIFT extraction and matching block. This block is responsible for calculating all the keypoints, the SIFT features and the number of common keypoints between vt and $vtr1$, $vtr2$ and $vtr3$. The output from this block is $K_{(vt,vtr1)}$, $K_{(vt,vtr2)}$ and $K_{(vt,vtr3)}$ which represents the number of common keypoints between vt and $vtr1$, $vtr2$ and $vtr3$

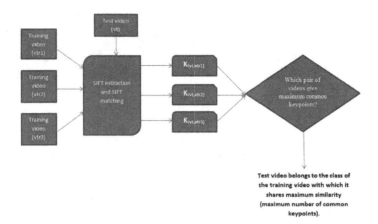

Fig. 2. The recognition strategy employed to recognise activities from videos using Algorithm 1. The SIFT matching and extraction block calculates the number of common keypoints $(K_{(vt,vtr1)}, K_{(vt,vtr2)}, K_{(vt,vtr3)})$ between the test video vt and the training videos $vtr1, vtr2$ and $vtr3$ respectively. vt is assigned the class of the training video with which it has maximum common keypoints.

respectively. The entire processing of the SIFT extraction and matching block is displayed in fig 3.

In Fig. 3, $vt(f_{t1})$, $vt(f_{t2})$, $vt(f_{t3})$, $vt(f_{t4})$ are the frames of a test video vt and $vtr1(f_{t1})$, $vtr1(f_{t2})$, $vtr1(f_{t3})$, $vtr1(f_{t4})$ are the frames of a training video $vtr1$. The SIFT extraction and matching block takes these frames as input and extracts keypoints and SIFT features from each frame of both the test and the training videos. $vt(\kappa_{ft1})$, $vt(\kappa_{ft2})$, $vt(\kappa_{ft3})$ and $vt(\kappa_{ft4})$ are the keypoints extracted from the test video vt and $vtr1(\kappa_{ft1})$, $vtr1(\kappa_{ft2})$, $vtr1(\kappa_{ft3})$, $vtr1(\kappa_{ft4})$ are the features extracted from the training video $vtr1$. Similarly, $vt(\delta_{ft1})$, $vt(\delta_{ft2})$, $vt(\delta_{ft3})$ and $vt(\delta_{ft4})$ are the SIFT features extracted from the test video vt and $vtr1(\delta_{ft1})$, $vtr1(\delta_{ft2})$, $vtr1(\delta_{ft3})$, $vtr1(\delta_{ft4})$ are the features extracted from the training video $vtr1$. After the keypoints and features are extracted, the keypoints in a frame of vt are matched with their counterparts in the $vtr1$. The keypoints common to both the videos are determined. $\kappa(ft1, ft1)$, $\kappa(ft2, ft2)$, $\kappa(ft3, ft3)$ and $\kappa(ft4, ft4)$ are the keypoints common to both the vt and the $vtr1$ videos in frames 1, 2, 3 and 4. The count of such keypoints in each frame is then added to obtain the final number of keypoints common to both vt and $vtr1$, represented as $K_{(vt,vtr1)}$. The $K_{(vt,vtr1)}$ is the output generated by the block.

Once, the count of common keypoints $(K_{(vt,vtr1)}, K_{(vt,vtr2)}$ and $K_{(vt,vtr3)}$ in Fig. 2) between a test video and a set of training videos is obtained, the recognition strategy moves to a decision block which takes $K_{(vt,vtr1)}, K_{(vt,vtr2)}$ and $K_{(vt,vtr3)}$ as input. The decision block then determines the training video that shares maximum number of common keypoints with the test video. The test

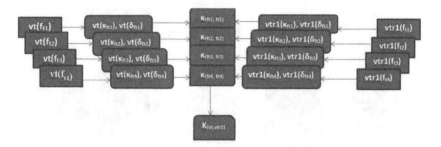

Fig. 3. The process inside the SIFT extraction and matching block of the overall recognition strategy. $vt(f_{t1})$, $vt(f_{t2})$, $vt(f_{t3})$ and $vt(f_{t4})$ are the frames of the test video vt. $vt(\delta_{ft1})$, $vt(\delta_{ft2})$, $vt(\delta_{ft3})$, $vt(\delta_{ft4})$ and $vt(\kappa_{ft1})$, $vt(\kappa_{ft2})$, $vt(\kappa_{ft3})$, $vt(\kappa_{ft4})$ are the SIFT features and keypoints extracted from the frames. $vtr1(f_{t1})$, $vtr1(f_{t2})$, $vtr1(f_{t3})$, $vtr1(f_{t4})$ and $vtr1(\delta_{ft1})$, $vtr1(\delta_{ft2})$, $vtr1(\delta_{ft3})$, $vtr1(\delta_{ft4})$ and $vtr1(\kappa_{ft1})$, $vtr1(\kappa_{ft2})$, $vtr1(\kappa_{ft3})$, $vtr1(\kappa_{ft4})$ are the frames, features and keypoints of a training video $vtr1$ respectively. $\kappa(ft1, ft1)$, $\kappa(ft2, ft2)$, $\kappa(ft3, ft3)$ and $\kappa(ft4, ft4)$ are the keypoints common to both vt and $vtr1$. $K(vt, vtr1)$ is the total number of keypoints common between vt and $vtr1$.

video is assigned the class of the training video with which it has the maximum number of common keypoints.

5   Initial Experimental Results

The recognition strategy described in the preceding section is tested with videos from the KTH and Weizmann action datasets. The KTH dataset consists of six action categories: box, wave, clap, run, walk and jog. Each of the actions have been performed by twenty five individuals under four different scenarios. Each of the action videos was further divided into four sub-videos. Thus, there were a total of 2400 sub-videos out of which only 720 sub-videos were randomly selected for experimentation. 289 videos (40.14%) out of 720 sub-videos were accurately classified using the proposed recognition strategy.

The Weizmann dataset consisted of ten action classes namely run, jump, walk, gallop, gallop sideways, bend, one hand wave, jumping jack, two hand wave, jumping in place and skip. These actions were performed by nine people and thus there were ninety videos. Forty three (47.78%) out of ninety videos were correctly classified. This performance of the strategy proposed in this paper on the Weizmann dataset was compared with the performance of Scovanner's strategy, which was reported in [5]. Scovanner et al. used three dimensional SIFT, two dimensional SIFT and multiple two dimensional SIFT along with SVM to recognise activities of the Weizmann videos. The different types of SIFT used by Scovanner et al. is represented in Fig. 4. The two dimensional SIFT is the standard SIFT proposed in [3] which is often applied to images, multiple two dimensional SIFT is the standard two dimensional SIFT applied to video data and three dimensional SIFT is the standard SIFT with a time dimension.

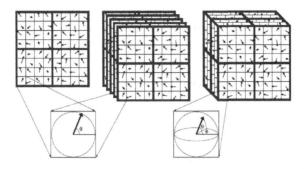

Fig. 4. Different types of SIFT as used in [5]. This figure was reproduced from the original article.

As Scovanner's method used SIFT in the recognition strategy, a comparison of their method with the one proposed in this paper was desirable. The performance of the recognition strategy proposed in this paper and Scovanner's strategy using different SIFT is shown in Table 1.

Table 1. Performance of different recognition strategies using SIFT descriptors on Weizmann dataset

Descriptor	Performance
Our recognition strategy	47.78%
Two dimensional SIFT	30.40%
Multiple two dimensional SIFT	47.80%
Three dimensional SIFT	82.60%

Results show that the strategy proposed in this paper performs better than two dimensional SIFT with SVM and performs in par with multiple two dimensional SIFT + SVM. The performances can be explained as below:

- Two dimensional SIFT with SVM performs poor with an accuracy of 30.40% because two dimensional SIFT ignores any form of time (temporal) aspect of the video data. As time is an important characteristics of videos, ignoring it leads to poor recognition of activities.
- Multiple two dimensional SIFT captures the time aspect to some extent and thus achieves an accuracy of 47.80% which is better than 30.40%. However, calculating two dimensional SIFT for each frame and then sampling them over time may not capture the true temporal information and thus, the recognition rate is not very high. The application of SIFT in the recognition strategy introduced in this paper is similar to Scovanner's use of multiple two dimensional SIFT with SVM. Hence, the performance of both the strategies are similar (47.78% achieved by the strategy described in this paper and 47.80% for Scovanner's strategy).

- Three dimensional SIFT considers the time dimension while computing the SIFT features and as this captures the time information better than multiple two dimensional SIFT, the action recognition rate is very high.

6 Conclusion and Future Work

The above application of Algorithm 1 to Weizmann and KTH videos and also its comparison with the strategy proposed by Scovanner et al. suggests the following:

- Different types of SIFT can be used to calculate feature based similarity measure. One such SIFT is the three dimensional SIFT introduced by Scovanner et al. The three dimensional SIFT incorporates in them the time dimension of the videos and thus using it may result in better activity recognition. Some other variants of SIFT that may also be used are dense-SIFT and colour-SIFT.
- In the above experiment, Scovanner's recognition strategy has not been applied on the KTH videos. A possible future work may be to apply Scovanner's strategy on KTH videos and study its performance.
- A comparison of the feature based similarity measure with the distance and similarity based measure is also desirable to further illustrate the effectiveness of the proposed measure.
- Currently, when the number of frames in the videos being compared differ, the longer video is truncated to the length of the shorter video. Attempts to avoid such ad-hoc truncation can be another possible future work.

References

1. Cha, S.H.: Comprehensive survey on distance/similarity measures between probability density functions. International Journal of Mathematical Models and Methods in Applied Sciences 1(4), 300–307 (2007)
2. Hirschberg, D.S.: A linear space algorithm for computing maximal common subsequences. Commun. ACM 18(6), 341–343 (1975)
3. Lowe, D.: Object recognition from local scale-invariant features. In: The Proceedings of the Seventh IEEE International Conference on Computer Vision, vol. 2, pp. 1150–1157 (1999)
4. Salvador, S., Chan, P.: Toward accurate dynamic time warping in linear time and space. Intell. Data Anal. 11(5), 561–580 (2007)
5. Scovanner, P., Ali, S., Shah, M.: A 3-dimensional sift descriptor and its application to action recognition. In: Proceedings of the 15th International Conference on Multimedia, MULTIMEDIA 2007, pp. 357–360 (2007)
6. Shashikanth, C.C., Kulkarni, P.: Article: Region based image similarity using fuzzy based sift matching. International Journal of Computer Applications 67(3), 47–50 (2013)
7. Wang, H.: All common subsequences. In: Proceedings of the 20th International Joint Conference on Artifical Intelligence, IJCAI 2007, pp. 635–640. Morgan Kaufmann Publishers Inc., San Francisco (2007)

Mining Multiple Discriminative Patterns
in Software Behavior Analysis

Hao Du[1], Chunping Li[1], and Hui Wang[2]

[1] School of Software, Tsinghua University, Beijing 100084, China
`duhao228@gmail.com, cli@tsinghua.edu.cn`
[2] Faculty of Computing and Engineering, University of Ulster,
Jordanstown BT37 0QB, UK
`h.wang@ulster.ac.uk`

Abstract. Sequence Classification has been a challenge task in recent years since sequence doesn't have explicit features and the high-order temporal characteristics make the number of patterns extremely massive. Pattern-based classification has demonstrated its power in recent studies by mining discriminative features efficiently. Both binary and numerical discriminative features have been utilized for effective sequence classification, but the effect of each type of features hasn't been analyzed separately. Our method selects the frequent closed unique iterative patterns as our candidate features, mined out the discriminative binary and numerical patterns for sequence classification, and given an insight into the discriminative power improvement by feature combinations. The experimental results on synthetic and real-life datasets reveal the validity of our approach.

1 Introduction

Software event sequence is a software behavior trace which is produced when software is running. Software behavior is the way that a program executes [1]. The sequence is distinct according to its various behaviors. Actually, a majority of the behaviors are normal but some abnormal behaviors fail to be expected by people. These abnormal behaviors are considered to be bugs, intrusions, malwares and so forth. All of these kinds of behaviors can be called software failures.

A series of events constitute software behavior which can be analyzed for finding out if software contains failures or not. Every event can correspond to the invocation of a method, the call of a module, and the execution of program statement, etc. These events can be recorded as the execution trace and series of these executions compose the sequence set which is the database of our analysis.

With the database of software event sequences, we consider the method of classification to distinguish normal and abnormal behaviors. Sequential data classification is a challenging topic. Some research works have been made in recent years. Classifying sequences is difficult because most classifiers deal with feature vectors but sequence data doesn't have explicit features. According to the current research, sequence

R. Hervás et al. (Eds.): UCAmI 2014, LNCS 8867, pp. 511–518, 2014.
© Springer International Publishing Switzerland 2014

classification methods can be divided into three categories, i.e., pattern based method, sequence distance method, and model based method [10].

Frequent pattern-based classification methods have shown their effectiveness for classifying large and complex datasets [1, 3, 4, 5, 6]. In pattern based classification, finding out discriminative patterns is crucial. Discriminative patterns occur with disproportionate frequency in some classes versus others, such patterns have demonstrated the considerable value for classification and subgroup discovery [2].

In this paper, we mine both binary and numerical discriminative patterns in software sequence classification. We use mutual information to find those patterns which occur in specific class but hardly in other classes, and we call them as binary discriminative patterns. As for numerical discriminative patterns, we find out those patterns with repetition time significantly distinguished from other classes using the Jensen-Shannon Divergence, and then use mutual information to find the best split number to distinguish the sequences by the repetition times. We also give insight into the independent additive pattern effect, by combining the patterns which doesn't have discriminative power itself, but the combined patterns sometimes have some significant discriminative power improvement.

The organization of this paper is as follows. Section II describes our method of mining binary, numerical and combined discriminative patterns to classify events sequences in details. Section III shows the experiment result and analysis with current existing work. Section IV gives the conclusion and future directions of our work.

2 Mining Binary, Numerical and Combined Discriminative Patterns

2.1 Problem Formulation

Let I be a set of distinct events. Let a sequence S be an ordered list of events. We denote S as $<e_1, e_2, ..., e_n>$ where each e_i is from I.

A pattern denoted as $<e_1, e_2, ..., e_n>$ is considered as a sub-pattern of another pattern $<f_1, f_2, ..., f_m>$ if there exists any integer which satisfies $1 \leq i_1 \leq i_2 \leq \cdots \leq i_n \leq m$ where $e_1 = f_{i_1}$, $e_2 = f_{i_2}, ..., e_n = f_{i_m}$. We write this relation as $P_1 \subseteq P_2$. And we say P_2 is a super-pattern of P_1.

Let $D = \{S_i, C_i\}_{i=1}^n$ where S_i represents the sequence and C_i represents the class label which has two values 0 and 1 (0 represents normal traces and 1 represents abnormal traces). The number of occurrences of a given pattern P in a sequence S is denoted as $occ(S, P)$. Based on the occurrence, we can define the function $ext(S, P)$ if pattern P exists in S as follows.

$$ext(S, P) = \begin{cases} 1 & (occ(S, P) > 0) \\ 0 & \text{otherwise} \end{cases} \tag{1}$$

In our method, the support of pattern P in sequence database D is denoted as $Sup(D,P)$, which is defined as $\sum_{S \in D} ext(S,P)$. A pattern P is frequent if $Sup(D,P) \geq \theta$, where θ is a minimum support threshold.

We choose frequent closed unique iterative pattern in [1] as our candidate pattern set. Given a frequency threshold min_sup, a pattern P can be defined as frequent closed unique pattern if P satisfies the following restraint:

(a) Sup(D,P) is higher than min_sup.
(b) P contains no repeated constituent events.

There exists no super-pattern of P which satisfies (a) and (b). The reasons we choose this approach include:

- Iterative pattern not only captures the high-order features, but also their frequencies.
- Iterative pattern considers repetition within one sequence and across multiple sequences.
- Frequent patterns are high quality features and have good model generalization ability.
- Frequent Closed iterative pattern would reduce the number of iterative patterns without any loss of information since they capture out all frequent iterative pattern.
- Frequent Unique closed iterative pattern would provide a compact set of closed iterative patterns that are composed of unique events.

We use all of the frequent closed unique patterns called *CondPatSet* in sequence database D as our candidate features. Based on these features, we would select out discriminative features of different types in the following section. During the generating process of *CondPatSet*, we also calculate the number of occurrence of each frequent closed unique iterative pattern in each sequence, represented by *nlist* = $\{occ(S_1,P),\ occ(S_2,P),...,\ occ(S_n,P)\}$ where $(S_i, C_i) \in D$ and $C_i = 0$ in normal traces and ablist = $\{occ(S_1,P),\ occ(S_2,P),...,\ occ(S_n,P)\}$ where $(S_i, C_i) \in D$ and $C_i = 1$ in abnormal traces.

2.2   Discriminative Binary Pattern Mining

There are several criteria to measure the discriminative power of pattern, such as Information Gain [11], Fisher Score [12] and Mutual Information, etc.

Mutual Information (MI) is used for filter feature selection as a measure of relevance between pattern and sequence category. Given the pattern *Pat* and class variable C, the MI between *Pat* and C is defined as:

$$MI(Pat, C) = \log \frac{P(Pat,C)}{P(Pat)P(C)} \tag{2}$$

MI can be considered as a statistic measure which reflects the dependency between *Pat* and C, We desire the selected patterns are highly dependent on the class category, but are independent between them.

2.3   Discriminative Numerical Pattern Mining

Using Mutual information, we can mine out the patterns which are highly relevant to the labeled class. But the repetition time of pattern in the sequence is ignored. However, the repetition time of pattern may be discriminative in some case. The overmuch or insufficient repetition of some pattern may denote some kind of failure.

To solve this problem, we record the repeat times of pattern P in each sequence during the pattern generation process and use Jensen Shannon Divergence (JSD) to evaluate the discriminative power of pattern by repetition. If the JSD value of repetition times between normal and abnormal classes exceeds given threshold value, we can view the pattern as Discriminative Numerical Pattern.

The Jensen-Shannon Divergence [13] is a function which measures distance between two distributions. While comparing samples by their empirical distributions, larger JS divergence indicates they may come from different classes. That's to say, the repetition time of pattern in different class differs much. The JSD is closed to the Kullback-Leibler (KL) divergence, which is a classical measure to compare two distributions. The JSD can be seen as a symmetric and smoothed variant of KL divergence since it's to the mean of distribution relatively. The JSD value between distributions P_1 and P_2 are defined as follows:

$$D_{JS}(P_1, P_2) = \frac{1}{2}D_{KL}(P_1, M) + \frac{1}{2}D_{KL}(P_2, M) \tag{3}$$

where

$$D_{KL}(P_1, P_2) = \sum_{e \in \Delta} P_1[e] \log \frac{P_1[e]}{P_2[e]} \quad \text{and} \quad M = \frac{1}{2}(P_1, P_2)$$

Through calculating the JSD value of each frequent closed unique pattern, we can choose the pattern which has a high JSD value as discriminative numerical pattern. But the repetition time bound is not explicit; the explicit bound means one of the repetition time value above or below may denote some failure. To apply the discriminative numerical pattern in the classifier, we would use mutual information to find out the proper bound. Different from the former section where the pattern exists or not, here we find out the relation between the repetitions less than or more than some value with the sequence class. The mutual information between pattern repetition time and sequence class of each split bound is shown as

$$MI(Pat_{below}, C) = \log \frac{P(Pat_{below}, C)}{P(Pat_{below})P(C)} \tag{4}$$

$$MI(Pat_{exceed}, C) = \log \frac{P(Pat_{exceed}, C)}{P(Pat_{exceed})P(C)} \tag{5}$$

2.4   Discriminative Combined Pattern Mining

In the former subsection, we have selected binary discriminative patterns and discriminative numerical patterns. But it only focused on the discriminative power of single type of patterns. In [2], the independent additive pattern and synergistic beyond independent additive pattern both have discriminative power than any of its sub-pattern. Applied in our classifier, a frequent closed unique pattern may be not discriminative binary or discriminative numerical pattern, but two kinds of patterns occurred together may have discriminative power than any one of them. The independent additive pattern set is a super-set of synergistic beyond independent additive pattern set. We would discuss the effect of independent additive pattern set here.

The Improvement Function (Imp) in the context of discriminative pattern mining based on MI is defined below, α represents the pattern set which contains two or more frequent closed unique iterative patterns:

$$\text{Imp}^c(\alpha) = \text{MI}(\alpha, C) - \text{Max}_{\alpha' \in \alpha}(\text{MI}(\alpha', C)) \tag{6}$$

Since the number of pattern combination in any size can be enormous, taking efficiency into consideration, we only select the pattern set of size 2, for example, $\alpha = \{Pat_a, Pat_b\}$, the definition for independent additive pattern is shown as:

MI (α, C) > MI_threshold, and MI (α, C) - Max(MI (Pat_a, C), MI $(Pat_b, C))$ > 0.

In the discriminative numerical pattern condition, the combined pattern can also give some more precise rules. We count the repetition time which a pattern occurs only when some specific pattern occurs, the specific pattern can be considered as conditional pattern. We calculate the Jensen-Shannon divergence value under the condition some specific pattern occurs. For example, $\alpha = \{Pat_a, Pat_b\}$, we calculate the JSD value of Pat_a only in the subset of D where Pat_b occurs in the sequence.

3   Experiment and Evaluation

3.1   Experiment Dataset

The datasets of our experiment include synthetic and real-life datasets. Synthetic datasets are CVS application and X11 windowing protocol, which are generated by using the simulator QUARK [7]. Given a software component model in the form of a probabilistic finite state automaton as input, QUARK can generate traces that represent the model following some coverage criteria. QUARK can also be able to inject errors to the synthetic traces. In this experiment, three types of errors are injected to the traces, i.e., addition bugs, omission bugs and ordering bugs. The meaning of 3 injected errors is explained in Table 1.

Table 1. Three Types of Errors

Type	Explanation
Omission bugs	Some method calls do not get called when they should have been
Additional bugs	Inject additional events resulting in failures
Ordering bugs	The order of events occurring is wrong

The real-world datasets come from Siemens Test Suite [8] and data race concurrency bugs from MYSQL [9]. There are also 3 types of errors in real-world datasets. For each sequence, the number at the end of the sequence denotes the sequence type, which 0 denotes a normal trace and 1 denotes a failing trace. In the real-world datasets, print_tokens and replace datasets are imbalanced datasets since the normal sequence number exceeds the failure sequence number a lot. The definite number of normal and failing traces and each type of errors are in the accuracy comparison table. We also perform 5-fold cross validation for each dataset, and the final result is the average accuracy average.

Since we consider both binary and numerical discriminative features in software event sequences, we select DDPMine [5] which considers only the binary patterns , SoftMine [1] and NDPMine [3] that both considers binary and numerical patterns but haven't distinguish the discriminative power of each type of pattern. Classification accuracy, defined as the number of true positives and true negatives over the total number of traces, is used as our evaluation measure. Accuracy is also the main measure used in related works. The three types of mining algorithms both have remarkable accuracy performance on sequence classifying problem, we compare the accuracy result of our algorithm MDPMine (Multiple Discriminative Pattern Mining) with three existing algorithms and analyze the effect of each type of pattern on sequence classification.

3.2   Experiment Result

We showed the accuracy of MDPMine with 3 other algorithms both on synthetic datasets (Table 2) and real-life datasets (Table 3). For each dataset, we perform 5-fold cross validation to guarantee there is no information leak, and average performance over 5-fold cross validation is reported.

We can conclude that the discriminative binary pattern plays an important role in most datasets (CVS omission, MYSQL, Schedule). The discriminative binary pattern is convenient to mine out, but it has some limitations. In some datasets, no matter how low the support threshold value is, the mined binary pattern only can detect software failure in very low accuracy. The combined discriminative patterns also show the accuracy improvement in some datasets (X11, CVS Ordering, CVS MIX and Print_tokens). For the overall results, the usage of several different types of discriminative pattern has remarkable failing trace detection accuracy with comparison with other pattern-based sequence classifying algorithms.

Table 2. Results on Synthetic Datasets

Dataset	Cor[a]	Error (|Traces|)		Accuracy			
		Add/ Omi	*Order*	*DDP Mine*	*Soft Mine*	*NDP Mine*	*MDP Mine*
X11	125	125	0	93.2	97.2	**100**	**100**
CVS Omission	170	170	0	**100**	**100**	**100**	**100**
CVS Ordering	180	0	180	96.4	96.7	96.1	**98.3**
CVS Mix	180	90	90	96.4	94.2	97.5	**98.4**

a.   Cor means Correct (|Traces|).

Table 3. Results on Real-life Datasets

Dataset	Cor[a]	Error (|Traces|)		Accuracy			
		Add/O mi	*Order*	*DDP Mine*	*Soft- Mine*	*NDP Mine*	*MDP Mine*
MYSQL	51	0	51	**100**	**100**	**100**	**100**
Tot_info	302	208	94	**92.8**	91.2	92.7	**92.8**
Schedule	2140	289	1851	92.2	92.5	90.4	**93.2**
Replace	1259	269	269	85.3	**90.8**	90.0	89.9
Print_tokens	3108	187	187	96.6	**100**	99.6	97.2

a.   Cor means Correct (|Traces|).

4   Conclusion and Future Work

Sequence classification is an important topic and has applications in many areas. It is also a challenging topic since it is hard and crucial to mine out discriminative patterns, especially for no explicit features of the high-order sequential characteristics. In this paper, by selecting frequent closed unique iterative pattern as candidate pattern sets, we recognize different types of discriminative patterns for software behavior sequence and compare the classifying results with current existing discriminative pattern-based sequence mining algorithms. We propose a novel approach to mine out discriminative numerical patterns and give an insight into the discriminative power improvement of combined features. The composition usage of these discriminative patterns results in remarkable accuracy and effect in software failure detection.

In the future work, to improve the efficiency and computation cost, we will consider converting the two-steps process of find these different features into one. We will also consider checking the validity of our approach in other application areas.

References

1. Lo, D., Cheng, H., Han, J.: Classification of Software Behaviors for Failure Detection: A Discriminative Pattern Mining Approach. In: KDD 2009 Proceedings of the 15th ACM SIGKDD International Conference on Knowledge Discovery and Data Mining, pp. 557–566 (2009)

2. Fang, G., Wang, W., Oatley, B.: Characterizing Discriminative Patterns. Computing Research Repository, abs/1102.4 (2011)
3. Kim, H., Kim, S., Weninger, T., Han, J., Abdelzaher, T.: NDPMine: Efficiently mining discriminative numerical features for pattern-based classification. In: Balcázar, J.L., Bonchi, F., Gionis, A., Sebag, M. (eds.) ECML PKDD 2010, Part II. LNCS, vol. 6322, pp. 35–50. Springer, Heidelberg (2010)
4. Cheng, H., Yan, X., Han, J., Hsu, C.: Discriminative Frequent Pattern Analysis for Effective Classification. In: Proceeding of the 2007 International Conference on Data Engineering (ICDE 2007) (2007)
5. Cheng, H., Yan, X., Han, J., Yu, P.: Direct discriminative pattern mining for effective classification. In: Proc. of ICDE (2008)
6. Fan, W., Zhang, K., Cheng, H., Gao, J., Yan, X., Han, J., Yu, P., Verscheure, O.: Direct Mining of Discriminative and Essential Frequent Patterns via Model-based Search Tree. In: Proceeding of the 14th ACM SIGKDD International Conference on Knowledge Discovery and Data Mining, August 24-27 (2008)
7. Lo, D., Khoo, S.: QUARK: Empirical Assessment of Automaton-based Specification Miners. In: Proceedings of the 13th Working Conference on Reverse Engineering (WCRE 2006), October 23-27, pp. 51–60 (2006)
8. Hutchins, M., Foster, H., Coradia, T., Ostrand, T.: Experiments on the effectiveness of dataflow- and control-flow-based test adequacy criteria. In: Proceedings of the 16th International Conference on Software Engineering, May 16-21, pp. 191–200 (1994)
9. Mysql atomicity violation, http://bugs.mysql.com/bug.pgh?id=169
10. Xing, Z., Pei, J., Keogh, E.: A brief survey on sequence classification. ACM SIGKDD Explorations 12(1), 40–48 (2010)
11. Ross Quinlan, J.: C4.5: Programs for Machine Learning. Morgan Kaufmann (1993)
12. Duda, R., Hart, P., Stork, D.: Pattern Classification, 2nd edn. Wiley Interscience (2000)
13. Fuqlede, B., Topsoe, F.: Jensen-Shannon Divergence and Hilbert space embedding. In: Proceedings of International Symposium on Information Theory (ISIT 2004), p. 31 (2004)

Person Detection, Tracking and Masking for Automated Annotation of Large CCTV Datasets

Marcos Nieto, Peter Leškovský, and Juan Diego Ortega

Vicomtech-IK4, Paseo Mikeletegi 57, San Sebastian 20009, Spain
{mnieto,pleskovsky,jdortega}@vicomtech.org

Abstract. In this paper we describe a real-time approach for person detection in video footage, joint with a privacy masking tool, in the framework of forensic applications in CCTV systems. Particularly, this paper summarizes our results in these domains within the European FP7 SAVASA and P-REACT projects. Our main contributions have been focused on real-time performance of detection algorithms using a novel perspective-based approach, and the creation of a methodology for privacy masking content such as the faces of the persons in the images.

Keywords: computer vision, real-time, detection and tracking, privacy masking.

1 Introduction

Analyzing large volumes of video footage in CCTV systems is troublesome and expensive for CCTV operators and law enforcement agencies. Companies, public institutions and the research community are pushing forward to provide technology solutions, especially in the field of video analytics, providing semantic-aware, remotely accessible, reduced-size annotations. These annotations can be stored and made accessible through VSaaS (Video Surveillance as a Service) with applications like the SAVASA system [1], or the P-REACT platform [2].

In this work we present our developments related to person detection, which can provide rich information of the scene and that can be used further by high-level semantic analysis to track persons or to recognise actions between persons. Our approach is based on a novel perspective-based for enhanced efficiency compared with traditional detection approaches.

Besides, the effective exploitation of this information must be compliant with the privacy and ethical rules of local jurisprudences, which may be very restrictive in some cases such as in Europe. In that sense, we have also worked on creating tools for masking private or protected content (e.g. detected faces in images) using standard tools and facilitating the protected reconstruction of the material with secure keys and a dedicated player.

2 Automatic Content Annotation

Figure 1 illustrates the conceptual architecture of the analysis modules of the automatic annotation scheme which includes the mentioned modules of person

R. Hervás et al. (Eds.): UCAmI 2014, LNCS 8867, pp. 519–522, 2014.
© Springer International Publishing Switzerland 2014

detection, tracking and privacy masking. Basically, this architecture shows the integration layers that can be used to connect to any CCTV system, using the proprietary SDKs of the NVR providers or standard interfaces like ONVIF. After a transcoding stage, the platform launches the person detection and tracking module, and additional feature extraction methods for high-level video analytics (more details can be found in [3]).

The detected persons are described in XML files that can then be used to build protected video files, using cryptographic methods and adding watermarking for providing digital evidence services.

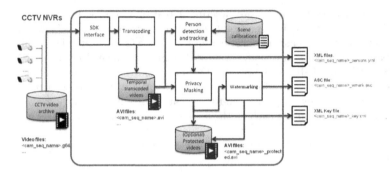

Fig. 1. Block diagram of the video analytic modules of the automatic annotation scheme

3   Person Detection

Using a default person model, we generate a grid of positions of parallelepipeds in the $3D$ world lying on a dominant plane, separated by defined steps (in metric units) [4]. The projection of the volumes defined this way provides the set of rectangles candidates to contain persons in the scene. The great advantage of this approach is that the hypotheses are all potentially correct compared to multiscale approaches, where there are a number of hypotheses whose sizes do not fit with their positions in the dominant plane. Hence the number of candidates is greatly reduced, and there is no more need to filter out absurd hypotheses (with respect to perspective) as it happens when using traditional scanning window approaches [5].

This grid-based approach can be used with any detector scheme (e.g. classifiers, foreground detection, etc) that provides a weighted output between 0 and 1. In our work, we have used two types of detectors: background subtraction and appearance-based detectors. The former are helpful to detect moving objects; the latter enhances the reliability of the system searching patterns of head-and-shoulder and full-body shapes. Analogously, when the perspective of the scene give a close view of the persons, it is possible to use face detection methods.

When densely sampling an image, several candidates partially represent each person. In Fig. 2 (right), the top view of the projected grid with the associated detection values, represented by the radius of each red circle at each cell position,

Fig. 2. Detection of 3D persons using the perspective grid (left) and an example top view of the grid (right)

is shown. Given this detection map, we obtain a refined map by removing noise and detections corresponding to figures larger or smaller than the person model. We do this by deconvolution of the map with a kernel corresponding to pixel occupancy of our person model at each grid cell.

The 3D detections are then mapped back to the image and a tracking stage associates them to existing tracks, which are then updated using the new position and size of the detections using a Kalman filter to smooth the trajectories.

The main achievement using the proposed perspective-grid detection approach is the reduction of the number of candidate regions in the images to be evaluated by the detector, along with the possibility to combine this methodology with any existing detector. To measure this feature, we have compared the use of the perspective-grid (PG) approach with a brute-force multiscale scanning window (BF-MSW) and a fine-tuned multiscale scanning window (FT-MSW) [4] in three different scenes with low, medium and far perspectives, respectively.

Table 1. Comparison of the number of candidates generated by the multiscale methods and the proposed perspective-grid (PG) method

Sequence	BF-MSW	FT-MSW	PG	PG improvement (%)
(a) TRECVID Cam1 [6]	27998	3051	2344	14,76
(b) UT-Interaction Dataset [7]	21105	2603	390	85,01
(c) IKUSI Cam3	27895	21588	8744	59,49

The fourth column of Table 1 shows the improvement of the proposed method over the results of the FT-MSW that also uses the perspective information of the scene to select the best parameters of the scanning window method. The datasets used correspond to a close view (a), an intermediate view (b) and a distant view of a parking area (c) scenes.

4   Privacy Masking

After personal or other privacy information (e.g. faces, license plates) is detected, we apply reversible occlusion of the corresponding regions in the video. We first extract the confidential regions from and occlude them in the main stream. The extracted regions are formed into privacy streams which are entirely encrypted once their encoding into desired video format has been obtained. Finally, all streams are encapsulated in common video container file. Upon video reply, we first decrypt the privacy streams and position them correctly within the main stream in order to reconstruct the original video.

Our approach to video encryption is non-standard due to the fact that there are no open or public standards which would define the application of encryption schemes to videos. We therefore followed general guidelines on encryption and key distribution applied to binary information. Especially, we followed the general cryptographic approaches applied in proprietary solutions like are DVD or Blue-ray media. The video is encrypted in its binary form with a symmetric AES cipher and the secret key used is then distributed in encrypted form, applying an asymmetric RSA encryption scheme. Private and public keys in the form defined by the OpenPGP standard protocol were used for the RSA encryption and distribution of the AES secret key among users.

5 Conclusions

We have presented an efficient methodology to exploit the perspective information of the scene to dramatically reduce the computational complexity of person detection algorithms for video surveillance applications turning it available for real-time processing. Moreover, our proposed method can conveniently be used with any existing input detector, such as background detectors, or detection-by-classification methods.

The privacy masking applied allows us to mask private information otherwise recognisable in the captured recordings and thus to comply to the strict privacy protection regulations set by the EU for distribution of surveillance videos. Nevertheless, it depends on the automatic detection of regions holding private information, which, for example for face detection, is still not 100% accurate.

References

1. FP7-SEC-2011-1 SAVASA project, http://www.savasa.eu
2. FP7-SEC-2013.7.2-1 P-REACT project, http://www.p-react.eu
3. Jargalsaikhan, I., Direkoglu, C., Little, S., O'Connor, N.E.: An evaluation of local action descriptors for human action classification in the presence of occlusion. In: MultiMedia Modeling, Dublin, Ireland (January 2014)
4. Nieto, M., Ortega, J.D., Cortes, A., Gaines, S.: Perspective Multiscale Detection and Tracking of persons. In: Gurrin, C., Hopfgartner, F., Hurst, W., Johansen, H., Lee, H., O'Connor, N. (eds.) MMM 2014, Part II. LNCS, vol. 8326, pp. 92–103. Springer, Heidelberg (2014)
5. Viola, P., Jones, M.: Robust real-time face detection. International Journal of Computer Vision, 3–7 (2008)
6. Smeaton, A.F., Over, P., Kraaij, W.: Evaluation campaigns and TRECVid. In: MIR 2006: Proceedings of the 8th ACM International Workshop on Multimedia Information Retrieval, pp. 312–330 (2006)
7. Ryoo, M.S., Aggarwal, J.K.: UT-Interaction Dataset ICPR contest on Semantic Description of Human Activities (SDHA) (2010)

Recognition by Enhanced Bag of Words Model via Topographic ICA

Min Jing[1,*], Hui Wang[1], Kathy Clawson[2], Sonya Coleman[1], Shuwei Chen[1],
Jun Liu[1], and Bryan Scotney[1]

[1] University of Ulster, UK
[2] Middlesbrough College, UK

Abstract. The Bag-of-Words (BoW) model has been increasingly applied in the field of computer vision, in which the local features are first mapped to a codebook produced by clustering method and then represented by histogram of the words. One of drawbacks in BoW model is that the orderless histogram ignores the valuable spatial relationships among the features. In this study, we propose a novel framework based on a topographic independent component analysis (TICA), which enables the geometrically nearby feature components to be grouped together thereby bridge the semantic gap in BoW model. In addition, the compact feature obtained from TICA helps to build an efficient codebook. Furthermore, we introduce a new closeness measurement based on Neighbourhood Counting Measure (NCM) to improve the k Nearest Neighbour classification. The preliminary results based on KTH and Trecvid data demonstrate the proposed TICA/NCM approach increases the recognition accuracy and improve the efficiency of BoW model.

Keywords: bag of words, topographic ICA, neighbourhood counting measurement, action recognition.

1 Introduction

Inspired from success in text categorization, the Bag-of-words (BoW) approach has been increasingly applied for human action recognition [10][8][6]. In BoW model the detected features are transformed into a representation that the positional arrangement is ignored. Such representation makes learning more efficient however discards the valuable spatial information among the features. To tackle this issue, some researchers propose to improve the clustering methods such as using Information Bottleneck (IB) [3] and diffusion distance [9]. Some methods are focused to capture the spatial-temporal structural information of visual words such as modified spatial correlogram [7], spatial-temporal pyramid matching [6] and spatial-temporal context via a local histogram within neighbourhood [4].

Recent studies have shown positive outcomes in applying the subspace-based methods for video content analysis, such as Non-negative Matrix Factorization

---

* Corresponding author.

R. Hervás et al. (Eds.): UCAmI 2014, LNCS 8867, pp. 523–531, 2014.
© Springer International Publishing Switzerland 2014

(NMF)[13], Independent Component Analysis (ICA) [21] and Topographic ICA [15], in which the new features are obtained by decomposition of the low level features into a number of components (or factors). Apart from dimension reduction, these methods enhance the discriminative features, and as the data driven model they can be used for unsupervised learning [15]. Most of these methods did not tackle the problems in BoW. A recent study [20] applied a graphic NMF to factorize the histogram of visual words generated by the locally weighted word context descriptors, in which the factors close to each other can be grouped together. In this work, we propose a topographic ICA which can group the geometrically nearby feature components thus helps to keep spatial information. Unlike [20] which applies NMF to histogram of words, we apply TICA to the low level features directly before learning the vocabulary, which leads a more efficient codebook for BoW model and reduces the computation cost in k mean clustering.

Finding nearest neighbours is the key idea for kNN classification, in which the neighbours are sorted by measuring the distance or similarity between the data points. Neighbourhood Counting Measure (NCM)[16] is a generic similarity measure that can be used for different types of data: multivariate, sequence (or time series) and tree structured [17][18]. Results from [16] show that NCM consistently provides better performance than state-of-art distance functions, such as Hamming distance and Value difference metric (VDM) (for categorical attributes) and Heterogeneous Value Difference Metric (for combining two distance functions). To date NCM has not been applied to image/video analysis, thus we extend NCM to action recognition by employing it as a similarity function in kNN classification.

The paper is organised as follows. Firstly the TICA and NCM are are explained. Then the proposed method is evaluated using KTH data and surveillance data Trecvid. The effect of NCM and neighbourhood function used in TICA are studied. The conclusion is provided in final section.

2   Proposed Method

Flowchart for the propose method is given in Fig. 1 and the details for method are explained in following sections.

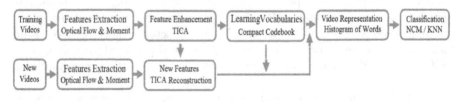

Fig. 1. Flowchart for the proposed method

2.1 Topographic ICA

In standard ICA, $\mathbf{V=AS}$, a data feature mixture $\mathbf{V}$ is decomposed into a number of statistically independent components (ICs) $\mathbf{S}$ and a mixing matrix $\mathbf{A}$ in which ICs have no particular order. In TICA model [5] the ICs geometrically far from each other are considered approximately independent but those close to each other are assumed to have certain dependencies. The dependency is defined by higher-order correlation between the estimated ICs, such as the correlation of their energies. The approximation of the joint density of the vector of component $\mathbf{s}$, denoted as $\tilde{p}(\mathbf{s})$, can be expressed as [5]

$$\tilde{p}(\mathbf{s}) = \prod_{j=1}^{n} exp(G(\sum_{i=1}^{n} h(i,j)s_i^2)) \tag{1}$$

where $h(i,j)$ is a neighbourhood function, $\mathbf{s} = [s_1, s_2, ..., s_n]^T$, n is the number of ICs, and $G(q) = -\alpha\sqrt{\epsilon + q}$ is a scalar function (ϵ set as 0.005 [5] and α is decided empirically). The neighbourhood function $h(i,j)$ that specifies the geometrical relationship between sources s_i and s_j in topography is usually defined as a monotonically decreasing function of some distance measurement. In this study, a simple neighbourhood function is applied, such that

$$h(i,j) = \begin{cases} 1 & if \ |i - j| \leq m \\ 0 & otherwise. \end{cases} \tag{2}$$

where m is the width of the neighbourhood. The approximation of the log-likelihood of TICA model, denoted as $\tilde{L}(\mathbf{W})$, is given as

$$log\tilde{L}(\mathbf{W}) = \sum_{t=1}^{T}\sum_{j=1}^{n} G(\sum_{i=1}^{n} h(i,j)(\mathbf{w}_i^T\mathbf{z}(t))^2) + Tlog(|det\mathbf{W}|) \tag{3}$$

where $\mathbf{z}(t)$ is the vector of features whitened by PCA, $\mathbf{W}$ is the unmixing matrix ($\mathbf{W=A}^\dagger$, $\dagger$ denotes pseudoinverse), T is the length of feature. The optimal solution $\mathbf{W}_{opt}$ can be obtained via maximization of the above log-likelihood function [5]. An example to demonstrate the effect of TICA is given in Fig. 2 using 13 nature image data (available at [11]) with a 3×3 neighbourhood area applied. The basis vector images obtained from ICA and TICA are compared, in which image patches from ICA are randomly located but after TICA those similar in location and orientation are grouped together.

2.2 Neighbourhood Counting Measure (NCM)

The NCM [16] is easy to implement and more flexible than Euclidean function as it can be used for both numerical and categorical data. The closeness between each data point is represented by all neighbourhoods covering both data points. Given two data points $\mathbf{x} = [x_1, x_2, ..., x_k]$ and $\mathbf{y} = [y_1, y_2, ..., y_k]$, the NCM can be calculated by

$$NCM(x,y) = \prod_{i=1}^{k} N_i \tag{4}$$

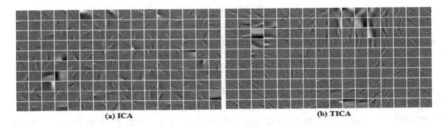

(a) ICA   (b) TICA

Fig. 2. The basis vector images obtained from (a) ICA and (b) TICA, in which the basis vectors similar in location and orientation are grouped together by TICA

where k is the dimension of features. N_i is the number of neighbourhoods covering both x_i and y_i, which can be obtained by:

$$N_i = \begin{cases} (max(a_i) - max(x_i, y_i) + 1) \times (min(x_i, y_i) - min(a_i) + 1), \text{numerical attribute} \\ 2^{m_i - 1}, \text{categorical attribute and } x_i = y_i \\ 2^{m_i - 2}, \text{categorical attribute and } x_i \neq y_i \end{cases}$$

$$(5)$$

where a_i denotes the ith attribute within the data space, m_i is the number of domain of a_i for categorical case. In this study the numerical case is applied, x_i and y_i are the ith attributes of two feature descriptors. In practice, to improve the computational efficiency, the logarithm was applied to Eq.(4) so the multiplication of N_i was replaced by summation of $log(N_i)$.

3   Experiments

The proposed method was evaluated by KTH [14] and Trecvid [12] data (Fig. 3). The accuracy is calculated as $(TP + TN)/N$, where TP denotes true positive, TN true negative and N is the number of cases under consideration.

Data. KTH data have 6 event classes: boxing, hand waving, hand clapping, walking, running and jogging. Each action is performed multiple times by 25 individuals with homogeneous background. For each class, 120 video sequences were used (outdoors and outdoors with different clothes). The Trecvid [12] data were extracted from 5 cameras in a UK airport. A subset data of four events was used: Cell2Ear, Object Put, PersonRuns and Pointing. For each event, the ground truth for regions of interest was manually annotated then the features were extracted per frame.

Feature Descriptors. We applied simple feature descriptor based on histogram of oriented optical flow (HOF) and motion feature based on Zernike moments of Efros optical flow channels. For each frame a normalized HOF magnitude (90 bins) is calculated where the magnitude of each bin corresponds to the sum of

Fig. 3. Examples of KTH [14] (left) and Trecvid [12] data (right)

magnitude of optical flow. The order of Zernike moments was 6. The calculated 2D Zernike moments of each channels were concatenated, resulting in a 64×1 vector per frame. The combined moment and HOF feature (denoted as HOFMO) is a 154×1 feature vector per frame. For TICA, the number of feature dimension was selected based on comparing their performance from dimension of 5 to 50, and based on the results, 25 for KTH and 45 for Trecvid were selected.

3.1 Effect of NCM

We first evaluated the performance of NCM comparing to three distance functions, correlation, Euclidean and Cityblock. (The function of "cosine" returns same results as Euclidean hence not included). The experiments were based on the HOFMO features of KTH without using TICA. Each class has 100 sequences for training and 20 for testing. The size of codebook was set as 100, 250 and 500. For classification, we run the weighted kNN under different number of neighbours. The results (Fig. 4) show that overall NCM achieves better performance than other distance functions in three cases.

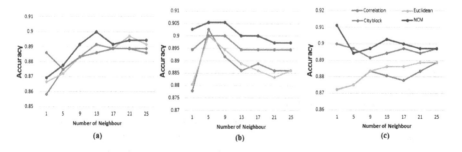

Fig. 4. Comparison of NCM with other distance functions, codebook size:(a) 100; (b) 250 and (c) 500

3.2 Neighbourhood Function in TICA

As defined in Eq.(2), the number of feature components to be grouped is affected by the width of neighbourhood m. To examine the effect of neighbourhood, we compared the performance by changing m from 1 to 5. The experiment was base on 6-folder cross validation for KTH data and results of mean accuracy from TICA/NCM and NCM are compared (Fig. 5). It can be seen that the overall performance is improved by using TICA. The optimal value for m can be determined empirically by training data. For the rest experiments, the best results of m from 3 to 5 were used in comparison.

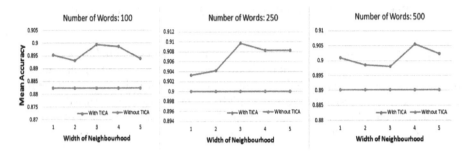

Fig. 5. Effect of width of neighbourhood m under different codebook size

3.3   Cross Validation

KTH. A 6-folder cross-validation was carried out. The comparison include four combinations: kNN via Euclidean (as it is commonly used in kNN), NCM, TICA/Euclidean and TICA/NCM. The results of mean accuracy under codebook size of 100, 250 and 500 are given in Fig. 6 (left). It can be seen that: 1) For both with and without TICA, NCM is better than Euclidean; even without TICA, using NCM alone may have better results than TICA/Euclidean; 2) TICA/NCM achieves the best results; 3) Because of compact feature from TICA, the codebook size can be small yet effective, such as size of 250 has better results than size 500.

Trecvid. A 9-folder cross-validation was performed and each folder has 40 sequences for training and 5 for testing. Because the number of training data for Trecvid is smaller than KTH, the codebook size of 50, 100 and 250 were used. The results Fig. 6(right) from Trecvid appear to be accordance with those from KTH: again NCM performces better than Euclidean and TICA/NCM achieves the best results comparing to the rest. The size of 50 returns the best performance than bigger size which suggest the proposed method improves the efficiency of BoW model.

3.4   Comparison and Discussion

We also compared the method to the approach using Hidden Markov Model (HMM) [1] and support vector machine (SVM) using the same HOFMO features. As in [1] 15 principal components of features were extracted and different events

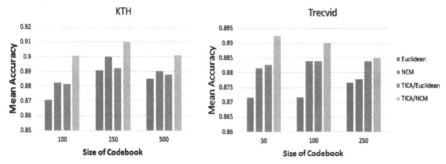

Fig. 6. Results of mean accuracy from cross validation for KTH and Trecvid

were represented by different HMM model parameters. The number of hidden states was 6 and the number of Gaussian under each state was 3. For SVM, the linear kennel function was applied as in our tests it had better results than other functions. The maximum iteration number was empirically set as 2000. The results in Table 1 show that the proposed method performs better than those from HMM and SVM.

Table 1. Comparison of methods using same HOFMO features

	HMM	SVM	Proposed
KTH	0.88±0.03	0.87±0.02	**0.91**±0.02
Trecvid	0.87±0.03	0.86±0.02	**0.89**±0.02

Comparing to other methods using different features of KTH, our best results of TP (0.83) is better that from [14] (0.71) and [10] (0.815), but still needs improvement to reach the state-of-art. At current stage, the method only applied HOF and moment features, which can be improved if using advanced features like SIFT. We will also explore more options for neighbourhood function in TICA in the future. Nevertheless, this work show positive outcome and improvement by considering the feature spatial information in BoW model. In addition it produces a more efficient codebook (size 250 for KTH) than most BoW based work that use much large size codebook, such as 500 [20], 1500 [10] or 4000 [19] [15].

4   Conclusion

In this paper we presented a new framework to improve the BoW model for video based recognition. A compact feature presentation is obtained by employing a topographic ICA to decompose the features of HOF and moment descriptors into a number of subcomponents, which not only enhance the discrimination of features but also enables a more efficient codebook. In addition, the TICA takes the BoW-ignored spatial information into account by grouping the geometrically nearby feature components. The results based on KTH and Trecvid demonstrate the improvement of BoW approach by the proposed TICA/NCM based approach. Further improvement can be made by applying the advanced feature descriptors and neighbourhood functions for TICA in the future.

Acknowledgments. This work is supported by FP7 projects SAVASA and Slandail.

References

1. Clawson, K., Jing, M., Scotney, B., Wang, H., Liu, J.: Human Action Recognition in Video via Fused Optical Flow and Moment Features – Towards a Hierarchical Approach to Complex Scenario Recognition. In: Gurrin, C., Hopfgartner, F., Hurst, W., Johansen, H., Lee, H., O'Connor, N. (eds.) MMM 2014, Part II. LNCS, vol. 8326, pp. 104–115. Springer, Heidelberg (2014)
2. Efros, A., Berg, A.C., Mori, G., Malik, J.: Recognizing action at a distance. In: Proc. ICCV (2003)
3. Fulkerson, B., Vedaldi, A., Soatto, S.: Localizing objects with smart dictionaries. In: Forsyth, D., Torr, P., Zisserman, A. (eds.) ECCV 2008, Part I. LNCS, vol. 5302, pp. 179–192. Springer, Heidelberg (2008)
4. Hu, Q., Qin, L., Huang, Q., Jiang, S., Tian, Q.: Action Recognition Using Spatial-Temporal Context. In: Proc. ICPR (2010)
5. Hyvärinen, A., Hoyer, P.O., Inki, M.: Topographic Independent Component Analysis. Neural Computation 13, 1527–1558 (2001)
6. Laptev, I., Marszalek, M., Schmid, C., Rozenfeld, B.: Learning realistic human actions from movies. In: Proc. CVPR, pp. 1–8 (2008)
7. Liu, J., Shah, M.: Learning human action via information maximization. In: Proc. CVPR (2008)
8. Liu, J., Luo, J., Shah, M.: Recognizing realistic actions from videos in the wild. In: Proc. CVPR (2009)
9. Liu, J., Yang, Y., Shah, M.: Learning Semantic Visual Vocabularies using Diffusion Distance. In: Proc. CVPR (2009)
10. Niebles, J.C., Wang, H., Fei-Fei, L.: Unsupervised learning of human action categories using spatial-temporal words. In: Proc. BMVC, vol. 3, pp. 1249–1258 (2006)
11. Hoyer, P.O.: Software Packages,
    http://www.cs.helsinki.fi/u/phoyer/software.html
12. Over, P., Awad, G., Michel, M., et al.: TRECVID 2013 - An Overview of the Goals, Tasks, Data, Evaluation Mechanisms and Metrics. In: Proc. TRECVID (2013)
13. Roth, P.M., Mauthner, T., Khan, I., Bischof, H.: Efficient Human Action Recognition by Cascaded Linear Classifcation. In: Proc. ICCV (2009)
14. Schuldt, C., Laptev, I., Caputo, B.: Recognizing human actions: a local svm approach. In: Proc. ICPR (2004)
15. Yang, Y., Shah, M.: Complex Events Detection using Data-driven Concepts. In: Fitzgibbon, A., Lazebnik, S., Perona, P., Sato, Y., Schmid, C. (eds.) ECCV 2012, Part III. LNCS, vol. 7574, pp. 722–735. Springer, Heidelberg (2012)
16. Wang, H.: Nearest neighbors by neighborhood counting. IEEE Transactions on Pattern Analysis and Machine Intelligence 28(6), 942–953 (2006)
17. Wang, H., Murtagh, H.: A study of neighborhood counting similarity. IEEE Transactions on Knowledge and Data Engineering 20(4), 449–461 (2008)

18. Wang, H.: Neighborhood counting measure and minimum risk metric. IEEE Transactions on Pattern Analysis and Machine Intelligence 32(4), 449–461 (2010)
19. Wang, H., Klaser, A., Schmid, C., Liu, C.: Action Recognition by Dense Trajectories. In: Proc. CVPR, pp. 3169–3176 (2011)
20. Wang, H., Yuan, C., Hu, W., Ling, H., Yang, W., Sun, C.: Action recognition using nonnegative action component representation and sparse basis selection. IEEE Trans. Image Processing 23(2), 571–581 (2014)
21. Zhou, J., Zhang, X.P.: An ICA mixture hidden Markov model for video content analysis. IEEE Trans. Circuit Syst. Video Technol. 18(11), 1576–1586 (2008)

A General Weighted Multi-scale Method for Improving LBP for Face Recognition

Xin Wei[2], Hui Wang[1], Gongde Guo[2], and Huan Wan[2]

[1] School of Computing and Mathematics
University of Ulster at Jordanstown, Belfast, UK
[2] Key Lab of Network Security and Cryptology
School of Mathematics and Computer Science
Fujian Normal University, P.R. China

Abstract. LBP (Local Binary Pattern) is a popular image descriptor (feature) that has been widely used in face recognition. LBP has some parameters, and different parameter values leads to different LBP feature vectors. In practice usually only one feature vector is used for one image, thus information about image content is not utilised fully by LBP. In this paper a novel way of utilising LBP features more fully is presented. Different LBP feature vectors are extracted for one image, corresponding to different combinations of LBP parameter values. These vectors are weighted and used in a distance function. Then the k-nearest neighbour classifier is used. Experiments have been conducted on the AR database. Results show this method does indeed produce better classification performance, suggesting that more information considered this way can have values.

Keywords: face recognition, LBP, weighting, multi-scale.

1 Introduction

Image representation is vital to face recognition, since it is a deciding factor for the recognition performance. Classic image representation methods include HOG[3], MSER[12], Gabor[9], SIFT[10] and LBP[13]. Among these is LBP (Local Binary Pattern), which has its prominent advantages.

LBP is a type of image descriptor (feature) able to capture image texture. It is conceptually simple, computationally efficient, yet very powerful in terms of performance; hence it has been widely used in face recognition and texture analysis, along with classifiers such as k-nearest neighbour and support vector machine. Therefore LBP has received a lot of attention in recent years, and many improvements and variants have been proposed [1,5,8].

LBP has some parameters: for example, the size of cells (typically 16×16), the radius of neighbourhood, the choice of patterns (LBP patterns) in constructing the histogram. Different combination of parameter values leads to different LBP feature vector. It is usual practice that only one feature vector is used for one image, which corresponds to one combination of parameter values. However a

R. Hervás et al. (Eds.): UCAmI 2014, LNCS 8867, pp. 532–539, 2014.
© Springer International Publishing Switzerland 2014

single combination of parameter values can only capture information about an image to some extent. It is then reasonable to expect more useful information to be captured by more than one combination of parameter values; hence better classification performance can be expected. This is a question that has not been explored in the literature, as far as the authors are aware.

In this paper a novel way of utilising LBP features more fully is presented. A *scale* variable is introduced, which applies to the radius of a neighbourhood [1]. A range of scales is considered, say $\{1, 2, 3\}$, resulting in different LBP feature vectors being extracted for one image. There are different ways of using multiple LBP feature vectors for one image. In this paper these vectors are weighted and used in a distance function. Then the k-nearest neighbour classifier is used. This approach to face recognition is evaluated on AR face database [11], where two LBP versions are used – Uniform LBP[13] and Hierarchical Multiscale LBP[6].

The rest of the paper is organised as follows. Section 2 reviews LBP and some of its variants. Section 3 presents the proposed method. Section 4 shows experimental results on the AR face database. Section 5 summarises and concludes the paper.

2 Brief Review of LBP

2.1 Circular LBP and Uniform LBP

The original LBP only considers 8 surrounding pixels of a center pixel. As a result, the LBP descriptors are sensitive to image rotating and image scaling. Therefore Ojala *et al* [13] proposed *Circular LBP*, which allows for different radius (R) and the number of sampling points (P), as shown in Figure 1.

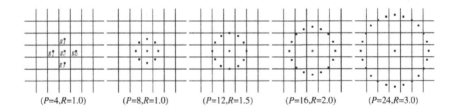

$(P=4,R=1.0)$ $(P=8,R=1.0)$ $(P=12,R=1.5)$ $(P=16,R=2.0)$ $(P=24,R=3.0)$

Fig. 1. Circularly symmetric neighbour sets for different (P;R)

However, Circular LBP has a problem: there may be too many LBP patterns if more sampling points are considered. An LBP operator with 8 sampling points has 2^8 patterns. As the number of sampling points increases, the number of LBP patterns increases exponentially. Therefore the LBP feature space is too sparse and so is not conducive to express image texture. In order to solve this

---

[1] For example, if the LBP algorithm adopts a radius value of 1 and scale 2 is applied, then the actual radius becomes 2.

problem, Ojala *et al* proposed *Uniform LBP* [13]. It takes the binary string of each pattern as linked with the head to the tail. In this method those patterns that have no more than two 0/1 transitions, called *uniform patterns*, are treated separately and are put into different bins for histogram statistics. However, all those patterns that have more than two 0/1 transitions, called *non-uniform pattern*, are put into one bin for histogram statistics. The 0/1 transition count can be computed by Equation 1.

$$U(LBP_{P,R}) = |s(g_{P-1} - g_c) - s(g_0 - g_c)| + \sum_{p=1}^{P-1} |s(g_p - g_c) - s(g_{p-1} - g_c)|. \quad (1)$$

where U denotes the number of 0/1 transitions. $LBP_{P,R}$ is the LBP value whose radius is R, and the number of sampling points is P. $s(x)$ is a function defined as follows. If x is not negative, $s(x)$ is 1; otherwise, $s(x)$ is 0. g_c denotes the value of the center pixel. g_p denotes the value of the pth pixel that is around the center pixel.

It is clear that the number of different Uniform LBP patterns is limited. Therefore, if the LBP patterns extracted from an image are mostly uniform patterns, then most of the useful information in an image can be captured by Uniform LBP vectors and different images can thus be separated by Uniform LBP vectors.

2.2   Hierarchical Multiscale LBP

In Uniform LBP all non-uniform patterns are placed in one bin of the histogram, so the information contained in these non-uniform patterns is lost. In order to capture such information to improve LBP, the *Hierarchical Multiscale LBP* is proposed [6]. This method first extracts LBP features with relatively large radius. For those pixels whose LBP values are non-uniform patterns, the LBP features with smaller radius are further extracted. For those pixels whose new LBP values are non-uniform patterns, the LBP features with even smaller radius are further extracted. This procedure is repeated until the LBP features with minimum radius are extracted. Figure 2 shows the basic process of this method.

3   Weighted Distance for Multi-scale LBP Features

In this section the proposed method for combining LBP features at different scales is presented. This method centres around a weighted distance function for two images. Each image is represented by an LBP vector using any LBP operator at a given scale. Here a *scale* is a natural number that is used to multiply the radius value(s) (the *base radius value(s)*) used by the chosen LBP operator (the *base LBP operator*) to produce the actual radius value(s) used in the computation. The base LBP operator can be the original LBP or any LBP variants. If the scale is 1, the actual radius value is the same as the base radius value.

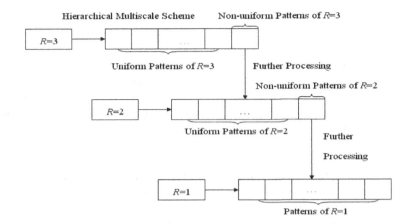

Fig. 2. An illustration of Hierarchical Multiscale LBP

Let m and m' be two images. Let $V_1, V_2, \cdots, V_n$ be the LBP feature vectors for image m extracted by the base LBP operator at scales $\{1, 2, \cdots, n\}$; $V_1', V_2', \cdots, V_n'$ be the LBP feature vectors for image m'. Let $w_1, w_2, \cdots, w_n$ be the weights of the scales. Then the distance between the two images is defined as follows:

$$d(m, m') = w_1 * ||V_1 - V_1'|| + w_2 * ||V_2 - V_2'|| + ... + w_n * ||V_n - V_n'|| \quad (2)$$

where $||V_i - V_i'||$ is the Euclidean distance of vectors V_i and V_i'.

If the base LBP operator is Uniform LBP, then there is only one radius to be scaled. Therefore the LBP feature vectors at different scales can be computed easily. If the base LBP operator is Hierarchical Multiscale LBP, then there are multiple radius parameters to be scaled. For example, if the Hierarchical Multiscale LBP has a hierarchy of depth 3, then there are 3 radius parameters. Suppose they have values of $2/3/4$ respectively – denote by $V_{2,3,4}$ the LBP vector of an image. If we apply scales of $\{1, 2, 3\}$, we will have three LBP vectors: $V_{2,3,4}$, $V_{4,6,8}$, $V_{3,9,12}$. Therefore the weighted distance of two images will be the following:

$$d(m, m') = w_1 * ||V_{2,3,4} - V_{2,3,4}'|| + w_2 * ||V_{4,6,8} - V_{4,6,8}'|| + w_3 * ||V_{6,9,12} - V_{6,9,12}'|| (3)$$

Discussion

It is clear that if the weights $w_1, w_2, \cdots, w_n$ take the values of $1, 0, \cdots, 0$ respectively, Eq.(2) becomes

$$d(m, m') = ||V_1 - V_1'|| \quad (4)$$

meaning that the image distance becomes the Euclidean distance of their LBP vectors at scale 1. By adjusting the weights, we allow LBP vectors at different scales to contribute toward the image distance.

There are three questions to answer. *The first question* is: Is there additional information obtained by considering LBP vectors at different scales? The answer to this question should be 'yes' as the LBP vectors at different scales are obtained under different parameter values so they should contain additional information. The important question is if such additional information can be utilised in some way that is useful or beneficial. There could be different ways of utilising the additional information, and this paper presents one way of doing so. This leads to *the second question*: Is the additional information utilised this way useful, such as by resulting in increased face recognition performance? The answer to this question is not obvious nor can it be obtained mathematically, so we have to be content with an empirical approach. Experimental results in the next section support a positive answer to this question.

The method here stipulates weighting the multiple LBP vectors and use them in an image distance function (Eq.2). Then, *the third question* is: How to select the weights? LBP is known as a *local texture* descriptor. At a small scale, say scale of 1, the LBP vector describes image texture at a small locality or, in other words, with fine details. At a large scale, say 3, the LBP vector describes image texture with coarse details. If we want to separate one human from one animal based on their images, it is reasonable to expect coarser texture details to be more useful than finer details. If we want to separate one person from another based on their images, it is reasonable to expect finer details to be more useful than coarser details. Since we focus on face recognition, we hypothesise LBP vectors at smaller scales should have higher weights than LBP vectors at higher scales. Therefore, if we consider LBP at scales $\{1, 2, 3\}$ we can consider weights $\{3, 2, 1\}$. The experimental results in the next section supports this hypothesis, and also supports a positive answer to the third question.

4   Experiments on AR Database

The weighted multiscale method for combining LBP vectors at different scales, or simply *Weighted Multiscale LBP*, has been evaluated through experiments on AR face database [11]. The AR face database includes more than 4000 images taken from 126 people, among which there are 70 men and 56 women. The images are divided into two sets where they are taken at different times. In our experiments a subset of the images is used, which consists 1400 images from 100 people with 14 images for each person. The face portion of each image is cropped out and normalized to the size of 100 * 80. The first seven images of each person in the first session are selected for training, which have the following characteristics: (1) neutral expression, (2) smile, (3) anger, (4) scream, (5) left light on, (6) right light on, and (7) all side lights on. The first seven images of each person in the second session are used for testing.

In one set of experiments we use Uniform LBP and Hierarchical Multiscale LBP as the base LBP operator. We represent images as Uniform LBP vectors or

Hierarchical Multiscale LBP vectors. We use the Euclidean distance to measure image distance and use 1-nearest neighbour classifier to classify images.

In another set of experiments we apply a base LBP operator at three or five scales, resulting in three or five base LBP vectors for each image. We use the weighted image distance function in Eq.(2) to measure image distance, and then use 1-nearest neighbour classifier. We consider three weighting schemes: (1) uniform (or equal) weighting of all scales; (2) fixed weighting – decreasing weights for increasing scales (e.g., weights of $3, 2, 1$ for scales of $1, 2, 3$); (3) optimal weighting of scales (i.e., consider all possible weight values in some range for different scales, and then select those weight values for the scales that give the best result). We also consider two scaling schemes: (1) 3 scales at $1, 2, 3$; (2) 5 scales at $1, 2, 3, 4, 5$.

To ensure fairness of comparison, PCA+LDA [15,4,2] is applied to all LBP vectors in all experiments to do dimension reduction.As a benchmark we also consider the well-known Principal Component Analysis (PCA) [15] and its variant 2D Principal Component Analysis (2DPCA) [16] as face recognition algorithms. They transform face images into a small set of characteristic feature images, called "eigenfaces", which are the principal components of the initial training set of face images[15,16].

Table 1 lists the recognition accuracy of different methods on AR database. It is clear from Table 1 that the recognition accuracy of Uniform LBP increased by up to 18.71% after applying weighted multiscaling with various types of weighting, and the recognition accuracy of Hierarchical Multiscale LBP increased by up to 2.43% after applying weighted multiscaling with various types of weighting. It is also clear that weighted multiscaling has led to increase in recognition accuracy for both base LBP operators under all three weighting schemes and two scaling schemes.

4.1 Discussion

Looking at the results from AR database we can observe the following.

- When multiple LBP vectors are used, face recognition accuracy has increased from the base LBP operator where only one LBP vector is used for each image. This observation strongly supports the expectation that utilising multiple LBP vectors through the weighted image distance does create value.
- Fixed weighting outperformed uniform weighting in 3 out of 4 cases, underperformed in 1 cases. This observation supports the expectation that finer details in images captured by LBP vectors at smaller scales are more useful than coarser details for face recognition. The fact that there are 1 out of 4 cases where fixed weighting underperformed uniform weighting suggests more research should be carried out about the relationship between the level of detail and the actual task.
- Optimal weighting substantially outperformed the base LBP operator where only one LBP vector is used for each image. This suggests that applying weighting can indeed make a difference when multiple LBP vectors are used.

Table 1. Recognition accuracy of different methods on AR database

Method	Recognition Accuracy
PCA	67.43%
2DPCA	72.14%
Uniform LBP	61.43%
Uniform LBP/UW3S	75.86%
Uniform LBP/FW3S	73.86%
Uniform LBP/OW3S	76.00%
Uniform LBP/UW5S	76.71%
Uniform LBP/FW5S	78.43%
Uniform LBP/OW5S	80.14%
Hierarchical Multiscale LBP	96.14%
Hierarchical Multiscale LBP/UW3S	97.14%
Hierarchical Multiscale LBP/FW3S	97.71%
Hierarchical Multiscale LBP/OW3S	98.00%
Hierarchical Multiscale LBP/UW5S	97.86%
Hierarchical Multiscale LBP/FW5S	98.14%
Hierarchical Multiscale LBP/OW5S	98.57%

5   Conclusion

In this paper a general weighted multiscale method is presented, which is aimed at utilising LBP information more fully by considering multiple LBP vectors at different scales. This method can be used to improve the existing LBP operators and their variants. Experiments on AR database confirm the usefulness of the proposed method and the expectation that utilising LBP information appropriately at multiple scales can indeed improve classification performance.

An interesting observation is that when weighted multiscaling is applied, Uniform LBP has achieved much higher improvement than Hierarchical Multiscale LBP consistently across all three databases. One explanation is that Uniform LBP considers only one scale whereas Hierarchical Multiscale LBP considers multiple scales in a hierarchical way, different from the way presented in this paper.

However this method comes at a cost as calculating more LBP vectors will certainly have a higher computation cost, although the increase in computation cost is only linear in the number of scales.

Future work will include studies on the relationship between the level of detail in image representation (via the scale of LBP operator) and the task, as well as the question of how to get an image distance function (2) in the style of *learning distance functions* [7,14].

References

1. Ahonen, T., Hadid, A., Pietikainen, M.: Face description with local binary patterns: Application to face recognition. IEEE Transactions on Pattern Analysis and Machine Intelligence 28(12), 2037–2041 (2006)
2. Belhumeur, P.N., Hespanha, J.P., Kriegman, D.: Eigenfaces vs. fisherfaces: Recognition using class specific linear projection. IEEE Transactions on Pattern Analysis and Machine Intelligence 19(7), 711–720 (1997)
3. Dalal, N., Triggs, B.: Histograms of oriented gradients for human detection. In: IEEE Computer Society Conference on Computer Vision and Pattern Recognition, CVPR 2005, vol. 1, pp. 886–893. IEEE (2005)
4. Using Discriminant Eigenfeatures. Short paper's. IEEE Transactions on Pattern Analysis and Machine Intelligence 18(8) (1996)
5. Guo, Z., Zhang, D.: A completed modeling of local binary pattern operator for texture classification. IEEE Transactions on Image Processing 19(6), 1657–1663 (2010)
6. Guo, Z., Zhang, D., Mou, X.: Hierarchical multiscale lbp for face and palmprint recognition. In: 2010 17th IEEE International Conference on Image Processing (ICIP), pp. 4521–4524. IEEE (2010)
7. Hertz, T., Bar-Hillel, A., Weinshall, D.: Learning distance functions for image retrieval. In: Proceedings of IEEE Conference in Computer Vision and Pattern Recognition, vol. 2 (2004)
8. Liao, S., Zhu, X., Lei, Z., Zhang, L., Li, S.Z.: Learning multi-scale block local binary patterns for face recognition. In: Lee, S.-W., Li, S.Z. (eds.) ICB 2007. LNCS, vol. 4642, pp. 828–837. Springer, Heidelberg (2007)
9. Liu, C., Wechsler, H.: Gabor feature based classification using the enhanced fisher linear discriminant model for face recognition. IEEE Transactions on Image Processing 11(4), 467–476 (2002)
10. Lowe, D.G.: Distinctive image features from scale-invariant keypoints. International Journal of Computer Vision 60(2), 91–110 (2004)
11. Martinez, A., Benavente, R.: The AR Face Database. CVC Tech.Report 24, Report 24 (1998)
12. Matas, J., Chum, O., Urban, M., Pajdla, T.: Robust wide-baseline stereo from maximally stable extremal regions. Image and Vision Computing 22(10), 761–767 (2004)
13. Ojala, T., Pietikainen, M., Maenpaa, T.: Multiresolution gray-scale and rotation invariant texture classification with local binary patterns. IEEE Transactions on Pattern Analysis and Machine Intelligence 24(7), 971–987 (2002)
14. Ramanan, D., Baker, S.: Local distance functions: A taxonomy, new algorithms, and an evaluation. IEEE Transactions on Pattern Analysis and Machine Intelligence 3(4), 794–806 (2011)
15. Turk, M.A., Pentland, A.P.: Face recognition using eigenfaces. In: Proceedings of IEEE Computer Society Conference on Computer Vision and Pattern Recognition, CVPR 1991, pp. 586–591. IEEE (1991)
16. Yang, J., Zhang, D., Frangi, A.F., Yang, J.-Y.: Two-dimensional pca: a new approach to appearance-based face representation and recognition. IEEE Transactions on Pattern Analysis and Machine Intelligence 26(1), 131–137 (2004)

Soft Sensing as Class-Imbalance Binary Classification – A Lattice Machine Approach

Huan Wan[2], Hui Wang[1], Gongde Guo[2], and Song Lin[2]

[1] School of Computing and Mathematics
University of Ulster at Jordanstown, Belfast, UK
[2] Key Lab of Network Security and Cryptology
School of Mathematics and Computer Science
Fujian Normal University, P.R. China

Abstract. Soft sensing is a class of problems that aim to sense some-thing of interest that cannot be measured directly through something else that can be measured directly. The problems are usually studied as separate topics in different fields, and there is little research studying these problems in a unified fashion. In this paper we argue that there are commonalities among these problems. They can all be formulated as class-imbalanced binary classification problems. We present an extension of Lattice Machine, which is binary classification and by focusing on characterising positive class to deal with class-imbalanced binary classification problems. We also present experimental results, where some public data sets from UCI data repository are turned into binary-class data and consequently they become class-imbalanced. These experiments show that the extended Lattice Machine outperforms the popular machine learning algorithms (SVM, NN, decision tree induction) when used as soft sensing engines, in terms of precision.

Keywords: Soft Sensing, binary classification, class imbalance learning, Lattice Machine.

1 Introduction

In this paper we focus on the topic of soft sensing, distil its characteristics, present our arguments, and propose a solution. *Soft sensing* is a class of problems that aim to sense "something of interest" (the *Interested Condition*) that cannot be measured directly through something else that can be measured directly. The result is *soft sensors* that do not depend on the use of physical sensor. Soft sensing seeks to answer the question: is the *Interested Condition* present in the data? This class of problems includes motion detection, object detection, anomaly detection, substance detection and many more. One example: given a video clip, is a known face pattern present in it? This is the face verification problem [1]. Another example: given a video clip, is an anomalous condition (e.g., obstacle on rail track) present? This is the anomaly detection problem [2]. Another example: given a sample of food, we measure its emission spectrum

R. Hervás et al. (Eds.): UCAmI 2014, LNCS 8867, pp. 540–547, 2014.
© Springer International Publishing Switzerland 2014

and ask the question: is a poisonous substance present? This is the substance detection problem [3].

These problems are usually studied as separate topics in different fields, and there is little research studying these problems in a unified approach with the aim of identifying new challenges to advance the state of the art. This paper represents a first attempt at studying soft sensing, a class of detection problems, in a unified approach. We take soft sensing as a binary classification problem which has positive and negative classes, with the positive class representing the interested condition. In data samples, the presence of the interested condition is usually rare so soft sensing as a binary classification problem is a class imbalance learning problem. For many learning algorithms class-imbalance learning reduces to majority class assignment – assign all data instances to the majority class. Two main strategies for dealing with class imbalance learning are: data sampling [4] and cost-sensitive learning [5]. The problem with these strategies is that there is substantial overhead or uncertainty, and the performance is less desirable. We take a different approach where, instead of trying to draw a line to separate positive/negative classes, we try to model or represent or characterise the positive, minority class, and use the negative, majority class as constraints in the modelling process. Our positive class modelling approach is based on Lattice Machine, a machine learning paradigm that aims to build hyper tuples as models that satisfy three principles: consistency, conservativeness and parsimoneousness. As such we do not need re-sampling or cost-sensitive learning, thus avoiding the overhead. More importantly, as shown later, the performance is even superior.

2   Soft Sensing

Soft sensing is to calculate in real-time an estimate of the quantity of interest that cannot be measured directly. It is used as a sensor to detect the presence of some interested condition. It is a class of problems where the focus of effort is the characterisation of the *interested condition* or the *identity* of interest. The problems in soft sensing include motion detection[6], object detection and recognition[7], person detection and recognition[8], event and scenario recognition[9], activity recognition[10], anomaly detection, and identity recognition and verification [11].

Soft sensing can be formulated as a two-class (binary) machine learning problem where the training data represents either the presence of the *interested condition* or not, corresponding to either positive or negative examples respectively. However, such a problem is usually class-imbalanced (i.e., very few positive examples in the training data), so solutions to soft sensing are those of class imbalanced machine learning.

3   Binary Classification and Class-Imbalanced Learning

Binary classification is classification with two classes. As a machine learning task, the training data set has data instances from two classes, usually called positive and negative classes. Any machine learning algorithm can be used for binary classification – SVM, KNN, decision tree induction, and Gaussian mixture model.

No matter how many classes there are, if the proportion of data in different classes is uneven or unbalanced (e.g., 1 : 20 or 1 positive instance for 20 negative instances), the data become class-imbalanced and the learning problem becomes *class-imbalance learning*. Many machine learning algorithms work well when the training data set is class-balanced, and do not as well as expected when data is class-imbalanced especially if the imbalanced ratio is very high.

There are many methods for improving performance of class-imbalance learning. Two most widely used methods are sampling and cost-sensitive learning. Other methods include kernel-based methods, active learning methods, one-class learning methods [12].

Sampling is a method that changes the training data set in order to artificially balance the data. Random oversampling and undersampling alter the training data set through repeating randomly selected examples in the minority class and removing randomly selected examples in the majority class respectively. Although useful, they come at a cost. Oversampling can lead to overfitting since it repeats minority class instances. And undersampling may lose potentially useful information since it uses a subset of the training data. Apart from random oversampling and undersampling, there are methods that use sampling in some complex ways to improve class-imbalance learning. Such as, The synthetic minority oversampling technique [13],the EasyEnsemble and BalanceCascade [14]etc.

Cost-sensitive learning is another method for improving the performance of class-imbalance learning. Instead of altering the training data, cost-sensitive learning uses cost matrix to describe the costs of misclassification and continually modifies the cost matrix by some strategies to solve class-imbalance learning problems. It assigns different misclassifying costs for different classes – the cost of misclassifying the minority class is set higher than the cost of misclassifying the majority class. A commonly used strategy is combining cost matrix with AdaBoost. AdaC1, AdaC2, and AdaC3 [15] put cost items into the weight updating strategy of AdaBoost. Other strategies include combining cost items with decision trees or neural networks.

4   Lattice Machine: Building Model for the Positive Class Only

4.1   Original Lattice Machine

Lattice Machine (LM) [16–18] is a learning algorithm based on the notion of hyper tuples (see Figures 1 and 2). It generates a model for each class as a set of hyper tuples, which together satisfies three learning principles: consistency (equi-labelled), conservativeness (supported) and parsimoneousness (maximal) (see Figure 3 for an illustration via a comparison with decision tree). LM is shown to be competitive with decision tree algorithm [16].

4.2   Extended Lattice Machine

Like any other learning algorithm, LM can be used for two-class data or multiple-class data. When applied to soft sensing, we are only interested in the positive class so the LM learning algorithm needs to be re-designed. The LM learning algorithm has three main steps:

1: create a hyper tuple with unused data instances from one class
2: check to see if this hyper tuple overlaps with any hyper tuple from another class; if so, throw away this hyper tuple and create another; if not, move to the next step
3: find all data instances from this class that are covered by this hyper tuple, and mark them as 'used'.

Now that there are only positive and negative classes and our interest is the positive class only, we need to replace the above algorithm outline by the following

1': create a hyper tuple with unused data instances from the positive class
2': check to see if this hyper tuple covers any data instance from the negative class; if so, throw away this hyper tuple and create another; if not, move to the next step
3': find all data instances from the positive class that are covered by this hyper tuple, and mark them as 'used'.

This extended LM learning algorithm ensures: (1) the resulting hyper tuples cover only positive data (thus consistent); (2) they are supported (thus conservative); (3) no hyper tuple is entirely covered by another hyper tuple (thus parsimonious). Therefore it still adheres to the three principles which LM is designed on.

5   Experiments

We conduct some experiments to evaluate the extended LM on class-imbalance learning and compare the extended LM with some popular learning algorithms: SVM, decision trees, and NN. We use precision as the main evaluation measure.

5.1   Experimental Settings

We select ten data sets from UCI data repository [19]: some are binary and class-imbalanced and have been used in class-imbalance learning studies; some are class-balanced but are transformed into class-imbalanced by keeping one class as positive and turning the rest classes into a single negative class.And the ten data sets are numeric, and have no missing value. Full details of these data sets are shown in Table 1.

x	y	z
a	0	α
a	1	α
b	2	β

(a)

x	y	z
{a}	{0, 1}	{α}
{b}	{2}	{β}

(b)

Fig. 1. (a) A set of simple tuples. (b) A set of hyper tuples.

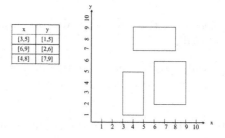

x	y
[3,5]	[1,5]
[6,9]	[2,6]
[4,8]	[7,9]

Fig. 2. Hyper tuples and their graphical illustration

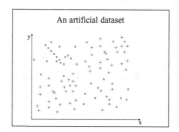

An artificial dataset

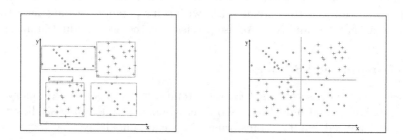

Fig. 3. A comparison of LM and decision tree on the same training data set – left: LM, and right: decision tree

We run Lattice Machine (LM), Support Vector Machines (SVM), Nearest Neighbour (NN), and Decision Tree on the above data sets to see how well they perform in class-imbalance learning. We implement LM by ourselves, and we use WEKA [20] implementations of all other classifiers: SMO – SVM, IB1 – NN and J48 – Decision Tree. Default settings are used for all algorithms. Evaluation strategy is five-fold cross validation and performance measure is *Precision*:

$$\text{Precision} = \frac{TP}{TP + FP}$$

where TP means True Positive and FP means False Positive.

We run two experiments with the above classifiers: one with oversampling (of minority class) and another without oversampling. Oversampling randomly repeats data instances in the minority class until the two classes reach a balance, i.e., they have the same number of data instances.

Table 1. Details of the UCI data sets used in this paper

Datasets	Size	Positive(number)	Pos/Neg	Level of imbalance
Ecoli	336	cp(143)	193/143	1.35
Iono	351	b(126)	225/126	1.79
Pima	768	Testedpositive(268)	500/268	1.87
Iris	150	virginical(50)	100/50	2
Wine	178	Class1(59)	119/59	2.02
Vehicle	846	van(199)	647/199	3.25
Hepatitis	155	Class(32)	123/32	3.84
Allpreriched	324	true(63)	261/63	4.14
Glass	214	headlamps(29)	185/29	6.38
Yeast	1484	ME3(51)	1433/51	28.1

5.2   Experimental Results

The experimental results without oversampling are shown in Table 2. We can see LM is comparable with SVM in terms of precision, but is better than NN and Decision Tree on most of the data sets. We can also see that LM is substantially better than the other three classifiers when the level of imbalance is higher than 5. The results with oversampling are shown in Table 3. We can see the performance of LM is significantly better than the performance of the other three classifiers on all data sets.

Therefore, from the results in Table 2 and Table 3, we can draw a conclusion that LM is a competitive classifier in class-imbalance learning and it has greater ability to deal with imbalanced data.

Table 2. Experimental results without oversampling

Datasets	SMO	IB1	J48	LM	Level of imbalance
Ecoli	0.945	0.931	0.958	0.959	1.35
Iono	0.947	0.925	0.867	0.977	1.79
Pima	0.734	0.581	0.585	0.625	1.87
Iris	0.958	0.936	0.887	0.93	2
Wine	0.932	0.894	0.951	1	2.02
Vehicle	0.918	0.851	0.847	0.876	3.25
Hepatitis	0.556	0.5	0.533	0.538	3.84
Allpreriched	0.714	0.472	0.622	0.591	4.14
Glass	0.821	0.833	0.846	0.929	6.38
Yeast	0.851	0.851	0.721	0.901	28.1

Table 3. Experimental results with oversampling

Datasets	SMO	IB1	J48	LM	Level of imbalance
Ecoli	0.954	0.944	0.953	0.97	1
Iono	0.933	0.972	0.922	1	1
Pima	0.77	0.792	0.77	0.933	1
Iris	0.952	0.962	0.951	0.964	1
Wine	0.95	0.944	0.967	1	1
Vehicle	0.939	0.949	0.946	0.966	1
Hepatitis	0.831	0.866	0.819	0.979	1
Allpreriched	0.875	0.859	0.855	0.996	1
Glass	0.949	0.984	0.949	1	1
Yeast	0.903	0.961	0.946	0.974	1

6   Conclusion

In this paper we study soft sensing, a class of detection problems. We formulate soft sensing as a class-imbalance binary classification problem where it is sufficient to model the minority, positive class. We propose an extension of Lattice Machine as an approach to the soft sensing problem. Experiments show that this extension of LM can indeed outperform other classifiers in their abilities to deal with class-imbalance learning, especially when the imbalanced ratio is higher.

References

1. Berg, T., Belhumeur, P.N.: Tom-vs-pete classifiers and identity-preserving alignment for face verification. In: BMVC, vol. 2, p. 7. Citeseer (2012)
2. Chandola, V., Banerjee, A., Kumar, V.: Anomaly detection: A survey. ACM Computing Surveys (CSUR) 41(3), 15 (2009)
3. Harding, G., Lanza, R.C., Myers, L.J., Young, P.A.: Substance detection systems. In: Substance Detection Systems, vol. 2092 (1994)
4. Chawla, N.V., Japkowicz, N., Kotcz, A.: Editorial: special issue on learning from imbalanced data sets. ACM SIGKDD Explorations Newsletter 6(1), 1–6 (2004)

5. Zhou, Z.-H.: Cost-sensitive learning. In: Torra, V., Narakawa, Y., Yin, J., Long, J. (eds.) MDAI 2011. LNCS, vol. 6820, pp. 17–18. Springer, Heidelberg (2011)
6. Hu, W., Tan, T., Wang, L., Maybank, S.: A survey on visual surveillance of object motion and behaviors. IEEE Transactions on Systems, Man, and Cybernetics, Part C: Applications and Reviews 34(3), 334–352 (2004)
7. Opelt, A., Fussenegger, M., Pinz, A., Auer, P.: Weak hypotheses and boosting for generic object detection and recognition. In: Pajdla, T., Matas, J(G.) (eds.) ECCV 2004. LNCS, vol. 3022, pp. 71–84. Springer, Heidelberg (2004)
8. Dalal, N., Triggs, B.: Histograms of oriented gradients for human detection. In: IEEE Computer Society Conference on Computer Vision and Pattern Recognition, CVPR 2005, vol. 1, pp. 886–893. IEEE (2005)
9. Vu, V.-T., Bremond, F., Thonnat, M.: Automatic video interpretation: A novel algorithm for temporal scenario recognition. IJCAI 3, 1295–1300 (2003)
10. Turaga, P., Chellappa, R., Subrahmanian, V.S., Udrea, O.: Machine recognition of human activities: A survey. IEEE Transactions on Circuits and Systems for Video Technology 18(11), 1473–1488 (2008)
11. Delac, K., Grgic, M.: A survey of biometric recognition methods. In: Proceedings of 46th International Symposium on Electronics in Marine, Elmar 2004, pp. 184–193. IEEE (2004)
12. He, H., Garcia, E.A.: Learning from imbalanced data. IEEE Transactions on Knowledge and Data Engineering 21(9), 1263–1284 (2009)
13. Chawla, N.V., Bowyer, K.W., Hall, L.O., Kegelmeyer, W.P.: Smote: synthetic minority over-sampling technique. arXiv preprint arXiv:1106.1813 (2011)
14. Liu, X.-Y., Wu, J., Zhou, Z.-H.: Exploratory undersampling for class-imbalance learning. IEEE Transactions on Systems, Man, and Cybernetics, Part B: Cybernetics 39(2), 539–550 (2009)
15. Sun, Y., Kamel, M.S., Wong, A.K., Wang, Y.: Cost-sensitive boosting for classification of imbalanced data. Pattern Recognition 40(12), 3358–3378 (2007)
16. Wang, H., Dubitzky, W., Düntsch, I., Bell, D.: A lattice machine approach to automated casebase design: Marrying lazy and eager learning. IJCAI, 254–263 (1999)
17. Wang, H., Düntsch, I., Gediga, G., Skowron, A.: Hyperrelations in version space. In: Proceedings of the 2002 ACM Symposium on Applied Computing, pp. 514–518. ACM (2002)
18. Wang, H., Düntsch, I., Trindade, L.: Lattice machine classification based on contextual probability. Fundamenta Informaticae 127(1), 241–256 (2013)
19. Blake, C., Merz, C.J.: Uci repository of machine learning databases. irvine, ca: University of california. Department of Information and Computer Science, vol. 55 (1998), http://www.ics.uci.edu/~mlearn/mlrepository.html
20. Hall, M., Frank, E., Holmes, G., Pfahringer, B., Reutemann, P., Witten, I.H.: The weka data mining software: an update. ACM SIGKDD Explorations Newsletter 11(1), 10–18 (2009)

Author Index